Found Sculpture and Photography from Contemporary Art

Taking its departure point from the 1933 surrealist photo
sculptures' by Brassaï and Dalí, *Found Sculpture and Photog* ... *to Contemporary Art* offers fresh perspectives on the sculptural object by relating it to both surrealist concerns with chance and the crucial role of photography in framing the everyday. This collection of essays questions the nature of sculptural practice, looking to forms of production and reproduction that blur the boundaries between things that are made and things that are found.

One of the book's central themes is the interplay of presence and absence in sculpture, as it is highlighted, disrupted, or multiplied through photography's indexical nature. The essays examine the surrealist three-dimensional object, its relation to and transformation through photographs, as well as the enduring legacies of such concerns for the artwork's materiality and temporality in performance and conceptual practices from the 1960s through the present. *Found Sculpture and Photography* sheds new light on the shifts in status of the art object, challenging the specificity of visual practices, pursuing a radical interrogation of agency in modern and contemporary practices, and exploring the boundaries between art and everyday life.

Anna Dezeuze is Lecturer in Art History at the Ecole Supérieure d'Art et de Design Marseille-Méditerranée in Marseilles, France.
Julia Kelly is a researcher at the University of Hull, UK.

Ashgate Studies in Surrealism

Series Editor:
Gavin Parkinson, The Courtauld Institute of Art, University of London, UK

With scholarly interest in Surrealism greater than ever, the Ashgate Studies in Surrealism series serves as a forum for key areas of Surrealist inquiry today. This series extends the ongoing academic and popular interest in Surrealism, evident in recent studies that have rethought established areas of Surrealist activity and engagement, including those of politics, the object, photography, crime, and modern physics. Expanding and adding various lines of inquiry, books in the series examine Surrealism's intersections with philosophical, social, artistic, and literary themes. Potential subjects to be examined in the context of Surrealism include but are not limited to: nature; queer studies; humor and play; science; theory in the 1950s and 1960s; the New Novel; Surrealist activities beyond Paris.

Proposals are welcomed for both monographs and essay collections dealing with the above subjects or with discussions of Surrealism in other aspects and genres. Monographic writings on artists and writers who have been generally overlooked by English-language scholarship (for instance, Victor Brauner, Toyen, Jorge Camacho) would also fall within the scope of this series.

Found Sculpture and Photography from Surrealism to Contemporary Art

Edited by
Anna Dezeuze and Julia Kelly

Routledge
Taylor & Francis Group
LONDON AND NEW YORK

First published 2013 by Ashgate Publishing

2 Park Square, Milton Park, Abingdon, Oxfordshire OX14 4RN
711 Third Avenue, New York, NY 10017

Routledge is an imprint of the Taylor & Francis Group, an informa business

First issued in paperback 2018

British Library Cataloguing in Publication Data
Found sculpture and photography from surrealism to
contemporary art. -- (Ashgate studies in surrealism)
1. Found objects (Art) 2. Sculpture. 3. Conceptual art.
4. Art and photography. 5. Photography, Artistic.
6. Surrealism.
I. Series II. Dezeuze, Anna. III. Kelly, Julia, 1970-
730.1-dc23

Library of Congress Cataloging-in-Publication Data
Found sculpture and photography from surrealism to contemporary art / edited by Anna Dezeuze and Julia Kelly.
pages cm -- (Ashgate studies in surrealism)
Includes bibliographical references and index.
ISBN 978-1-4094-0000-4 (hardcover) 1. Surrealism. 2. Found objects (Art) 3. Sculpture, Modern--20th century--Themes, motives. 4. Vernacular photography. I. Dezeuze, Anna, editor of compilation. II. Kelly, Julia, 1970- editor of compilation.
NB198.5.S8F67 2012
735'.23--dc23

2012012888

ISBN 978-1-4094-0000-4 (hbk)
ISBN 978-1-138-54808-4 (pbk)

Contents

List of Figures *vii*
Notes on Contributors *xi*
Acknowledgements *xv*

Introduction: Involuntary Sculpture: Process, Photography and the Ephemeral Object **1**
Anna Dezeuze and Julia Kelly

1 **Voluntary and Involuntary Sculpture** **13**
Steven Harris

2 **The Found, the Made and the Functional: Surrealism, Objects and Sculpture** **39**
Julia Kelly

3 **Close-Up on the Object: Attending to the Films of Man Ray** **59**
Samantha Lackey

4 **Kaprow's Vector** **77**
Martha Buskirk

5 **Richard Wentworth's *Making Do, Getting By* and the Elusive Everyday** **99**
Anna Dezeuze

6 **In Formation: On Terry Fox's *Children's Tapes*** **119**
Carrie Lambert-Beatty

7 **Documents, Dreams and Fantasies: Passages through the Involuntary from Photography to Sculpture in the Work of Mike Kelley** **137**
John C. Welchman

8 **Chance/Lens (Subversive Translation)** **157**
Simon Baker

9 **Involuntary Photography** **171**
Margaret Iversen

Bibliography *185*
Index *195*

List of Figures

I.1 Brassaï (pseud.) Gyula Halász, *Sculptures involontaires*, page from the journal *Minotaure*, nos. 3–4, 1933 © Estate Brassaï-RMN. Photograph © RMN/Jean-Gilles Berizzi. Private collection

1.1 Alberto Giacometti, 'Objets mobiles et muets', *Le Surréalisme au service de la révolution*, no. 3 (December 1931), pp. 18–19 © DACS and ADAGP

1.2 Man Ray, *Woman Holding Giacometti's* Objet désagréable, silver gelatin print, 1932, Musée National d'Art Moderne, Centre Georges Pompidou, Paris © Man Ray Trust/SODRAC (2009). CNAC/MNAM/ Dist. Réunion des Musées Nationaux/Art Resource, NY

1.3 Hans Arp, *Trois objets désagréables sur une figure*, plaster, 1932, 37 × 29.5 × 19 cm (base), Silkeborg Kunstmuseum, Silkeborg © Jean Hans Arp Estate/SODRAC (2009). Photo: Lars Bay

1.4 Hans Arp, *Nombril et deux idées*, plaster, 1932, 14.5 × 22 × 21.5 cm (base), Musée d'Art Moderne et Contemporain de la Ville de Strasbourg © Jean Hans Arp Estate/SODRAC (2009). Photo Musées de la Ville de Strasbourg, M. Bertola

1.5 Hans Arp, *Concrétion humaine*, plaster, 1934, 32 × 39 × 40 cm, Fondation Arp, Clamart © Jean Hans Arp Estate/SODRAC (2009). Photo: Michel Nguyen

2.1 Man Ray, *Aeneas carrying his father*, in *Minotaure*, 1(5) (1934), p. 12 © Man Ray Trust/ADAGP-DACS 2011

2.2 Alberto Giacometti, *Vide-Poche*, plaster, 1930, 17.5 × 19.5 × 29.5, Kunsthaus Zurich, Alberto Giacometti Foundation. Photograph courtesy Kunsthaus Zurich. © ADAGP-DACS 2011

2.3 Paule Vézelay in Paris, c.1934–35 © The estate of Paule Vézelay. Leeds Museums and Galleries (Henry Moore Institute Archive)

2.4 Paule Vézelay, *Garden*, plaster, 1935 © The estate of Paule Vézelay. Leeds Museums and Galleries (Henry Moore Institute Archive)

3.1 Man Ray, *Photogram* (still from the film *Le Retour à la raison*), 1923 © Man Ray Trust/ADAGP-DACS/Telimage-2011

3.2 Fernand Léger, still from *Ballet mécanique* (1924) © ADAGP-DACS 2011. Photograph courtesy BFI, London

4.1 Allan Kaprow, *Yard*, 1961. Courtesy Allan Kaprow Estate and Hauser & Wirth. Photo: Ken Heyman, licensed by Woodfin Camp Associates

4.2 Allan Kaprow, page spread from *Assemblage, Environments and Happenings*, 1966. Courtesy Allan Kaprow Estate and Hauser & Wirth. Photo of Jackson Pollock painting by Hans Namuth, 1950, licensed by Center for Creative Photography; photo of *Yard*, 1961 by Ken Heyman, licensed by Woodfin Camp Associates

4.3 Allan Kaprow, *Yard*, 1991, reinvented for *7 Environments*, Fondazione Mudima, Milan. Courtesy Allan Kaprow Estate. Photo: Jeff Kelley

4.4 Allan Kaprow, *Yard*, 1998, reinvented for *Out of Actions*, Museum of Contemporary Art, Los Angeles. Courtesy Allan Kaprow Estate and Hauser & Wirth. Photo: Alex Slade

5.1 Richard Wentworth, *Kings Cross, London*, colour print made from transparency, 11 × 7 cm, 1978, from the *Making Do, Getting By* series. British Council Collection © Richard Wentworth

5.2 Richard Wentworth, *South West France 2007*, unique colour photograph, 29.6 × 42 cm, 2007, from the *Making Do, Getting By* series. Courtesy the artist and Lisson Gallery. © Richard Wentworth

5.3 Richard Serra, *Prop*, lead antimony, sheet, 152.4 × 152.4 cm, 1968, Walker Art Center, Minneapolis. Gift of Penny and Mike Winton, 1977. © 2011 Richard Serra / Artists Rights Society (ARS), New York

5.4 Richard Wentworth, *London 1994*, unique photographic print, 43.5 × 51 × 6.5 cm, 1999, from the *Making Do, Getting By* series. Courtesy the artist and Lisson Gallery. © Richard Wentworth

6.1 Sol LeWitt, *Incomplete Open Cubes*, gelatin silver prints, and drawings on paper, painted wood structures, 1974, sculptures: 20.3 × 20.3 × 20.3 cm, framed works: 66 × 35.6 cm, base: 30.5 × 304.8 × 548.6 cm. San Francisco Museum of Modern Art, Accessions Committee Fund: gift of Emily L. Carroll and Thomas Weisel, Jean and James E. Douglas, Jr., Susan and Robert Green, Evelyn Haas, Mimi and Peter Haas, Eve and Harvey Masonek, Elaine McKeon, the Modern Art Council, Phyllis and Stuart G. Moldaw, Christine and Michael Murray, Danielle and Brooks Walker Jr., and Phyllis Wattis. Photo: Ben Blackwell © The LeWitt Estate/Artists Rights Society (ARS), New York

6.2 & 6.3 Terry Fox, *The Children's Tapes*, video stills, 1974 © Estate of Terry Fox

6.4 & 6.5 Terry Fox, *The Children's Tapes*, video stills, 1974 © Estate of Terry Fox

7.1 Mike Kelley, *The Poltergeist*, framed photographic prints, 1979. Seven parts: two photographs, 40 × 27.5 inches, 40 × 62.5 inches; text photograph, 40 × 33 inches; four photographs, 40 × 30 inches each. Photo: Roberto Marossi. Courtesy Mike Kelley Studio

7.2 Mike Kelley, *Untitled (Dust Balls) #11*, black and white photograph on museum board, 31 × 22.5 inches, 1994. Edition of 5. Courtesy Mike Kelley Studio

7.3 Mike Kelley, *Niobe's Tear (from The Poetry of Form: Part of an Ongoing Attempt to Develop an Auteur Theory of Naming)*, gelatin silver print, title text on mat, 16 × 12 inches, 1985/1996. Edition of 5. Courtesy Mike Kelley Studio

7.4 Mike Kelley, *The Gateway to Freedom*, black and white photograph, 8 × 10 inches, 1989. Courtesy Mike Kelley Studio

7.5 Mike Kelley, *John Glenn Memorial Detroit River Reclamation Project (Including the Local Culture Pictorial Guide, 1968–1972, Wayne/ Westland Eagle)*, mixed media installation, 137 × 216 × 249 inches, 2001. Photo: Fredrik Nilsen. Courtesy Mike Kelley Studio

7.6 Mike Kelley, *Extracurricular Activity Projective Reconstruction #10 (Group Portrait)*, chromogenic print and black and white Piezo print on rag paper, 73.5 × 37.5 inches, 2004–2005. Edition of 5. Courtesy Mike Kelley Studio

8.1 Installation shot of Melissa McGill's *Inside the White Cube* exhibition, White Cube, London, 6 May – 1 June 2003; *Untitled*, porcelain (foreground), 2002, and *Shadow of Ecstasy* (rear left on wall), 2003. Courtesy the artist

8.2 Man Ray, photographs for André Breton's essay 'Equation of the Found Object', *Documents 34*, 1934

8.3 Melissa McGill and Ellis Michael Quinn, *Untitled*, C-print, 2000. Courtesy the artist

8.4 Melissa McGill, *Untitled*, porcelain, 2000. Courtesy the artist

9.1 Christian Boltanski, *Vitrine de réference*, white painted wood, playdough, ball of dirt, Xerox, black and white photographs, sugar cubes, trap, hand written letter, Gillette razor blade mounted on wood, 120 × 70 × 15 cm, 1972. Courtesy the artist and Marian Goodman Gallery, New York/Paris

9.2 Christian Boltanski, *Monument*, black and white photographs, colour photographs, colour collage and light, 114.9 × 280 × 7 cm, 1986. Courtesy the artist and Marian Goodman Gallery, New York/Paris

9.3 Gabriel Orozco, *Yielding Stone*, plasticine, 35.6 × 43.2 × 43.2 cm, 1992. Courtesy the artist and Marian Goodman Gallery, New York

9.4 Gabriel Orozco, *Extension of Reflection*, chromogenic colour print, 40.6 × 50.8 cm, 1992. Courtesy the artist and Marian Goodman Gallery, New York

Notes on Contributors

Dr Simon Baker is Curator of Photography and International Art at Tate. He completed his PhD at University College, London, on surrealism and revolution, and was the recipient of a Henry Moore Foundation postdoctoral Fellowship and a Gould Research Fellowship at the Department of Art & Archaeology, Princeton University, before lecturing at Nottingham University. He co-curated, with Dawn Ades, the major exhibition *Undercover Surrealism* at the Hayward Gallery, London, in 2006, and the exhibition *Close Up* at the Fruitmarket Gallery, Edinburgh, 2008. His book *Surrealism, History and Revolution* was published by Peter Lang in 2007.

Dr Martha Buskirk is Associate Professor of Art History and Criticism at Montserrat College of Art. She has been the recipient of a 2000–2001 Bunting Fellowship at the Radcliffe Institute for Advanced Study and a 2004 Clark fellowship. She is the co-editor of *The Duchamp Effect* and *The Destruction of Tilted Arc: Documents* (both MIT Press), and her articles and reviews have appeared in many publications, including *Art in America* and *October*. *The Contingent Object of Contemporary Art* was published by MIT Press in 2003, and her book *Creative Enterprises: Contemporary Art between Museum and Marketplace* came out with Continuum in 2012.

Dr Anna Dezeuze is Lecturer in Art History at the École Supérieure d'Art et de Design, Marseille-Méditerranée. She obtained her PhD from the Courtauld Institute of Art, London, in 2003, and held a number of postdoctoral research fellowships at the University of Manchester, as well as the Smithsonian American Art Museum in Washington, D.C. She has published essays on Fluxus, on Bruce Nauman, on the Brazilian artist Hélio Oiticica, on spectator participation in kinetic art and on Neo-dada and assemblage. She also writes for the art magazines *Art Monthly* and *Mute,* and co-curated with David Lomas the 2009 travelling exhibition *Subversive Spaces: Surrealism and Contemporary Art*. Her edited book on *The 'Do-it-yourself' Artwork: Participation from Fluxus to New Media* was published by Manchester University Press in 2010.

Dr Steven Harris is Associate Professor at the University of Alberta. He completed a PhD on the surrealist object at the University of British Columbia, and held a Postdoctoral Fellowship at the University of Essex. His *Surrealist Art and Thought in the 1930s* was published by Cambridge University Press in 2004. His current research project concerns 'The Poetics of Disenchantment: The European Avant-Garde at Mid-Century'.

Professor Margaret Iversen is Professor in Art History and Theory at the University of Essex. Her book *Beyond Pleasure: Freud, Lacan, Barthes* was published by Penn University Press in 2007. She has written about Aloïs Riegl (1993), Mary Kelly (Phaidon, 1997), Edward Hopper (Tate, 2004) and the relations between art history and aesthetics (with Stephen Melville, Chicago University Press, 2010). She has edited a book about chance (MIT Press/Whitechapel, 2010). She also writes about photography and was the director of the AHRC Research Project on *Aesthetics after Photography*, 2007–2010.

Dr Julia Kelly is a Researcher at the University of Hull. She was part of the AHRC Research Centre for the Study of Surrealism and its Legacies at the University of Manchester, and she has published on surrealist art writing and modern sculpture, including essays on Joseph Cornell, Henry Moore's surrealist sculpture and the Bureau of Surrealist Research. Her book *Art, Ethnography and the Life of Objects, Paris c.1925–35* was published in 2007 by Manchester University Press. She guest-edited, with Anna Dezeuze and Jo Applin, the Spring 2008 issue of the *Art Journal* on the theme of 'assemblage/bricolage'. She was co-editor of the volume *Alberto Giacometti: Critical Essays* with Peter Read (2009). She is currently co-authoring, with Jon Wood, a monograph on Bill Woodrow, and co-editing *The Studio in the Gallery*, forthcoming with Ashgate.

Dr Samantha Lackey is Curator at The Hepworth Wakefield Gallery, Yorkshire. She previously held the posts of Assistant Curator and Curatorial Research Fellow at The Whitworth Art Gallery, The University of Manchester where she worked on the exhibition *Subversive Spaces: Surrealism and Contemporary Art*. Previous to this appointment she was Senior Research Fellow for the AHRC Research Centre for Studies of Surrealism and its Legacies, a partnership between the universities of Manchester and Essex and Tate. Her research interests include the relationship between surrealism and contemporary art and current art practice utilising the moving image.

Dr Carrie Lambert-Beatty is Assistant Professor of Visual and Environmental Studies at Harvard University. Her writing on performance art, postmodern dance, and minimalism has been published in journals such as *Trans*, *October*, and *Art Journal*, and in the catalogues for the exhibitions *A Minimal Future? Art as Object 1958–68* (MIT Press, 2004) and *Radical Juxtapositions: Yvonne Rainer 1961–2002* (Rosenwald-Wolf Gallery, University of The Arts, Philadelphia, 2003). Her book *Being Watched: Yvonne Rainer and the 1960s* was published by MIT Press in 2008, and part of a new project on intersections of art and activism was published in *Signs: Journal of Women in Culture and Society* in the Winter 2008 issue.

Professor John C. Welchman is Professor of Art History, Theory and Criticism in the Visual Arts department at the University of California, San Diego. His books on art include *Modernism Relocated: Towards a Cultural Studies of Visual Modernity* (1995), *Invisible Colours: A Visual History of Titles* (1997) and *Art after Appropriation: Essays on Art in the 1990s* (2001); he is co-author of *The Dada and Surrealist Word Image* (1989) and of *Mike Kelley* (1999); and editor of *Rethinking Borders* (1996), *Institutional Critique and After* (2006), *The Aesthetics of Risk* (2008); and *Black Sphinx: On the Comedic in Modern Art* (2010). *XX to XXI: Essays on European Art* is forthcoming with Akal, Madrid, in Spanish, and as a related volume in German with Philo, Hamburg. He is the editor of the volume *Sculpture and the Vitrine*, to be published by Ashgate in 2013.

Acknowledgements

The one-day symposium that was the starting point for this volume, *Involuntary Sculpture*, held at the Henry Moore Institute in November 2004, was a collaboration between the Henry Moore Institute and the AHRC Research Centre for the Study of Surrealism and its Legacies. We would like to thank former and current staff at the Henry Moore Institute for their kind support for this project and the ensuing publication: Jon Wood, Martina Droth, Penelope Curtis, Ellen Tait, Claire Sawyer, Jackie Howson, Ann Sproat and Kirstie Gregory. We would also like to thank the directors of the AHRC Research Centre for the Study of Surrealism and its Legacies: Dawn Ades, David Lomas and Jennifer Mundy.

The Henry Moore Foundation very generously awarded us a subvention towards the image costs for this book, and we would like to thank them for this. On behalf of our authors, we would also like to thank the artists and copyright holders who kindly agreed to waive their copyright fees.

This publication has long been in preparation, and our most heartfelt thanks go to our authors for their patience, hard work, and commitment to this project over the last years and months.

Introduction
Involuntary Sculpture: Process, Photography and the Ephemeral Object

Anna Dezeuze and Julia Kelly

Involuntary Sculpture

At first consideration, sculpture might be thought of as the most willed of artistic media. Requiring serious physical commitment, sculptural activity is marked traditionally by labour-intensive processes like hewing, hacking, welding and casting, both on an individual and an industrial scale. The mythology of direct carving certainly carries associations of hard physical graft, clearly linked to personal volition, the sculptor locked in a 'heroic' struggle with stone, wood or marble. The fact that sculpture is seen to engage directly with the material world reinforces this, making it an activity devoted to 'taming' the obdurate stuff around us, shaping and bending it according to our will.

This anthology, however, presents a very different vision of sculptural processes. What happens when sculpture ceases to be quite so controlled, when it lets itself be dictated by principles of chance, determined by its environment or by the circumstances of its reception and documentation? For the brute activities listed above we could substitute a different set of much less 'voluntary' ones: fingering, fiddling, propping and shuffling, to which should be added the instantaneous snapping of the camera lens. Where sculpture is 'found' and not 'made', or indeed exists somewhere between the two, it can also become less material and more obviously contingent – a form of a thing, or a formation of things, captured at a specific time. If 'voluntary' sculpture suggests the production of a deliberate material configuration, set forever in hard matter, 'involuntary' sculpture points to its own transience or its role as part of an ongoing process, where it exists beyond a serendipitous photographic image.

This volume takes its cue from a selection of photographs by Brassaï with captions by Salvador Dalí published in the surrealist periodical *Minotaure* in 1933 and bearing the title 'Involuntary Sculptures' (Figure I.1). Scraps of everyday debris – including rolled-up bus tickets, a piece of bread roll, a curl of soap from a sink and a blob of toothpaste – featured in photographic close-up as 'automatic' sculptural configurations. These banal and non-artistic objects (one of the tickets was allegedly found screwed up in the pocket of a bank employee) were intended at least in part as a riposte to the prevailing perception of sculpture at the time, represented in the same journal by another selection of photographs by Brassaï

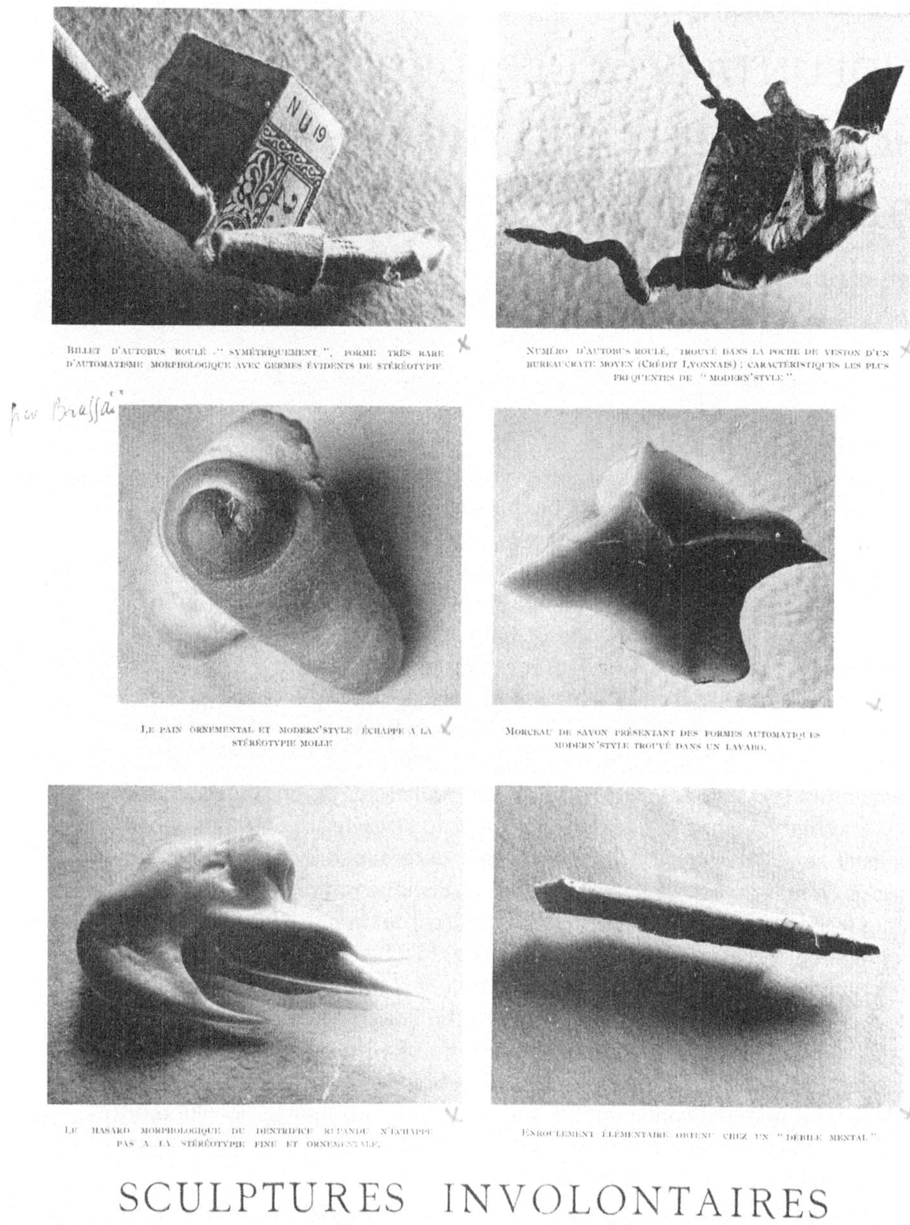

Billet d'autobus roulé " symétriquement ", forme très rare d'automatisme morphologique avec germes évidents de stéréotypie.

Numéro d'autobus roulé, trouvé dans la poche de veston d'un bureaucrate moyen (Crédit Lyonnais) ; caractéristiques les plus fréquentes de " modern'style ".

par Brassaï

Le pain ornemental et modern'style échappe à la stéréotypie molle

Morceau de savon présentant des formes automatiques modern'style trouvé dans un lavabo.

Le hasard morphologique du dentrifice répandu n'échappe pas à la stéréotypie fine et ornementale.

Enroulement élémentaire obtenu chez un " débile mental ".

SCULPTURES INVOLONTAIRES

I.1 Brassaï (pseud.) Gyula Halász, *Sculptures involontaires*, page from the journal *Minotaure*, nos. 3–4, 1933 © Estate Brassaï-RMN
Photograph © RMN/Jean-Gilles Berizzi. Private collection

of the studios of Aristide Maillol, Charles Despiau, Alberto Giacometti, Jacques Lipchitz and Henri Laurens, as Steven Harris's essay in this volume makes clear. There was no agreed definition of 'surrealist' sculpture, however: indeed, such a thing could be argued to be impossible in itself, while surrealist interests in three-dimensional production became much more closely oriented towards the complex category of the surrealist object.

Brassaï and Dalí's photo-essay provides a tantalising evocation of sculptural possibility, where forms are both shaped by human hands, sometimes with little conscious thought (the rolled bus ticket), and subject to 'organic' growth (the piece of bread rising and changing shape in the oven). It also freezes its array of objects at a given moment, before they are discarded, swept or wiped away, dissolved or eaten. Nevertheless, their photographic capturing does give them a certain solid presence, particularly through Brassaï's characteristic use of dramatic chiaroscuro. In this sense their effect is unlike that of another surrealist image on a related theme, Man Ray's photograph *Moving Sculpture* for *La Révolution surréaliste* in 1926, a film-still-like scene of pale-coloured washing fluttering on the breeze. The title of Man Ray's photograph, originally taken in 1920, suggests that this is a record of a particular phenomenon: the drying laundry as kinetic sculpture, its soft fabric billowing and bulging. In both images, though, the parameters of 'sculpture' are challenged and expanded, while photography fulfils simultaneous (and potentially contradictory) functions of auratic reproduction and quasi-scientific documentation. In her essay in this volume, Samantha Lackey argues that the film from which this image of washing was drawn, *Le Retour à la raison*, was a crucial example of a specific mode of cinematic distraction, where the constant progression of moving object-tableaux and fragmented scenes served to disrupt rather than focus the spectator's attention.

Rather than looking to avoid or resolve them, this volume seeks out the contradictions and pressure points inherent in the concept of 'involuntary sculpture', and in the relations between sculpture and photography that often accompany it. It is here, we argue, that modern and contemporary sculpture can be of continued and renewed interest, by operating against the grain of established categories and conventions.

Sculpture and Photography

Sculpture's relationship to photography has become a focus of scholarly interest since the late 1990s.[1] The two media at first seem to have little in common, one dealing with three-dimensional presence, the other with two-dimensional image. While the interrelation between painting and photography tended to be antagonistic in the late nineteenth and early twentieth centuries, as each competed with and fed off the advantages of the other, sculpture seemed to provide, however, particularly successful subject matter for photography from its emergence in the late 1830s. Like the still life, a sculpture did not move and thus lent itself well to long exposure, as exemplified in images of antique statuary and busts by Hippolyte Bayard and William Henry Fox Talbot in the 1840s. Such images carried further symbolic resonances: sculpture's traditional associations with death and the deathly found a parallel in the immortalising processes of the photograph, a central concern in photographic theory from the writings of Walter Benjamin to those of Roland Barthes.

Sculpture also, especially in the case of antique copies and casts in white plaster, stone and marble, had exceptional photogenic qualities, setting up striking contrasts of light and shade as well as nuances of texture. In this sense, both media share a manipulation of effects of light, as well as a concern, potentially, with framing and apprehending an object from specific points of view. Through photographic representation, sculptures can take on another life, eternalised as images in their own right in what André Malraux would call the 'museum without walls'. The ways in which Auguste Rodin's sculpture was photographed by Eugène Druet, Edward Steichen and others around the 1900s set a particular precedent for this, while the play of light on polished surfaces and the use of photography to explore interrelationships between sculptural pieces is associated above all with the experimental photographic practice of Constantin Brancusi, as several scholars have pointed out.[2] The work of these two sculptors and its photographic representation can be said to have established certain paradigms in the relationship between sculpture and photography, extending beyond the concerns of materiality, light and volume to those of sculptural installation and the conceptualisation of the *work* of the sculptor him- or herself.

In the interplay of sculpture and photography, the physical practices normally associated with making sculpture and the 'mechanical' processes of the photograph clash and challenge one another. This volume treats such tensions as generative, as ways of complicating historical distinctions and categories. Thomas McEvilley, in his analysis of the growing prominence of sculptural tendencies in art from the 1960s onwards, characterises what he sees as sculpture's 'ethical' superiority as follows: 'Painting means escapist fantasy; sculpture means direct dealing with the material world.'[3] This volume, however, seeks to complicate such oppositions, taking its starting point from surrealism (perhaps the modern movement most readily associated with 'escapist fantasy'), but also exploring the multiple roles of photography as both artwork in its own right and documentation, as object and image, as material evidence and the dematerialising frame for the absent, the lost, the imagined.

Surrealist Object, Surrealist Photography

Surrealist practice in three dimensions is most commonly understood in terms of the surrealist object, whose radical hybridity and innovative engagement with everyday commodities have made it a seminal precursor for contemporary three-dimensional practices as well as installation art. The surrealist objects that have attracted the most attention are those which manifest a fetishistic concern with the body or a confusion of animate and inanimate elements, such as Meret Oppenheim's famous *Fur-covered Cup, Saucer and Spoon*, or Dalí's *Lobster Telephone*. Accordingly, the legacy of surrealism in later twentieth- and twenty-first-century art has been seen predominantly in terms of expressions of visceral eroticism and 'uncanny' physicality, in the work of Louise Bourgeois, Robert Gober, Cathy de Monchaux and Sarah Lucas, amongst others. However, this emphasis has obscured the more subtle ramifications of surrealism's concerns with objects and sculpture. The surrealist object itself presents a tension between chance encounters with and of unfamiliar things on the one hand, and the artist's processes of intervention and control on the other. In fact, there are many types of surrealist objects, including natural objects, the Duchampian readymade, as well as found objects known through photographs (in André Breton's 1928 novel *Nadja* for example), and collaborative, ephemeral constructions. While both Simon Baker and Margaret Iversen return to Breton's use of photographs in this volume, ephemeral constructions are central to Anna Dezeuze's and Martha Buskirk's essays, and an interest in natural geological configurations appears to link practices as different as Giacometti's (discussed by Julia Kelly) and Mike Kelley's (the focus of John Welchman's essay). In the proofs for the project, Brassaï actually refers to the *Involuntary Sculptures* as 'automatic objects', blurring the distinctions between found object and photography, while referring to the surrealist practice of automatic writing as a means to channel unconscious thoughts. As a repository for unconscious psychic urges, the surrealist object as a whole sets in motion an interplay between artist and creator, and between object and viewer, whose encapsulation within a discrete physical thing can only be ambivalent.

The crucial role of photography in surrealism has been increasingly acknowledged and studied, starting with Rosalind Krauss's 1981 essay, in which the *Involuntary Sculptures* are discussed as typical of the surrealists' use of the camera as a privileged means of accessing the 'surreality' of the world, that is, its nature as representation to be probed in search of the marvellous. 'As it signals that experience of reality the camera frame also controls it, configures it', explains Krauss: in the *Involuntary Sculptures*, it is the close-up that extends the capacity of the eye and brings into being these hitherto invisible 'sculptures'.[4] Dalí himself had pointed out as early as 1929 that 'the mere fact of photographic transposition [of the world around us] already implies a total invention: the registering of an UNKNOWN REALITY'.[5] As Dawn Ades and Simon Baker have suggested, the very practice of the photographic close-up embodies the historical ambivalence of photography between scientific objectivity and defamiliarisation or disorientation. While the glass shelf used by Brassaï to photograph the *Involuntary Sculptures* recalls the glass slides used in the microscopic preparations that were the subject of early scientific photography,[6] the enlargement of such small objects robs them of their recognisability, triggering powerful 'alienating effects'.[7] The new modes of attention required by the cinematic close-up are extensively discussed in this book by Samantha Lackey, while Carrie Lambert-Beatty refers to their performance of a child-like view of the world.

For Margaret Iversen and Simon Baker, writing in this volume, the interaction between the found object and the surrealist photograph is crucial. Where Baker sees the photograph as participating actively in the introduction of the found object into a 'perceptual regime' that will guarantee its significance as a meaningful find for viewers to come, Iversen goes one step further and directly compares the operation of the found object to that of photography itself. The 'involuntary' nature of photography, she argues, exists at the moment in which a detail in the most banal photograph – what Barthes has called the 'punctum' – can unexpectedly reach out directly to the viewer's unconscious, just as an object can be found to answer its finder's most intimate desires and fears. In theories of photography, this 'involuntary' account counters the simulacral model of the photograph as a blank, free-floating, empty signifier. In artistic practices, Iversen demonstrates how Christian Boltanski and Gabriel Orozco bring together the found object and the photograph in order to complicate the relations between reality and simulation. In this way, Iversen is returning us to what Robin Kelsey and Blake Stimson have described as the original 'dream of photography' – a desire to reconcile the extremes of a 'seemingly unconditional transcriptive fidelity' and 'seemingly unconditional inner revelation'.[8]

Process and 'Dematerialisation'

Elusive desires and intimations of death are captured in the web of relations between surrealist objects, photography and autobiographical narratives. Along with other surrealist techniques such as automatic writing or the practice of the exquisite corpse, this type of process is what constitutes, according to Simon Baker, one of the most important legacies of surrealism in contemporary art. If Baker refers to the specific contemporary practice of Melissa McGill, in which the creation of physical sculptures is mediated through photography, the notion of process became a particularly significant characteristic of sculpture and conceptual art in the 1960s and 1970s. In fact, the 'process art' of Richard Serra involves, as Anna Dezeuze points out, the very gestures of tearing, spilling or rolling involved in the creation of the *Involuntary Sculptures*. Other, more everyday processes were evoked in Terry Fox's *Children's Tapes* (discussed by Carrie Lambert-Beatty in this volume), in which the artist recorded simple physics experiments using humble household objects in his kitchen.

Other conceptual artists interested in process turned to spaces outside the studio and the gallery in their desire to engage with natural landscapes or the urban everyday. In all these forms, photography and video became essential tools for documenting process, whether ephemeral constructions in the studio or site-specific interventions in the landscape. Douglas Fogle has celebrated the *Involuntary Sculptures* as forerunners of conceptual photography, which is used as a means to an end rather than an end in itself, thus evading the two dominant categories in the history of photography: 'photographic Pictorialism' and documentary photography.[9] An 'extraphotographic impulse' which disrupts modernist notions of photography does indeed characterise a certain type of surrealist photography as well as conceptual practices such as Terry Fox's or Mike Kelley's, along with those of Robert Smithson and Dan Graham. As Dezeuze suggests, Richard Wentworth's series of photographs *Making Do, Getting By*, started in the 1970s, is indebted to this kind of understanding of conceptual photography as a tool to document other overarching concerns – in his case, the 'sculptures' that we spontaneously create in everyday situations.

The emphasis on process naturally led artists away from the production of objects and sculptures and towards a combination of photographic and textual documentation which Lucy Lippard described as a 'dematerialisation of the art object' in 1968. 'Dematerialised' practices involved a general 'de-emphasis' of the 'material aspects' traditionally associated with artworks, including 'uniqueness, permanence, decorative attractiveness'.[10] The *Involuntary Sculptures* bring together two forms of 'dematerialisation': the emphasis on the ephemeral, and the use of photography as a record of these impermanent objects. In this sense, they also relate to a variety of 'dematerialising' practices at different historical moments. As Martha Buskirk's essay shows, 'proto-conceptual' artists such as Allan Kaprow developed photography alongside ephemeral environments using junk materials. Though aware of their intrinsic connection, Kaprow never privileged photography over the material creation of the environments, unlike the conceptual artists who would follow him. Kaprow's work embodies a transitional moment before photography established itself as the language of dematerialisation. Some 20 years later, Mike Kelley returned to Kaprow's suspicion of the documentary function of performance photographs, but set out to explore the very relations between reality and fantasy through the use of found and accidental photographs, sometimes in parallel, and sometimes in dialogue, with his performance and installation practice. Kaprow's and Kelley's practices thus appear to bracket a seminal moment of conceptual photography in the 1960s and 1970s, in which the model was the figure of the amateur photographer, and the medium was considered to be untainted, so to speak, by the history of art, thus facilitating a more direct access to reality.

This turn to new fields of everyday life was not so much a dematerialisation, as an 'expansion or diminution of art as a solid structure', as Lawrence Alloway suggested in 1969, as the 'interface' between art and other fields became 'blurred'.[11] Whether interpreted in an 'expansionist' or a 'reductivist' model, to use Alloway's words, this shift served to radically challenge the fetishisation of the art object – after all, as William Pietz has explained, the fetish is premised on a 'irreducible, untranscended materiality'.[12] Rather than negating materiality in itself, then, the cross-overs between process art and conceptual photography discussed in this volume recast the materiality of both the fetish and object-based sculpture, traditionally defined as stable, if not monumental. In this sense, the precarious balancing acts involved in Fox's *Children's Tapes*, in Wentworth's *Making Do, Getting By* series (Figures 5.1 and 5.2) or in Orozco's more recent ephemeral arrangements, all serve to dramatise a materiality that is both literally and ontologically contingent.

Re-Reading the History of Sculpture

Where Douglas Fogle's study of photoconceptualism outlined a new trajectory of conceptual art within the medium of photography, Helen Molesworth's 2005 exhibition, *Part Object Part Sculpture*, sought to retrieve a 'space of fantasy and desire' within the production of sculpture and painting from the 1950s to the present, through erotic logics of repetition and displacement.[13] The present book can be situated in an intermediate space between these two projects. We certainly share with Molesworth a desire to displace the dominance of minimalism in 'accounts of the scope and aim of late twentieth-century sculpture', and its attendant privileging of both Duchamp's readymades as foundational models and the emphasis on a 'logic of industrial production' (prevalent in minimalism and pop art). While we also believe that reflection on bodily gestures and unconscious desires can fruitfully be brought forward to counter these pervasive narratives, the kind of works discussed in the present book do not evoke seductive or repulsive body parts, sexual organs or skin in the same direct way as the sculptural works of Louise Bourgeois, Eva Hesse, Yayoi Kusama, Lynda Benglis or Alberto Burri. Tactility does figure prominently in Julia Kelly's essay, for example, but it is mediated by forms evoking archaic implements or imaginary inventions as much as bodily shapes. The *Involuntary Sculptures* may share the ghostly presence of absent bodies with Rachel Whiteread's casts, but they are much less physical and 'resistant to words' (as Molesworth would put it): the mediation of Brassaï's photography has the effect, as we have suggested, of introducing other types of polarity between matter and the immaterial, between singular ephemeral event and banal repetition, between form and formlessness.[14] That Gabriel Orozco's practice figures as a paradigmatic project in both this book and Molesworth's show suggests how the two fields can be combined productively. Inspired by Orozco's 'work tables' scattered with objects, Briony Fer's discussion of 'sculpture as leftover' in *Part Object Part Sculpture* could usefully be brought to bear on the *Involuntary Sculptures* themselves.[15] Particularly suggestive is Fer's analysis of leftovers as 'part objects in time rather than space', thus highlighting a fractured, discontinuous time. Her opposition between the 'economy of leftovers' and the 'economy of collecting', in the sense that the latter is a means of controlling a kind of 'dispersion' that the former encourages, is also very fruitful.[16]

In *Part Object Part Sculpture*, it is Duchamp's 1950s cast objects that provide an alternative trajectory to his mass-produced readymades; in Fogle's *The Last Picture Show* the main reference is *Dust Breeding*, the photograph taken by Man Ray of the dust gathered on Duchamp's *Large Glass*, a 'hybrid object caught somewhere between the realms of photography and sculpture'.[17] This book explores the field of the surrealist object as it emerges at the intersection of these different approaches to matter and process. Perhaps the connecting link within the Duchampian field is the '*infra-mince*' – this notion, developed by Duchamp in his notes, seems to oscillate itself between matter and immaterial, bodily presence and absence. The *infra-mince* can be found in the difference between two casts from the same mould as much as in the 'heat of a seat (that has just been left)'; the folds in a pair of trousers are, according to Duchamp, 'a sculptural expression of the person who has worn them', in much the same way, we may add, as the curled bus ticket found in his or her pocket … .[18] The more political dimensions of such *infra-mince* phenomena become clearer if we follow Benjamin Buchloh's suggestion that the 'desire to demarcate one's somatic existence in space' animating the *Involuntary Sculptures* can be linked (in Orozco's work for example) to an exploration of 'the collective dormant symbolic resistance against the total reification, if not the extinction, of subject/object relationships'.[19]

Agency and Memory

Subject/object relations certainly lie at the heart of this volume, in which André Breton's concern with the 'objectification of the subjective' runs like a thread. The *Involuntary Sculptures* 'inhabit a space at once real and phantasmatic', concludes Iversen; they 'act as attentional bridges between the everyday and the fantasmatic' according to Lambert-Beatty. As the aura of objects is challenged – through an appeal to touch, as Harris and Kelly demonstrate, and through the mediation of photography, as Iversen and Baker suggest – the very definition of subjectivity is questioned.

In a late essay, Brassaï would argue that the photograph developed in the darkroom acted as a metaphor for Marcel Proust's well-known accounts of 'involuntary memory', a latent remembrance suddenly triggered by an everyday object or experience, such as the taste of a *madeleine* dipped in tea. In that kind of moment, past and present locations are telescoped, and, according to Proust, 'our whole person ... totters between them ... in the vertigo of an uncertainty like the kind we sometimes experience before an ineffable vision, at the moment of falling asleep'[20] – a state of *demi-sommeil* that Samantha Lackey relates to experimental film techniques in this volume. This vertigo can be heightened not only by alternating states of attention and distraction in film, but also by the very slippery relation between photography and reality in which, as Buskirk and Iversen point out, the photograph can shape, and even corrupt, our very memory of an ephemeral object.

Memory involves collective as well as individual forms of agency. Dezeuze relates it to biological instincts and everyday practices, while Kelly and Harris invoke archaic encounters with nature. Welchman focuses on the vast collective unconscious that Mike Kelley mines through his explorations of American popular culture. In this sense, the 'involuntary' is identified with the 'anonymous' or the 'impersonal', as Paul Eluard would in his 1942 book of *Poésie involontaire et poésie intentionnelle*, a collection that includes, alongside extracts from writers such as Francis Ponge or Raymond Queneau, a selection of children's tales and questions, as well as found items including names of flowers, a description from a magician's catalogue, and a bizarre news item.[21] Just as Eluard sought to demonstrate that poetry has never been the property of poets alone, the *Involuntary Sculptures* raise crucial issues of authorship and agency, and the broader question of how exactly such individual and collective unconscious desires can be embodied in objects and photographs. Whether approaching them through anthropology or psychoanalysis, through educational theories or studies of everyday life, the essays in this book probe these complex questions. Rather than providing a final and unified answer, what we hope to demonstrate is that the ramifications of the *Involuntary Sculptures* can extend from the beginnings of sculpture to contemporary practices, and into fields outside the history of art itself – a true testimony to the lasting impact of surrealism.

Notes

1 Instances of this include Michel Frizot and Dominique Païni (eds), *Sculpter Photographier/Photographie Sculpture* (Paris, 1993), Erika Billeter (ed.), *Skulptur im Licht der Fotografie* (Duisburg, 1997) and Geraldine Johnson (ed.), *Sculpture and Photography: Envisioning the Third Dimension* (Cambridge, 1998).

2 See for example Hélène Pinet, 'La Sculpture, la photographie et le critique', Jacques Leenhardt, 'Au-delà de la matière: Brancusi et la photographie', and Elizabeth A. Brown, 'L'atelier métaphorique', in Frizot and Païni (eds), *Sculpter Photographier*, pp. 85–91, pp. 33–9 and pp. 41–55; Paul Paret, 'Sculpture and its Negative: The Photographs of Constantin Brancusi', and Hélène Pinet, '*Montrer est la question vitale*: Rodin and Photography', in Johnson (ed.), *Sculpture and Photography*, pp. 101–30 and 68–85.

3 Thomas McEvilley, *Sculpture in the Age of Doubt* (New York, 1999), p. 42.

4 Rosalind Krauss, 'The Photographic Conditions of Surrealism', *October* 19 (Winter 1981), p. 31.

5 Salvador Dalí, 'Photographic Data' [1929], quoted by Simon Baker in 'Watch Out for Life: The Conceptual Close-Up, 1920–2006', in Dawn Ades and Simon Baker, *Close-Up: Proximity and Defamiliarisation in Art, Film and Photography* (Edinburgh, 2008), p. 78.

6 Dawn Ades, 'Little Things: Close-up in Photo and Film, 1839–1963', in Ades and Baker, *Close-Up*, p. 48.

7 Baker, 'Watch Out for Life', in Ades and Baker, *Close-Up*, p. 95.

8 Robin Kelsey and Blake Stimson, 'Photography's Double Index (A Short History in Three Parts)', in Kelsey and Stimson (eds), *The Meaning of Photography* (Willliamstown, MA and New Haven, 2008), p. xvii.

9 Douglas Fogle (ed.), *The Last Picture Show: Artists Using Photography, 1960–82* (Minneapolis, 2003).

10 Lucy Lippard, 'Preface', in *Six Years: The Dematerialization of the Art Object from 1966 to 1972* (London, 1973), p. 5.

11 Lawrence Alloway, 'The Expanding and Disappearing Work of Art', *Auction*, III/2 (October 1969), reprinted in Alloway, *Topics in American Art since 1945* (New York, 1975), p. 207.

12 William Pietz, 'The Problem of the Fetish, Part I', *Res*, 9 (Spring 1985), p. 6.

13 Helen Molesworth, 'Introduction: Part Object, Part Sculpture', in H. Molesworth (ed.), *Part Object Part Sculpture* (Columbus, OH, 2005), p. 25.

14 Ibid., p. 25.

15 Briony Fer, 'The Scatter: Sculpture as Leftover', in Molesworth (ed.), *Part Object Part Sculpture*, pp. 222–33.

16 Ibid., p. 231.

17 Fogle, 'The Last Picture Show', in *The Last Picture Show*, p. 10.

18 Marcel Duchamp, *Notes* (Paris, 1999), pp. 21, 34 (our translation).

19 Benjamin Buchloh, 'Gabriel Orozco: Sculpture as Recollection', in Yve-Alain Bois (et al.), *Gabriel Orozco* (London, 2006), p. 178.

20 Brassaï, *Proust in the Power of Photography* [1997], trans. R. Howard (Chicago, 2001), p. 137.

21 Paul Eluard, *Poésie involontaire et poésie intentionnelle* (Paris, 1942).

1

Voluntary and Involuntary Sculpture

Steven Harris

The *Involuntary Sculptures* which appeared anonymously in *Minotaure* nos. 3–4 in December 1933 (Figure I.1) can be seen as instances or symptoms of conflict on numerous levels: within the editorial committee of *Minotaure* over the direction of the review; within the surrealist group over the definition of automatism, and thus of surrealism itself; and within contemporary art over the direction that sculpture would take, as sculpture became an increasingly important category for the surrealist group in the 1930s. Rather than assimilate the *Involuntary Sculptures* to modernist primitivism, as Katharine Conley has done in a 2003 essay, I would like to discuss them in the light of surrealism's own critical relation to modern art, which I think is necessary if we are to find our way towards an understanding of surrealist sculpture.[1] This essay will focus initially, then, on the intervention of the *Involuntary Sculptures* into the economy of *Minotaure* nos. 3–4, then on some ideas of what sculpture might have represented for surrealism in the 1930s, with particular attention to Hans Arp's ideas about sculpture following his decision to begin modelling in plaster in 1930.[2]

The issue of *Minotaure* in which the *Involuntary Sculptures* appeared, like all but one of the issues up to director E. Tériade's departure in 1937, is an unstable compound of modernist and surrealist interests and investments, which intersect and collide in rather interesting ways. The alliance struck in 1933 between Tériade and the surrealists, his fellow critic Maurice Raynal, and the review's publisher Albert Skira occurs at a time when a more sustained political engagement on the part of the surrealists was temporarily foreclosed with their expulsion or resignation from the Association des Ecrivains et Artistes Révolutionnaires (AEAR).[3] Collaboration on the magazine is conceived by both parties as an alliance of the 'modern spirit', a '*unity of differences*', as the editorial note that opens *Minotaure* nos. 3–4 puts it:

> Each collective publication published under the title MINOTAURE is justified in our eyes insofar as we attain through it the determination, from an intellectual point of view, of an undeniable nerve centre, and as we attempt to make of this centre an equilibrium, that is to say a *unity of differences* in order to give to a thought always in formation its new and true shape.[4]

In this statement, moreover, both art and thought (including scientific thought) are conceptualised as forms of experimental research which are both preserved and advanced; such are the stakes of the unity of differences upon which the review is premised, presumably for both parties.

Contemporary art, in the form of a deluxe tribune like *Minotaure* (and to a lesser extent *Cahiers d'art*, with which the surrealists collaborated in 1935–36), has become the site for the advancement of experimental knowledge so far as the surrealists are concerned, now that the possibilities for political action in alliance with the revolutionary avant-garde of the French Communist Party have been blocked. There is an alliance forged and a compromise made with that part of bourgeois culture that supports new forms of art and thought; this is rather different from the maintenance of an independent position antithetical to bourgeois culture, such as was represented by the review that *Minotaure* in some senses succeeded, *Le Surréalisme au service de la révolution* (whose final two issues were published simultaneously just two weeks before the double appearance of the first two issues of *Minotaure*). While financial difficulties contributed to the end of the surrealists' own journal, and while they decided after some hesitation to take up the opportunity offered them by Skira, this decision was undoubtedly made in the light of their exclusion from the leading organisation for revolutionary artists and intellectuals of the day, the AEAR.[5] At the same time, their participation in *Minotaure* was premised on the expanded conception of 'the modern movement' offered by *Minotaure*'s directors, Skira and Tériade; it would never simply be an art review of the kind represented by *L'Amour de l'art*, *L'Art vivant* or even *Cahiers d'art*, but would always be, and in fact was, something rather more complex.

If the ideal to be attained by the review was an equilibrium, however, the alliance of modernist critics and surrealists resulted in a heterogeneous publication that was not necessarily the product of a mutual respect for one another's point of view, but rather of an intense internal conflict.[6] The *Involuntary Sculptures*, for instance, which were one of five contributions made by Salvador Dalí to this issue of *Minotaure*, were thought of and argued for by Paul Eluard, one of the surrealist editors of *Minotaure*, as necessary antitheses to 'Dieu-table-cuvette', the essay contributed by Maurice Raynal (and illustrated, significantly, by Brassaï's photographs) on the sculpture studios of Constantin Brancusi, Charles Despiau, Alberto Giacometti, Henri Laurens, Jacques Lipchitz and Aristide Maillol.[7] Brassaï is named as photographer in this instance in the table of contents, as he is not for the photographs of the *Involuntary Sculptures*, though we know from Brassaï's contact sheets and from anecdotal evidence that he made these photographs too, just as we know that Salvador Dalí was responsible for their captions.[8] However, neither artist is named in association with them; rather, the *Involuntary Sculptures* are attributed to 'XXX', as if they are anonymous, of unconscious or popular origin (or perhaps both), and in my view this is a key to their significance.[9]

In a letter of September 1933 to his former wife Gala Eluard, now living with Dalí, and to Dalí himself, Paul Eluard complains about the difficulty he has had in having the *Involuntary Sculptures* accepted by the other editors of *Minotaure*; he writes, after noting several of the other compromises necessary in a publication of this nature:

> Reproductions of sculptors' studios (Laurens, Maillol, Brancusi, Giacometti). Which is not serious if we manage to push through the involuntary sculptures, a page of 4. I am just about the only one to defend these involuntary sculptures *tooth and nail*. Support me, insist. Breton is lukewarm, doesn't find that they can be attractively reproduced. It's a great shame that the photographs are bad, because I know how difficult it will be for me to have them redone. In general, I have to admit that Brassaï does not show much enthusiasm for anything that is not his photography, his own work. Couldn't Dali do a few new sculptures in Barcelona and have them well photographed himself, either by Man Ray or by a photographer. It's *essential* in order to fight the nuisance of the other sculptures.[10]

This passage raises several interesting points apart from the one I am emphasising: for instance, Breton's lukewarm attitude towards the *Involuntary Sculptures*, or the general dislike of the photographs Brassaï made of them, despite the praise and fascination they have elicited in more recent times (including at the 2004 *Involuntary Sculpture* symposium in Leeds, at which an earlier version of this essay was presented). There is nothing, by the way, to indicate that Brassaï retook these photographs, and two of those found on the contact sheets in Alain Sayag and Annick Lionel-Marie's 2000 monograph were published in *Minotaure*.[11] Yet Eluard's comments also serve to resituate Brassaï's role here as hired photographer rather than as artist or collaborator, the role he also played in photographing sculptors' studios for Raynal.[12]

If Eluard writes that the *Involuntary Sculptures* are '*essential* in order to fight the nuisance of the other sculptures', and asks that Dalí insist on their presence in the issue, it is because they are a necessary part of this issue's economy so far as Eluard is concerned, in their antithetical relation to the voluntary sculpture on display in the photographs that accompany Raynal's essay. Thus two different conceptions of the possibilities for contemporary sculpture are revealed here, the second of which follows and implicitly negates the first.[13] Rather than including surrealism among the other modern movements, then, as Conley and others have done, I wish to separate them out, despite their temporary alliance in *Minotaure* in a 'unity of differences'. I wish to do so in order to think through the possibilities of a surrealist sculpture for artists such as Dalí, Giacometti and Arp, as well as for those artists coming after surrealism who have thought of their work in terms of the *mise-en-scène*, of the encounter, or of an 'objectification of the subjective' or an 'inner necessity'. While such terms were of course theorised earlier by the symbolists and by Wassily Kandinsky, they now supersede the formal and ethical imperatives of modern art as these were understood and accepted by Paul Gauguin and Kandinsky.

The *Involuntary Sculptures* are one instance of a series of essays and visual presentations in *Minotaure* nos. 3–4 organised around the themes of the automatic and the popular, which sometimes overlap: these include Brassaï's illustrated essay 'Du mur des cavernes au mur d'usine', which concerns popular graffiti; Jacques Lacan's essay on the crimes of Léa and Christine Papin; Benjamin

Péret's 'Au paradis des fantômes', concerning automatons; Breton's 'Le Message automatique', which in part concerns mediumistic writing, but which is also an important revision of the theory of automatic writing; Dalí's 'De la beauté terrifiante et comestible, de l'architecture Modern'style', concerning an art nouveau architecture that Dalí and Breton both identify with automatism; the photo-collage *Le Phénomène de l'extase*, attributed to and commented upon by Dalí; Tristan Tzara's 'D'un certain automatisme du goût', on women's fashion, and finally Eluard's 'Les plus belles cartes postales'.[14] There are many other contributions to the issue as well, including several more by surrealists or their allies, and I do not wish to claim that the issue is solely oriented to these two themes. However, they do stake out a position rather different from that proposed by Tériade and Raynal in their contributions to the issue; in general, in the surrealist or surrealising contributions, a popular and unconscious expression works against the notion of mastery invoked by the photographs of sculptors' studios, which despite the emphasis on spontaneity in Raynal's text (and in Tériade's as well), still remain within the province of professional art production. In this context, the *Involuntary Sculptures* become instances of an automatic popular expression, as well as one bracket of a parenthesis framing Dalí's discussion of a hysterical and automatic 'modern-style' architecture that is in his own terms 'extra-plastic' in nature.[15]

Interpolated in Briony Fer's valuable discussion of surrealist hysteria in *Realism, Rationalism, Surrealism* is a photo-essay which remains undiscussed as such, but which serves to demonstrate the notion of the surrealist image as the visual manifestation of a symptom or thought, in the same way that the hysteric makes visible her psychical disorder through her passional attitudes.[16] To this extent, the *Involuntary Sculptures* are symptomatic, in the sense understood by Sigmund Freud in *The Psychopathology of Everyday Life*; they are signs of an interior mental life, expressed as nervous habits that betray themselves in visible signs, like tics or slips of the tongue that would otherwise go unnoticed. They are refuse or residues, symptoms of unconscious thought. It becomes a question of looking at the overlooked, and Brassaï and Dalí isolate and magnify their objects to this end.

Even so, they are haptic, the result of unconscious manipulations of materials by hand or mouth, and in this sense they are mischievously brought by Dalí into the category of sculpture, in order to trouble craft, intention and beauty.[17] They are haptic, yet they are, as Dalí insists art nouveau architecture is, also extra-plastic, which is to say they are oriented against the 'straight line' of plasticism, as he claims in the article that immediately follows the *Involuntary Sculptures*.[18] In other words, they are oriented both against modernist architecture as it is practised by someone like Le Corbusier (one of surrealism's *bêtes noires*), and against a concern for form and materials as such. Dalí understands the surrealist object in the same way, as a category that is 'extra-plastic' by definition: it exists outside the concerns of either traditional or modern sculpture, yet like the *Involuntary Sculptures* it is a critique of the limitations of even modern sculpture, which is insufficiently radical in surrealism's view insofar as it retains the specialised division of labour inherent in class culture.[19] The skills and training necessary for the professional practice of painting or sculpture preclude the notion of a 'poetry made by all, not by one', the Comte de Lautréamont's watchword adopted by the surrealists, and are themselves a symptom of class culture.

The *Involuntary Sculptures* are thus both sculpture and not-sculpture, plastic by the very manipulation of their materials, and extra-plastic in their lack of concern for the shaping of those materials. They are material signifiers of unconscious mental processes, which is something rather different from plastic sculpture. They are formless, as it were, since they are an unmediated expression of interiority, which is the same position that automatic writing occupies in relation to more consciously crafted works of literature. They are, in Dalí's terms, 'concrete irrationality'.[20]

At the same time, there is a difference between these objects and automatic writing, which is perhaps the reason that Breton remained lukewarm towards them: they may be expressions of unconscious thought, but they do not appear to depend on language. Automatic writing is indeed a negation of existing categories of literature, but it is valuable to Breton not simply as negation (though negation is indeed an important concern), but for the production of images that were not obtainable by other, more deliberate means; it is superior to other kinds of literature precisely because it is capable of producing such images, which are in principle an unsuspected *rapprochement* of contraries, an encounter on the model of collage.[21] This, I believe, is the stake of Breton's *Surrealism and Painting*, which attempts to situate surrealism in a critical relation to contemporary art through the revaluation of collage from formal innovation in cubist painting to the creation of poetic images; this is the primary reason, I think, for the focus in its pages on Pablo Picasso and Max Ernst, as these two artists are made responsible first for the invention of collage, then for its revaluation away from form and metonym towards more surprising uses, which are akin to the kinds of images that had already been produced in automatic writing. Surrealism's critical relation to modern art and literature turns on the revaluation of collage as the *rapprochement* of distant realities to produce an image; this image is not, however, crafted in a premeditated fashion, but appears automatically, without labour and in the absence of formal concerns. This in turn is related to the production of similar images in dreams, wherein it is the strange beauty of the image itself that is of chief concern, and not the means by which it is made manifest.

In this way, the major formal innovation so far produced by modern art, collage, is sublated into the post-formal practice of automatic writing, which locates surrealism in its own terms as a dialectical supersession of modern art. In a well-known passage in the first section of *Surrealism and Painting*, Breton aligns surrealist cultural revolution with political revolution, and claims that this is not the time to focus on formal issues:

> The revolutionary significance of a work, or quite simply its significance, should never be subordinated to the choice of elements that the work brings into play. Whence the difficulty of setting up a rigorous and objective scale of plastic values at a time when a radical overhaul of all values is about to be overtaken, and when perspicacity obliges us to recognize only those values likely to hasten this overhaul.[22]

Just prior to this passage, Breton deplores, as he will continue to deplore throughout his life, the domination of the signified by the signifier in modern art, which surrealism is pledged to reverse in its concern for the unmediated expression of content:

> Painters share a responsibility with all others to whom the formidable lot has fallen of preventing, in the mode of expression that is theirs, the survival of the sign over the thing signified; at the present hour, this responsibility appears to me to be heavy and, in general, quite poorly borne.[23]

This critique of the formal imperatives of modern art and literature, which is echoed in the writings of Dalí, Louis Aragon, Tristan Tzara, René Crevel and Claude Cahun, makes it difficult for this writer to see surrealism as another modern movement, despite its critical relation to past and contemporary forms of art and literature.[24] Surrealism positions itself as a supersession of such concerns, and this supersession turns on the revaluation of collage from formal innovation to poetic practice. Formal values, which are superfluous to automatic modes of expression, are not only incidental to the expression of content, they will be subject to radical revision in the new society.

Moreover, Breton, in keeping with a Hegelian understanding of the trajectory of art, and with a symbolist viewpoint that is itself informed by Hegelian aesthetics, sees the creative process as an 'objectification of the subjective', that is, as an externalisation of poetic thought in material form, in opposition to the bulk of abstract art and to an art of imitation; as he says in 'Crise de l'objet' of 1936:

> Let us observe, in passing, that the philosophy which gave life to poetic objects moved with a steady rush from abstract to concrete, when one part of contemporary art (abstraction) persisted in taking the opposite direction, and ... put itself in the position of seeing its realizations decisively outclassed.[25]

Breton is speaking specifically of surrealist objects here, which are products of a process of objectification that does not abstract from or imitate an external model, but which is a manifestation of interiority, and which is also, by definition, 'extra-plastic', even as the objects are fabricated on the basis of collage methods. It is, in fact, largely because they are assemblages of found materials that they are considered to lie outside the category of sculpture, since – apart from dadaists and constructivists – sculptors had not yet recognised and incorporated construction into their own working procedures. Yet it is also crucial to the conceptualisation of the objects as appropriate vehicles for the externalisation of interior thought that collage had already been revalued by surrealist theoreticians like Breton and Aragon as a poetic procedure that works against formal concerns, to the extent than an image forms itself through the juxtaposition of distant realities.[26] In this context, there could be no more suitable medium for the objectification or materialisation of thought than assemblage, which is informal by nature, and which anyone can make.

If Breton is lukewarm towards the *Involuntary Sculptures*, I suspect it is due to the fact that, although they are automatic, they do not produce the images he values as the fruit of the automatic process. They are opaque material signifiers, but they are not poetic. They may undermine the more determinate forms of sculpture featured elsewhere in the issue, but they do not provide an alternative to them that is superior in kind or quality; they are not a supersession in this sense, even though they are indisputably objectifications of interior states of mind. Rather, they remain symptomatic. To this extent, the idea of automatism they represent is by no means identical to Breton's own, although they are both a popular and an unconscious form of expression. They may even be an implicit critique of automatism as the founding method of surrealism, in their stereotypical forms of expression; certainly Dalí, Tzara and Roger Caillois were engaged in a critique of automatism at that time within the group, in an attempt to broaden or reformulate surrealist activity along other lines.[27] While automatism is definitely the subject of Dalí's and Tzara's essays in this issue of *Minotaure*, it is not conceived in quite the same way as Breton's understanding of a procedure that makes possible the production of astonishing images; it is, rather, a consideration of the production of symptomatic traces of unconscious mental processes in architecture or in women's fashion. Indeed, Dalí identifies automatism with stereotypy on several occasions, including 'De la beauté terrifiante et comestible, de l'architecture Modern'style'.[28]

If the surrealist object explicitly lies outside the category of sculpture, in the rationales given by Dalí, Breton and others for its invention and circulation from 1931 on, this is because it was both construction and 'extra-plastic'.[29] Most of Joan Miró's early sculptures fit into this category, and were explicitly aligned with the surrealist object between 1931 and 1933. Giacometti's sculptures in his surrealist period, which sometimes fit the category of the object, are largely conceived in terms of a *mise-en-scène* or an encounter, or both, and the issues of skill and the artist's hand are also often minimised, as they are for Arp, by having craftsmen manufacture his works to his specifications (although rough plaster versions were usually made by the artist first). This is of course a division of labour, but the manual effort and skills needed for the sculptures' successful resolution are contributed by others, leaving to the artist the mental labour of imagining the work into existence – which then appears fully made. As Rosalind Krauss, Christian Klemm and Anne Umland have each noted, Giacometti's cages frame scenes in which something is about to occur, or the landscape format of his base sculptures creates a *mise-en-scène* for play, which is itself a form of encounter.[30] These are types of construction that are in accord with a surrealist emphasis on the poetic image imagined as a chance encounter, which are to be completed in a sense by the presence of the beholder as player or manipulator of these objects. Such works are most usefully considered, as they have been by Krauss and others, in their intertextual and critical relation to other contemporary modes of sculpture, and certainly they differ significantly from the examples of work by Despiau, Laurens, Lipchitz and Maillol in Raynal's essay for *Minotaure*.

Although several of Giacometti's sculptures stage an encounter, others, like his *Objet désagréable* of 1931 are meant to be handled by the beholder, in what can be thought of as a regression to the haptic dimension of the object from the more distanced optical dimension of a work of art. (That is, the hand in question is the beholder's rather than the artist's, who has commissioned another to make it.)

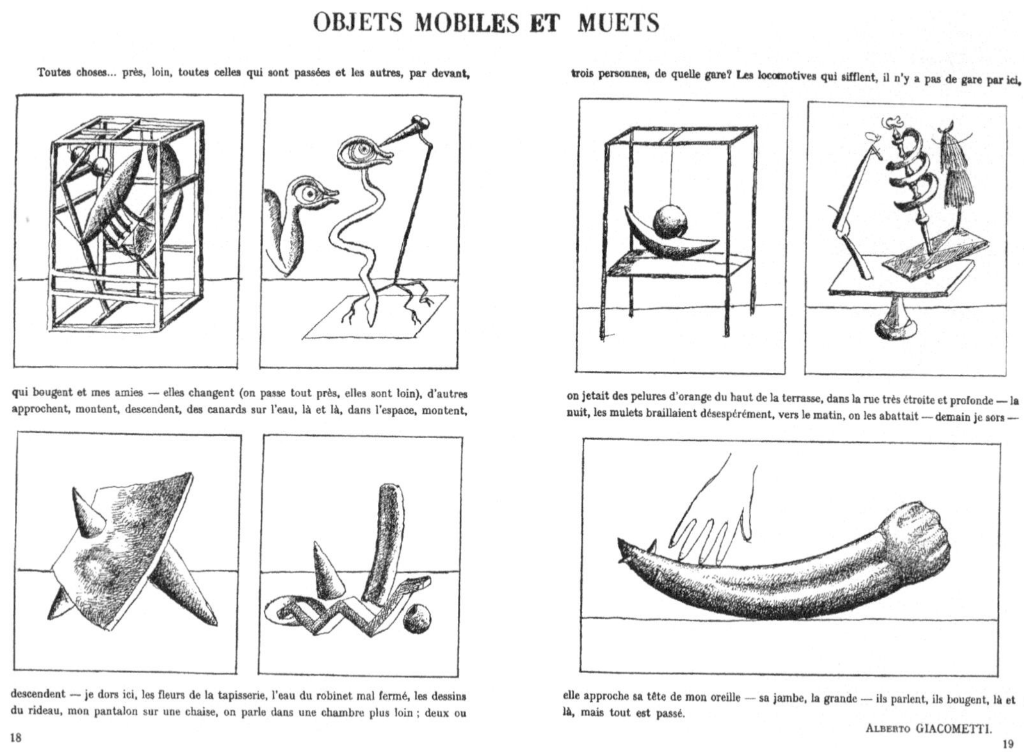

OBJETS MOBILES ET MUETS

Toutes choses... près, loin, toutes celles qui sont passées et les autres, par devant,

qui bougent et mes amies — elles changent (on passe tout près, elles sont loin), d'autres approchent, montent, descendent, des canards sur l'eau, là et là, dans l'espace, montent,

descendent — je dors ici, les fleurs de la tapisserie, l'eau du robinet mal fermé, les dessins du rideau, mon pantalon sur une chaise, on parle dans une chambre plus loin ; deux ou

18

trois personnes, de quelle gare? Les locomotives qui sifflent, il n'y a pas de gare par ici,

on jetait des pelures d'orange du haut de la terrasse, dans la rue très étroite et profonde — la nuit, les mulets braillaient désespérément, vers le matin, on les abattait — demain je sors —

elle approche sa tête de mon oreille — sa jambe, la grande — ils parlent, ils bougent, là et là, mais tout est passé.

ALBERTO GIACOMETTI.

19

1.1 Alberto Giacometti, 'Objets mobiles et muets', *Le Surréalisme au service de la révolution*, no. 3 (December 1931), pp. 18–19 © DACS and ADAGP

This haptic dimension is emphasised in Giacometti's drawing of this object in *Le Surréalisme au service de la révolution* no. 3 (Figure 1.1), in which a hand is drawn just above the object itself, and in Man Ray's photograph of a nude model holding the object to her breast (Figure 1.2), where the gendered difference between object and subject is emphasised in order to eroticise the intimately sensuous dimension of touch (even as this regression to touch, intimacy and sexuality is indicated through the highly optical medium of photography).[31]

The use of the term 'haptic' refers to Aloïs Riegl's theorisation of a development in sculpture from haptic to optical modes of perception, most notably in his 1901 book *Late Roman Art Industry*. While Riegl's theory is not entirely relevant to my discussion here, Walter Benjamin's adaptation of it in his 1936 essay 'The Work of Art in the Age of Mechanical Reproduction' is, and it is from this perspective that I wish to briefly discuss the pertinence of touch to surrealist sculpture. Benjamin's essay, like Riegl's book, is concerned more with perception rather than with the literal handling of objects, in Benjamin's case with the implications of new reproductive media for a mass audience. Benjamin effects a theoretical reversal of Riegl's shift from haptic to optic in class terms, through what he calls the 'tactile appropriation' of the new media by the masses, which they master by habit in the same way they master a trade.[32] If, in Benjamin's terms, the aura of an artwork always involves a notional distance from it, however close one is to it physically – so that one's experience of it is always optical and contemplative – the new reproductive media, which no longer partake of this aura, enable

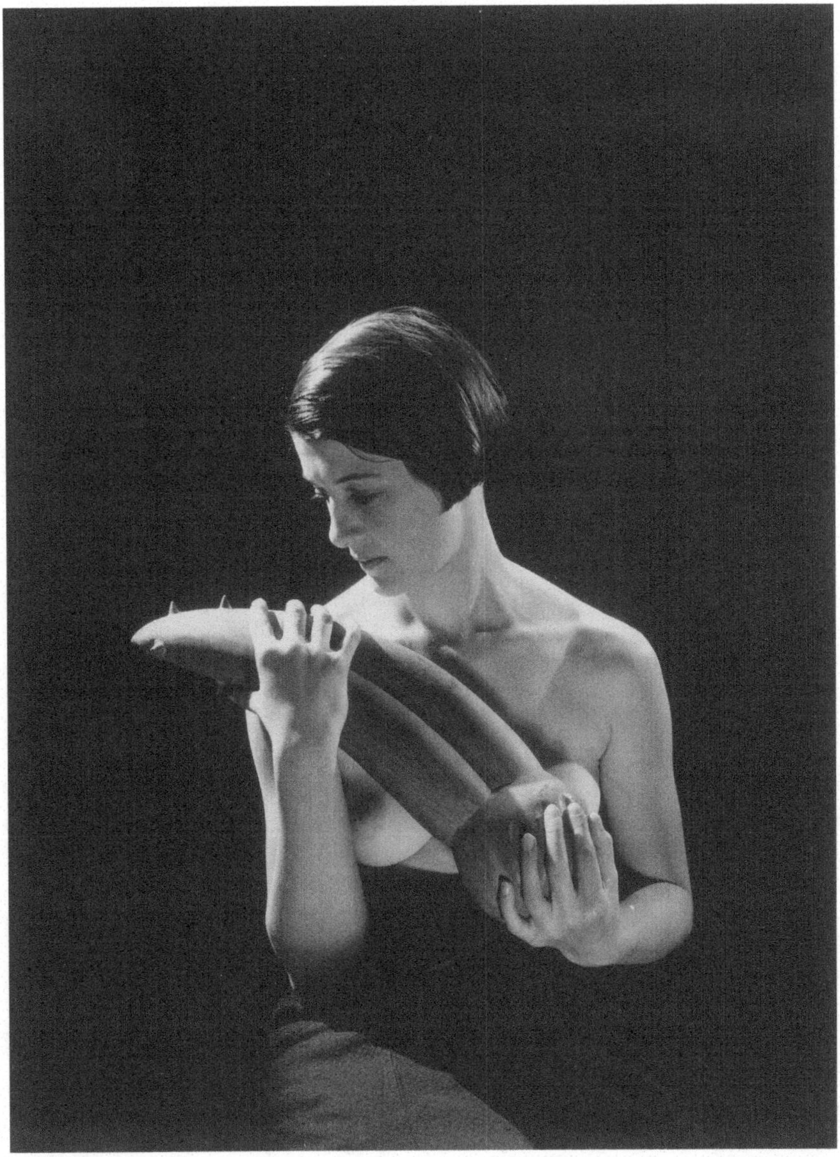

1.2 Man Ray, *Woman Holding Giacometti's* Objet désagréable, silver gelatin print, 1932, Musée National d'Art Moderne, Centre Georges Pompidou, Paris © Man Ray Trust/ SODRAC (2009). CNAC/MNAM/ Dist. Réunion des Musées Nationaux/Art Resource, NY

the masses to 'bring things "closer"', to master them through use.[33] Although perception quite literally remains optical, given the imagistic nature of the film and photography that, as reproductive media, are the focal point of Benjamin's analysis, the mode of their reception or 'appropriation' is 'tactile' or haptic, rather than optical; 'the unique phenomenon of a distance, however close the object may be' has been eliminated by a progressive mode of reception that, while predicated on technological development, is fundamentally social in character.[34] It is 'regressive' in its movement from optic to haptic, but 'progressive' in its ability to master new media, and in the mass nature of its reception, which is identified with the proletariat.

I am not claiming that the surrealists were in any way aware of Benjamin's essay, which remained little known until the 1950s at least. What I wish to focus on here is the overcoming of a contemplative and sublimated notion of art – which is optical in nature, distanced and auratic – through the sense of touch. When the sense of touch is evoked, as we have already seen by way of Giacometti's *Objet désagréable*, it is focused not so much (or not at all) on the expressive artist, on the visible traces of his or her own hand, as it is on the beholder, who does not simply gaze at the object but who handles, plays or caresses it.

Benjamin is most interested in the mode of reception appropriate to the mass media, by the masses which are the political focus of his attention. For the surrealists, the production of images, objects and sculpture remains an individual one, and these objects and images are still intended to be received individually; if they are produced in a certain state of distraction, they are to be received with attention rather than in the distracted mode of reception Benjamin thought appropriate for the mass media (in order not to be taken in by the messages they conveyed).

The surrealists did not concern themselves with the implications of reproductive media in the same way that Benjamin did, although they did put forward democratic models of production through automatic writing, collage and assemblage, frottage, decalcomania, and so on. In these two paradigms, art is either taken out of the connoisseur's hands through reproduction, or is to be produced individually by everyone. In either case, however, the objects are intended to be brought close, *handled* figuratively or literally, which is something to which both Tristan Tzara and Claude Cahun refer explicitly in their writings on 'primitive' and surrealist objects.[35] My point here, through this discussion of Benjamin's own reversal of Riegl's thesis in class terms, is that a regression from optic to haptic is effected in surrealist practice as a point of difference with conventional, even modern sculptural practice, where an apprehension of touch remains centred on the *artist's* hand. In the case of surrealist objects specifically, the beholder is invited to handle them, or even to begin producing them him- or herself.

Hans Arp and Henry Moore were both situated between abstract and surrealist tendencies in contemporary art, in other words between groups of artists who were publicly opposed to one another's views.[36] I want to focus in the last part of this essay on a few works by Arp in the light of this situation. His work is typically described as a kind of natural growth or expression, a view encouraged by Arp himself in numerous statements. This point of view has a long history in modern art, and derives from the symbolist notion of an 'objectification of the subjective', which was taken over by surrealism; rather than an imitation of nature, which moves from concrete to abstract, expression will move from abstract to concrete, in an unfolding of the imagination akin to natural growth.[37] As Arp wrote in *Cahiers d'art* in 1931:

> Art is a fruit growing out of man like a fruit out of a plant or the child in its mother. While the fruit of the plant grows independent forms and never resembles a balloon or a president in a dress suit, the artistic fruit of man shows for the most part a ridiculous resemblance to the appearance of other things.[38]

As we can see, such a statement is not simply a positive expression, but is oriented against an art of imitation, against which Arp's collages, reliefs and sculpture were always posed.

Yet this text, as its title 'A propos de l'art abstrait' makes clear, is not simply critical of mimetic art, but also situates his work in relation to contemporary forms of abstraction. Arp had been in touch with Theo van Doesburg from 1922, when he attended the dada-constructivist congress in Weimar along with other dadaists like Tristan Tzara and Hans Richter, and where he met El Lissitzky, László Moholy-Nagy and others; he also worked on the design of the Café Aubette in Strasbourg from 1926 to 1928 with van Doesburg and Sophie Taeuber.[39] At the same time as he was participating in surrealist exhibitions and reviews, from 1925 on, he was close to Michel Seuphor, and his work appeared in *Documents internationaux de l'Esprit nouveau*, edited by Seuphor and Paul Dermée in 1927, in *Cercle et Carré* and its accompanying exhibition in 1930, and in *Abstraction création art non figuratif* from 1932 to 1934.

All of these publications were explicitly oriented against surrealism, and one of the rare critical essays in the first issue of *Abstraction création* – a review mostly given over to reproductions and artists' statements – was Seuphor's 'L'Art nouveau et le surréalisme', wherein surrealism was pilloried as reactionary in relation to the rationalist and modernist orientation of the review.[40] Arp was nevertheless represented in the issue by two illustrations and an essay by Hans Schiess, and his sculptures with moveable objects, such as *Navel and Two Thoughts*, 1932, appeared in the 1933 and 1934 volumes. That is, he was closely associated in the 1920s and 1930s with many of the most significant representatives of modernist tendencies, who were as hostile to surrealism as the surrealist group was to modern art, in spite of its tactical alliance with Raynal and Tériade from 1933 to 1937. Abstraction was a particular culprit in surrealist eyes, precisely for its trajectory from concrete to abstract, although of course only a minority of non-figurative artists actually abstracted from an external model; in any case, *Minotaure* was not open to contemporary forms of abstraction, and restricted itself to figurative forms of modern and surrealist art, in addition to the wealth of other imagery that made its appearance in the review.[41] *Abstraction création*, for its part, was *exclusively* devoted to the promotion of non-figurative art, and is the plasticism Dalí had in mind in 1933 (not to say in 1935, the date of his 'Abjection et misère de l'Abstraction Création').[42]

Arp's relation to abstraction, to modern art and to surrealism begins to become clear in the light of this double orientation; it is in fact conceived in very similar terms to those promoted by surrealism, which were already found to some extent in Kandinsky, the great exception to the rule of geometry in abstract art.[43] To the notion of abstraction, Arp opposed the term 'concretion':

> Man calls abstract that which is concrete. That's admirable all the same, for ordinarily he confuses what's in front of him and behind him even when using his nose, his mouth and his ears, that is to say six of his eight openings. I understand that he should call a cubist picture abstract because some parts have been abstracted from the object that served as a model for this picture. But I find that a painting or a sculpture that have not had an object for a model are just as concrete and sensual as a leaf or a stone.[44]

While *Abstraction création* proposed two routes to the non-figurative in its editorial for the first issue of its review – the abstraction from natural forms, and an ordering of geometric forms that were independent of nature – Arp proposed a third one in *Cahiers d'art*: the concrete, or the externalisation in material form of subjective thought processes as this was theorised by Kandinsky and by the surrealists. The concrete, in other words, is the expression of spirit, akin to the life-spirit that causes natural growth.

The nature of Arp's intervention into the debate on abstraction is further clarified when one realises that he took his term 'concrete art' from van Doesburg, who first used it in an editorial for his ephemeral review *Art concret* (whose single issue appeared in April 1930). van Doesburg too conceives of a concrete art as the product of spirit, but in this case it is a rationalised and premeditated art: 'Before it is physically made material, the work of art is fully conceived by the spirit.'[45] In other words, it moves from a similar basis in a similar direction, but its foundation is reason rather than instinct: 'We are painters who think and measure.'[46] Arp revalues van Doesburg's term in 'A propos de l'art abstrait' away from what he will later call, in 'Dadaland', 'a profession of faith in the machine and technology' towards a conception of art as a natural process. (While this view was already present in the essay by 'Alexander Partens' in the *Dada Almanach*, it had not yet been named 'concrete'.)[47] Arp's appropriation of the term 'concrete art' is both a homage to his friend van Doesburg following his early death in 1931, and a *détournement* of its initial meaning, which revalues it in keeping with Kandinsky's understanding of 'the spiritual in art', and which counters the rationalist emphasis in contemporary abstraction that van Doesburg had supported. It is thus a very dialectical move, one taken at the moment when Arp is turning to the traditional category of sculpture for the first time in his career (if we concede that the reliefs that he had been making since 1917 were situated *between* painting and sculpture); it even clarifies the meaning of this turn.[48]

In her essay on Arp's chance collages, Jane Hancock sees Arp's return to his dada drawings as source material for his *papiers déchirés* as an implicit criticism of surrealism, which is confirmed by his remarks to Jan Brzekowski published in *L'Art contemporain* in 1930.[49] The simultaneous turn to the *papiers déchirés* and to three-dimensional sculpture, remarked upon by several of Arp's commentators, would in this reading thus signal a turn away from surrealism towards both older and newer modes of production.[50] While Arp extols dada in remarks made at this time, while he turns to a very traditional material and mode of sculptural production (modelling in plaster), and while he voices certain criticisms of surrealism in 1930, the way in which Arp's sculptural practice develops in the early 1930s leads me to think that he was positioning himself between surrealism and abstraction, bringing the good news of expressionist and surrealist values to a non-mimetic and non-figurative art; or, to put it another way, that he saw the surrealist endorsement of the trajectory of art from subjective to objective as a confirmation of views he had expressed earlier, rather than inimical to them.[51] From this perspective, Arp's explicit return to his dada past in both his writings and his *papiers déchirés* would not signal a rejection of surrealism so much as a recognition of what the two movements shared. In any case, Marcel Duchamp saw Arp's concretions as his contribution to surrealism rather than a departure from it, and this insight should be taken seriously.[52]

If we look at early examples of Arp's sculpture in the round, such as *Trois objets désagréables sur une figure*, better known as *Head with Annoying Objects* (whose initial title was *Tête couverte de trois objets désagréables: une mouche, une mandoline et une paire de moustaches*) and *Navel and Two Thoughts* (*Nombril et deux idées*) (Figures 1.3 and 1.4), both likely made in 1932, we can see that they, like Giacometti's works from the same period, are transactional sculptures which the beholder is encouraged to handle. In neither sculpture is there an established 'composition', since the smaller forms are subject to rearrangement: a fact confirmed by photographs of the former sculpture in different configurations in *Cahiers d'art*.[53] They are also encounters, of the kind that interested Giacometti. As the title of the *Navel and Two Ideas* makes clear, and as the later publication of the scenario related to *Head with Annoying Objects* confirms, these sculptures can also be read as expressions, whether of ideas from a matrix, or as objects which appear on the face or surface of the sculpture as in a dream or reverie.[54] That is, they refer to the process of the objectification of subjective thought, whose consequence is the appearance of small objects on a larger form, as if they were generated from the latter. Moreover, the use of the term 'objets désagréables' in the title of *Head with Annoying Objects* makes the relation of Arp's transactional sculptures to Giacometti and to the surrealist object explicit, as an act of identification with the orientation of this group and its recent theorisation and invention of surrealist objects – even if these works are sculptures, since they are shaped by human hand.

For a long time, Arp had rejected the hand of the artist, as he had rejected traditional media in his work in collage, embroidery, tapestry and wood relief. In a move that predates Robert Morris and even László Moholy-Nagy, the pseudonymous 'Alexander Partens' tells of Arp giving the specifications for his reliefs to a carpenter over the phone.[55] His decision to begin modelling directly in plaster in 1930 involved a turn to the kind of traditional medium he had rejected in 1915. In other words, Arp shifts his practice from not-handling (the collages cut with paper-cutters, the reliefs sawn by carpenters) to handling, a shift which encompasses both the torn-paper reliefs and the plaster sculptures despite their other differences. The transactional sculptures in particular are subject to handling by both beholder and artist.

While this return to a traditional medium and a traditional way of working can be understood in part as Arp's acceptance of his status as a professional artist, which he had resisted for so long, and his acceptance of the permanence of the art object which is a part of that practice (modelled in plaster, his sculptures when purchased were then carved or cast by others in more durable materials), it is also related to some thematic concerns in his work that I wish to address at this point. One is the haptic dimension of working in soft materials – which, Gaston Bachelard claims in *Water and Dreams*, produces very different results than working with hard substances like wood or stone. In Bachelard's view, working with viscous matter allows the hand to dream, to deform as well as form, through a process that both adds and subtracts – which is literally inside matter and not external to it, as is the case with the carver and his or her

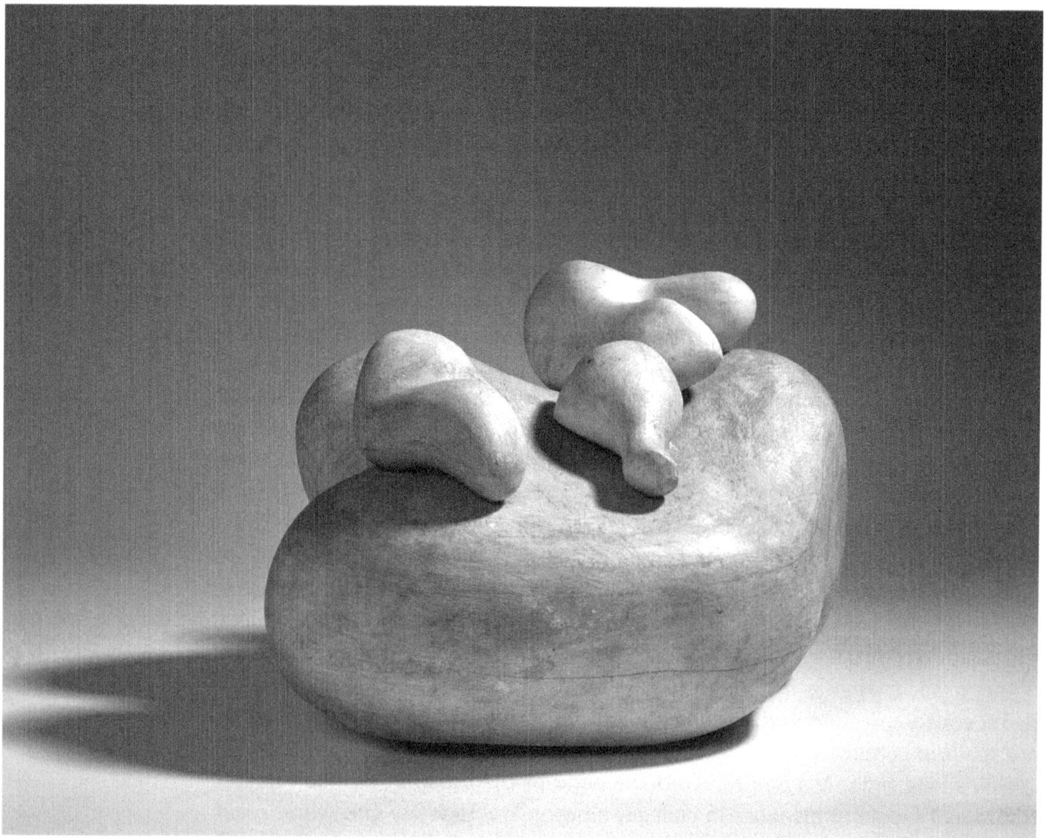

1.3 Hans Arp, *Trois objets désagréables sur une figure*, plaster, 1932, 37 × 29.5 × 19 cm (base), Silkeborg Kunstmuseum, Silkeborg © Jean Hans Arp Estate/ SODRAC (2009). Photo: Lars Bay

uni-directional elimination of the incidental. Indeed, Bachelard identifies this way of working with the dream, as well as with the deformation of objects found in Dalí's paintings:

> When we mold, and knead, and shape, there is no longer any geometry, nor any sharp edge or interruption. It is indeed an endless dream, an activity in which we close our eyes, an inward reverie.[56]

In this argument, we have a haptic process that is primarily dedicated to the process of reverie, rather than to the resolution of an object, yet this reverie is achieved through working with earth and water, rather than through dreaming, or spirit, alone. Bachelard, who by this time had had a long acquaintance with surrealist theory, poetry and visual art, was thinking in terms of an automatic practice that would produce a kind of involuntary sculpture, albeit one that was still focused on the artist and craftsperson rather than on unconscious popular expression.

Arp acknowledged the difference between his and Brancusi's approaches to sculpture in a remark made to Pierre Schneider in 1958, and William Rubin extrapolated on this difference between modelling and carving, abstraction and concretion in his remarks on Arp in *Dada and Surrealist Art*, noting 'the

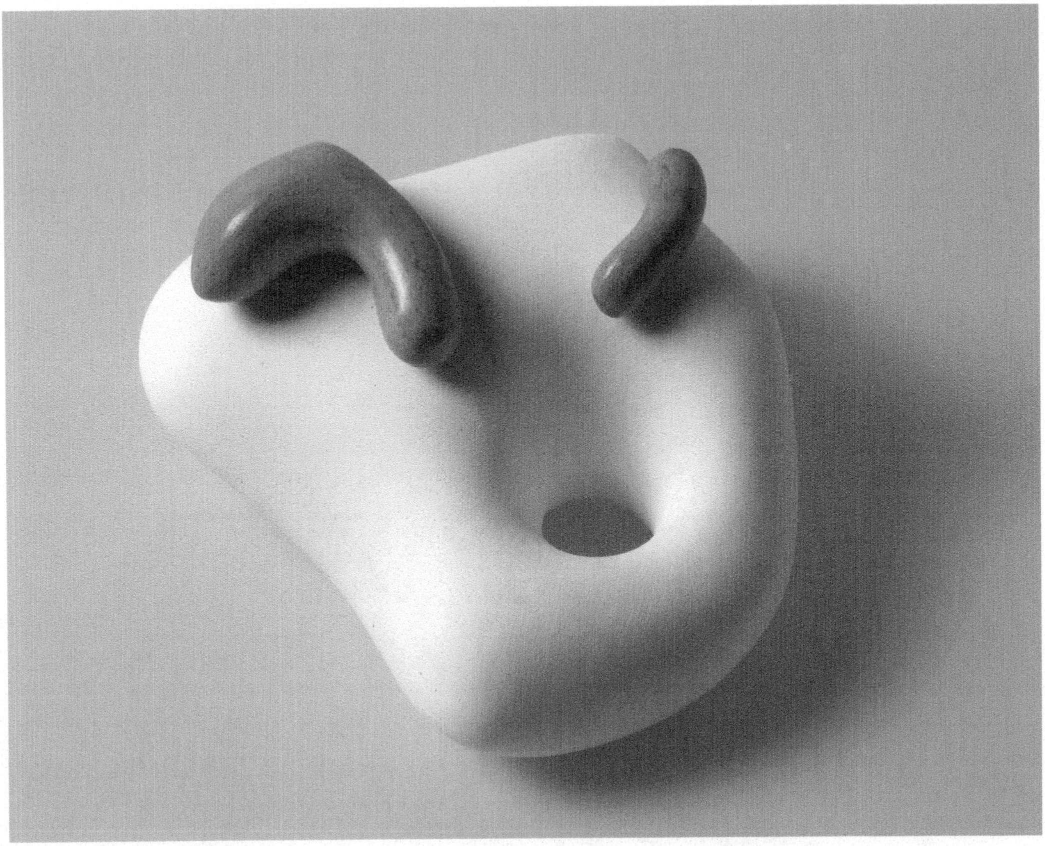

1.4 Hans Arp, *Nombril et deux idées*, plaster, 1932, 14.5 × 22 × 21.5 cm (base), Musée d'Art Moderne et Contemporain de la Ville de Strasbourg © Jean Hans Arp Estate/SODRAC (2009). Photo Musées de la Ville de Strasbourg, M. Bertola

metamorphosis and improvisation which Arp's fundamentally additive way of composing demands'.[57] As a consequence of his procedures, Rubin added: 'Arp's work is centrifugal, the work growing outward, seemingly organically, from a nucleus'.[58] While Rubin was writing in full knowledge of Arp's own descriptions of his work, he was also identifying the formal logic of Arp's concretions of the 1930s, such as *Human Concretion* (*Concrétion humaine*), 1934 (Figure 1.5), as an additive process which takes on the appearance of buds or new growth (vs. Brancusi's search for essential form, which involves reduction or removal). This was a property that Arp had of course described in 'A propos de l'art abstrait'.

Carola Giedion-Welcker has noted the importance of surface in Arp's works, whether this be the accretion of surfaces in his reliefs, or the roundness of the concretions that have been smoothed by human hand.[59] To the extent that this is true – and I think it is – it can be identified with Arp's understanding of the artwork as a kind of organic growth, pushing out from the inside as an expression of spirit. The surface would then be what is revealed of this spirit, in a relation of essence and appearance that, while optical for the viewer, nevertheless embodies or incarnates an experience of unfolding, of a movement from internal to external that retains as well an element of the haptic. In this process, one would not discover essence through reduction or subtraction, since this results in forms abstracted from nature (a movement from objective to subjective, in

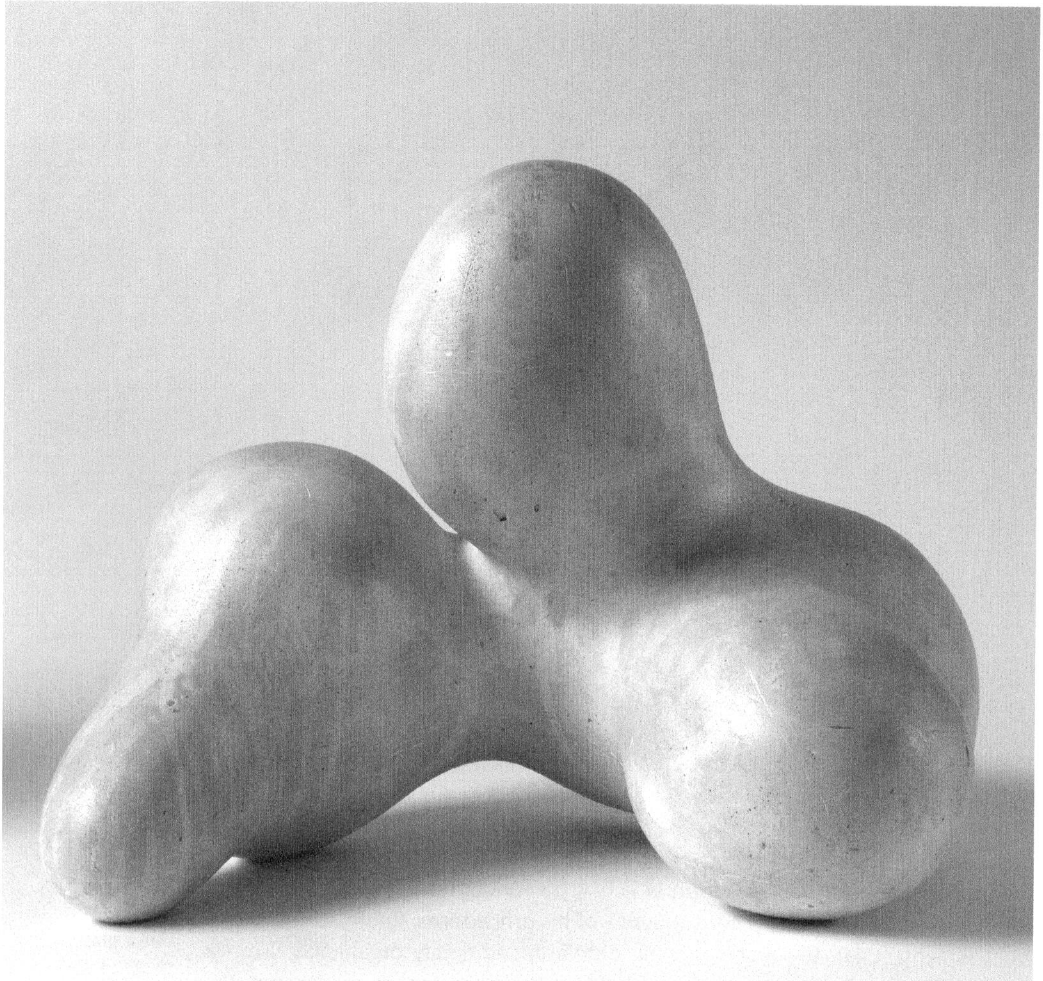

1.5 Hans Arp, *Concrétion humaine*, plaster, 1934, 32 × 39 × 40 cm, Fondation Arp, Clamart © Jean Hans Arp Estate/SODRAC (2009). Photo: Michel Nguyen

Breton's terms, which Arp and Rubin identify in Brancusi's work); essence would be understood, rather, as an internal force giving shape to objects, which are spirit made concrete.

For a number of Arp's commentators, including old friends like Richard Huelsenbeck and Michel Seuphor, his work suggested the maternal: 'Arp's rhythms are those of rocking, of an infinite tenderness'.[60] This raises the question of the quality or nature of touch at issue in Arp's sculpture, which in this reading is an intimate one that is more closely related to the mother-child relation than it is sexual (for a counter-example, we can recall Giacometti's *Objet désagréable*, which is provocatively phallic). If this is so, it would be another instance of a regression to the haptic from the optic, in a recollection of a time before separation from the dyad. The ground of the encounter in Arp's early transactional sculptures is then a maternal one, in which there is little or no distance between major and minor components.

Margherita Andreotti and Briony Fer identify and discuss this maternal dimension of Arp's work as well, which Fer relates to the image of the navel that recurs so frequently in Arp's imagery, including in *Navel and Two Thoughts*. In Fer's view, the navel is the liminal point of separation from the mother, and Andreotti quotes Arp as asking, in 1952: 'why have we torn the umbilical cord that tied us to the original foundation'.[61] If we think of *Navel and Two Thoughts* and *Head with Annoying Objects* in this light, we can perhaps see the larger shapes as the maternal forms out of which the thoughts or objects emerge. The navel shape would be particularly closely related to this theme, since it condenses a number of closely related concepts – natural growth, expression of thought, the maternal – in one object. What is explicit in these early transactional sculptures remains implicit in the later single-form concretions.

Not only is concretion in keeping with the trajectory of surrealist theory, but Arp linked it to the unconscious and to the surrealist object (which he also described as a concrete art) in his writings. In his 1942 contribution to Peggy Guggenheim's *Art of This Century* catalogue, which at this point in time aligned surrealism and abstraction as complementary forms of modern art, Arp situated a concrete art between the surrealism of Breton and the abstraction of Mondrian, the other two contributors to the catalogue. He wrote there:

> ... certain works by Duchamp, Man Ray, Masson, Miró, and Ernst, and a number of 'surrealist objects', are also concrete art. Devoid of any descriptive, dreamlike, literary, or polemical content, the works of these artists are, it seems to me, highly important in the evolution of concrete art, for, by allusion, they manage to introduce into that art the psychic emotion that makes it live.[62]

Later, in 'Danger de mort', Arp would write:

> The process of abstraction in painting is sufficiently known through cubism, so I needn't talk about it. The process of concrete art, with its point of departure in the artist's unconscious, is infinitely more dangerous.[63]

In each of these instances, it seems to me, Arp is aligning concrete art sufficiently with surrealism as to suggest a non-contradiction with it, rather than the rejection of surrealism and return to dada suggested by Hancock. While Arp certainly had his criticisms of the illusionist approach to painting taken by Dalí, or of the surrealist group's relations with the French Communist Party, which were voiced in writings published in 1930 and 1932, he never broke with the surrealist group as he felt he had to, for instance, with Abstraction-Création in 1934 over that group's leadership.[64]

The 'concrete' is that which is hard, it need hardly be said; there is a reification of thought in this conception of art's realisation, which is literalised in Arp's sculpture – in the stone-like density of his objects – more explicitly than it is in Giacometti's surrealist sculpture or in the surrealist object generally. Arp's sculpture is not merely something that has grown, but also something that has congealed or solidified, which Arp is well aware of and which he discusses in 'Looking', his text for the 1958 Museum of Modern Art catalogue: 'Concretion signifies the natural process of condensation, hardening, coagulating, thickening, growing together. Concretion designates the solidification of a mass.'[65] In her essay on Arp in *On Abstract Art*, Briony Fer relates this coagulation of forms to the death drive, in reading Arp's *papiers déchirés* through Hal Foster's reconsideration of this concept in *Compulsive Beauty*.[66] In doing so, she intends to read against the grain of a traditional reception of Arp's work focused on metaphors of growth and nature. Other scholars like Harriet Watts and Andreotti have written of the *papiers déchirés* as the necessary complement to Arp's turn to three-dimensional sculpture (with its references to birth and growth), in their explicit invocation of decay, decomposition and impermanence; that is, as two aspects of a single natural process.[67] There is an indistinction between organic and inorganic, animate and inanimate in these works, which is a sign of the uncanny. As much as intimations of natural growth, Arp's sculptures may suggest its opposite – the petrifaction of life in sculptural objects, or reifications of thought – that equally signal the decision to take up a professional career.

This is not an issue I can explore further here, though it is an interesting and important one. I would, however, like to take a last look at one of the *Involuntary Sculptures*, by way of closing: the second row down, on the left. It's a roll, which is different in kind from the other involuntary sculptures on display, which have been manipulated unconsciously by human hand or mouth. This one too was evidently shaped by human hands, but assumed its present form in the baker's oven. It is an instance of the kind of internal and unconscious growth advocated by Arp in his 1931 essay, as opposed to the deformations visited on tickets, soap or toothpaste by distracted hands and minds. This too is a model for surrealist sculpture, which by definition sidesteps the question of craft, given that craft had been so completely identified with the traditional means and values of sculpture.

Notes

1 Katharine Conley, 'Modernist Primitivism in 1933: Brassaï's "Involuntary Sculptures" in Minotaure', *Modernism/modernity*, 10(1) (2003), pp. 127–40. Conley reads the *Involuntary Sculptures* from a perspective informed by recent writings on surrealist ethnography.

2 Since Hans Arp only began signing his works 'Jean Arp' in 1939 as a protest against German bellicosity, I will use the first version of his name here to discuss sculptures made in the 1930s.

3 I make this argument in *Surrealist Art and Thought in the 1930s: Art, Politics, and the Psyche* (Cambridge, 2004), pp. 144–6. There, I discuss the surrealists' relations with the AEAR on pp. 77–83. The AEAR was a united-front organisation controlled by the French Communist Party, but not limited to its members. Breton was expelled from the AEAR on 27 June 1933, the month in which the first two issues of *Minotaure* appeared, and the other surrealist members of the organisation resigned shortly thereafter, along with a number of sympathisers. See also the chronology for André Breton, *Oeuvres complètes*, ed. Marguerite Bonnet (Paris, 1992), vol. 2, pp. xxxviii–xl, and the commentary, pp. 1492–93. For what is in my view the best extended discussion of the surrealists' political involvements, see Carole Reynaud Paligot, *Parcours politique des surréalistes 1919–69* (Paris, 1995).

4 Unsigned editorial preface to *Minotaure*, 3–4 (December 1933), n.p. So far as an alliance of the 'modern spirit' is concerned: in the prospectus that opens *Minotaure*, 1 (June 1933), as well as in the preface signed by Skira and Tériade to the catalogue for the *Exposition Minotaure* held at the Palais des Beaux-Arts in Brussels in May–June 1934, the precise words used are 'l'esprit du mouvement moderne'. Unless otherwise specified, all translations are mine.

5 See the chronology to Breton, *Oeuvres complètes*, vol. 2, pp. 197–8, 202–203, 208–11. On the surrealists and their collaboration on *Minotaure*, see also José Pierre, 'André Breton et/ou "Minotaure"', in *Regards sur Minotaure: La Revue à tête de bête* (Geneva, 1987), pp. 95–119.

6 In a letter to Gala, Eluard writes of 'the inertia, the concealed and dissimulated ill will of Tériade'. Eluard, undated letter (early September 1933), in *Lettres à Gala*, p. 221; *Letters to Gala*, trans. J. Browner (New York, 1989), p. 178.

7 Maurice Raynal, 'Dieu–table–cuvette', *Minotaure*, 3–4 (December 1933), pp. 39–40, with photographs by Brassaï and Constantin Brancusi (of his own studio), pp. 41–53. For a discussion of Raynal's essay, as well as a translation, see the title essay by Jon Wood in *Close Encounters: The Sculptor's Studio in the Age of the Camera* (Leeds, 2001), pp. 8–27, and the translation by Charles Penwarden on pp. 92–3. The latter can also be found in Jon Wood, David Hulks and Alex Potts (eds), *The Modern Sculpture Reader* (Leeds, 2007), pp. 109–12.

8 Two contact sheets for the *Involuntary Sculptures* are reproduced in Alain Sayag and Annick Lionel-Marie (eds), *Brassaï: The Monograph* (Boston, 2000), p. 134. On them is written: 'Automatic objects photographed in collaboration with Dali in 1933' ['Objects [*sic*] automatiques photographiés en collaboration avec S. Dali en 1933']. The captions that accompany the photographs in *Minotaure* use the same vocabulary employed by Dalí in 'De la beauté terrifiante et comestible, de l'architecture Modern'style', the essay that immediately follows the *Involuntary Sculptures*. Later, Brassaï will briefly mention his collaboration with Dalí on the *Involuntary Sculptures* and on *Le Phénomène de l'extase* (the photo-collage that appeared in the same issue), though he does not say much about them. Brassaï, *Picasso and Company* [1964], trans. F. Price (Garden City, NY, 1966), p. 36.

9 Paul Eluard informed Dalí in a letter to his former wife Gala that it would be necessary to leave the *Involuntary Sculptures* unsigned, as otherwise Dalí would figure in the issue too many times. Paul Eluard, undated letter to Gala Eluard (*c.*20 September 1933), in *Lettres à Gala*, p. 226. In fact, Dalí was featured in E. Tériade's 'Emancipation de la peinture', pp. 18 and 20, saw four of his etchings for *Les Chants de Maldoror* reproduced on p. 37, and published his important essay 'De la beauté terrifiante et comestible, de l'architecture Modern'style' immediately following the *Involuntary Sculptures* on pp. 69–76. This essay was in turn followed by a full-page reproduction of *Le Phénomène de l'extase* and a commentary pp. 76–7. However, only the essay appears under his name in the table of contents.

10 Eluard, undated letter to Gala Eluard (early September 1933), in *Lettres à Gala*, p. 222; *Letters to Gala*, p. 179. The other compromises Eluard mentions as a result of the surrealists' association with Tériade and Raynal are 'Emancipation de la peinture', the article by Tériade mentioned in the previous note; reproductions of works by Francisco Borès, André Beaudin, Gaston-Louis Roux and André Masson (which he qualifies as serious – Masson was not reconciled with his former surrealist comrades until 1936, and the others were artists championed by Tériade since his days at *Cahiers d'art*); an article by Michel Leiris on Roussel (not too serious), and another by Pierre Reverdy (*quite* serious). It is Raynal's article on sculpture which gets the most attention in this letter, however, and against which the *Involuntary Sculptures* are oriented.

11 Curiously, drawings of two of the other photographs are found on the contact sheets as well.

12 Brassaï also figured in *Minotaure* nos. 3–4 as artist and contributor with his essay and photo-collage 'Du mur des cavernes au mur d'usine' and 'Graffiti parisiens', pp. 6–7. This double role was also played by Man Ray, who like Brassaï did much of the photographic work for *Minotaure* nos. 3–4, but who contributed an essay, 'L'Age de la lumière', to this issue of the review on p. 1 opposite his colour frontispiece for the issue; the essay was then followed by three pages of his own photographs. In raising the issue of the secondary role played by Brassaï in the conception of the *Involuntary Sculptures* (which I wish to keep separate from that of the quality of their execution, which is a different issue), I am questioning the assumption Katharine Conley makes about Brassaï's authorship, which conditions her essay on the photographs. In his lucid exposition of the uses of documentary photography in surrealist books and journals, Ian Walker refers to a retroactive authorial function attributed to Eugène Atget once his work had become known posthumously, and I think something similar is happening in Conley's discussion of Brassaï as author of the *Involuntary Sculptures*. Conley acknowledges, however, that the photographs were published anonymously. Ian Walker, *City Gorged with Dreams: Surrealism and Documentary Photography in Interwar Paris* (Manchester, 2002), p. 96.

13 Giacometti has likely been included in Raynal's article as a pluralistic gesture in relation to the alliance of modern art and surrealism effected in *Minotaure*, and is only incidentally a target of Dalí's editorial intervention, which is oriented against the craft, labour, and formal and thematic concerns of modern sculpture in general. A similar gesture was made by Tériade in 'Emancipation de la peinture', in giving Dalí such a prominent place amongst the other artists featured: Matisse, Braque, Picasso and Borès were, like Dalí, quoted, and paintings, prints and drawings by Derain, Matisse, Braque, Miró, Borès, Beaudin, Picasso and Dalí were reproduced.

14 Conley also recognises this thematic consistency.

15 The other bracket is the photo-collage of images of hysterical, religious and sexual ecstasy found in *Le Phénomène de l'extase*. On the changing terms of art-critical discourse in response to surrealist theory and practice, see Kim Grant, *Surrealism and the Visual Arts: Theory and Reception* (Cambridge, 2005). Her discussion of *Minotaure* nos. 3–4 can be found on pp. 328–39.

16 Briony Fer, 'Surrealism, Myth and Psychoanalysis', in Fer, David Batchelor, and Paul Wood, *Realism, Rationalism, Surrealism: Art between the Wars* (New Haven, 1993), pp. 170–249. The section on hysteria, which includes the visual essay to which I am referring, is found on pp. 209–18. It includes several images from *Minotaure* nos. 3–4: the *Involuntary Sculptures*, Brassaï's *Graffiti parisiens*, photographs by Man Ray and Brassaï which illustrated Dalí's 'De la beauté terrifiante et comestible, de l'architecture Modern'style', and Dalí's *Le Phénomène de l'extase*, in addition to photographs from Jean-Martin Charcot's *Iconographie photographique de la Salpêtrière* reproduced in *La Révolution surréaliste* no. 11 in 1928, and photographs taken by Brassaï and Man Ray for André Breton's essay 'La Beauté sera convulsive' in *Minotaure*, 5 (1934).

17 Conley references Dawn Ades on this point, who notes that the *Involuntary Sculptures* are sculptures and not objects, because they are shaped rather than found. Conley, p. 134, citing Ades, *Dalí* (London, 1995), p. 62.

18 Salvador Dalí, 'De la beauté terrifiante et comestible, de l'architecture Modern'style', *Minotaure*, 3–4 (December 1933), p. 70. The term 'modern'style' refers to what in English is known as 'art nouveau'; that is, each language designates the style as

foreign in nature, by referring to it through a term that is either English in French, or French in English.

19 Dalí uses the term 'extra-plastic' to describe surrealist objects, which consequently are situated outside the category of sculpture, in his 'Objets surréalistes', *Le Surréalisme au service de la révolution*, 3 (December 1931), p. 16.

20 This phrase is used in Dalí's *La Conquête de l'irrationnel* (Paris, 1935), p. 12, but it is implicit throughout his writings on the objectification of irrational states of mind.

21 I rehearse these arguments at greater length in the first chapter of *Surrealist Art and Thought in the 1930s*. For a very different account of the importance of the visual arts to surrealism, which is nevertheless excellent in its own way, see Grant, *Surrealism and the Visual Arts*.

22 André Breton, *Surrealism and Painting*, trans. S. Watson Taylor (Boston, 2002), p. 8; André Breton, *Le Surréalisme et la Peinture* (Paris, 1965), p. 8. This passage is from the first section of the book, first published *La Révolution surréaliste* no. 4 in 1925.

23 Ibid. Breton's critique of a formalist approach to art, in which form is appreciated at the expense of content, recurs throughout his writings, and can be found for instance in 'Seconde Arche', his 1947 preface to the catalogue for a surrealist exhibition in Prague. André Breton, *Oeuvres complètes*, ed. Marguerite Bonnet and Etienne-Alain Hubert (Paris, 1999), vol. 3, p. 762.

24 Surrealist statements that take modernism to task are made, for instance, by Louis Aragon in 'Introduction à 1930', *La Révolution surréaliste*, 12 (December 1929), pp. 62 and 64; Aragon, 'La Peinture au défi' [1930], in *Les Collages* (Paris, 1980), pp. 37–77; Tristan Tzara, 'Essai sur la situation de la poésie', *Le Surréalisme au service de la révolution*, 4 (December 1931), pp. 15–23 and 'Note relative à l'Essai sur la situation de la poésie', *Le Surréalisme au service de la révolution*, 5 (15 May 1933), pp. 39–40; René Crevel, *L'Esprit contre la raison* [1927], in *L'Esprit contre la raison et autres écrits surréalistes* (Paris, 1986), pp. 60–61; Crevel, *Dali ou l'anti-obscurantisme* [1931], in ibid., p. 115; Breton, 'Il y aura une fois', *Le Surréalisme au service de la révolution*, 1 (July 1930); Dalí, 'Lettre à André Breton' [1933], in *Oui 2: L'Archangélisme scientifique*, ed. Robert Descharnes (Paris, 1971), pp. 17–18; Dalí, *La Conquête de l'irrationnel*, pp. 7–8 and 19–20; Claude Cahun, *Les Paris sont ouverts* [1934] in *Écrits*, ed. François Leperlier (Paris, 2002), pp. 8–9.

25 André Breton, 'Crisis of the Object' [1936], trans. L.R. Lippard, in Lippard (ed.), *Surrealists on Art* (Englewood Cliffs, NJ, 1970), p. 55; Breton, *Le Surréalisme et la Peinture*, p. 280.

26 With regard to Aragon, I am referring to his seminal text 'La Peinture au défi', which was first published as a preface to the catalogue for an exhibition of collages at the Galerie Goemans in 1930.

27 See my discussion of Dalí's, Tzara's and Caillois's critique of automatism in chapters 3 and 5 of *Surrealist Art and Thought in the 1930s*, which is too complex to rehearse here.

28 Dalí, 'De la beauté terrifiante et comestible', p. 73. Automatism is mentioned twice in the captions to the *Involuntary Sculptures*, and stereotypy three times, once in conjunction; 'modern'style' is mentioned three times as well, the three terms being interrelated if not quite interchangeable. Note, however, that Breton mentions the 'captivating stereotypy' of 'modern'style' architecture as a mediumistic mode of art in 'Le Message automatique' (in the same issue of *Minotaure*), lest we think of constructing too simple an opposition here. Breton, 'Le Message automatique', in *Oeuvres complètes*, vol. 2, p. 384.

29 See the essays by Breton and Dalí in *Le Surréalisme au service de la révolution*, 3 (December 1931) and those by Breton, Marcel Jean and Claude Cahun in the special issue of *Cahiers d'art* (11e année) devoted to the object in 1936, as well as Dalí, 'The Object as Revealed in Surrealist Experiment' [1932], in Lippard (ed.), *Surrealists on Art*, pp. 87–96, and Roger Caillois, 'Le Décor surréaliste de la vie', *Documents 33, 5* (August 1933), pp. 16–17.

30 On Giacometti's surrealist period, see the essays by Anne Umland and Christian Klemm in Klemm (ed.), *Alberto Giacometti* (New York and Zurich, 2001), as well as Rosalind Krauss's important 1984 essay on Giacometti collected in *The Originality of the Avant-Garde and Other Modernist Myths* (Cambridge, MA, 1985), pp. 42–85.

31 Alberto Giacometti, 'Objets mobiles et muets', *Le Surréalisme au service de la révolution*, 3 (December 1931), p. 19. For another discussion of touch in Giacometti's sculpture, see Chapter 2 below.

32 Walter Benjamin, 'The Work of Art in the Age of Mechanical Reproduction' [1936], in Benjamin, *Illuminations* [1955], ed. Hannah Arendt, trans. H. Zohn (New York, 1969), p. 240.

33 Ibid., p. 223.

34 Ibid., p. 222.

35 Tristan Tzara, 'D'un certain automatisme du goût', *Minotaure*, 3–4 (December 1933), pp. 209–10; Claude Cahun, 'Prenez garde aux objets domestiques', *Cahiers d'art*, 11e année (1936), p. 46.

36 For an excellent discussion of Henry Moore's relations to surrealism, which I can't explore here, see Julia Kelly, 'The Unfamiliar Figure: Henry Moore in French periodicals in the 1930s', in Jane Beckett and Fiona Russell (eds), *Henry Moore: Critical Essays* (Aldershot, 2003), pp. 43–65.

37 The reader is referred to the passage from Breton's 'Crise de l'objet' cited in n. 25.

38 Hans Arp, 'A propos de l'art abstrait', *Cahiers d'art*, 6e année, 7–8 (1931), p. 358. This is to my knowledge the first appearance of this statement, which is repeated later on several occasions. The essay is also Arp's first statement of his artistic principles since 1915 – or 1920, if 'Alexander Partens' is a pseudonym for, among others, Arp in the essay on dada art in the 1920 *Dada Almanach*. (A note in the 1993 English edition of the *Almanach* states that 'Partens' was a pseudonym for Arp, Tzara and Walter Serner. Editorial note to Alexander Partens, 'Dada Art', in Richard Huelsenbeck (ed.), *Dada Almanac* [1920], new edn, ed. Malcolm Green and Alastair Brotchie [London, 1993], p. 91.)

39 See, most recently, Emmanuel Guigon, Hans van der Werf, and Mariet Willinge (eds), *L'Aubette ou la couleur dans l'architecture: Une Oeuvre de Hans Arp, Sophie Taeuber-Arp, Theo van Doesburg* (Strasbourg, 2006).

40 Michel Seuphor, 'L'Art nouveau et le surréalisme', *Abstraction création art non figuratif*, 1 (1932), p. 11. Seuphor's essay is structured around several binaries: health/disease, reason/irrationality, construction/destruction, Christianity/Communism. Needless to say, the 'new art' of his title is not surrealism, but becomes aware of what it can be through the need to develop an alternative to surrealism. In this way, surrealism has the role of a necessary evil, but an evil nonetheless, which he describes as 'this belt of impurity and nonsense' ['cette ceinture de l'impureté et du non-sens'], against which one brandishes the weapons of wisdom and faith.

41 In the anonymous editorial to the first issue of *Abstraction création art non figuratif*, two kinds of non-figurative art were described: those which abstracted from nature, and those which were constructed along geometric lines. Any artists whose work had figurative associations were not to be admitted, though in practice there are figurative associations in a minority of the works reproduced in the review, including those by Arp. *Abstraction création art non figuratif 1932*, p. 1.

42 'Abjection et misère de l'Abstraction Création' is one of four texts that constitute *La Conquête de l'irrationnel*, cited in n. 20.

43 Kandinsky and Arp had known each other since 1912, when Arp contributed to the *Blaue Reiter Almanach*, and Arp was the first artist Kandinsky visited when he relocated to Paris in 1933. On their relations, see Harriet Watts, 'Arp, Kandinsky, and the Legacy of Jakob Böhme', in *The Spiritual in Art: Abstract Painting 1890–1985* (Los Angeles and New York, 1986), pp. 239–55.

44 Arp, 'A propos de l'art abstrait', p. 358.

45 Theo van Doesburg, 'Comments on the Basis of Concrete Painting' [1930], trans. Joost Baljeu, in Baljeu, *Theo van Doesburg* (New York, 1974), p. 182.

46 Ibid.

47 Jean Arp, 'Dadaland' [1938], trans. R. Manheim, in Lucy R. Lippard (ed.), *Dadas on Art* (Englewood Cliffs, NJ, 1971), p. 24; Partens, 'Dada Art' [1920], trans. M. Green, in *Dada Almanac*, p. 93.

48 Jane Hancock plausibly suggests 1917 rather than the generally-accepted 1916 as the earliest date for the reliefs, given that geometrical compositions were Arp's primary preoccupation through most of 1916, as we know from his correspondence. The reliefs, which like most of his production were not dated by the artist, were first exhibited in 1918. Jane Hancock, 'The Philosophy in Arp's Formal Language: Toward an Interpretation', in *Arp 1886–1966* (Cambridge, 1987), p. 62.

49 Jane Hancock, 'Arp's Chance Collages', in Stephen C. Foster (ed.), *Dada/Dimensions* (Ann Arbor, 1985), p. 64. In Jean Arp, *Jours effeuillés: Poèmes, essais, souvenirs 1920–65*, ed. Marcel Jean (Paris, 1966), Arp's letter to Brzekowski is dated to 1927, but this is impossible given that Brzekowski only arrived in Paris in 1928, and only started his review in 1929. Moreover, Arp's remark that 'more recently the surrealist painters have been using illusionist descriptive academic means which would warm the cockles of rops' heart' [*sic*] would appear to refer to Dalí's tumultuous entry into the surrealist group in November 1929, rather than to any developments in 1927. Arp, 'Cher Monsieur Brzekowski', in *Jours effeuillés*, p. 63; Jean Arp, *Arp on Arp: Poems, Essays, Memories*, ed. Marcel Jean, trans. J. Neugroschel (New York, 1972), p. 35.

50 Hancock, 'Arp's Chance Collages', pp. 79–80 (n. 65); Harriet Watts, 'Hans Arp and the Principle of Constellation', in J. Hancock and S. Poley (eds), *Arp 1886–1966* (Cambridge, 1987), p. 112; Margherita Andreotti, *The Early Sculpture of Jean Arp* (Ann Arbor, 1989), p. 84.

51 Arp's views on surrealism are expressed in Jean Arp, 'Cher Monsieur Brzekowski' [1930], in *Jours effeuillés*, p. 63; Hans Arp, 'Notes from a Diary' [1932], trans. E. Jolas, in Hancock and Poley, *Arp 1886–1966*, p. 11; Arp, 'Art concret' [1944], in *Jours effeuillés*, p. 184; Jean Hans Arp, 'Looking', in *Arp*, ed. James Thrall Soby, trans. R. Manheim (New York, 1958), p. 14; Pierre Schneider, 'Arp Speaks for the Laws of Chance', *ARTnews*, 57 (November 1958), pp. 50–51. Arp's 'Notes from a Diary', while largely concerned with dada, also protest Aragon's defection from surrealism the previous month.

52 Marcel Duchamp, entry on Arp in *Collection of the Société Anonyme* (1950), in Michel Sanouillet and Elmer Peterson (eds), *The Writings of Marcel Duchamp* (New York, 1989), p. 144.

53 In her catalogue of Arp's early sculpture, Margherita Andreotti proposes 1932 as the most likely date of fabrication for these two undated sculptures, although *Head with Annoying Objects* has sometimes been dated to 1930. *Head with Annoying Objects* was first seen at the *Exposition surréaliste* at the Galerie Pierre Colle in 1933, and reproduced in *Cahiers d'art*, 8e année, 5–6 (1933), and *Navel and Two Thoughts* was reproduced in *Abstraction création art non figuratif* no. 2 (1933). Andreotti, *The Early Sculpture of Jean Arp*, pp. 269 and 275–6.

54 'La grande mouche la moustache et la petite mandoline', a poem describing the objects named in the 1932 sculpture and their appearance on Arp's face upon awakening from a dreamless sleep, was first published in 1946 in the 1917–35 section of Arp's major collection of poetry, *Le Siège de l'air*. We can thus infer that it was written around the time of the sculpture. Arp, *Jours effeuillés*, pp. 249–50. Aimée Bleikasten discusses this text in 'Arp the Poet, or, The Voice of Origins', in Hancock and Poley, *Arp 1886–1966*, p. 22.

55 Partens, 'Dada Art', p. 95.

56 I am using Mary McAllester Jones's translation of a passage from chapter 4 of *L'Eau et les rêves*, first published in 1942. Mary McAllester Jones, *Gaston Bachelard: Subversive Humanist* (Madison, 1991), p. 105. The reference to Dalí is on p. 104. The whole book has been translated by Edith R. Farrell as *Water and Dreams: An Essay on the Imagination of Matter* (Dallas, 1983).

57 Schneider, p. 50; William Rubin, *Dada and Surrealist Art* (New York, 1969), p. 261.

58 Ibid.

59 Carola Giedion-Welcker, 'The World of Forms and Phantoms in Arp's Work', *Quadrum*, 11 (1961), p. 188.

60 Michel Seuphor, *L'Art abstrait* [1949], as quoted by Briony Fer in 'The Laws of Chance' in Fer, *On Abstract Art* (New Haven, 1997), p. 61. Richard Huelsenbeck noted the maternal nature of Arp's art twice, in 'The Sculptor Jean Arp' [1954], included in *Memoirs of a Dada Drummer* [1957], ed. Hans J. Kleinschmidt, trans. J. Neugroschel (New York, 1974), p. 100, and in the *Memoirs* themselves, p. 15.

61 Fer, *On Abstract Art* p. 76; Andreotti, p. 139. Andreotti is translating from the French version of Arp's 'Les Pis sont desséchés', originally published in English by the Curt Valentin Gallery as part of *Dreams and Projects* in 1951. Neugroschel's version in *Arp on Arp* differs slightly.

62 Arp, 'Concrete Art', in *Arp on Arp*, p. 140. This is a revised version of the essay first published in *Art of This Century*.

63 Arp, 'Danger de mort' [1954], in *Jours effeuillés*, p. 403; 'Mortal Danger', in *Arp on Arp*, p. 315. The text first appeared in *XXe siècle* in January 1954.

64 In a letter of 2 June 1934 reproduced in facsimile in *Abstraction–Création 1931–36* (Münster and Paris, 1978), pp. 54–5, Louis Fernandez, Jean Hélion, Arp and Sophie Taeuber resigned from Abstraction–Création over what they took to be Auguste Herbin's high-handed direction of the organisation.

65 Arp, 'Looking', pp. 14–15.

66 Fer, 'The Laws of Chance', *On Abstract Art*, pp. 55–76. Hal Foster's *Compulsive Beauty* (Cambridge, MA, 1993), is a deconstructive reading of surrealism through the logic of the death drive, as this is theorised in psychoanalytic thought.

67 Watts, 'Hans Arp and the Principle of Constellation', in Hancock and Poley, *Arp 1886–1966*, p. 112; Andreotti, p. 84.

2

The Found, the Made and the Functional: Surrealism, Objects and Sculpture

Julia Kelly

When in the early 1930s Salvador Dalí famously declared the surrealist object to be 'extra-plastic and made by all', these terms appeared to challenge head on the fundamental tenets of western art-making in the early twentieth century.[1] Pitted against the individual 'professional' artist, against concerns of technique and material and against artistic medium specificity, surrealism in principle was at odds with the notion of 'sculpture' as a special kind of practice, and with the production of 'sculptures' as special three-dimensional works of art. Yet the surrealist object proved to be a notoriously open category, covering a wide variety of different 'things': not only so-called found objects issuing from an industrial production line, but also objects 'shaped' by the forces of nature, objects made by the hand either of an artist, a self-defining non-artist or indeed an anonymous artisan, as well as objects whose origins were deliberately obscure.

From our perspective now, instead of implying a simplistic opposition between modernist 'high' art and its unruly other, the surrealist object in practice, particularly with regard to the work of 'trained' artists involved with surrealism, presents a complex knot of technical, material and conceptual concerns, compounded by its mediation through photographic reproduction. In particular, the so-called object existed in intriguing proximity to sculpture being made by artists affiliated with surrealism. The works I will address in the second half of this essay, by Alberto Giacometti and Paule Vézelay, were made to look like found objects, or incorporated found objects into tabletop assemblages which themselves had a functional appearance, as if made for other purposes than artistic 'contemplation'. Moreover, I am arguing that these works complicate the distinctions between sculptural practice and the surrealist project, to the advantage of both.

For André Breton, one of surrealism's main early theorists, objects were glimpsed in dreams, and the artist's task more generally was to 'trace' visual apparitions and images, both concepts pointing to a realm of intangibility and fragility, rather than the material certainty of sculpture.[2] The sculptures produced by Giacometti and Vézelay during the 1930s, however – small, hand-sized pieces made of plaster, and experimental works using strings and wires in combination with solid sculptural forms – explored the tensions between 'spontaneous' drawings in space and concretely realised forms. If sculpture for surrealism was too lumbering and unwieldy to be truly 'automatic', the works of these two artists arguably complicated such distinctions by playing with sculptural form and function in subtle but radical ways. Like the slight bits of fingered debris that found their way under Brassaï's lens in the page of 'Sculptures involontaires' in 1933 (Figure I.1), these works referred to everyday tactility and the impulses of the hand.

Involuntary Contraptions in Dada and Surrealism

The practice of making sculpture could not easily find a place in the collection of activities and aspirations that coalesced under the heading 'surrealism' in the mid 1920s. Surrealism's intellectual allegiances were primarily with literature, as the model for what André Breton termed 'thought-writing'.[3] Modern 'sculpture' appeared to play no role here, save in the guise of three-dimensional artefacts: tantalising found objects or the pre-existing 'modern mannequins' that intrigued Breton.[4] The paintings of Giorgio de Chirico provided evocations of traditional municipal statuary, now imbued with disturbing psychic associations, as well as Greco-Roman style fragments, like the headless torso in *The Uncertainty of the Poet* (1913). An isolated torso floating in the Seine appeared in Breton's 1924 *Soluble Fish*, while the cast of a headless and armless woman's body, presumably a close relation of the 'modern mannequin', hung from the ceiling of the 'Bureau de recherches surréalistes'.[5]

While the first wave of surrealist activity centring around the short-lived Bureau in 1924–25 pointed towards the 'discovery' of objects, either by actively hunting them in the Paris flea markets, or by eliciting donations from the 'public', like the bronze glove given to the Bureau by Lise Deharme, the few three-dimensional works published in *La Révolution surréaliste* did include things not just found, but also made.[6] Works by Man Ray such as the cork *Object* and the card and feather assemblage *De quoi écrire* (1922) took found elements but combined and altered these to form new configurations. These pieces did engage to some degree with more properly sculptural concerns of materials and technique: paper folding and carving in cork. If such concerns were not explicit in 1920s surrealism, this may have been in part due to the deliberate distancing of Breton and his then affiliates from dada, and particularly from the work and interests of Tristan Tzara. In dada, arguably, could be found the seeds of many of the ideas that would inform both the development of the surrealist object, and the production of what might be called surrealist sculpture.

Dada's 'anti-art' spirit encouraged the use of 'low' materials like wood and paper, employed in rough techniques, like the pieces of wood roughly nailed together in Hans Arp's reliefs. Tzara described these new processes as defiantly anti-painting, in terms that suggested sculptural interventions: 'The new artist protests; he no longer paints (symbolical and illusionist reproduction) but creates directly in stone, wood or iron, rocks which are locomotive organisms capable of being turned in any direction by the limpid wind of momentary sensation.'[7] The imagery used by Tzara here appeared to oppose the cerebral and distanced act of painting with something much more immediate and visceral which would have a direct bodily relationship to its maker or viewer. Tzara's description also cast dada production as kinetic, culminating in objects subject to arbitrary and involuntary movements.

While Arp's reliefs of the 1910s appeared to some extent to reflect the artist's careful control of the material as a wood-carver, despite their iconography of free-flowing shapes, sculptural constructions by Marcel Janco were more arbitrary in appearance and thus closer to Tzara's evocation of three-dimensional art making activity. In the first issue of the Zurich-based *Dada*, Tzara described some pieces by Janco in the following poetic terms:

> he has made some surface sculptures until him people made superimpositions of bodies and used wire as drawing in space (for the first time) the upper part of construction 3 allows matter to show its life wire trembles sensitive moon sun blue sea horse at the bottom of the sea [*sic*].[8]

Striking in this statement is the emphasis less on a strident and aggressive form of 'anti-art' as protest, but Tzara's appreciation of the delicate and contingent qualities of Janco's work. Janco's *Construction 3*, reproduced to accompany Tzara's commentary, can only be imprecisely apprehended from the black and white photograph of it that exists in facsimiles of the periodical and in a postcard reproduction of the period, but it seems to have played upon a contrast between solid volumes and the insubstantiality of loops of fine wire (its use of wire, with its reference to forms of jewellery such as earrings, is reminiscent of the work of the Baroness Elsa von Freytag-Loringhoven at about the same time in New York, whose tendency towards the ephemeral and bodily interactivity has been analysed by Amelia Jones).[9]

This work by Janco, possibly a deliberately impermanent piece, sets up a very different precedent in dada for surrealist sculptural activity than the reliefs of Arp or the dolls and puppets of his partner Sophie Taeuber-Arp. Instead of referring to the human figure, whether directly through an uncanny wooden double, or through carved figurative forms such as navels or moustaches, Janco's construction was a kind of contraption, perhaps a measuring instrument vibrating in response to touch or atmospheric changes. Its orientation was as much to the hand (and perhaps even the ear) as to the eyes: intended for some kind of interaction and use as well as visual contemplation. This meant too that a work of this nature might change its physical appearance due to manipulation or movement, no longer fixed at the moment of its completion by the artist but open to further development. The early objects of Marcel Duchamp like the 1913 *Bicycle Wheel* come to mind here, but also the work of constructivist sculptors like Vladimir Tatlin, working on open-ended three-dimensional projects such as the *Corner Counter-Reliefs* (*c.*1914).

In the surrealist context, Giacometti's *Suspended Ball* (1930–31) was celebrated as a model for the surrealist object, but it also resembled a contraption to be manipulated, or at least set in motion, with its hanging sphere suggesting the mechanism of a clock. One potential model for it was the pendulum of the nineteenth-century scientist Léon Foucault housed in the Musée des Arts et Métiers in Paris, a spherical device for demonstrating the earth's revolution, which in its original incarnation had brushed against a bed of wet sand, as

Giacometti's ball might be imagined to brush against the curved wedge beneath it. *Suspended Ball*'s reference to temporal measurement was made explicit in Giacometti's *L'Heure des traces* (1931), whose pointed sliver mounted on a thin vertical wire, often read as a dagger, additionally suggested the curved slides of measuring instruments such as compasses or octants. The production of new surrealist *contraptions* rather than objects had been encouraged by Louis Aragon in his article for the first issue of *La Révolution surréaliste*, 'The Shadow of the Inventor'.[10] Aragon had lamented the banality of the new gadgets paraded at the Concours Lépine, the Parisian inventors' fair, and had called for the creation of more interesting inventions which could dazzle their owners and spectators with a display equivalent to the ingenuity of parlour tricks. Aragon praised, for example, the swinging mechanism of 'two wood cutters ... striking in turn a tree trunk' (that he had perhaps seen on a cuckoo clock), a folding axe he had seen in an ironmonger's window with the caption 'the only one that opens like a book', and a toy goldfish mounted on a pole with a semi-circle of metal fixed to it, which when spun created the illusion of a spherical bowl (the latter example with its optical illusion reminding us that Duchamp took his *Rotoreliefs* of the mid-1920s to the same inventors' fair Aragon was haunting).[11] For Aragon, these seemingly 'minor' objects and amusements with their swinging and spinning movements were equivalent to the 'great' technological insights, such as Galileo's pendulum experiments. The surrealist interest in new object-inventions, also one of the areas of concern of the Bureau of Surrealist Research, seems to have been lost in the articulation of the dream-object by Breton, and arguably only re-emerged in Giacometti's early 1930s works.

The concept of a 'contraption', of course, implies the construction of a deliberate mechanism. Giacometti's early 1930s sculptures in this vein, which include *Point to the Eye* and *Caught Hand*, have no obvious 'function', resembling instead the absurd machines of dadaist imagination. Aragon's essay, however, suggested a process of invention, a spark of ingenuity in the objects he identified, which went beyond any banal function, whether intended by their makers or not. It was significant that one of the contraptions he described, the fish appearing to hover in the 'bowl' of a strip of rotating metal, was a kind of toy, although not necessarily exclusively a children's toy, just as the parlour tricks he praised were games for adults. In this sense, the surrealist contraption might occupy a space between the strictly functional object and the 'curiosity', maintaining an experimental openness through manipulation and interaction. Spontaneous invention and reinvention through 'use' constituted one form of three-dimensional 'automatism', where both the maker and the viewer-handler of the object participated in chance configurations and reconfigurations of form and function.

Surrealist Objects, Rocks and Roots

When Giacometti's sculpture began to be celebrated by the surrealists in the early 1930s, this reception came with an important caveat. In his article on 'Symbolically Functioning Objects' for *Le Surréalisme au service de la révolution*,

Dalí praised Giacometti's *Suspended Ball*, but also pointed out its shortcomings for the surrealist conception of the object. Giacometti's work, Dalí complained, 'kept within the means proper to sculpture'. Subsequent surrealist objects should avoid considerations of material, technique and form: 'Objects with a symbolic function', he argued, should 'leave no room for formal preoccupations'.[12] Here, Dalí set out a clear refusal of anything that could properly be called 'sculpture', because its insistence on intentional technical fabrication could not for him be reconciled with the spontaneous, 'automatic' discovery of the object. Alongside the work of Giacometti, with his background as a trained sculptor (in the studio of Emile-Antoine Bourdelle), were reproduced objects by writers with no formal training in the visual arts at all, such as Gala Eluard and André Breton.

If 'automatic' sculpture seemed like an unrealisable proposition, surrealist 'automatic' writing in fact was itself in an impossible position. Laurent Jenny has shown how 'authentic' automatism was tempered by the demands of rhetorical expression.[13] Raising the same problems that appeared to pertain to surrealist painting and indeed sculpture, automatic writing represented an ideal moment before the intervention of speech and linguistic or artistic form. The concerns of linguistic style might be said to feature more strongly in the case of individual expression, hence, presumably, the surrealist interest in collective artistic invention. If automatic writing aspired to a lost state of pure 'spoken thought', the equivalent of this in sculptural terms is difficult to identify. The found object, as something potentially 'free' from conscious artistic intervention, often came loaded with cultural connotations (the cylindrical graph reproduced in *Nadja* with its obscure three-dimensional charts as an example of 'weird science', the folkloric wooden 'slipper-spoon' photographed by Man Ray for Breton's *L'Amour fou*, the black magic 'tabernacle' allegedly found by Yves Tanguy at a flea market). But the surrealist interest in found *natural* objects might provide a more promising line of enquiry, where 'automatism' could signal a broader realm of collective experience from an anthropological perspective.

Surrealism's deliberate focus on the object as an anti-artistic activity was clearly significant in opening up a much broader arena of sculptural practice than previously available. That poets or writers could make objects, that objects could be 'found' and presented, that they could consist of rough or throwaway materials, and be part of an ongoing process (without necessarily being 'finished' for posterity and preservation), all of these factors expanded the remit of sculptural activity in ways that have been highly influential. However, the surrealist object also varied widely, not only in the obvious sense of the content and connotations of individual objects, but also in the differing degrees of artistic intervention and manipulation that these involved. It is at this point that the fraught relationship between the terms 'object' and 'sculpture' most strongly comes to the fore.

The found natural object, potentially the 'degree zero' of object production, in fact belongs to a relatively common and traditional category of 'artistic' collecting: the strangely shaped stone, the unusual shell found on the beach, the exceptional crystal formation. Items like these featured in the personal collections of several surrealists, including Breton, but also referred back to traditions of Renaissance collecting and the cabinets of curiosity of the sixteenth and seventeenth centuries.[14] Their principle attraction was their embodiment of the 'mysterious' or 'wondrous' workings of nature in producing, without human intervention, intriguing forms that seemed to rival human artistic inventiveness or complexity. Such objects could be seen as 'automatic' sculptures in the sense that some kind of primal material urge or volition was immanent in them, causing them to produce spectacular forms unconsciously.

The interpretation of found objects in these terms had a clear relationship to the surrealist interest in psychoanalytic theory, as the externalisation of hidden drives and desires, as several commentators have shown.[15] Here, however, I would like to frame them with a different discourse drawn from anthropology, in order to address their material and technical qualities, that is to say, the *sculptural* concerns that I feel have been overlooked. In anthropological analyses of the earliest forms of art-making, early humans were seen to have been struck by the anthropomorphic or zoomorphic features of natural found objects, as evidence of their animistic life-force, and hence to have singled these objects out as particularly significant and worthy both of collection, and of deployment as the basis for further artistic intervention. I will draw here in particular on the work of the late nineteenth-century British anthropological theorist Henry Balfour, whose highly influential work in this field underpinned many of the developments in the early twentieth-century 'anthropology of art', but who was also one of the few theorists to refer explicitly to sculpture.[16]

Balfour's 1893 *The Evolution of Decorative Art* provided an especially interesting examination of the development of sculptural forms, a topic rarely discussed specifically in texts of this period, which focused largely on the 'evolution' of linear motifs.[17] While discoveries of cave art during the nineteenth century had provided the materials for discussions of the development of graphic production, there was no real equivalent for sculpture.[18] Cave paintings could be more readily re- (and mis-) interpreted by the modern age as 'art', but ancient stones and bones bearing the marks of human intervention had a more ambiguous status, being too close to tools and implements. Balfour, however, saw such objects as the first kind of sculptural practice, and he used the term 'sculpture' explicitly. The transition between tools and art was, for Balfour, the consequence of a purely accidental procedure: the recognition of chance resemblances in found or made objects to human or animal forms. He stressed: '... there is far more reason for believing that art owes its absolute origin to *accident* in this manner than that it is the direct outcome of the intelligence, the application of matured reasoning'.[19] Such a recognition of a coincidental likeness, in Balfour's terms, led to 'the application of artificial means in order to increase the effect of this accidental resemblance', that is to say, to carving or incising extra features, like adding an eye to a piece of wood shaped like an animal's head.

One of the examples Balfour used in his analysis of the beginnings of sculpture anticipated an important found object in Breton's own collection: the mandrake root (Figure 2.1). Balfour pointed to the wealth of superstitions and spiritual power bestowed upon the mandrake due to its anthropomorphic qualities (its forked root resembling two legs). But he also drew attention to the interplay of

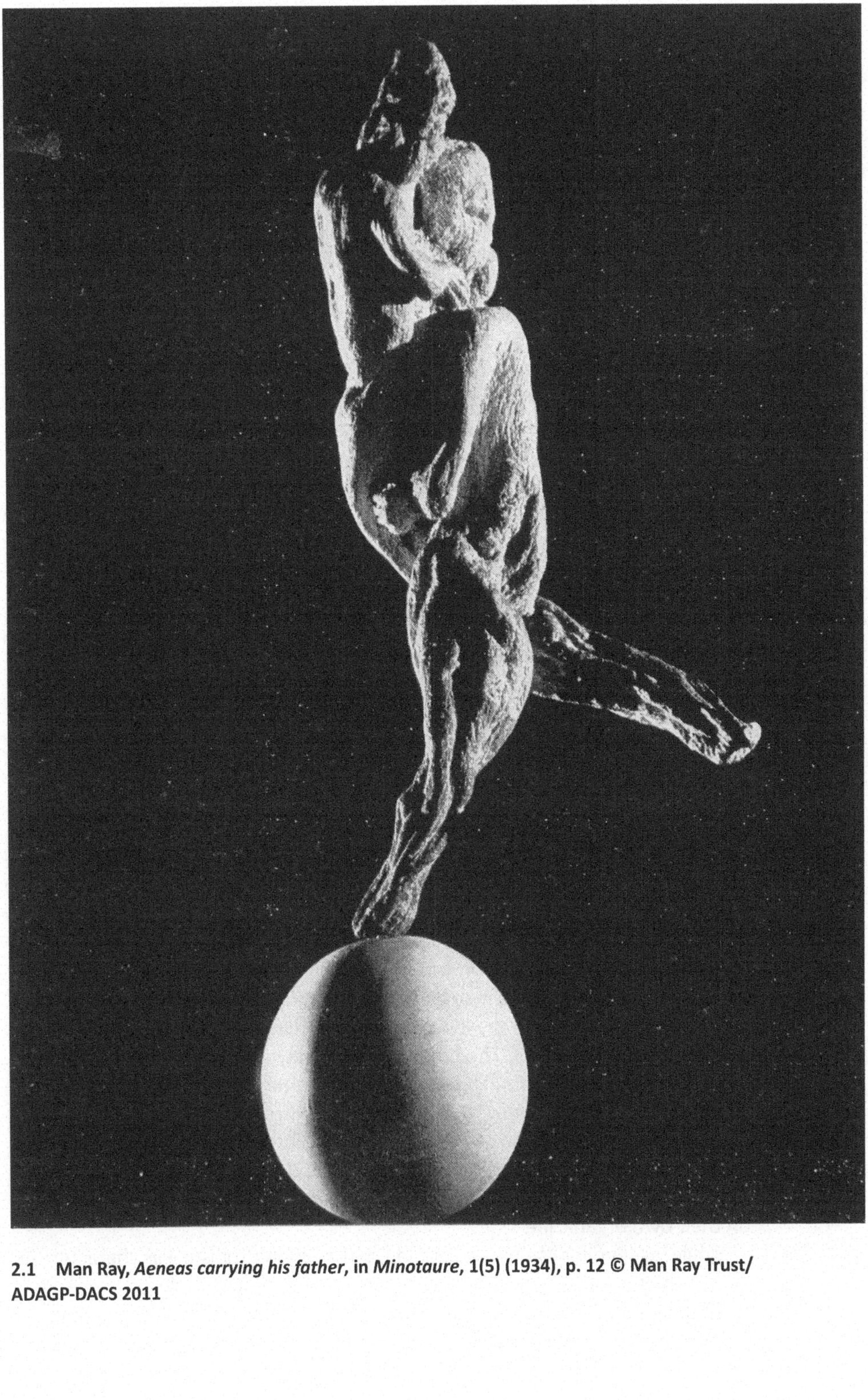

2.1 Man Ray, *Aeneas carrying his father*, in *Minotaure*, 1(5) (1934), p. 12 © Man Ray Trust/ ADAGP-DACS 2011

accidental likeness and human intervention in the perception of the mandrake's significance:

> The likeness ... is frequently aided by art, the living root being carved so as to further resemble a man or woman, with well-formed face and limbs ... and being subsequently allowed to go on growing for a while, is then traded off upon the confiding public as a curiosity in natural growth, with a corresponding endowment of super-natural potency.[20]

The mandrake, then, was a striking instance of the combination of a 'found' natural (and spectacular) form, with sculptural processes like carving employed to 'improve' upon its appearance. The mandrake root owned by Breton, which for him resembled Aeneas carrying his father and became one of the subjects of his text 'La Beauté sera convulsive', was further enhanced in the photograph of it taken by Man Ray for *Minotaure*, where the mandrake was shown balanced upon a pale sphere and dramatically lit against a black background.[21] That Breton could read into his mandrake root an implied mythological narrative of trauma and loss demonstrates the collaboration and interdependence between the object and its finder/owner, heightened in this instance by the mandrake's material properties.

The mandrake was a significant example of a potentially 'automatic' sculpture: a natural object whose initial anthropomorphism was already notable, heightened by carving and by the fact that it would continue to grow while still being worked upon, giving its final appearance an essential unpredictability. The contemporary anthropological theorist Tim Ingold has used the term 'autopoiesis' to challenge the prevailing distinction that 'artefacts are made, organisms grow'.[22] In an analysis drawing upon early twentieth-century animist theories (for instance, D'Arcy Thompson's *On Growth and Form*, 1917), Ingold describes this concept as 'the self-transformation over time of the system of relations within which an organism or artefact comes into being'.[23] While Ingold's object of study is a more ostensibly functional one, the coiled basket, the mandrake root could similarly be thought of as a 'self-generating' form, emerging from an interactive process with its finders, carvers or owners.

The concerns underlying Balfour's late-nineteenth-century study, which included a strong emphasis on 'primitive' beliefs in the animism of inanimate objects, also informed the work of his peer Alfred Haddon, who coined the term 'biomorph' to evoke the living qualities of things which grew, changed and developed (or 'evolved').[24] The biomorph's 'borrowed vitality', as Haddon put it, pointed to the fact that its 'life' was a perceived rather than actual feature of it.[25] 'Biomorphism', itself a highly slippery term, took on a further set of connotations when it was applied to artistic production in Europe in the 1930s, finding a particular application to a range of sculptural production, in the work of Arp and Henry Moore above all, where plaster, wood and stone forms appeared to take on their own organic life.

While, as Jennifer Mundy has argued, artistic biomorphism was characterised by 'an imagery of irregularly curvilinear shapes that are closed or tending towards closure', its anthropological definition suggested instead an openness of form in the interaction of object and viewer/user as part of an ongoing process.[26]

The British critic Geoffrey Grigson was the first to use the term 'biomorphism' in relation to western art in his anthology *The Arts To-Day* in 1935, but his discussion of it in relation to three-dimensional production strongly echoed Balfour's analysis of the recognition of form in natural objects. The first three-dimensional artist, Grigson claimed:

> ... may have recognised in a tool, while shaping it, or in a stone or other fragment which he picked up, an accidental likeness to creatures that filled his mind ... or ... he may simply have read into objects the shape of which affected him the important memory images of animal or woman. The chance likeness, or the imagined likeness could then be deliberately or accidently [*sic*] increased, or made 'real', and the figure in this way would have been an act of creation by himself.[27]

If the mandrake had anthropomorphic potential due to its status as a living, growing plant, the stones and crystals that the surrealists collected could also be seen to have animistic properties. Indeed, this aspect of surrealist activity, I would argue, contributed on one level to the connection made by Grigson between imagined archaic art-making and modern art practice.[28] Breton collected throughout his life examples of stones, roots and pieces of wood with 'accidental' anthropomorphic properties. Some of these may have been deliberately manipulated in the manner of the mandrake root (another good example of this are the highly prized Chinese scholars' rocks with their extraordinary formations, believed for centuries to be 'natural' occurrences but in fact often enhanced by carving).[29] Beyond the anthropological concept of 'nature worship', the surrealists could also draw upon German romantic literature for instances of this theme, in particular Ludwig Tieck's *Der Runenberg* (1802), in which underground crystals and geological formations were construed as living. The 'desert rose' that Max Ernst owned, a gift from Roland Penrose that he conserved in a special box, was such an example of a natural concretion which had taken on a spectacular form 'involuntarily' (Michel Leiris also later used the image of this stone to evoke Giacometti's post-war sculpture).[30]

In relational theories of art, for example Alfred Gell's 'anthropology of art', found objects such as natural forms, as well as Duchamp's readymades, are instances of an interaction between the artist and the object, rather than existing purely in themselves.[31] Citing the example of Buddhist garden designers, selectors of the most striking natural boulders, who are considered as creatively superior to stone carvers or sculptors, Gell emphasised the artist's role in choosing the 'right' object:

> ... even the purportedly 'arbitrary' ready-mades of Duchamp, forced themselves on the artist (as patient) who responded to the appeal of their arbitrariness and anonymity, just as the Buddhist landscape artists responded to their mutely speaking boulders.[32]

In this reading, the strangely shaped rock or root of surrealist imagination could only become 'involuntary' or 'automatic' through its reception as such, through the artist's response and involvement, assuming a role as a kind of interlocutor. Moreover, the artist's selection had important consequences for the object's further reception by a spectator, as part of what Gell has called elsewhere 'the technology of enchantment'.[33] The function of a particular object in these terms is inseparable from the spectacular form 'harnessed' by its finder: surely this is the significance of the 'convulsive beauty' of Breton's mandrake. But more significantly here, the object in its engagement with its finder by definition had a function or use that was an integral part of its 'artistic' impact, just as the sculptural objects discussed by Balfour were both tools and also decorative pieces.

Giacometti's Surrealist Tools

Amongst the variety of surrealist objects, there was one which had an intriguing relationship to ideas of function: the wooden 'slipper-spoon' supposedly found at a flea market by Breton and aligned by him with the work of Giacometti in his essay 'Equation de l'objet trouvé' (see Figure 8.2).[34] This wooden spoon, decorated with a small boot at the end of its handle, suggested the folk carving traditions of Central or Eastern Europe, and was a good example of something with an ostensible use which also carried a symbolic charge – its tiny shoe prompting Breton to contemplate the fairytale *Cinderella*. The spoon's potential function as an implement was made more effective by its unusual form (the theme of magical transformation in Charles Perrault's tale was surely not a coincidental factor in Breton's choice of it). This implies, of course, a very different conception of the surrealist found object often described as essentially 'diverted' from its original use. Instead, we might place an emphasis on the process of 'discovering' the found object as the automatic gesture, allowing the potency of the object itself to impress itself upon its finder, despite their intentions.

Giacometti had in fact just prior to the appearance of Breton's text published an account of his own production of sculpture that called attention to his own surrender of conscious control (a rare trope in sculptors' writings):

> For years I have only given form to sculptures which offered themselves complete to my mind, I have limited myself to reproduce them in space without changing anything or asking myself what they could mean … Attempts I have sometimes made to consciously give form to a painting or even to a sculpture have always failed.[35]

Giacometti's description, in his essay 'I can only speak *indirectly* about my sculptures', of a process of 'finding' sculptures ready made in his mind is clearly highly ambiguous, given that he rarely used actual found objects in his early 1930s works, instead creating forms that *resembled* found things (small skeletons, marble-like spheres, game board pieces). But his statement did encapsulate the tensions existing between objects and sculpture in surrealism that his works would also play out. In particular, the *Disagreeable Objects* and related works from 1930 to 1931, which did away altogether with the built-in mini pedestals and framing devices of earlier pieces, functioned as freestanding sculptures viewed potentially from many perspectives and amenable to tactile intervention. Like many surrealist objects, these works too posed a challenge to the distanced preciousness of the 'high' artwork, deliberately allying themselves with the realm of the overlooked artefact.

In this respect we could read Giacometti's *Disagreeable Object* of 1931, produced first in plaster then in wood, as the hidden counterpart to Breton's 'slipper-spoon': both prostrate objects intended to be handled, and both carrying phallic connotations (see Figures 1.1 and 1.2). Like the folk spoon, Giacometti's tusk-shaped object also appeared to have some kind of use, with conical protrusions at its narrow end and grooves in its bulbous 'handle', suggesting the wear of fingers. The forms of this sculpture cleverly evoked a piece of found natural material – a tusk, horn, or even a length of bone, stone or driftwood – which had been minimally transformed in order to improve its efficacy, in the manner of the archaic tool-maker. This object also, like some of the prehistoric tools discussed by Balfour, had an anthropomorphic aspect that has been relatively overlooked. The hollows in its 'handle' can be read as facial features, while the sharp points resemble vestigial limbs. In the small drawing Giacometti made of the work for his 1948 letter to his dealer Pierre Matisse, it appears much more fragile than its wooden or plaster variants, closer in shape to a diminutive prone figure.[36] Disturbingly, the 'disagreeable object' becomes an (unwanted) baby or foetus as well as a proto-weapon.

Giacometti's work, of course, was the knowing and sophisticated product of a skilled training, and he was also seen by the rare few, in the early 1930s, as a 'real' sculptor pursuing sculptural concerns. In an article on Giacometti for *Cahiers d'art* in 1932, the critic Christian Zervos stressed the artist's quest for sculptural perfection, arguing that he was increasingly 'eliminating anything that can harm its pure plasticity'.[37] Zervos claimed in this respect that Giacometti's work *Caress* of 1932 was to undergo a revision: the shape of the hand traced in the plaster was to be eliminated from the final stone version as it had no formal role, being irrelevant and even an annoyance ('son rôle plastique étant nul, même gênant'). It was no coincidence that the incised feature Zervos identified as extraneous (and which Giacometti did *not* ask to be eliminated in the marble version executed by his brother Diego, after all appearing on both sides of the sculpture), represented the tactile interaction that the surrealist object was beginning to intimate. In 1932, at the time of the publication of Zervos's article in *Cahiers d'art*, Giacometti gave the work later known as *Caress* a different title: 'Malgré les mains', 'In spite of the hands', a phrase that perhaps literally referred to the 'annoying' incised hands discussed by Zervos, but which also suggested the tensions implicit in the sculptor's ways of working.

Caress also represented an urge to touch and stroke the rounded and swollen forms of modern sculpture. If a discourse of sculptural autonomy in the early twentieth century proposed the separation of viewer and work, Giacometti's *Caress* suggested an atavistic return to a 'forbidden' tactility. In the work of Arp or Henry Moore, so-called biomorphic sculptures which evoked organic bodily swellings were those most likely to be included in surveys of surrealist art in the 1930s, in exhibition or book form.[38] Giacometti's *Caress* served to say: 'look, these works are meant to be held and handled'.

Questions of tactile intervention and 'use' informed several of Giacometti's early 1930s sculptures. His *Vide-Poche* of 1930 played with the idea of a place to put small everyday odds and ends, reconfigured as two sculptural forms within a shallow bowl (Figure 2.2). Here, instead of holding actual pocket debris or loose

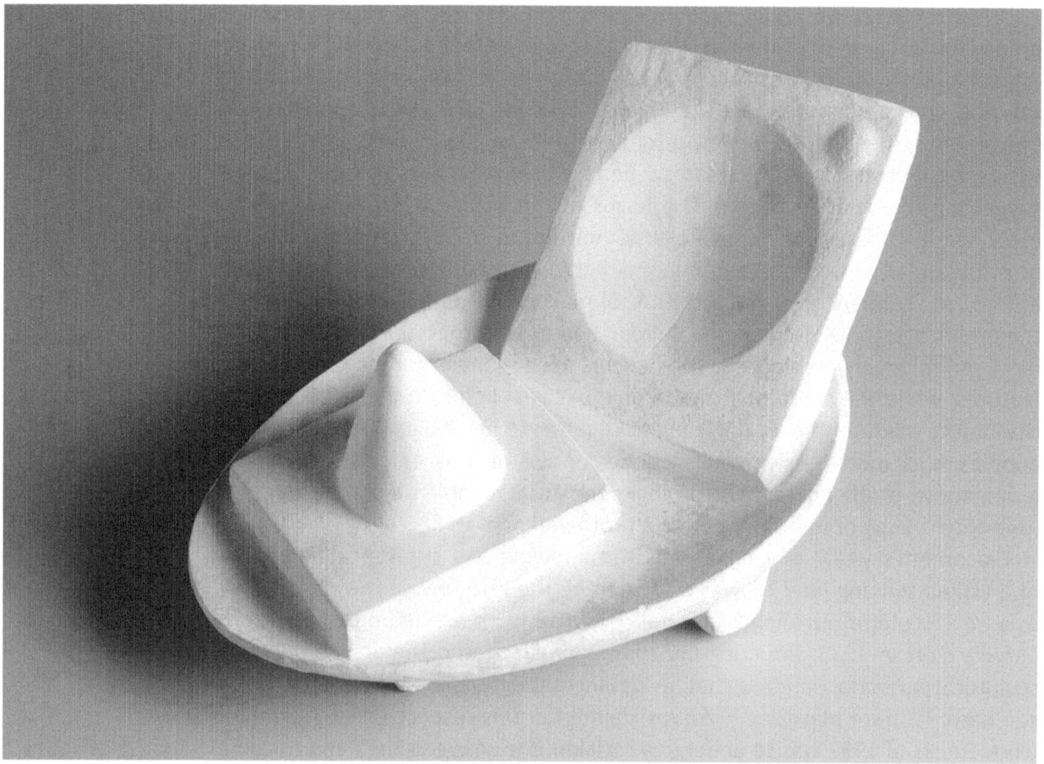

2.2 Alberto Giacometti, *Vide-Poche*, plaster, 1930, 17.5 × 19.5 × 29.5, Kunsthaus Zurich, Alberto Giacometti Foundation. Photograph courtesy Kunsthaus Zurich. © ADAGP-DACS 2011

change (the plaster being too fragile for literal 'use', one suspects), the *vide-poche* held two small forms by Giacometti himself, as if they too, like the 'Involuntary Sculptures' photographed by Brassaï, were the product of unthinking processes of fiddling and thumbing, further shaped by everyday wear and tear. This piece was reproduced in a contemporary periodical on top of a collector's dresser, as if it *could be* a functioning object, but where it also appeared as a decorative addition to an interior design scheme.[39] Giacometti himself was concerned about the potential slippage between 'art' objects and design pieces in his work, where the exigencies of 'function' could trouble the role of 'sculpture'.[40]

Several of Giacometti's so-called 'game boards' too had an apparently ambiguous relationship to 'sculpture' proper. *Man, Woman and Child* (*c.*1931) and *Point to the Eye* (1931–32) both had bases that resembled items of artisanal manufacture (and indeed were conceived initially in plaster and then in wood by the Basque craftsman Ipoustegui, Giacometti's neighbour and collaborator during this period). In their wooden variants, these works appeared more 'found' than 'made', particularly in *Man, Woman and Child*, where a sliding mechanism could alter the positions of a metal figure with outstretched arms and a blade-like triangle. These were sculptures returning towards the status of objects, absurd amusements or toys for adults. In *Circuit* (1931–32), the 'game' appeared to consist in no more than pushing a small ball, once removed from a special indented holder, around a curving track. But this piece also had an intriguing relationship to avant-garde sculpture at the time: the little sphere and biomorphic shape of the 'circuit' both were resonant of the articulation of the body in works by Picasso, for example (such as the *Head of a Woman* of 1931 and numerous studies and drawings for sculpture), as well as of the forms of Arp's 1931 *Bell and Navels*. In this way, *Circuit* played on a developing three-dimensional language, reducing it to a seemingly simple object for fiddling with, deflating the tumescent forms of sculptural biomorphism.

Vézelay's Everyday Ensembles

Paule Vézelay is much less well known than Giacometti, either as a sculptor or a surrealist.[41] This British-born artist, who had contact with surrealism through her relationship with André Masson in the late 1920s, and later through her long friendship with Arp, did, however, produce a body of sculptural work in the 1930s that presents intriguing parallels with Giacometti's output at the time. This work also suggested the role of tactility, in the handling and rearrangement of sculptural ensembles, whose forms similarly evoked basic tools. Vézelay was known at the time primarily for her paintings and box constructions using wire and cut-out two-dimensional shapes. In a preface written for her 1936 exhibition at the Lefevre Galleries in London, the British surrealist Paul Nash referred only to her paintings, but in terms that had a clear sculptural application:

> Here are only sensibility, tact, and a gentle but firm persuasiveness. I use the word 'tact' to mean, literally, touch; for these pictures, with few exceptions, appeal to me, as things first clearly seen and then felt with both delicacy and decision, in the actual process of painting.[42]

A photograph in the exhibition's brief catalogue showed the artist handling one of her plaster sculptures.[43] Despite the gendered connotations of Nash's language, his emphasis on the 'delicacy' of Vézelay's works also points to their potential fragility and impermanence, as objects caught between materiality and immateriality.

Small-scale ensembles with potentially movable parts were also created by Vézelay in the mid 1930s, for whom Arp's work was a conscious point of reference, in the context of their close friendship from about 1934 onwards. But the series of plaster pieces produced by Vézelay in 1935 appeared to owe just as much to Giacometti, particularly in their use of a horizontal board- or bowl-like format. While Giacometti's works were frequently sexualised, and even in the work of Arp, 'buds, breasts and biomorphs are thrusting, curious', as Sarah Wilson has put it, Vézelay's sculptures appeared more obviously oriented towards the domestic, towards the domain of the tabletop.[44] A photograph of Vézelay in her Paris studio shows plaster pieces set out on a long table like so many things to be shuffled and rearranged (Figure 2.3). Bowl forms featured in several of these pieces, containing collections of plaster shapes that might evoke fruit still lives (one possible reading, of course, of Giacometti's *Suspended Ball*). This reference to fruit, made explicit in the work *Boat and Fruit*, where a small object lay in the hollow of an elongated

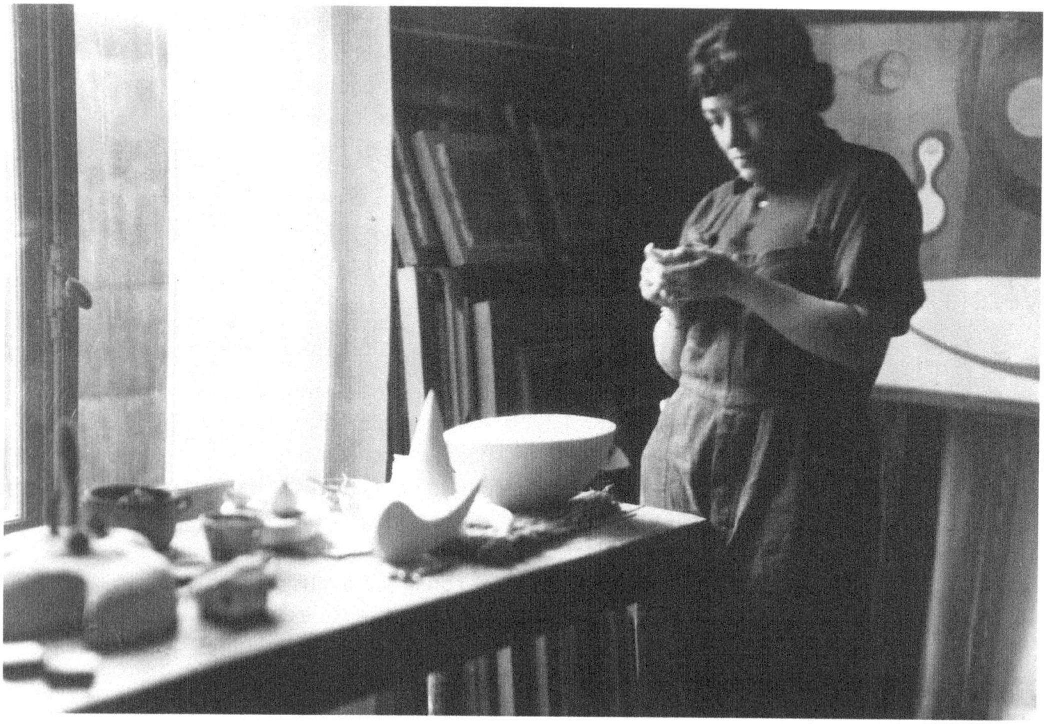

2.3 Paule Vézelay in Paris, c.1934–35 © The estate of Paule Vézelay. Leeds Museums and Galleries (Henry Moore Institute Archive)

receptacle, had clear overtones of Arp's own evocations of sculpture as a kind of metaphorical 'fruit' bursting with its own life.[45] However, Vézelay's pieces seemed less informed by these vitalist concerns, and much more 'relational' in their orientation, playing with the tensions between the 'found' and the 'made', and suggesting rearrangement and manipulation.

Vézelay hardly commented herself on these sculptural pieces, preferring instead to account mainly for her so-called 'space constructions', wooden boxes with criss-crossing fragile wires and thread and cut-out paper shapes. But in writing about her own notion of 'living lines' as part of her 'research in three dimensions', she did reveal their potentially 'automatic' role, albeit in rather conventional terms:

> ... they answered my every demand with all the flexibility I would allow them, and in my most optimistic moments I was content, feeling that these lines did indeed come from my hand and my Spirit ... that they were inevitable ... yet I had to confess that they were in some degree controlled by a power far greater than any I could claim as my own. This was disquieting ... [46]

As in Giacometti's work, there was an interplay in Vézelay's sculptural work between the 'automatic' line and its three-dimensional projection, so that her small tool-like ensembles bore a close relationship to both paintings and drawings with curving biomorphic forms and constructions 'using various kinds of wire which gave me the three-dimensional lines which could be curved and undulated in any direction I desired'.[47]

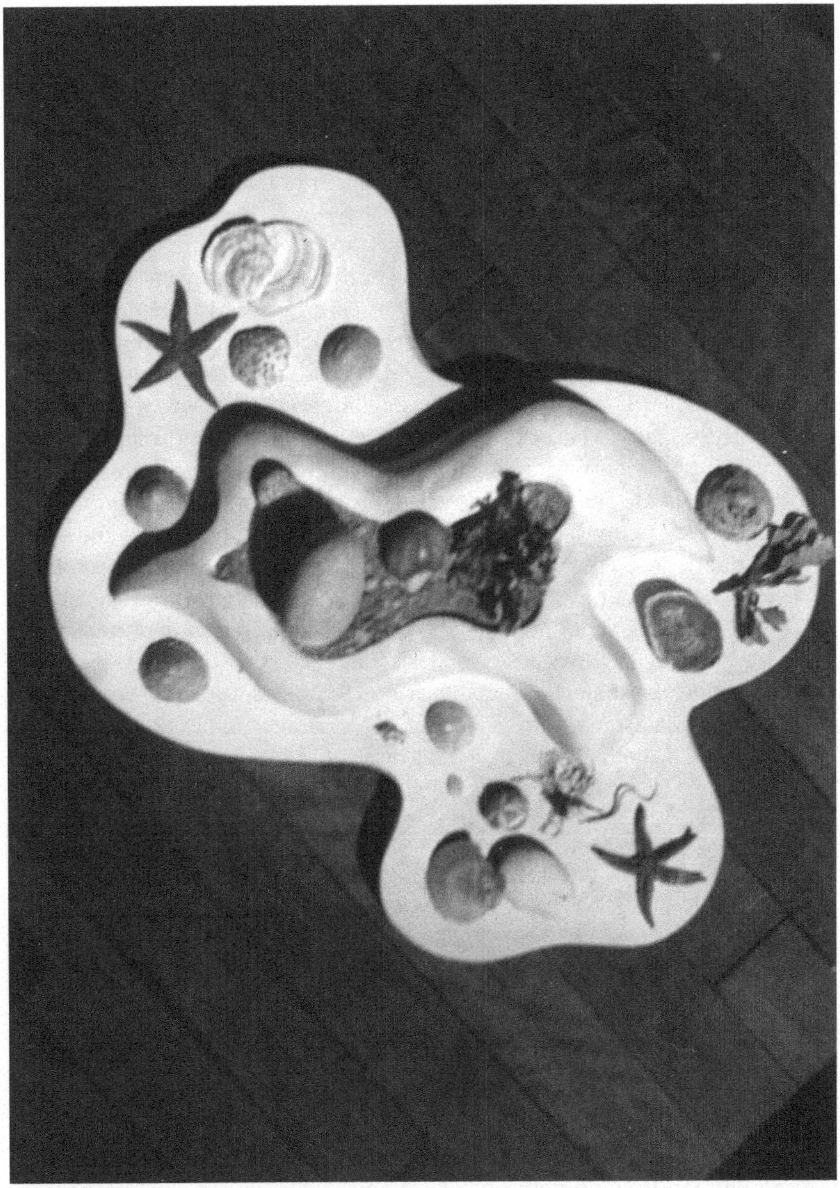

2.4 Paule Vézelay, *Garden*, plaster, 1935 © The estate of Paule Vézelay. Leeds Museums and Galleries (Henry Moore Institute Archive)

The interplay between sculpture and functional object was perhaps most pronounced in Vézelay's *Garden* piece of 1935, in which a flat curving plaster receptacle was mounted on a large undulating plaster base. The extreme horizontal orientation of this piece was to some degree reminiscent of Giacometti's works, but its most obvious reference was to landscape, pointing, through its title, to garden design. Photographs of this sculpture show it 'in use': in one version, its central cavity contains sand and four small cacti; in another, a collection of rocks, seaweed, shells and starfish litter its surfaces (Figure 2.4).[48] The potentially random forms and configurations of these found and cultivated things were held in tension with the fixed but suggestively organic shapes of the plaster, pointing to co-existing but different temporal orders of 'natural' growth and decay: plants versus stones versus fragile dried pieces of seaweed and even the fragility and impermanence of plaster itself. Beyond the harnessing of 'involuntary' natural forms, like the principles of Buddhist garden design discussed by Gell, Vézelay's piece was significant in its changing appearance, as a kind of container to be worked with.

The process and manipulation inherent in Vézelay's *Garden* allow us to read other plaster works based on receptacle forms in similar terms, such as *Sculpture* and *Four Objects on an Oval Form* (both also 1935). In these sculptures, collections of tusk-like objects are grouped around hollowed-out bases. In *Sculpture*, as in Giacometti's *Vide-Poche*, a *mise en abyme* effect is created as smaller receptacles nestle inside larger ones; one tool held within another. The apparently artless configurations of elements in these two works kept in play the important ambiguity in the status of these plaster objects, evoking implements neither completely deliberately crafted for their intended use, nor merely 'found' as such, but something in between. Like the shells and sea debris in *Garden*, these pointed plaster pieces also appeared open to rearrangement, but not of a definitive or forceful kind, rather suggesting a process of pottering about, fiddling and playing with a collection of small-scale things.

The manipulable object-like qualities of 1930s sculptures by Vézelay and Giacometti echoed some of the ideas set out by Aragon in his 1924 essay 'The Shadow of the Inventor', in particular his discussion of 'little familiar objects' as 'pure imagination, escaping from reason':

> Such are those social turns, whose subject is a handkerchief, a match, a piece of string, some keys ... which neither make us laugh nor cry, which scarcely occupy our eyes, but occupy our hands a little, and seem at first indifferent to our minds.[49]

The kind of role for the surrealist object suggested in Aragon's essay, which, as I have argued, was largely obscured and overlooked due to the dominance of the theoretical formulations of Breton and Dalí, opens up a range of alternative readings with significant implications for sculptural 'automatism'. In the objects and interactions I have examined in this essay, distinctions between 'finding' and 'making' sculptural things become less pressing than their relationships with their 'users'. The 'automatic' and the 'involuntary' are not inherent qualities, but can be read from an anthropological perspective on the origins of three-dimensional artefacts in relation to 'natural' configurations of stone or organic matter. The apparently 'regressive' character of such references is misleading. Instead of pointing towards a lost archaic realm of object animism, the complex dynamics explored by Giacometti and Vézelay suggest new varieties of sculptural interactivity, of invention through touch and use, and of the extension of sculpture into everyday object relations, all of which continue to inform sculptural practice today.

Notes

1 Salvador Dalí, 'Objets surréalistes', *Le Surréalisme au service de la révolution*, 3 (December 1931), p. 16.

2 André Breton, 'Manifesto of Surrealism' [1924], in *Manifestoes of Surrealism*, trans. R. Seaver and H.R. Lane (Ann Arbor, 1972), p. 21.

3 Breton, *Manifestoes of Surrealism*, p. 24.

4 Ibid., p. 34 and p. 16.

5 Ibid., p. 57.

6 On the role of the object in the activities of the Bureau, see Julia Kelly, 'The Bureau of Surrealist Research', in Therese Lichtenstein (ed.), *Twilight Visions: Surrealism and Paris* (Berkeley and Los Angeles, 2009), pp. 79–101.

7 Tristan Tzara in Hans Richter, *Dada, Art and Anti-Art* (London, 1965), p. 33.

8 Tristan Tzara, 'Marcel Janco', *Dada* 1 [July 1917] (Paris, 1981), p. 110.

9 Amelia Jones, *Irrational Modernism: A Neurasthenic History of New York Dada* (Cambridge, MA, 2004), p. 143 and pp. 190–99.

10 Louis Aragon, 'L'Ombre de l'inventeur', *La Révolution surréaliste*, 1(1) (1924), pp. 22–4.

11 The goldfish bowl illusion had also been the subject of an essay by André Salmon comparing modern sculpture to products of industrial and artisanal manufacture. See 'Apologue du petit poisson de fer blanc', *La jeune sculpture française* (Paris, 1919), pp. 8–19.

12 Dalí, 'Objets surréalistes', p. 16.

13 Laurent Jenny, 'From Breton to Dalí: The Adventures of Automatism', *October*, 51 (Winter 1989), pp. 106–9.

14 For a sustained analysis of the resonances between historical cabinets of curiosities and their twentieth- and twenty-first-century variants, see Marion Endt, *Nature and the Marvellous in Surrealism and Contemporary Art*, PhD thesis (University of Manchester, 2009).

15 The most sustained example of this is Hal Foster's *Compulsive Beauty* (Cambridge, MA, 1993).

16 Henry Balfour, *The Evolution of Decorative Art* (London, 1893).

17 For instance in his compatriot Alfred Haddon's *Evolution in Art: As Illustrated by the Life-histories of Designs* (London, 1895).

18 Although the role of relief in cave art, and the way that the cave wall can be apprehended through touch, offer a means of complicating this distinction between sculptural and linear forms, which I do not have room to address here. My thanks to Dario Gamboni for this insight.

19 Balfour, *Evolution of Decorative Art*, p. 79.

20 Ibid., p. 86.

21 André Breton, 'La Beauté sera convulsive', *Minotaure*, 1(5) (1934), pp. 9–16.

22 Tim Ingold, 'On Weaving a Basket' [2000], in Fiona Candlin and Raiford Guins (eds), *The Object Reader* (London, 2008), p. 80.

23 Ibid., p. 87.

24 Haddon, *Evolution in Art*, pp. 126–7.

25 Ibid., p. 127.

26 Jennifer Mundy, *Biomorphism*, PhD thesis (University of London, 1986), p. 14. See also Mundy, 'Comment on England' in Chris Stephens (ed.), *Henry Moore* (London, 2009), pp. 22–37.

27 Geoffrey Grigson, 'Painting and Sculpture', in *The Arts To-Day* (London, 1935), pp. 76–7.

28 For a detailed discussion of Grigson's use of currents in modern art to interpret prehistoric images and forms, see Mundy, 'Comment on England', pp. 24–8.

29 See Robert D. Mowry, *Worlds within Worlds: The Richard Rosenblum Collection of Chinese Scholars' Rocks* (Cambridge, MA, 1997), and *Objects of Contemplation: Natural Sculptures from the Qing Dynasty* (Leeds, 2009).

30 See *Max Ernst: Sculptures, maisons et paysages* (Paris, 1998), cat. no. 28 (*Rose de sable, Oeil de sphinx*, 1929), and Michel Leiris, *Pierres pour un Alberto Giacometti* (Paris, 1991), p. 23.

31 Alfred Gell, *Art and Agency* (Oxford, 1998), p. 30.

32 Ibid., p. 30.

33 See Gell, 'The Technology of Enchantment and the Enchantment of Technology', in Jeremy Coote and Anthony Shelton (eds), *Anthropology, Art and Aesthetics* (Oxford, 1992), pp. 40–67.

34 André Breton, 'Equation de l'objet trouvé', *Documents*, 10 (February 1934), and *L'Amour fou* (Paris, 1937), pp. 38–57. For a discussion of the slipper-spoon in relation to photography, see Simon Baker's essay in this volume, Chapter 8.

35 Alberto Giacometti, 'Je ne puis parler *qu'indirectement* de mes sculptures', *Minotaure*, 3–4 (December 1933), p. 46.

36 See Alberto Giacometti, *Ecrits* (Paris, 1995), p. 41.

37 Christian Zervos, 'Quelques notes sur les sculptures de Giacometti', *Cahiers d'art*, 7 (1932), p. 342.

38 See Julia Kelly, 'The Unfamiliar Figure: Henry Moore in French Periodicals in the 1930s', in Jane Beckett and Fiona Russell (eds), *Henry Moore: Critical Essays* (Aldershot, 2003), pp. 43–65.

39 See *Art et Industrie* (April 1936), p. 11. The dresser was designed by Jean-Michel Frank.

40 See Alberto Giacometti, 'Entretien avec André Parinaud', in *Ecrits*, p. 272, and Robin Spencer, 'Giacometti's Break with Surrealism: Abstraction, Hegelianism and the Communicating Vase' in Peter Read and Julia Kelly (eds), *Giacometti: Critical Essays* (Farnham, 2009), pp. 63–86.

41 Studies of her work include Ronald Alley, *Paule Vézelay* (London, 1983), Sarah Wilson, *Paule Vézelay/Hans Arp: The Enchantments of Purity* (Leeds, 1995) and *Paule Vézelay Retrospective* (London, 2000).

42 Paul Nash, 'Foreword', *Catalogue of Paintings and Sculpture by Paule Vézelay*, Lefevre Galleries (London, 1936), n.p. [p. 2].

43 Ibid., n.p. [p. 1].

44 Sarah Wilson, *Paule Vézelay/Hans Arp*, p. 4.

45 See the discussion by Steven Harris in Chapter 1, above.

46 Paule Vézelay, 'Recherches en Trois Dimensions, tableaux de Fils et Ficelle tendu', notes from January 1964 (Tate Archive 8615.1).

47 Paule Vézelay, interview with William Lipke, 1964–65 (Tate Archive 8223 LIPKE).

48 Wilson, *Paule Vézelay/Hans Arp*, p. 4.

49 Aragon, 'L'Ombre de l'inventeur', p. 24.

3

Close-Up on the Object: Attending to the Films of Man Ray

Samantha Lackey

A Sprinkling of Salt

Jumping, dancing and agitating a hundred paths across the screen, a crowd of unidentifiable grains of black, white and grey constitute the first images in Man Ray's 1923 film, *Le Retour à la raison*. This cacophony of multiple forms shifts to a tumbling black disk with a dark and then light narrow spike protruding from its centre: a drawing pin. Suddenly the pin is accompanied by the unmistakable black shapes of dozens of sharply pointed nails, appearing to fall over and around each other (Figure 3.1). The grains return, followed by other objects of everyday use, this time as white negatives on a black background. A field of white disks with black centres precedes indistinct shots of moving lights: the carousel of a fairground, filmed from a distance. Smoke, blowing across Man Ray's *Dancer/Danger* (1920) painting of immobile mechanical cogs on glass, is superseded by tight white coils of springs, encompassing the screen and returning the image to the gradiated shades of moving objects, and then in turn indistinguishable shapes, springs and nails. A white tubular form, truncated at its top and bottom, consumes the visual field, twisting and turning. Next is a white page marked with horizontal black lines like a poetic rendition in written semaphore; then a scribble (of a signature – '*Man Ray à tirer 5 fois*'). The image returns to the suspended spiralling cone of paper, then a three-dimensional grid of card or wood, twisting round in the air, casting a spinning shadow and finally a woman's naked torso, striated with shadow, her unseen arms raised above her head, her body also twisting and turning from side to side.

This extraordinary film was created at the last-minute behest of Tristan Tzara who had informed Man Ray that a small film by him had already been included in the programme of the dada *Soirée du Cœur à Barbe* (held at the Théâtre Michel in Paris on 6 July 1923). In response, Man Ray hastily composed a work combining certain pre-filmed images (including the torso, the gridded 'eggbox' sculpture and spiral) and a filmic development of his photographic rayograph process in which objects were placed directly on photographic paper and exposed to light, thus producing the objects' negative shapes on the paper (this includes the grains of salt and pepper, drawing pins, nails and coils).[1] The resulting film is a composite of these elements, and shifts between the objects' indexical materiality and their

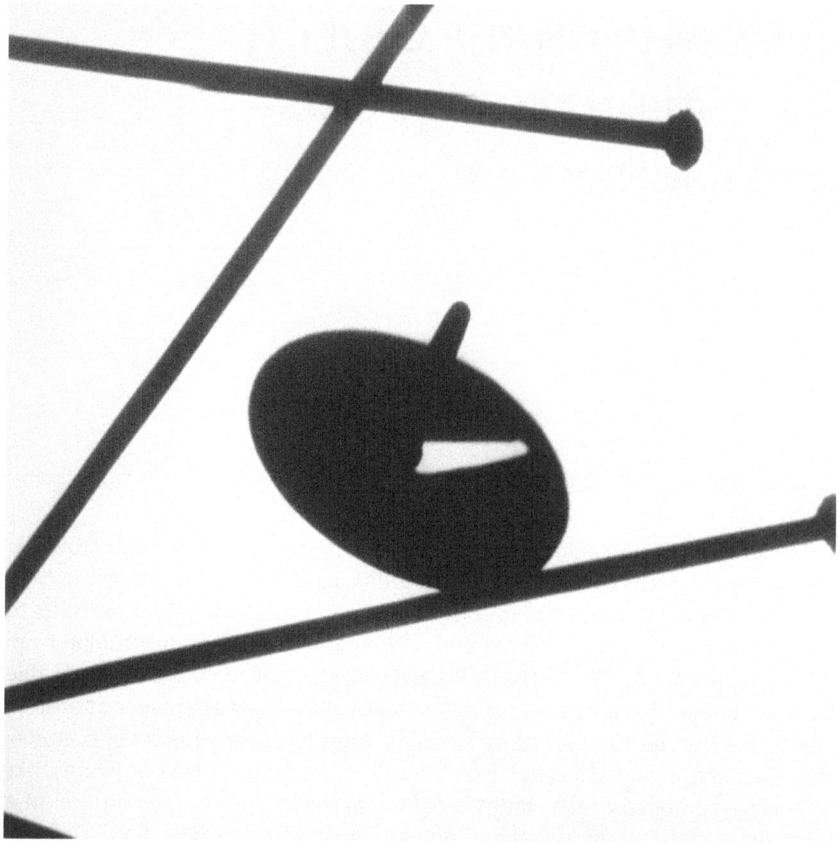

3.1 Man Ray, *Photogram* (still from the film *Le Retour à la raison*), 1923 © Man Ray Trust/ ADAGP-DACS/ Telimage-2011

mediation through filmic and photographic technologies. Constructed at that period of nascent surrealism when dada's death throes were both spectacular and nearing their inevitable conclusion, the film is informed by a set of cultural and historical conditions which include the emerging field of film theory and the developing surrealist rhetoric of automatism. This essay is concerned above all with situating *Le Retour à la raison* within the post-WWI milieu of avant-garde practice, using the close-up as a point of orientation. I propose that the close-up operates in a specific manner during this inter-war period. As a formal device it stands for a shift in visual culture which enacts both a response to, and a critique of, modes of spectatorship. To explore this contention I will consider three particular points of congruence. Firstly, I will examine the resonances between the attentive effects of Man Ray's *Le Retour à la raison* and the proto-surrealist explorations of early psychology and spiritualism of the same period. Secondly, I will isolate and examine early film theory's exposition of the close-up as paradigmatic of an analogy between film and mental operations. Finally, I make use of Fernand Léger's *Ballet Mécanique* (1924) as consolidation of my argument for the importance of the close-up and attention in an understanding of early European avant-garde practice and its relation to the attentive practices of modernity.

The Active Spectator: Caught between Attention and Distraction

Projected onto a screen in a theatrical auditorium, the images of objects in Man Ray's films are a strange manifestation of the filmic close-up. The photographic close-up was predicated on microscopy and magnification's potential for revealing detail invisible to the human eye. Conversely, the huge grains of salt and pepper, drawing pins, nails and springs in *Le Retour à la raison* lack this elaboration of detail in their solid shading on the film strip. In fact, they operate neither as orthodox close-up, nor as conventional film; the still images on each frame of the film, when run together, produce a visibly legible, yet discontinuous and unfamiliar rendition of animated and ghostly objects.

That the close-up played a significant role within surrealism is certain. The 2008 exhibition and accompanying catalogue, *Close-Up: Proximity and Defamiliarisation in Art, Film and Photography*, curated by Dawn Ades and Simon Baker, affirmed the importance of this technical device.[2] The curators drew attention to the juxtapositional close-ups in Luis Buñuel and Salvador Dalí's 1929 film, *Un Chien Andalou* (sea-urchin cut to armpit hair, moon to eye) and Georges Bataille's inclusion in the journal *Documents* of Karl Blossfeldt's photographs of botanical close-ups, Jacques-André Boiffard's highly magnified big toe photographs and the magnified underwater scene stills from natural history films. Both scholars also pointed to the remarkable results of the collaboration in the early 1930s between Salvador Dalí and Brassaï: a series of close-up photographs of found objects reproduced in 1933 under the title 'Involuntary Sculptures' in the surrealist journal *Minotaure* (Figure I.1). Ades and Baker's investigation of the close-up is the latest in a line of readings which have accorded photography a central role within the surrealist movement. As critics have consistently noted, photography is intimately connected to the surrealist tenet of automatism. This assertion subscribes to a now-familiar theory which resolves the contradictions of surrealist visual practice (namely the antinomy between the representation of dream and automatist methodologies) on the grounds of the seemingly automatic processes of photography and the privileged relationship between the photograph and reality.[3]

The conditions of watching the moving film strip, rather than looking at a static rayograph, insist on a re-evaluation of the role of the viewer in this process. As is well known, André Breton clearly outlined a surrealist preoccupation with the film spectator's disorientation in a recollection of his and Jacques Vaché's cinematic viewing practices:

> There was nothing we enjoyed as much as to choose a theatre at random, barge in when the movie had already started, and leave at the first sign of boredom – of surfeit – to rush off to some other theatre where we behaved in exactly the same way and so on.[4]

This description overtly operates against a tenacious tradition of film theory which has described the surrealist relationship to film through the analogy to dreams. Through these kinds of readings the typical trope of avant-garde film, disruption of diegesis, is aligned to the narrative disruptions of the unconscious – most typically encompassing Freudian concepts of condensation and displacement. Yet, Breton's reference to 'boredom' and the following statement that focuses on the effects of *dépaysement* (disorientation), point towards a more complex conception of cinematic experience:

> I have never known anything so magnetizing ... We saw in the cinema then, such as it was, a lyrical substance simply begging to be hauled in en masse, with the aid of chance. I think that what we valued most in it, to the point of taking no interest in anything else, was its *power to disorientate*.[5]

In moving between cinemas – and boredom and a renewed attention – the two friends proposed an active mode of spectatorship. Furthermore, in emphasising the importance of an unstable or 'disorientated' viewing subject, Breton conferred upon film the power to shock, provoke or dismay.

The analysis of the film audience's experience has proved to be a central concern in the development of film studies as a discipline. Influentially, in the 1970s and 1980s the work of theorists such as Christian Metz and Laura Mulvey utilised psychoanalytic models for their investigations of the film form which sought to account for the operations of the medium. The subsequent turn to the semiotics of film (which has a parallel in Rosalind Krauss's examination of surrealist photography) has more recently been supplemented by the work of Tom Gunning, whose accounts of early film offer a highly nuanced return to the social and historical context of filmmaking. In his discussions of the congruencies between avant-garde film (including films made by the surrealists) and early film (defined as films made and shown between 1895 and 1906 before the advent of narrative structure), Gunning suggested that certain strategies of spectatorship were common to both.[6] Describing these mutual tropes he used the term 'cinema of attractions' to characterise a form of filmmaking orientated around the display of filmic properties and the solicitation of spectator attention. Common devices were used to draw attention to the defining quality of film – the ability to demonstrate movement – and included the use of camera trickery, slow-motion and fast-forward. Here the solicitation was achieved through methods which played on the knowing viewer, who was already cognisant with a wide variety of optical devices and aware of the type of spectacle with which they were to be presented. [7] A further harnessing of the spectator was identified in the model of early film, which used as its structure a series of small shocks, directing attention and rousing the audience from a position of distraction. Gunning described these as revolving 'around the act of display and the anticipations that can be heightened by delaying or announcing it (or both) and its inevitable disappearance'.[8] In this respect Gunning uses the phrase 'Now you see it. Now you don't' to characterise this succession of instants that are implicated in the cinema of attractions' temporal construction.

What is interesting in Gunning's account of the temporality of the cinema of attractions is the way this phrase is reminiscent of nineteenth- and early twentieth- century psychological investigations that attempted to demonstrate, through differing modes of attention (hypnosis, hysteria, automatism), the existence of a stratified consciousness. The oscillation between presence and absence, and the attention and distraction of the viewing subject recalls the alternately distracted and attentive subject of the psychological experiment, caught between conscious awareness and passivity.

Scientific explorations of the unconscious had, by the early twentieth century, been assimilated into the wider cultural field. In particular the spectacular manifestations of these experiments had transferred to theatres and music halls as highly popular demonstrations of hypnosis, hysteria and mediumistic connections with other worlds. The embryonic surrealist group recognised the epistemological consequences of this challenge to the unity of the self and experimented enthusiastically with hypnotism and somnambulism during the '*époque de sommeils*' (period of trances) in late 1922.[9] As surrealism gestated, slowly developing its intellectual rationale in relation to the expression of pure psychic automatism, it drew as much sustenance from early psychiatry and its various adaptations in popular culture as it did from the only partially translated writings of the psychoanalyst Sigmund Freud. In the *Manifesto of Surrealism* of 1924 Breton wrote plainly of his indebtedness to Freud but also invoked the less theoretically determined milieu of experimental psychology: he related an experience that appears to exist *between* the states of attention and distraction. He wrote of a moment that was '*neither sleep, nor wakefulness*' when he perceived a clearly articulated phrase that was something like: 'There is a man cut in two by the window'. This phrase was accompanied by the 'faint visual image of a man walking cut half way up by a window perpendicular to the axis of his body'.[10] Although Breton identified this as an image of a rare sort, this apparent singularity should be read as referring to the particulars of the image, rather than the imaging process itself. In fact, entire investigations had been dedicated to the study of images which appear at that same interstitial moment which produces a fleeting encounter with consciousness.[11] Accounts of this state of *demi-sommeil* related the difficulty of maintaining the image, describing instead a succession of such visions, which appear, exist and are then withdrawn. Continually thwarted in attempts to retain the imagery of the unconscious, the spectator of night visions and early film is caught in the same position.

That Breton was occupied by these accounts comes as no surprise. His later representations of the role of automatism within early surrealism reference the best-selling accounts of the celebrated medium Hélène Smith by the Swiss psychologist, Théodore Flournoy (the last of which is entitled, *New Observations Regarding a Case of Somnambulism*, 1902) and the British psychologist and spiritualist Frederic William Henry Myers' 1903 book, *Human Personality and its Survival of Bodily Death*.[12] Indeed Breton's interest in early psychiatry was wide-ranging, as the 1993 sale of the contents of his library revealed. One notable volume in his collection was the French translation of a work by a collective of British psychologists and spiritualists: Edmund Gurney, Myers and Frank Podmore's *Phantasms of the Living*, published in 1886. The book reproduced case studies of psychic experience which were intended to prove the existence of an afterlife, but also contributed significantly to a growing body of research on the activities of the unconscious. One account included in the book typically describes a subject's experience of dream phantasms:

> For many years I have been accustomed to seeing multitudes of faces as I lie awake in bed, generally before falling asleep at night, after waking up in the morning or if I should wake in the middle of the night. They seem to come out of the darkness as a mist, and rapidly develop into sharp delineation, assuming roundness, vividness and living reality. Then they fade off only to give place to others, which succeed with surprising rapidity and in enormous multitudes.[13]

In this dream account in *Phantasms of the Living*, as soon as a resolution of the image is achieved, it disappears to be replaced with another. Similarly, viewers of both early and dada/surrealist film were perpetually thwarted in the desperate attempt to impose a clear narrative onto the images appearing before them.

The validity of such a claim for surrealist film can be further strengthened through contemporaneous criticism. Robert Aron, an early film theorist, wrote in his article 'Films of Revolt' (1929) of the superiority of films by Buñuel and Man Ray to those filmmakers who utilised a narrative technique, suggesting instead that they:

> ... condemn the spectator to a far deeper sense of disorder. Again and again everything is put in question. The familiar determinism which governs the ordinary succession of actions is unsettled – in that Man Ray and Buñuel create peculiar breaks in the narrative, each of which strangely never returns to what went before.[14]

Such an experience brings to mind the description of Man Ray's *Le Retour à la raison*.[15] Here the proliferation of the shapes left by the multiple objects on the film stock give the appearance of dancing, ghostly objects which disrupt conventional vision and metamorphose in the blink of an eye from one object to another. Each time these images threaten to assert a sense of their own sensibility, pattern, identification and aesthetic appeal, they change to the next, finally showing the naked female torso, which is also withdrawn from the viewer. This mode of cinematic temporality is absolutely opposed to any kind of explicit narrative. Instead it positions itself as a short film of attractions, a series of small jolts, described by Man Ray himself as 'a series of fragments ... with a certain optical sequence that makes up a whole that remains a fragment'.[16] In offering and withdrawing different types of image the film denies attempts to read it either as a cohesive abstract work or a narrative. Instead, it consistently presents only movement which forms the visual context for the objects' inassimilable forms, producing a spectatorial experience of interruption and disavowal, distraction within the hypnotic attraction to the kinetic effects of the film.

It is evident that Man Ray deliberately attempted strategies of attentive disruption in his own viewing process, telling his muse Kiki that:

> If a film bored him, he transformed it voluntarily by blinking his eyes at a rapid pace, by passing his fingers in front of his eyes, by forming grates, or by placing a semi-transparent cloth over his eyes.[17]

These devices infer a deliberate manipulation of film in a pattern of disruption; a literal 'now you see it, now you don't'. In his other films – *Emak Bakia* (1923),

L'Étoile de mer (1926) and *Les Mystères du château du dé* (1928) – the attention and distraction of the spectator is similarly controlled through interference with the screen image. By using refracting or gelatine covered lenses, split screens, images from moving vehicles and a direct look at the camera by the actor, the fictional unity of the screen is disregarded and replaced with an attempt to stimulate varying degrees of attention. This spectator's attentive oscillation produced by the films operates in terms which parallel the hypnogogic state. The interstitial state implicated in such a production withdraws the imagery after it has been perceived, thus denying any control to the viewer or dreamer. Thus Man Ray's films are emblematic of a historical moment when scientific and quasi-scientific understandings of attention and their relationship to a burgeoning understanding of subjectivity resonated with avant-garde experiments with perception and vision.

Close-Up on the Modern Marvellous

> Reception in distraction – the sort of reception which is increasingly notable in all areas of art and is a symptom of profound changes in apperception – finds in film its true training ground.[18]

As Walter Benjamin observed, the conditions of modernity produced a paradigmatic shift in modes of perception. Film both produced and reproduced the conditions of the subject's changing environment and experience. Benjamin's thesis of a new 'optical unconscious' revealed through the operations of the camera relied on film's ability – particularly through slow motion and the close-up – to expose what went unseen in everyday life and to parallel the operations of the psychoanalytic unconscious. That this was intimately connected to issues of attention and distraction was also clear to Benjamin as he dissected descriptions of urban experience by other authors (Charles Baudelaire and Edgar Allan Poe). For Benjamin the city walker or *flâneur* must be constantly aware of demands on his attention, the observational stroll necessarily encompassing multiple views of his surroundings in quick succession. Film responded directly to this crisis: 'There came a day when a new and urgent need for stimuli was met by the film.'[19]

Benjamin was not alone in his identification of a relationship between modern subjectivity and film. Contemporaneous film criticism proposed an occasionally woolly analogy between film and the operations of the mind which was manifested within two major debates: firstly the use of film's attention-grabbing properties to distinguish it from other mediums; and secondly the use of these properties to develop and comment on the practice of attention within contemporary life.

One point of intersection between avant-garde explorations of modernity and the elucidation of the film form lies in the early film criticism of the author and poet Louis Aragon, who at the time of writing was deeply involved with the proto-surrealist group responsible for the journal *Littérature*. Aragon's essay of 1918, 'Du décor', published in the specialist magazine *Le Film*, celebrated the new medium and combined the germs of a surrealist theory of film with the clear influence of contemporary filmic discourse. Aragon's thesis in this essay resonated with the struggle for the definition of film's essential qualities as an art, proposing the absolutely contemporary nature of the medium and its ability to stand in for and depict 'the modern'. Intrinsic to this argument was the transformative power of the cinema:

> Poets without being artists, children sometimes fix their attention on an object to the point where their concentration makes it grow larger, grow so much that it completely occupies their visual field, assumes a metaphysical aspect and loses all relation to its purpose. Or they repeat a word endlessly, so often it divests itself of meaning and becomes a poignant and pointless sound that makes them cry. Likewise on screen objects that were a few moments ago sticks of furniture or books of cloakroom tickets are transformed to the point where they take on menacing or enigmatic meanings. The theatre is powerless where such emotive concentration is concerned. To endow with poetic value that which does not yet truly possess it, to wilfully restrict the field of vision so as to intensify expression: these are the properties that help make the cinematic décor the adequate setting of modern beauty.[20]

This description of cinema's powers linked together the modern, the visual field and film's ability to focus the spectator's concentration upon an object. The objects described by Aragon were detached from their usual patterns of signification as part of those filmic processes which direct and control not only the visual but also the psychological. Hungarian film theorist Béla Balázs similarly stressed the cinema's ability to focus on an object and to re-present it to the viewer. More specifically he suggested that the close-up offered a method of renewing the spectator's relationship to life and to the objects of that life:

> The close-up can show us a quality in a gesture of the hand we never noticed before when we saw that hand stroke or strike something, a quality which is often more expressive than any play of the features. The close-up shows you your shadow on the wall with which you have lived all your life and which you scarcely knew; it shows the speechless face and fate of the dumb objects that live with you in your room and whose fate is bound up with your own.[21]

In these two examples the emphasis placed on the defamiliarisation of the object by the close-up recalls the later surrealist technique of disorientation or *dépaysement*. In noting the affective results of cinematic proximity to the object, Aragon and Balázs appropriately acknowledged the importance of differing levels of attentiveness in the viewing process. Furthermore such a position presumed an awareness of the close-up's power as a means of directing the spectator's attention onto a particular aspect of the film, and thus the construction of a controlled vision through cinema.

Likewise, in the textbooks of the Russian filmmaker Vsevolod Pudovkin, emphasis was placed upon the director's ability to control the attention of the spectator through his use of directing techniques. In a comparison between theatrical and film direction he conferred upon the film director a new power of focus: 'The film technician, equipped with his camera, is infinitely more powerful. The attention of the spectator is entirely in his hands.'[22] Pudovkin insisted on the use of the close-up as a means of releasing the viewer from unnecessary superfluities in the visual field, thus controlling the amount of energy expended and encouraging an emotional intensity focused on a particular object or figure – an effect unattainable in the theatre.

The close-up then stands as paradigmatic of the real importance accorded to issues of attention within early attempts to theorise film. The writings on this subject of the German film theorist Hugo Münsterberg attest to this. He postulated that attention operated as a constitutive factor in defining the new medium. If previous arts held movement in their remit, he contended, none had been so able to focus the spectator explicitly onto an intended detail. Münsterberg used the example of a hand clasping a deadly weapon to illustrate this point. He maintained that the focus on the hand and the object ensured the disappearance of everything extraneous to the object at that moment. For him, '*The close-up has objectified in our world of perception our mental act of attention and by it has furnished art with a means that far transcends any power of the stage.*'[23] That this underlined the superiority of the film to theatre is clear. However, the implication of Münsterberg's italicised sentence is that the close-up had a role far greater than that of focusing the audience's attention. It was an objectification of the act of attention, a mental act made visible.

The analogy between the machinations of the mind and the operations of the cinema proposed a means of codifying the aesthetic effects of film and resulted in sophisticated attempts to propose complex cognitive film theories. The French filmmaker and theorist Jean Epstein coined the term *lyrosophy* in his particularly dense brand of film theory based around psychological/philosophical concepts. Epstein believed that the unconscious contained a pre-formulated syntax of knowledge, which in turn could provide a structural basis for the development of both a film art and a radical, new, contemporary poetry.[24] This focus on vision as a point of knowledge cast the cinema as producer rather than product of knowledge, part of a process of making aware; 'The cinema is a particular form of knowing, in that it represents the world in its continuous mobility.'[25] More specifically, the close-up had its own particular role to play. In his essay 'Grossissement' ('Magnification'), Epstein explored the emotional and physical effects of the close-up:

> The close-up limits and directs the attention. As an emotional indicator, it overwhelms me. I have neither the right not the ability to be distracted. It speaks the present imperative of the verb to understand. Just as petroleum potentially exists in the landscape that the engineer gropingly probes, the photogenic and a whole new rhetoric are similarly concealed in the close-up.[26]

It is my contention that filmmakers working in the 1910s and 1920s recognised and appropriated the cinematic close-up as a trope to focus the spectator's attention. The augmentation of concentration controlled by the filmmaker enabled the spectator's direct manipulation, utilising the 'cinema of attractions' in order to shore up the validity of this new art. At the same time, however, the disruption of the model of contemplative viewing by the cinema's new attentive practices was also the subject of critical disapprobation, if not outright contempt. Consider, for example, Paul Valéry's essay on the pernicious effects of the cinema, 'L'Écran' ('The Screen').[27] In this mini-essay, explicitly anti-cinema in its premise, he began by alluding to the similarity between the screen of the cinema and the canvas of a painting. In this comparison it was the cinema's lack of permanence, the transience of its effects that was to receive the thrust of Valéry's critical disapproval, 'where neither life, nor blood itself leaves traces ... Everyone can see with his own eyes that all that is, is surface'. Valéry, did, however, point succinctly to the tropes of early filmmaking. 'Actions are speeded up or slowed down. Their order may be reversed. The dead revive and laugh.' In this poetic rendering of surface he correctly identified the meaning of a certain type of filmmaking; his referencing of specific filmic episodes recognised the exposition of a symptomatic cinema involved in an aesthetics of display and very much concerned with its own surface features, its technical tricks, and the properties of movement that differentiated it from the static canvas.

Valéry continued in 'L'Écran' to discuss the transformative relationship between cinema and the real, which he interpreted as a cheapening, a falsification of reality: 'It is an artificial dream. It is, too, an external memory, endowed with mechanical perfection. *Finally, by means of stills and close-ups, the act of attention itself is represented*.' Here, the cinema's ability to replicate the act of attention is perceived as a constituent of its debasement of art as it replaced representation with a simulation of reality.

The operations of the close-up, whereby the alternatively attentive and distracted spectator could be forced to attend to an image for a period of time dictated by the filmmaker, perpetuated the role which the proto-cinematic machines of the visible had already taken on, reflecting the new (and often unwelcome) understandings of the relationship between perception, subjectivity and the unconscious. As such I would like to argue that the cinema operated as another iteration of the attempted control of the subject's visual field in the modern urban environment. The acknowledgement of these underlying social imperatives is carried out through a recognition by filmmakers that it was the objects of modernity, of the shop window, which provided the optimum examples for any discussion of the close-up that directly related cinema to modern everyday experience. Film theorists repeatedly invoked the department store's transparent window as screen and the carefully arranged displays of objects as directly analogous to the film's presentation of the object in close-up. For example, Siegfried Kracauer in his 1947 account of the relationship of film to urban existence and spectacle pointed to the use of the details of life:

> In the course of their spatial conquests, films of fiction and films of fact alike capture innumerable components of the world they mirror: huge mass displays, casual configurations of human bodies and inanimate objects and an endless succession of unobtrusive phenomenon. As a matter of fact the screen shows itself particularly concerned with the unobtrusive, the normally neglected ... Films seem to fulfil an innate mission in ferreting out minutiae.[28]

Epstein in his discussion of the close-up pointed only to the objects of modern urban experience: '*Shop windows*, cafés, quite wretched urchins, a cashier ... a fair, the dust of automobiles.'[29] Münsterberg too in his chapter on 'Attention', used the same analogy: 'As we are passing along the street we see something in the shop window and as soon as it stirs up our interest, our body adjusts itself, we stop, we fixate it, we get more of the detail in it.'[30] Here the film theorists invoked the consumer object and its associated control of the subject without criticism. This observation of course operates quite differently from the critical dada/surrealist adaptation of the found object through its removal from chains of circulation and subsequent elevation from everyday to art object.[31] However, it does open up the possibility that the crucial relationship to be explored is that between object, attention and context, the latter being constituted by those cousins of visual modernity, the projected spaces of the shop window and the cinema screen.

'Beautiful, Manufactured Objects'[32]

These two locations collide once more via the filmic close-up and its congruent isolations of objects in Fernand Léger's film *Ballet Mécanique* (1923–24). Originally intended as a collaborative work with the American composer George Antheil, who wrote a musical score of the same name which remained separate from the film until the 1990s, *Ballet Mécanique* was produced from footage shot largely by Man Ray and the American filmmaker Dudley Murphy. It is widely held that Léger produced the film, drawing storyboard sketches, directing subject matter and overseeing the complex editing process.[33] The black and white film is 16 minutes long and is a sharply edited collision of over 300 separate shots. It opens with an animated Charlie Chaplin composed from a cubist-inspired collage of geometric shapes, identifiable by his cane and hat, presenting the titles of the film. Next comes a woman swinging backwards and forwards on a garden swing, introducing a rhythmic pulse, which is sustained throughout. This woman reappears later (the second time the film strip is inverted so the image is shown upside down) and is one of only four human bodies present in *Ballet Mécanique*: the others are the slowly smiling mouth and the opening and closing eyes of Kiki de Montparnasse; a man holding a newspaper up to his face who rises from the bottom of the screen among a kaleidoscopic background of moving objects; and a heavy-set woman, often described as a washerwoman, dressed in inexpensive, plain clothing, climbing a set of stairs.

The cacophony of objects which are interspersed throughout the film include: the wheels and cogs of fervently productive machinery; 'dancing' wine bottles; a cropped shot of the feet of tens of hurrying people walking along a pavement; a fairground scene; an inserted textual narrative about a recent jewellery theft illustrated by a shot of a pearl necklace; isolated two-dimensional shapes of a circle, a square and a triangle; rotating saucepan lids (Figure 3.2); a straw hat; moving cake moulds; and a horse girdle. Repetition, diffracted images and the speed of the montage contribute towards an exhilarating cinematic experience of movement, visual rhythm and dynamism. As a mechanical ballet it produces analogies between machines, objects and bodies without any hierarchy of superiority.

This equivalence of corporeality with machinery was an already familiar trope of the avant-garde; the early 1920s artistic project of mechanomorphism

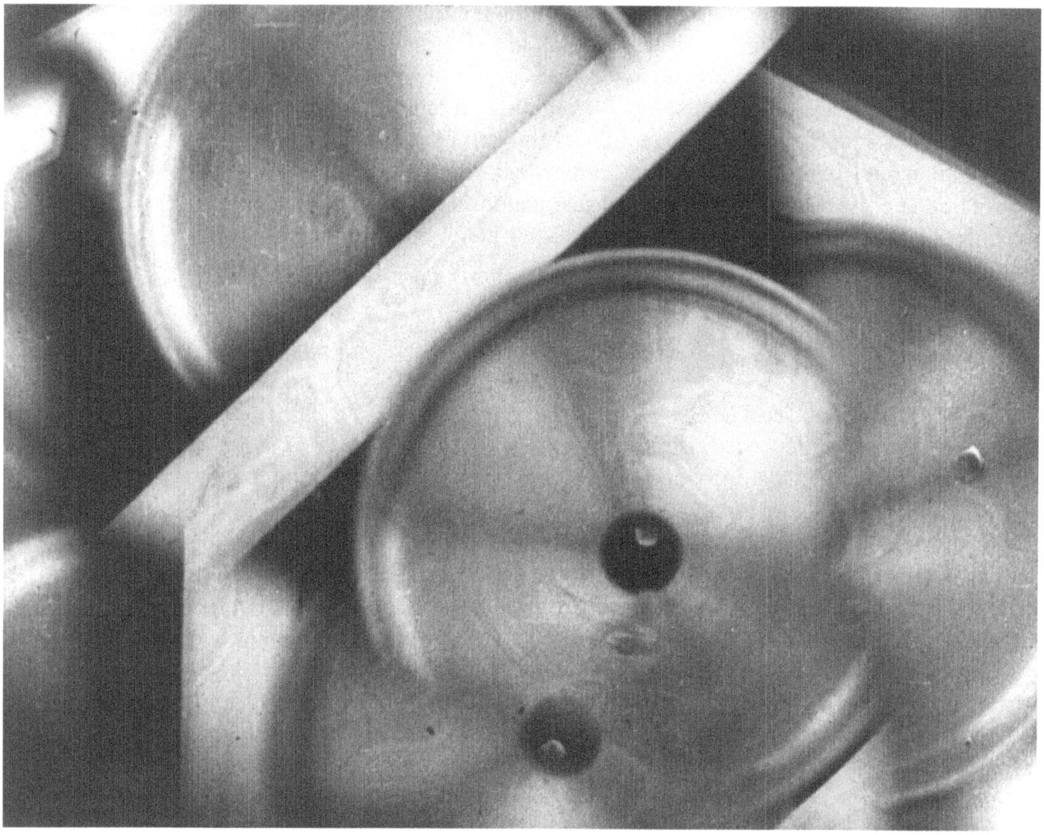

3.2 Fernand Léger, still from *Ballet mécanique* (1924) © ADAGP-DACS 2011. Photograph courtesy BFI, London

exemplified in Francis Picabia's mechanical portraits and Marcel Duchamp's substitution of bodily congress for mechanical operations suggests a context for a sexualised reading of the film. There are visual grounds for this, as in *Ballet Mécanique* the machinery's pulsing, thrusting movement combines with the part-object-like appearance of 'nippled' saucepans and vulva-like horse girdles. Yet viewing the film produces an experience that distinctly lacks the copulatory pulse apparent in Duchamp's film collaboration with Man Ray, *Anémic Cinéma* (completed in 1926 after several years of experimentation), where the oscillating spirals of rotoreliefs take on unambiguous allusions to breasts and penises, producing the illusion of depth and the impression of penetration as they recede and protrude into space. Conversely, the objects in *Ballet Mécanique* resist any projective identification of the body because of the film's adherence to the paradigms of Gunning's cinema of attractions. That is to say that the film emphasises modes of presentation and qualities specific to the medium of film – movement, speed, diffracted lenses, an emphasis placed on the self-reflexive presentation of the film by Chaplin – at the expense of any passive identification with the screen image. Writing in 1924 Léger described his intention to '*amaze* the audience first, then make them uneasy, and then push the adventure to the point of exasperation', an objective most clearly manifested in the repeated shots of the washerwoman climbing the stairs which are visually reiterated over and over again to a point past counting.[34] Frustration on the part of the audience is maintained through the relentless speed of the filmic cuts, the impossibility of immersion within the film and the persistent and repeated attempts to confuse the viewer through the use of close-up or multiplication of objects, which render them unrecognisable in the first instance.

Léger's essay on the film provides further context for the domination of the isolated object as the constituent element of *Ballet Mécanique*. He recounts an experiment when he filmed a woman's polished fingernail in close-up. This part-bodily, part-artificial object was presented to an unsuspecting audience who mis-recognised the image as some kind of planetary surface, a whole new world proposed from a detail. The particulars of this described example in fact bear little resemblance to the actual close-ups in *Ballet Mécanique*, which avoided the distantiation effect produced by unrecognisable detail in favour of the isolation of singular objects. Léger himself addressed this discrepancy in his writings, explaining that:

> I took very ordinary objects that I transferred to the screen by giving them a very deliberate, very calculated mobility and rhythm. Contrasting objects, slow and rapid passages, rest and intensity – the whole film was constructed on that. I used the close-up which is the only cinematographic invention.[35]

This emphasis on the possibilities of the ordinary object was a theme to which Léger repeatedly turned in his writings on art. Léger proposed the mass-produced industrial object as exemplary modern subject, rejecting the artist's chase for the 'beautiful subject' on the paradoxical grounds that 'If an object, a subject is beautiful, it is no longer raw material; it has a plastic value and is therefore unusable; one can only look at and admire it. It is not even "copiable". The experience of it is complete.'[36] Mass-produced industrial wares are the 'beautiful objects that are slowly being revealed and perceived by man; they are occupying an increasingly important place around us, in our interior and exterior life', and it is this new subject matter that provokes Léger to extort: 'Cultivate this possibility, release it, direct it, extend its consequences.'[37] The role of the artist is clear then: it involves a transformative practice of revealing the hidden beauty of the everyday. This effort of concentration on the object has been noted particularly in Léger's painting of this period, and it has been suggested that such works may be productively considered as exhibiting a cinematic aesthetic of fragmentation (the cut) and isolation of objects (the close-up).[38]

Like Aragon, Léger valued the close-up as a means for the artist/filmmaker to disclose the overlooked beauty of the object. And again like Aragon, Léger related this power to the possible representation of modernity. Politically committed to socialism, Léger celebrated the potential offered by the manufactured object and the mechanisation of the workforce to free the working class from the deadening experience of manual labour. Yet, the effects of modernity were recognised for their complexity, as Léger clearly described in his proto-Benjaminian analysis of the scopic and physical demands of modernity which, he suggested, produce a new subject, the masses who 'crave distraction at any price', and rush towards the screen.[39] The sensory overload produced by experiences such as the train journey, the automobile ride and the movement of the individual through the city resulted, according to Léger, in the need for the modern existence to produce for itself an art of 'dynamic divisionism'.[40] For Léger this was resolved quite evidently: 'the perfect emblem of modernity and the modern city', as Matthew Affron has pointed out in reference to the artist's work, 'is the billboard'.[41] The inclusion of signs and posters in his paintings and the inclusion of an image of the Cadum baby (a famous advertisement showing a huge, smiling disembodied head which was used to sell soap) in *Ballet Mécanique* attest to this evocation of the billboard as an exemplar of modern representation. Playing into a much wider discourse on the role of poster advertising as decoration or disruption, Léger's approbation also intersected with the surrealist enthusiasm for the poster as a source for the marvellous. Here the everyday object could be isolated and celebrated in a response to the fragmentary experience of the city, thus addressing the singular problem of the overloaded senses of the individual.

While the newly developed typographical conventions of the billboard present themselves squarely in the midst of both Léger's paintings and writings, I would like to argue that he focused even more forcefully on another aspect of visual culture in order to challenge the newly developing conventions of consumerist circulation and desire. Having identified the problem produced by the speed and fragmentation of modern life – namely that '[t]he thing that is imagined is less fixed, the object exposes itself less than it did formerly'[42] – Léger recognised one solution in the concomitant development of a space in which to display these objects in 'the lighted, coloured display counter'.[43] The counter and the shop window operated to divert the attention of the subject away from the multifarious demands made by the sounds, smells, speed and confusion of everyday urban life, in order to focus on particular items. This detail of the consumer object finds its way back to Léger's own account of *Ballet Mécanique* in which he made the somewhat hyperbolic claim that the film had influenced 'the development of modern film (in Russia and Germany), the *art of window display*, and the development of photographic collections'.[44] Thus, the film apparently and productively returned its solicitation of attention back from the cinema screen onto the shop window. Anne Friedberg suggests that the concept of 'window shopping' is especially pertinent to analyses of early cinema as both imply 'a mode of consumer contemplation'. In the case of the window this is manifested in a 'speculative regard to the *mise-en-scène* of the display window without the commitment to enter the store or make a purchase'. In the case of cinema spectatorship there is a reliance on 'an equally distanced contemplation: a tableau, framed and inaccessible, not behind glass but on a screen'.[45] In *Ballet Mécanique* the spectator is presented with all the signs of the contemporary shop window in the isolation and repetition of objects and most startlingly in the image which shows two stocking-clad mannequin legs on top of an armoire with a clock resting between them. To negotiate a relationship between art and shop window was not problematic for Léger; both arenas were, in his thesis, searching for an intervention into the intensity of everyday life and both had direct recourse to the display of the manufactured object aligned with a need to both attract and produce attentiveness within the spectator.

In highlighting Léger's specific concern with the close-up alongside Man Ray's use of the same technical device I have placed the two squarely in the same discursive field. Although surrealism and purism are traditionally understood as opposed to each other, the status of *Le Retour à la raison* and *Ballet Mécanique* as both tangentially connected to these movements ideally situates the films as complementary strategies for confronting the experiences of modernity via the attentive properties of the object.

Man Ray and Léger's films activate a stimulating and disorientating solicitation of the spectator. As such they expose a dynamic between the object and attention that is manifested in both the provocations of early cinema and everyday life. The audience must be encountered and engaged, not just by an aesthetic gesture in the form of shock, but a temporary splitting of the subject. The reorganisation of perception within modernity is hereby exposed and contained. The onslaught of visual stimuli familiar from descriptions of urban life is caught within the new space of the darkened cinema auditorium. For a short while the avant-garde film finds a way of warding off the passive audience of the future through the defamiliarisation of the familiar. The mundane objects of modernity, the nails, drawing pins and saucepan lids are celebrated and simultaneously integrated back into the perceptive experiences already provided by everyday life.

Notes

1 Man Ray's description of the film is at odds with the extant version and there is some confusion as to the actual content of the film. Within this essay I will be referring to the version released on video to accompany the seminal exhibition mounted by the Centre Georges Pompidou in 1998, *Man Ray: directeur de mauvais movies*.

2 Dawn Ades and Simon Baker, *Close-Up: Proximity and Defamiliarisation in Art, Film and Photography* (Edinburgh, 2008). The eponymous exhibition was held at The Fruitmarket Gallery, 24 October 2008 – 11 January 2009.

3 Rosalind Krauss, 'The Photographic Conditions of Surrealism', *October*, 19 (Winter 1981), pp. 3–34.

4 André Breton, 'As in a Wood', in Paul Hammond (ed.), *The Shadow & Its Shadow* (San Francisco, 2000). First published as 'Comme dans un bois', in *L'Âge du cinéma*, 34 (August–November 1951), pp. 26–30.

5 Ibid.

6 Tom Gunning, 'The Cinema of Attractions. Early Film: Its Spectator and the Avant-Garde' [1986] in Thomas Elsaesser (ed.), *Early Cinema: Space – Frame – Narrative* (London, 1999), pp. 56–62. An expanded account of 'the cinema of attractions' is given by Gunning in 'An Aesthetics of Astonishment: Early Film and the (In)Credulous Spectator' [1989], in Linda Williams (ed.), *Viewing Positions: Ways of Seeing Film* (New Brunswick, 1995), pp. 114–33.

7 Gunning, 'An Aesthetics of Astonishment', pp. 119–21.

8 Tom Gunning, '"Now You See It, Now You Don't": The Temporality of the Cinema of Attractions', *The Velvet Light Trap*, 32 (Fall 1993), p. 9.

9 For further information on this period see Dawn Ades, 'Between Dada and Surrealism: Painting in the *Mouvement flou*', in Terry Ann R. Neff (ed.), *In the Mind's Eye: Dada and Surrealism* (New York, 1985), pp. 23–41.

10 André Breton, 'Manifesto of Surrealism', in *Manifestoes of Surrealism* (Ann Arbor, 1972), p. 22. First published as *Manifeste du surréalisme, Poisson soluble* (Paris, 1924).

11 In particular I am thinking of Eugène B. Leroy's *Les Visions du Demi-Soleil,* Auguste Liébault, *Du sommeil et des états analogues considérés au point de vue de l'action du moral sur le physique* (Paris, 1866) and Auguste Liébeault, *Le sommeil provoqué et les états analogues* (Paris, 1889).

12 André Breton, *Conversations: The Autobiography of Surrealism* (New York, 1993), p. 60 and p. 108. First published as *Entretiens* (Paris, 1969).

13 Edmund Gurney, Frederic W.H. Myers and Frederick Podmore, *Phantasms of the Living*, vol. 1 (London, 1886), p. 473. The legitimacy of placing this quotation in the same discursive field as the discussion of the *demi-sommeil* state is confirmed by the presence of the French translation of the work, *Les Hallucinations télépathiques* (Paris, 1891), in Breton's library. See *André Breton, 42, Rue Fontaine*, Calmels Cohen Book Catalogue (Paris, 2003), n.p.

14 Robert Aron, 'Films of Revolt', in Richard Abel (ed.), *French Film Theory and Criticism: A History/Anthology 1907–1939*, vol. 1 (New Jersey, 1988), p. 432. First published as 'Films de révolte', *La Revue du cinéma* 5 (15 November 1929), pp. 41–45.

15 The apocryphal story relating to the making of the film recounts how Picabia informed Man Ray that a small film by him had already been included in the programme of the dada evening.

16 Man Ray quoted in Frank Stauffacher (ed.), *Art in Cinema* (New York, 1968), p. 25.

17 Kiki as quoted in Stephen Kovács, *From Enchantment to Rage: The Story of Surrealist Cinema* (New Jersey, 1980), p. 273.

18 Walter Benjamin, 'The Work of Art in the Age of Its Reproducibility' [1936], in Howard Eiland and Michael W. Jennings (eds), *Walter Benjamin: Selected Writings Volume 3: 1935–1938* (Cambridge, MA, and London, 2002), p. 120. My italics.

19 Walter Benjamin, 'On Some Motifs in Baudelaire' in *Illuminations* (London, 1973), trans. H. Zohn, p. 171. First published in *Zeitschrift für Sozialforschung*, 8(1–2) (1939).

20 Louis Aragon, 'On Décor', in Richard Abel (ed.), *French Film Theory and Criticism*, vol. 1, p. 166. First published as 'Du décor', *Le Film*, 131 (16 September 1918), pp. 8–10. For another discussion of the relation between the child's perspective and the filmic close-up, see Chapter 6 below.

21 Béla Balázs, *Theory of the Film (Character and Growth of a New Art)* (New York, 1970), trans. D. Dobson, p. 55. This work was acknowledged by Balázs to be a synthesis of his two earlier works: *Der Sichtbare Mensch oder die Kultur des Films* (Vienna, 1924) and *Der Geist des Films* (Saale, 1930).

22 Vsevolod I. Pudovkin, *Film Technique and Film Acting*, ed. and trans. Ivor Montague (London, 1958), p. 92. This book is based on a series of lectures given to the State Institute, Moscow in 1927 and first published as *Filmregie und Filmanuscript* (Berlin, 1928).

23 Hugo Münsterberg, *The Photoplay: A Psychological Study* (New York, 1916); facsimile (New York, 1970), p. 38. Emphasis in the original.

24 For an account of the film philosophy of Jean Epstein see Malcolm Turvey, 'Jean Epstein's Cinema of Immanence: The Rehabilitation of the Corporeal Eye', *October*,

83 (Winter 1998), pp. 25–50. In this delicately nuanced argument Turvey suggested that Epstein posited an ideal of the cinema as ocular prosthetic, which imbued the spectator who used it with a new vision. This operated as part of an anti-Cartesian vision that is based in the corporeal, rather than the disembodied eye.

25 Jean Epstein, 'The Cinema Continues', in Richard Abel (ed.), *French Film Theory and Criticism, vol. 2: 1929–1939* (New Jersey, 1988), p. 64. First published as 'Le Cinématographe continue', *Cinéa-Ciné*, 1 (November 1930).

26 Jean Epstein, 'Magnification', in Abel (ed.), *French Film Theory and Criticism*, vol. 1, p. 239. First published as 'Grossissement', *Bonjour Cinéma* (Paris, 1921), pp. 93–108.

27 Paul Valéry, 'The Screen', in *The Collected Works of Paul Valéry, vol. 2: Poems in the Rough*, ed. Jackson Matthews and trans. H. Corke (London, 1969), p. 202. First published as 'L'Écran', in *Modes et manières d'aujourd'hui* (Paris, 1923).

28 Siegfried Kracauer, *From Caligari to Hitler: A Psychological History of the German Film* (Princeton, 1947), p. 7.

29 Epstein, 'Magnification', p. 238. My italics.

30 Münsterberg, *The Photoplay*, p. 37.

31 For two excellent accounts of the role of surrealist objects as producers of meaning within the political and economic registers see Johanna Malt, *Obscure Objects of Desire: Surrealism, Fetishism and Politics* (Oxford, 2004) and Steven Harris, *Surrealist Art and Thought in the 1930s: Art, Politics and the Psyche* (Cambridge, 2004).

32 Fernand Léger, 'The Spectacle: Light, Color, Moving Image, Object-Spectacle' [*c.*1924], in *Functions of Painting*, ed. Edward F. Fry and trans. A. Anderson (London, 1973), p. 45.

33 For details of the collaborative input into *Ballet Mécanique*, especially the contribution of Dudley Murphy, see William Moritz, 'Americans in Paris: Man Ray and Dudley Murphy', in Jan-Christopher Horak (ed.), *Lovers of Cinema: The First American Film Avant-Garde 1919–1945* (Wisconsin, 1995), pp. 118–36.

34 Fernand Léger, 'Ballet Mécanique', *Functions of Painting*, p. 51. Unpublished essay *c.*1924. A truncated version of the essay was published as 'Mechanical Ballet', *The Little Review* (Autumn/Winter 1924–5), pp. 42–4.

35 Léger, 'Ballet Mécanique', p. 50.

36 Fernand Léger, 'Notes on Contemporary Plastic Life' [1923], *Functions of Painting*, pp. 26–7.

37 Fernand Léger, 'The Spectacle' [1924], *Functions of Painting*, pp. 44–5.

38 Christopher Green has suggested that Léger's close working relationship with the poet Blaise Cendrars, who had pointed out the importance of the close-up in his paean to cinema, 'L'ABC du cinéma' (1919) may well have contributed to the development of a film aesthetic within his paintings. The two collaborators also worked together on a 'film-book' with illustrations by Cendrars and text by Léger; *La Fin du Monde: Filmée par L'Ange N-D* (Paris, 1919). See Christopher Green, *Léger and the Avant-Garde* (New Haven and London, 1975), p. 166.

39 Fernand Léger, 'The Spectacle: Light, Color, Moving Image, Object Spectacle' [1924], *Functions of Painting*, p. 37.

40 Fernand Léger, 'The Origins of Painting' [1913], *Functions of Painting*, p. 8.

41 Matthew Affron, 'Léger's Modernism: Subjects and Objects', in Carolyn Lanchner (ed.), *Fernand Léger* (New York, 1998), p. 75.

42 Fernand Léger, 'Contemporary Achievements in Painting' [1914], in *Functions of Painting*, p. 11.

43 Léger, 'The Spectacle', p. 36.

44 Léger, 'Ballet Mécanique', p. 48. Italics in original.

45 Anne Friedberg, *Window Shopping and the Postmodern* (Berkeley, 1994), p. 68.

4

Kaprow's Vector

Martha Buskirk

Ruminating on Jackson Pollock's legacy, following his death in 1956, Allan Kaprow was both elegiac and subversive. Looking past Pollock's elaborate surfaces, and the modernist readings they inspired, he focused on the process of creation, presciently finding, in his identification with the act of painting by the artist who famously worked 'in' his canvas, the dissolution of modernist categories, and indeed art as a distinct sphere of activity in general.[1] During the years that followed, Kaprow's unfolding critique of art and art making took him ever further away, first from the object, then from events that might devolve into spectacle, and finally from almost anything understood as a bounded activity, much less as art presented for static display.

Some 50 years later, and shortly after Kaprow's own passing, a travelling retrospective of Kaprow's work presented multiple strategies for dealing with his evasions, essentially circling around work that remains elusively beyond the museum's grasp. Voluminous documentation appeared in rows of horizontal display cases, supplemented by films or videos generated as part of the happenings and other event-based work. Many happenings were reinvented, with new versions scattered throughout each community. Within the museum walls, Kaprow's lifetime insistence that his environments change as his own concerns evolved was carried on by turning them into collaborations with curators or other artists who took up the process of transformation. 'Look at the documentation and reinvent the pieces' was Kaprow's charge to later generations, as recounted by Paul McCarthy.[2]

The gap between the documents in the display cases and the redirected environments was in some sense a brilliant demonstration of the divide separating the museum's early twenty-first century audience from these historically important works originating in the previous five decades. The split reflected a desire to be true to two conflicting agendas – a devotion to points of origin, and respect for the stated philosophy of an artist dedicated to thwarting this archival impulse. Seeing contemporary artistic interpretations of such key works as the 1960 *Apple Shrine*, 1962 *Words*, or 1963 *Push and Pull* (the last already an oblique homage on Kaprow's part, indicated by its subtitle *A Furniture Comedy for Hans Hofmann*) made for an interestingly diverse experience, but these radical reinventions also wilfully frustrated the retrospective desire that exhibitions of this sort usually fulfil.[3]

The restaging of *18 Happenings in 6 Parts* was the odd exception to the rule, meticulously re-enacted in accordance with the documentary record (and with the literal remake justified by the existence of this detailed documentation).[4] A new viewing public had the opportunity to witness a studied attempt to channel the consciously anti-theatrical gestures of an earlier avant-garde. But the experience, at least to this member of the New York audience, was a double removal – with the viewers separated from the performers in a way Kaprow would later reject for his participatory happenings, plus an acute awareness that, because the entire event was being restaged, even the spectators were playing a role in a revival production. One learned from the remake, as one would learn from reconstructing the scene of a crime, but there was no going back, no way to experience as new an event so thoroughly historicised (a problem Kaprow certainly recognised). The happening also had a greatly expanded audience for its multi-city tour, often playing to sold-out houses, as opposed to the spotty attendance suggested by empty seats visible in some of the photos from the original 1959 event.

Kaprow's prescience, in his essay on Pollock, about the breakdown of distinctions between different forms of artistic activity, was accompanied by an equally acute awareness of the contradictions inherent in operating across the boundaries between art and everyday life, and the implications of this for the artwork's recuperation by the museum or gallery. Where art has imitated life, there is also the potential for a reversal once the work becomes historically significant: 'All snow shovels in hardware stores imitate Duchamp's in a museum' was Kaprow's assessment by 1972.[5] And Kaprow recognised an incongruity running through the work of his contemporaries in the 1960s and 1970s with regard to the role of the document, as 'those who consistently, or at one time or other have chosen to operate outside the pale of art establishments ... have informed the art establishment of their activities'.[6] While Kaprow saw a debt to Marcel Duchamp's readymades as part of the history his happenings shared with later conceptual art, earthworks, and body art, he did not necessarily employ the same strategies as his contemporaries to convey the work.[7] One such response to the tension between act or situation and document appears as a heightened emphasis on the latter, ranging from Bruce Nauman's simple, often repetitive movements before a stationary video camera in his studio to the subtle wrinkles in the texture of everyday life that Gabriel Orozco captures in still photographs. Kaprow, by contrast, became increasingly suspicious of the relay function of photography, whether as a stand-in for the otherwise ephemeral or a template for its reconstruction as part of the museum's historicising project.

The retrospective was hardly the first time that Kaprow's work had been remade, however, meaning that he actually had many opportunities to develop tactics to frustrate the impulse to produce simulations of non-repeatable situations. Such strategies are also bound up in his sustained critique of the museum; yet Kaprow's insistence that his early environments not simply be remade, as interest in his work grew, meant that he remained deeply enmeshed in a dialogue with museum curators. There is also the related issue of how the subsequent history of a work shapes our understanding of what we take to be qualities inherent at its point of origin. The retrospective fortunes of Kaprow's work seem to be just beginning, if one is to judge by the staging of not one, but three new versions of *Yard* to mark the 2009 inauguration of the New York branch of the Hauser & Wirth Gallery in the very same townhouse where the work was originally created in 1961.[8] But there is also a great deal to be learned from the saga of *Yard* during the four decades immediately following its initial appearance, as Kaprow's life-long insistence on his own process of reinvention yielded multiple versions of a work that continued to be identified by later audiences with the photographic records of its initial installation.

Photographic Memories

There can be little question that Kaprow's 1961 environment called *Yard* (Figure 4.1) is now firmly ensconced in the history of the post-war avant-garde, with this early installation by an artist who was a central figure in the development of happenings deriving its significance from his use of everyday materials as part of an effort to redirect the traditional relationship between art and viewer through audience participation. Yet there are many assumptions operating in the presumed familiarity the work enjoys, including what it means to base our understanding of this ephemeral installation on the evidence provided by the extensive series of photographs of the environment that Kaprow created in 1961, how *Yard* achieved its status as one of Kaprow's best-known works, and the identification of *Yard* with the 1961 configuration given Kaprow's commitment to refashioning the work for its appearances in subsequent exhibitions. It is therefore crucial to examine both the role of the photograph in allowing subsequent audience partial access to a work tied to a particular place and time, and the operations of authorship over the work's extended history.

Despite, or perhaps even because of, his suspicions about the impact of photography as well as the entry of the work into the context of the museum, Kaprow's ongoing engagement with both draws attention to how the circulation of reproductions helps secure the identity of the work through its various physical configurations. This key example suggests some of the issues raised as now canonical site-specific, performance-based, or otherwise ephemeral works of the 1960s become part of a retrospective project. Specifically, the ongoing history of *Yard*, which can be traced through the process of definition suggested by publications and exhibitions subsequent to *Yard*'s initial appearance in 1961, demonstrates certain tensions in the work's historicisation, as well as its life-long connection to Kaprow. The fortunes of this environment also point to a broader series of questions about the shifting significance of an avant-garde gesture as it moves from relatively humble initial statement to canonical status, drawing attention to operations that may be less noticeable when associated with the assumed continuity of a self-contained physical object.

For ephemeral activities or environments, a diverse array of information may be employed in the retrospective reading of the work by an audience not present for the initial gesture. Such material can include plans for the work, supplementary data prepared for the initial audience, photographs and other audio or visual records of ephemeral events or arrangements, retained physical

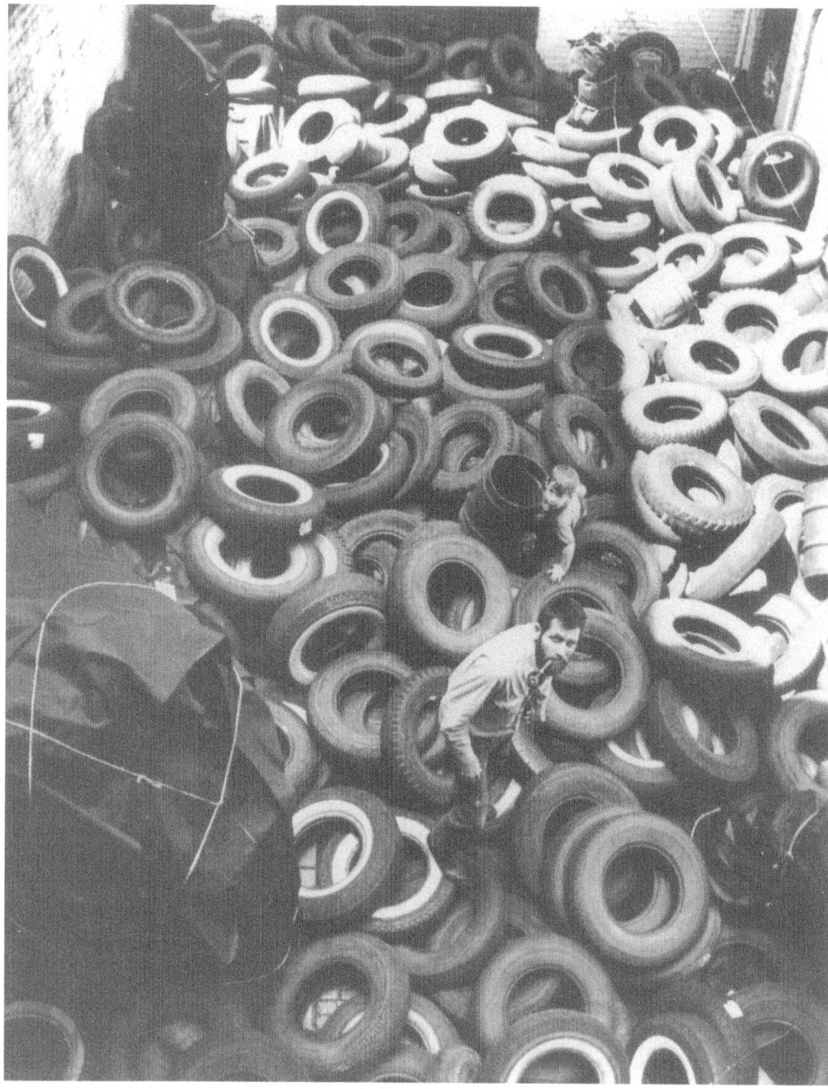

4.1 Allan Kaprow, *Yard*, 1961. Courtesy Allan Kaprow Estate and Hauser & Wirth. Photo: Ken Heyman, licensed by Woodfin Camp Associates

elements (for example, the encased relics preserved from Chris Burden's early performances), the artist's own statements, and accounts by others recollecting the experience. Brian O'Doherty, who also paid early attention to the far from neutral dynamics of the 'white cube', has asserted that 'avant-garde gestures have two audiences: one which was there and one – the rest of us – which wasn't'. This 'original audience', he continues, 'is often restless and bored by its forced tenancy of a moment it cannot fully perceive', and is therefore 'in advance of itself', in relation to a work completed through memory or rumour, and with the aid of photographic evidence, years later.[9]

The dynamic at play received a telling demonstration in Silvia Kolbowski's 1998–99 video installation, *an inadequate history of conceptual art*, where viewers encountered an out-of-sync juxtaposition of video images of speakers' hands and audio recollections of striking encounters with a range of ephemeral works. The artist, while holding onto her role as such, annexed research methods associated with art history and criticism. Yet the obvious inadequacy indicated by the title – the evidently vague or tentative descriptions – drew attention both to the obvious limitations of the eye-witness verbal account and the inherent fallibility of the memories thus recounted.[10] At the same time, the descriptions suggest a sense of scope or duration, in contrast to the impression that might be conveyed by photographic images of a frozen moment.

The promulgation of the work through a few iconic images can also help erase some of the rough edges that might suggest a goofy amateurism to an initial audience. And of course the photograph is likely to play havoc with more inchoate memories, a process familiar to anyone whose recollections of the open-ended experience of a trip are first reorganised around, and eventually reduced to little more than the evidence provided by a haphazard collection of tourist snapshots. The memory of seeing any work of art, with the full variety of effects discovered in its physical presence, may be gradually corrupted by the introduction of the reproduction – a potentially reversible process for art that one can revisit, and a more definitive reduction for one's recollection of the ephemeral. And, taking the implications of this process one step further, Mignon Nixon makes a provocative connection, in her analysis of the dynamics of unconscious desire she finds in Kolbowski's *inadequate history*, between strategies associated with conceptual art and the role of the screen memory – that photo-like image that can so convincingly provide evidence of an event that may or may not have even occurred.[11]

The increasing popularity of the happenings during the 1960s forced Kaprow to consider the danger of their transformation into spectacle, evident not only in their sometimes sensational media coverage, but also in the impact of documentation on the event itself, as the temptation to act for the camera externalised the experience of the immediate action.[12] Recording devices were allowed to remain only if they were integral to the action itself, with photography incorporated, for example, in the 1968 *Transfer*, as participants posed with the stacks of barrels that were successively painted and moved from site to site, or, from that same year, in *Record II*, as university students in Austin, Texas, interacted with the rocks in a quarry and then circulated photographs of the activity the next day. Taking a different tack, the staged photographs used as illustration for his 1975 publication *Air Condition*, which evoke the intervening conceptual engagement with the snapshot, function as instructions rather than records in the context of increasingly low-key and often private activities that, once realised, are known through the fragmentary verbal accounts or 'gossip' that Kaprow turned to in the place of the false transparency of other forms of documentation.[13]

Step Right In

Yet that would all come later, not at the time of the initial appearance of the happenings and environments during the late 1950s and early 1960s, but as Kaprow became known for that work. So it is important to look back to that earlier moment, when *Yard* was created in a courtyard adjoining the Martha Jackson

Gallery as part of a 1961 exhibition entitled *Environments, Situations, Spaces*. This was the third in a group of exhibitions that broke with Jackson's established focus on contemporary painting in order to showcase experimental work incorporating a wide variety of materials – and thus brought art more commonly associated with downtown venues to a gallery operated out of a town house on New York's upper east side. *Environments, Situations, Spaces* was preceded by two 1960 exhibitions entitled *New Forms – New Media* 1 and 2, which gathered together a range of assembly-based constructions. Kaprow was represented in the first 1960 exhibition with a collage-based work; he was also present as the author of a short catalogue essay, 'Some Observations on Contemporary Art', where he anticipated the possibility that 'These agglomerates may grow, as if they were some self-energised being, into rooms-full and become in every sense of the word environments where the spectator is a real part, that is, a participant rather than a passive observer.'[14]

Kaprow had by this time already produced his first environment at the Hansa Gallery in 1958, but with *Environments, Situations, Spaces* this ambition was realised in the context of a group endeavour that required the gallery space to be divided into different areas and handed over to the six artists who participated in the 1961 show. Not only did Kaprow fill the entire space of the courtyard behind the gallery, but he temporarily swallowed up the more traditionally modernist sculptures already on the site (later identified by Kaprow as works by Barbara Hepworth and Alberto Giacometti), which, hidden behind protective coverings and tied up like packages, remain visible in photographs only as an amorphous presence punctuating the sea of tyres.[15] In addition to Kaprow's *Yard*, the 1961 exhibition included an untitled installation by Robert Whitman, Jim Dine's *Spring Cabinet*, a work by Walter Gaudnek called *Unlimited Dimensions*, George Brecht's *Iced Dice* (a realisation of his *Chair Events* score), and an early version of Claes Oldenburg's *Store*, with the various painted reliefs hung close together along a wall in a configuration that Oldenburg described as 'a kind of mural', in contrast to the full environment he would create in the subsequent and better-known version of the *Store* that opened downtown later the same year.[16]

This 1961 exhibition has been described as important, radical, even a landmark. Yet at the time it was part of a rather brief digression in the programming at this particular gallery that inspired relatively short and indifferent descriptions by the few critics who saw fit to review the show, and a response of a rather different kind by a neighbour who (either not recognising the tyres as art, or not caring) lodged complaints that forced Jackson's nephew to go to court to contest the resultant fine.[17] The only review in the art press was Jack Kroll's paragraph in *Art News* on this exploit by the 'Happening Boys', whom he relates to Gregory Corso and Yves Klein, but deems regressive by comparison.[18] And none other than O'Doherty, writing about the exhibition for the *New York Times*, might have been illustrating his later hypothesis about delayed understanding, with a description of incomprehension that included his failure to find the information to identify the artist responsible for 'what looks like candy wrappings removed from gigantic toffees, and strung up on thick, inelegant strings' (presumably Oldenburg's *Store* mural), and no indication that he was even aware of the tyre-filled courtyard.[19]

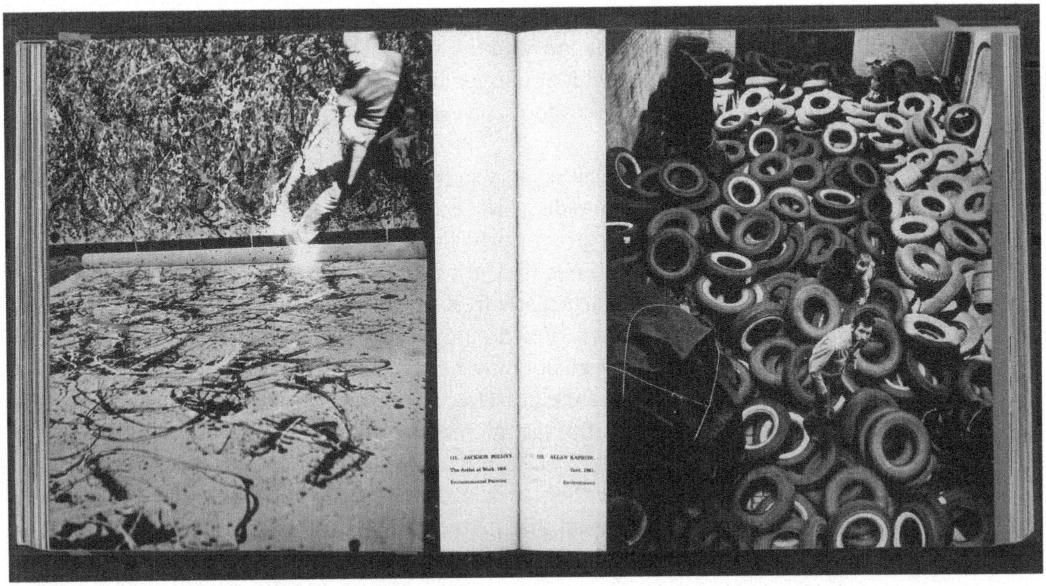

4.2 Allan Kaprow, page spread from *Assemblage, Environments and Happenings*, 1966. Courtesy Allan Kaprow Estate and Hauser & Wirth. Photo of Jackson Pollock painting by Hans Namuth, 1950, licensed by Center for Creative Photography; photo of *Yard*, 1961 by Ken Heyman, licensed by Woodfin Camp Associates

Nonetheless, for Kaprow *Yard* was a work that he would later term a 'signature' piece – with evidence of its importance for him suggested by the well-known juxtaposition in his 1966 book *Assemblage, Environments and Happenings* of *Yard* and a photograph of Pollock in the act of painting that creates a visual echo of the arguments he had outlined nearly a decade earlier in his essay 'The Legacy of Jackson Pollock' (Figure 4.2). Moreover, the prominence of the work is certainly due in large part to the extensive series of installation photographs by Robert McElroy and Ken Heyman from which the images in the book were selected. *Yard* as known through these photographs has been contextualised, in retrospect, as one of a key series of environments that opened onto Kaprow's articulation of the happening. And Kaprow's attention to securing *Yard*'s renown is also consistent with a kind of avant-garde professionalism already evident in the 1959 *18 Happenings in 6 Parts* at the Reuben Gallery, with its controlled choreography of an audience dotted with art world notables.[20] Accounts of a disagreement between Kaprow and Oldenburg around the time of the Jackson Gallery exhibition present another demonstration of the perceived stakes in the sometimes competing attempts to define the emerging aesthetic forces of the period.[21]

Given Kaprow's later ambivalence about photographic documentation, it is worth considering the structure of *Assemblage, Environments and Happenings* with respect to the role of the photograph generally and its presentation of *Yard* in particular. The book is divided into three sections, the first beginning, without front matter or preamble, with a succession of over 100 photographs devoted mainly to environments and happenings by Kaprow and others. The sequences of photographs in the first section are punctuated by different combinations of all black or white pages, as well as pages with just a dot in the centre, and Kaprow has orchestrated the photographs with rather cryptic words or phrases in a much more prominent type than the small captions that identify each image.

Not until the second section, Kaprow's text, does one encounter a title page and publication information; and the survey text is followed by a third selection of more than 40 individual happenings presented through a combination of photographic documentation and various text-based scripts, scenarios, or instructions.

Within the first section, it is only after the twentieth page that Kaprow presents, under the heading 'Note on the Photographs', a couple of short paragraphs about their structure, beginning 'Photographs of art works have their own reality and sometimes they are art in turn. Those taken of the subject of this book tend to be particularly free. They refer to their models, but strangely, as would a movie taken of a dream, stopped at unexpected intervals.' Their order is not chronological, but rather, he suggests, one that will inspire reverie.[22] *Yard* makes its appearance in the conclusion to the first section, as part of a progression, following the last all-monochrome break on pages 128 and 129, that builds up to the tyre environment through a number of other works that could be described as thematically or materially related. This final sequence begins with a page spread that juxtaposes George Segal's 1962 *Bus Driver* and Oldenburg's 1961 *Fotodeath* happening. Next, two views of Jim Dine's 1960 *Car Crash* appear opposite a view of Oldenburg working on his *Store* (captioned as 'environment in progress'). These are followed, in succession, by Kaprow's 1962 *Courtyard* happening (with its swinging tyre) on two pages; then *Courtyard* again, opposite Robert Rauchenberg's 1959 *Monogram*; Dine's *Car Crash* again (this time in rehearsal) opposite the first appearance of *Yard*, in a photograph that presents Kaprow himself front and centre; then *Yard* again, with Kaprow throwing one of the tyres, opposite another view of Oldenburg working on *Store*; the well-known juxtaposition of Pollock at work (labelled in the caption as 'environmental painting') with *Yard*, again, this time with Kaprow and his son; and as the final image in the book's first section, *Yard* for the last time opposite the back of the first page of the text section, which is set off by a black dot as well as the brown paper used for that part of the book.

A second invitation to step right in (repeated from the opening pages of the book) takes the reader into the text section. But it also appears, tellingly, below a photograph of *Yard* that has a compositional structure familiar from certain German romantic paintings, where a foreground figure seen from behind encourages us to identify with the act of viewing – though of course with the twist that what we are thereby encouraged to experience photographically is an environment meant to be entered and actually completed through participation rather than disembodied sight. In fact, the black and white photographs of *Yard*, seemingly more than similar documents of the happenings, promote the illusion that one can understand the work through these visual records – along with the assumption we are indeed talking about a work with a continuous identity. 'In answer to their appeal, the plastic arts have produced their printing press', wrote André Malraux in a description of how sculpture is more likely than painting to be conveyed effectively by black and white photographs – a point that seems to apply equally to an understanding of the impact of the photographs of *Yard*.[23] This environment clearly partakes of sculpture's susceptibility to the photograph, despite a quite literal effacement of the more self-contained exemplars already in the courtyard.

While Kaprow's increasing fame as the originator of the happening would undoubtedly have ensured attention to his environments, it is also evident that Kaprow, as the author of the history presented in *Assemblage, Environments and Happenings* through images and words, took the opportunity to consolidate the importance of an early environment and therefore to ensure it a presence not immediately secured by its initial physical form in 1961. It is equally striking how Kaprow uses his selection of photographs to support the case he had already laid out with the 1958 publication of 'The Legacy of Jackson Pollock'. There Kaprow's description evokes both his experience of Pollock's early exhibitions and the power of Hans Namuth's photographs of the painter in action: 'I am convinced that to grasp a Pollock's impact properly, we must be acrobats, constantly shuttling between an identification with the hands and body that flung the paint and stood "in" the canvas and submission to the objective markings, allowing them to entangle and assault us.' Kaprow's lesson took the form of a prediction of a different kind of art: 'Pollock, as I see him, left us at the point where we must become preoccupied with and even dazzled by the space and objects of our everyday life, either our bodies, clothes, rooms, or, if need be, the vastness of Forty-second Street.'[24] And, looking back 10 years later, he reiterated the idea of the emergence of his own and related practices from abstract expressionism, suggesting that the 'preponderance of fragile, soft, and irregular materials' in early environments and settings for happenings were an outgrowth of the 'sprawling, limitless impulses' of the earlier movement.[25] It is therefore significant that Kaprow's book presents a comparison between a photograph of Pollock in action, within the space defined by the horizontal canvas before it goes up onto the wall, and a photo of an environment meant to be entered that shows Kaprow himself as participant. Whereas the possibility of entering into the horizontal canvas was, with rare exceptions, Pollock's alone, Kaprow was occupying a position that he envisioned for others. Yet the historical distance gives them a greater equivalence, in the impossibility of experiencing either position other than through an imaginary traversing of the photo.

What the identification of this work with the series of 1961 installation photographs masks is the degree to which Kaprow defined *Yard* and his other early environments as ongoing works that he insisted upon reconsidering each time they were exhibited. To the extent that *Yard* was a work not fully appreciated at first, only gradually achieving its status as a 'signature piece' for Kaprow, it can be understood against many other stories of initial incomprehension later replaced by close attention and high regard. In this familiar story, the work is understood differently by successive audiences, with its significance changed by these subsequent readings. Yet Kaprow's *Yard* presents an added element, in the form of an environment that has been realised at a number of uneven intervals, and one that changes not only in reading or significance, but also in physical configuration. Indeed, *Yard* is not simply a 1961 work, but an environment with a surprisingly extended history that spans five decades and three continents, with reappearances in contexts that include solo shows, thematic exhibitions, and the type of retrospective attempt to define a broad historical context evident in the 1998 *Out of Actions* exhibition at the Los Angeles Museum of Contemporary Art. While Kaprow's insistence on reinterpretation was particularly evident in the dialogue between artist and curator around the Los Angeles Museum of Contemporary Art exhibition, he had already created nine versions of the work preceding this 1998 display, each under somewhat different circumstances.

Yard, Redux

The first reappearance of *Yard* was in the survey of Kaprow's work organised by the Pasadena museum in 1967 (thus one year after the publication of *Assemblage, Environments and Happenings*) – with the familiar image of Kaprow and his young son peering up from the sea of tyres featured both on the cover of the catalogue and on a two-page spread where it was juxtaposed with the image showing the participant's back in the foreground. Kaprow declared his ambivalence about this museum project with a statement on the third page of the catalogue in which he associated the museum with a 'reek of holy death', even as he acknowledged its practical function, in the absence of other 'agencies or means for otherwise making art accessible to the public'. He also indicated a plan to 'camouflage the museum environment as much as possible', which he achieved at the Pasadena museum in part by having the walls covered with tarpaper.[26] And it was on the occasion of this exhibition that he produced his last major happening, *Fluids*, for which he used the museum as an agent to create an off-site work in the form of large-scale rectangular ice constructions built and left to melt at various sites throughout the region.

The Pasadena exhibition therefore marks the point when *Yard*'s identity began to bifurcate, with Kaprow involved in its ongoing permutations as he reconceptualised the work for different venues, even as it has continued to be known largely through the same set of fixed historical images. Moreover, the Pasadena catalogue structure is repeated in many subsequent publications, as the work included in the exhibition is reconfigured to varying and sometimes even radical degrees even as the environment is reproduced, both in the catalogue and many of the press accounts, with the 1961 installation views. This temporal lag reflects the practical difficulty of documenting a work made on site for a publication prepared in advance, but the practice also contributes to an overall tendency to revert back to the 1961 photos as a basis for defining the work.

After 1967, *Yard* moved overseas for the 1971 *Happenings und Fluxus* exhibition in Cologne, with its configuration hinted at by a drawing used as a wrapper for the exhibition's checklist, followed by its inclusion in a 1981 exhibition called *Schwartz* in Düsseldorf, and *Kunst wird Material* in West Berlin in 1982. Then, in 1984 it appeared in New York for the Whitney Museum's *Blam! The Explosion of Pop, Minimalism, and Performance, 1958–64* exhibition, where the early importance of the Jackson Gallery show was affirmed by the inclusion of five of the six artists from *Environments, Situations, Spaces* as key players in the now historical story of the transition from pop to minimalism. In addition to *Yard*, for which Kaprow took advantage of the basement well of the Breuer building to create a confined piling of tyres with strong visual similarities to the original courtyard configuration, the exhibition included a version of Oldenburg's *Store* where the now valuable objects loaned from various individual and institutional collections were set up in a partial approximation of the storefront installation, as well as examples of works by Brecht, Dine, and Robert Watts that were either borrowed or newly reconstructed for the exhibition.[27]

At another exhibition only two years later, a 1986 survey of Kaprow's work at the Museum am Ostwall, Dortmund, *Yard*'s new configuration was uncharacteristically reproduced in the catalogue, perhaps thanks to the flexible publication format offered by its loose-leaf binding – though even here the new version was in a supplement at the end, secondary to the 1961 installation shots in the body of the text. After that it turned up at a 1990 biennale in Sidney, organised around the theme of the *Readymade Boomerang*, where Eleanor Heartney described how its location, visible from the gallery through plate glass windows, emphasised 'a certain Minimalist elegance of the tires and their arrangement'.[28] And the very next year, on the occasion of the 1991 *7 Environments* in Milan, *Yard* underwent its most radical transformation, with the pile of used tyres and oil barrels replaced by orderly racks arranged in front of hot pink walls, and a Fiat parked square in the middle (Figure 4.3).

Kaprow took the occasion of the 1991 survey of his environments to create new versions of other such often reproduced environments as *Apple Shrine* or *Push and Pull* in forms that bore an equally tangential *visual* relationship to their initial presentation. The series of shifts, Jeff Kelley suggests, conveys an acknowledgement of the intervening three decades, as 'bohemian street junk was replaced by synthetic materials and standardised, easily consumable units; cardboard, chicken wire, broken glass, and tar were largely supplanted by rolls of carpet, etched glass, sheets of plastic, and walls of silk'.[29] Some of the material differences were inevitable, and point outward, to the shifting time and place within which each installation was realised (for example, the use of a smaller Italian tyre, in contrast to the American castoffs with which the work was initiated), and others might even be considered within an expanded definition of style. Kaprow's 1991 interpretation of the work presented a very different aesthetic of arrangement; yet it does retain an element of viewer interaction, with the 1961 possibility of tossing about the randomly piled tyres replaced 30 years later by an absurd version of a more practical act, that of attempting to change a tyre on the immobilised Fiat jacked up in the middle of the surrounding racks. At the same time, evidence of the visual distinction between the first versions of the environments and Kaprow's 1991 conceptualisation was provided by blown-up photographs of the initial configuration, such that, in *7 Environments*, the juxtaposition of the photographs and reconfigured 1991 installations brought into the exhibition itself the contrast usually present between catalogue and specific example.

It is also evident, from the correspondence relating to the appearance of *Yard* in the 1998 *Out of Actions* exhibition, that the obvious contrast between the 1961 photographs and the 1991 configuration of *Yard* was giving curator Paul Schimmel nightmares as he tried to organise a retrospective survey of performance-based practices – and therefore wanted to include the work familiar from the initial installation views that ensured its historical significance. What Schimmel most decidedly did not want was something like the version of the work in Italy, which, in his assessment, 'looked like a car repair shop'.[30] After much back and forth, what emerged was a free-standing configuration, encased by a chain link fence

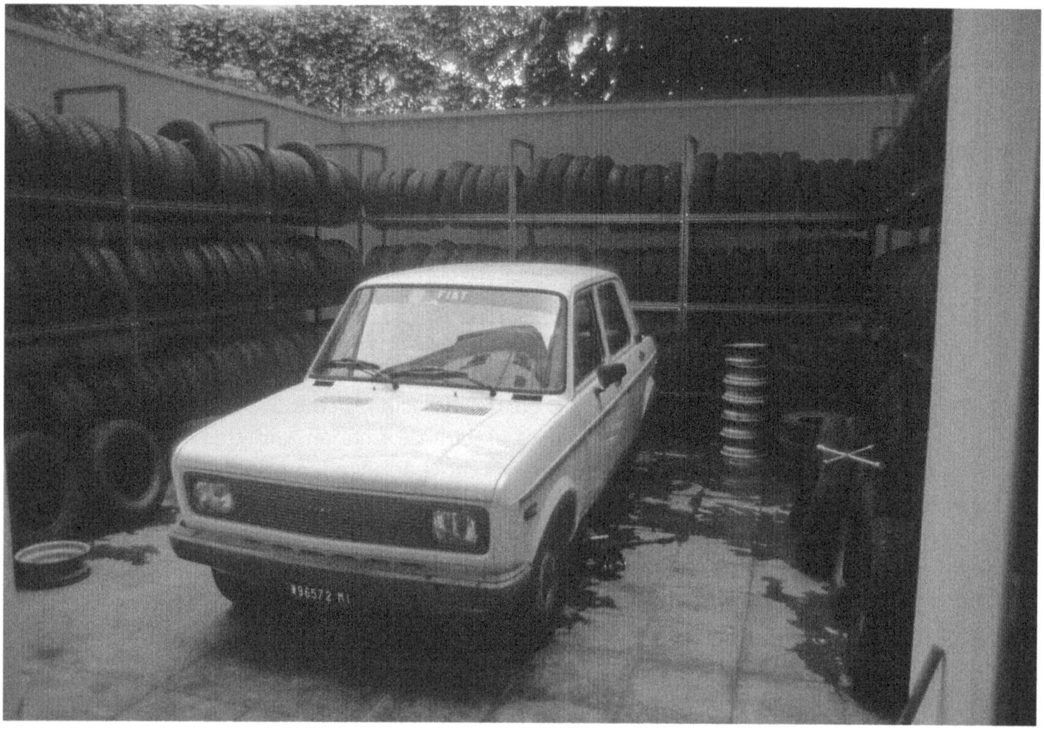

4.3 Allan Kaprow, *Yard*, 1991, reinvented for *7 Environments*, Fondazione Mudima, Milan. Courtesy Allan Kaprow Estate. Photo: Jeff Kelley

enclosure erected in the parking lot in front of MOCA's Geffen Contemporary building – with audience participation incorporated via the invitation to enter as well as climb over the low fences separating the interior spaces (Figure 4.4).

Kaprow's insistence on reconceptualisation therefore introduced an added element in what was an already complex process of historical definition, as the work's reception history is inescapably intertwined with Kaprow's own process of reinterpreting his early gestures. Yes, *Yard* is a work that can be dated to 1961, and viewed as an outgrowth of the environments and events Kaprow had begun establishing in the late 1950s; and it is a work with an evolving existence that continues through its subsequent reappearances. But *Yard*'s later fame is also closely tied to its fortunes in 1966 and 1967, the years, respectively, of Kaprow's major book publication and the beginning of *Yard*'s museum career. In this regard, the process of definition that takes place retrospectively, after the work's initial appearance, intersects with, and has to be understood as inflected by ideas articulated in the second half of the 1960s, including theories of authorship and, in the context of conceptual art, the expansions of artistic practice to include such secondary realms as archivist, critic or historian.

Along the Way

If the establishment of *Yard* as one of Kaprow's significant works can be dated not just to its initial appearance in 1961, but also to 1966 and 1967 as key years

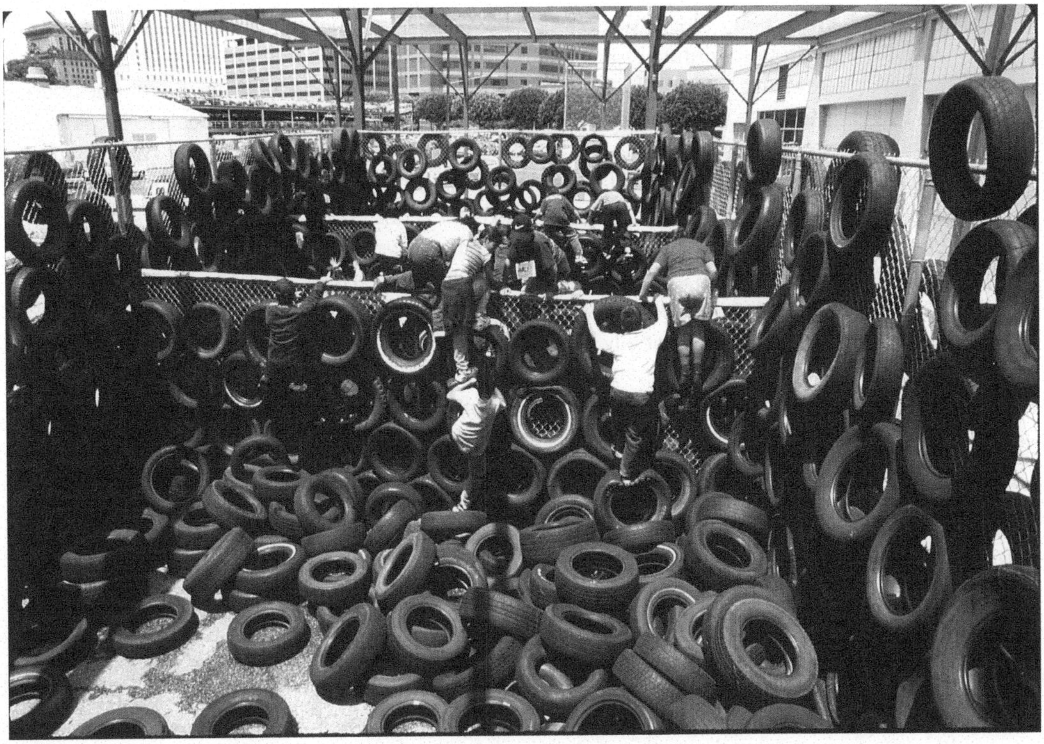

4.4 **Allan Kaprow, *Yard*, 1998, reinvented for *Out of Actions*, Museum of Contemporary Art, Los Angeles. Courtesy Allan Kaprow Estate and Hauser & Wirth. Photo: Alex Slade**

for the retroactive process of securing the work's significance, then it is equally important to consider the work's ongoing fortunes in relation to this slightly later historical moment. There would, of course, be countless ways one could take on this expanded task of contextualisation, but one suggestive point of entry is provided by *Aspen*, 'the magazine in a box', which was conceived as a kind of time capsule by publisher Phyllis Johnson. Kaprow makes an appearance in issue 6A, the performance art issue edited by Jon Hendricks and published in the winter of 1968–69, via a typescript of the instructions and notes for his 1963 *Push and Pull: A Furniture Comedy for Hans Hofmann*. But in many respects issue 5+6 from fall-winter 1967, which was billed as the minimalism issue and edited by none other than O'Doherty, provides a more suggestive backdrop, with critical and poetic texts, audio recordings, film clips, documents, and even the component parts for one do-it-yourself sculpture in a provocative intermix that testifies to the editor's by then significant immersion in the avant-garde dialogue of the mid 1960s.[31]

One of the interesting issues raised by Kaprow's ongoing refashioning of his earlier work is the relationship of that trajectory to his renunciation of new work of the same kind. 'Once, the task of the artist was to make good art', he asserts in the opening of his 'Manifesto' of 1966; 'now it is to avoid making art of any kind'. As it happens, the main text section of *Aspen* 5+6 included an essay by Susan Sontag, 'The Aesthetic of Silence', that addressed how the act of renunciation, in the examples of Arthur Rimbaud, Ludwig Wittgenstein, and Duchamp, 'imparts retroactively an added power and authority to what was broken off'. She also cites John Cage to the effect that 'there is no such thing as silence', and indeed Kaprow's later career, like that of Duchamp, shows ample evidence of the extensive activity that may indeed be hiding behind an ostensible renunciation.[32] The artist's own involvement in the further refashioning of earlier work is but one way that the act of making becomes enmeshed in what otherwise might be understood as secondary forms of contextualisation. Kaprow would later refer to Duchamp's claim that the 'creative act is not performed by the artist alone', and also credit Duchamp's influence for the development, particularly in the context of conceptual art, whereby 'critical discourse is inseparable from whatever other stuff art is made of'.[33]

Duchamp originally articulated the idea of the 'art coefficient' in his 1957 statement 'The Creative Act', a declaration which reappeared in this issue of *Aspen*, together with a selection from 'A L'Infinitif', as a floppy phonograph recording of Duchamp reading these texts. Moreover, the same text section as Sontag's essay also included the first English language appearance of Roland Barthes's 'Death of the Author', with its critique of the idea that an explanation of the work can be found in its producer, in 'the voice of a single person, the *author*, "confiding" in us'.[34] The format of Duchamp's audio contribution to 5+6 notwithstanding, there are obvious parallels between the approach Duchamp pioneered with the readymades and Barthes's articulation of a text 'as a multi-dimensional space in which a variety of writings, none of them original, blend and clash'.[35] A pile of used tyres might also seem to fit rather nicely as a three-dimensional parallel to this proposition, sharing, as the tyres do, the condition of the readymade, arranged rather than formed by the artist, and carrying a host of multivalent associations through the prior familiarity of the object thus selected. And yet, as the far from quiet silences of both Duchamp and Kaprow serve to demonstrate, it is perhaps more a matter of redirection, as the author doesn't disappear, but instead moves over into activities that contribute to the further framing or interpretation of an initial recontextualisation. The turn that Kaprow makes, and one that links his enterprise to the many ways that the definition of the artist, and artistic activity, have been extended over the course of the twentieth century, is Kaprow's assumption of what had been secondary functions, applied by others to the process of defining or constructing the interpretive context for the work, so that the role assumed for the reader is deflected onto the birth of the artist as organiser, critic, historian, or, as Kaprow would later describe himself, provider of services.[36]

George Kubler's 'Style and Representation of Historical Time', the third text bound together with those by Sontag and Barthes in *Aspen* 5+6, points to the other important dimension implicit not only in the initial audience experience of Kaprow's spatial configuration, but also in its extended history. In his 1962 *The Shape of Time: Remarks on the History of Things* (which was read by a number of artists in the 1960s), Kubler had posited the work of art as 'the residue of an event' and also a form of signal or relay that would inspire additional works and in turn be read through those subsequent acts.[37] Although Kubler does not make an appearance in the index to Kaprow's *Essays on the Blurring of Art and Life*, Robert Smithson was reading his work, and there is a suggestive echo, in a comparison between museums and mausoleums, that Kaprow made in a dialogue with Smithson, of a statement by Kubler about parallels between tomb furniture and the museum that Smithson used as the epigram to 'Some Void Thoughts on Museums' (a brief essay that appeared on the same page of *Arts Magazine* as the concluding paragraphs to Kaprow's 'Death in the Museum').[38]

Kubler's contribution to *Aspen* returns to the specific problem of stylistic unity in the face of temporal overlays such that 'every work of art is a fragment of some larger unit ... a bundle of components of different ages'. Yet, in the contrast Kubler puts forward between painting ('about the world of vision') and history ('about duration'), it is the comments about history rather than art that could function as a direct description of the problems presented by the desire to remake Kaprow's ephemeral actions or arrangements. 'Past events', Kubler asserts, 'are no longer available to observation save as artefacts or contingent traces of the activity under study, which we can know only in documents, chronicles, and histories.' If Duchamp as well as later conceptual practices took the artist into the terrain of the historian or critic, then it is perhaps fitting that Kubler's five axioms about historical duration are most resonant with Kaprow's work:

1. Similar actions by the same agent cannot occupy the same time. If they do, the recipient is different and the action also.
2. No one agent can perform the same action more than once without ageing.
3. Actions can only be similar, but not identical, being different as to agent, or as to time, or as to location.
4. Actions repeated undergo change.
5. The agent changes with each repeated action.[39]

According to Kubler, the challenge of duration extends the question of style to the full range of works that have been analysed according to such terms. It is therefore interesting to note how the early and eager adaptation of photographs as a tool for connoisseurship represents an attempt to defeat problems of duration on the level of reception, characterised by Malraux as the 'comparison of a present vision with a memory' prior to the widespread circulation of reproductions.[40] Yet Kubler is also addressing the issue of duration in production, not only through the incorporation of references drawn from different eras within any given work, but also as the artist moves through time and therefore necessarily returns to a problem with a different set of coordinates.

Kaprow's remakes of *Yard* serve to dramatise this instability by introducing an aspect of change typically discovered in a comparison of works from an artist's different periods into a single work rendered inherently multiple through his intermittent exercise of authorial power. The 1961 photographs of *Yard*, while in large part responsible for the ongoing interest in this assembly of used tyres, are also involved in a rather different operation than the use of photography in art history's comparative method, and in particular for the imperatives of connoisseurship centred upon the identification of unique stylistic traits. Photographs of later installations, by contrast, enable comparisons among the temporally and geographically dispersed examples of what Kaprow nonetheless identifies as the ongoing interpretations of a single work. *Yard* is a continuous work to the extent that variants were declared as such by the artist Kaprow –

even as its transformations over the years testify to the changing concerns of the individual occupying that proper name. Thus the photograph is part of a process that is both fixed and fluid, allowing comparison of the far flung examples of a work that cannot be understood as singular, even as the work has, after each disturbance, largely settled back into its identity with the 1961 photographs.

'The viewer of today not only sees things in a different way but also sees different things', is Michael Ann Holly's succinct formulation in the introduction to *Past Looking* – in the context of a discussion of the deferred action whereby our understanding of the past is revised in light of the present. Yet Holly identifies this mobility in a discussion largely centred upon painting, where barring damage or radical conservation treatments one can assume at least a certain continuity in the physical artefact under reconsideration.[41] Work that has to be reinstalled or remade each time it is shown is in some respects more evidently subject to passage of time, but in other ways evades this process of historical definition. Instead of a continuous physical object, relatively unchanged except for wear or conservation efforts, the work's appearance reflects an ongoing process of reinterpretation. Of course Sol LeWitt pointedly addressed the issue of physical contingency with his series of wall drawings begun in 1968, where he developed an explicit strategy for creating works based on a set of instructions carried out by others and remade each time the work is exhibited. In contrast to obviously conceptual works by LeWitt and others, where procedures for remaking are explicit in the initial plans, impetus for Kaprow's remakes came after the initial installation, with later interpretations emanating not from the single point of the plan, but in the intersection between Kaprow's evolving motivations and a range of forces that includes the equally mobile series of curatorial contexts within which *Yard* has been summoned to reappear.

Intent

In the case of the 1998 *Out of Actions* exhibition, one interesting side effect of organising a retrospective of performance-based works from the 1960s and 1970s was the motivation for the museum to go into the business of creating replicas. Another form of copy, the plaster casts that had been valued in part because of their educational function, had long been banished from most museum collections. Here, however, the curator wanted a replica not to represent a canonical sculpture located in another collection, but in order to display a by-now canonical environment without a continuous physical existence. In a subsequent essay about *Out of Actions*, Schimmel recounted his difficulty as a curator of a historical exhibition when faced with Kaprow's insistence that the work reflect his ongoing interests as an artist. And the correspondence files related to this exhibition indicate that Kaprow was adamant that the work could not simply be remade from the photograph.[42]

Kaprow's argument that the work had remained in flux left the curator in the bind of needing the artist's endorsement to create the work, but wanting something rather different than what Kaprow was interested in authorising.

Whereas Schimmel did not want a new work, Kaprow did not want to create a remake based on a close reprise of the 1961 photographs, and the organisation of the collection around original works of authorship is one reason why Schimmel needed Kaprow's permission and participation, nearly four decades later, to reconstitute this historical work. One of the most striking points in the published account of the negotiation process connected to *Yard* is Schimmel's own assertion of artistic intent in his suggestion that the version of the work in Italy was inconsistent with *Kaprow's* original intention for the work. His description of the MOCA version was similar: 'With much discussion and a great deal of struggle, I convinced him to make a piece that I think also has only a passing resemblance to his original intention.'[43]

In his comments on Duchamp's 'Creative Act' (and with decided overtones of Barthes), Kaprow posited certain circumstances where the author would recede: 'According to some of my friends, the freeways of Los Angeles are great theater, modern theater, with no beginning or end, full of chance excitements and plenty of the sort of boredom we all love ... Their future as Readymade art depends on the reader.'[44] When it came to *Yard*, however, Kaprow was not willing to cede his authorial position to Schimmel, closely controlling the process of interpretation that is part of the reinstallation of the early environments, and even using his grip on their identity as another way of continuing his resistance to the mandates of museum contextualisation. In this example, as in many others, one after-effect of the readymade is evident in the role thus opened for the artist to continue to establish the context for the act, not just at the initial moment of selection, but over time, in the ongoing process through which the work's significance is secured. Furthermore, if earlier commission procedures were for a time supplanted by the romantic model of the easel painting, produced on an independent basis by the artist in the studio, then the increasingly popular procedure of inviting artists to create site-specific works for particular installations suggests a curious return that brings together certain of the logistics of the former while still holding to an ideal of artistic independence associated with the latter. In the negotiations over *Yard*, the curator's attempts to commission a work that in many respects already existed opens onto a process of interpretation where readings of a past point of origin are articulated in debates pointing forward, toward the outcome of the work's future reinstallation. Moreover, the prolonged, elaborate discussions between curator and artist demonstrate from a practical standpoint how nearby indeed the artist may be – not an imagined figure, to be discovered through the work, but a very insistent actual presence.

The issues raised by the intersection of authorship and photograph are important not only for *Yard*'s history, but in work produced by many other artists during the historical period spanned by the multiple versions of Kaprow's environment. Kaprow's comment about the reading of the Los Angeles freeway as a kind of readymade, as well as an alternate idea for bypassing the gallery entirely and simply inviting spectators to the dump, evoke a well-known description by Tony Smith of his experience of the vastness of the newly built New Jersey turnpike or, even more apropos, the take on the industrial landscape articulated by Smithson in his 1967 *Artforum* essay 'The Monuments of Passaic'.[45]

Smithson's published account of his discovery of monuments in the residue of utilitarian forms describes a journey taken alone; when he went back later with friends, however, it hardly seems coincidental that he made one such trip in 1968 with Nancy Holt, Oldenburg, and Kaprow.[46] But neither Smithson's narrative nor Kaprow's alternate plan to direct viewers to the dump actually releases the process of definition; instead Smithson's reader or Kaprow's hypothetical viewer experiences the found readymade through this authorial intervention. And, for the much larger audience that encounters Smithson's monuments only through the published account, the photographs give these immobile readymades a kind of parity with other works represented in the imaginary museum of the reproduction.

Yard's prolonged history clearly has many implications for other practices, including how questions raised by the role of the photograph for Kaprow's later audience intersect with both conceptual procedures of the 1960s and the widespread integration of photographs and other forms of documentation in contemporary practice, where such uses are now established as a means to convey distant, private, or ephemeral works that the artist nonetheless defines as art.[47] And even Kaprow's strategies for resisting object making have been assimilated into an extended definition of artistic production centred on negotiated interventions. Kaprow concluded his 1971 essay 'Education of the Un-Artist, Part I', with a plea: 'Artists of the world, drop out! You have nothing to lose but your professions!'[48] His alternative, articulated in his correspondence with Schimmel, was to insist on his identity as a provider of services rather than a producer of objects. Yet the model of the service provider has proven compelling for artists engaged in performance practices that activate the idea of the tour Smithson only playfully suggested – including Andrea Fraser's attention to the rhetoric of the museum, or Carey Young's focus on corporate strategies.[49] With the institutional embrace of site-specific projects, the return of certain aspects of the negotiated commission is linked to the rise of a new form of artist professional who may work in close coordination with curators and a range of other experts necessary for the realisation of any given work.

Perhaps the most compelling legacy of *Yard* can therefore be found in the irresolvable contradictions its extended history presents. The photograph records, isolates, and fixes a historical moment that cannot be retrieved – dependent as the event thus recorded was on the particular circumstances of place and time. But to the extent that the work it documents has an ongoing existence, the photographic record falsely locked into place a conception of the work at a single, now inaccessible moment, even as installations identified as *Yard* by the artist called Kaprow continued to reappear in a variety of guises. For this and many other works that do not have an enduring physical form, the photograph can function as much more than a secondary document that transmits information about an absent object bound by time and space. It provides the basis for the work's apparent continuity, with the reproduction enduring as the physical configuration comes and goes. Kaprow was insistent that he did not want new installations simply to recreate the photographs of the initial environment; yet without those same photos *Yard* would not have achieved its status as an important and seemingly familiar work, and Kaprow would not have had the opportunity to introduce strategies of resistance only made possible by the work's embrace. There is obviously no going back to recreate the circumstances that framed Kaprow's original undertaking, despite the expanding interest in participatory work witnessed by few in its first incarnation. Kaprow's decision to consider the early works ongoing therefore addressed the ambiguity of trying to revive a gesture that the work's later audience, upon viewing the photographic evidence, interprets as clearly dependent on its initial context.

Notes

1 Allan Kaprow, 'The Legacy of Jackson Pollock' [1958], in *Essays on the Blurring of Art and Life*, ed. Jeff Kelley (Berkeley and Los Angeles, 1993), pp. 1–9.

2 Paul McCarthy, in 'Allan Kaprow: Art & Life', *Art in America* (March 2008), p. 136 (transcript of panel discussion held at the Jewish Museum, 8 November 2007). The retrospective, *Allan Kaprow – Art as Life*, opened in 2006 at the Haus der Kunst, Munich, and subsequently travelled to the Van Abbemuseum, Eindhoven; Kunsthalle Bern, Berne; Museo Villa Groce Genova; and the Museum of Contemporary Art, Los Angeles.

3 For the 2008 version of the retrospective at LA MOCA, Allen Ruppersberg reinvented *Words*, John Baldessari and Skylar Haskard took on *Apple Shrine*, and Barbara T. Smith was responsible for *Push and Pull*.

4 On the justification for re-enacting *18 Happenings in 6 Parts*, see André Lepecki, 'Redoing 18 Happenings in 6 Parts', in *Allan Kaprow – 18 Happenings in 6 Parts – 9/10/11 November 2006* (Göttingen, 2007), pp. 45–50, and Stephanie Rosenthal, 'Agency for Action', in Eva Meyer-Hermann, Andew Perchuk and Stephanie Rosenthal (eds), *Allan Kaprow – Art as Life* (Los Angeles, 2008), p. 66. *18 Happenings in 6 Parts* was restaged in various locations in conjunction with the travelling retrospective, and also in New York as part of Performa 07.

5 Allan Kaprow, 'The Education of the Un-Artist, Part II' [1972], in *Essays on the Blurring of Art and Life*, p. 111.

6 Allan Kaprow, 'The Education of the Un-Artist, Part I' [1971], in ibid, p. 98.

7 Allan Kaprow, 'Doctor MD' [1973], in ibid, p. 127.

8 The September 2009 inaugural Hauser & Wirth New York exhibition, curated by Helen Molesworth, included William Pope.L's reinvention of *Yard* within the former Martha Jackson Gallery, along with off-site reinventions by Josiah McElheny and Sharon Hayes in public spaces in downtown Manhattan and Queens. In addition to inhabiting the site of *Yard*'s original appearance, the gallery also represents the Kaprow estate.

9 Brian O'Doherty, 'The Gallery as Gesture', in Reesa Greenberg, Bruce W. Ferguson, and Sandy Nairne, *Thinking about Exhibitions* (London, 1996), p. 322.

10 For transcriptions from this work, see Silvia Kolbowski, 'an inadequate history of conceptual art', *October*, 92 (Spring 2000), pp. 53–70, and *Silvia Kolbowski, inadequate ... Like ... Power at the Secession* (Cologne, 2004), pp. 6–17.

11 Mignon Nixon, 'On the Couch', *October*, 113 (Summer 2005), p. 72.

12 On this dynamic, see Judith F. Rodenbeck, 'Foil: Allan Kaprow before Photography', in Benjamin H.D. Buchloh and Judith F. Rodenbeck, *Experiments in the Everyday: Allan Kaprow and Robert Watts – Events, Objects, Documents* (New York, 2000), pp. 47–67.

13 For descriptions of various works involving the incorporation of photography, see Jeff Kelley, *Childsplay: The Art of Allan Kaprow* (Berkeley, 2004), pp. 130, 133, 144–5, and 188–9.

14 *New Forms – New Media 1* (New York, 1960), n.p.

15 See Kelley, *Childsplay*, p. 58, referencing Kaprow's recollections to Kelley in a conversation from May 1995.

16 Claes Oldenburg, interview by Paul Cummings, December 4, 1973 – January 25, 1974, transcript, Archives of American Art, New York, quoted in Julie H. Reiss, *From Margin to Center: The Spaces of Installation Art* (Cambridge, MA, 1999), p. 40.

17 See Reiss, *From Margin to Center*, pp. 36–41, for an account of these responses to the 1961 Jackson Gallery exhibition. Reiss cites reviews from four sources: *Art News*, *New York Times*, *Village Voice*, and *Newsweek*.

18 Jack Kroll, review of *Environments, Situations, Spaces*, *Art News* 60 (September 1961), p. 16.

19 Brian O'Doherty, 'Art: 3 Displays Run Gamut of Styles', *New York Times* (6 June 1961), p. 43.

20 Kelley cites a 14-page guest list that included David Tudor, Claes Oldenburg, Jim Dine, Jasper Johns, Leo Castelli, Ivan Karp, Dan Flavin, Meyer Schapiro, Richard Bellamy, and Fairfield Porter. See Kelley, *Childsplay*, p. 34.

21 The disagreement is addressed in interviews Susan Hapgood conducted with Kaprow and Oldenburg in 1992 and 1993 respectively. See the interview section in Susan Hapgood, *Neo-Dada: Redefining Art, 1958–62* (New York, 1994), particularly pp. 120 and 125.

22 Allan Kaprow, *Assemblage, Environments and Happenings* (New York, 1966), p. 21.

23 André Malraux, *Museum without Walls*, trans. S. Gilbert and F. Price (Garden City, New York, 1967), p. 12.

24 Allan Kaprow, 'The Legacy of Jackson Pollock' [1958], in *Essays on the Blurring of Art and Life*, pp. 5, 7. For a more recent analysis of this dynamic, see William Kaizen, 'Framed Space: Allan Kaprow and the Spread of Painting', *Grey Room* 13 (Fall 2003), pp. 80–107.

25 Kaprow, 'The Shape of the Art Environment' [1968], in *Essays on the Blurring of Art and Life*, p. 92.

26 Allan Kaprow, introductory text in *Allan Kaprow* (Pasadena, 1967), p. 3. On the specific decision to use tarpaper, see Robert E. Haywood, 'Critique of Instrumental Labor: Meyer Schapiro's and Allan Kaprow's Theory of Avant-Garde Art', in Buchloh and Rodenbeck, *Experiments in the Everyday*, p. 42.

27 See Barbara Haskell, *Blam! The Explosion of Pop, Minimalism, and Performance, 1958–64* (New York, 1984). The checklist on pages 157–60 indicates that works by George Brecht, Walter De Maria, Red Grooms, Allan Kaprow, Robert Morris, Robert Watts, and Robert Whitman were reconstructed for the 1984 exhibition.

28 Eleanor Heartney, 'Report from Sydney: The Expanded Readymade', *Art in America*, 78 (September 1990), p. 91.

29 Kelley, *Childsplay*, p. 220. See also Allan Kaprow, *7 Environments* (Milan, 1992), for extensive photographs of the reconstruction of all seven environments.

30 Paul Schimmel, 'Intentionality and Performance-Based Art', in Miguel Angel Corzo (ed.), *Mortality Immortality? The Legacy of 20th-Century Art* (Los Angeles, 1999), p. 138. The correspondence between Kaprow and Schimmel appears in the Kaprow Papers, Box 34, in the Special Collections of the Getty Research Library at the Getty Research Institute. For the exhibition overview, see Paul Schimmel, *Out of Actions: Between Performance and the Object, 1949–79* (Los Angeles and London, 1998).

31 See www.ubu.com/aspen (accessed: 10/01/2011) for a survey of the contents of all 10 issues of *Aspen* that, while failing to provide the important tactile experience of sifting through the loose pieces that constitute this magazine, does have the advantage of comprehensiveness not necessarily found in the sometimes fragmentary condition of library holdings, as well as access to audio and film components from 5+6.

32 Susan Sontag, 'The Aesthetics of Silence', *Aspen*, 5+6 (1967), section 3.

33 Kaprow, 'Doctor MD,' in *Essays on the Blurring of Art and Life*, p. 127.

34 Roland Barthes, 'The Death of the Author' [1968], in *Image Music Text*, trans. S. Heath (New York, 1977), p. 143.

35 Ibid, p. 146.

36 Kaprow tells Schimmel that he provides services rather than making objects in a note dated 16 September 1997 in the Kaprow Papers.

37 George Kubler, *The Shape of Time: Remarks on the History of Things* (New Haven, 1962), p. 21.

38 See 'What is a Museum? A Dialogue between Allan Kaprow and Robert Smithson' [1967], reprinted in *The Writings of Robert Smithson*, ed. Nancy Holt (New York, 1979), p. 59, as well as Allan Kaprow, 'Death in the Museum', and Robert Smithson, 'Some Void Thoughts on Museums', *Arts Magazine*, 41 (February 1967), pp. 40–41. On the importance of Kubler for Smithson and other artists, see Pamela M. Lee's chapter 'Ultramoderne: Or, How George Kubler Stole the Time in Sixties Art', in *Chronophobia: On Time in the Art of the 1960s* (Cambridge, MA, 2004), pp. 218–56.

39 George Kubler, 'Style and the Representation of Historical Time', *Aspen*, 5+6 (1967), section 3.

40 Malraux, *Museum without Walls*, p. 11.

41 Michael Ann Holly, *Past Looking: Historical Imagination and the Rhetoric of the Image* (Ithaca, 1996), p. 26.

42 See in particular Kaprow's 8 February 1997 letter to Schimmel in the Kaprow Papers.

43 Schimmel, 'Intentionality and Performance-Based Art', p. 138.

44 Kaprow, 'Doctor MD', in *Essays on the Blurring of Art and Life*, p. 129.

45 References to the junkyard alternative appear in Kelley, *Childsplay*, p. 59, and a 4 June 1997 letter from Kaprow to Kristine Stiles in the Kaprow Papers.

46 On Smithson's 'Monuments of Passaic', see Ann Reynolds, *Robert Smithson: Learning from New Jersey and Elsewhere* (Cambridge, MA, 2003). The reference to Kaprow appears on page 265, note 86.

47 On the role of the photograph within a range of practices from the 1960s to the present, see Martha Buskirk, *The Contingent Object of Contemporary Art* (Cambridge, MA, 2003), particularly chapter 5, pp. 211–58.

48 Kaprow, 'The Education of the Un-Artist, Part I' [1971], in *Essays on the Blurring of Art and Life*, p. 109.

49 See, for example, Andrea Fraser, 'How to Provide an Artistic Service: An Introduction' [1994], in Zoya Kocur and Simon Leung (eds), *Theory in Contemporary Art since 1985* (Malden, MA, 2005), pp. 69–75.

5

Richard Wentworth's *Making Do, Getting By* and the Elusive Everyday

Anna Dezeuze

As an artwork, the status of Richard Wentworth's series of photographs entitled *Making Do, Getting By* is, in many senses, uncertain. Wentworth is a sculptor, and it is alongside his sculptural work, rather than as part of it, that he has been taking, since 1970, thousands upon thousands of photographs of human interventions in their environment as he encounters them randomly in the street: the headlight of a red Austin Mini kept in place by a diagonal piece of red tape, a chair and broomstick used to reserve a parking space (Figure 5.1), a coffee cup propping a window open (Figure 5.2), a lost leather glove arranged on the spike of a London street railing (Figure 5.4). An early batch was first included in an article for *Artscribe* in 1978 under the title 'Making Do and Getting By'; a video was made with them in 1985, many of them have been shown by Wentworth in his talks and lectures, and they have even been exhibited in museums and galleries.[1] Yet Wentworth remains ambivalent about them – he refuses to see them as artworks, but he often uses them as a way of speaking about his interests without discussing his sculpture; he is frank about their low market value, but admits they have acquired an 'iconic' status over the years.[2]

Brassaï and Dalí's *Involuntary Sculptures* (Figure I.1) are similarly ambivalent – anonymously published, they cannot be considered as 'works' by either artist in the same way as their photographs or painting respectively. Dismissed at the time as bad photographs (Paul Eluard had to plead to have them included in *Minotaure*), they have also acquired a 'mythic' status, not least for Wentworth, who included them in an exhibition that he curated.[3] Rather than try to fix the status of these works, this essay will explore these ambiguities by focusing on a set of intertwined issues including the notion of automatism and our relation to everyday objects. Although Wentworth's sculptural practice will be referred to, it is his photographs that interest me here, as I explore some of the ways in which his photographic practice and statements shed light on his relation to sculpture, found objects and the everyday. By presenting Wentworth's *Making Do, Getting By* series as an update of Brassaï and Dalí's joint project, I wish both to demonstrate the radicality of the *Involuntary Sculptures* and point to their shared preoccupations. In turn, Wentworth's series can be seen as a forerunner for many artistic practices exploring the everyday since the late

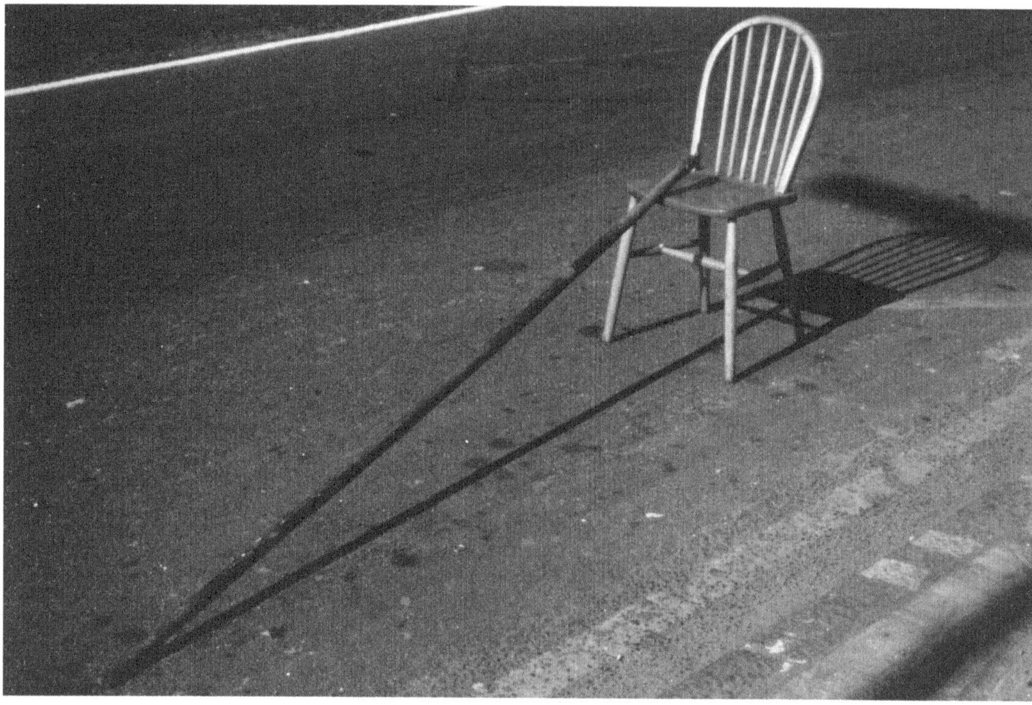

5.1 Richard Wentworth, *Kings Cross, London*, colour print made from transparency, 11 × 7 cm, 1978, from the *Making Do, Getting By* series. British Council Collection © Richard Wentworth

1980s and early 1990s.[4] The specific kind of approach to the everyday will be discussed here in relation to theories of everyday life, in particular Michel de Certeau's 1980 *Practice of Everyday Life*.

Anonymous Sculptures

Describing the *Involuntary Sculptures*, Wentworth immediately relates the everyday objects to art: the image of the bread, he says, is 'almost more like a photograph of a ceramic, because baking and ceramics are really the same thing' (C, p. 13), and the 'twirls' of the bus ticket are described as architectural 'volutes' (C, p. 13) (with this comparison, Wentworth is intuitively pointing to the art nouveau architecture evoked in Dalí's captions). For Wentworth, the world is already full of sculpture. A wall is an 'amazing piece of sculpture', 'worth a lot of Henry Moores' (C, p. 8) and he finds 'empty cigarette packets folded up under table legs more monumental than a Henry Moore'.[5] The repeated reference to Moore is not coincidental: Wentworth used to work as his assistant. Unlike Moore, however, it is not in the natural world that Wentworth finds his everyday sculptures but in the resolutely man-made field of the architectural, the artisanal, and the do-it-yourself. Rather than reiterating the traditional trope of life imitating art, Wentworth claims his motive for taking his photographs extends beyond the field of his specific sculptural practice: 'I think I'm just trying to remind myself that the world is made' (C, p. 16). The idea of the world

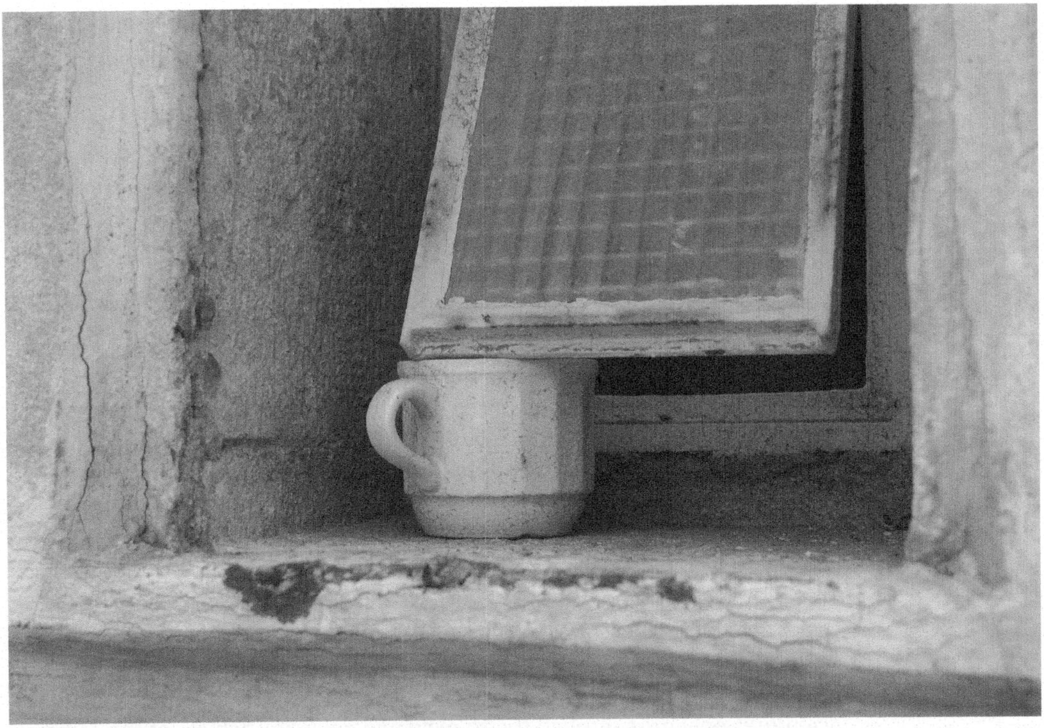

5.2 Richard Wentworth, *South West France 2007*, unique colour photograph, 29.6 × 42 cm, 2007, from the *Making Do, Getting By* series. Courtesy the artist and Lisson Gallery. © Richard Wentworth

as 'made' relates to two different ideas: that very little of the world has been spared human intervention (even landscape, Wentworth reminds us, is a human invention), and that all our perceptions are culturally defined (we can see Pop art everywhere because it has infiltrated so many spheres of our lives). One-to-one comparisons of artworks and everyday objects are 'babyish', Wentworth admits (C, p. 16), and none of his photographs refer to specific artists or artworks directly. Wentworth's 'reminders' are more general: they point to the age-old, infinite, teeming activity of humans coming to grips with the world.

This process is necessarily performative. Just as the bread in the *Involuntary Sculptures* was 'flat at some point' before being 'rolled and ... put in the kiln' (C, p. 13), the pieces of paper have been 'rolled', and the toothpaste 'spread', as the captions themselves suggest. The concrete, material actions embodied by these past participles bring to mind American sculptor Richard Serra's 1967–68 *Verb List* related to the kind of 'process art' that he was developing at the time. Indeed, Serra's list not only starts with the verb 'to roll', and includes 'to spread', but also introduces infinitives that could describe other activities involved in the *Involuntary Sculptures*, such as 'to tear', 'to twist', 'to spill', 'to discard' ... In this context, it is not surprising that Wentworth cites Serra's series of works involving molten lead being thrown onto the floor and walls of the gallery as an example of 'automatic sculpture' (C, p. 15). (The series included the 1968 *Splashing* and the 1969 *Casting*, both made at the Leo Castelli Warehouse in New York.) What is 'automatic' about Serra's work, according to Wentworth, is its reliance on gravity and the very physical process of change in the material itself. It is about the direct relation between the human gesture and its material embodiment – as Serra laconically put it: 'It's how we do what we do that confers meaning on what we've done.'[6]

The *Involuntary Sculptures* may share the same vocabulary as Serra's monumental works, but are decidedly less spectacular: unlike Serra's spilled liquid metal (*Splashing*) or rolled sheet of lead (*Thirty-five Feet of Lead Rolled Up*, 1968), the gob of toothpaste or rolled-up piece of paper in Brassaï's photographs are products of everyday activities which we hardly notice (let alone produce wearing a 'heroic' working attire including leather gloves and a helmet). Similarly, Wentworth's description of how '"[p]utting" and "placing" encompass a hierarchy of alignments – laying, leaning, propping, wedging, chocking, jamming' may evoke a range of 'prop' works realised by Serra (Figure 5.3), but he is in fact speaking of the ways in which we use objects in everyday life, from the 'out-of-work domestic broom' casually propped in a corner, to the apparently endless variety of objects wedged under doors and windows to keep them open (MD, p. 23) (Figure 5.2).

By highlighting the physical qualities of each fragment, the close-up photography of Brassaï brings out the close relation between gesture and object. These photographs, argues Wentworth, are 'like *very* good animation' (C, p. 13); they bring these objects to life, and suggest the movements of rolling, spreading, baking. Rosalind Krauss has discussed the crucial role of photography in framing reality and presenting it to our attention; she argues that the *Involuntary Sculptures* only exist through the framing and enlarging activity of the camera.[7] This is closely related to Walter Benjamin's discussion of the way photography reveals an 'optical unconscious' through such means as enlargement and the slowing of motion which extend our perceptive capacities. As an example, Benjamin suggests that only photography can tell us 'what happens during the fraction of a second when a person *steps out*'.[8] Wentworth turned to photography precisely because he was interested in such 'momentary and fleeting' gestures which are 'rarely "seen," just caught in a glimpse'. The optical unconscious, then, that the camera reveals in Brassaï's and Wentworth's 'involuntary sculptures' is not only an extension of our conscious perception. As Krauss has put it, 'what the camera frames and thereby makes visible is the automatic writing of the world: the constant, uninterrupted production of signs'.[9] It is photography that 'reminds us that the world is made', in Wentworth's terms, that allows us to see 'things that are in the world, that are made by us, that we don't quite see' (C, p. 13).

In contrast to the dramatically lit and enlarged *Involuntary Sculptures*, however, Wentworth's snapshots are spontaneous, lacking according to him 'any degree of control over lighting, and the other unpredictable context factors' (MD, p. 21). They are more 'banal', and seek to 'celebrate' what they show rather than impose a specific authorial style. These characteristics are inherent to amateur photography, which models itself largely on the documentary tradition. Wentworth's photographs embody the point at which surrealist, documentary and amateur photography coincide. As Ian Walker has suggested, surrealist photography is characterised by a documentary impulse, which is predicated on the belief that the marvellous is inherently present in reality, and hence needs only to be revealed.[10] The amateur photographer, according to Julian Stallabrass,

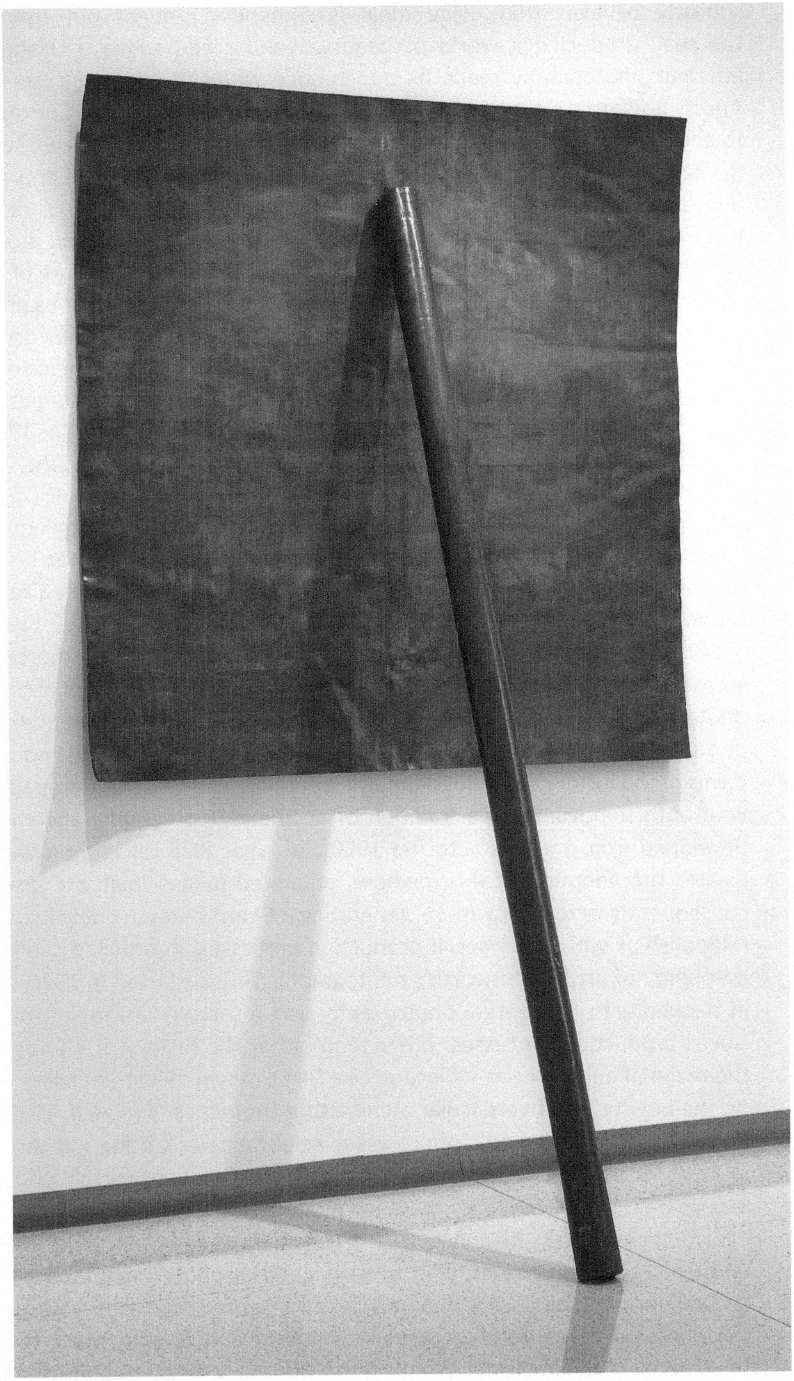

5.3 Richard Serra, *Prop*, lead antimony, sheet, 152.4 × 152.4 cm, 1968, Walker Art Center, Minneapolis. Gift of Penny and Mike Winton, 1977 © 2011 Richard Serra / Artists Rights Society (ARS), New York

similarly believes that '[t]he ideal is somehow brought out from behind the real, producing a world of beauty, wonder and sense'.[11] Unsurprisingly, amateur photography made its appearance within surrealism, from Jacques-André Boiffard's deliberately deadpan illustrations for André Breton's *Nadja* to the many found images scattered throughout surrealist reviews such as *La Révolution surréaliste* and *Documents*. Moreover, the image of the snapshot (*l'instantané*), with its connotations of photographic immediacy, is referred to more than once in surrealist writings. In the text on art nouveau architecture which follows the *Involuntary Sculptures*, Dalí for example speaks of columns which 'emerge for the first time in the world of the hard undulations of *sculpted water* with the photographic concern of the snapshot'.[12] The 'ornamental automatism' of these columns, like that of the bus ticket or the piece of soap, is thus closely linked to the ways in which they seem to fix these energies *as if in a snapshot*, thus emerging as the 'realisation of solidified desires'.[13] As Walker has pointed out, a comparison was implied between the immediacy of the snapshot, with its connotations of authenticity and innocence, and surrealist automatic writing, which is written so quickly as not to be contrived.[14] Similarly, despite his awareness of photographic traditions, Wentworth insists that he remains an amateur photographer who takes his pictures very quickly, in a mode that cannot be 'knowing'.[15]

If the amateur photographer appeared only sporadically in the context of surrealism, (s)he would become a crucial model for the development of conceptual photography in the late 1960s and early 1970s. As Jeff Wall has argued, amateur photography came to serve a variety of pivotal functions at that moment.[16] In terms of the history of the medium, the adoption of amateur photography broke with both the avant-garde tradition of aesthetic photography and the canon, developed from the 1920s to the 1950s, of what Wall calls 'photojournalism-as-art'. The adoption of this medium, untainted by any 'high art' credentials, consequently acted as a more general avant-garde ploy to develop 'mimetic relationships with other social production processes' in order to challenge the autonomy of art.[17] Wentworth's photographic series, started in 1970, emerged in parallel with conceptual photography and resolutely affirmed a relation to 'social production processes' other than either the history of photography or the realm of autonomous sculpture. Like Dan Graham's illustrations for his essay on the new types of vernacular architecture (*Homes for America*, 1966–67), or Robert Smithson's parodic photo-essay celebrating a 'rotting industrial town' in New Jersey (*The Monuments of Passaic*, 1967), Wentworth's photographs occupy a grey zone between the documentation of existing places, objects and activities, and works of conceptual art. If Wentworth's snapshots thus easily find a place in the photographic arena opened by photoconceptual works such as Graham's or Smithson's, they are less concerned, however, with parodying the photojournalist tradition. Where Smithson and Graham were responding to American minimalism, Wentworth's formal preoccupations focused on general sculptural processes involved in everyday arrangements of found and readymade objects. In this sense, he has been extending the conceptual artists' project to locate 'the impulse toward self-sufficient and non-objective forms of art in concrete, personal responses to real life, social experiences'.[18]

For Wall, the 'amateur' style appeared as the most appropriate tool for undermining the 'objectivist and positivist' styles of both minimalism and photojournalism because '[t]he pictures are, as reductivist works, models of our actual relations with their subjects, rather than dramatized representations that transfigure those relations by making it impossible for us to have such relations with them'.[19] The issue of 'transfiguration' is an ongoing problem of photography – Benjamin himself complained as early as 1937 that German avant-garde photographers could 'no longer photograph a tenement block or a refuse heap without transfiguring it'.[20] This transfiguration operates at different levels: making the photographed object look more beautiful than it is (in the aesthetic picture), or making it stand as a symbol for a wider message (for example, in the humanism of documentary-as-art photography), and generally transforming the object into the expression of the individual photographer's style. These processes are encapsulated by the most basic term of framing – *how* you frame reality will decide how it is transfigured. Wentworth's refusal to 'transfigure' objects was expressed in his vehement objection to psychologist Richard Gregory's suggestion that going around and leaning frames on found objects would be the same thing as taking photographs (C, p. 17). For Wentworth, the photographs are only interesting because they are not isolating objects from reality so much as capturing the 'involuntary sculptures' *as they are being produced* in everyday life. Since these sculptures are context-specific, any framing would be a transfiguration; it would distort 'our actual relations with their subjects', to use Wall's terms. Brassaï's *Involuntary Sculptures*, Wentworth remarks, seem to float in 'outer space': in the process of being framed, lit and presented to our scrutiny on glass plates, they have been wrenched out of their context.[21] Finding the marvellous behind the surface of the everyday may be the aim of both the amateur photographer and the surrealist, but once the marvellous is revealed, its dialectical relation with the everyday threatens to be forever lost.

In addition to its deadpan style, conceptual photography often focuses on deliberately bland, banal, or trivial subject matter. If Wentworth's photographs share an interest in the trivial, their subject matter remains nonetheless less aggressively boring, so to speak, than Ed Ruscha's 1962 photographs of 26 petrol stations along Route 66 between Los Angeles to Oklahoma City, for example, partly because the processes that they record systematically introduce a narrative within the image, however discreet. How far these narratives involve the transfiguration of the everyday hinges on two issues that I shall examine in the next sections: the ways in which objects are invested with psychic drives, and the definition of everyday life itself.

'Neurotic' Objects

Wentworth's world is filled with the murmur of objects. In the same way as materials are handled to create objects, objects are named and arranged to construct what Wentworth has called 'a whole language of low-level message-sending'.[22] For example, buildings used to be inscribed with inlaid letters, because 'people were very busy telling you who they were' (C, p. 6); the names of four-by-four cars – 'Warrior', 'Shogun', 'Patrol', 'Cherokee' – evoke the American and Japanese military (C, p. 7); even walls 'express different kinds of power' (C, p. 22) (one need only think of the wall built in Israel). In contrast with these very public statements of power, Wentworth's photographs tend to focus on the equally talkative 'mundane improvisations' of everyday life (MD, p. 21) by which a 'discarded cardboard box' – or a household chair (Figure 5.1) – positioned in the middle of a parking place may be too flimsy to physically prevent someone from parking, but 'by deliberate placement it can form a sign which matches any neon directive' (MD, p. 23).

Speaking about the Brassaï and Dalí *Involuntary Sculptures*, Wentworth exclaimed: 'the one that I really adore is a kind of neurotic furling of a bus ticket' (C, p. 13). Other comparable everyday 'neuroses' according to him include the 'area of the chewed pencil' (Krauss, for her part, evokes 'those pieces of eraser that we unconsciously knead').[23] Dalí's ironic introduction of the term *'débile mental'* ('mentally defective' person) into the caption for the rolled-up piece of paper belongs to the range of pathological vocabulary that he mobilises in his text on art nouveau architecture. Amid pseudo-scientific references to such psychoanalytical terms as megalomania, hysteria, onanism, coprophagia, and the 'sadistic-anal complex', Dalí seems to define *'débilité mentale'* as the opposite of 'the act of reason' (*l'activité raisonnante*) and sets up a connection, established in studies of the art of the mentally ill, between 'pathological communications' and an 'ornamental exacerbation'.[24] These seem to be brought together in the comical phrase 'positive lyrical imbecility'. Though not following Dalí's exaggerated use of psychoanalysis, Wentworth's reference to 'neurosis' in its contemporary vulgarized sense brings to the fore the psychological dimensions of our relations to objects. Like Freud's 'psychopathology of everyday life', Wentworth and Dalí find evidence of unconscious behaviour in our most banal actions. Indeed, in some everyday scenarios described by Freud, people's relation to objects speak volumes – a mislaid bunch of keys postpones a dreaded departure, while an acquaintance's overcoat thrown on the back of a chair proclaims to Freud: 'There's no room for you here, you're superfluous now'.[25] Evidence of what Wentworth describes as everyday 'psycho-sexual' behaviour is given by the artist as he ends his discussion of the *Involuntary Sculptures* by describing the way in which one of his teenage sons used to put the remote control in his mouth when he watched television (C, p. 14). The 'little teeth marks' on the remote control betray an oral fixation which, we imagine, is only slightly more unusual than the compulsion to chew the end of a pencil. Indeed, for Wentworth, it seems that *any* object can be potentially psychologically charged as long as it triggers a reaction in what he calls his 'nervous system' (C, p. 3). When his other son phoned him to say that he had found an abandoned wooden staircase, Wentworth admits that the description was 'quite erotic' but that once he saw the object he realised it 'was absolutely no good' for him because he hadn't found it himself (C, p. 18). In the same way, Wentworth explains, 'you don't want people sent to you because somebody says "this is your kind of sexual treat"' (C, p. 18). What this suggests is that a general field of desire brings together actions as apparently different as chewing a remote control and holding a pencil in one's mouth to free one's hands to do something else.

The potentially erotic nature of the found object was most strikingly celebrated by André Breton in his 1937 *L'Amour fou*, in which he recounts how he purchased a wooden spoon decorated with a tiny shoe at the flea market, only to realise that it provided an unexpected resolution to a whole string of desires (see Figure 8.2).[26] The surrealist belief in 'objective chance' as an external phenomenon that revealed internal repressed desires certainly opened up new ways of perceiving everyday objects. Unlike Breton, however, Wentworth never explains exactly why this wooden staircase was 'no good' or why, conversely, this or that other object fulfils a quasi-erotic desire. The nature of this desire may be as idiosyncratic as Breton's personal associations of the spoon and its slipper with Cinderella and with genital imagery, but it remains enigmatic. In contrast, the series of photographs by Wentworth, which show the results of people arranging and placing objects in the world in response to functional needs rather than personal obsessions, seem to map out more transparently a web of collective 'neurotic' desires and anxieties through the repetition of patterns of behaviour. But to what, then, do these desires and anxieties relate?

Wentworth himself points out that certain aspects of 'fiddling' can lead to a 'rather sexual' kind of pleasure. 'Discovering that things fit' – like a bottle cap on the bottom of a walking stick – is a case in point for him (C, p. 20). This kind of fiddling evokes an image discussed by Breton in relation to his slipper-spoon – that of Cinderella's foot fitting perfectly into the glass slipper presented to her by Prince Charming.[27] For Breton, the sexual content of this image evokes the bliss of being united with the 'lost object' that he had been longing for, thanks to the encounter with the 'unique' woman who could love and be loved by him (according to Hal Foster, this woman is ultimately revealed to be the phallic mother).[28] If Wentworth clearly distances himself from the surrealists' quasi-mystical belief in the conjunction of love, 'objective chance' and the marvellous, the avowedly 'sexual' nature of his interest in objects could be situated in the area of a similarly pleasurable construction of meaning within the chaos of everyday life. I would suggest that in Wentworth's universe, the *trouvaille* that perhaps comes closest to Breton's purchase of the slipper-spoon is the instance in which an artist friend of his once threw down to him, from her window, the keys to her flat concealed inside a rubber glove: 'as it fell to earth it looked like a greeting or the hand of God smiting me from on high', he recalls.[29] Conceived as a simple device to deal with a broken door buzzer, the 'key-glove' object becomes a new entity, bringing together the ideas of 'hand, warmth, salute, entrance', and creating, according to Wentworth, 'a visual event with a metaphorical charge which is inevitable, dense with meaning'. Wentworth's notion of 'inevitability' seems to be a version of Breton's 'objective chance', stripped of any belief in fate or of a longed-for return to a state of happiness.

The surrealist *trouvaille* is not, however, only related to the fulfilment of desire. As Foster has pointed out, its uncanny characteristics reveal an undertow of irretrievable loss and, ultimately, death. If the lost object signals an impossible return to the womb, it is necessarily condemned to be sought again and again, and never found. Similarly, while Wentworth celebrates the pleasures of 'making do and getting by', his photographs also point to the precariousness and fragility of these endeavours, as human constructions are constantly destroyed. 'I like to be near things that are falling – actually sometimes physically. I like to be near

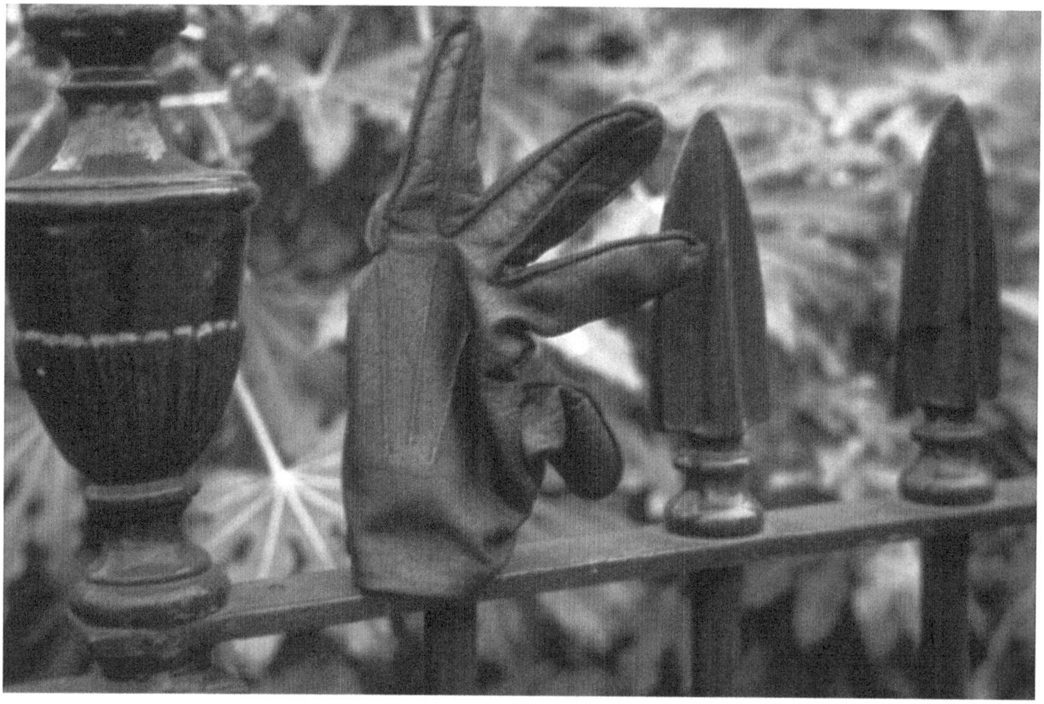

5.4 Richard Wentworth, *London 1994*, unique photographic print, 43.5 × 51 × 6.5 cm, 1999, from the *Making Do, Getting By* series. Courtesy the artist and Lisson Gallery. © Richard Wentworth

things at the end of their social life', explains Wentworth (C, p. 18). Describing a flea market in Berlin, Wentworth finds himself thinking of refugee camps during the war, before returning to the topic of how one can rescue 'that plate lying in the gutter' or let it disappear into the landfill, and then evoking his fascination with cemeteries (C, p. 19). Many photographs show objects caught in a perilous balance – a cup keeping a window open (Figure 5.2), a leather glove impaled on street railings (Figure 5.4), a whole choreography of 'resistance to gravity'.[30] Falling is of course associated with death and destruction. 'One of the primary things about being alive is trying to stand upright, which is why the act of falling over is really quite a catastrophe', explains the artist (C, p. 24). From this basis Wentworth relishes the possibility of balancing objects audaciously and 'getting away with it', while acknowledging that this exhilaration operates at this brief, transient moment that reminds us that 'we're all going to die' (C, p. 25).

With the idea of the 'falling object', Wentworth thus brings together two characteristics of both his photographic and sculptural work: the frequent inclusion of (metaphorically fallen) used, outmoded or discarded objects, and the recurrent gestures of spilling and dropping objects (which have literally fallen). The sculptural activities of propping, balancing, spreading, and rolling materials relating to the *Involuntary Sculptures* and Serra's process art thus become laden with the psychological connotations associated with the precarious birth and death of forms. Moreover, in the photographs, objects are often found on pavements and floors, in corners or at the interstices of windows and doors, squeezed between railings or behind a drain, suspended in spaces of transition between value and junk, between existence and disappearance.

The 'neurotic' behaviours described by Wentworth and Dalí merge with the background noise of the everyday activities with which we engage with the world of objects. Just as Georges Perec spoke of the written traces that we all leave behind in our daily shopping lists, tax returns and scribbles on 'a metro ticket, the margin of a newspaper, a cigarette packet, the back of an envelope',[31] the sculptures unearthed by Wentworth or Dalí and Brassaï are residues of our existence in the world. Like Perec, who considers the empty page less as a *tabula rasa* than as a space of inscription, Wentworth resolutely locates the sculptor's activity in a world already teeming with man-made objects and interventions, as compulsive as fiddling, biting a remote control or kneading pieces of erasers. 'The constant, uninterrupted production of signs' associated by Krauss with surrealist photography is the very texture of the everyday, and Wentworth the sculptor/photographer, rather than working in the isolation of the studio, eagerly joins in the general conversation. As Maurice Blanchot put it, the everyday is 'the soft human murmur in us, around us' which disappears as soon as we try to listen to it, but can be heard when we also start to chatter.[32]

Ways of Doing

'I feel very strongly they don't belong to me', Wentworth explained about his photographs, 'it's a linguistic space, if you like' (C, p. 16). This definition of the everyday as a linguistic space was most systematically pursued by Michel de Certeau in his *Practice of Everyday Life*. Just as Certeau argues that our 'ways of doing' are comparable to our 'ways of speaking',[33] Wentworth explains that an arrangement of objects in order to hold a parking place is 'like somebody who just puts together a really decent sentence and you think: "well, I actually liked hearing that"' (C, p. 11). The linguistic theories that Certeau deploys focus on the performative nature of language. Language is shared by all but used differently by each; what these theories emphasise is the ways in which each speaker operates within this field, appropriating it for his or her own purposes, situating it in a specific context (which includes a place, a moment and an audience). Similarly, Certeau focuses on the new '*ways of using* the products imposed by a dominant economic power'.[34]

'Making Do' ('*Faire avec*') is, in fact, the title of chapter 3 of *The Practice of Everyday Life*. In this chapter, Certeau develops his most important contribution to studies of the everyday – a definition of the fundamental characteristics of everyday life as a 'practice'. Wentworth's series of photographs share more than a title with Certeau's work: the sculptor's succinct definition of what 'making do' means – '[p]redicaments will always provoke idiosyncratic responses and solutions' (MD, p. 22) – constitutes the very starting point for Certeau's conception of everyday life. For Certeau, everyday life is indeed a 'predicament' to which people react, as they 'tinker with and within the dominant cultural economy to obtain innumerable and infinitesimal metamorphoses of its law into their interests and their own rules'.[35] The French term used by Certeau is *bricoler*, which is related to *bricolage*, the activity of repairing or constructing objects by using whatever parts are at hand, in the way of handymen or do-it-yourself enthusiasts. *Bricolage* is of course what Wentworth's 'fiddlers' do, as they use the odds and ends around them to respond to a specific situation. Wentworth's idea of resourcefulness is the equivalent of what Certeau calls 'ruses' – the tricks employed by users of a given order to make it their own. *Bricolage* is a site of pleasure: the 'erotic' thrill of fiddling mentioned by Wentworth echoes the *plaisir* and *jouir* that Certeau associates with everyday practices.

The central distinction introduced by Certeau to describe the relations between producers and *bricoleurs*/users, between language and individual acts of speaking, is his well-known opposition between 'strategies' and 'tactics'.[36] Strategies operate in a space that has been circumscribed as an isolated whole to be defended against exterior threats, whereas tactics exist within a space which is not their own, and need to fight this more powerful entity from within a space over which they have no control. The only means, then, for tactics to counter this imposed order lie in taking advantage of specific moments in which 'breaches' open within the architecture of surveillance and strategies. Tactics thrive in a temporal, rather than a spatial, sphere – they require agents to be nimble, alert, quick to seize opportunities as and when they arise.

The temporal dimension of these practices lies at the heart of Wentworth's photographs, which capture ephemeral, transient situations, in a given context. As a photographer, he himself has to take notice of what is presented to him and turn it to his advantage. Strikingly, the 'out-of-work domestic broom' leaning in a doorway mentioned by Wentworth was a favoured motif for the nineteenth-century British photography pioneer William Henry Fox Talbot, who used it as an illustration of the photographer's skill at spotting an interesting visual arrangement in his everyday surroundings. As Robin Kelsey has suggested, the propped broom evokes the gnomon of a sundial, visualising the precise moment in time at which the photographer encountered his composition.[37] While Kelsey suspects that Talbot in fact deliberately arranged these brooms in their doorways, Wentworth's photographs appear to be more genuinely spontaneous, and the sculptor never directly uses the arrangements and 'events' that he witnesses in the street, either by exhibiting them as his own artworks, or making works based on them. As Certeau explained, the temporal order of tactics never allows any gain to be kept, as there is nowhere to 'stock' any new 'benefits'. The snapshot captures the practices at the very moment when they operate a tactical move, as they are 'hijacking' found and readymade objects to fulfil an urgent function, just as a guerrilla fighter organises punctual raids, kidnappings and targeted attacks ('to hijack' is one of the more dramatic translations of *détourner*, the French term used by Certeau).

The relation between tactics and guerrilla fighting suggests a political dimension of resistance in everyday practices. If Certeau sees political ramifications to practices of everyday life – in particular with the turn to 'punctual actions', 'local operations' and 'ecological groups'[38] – his notion of 'tactical' behaviours remains a far cry from any traditional political activism. Indeed, most 'tactical' activities described by Certeau are hardly subversive – shopping, cooking, walking are things that most of us have, after all, little choice in doing. It is only within constraints that ruses can emerge. This process is captured by a paradoxical term used by

Certeau as he speaks of a 'common and silent, almost sheeplike subversion' (*une subversion commune et silencieuse, quasi moutonnière*).[39] Wentworth, for his part, has couched his interest in the 'rub' between what he calls 'formalism' and the 'ripostes to formalism' as a general form of 'resistance'.[40]

Notions of agency and intention appear central to our understanding of Certeau's politics and Wentworth's photographs. Certeau goes as far as comparing everyday tactics with the 'simulations' and 'tricks' of fish and plants – the 'art' of 'making do' goes back beyond 'the institution itself of consciousness', it has survived through 'a memory without language, from the bottom of the oceans to the streets of our megalopolises'.[41] In his conversation with Wentworth, brain scientist Mark Lythgoe introduced a similar kind of reasoning as he suggested that the artist's photographs relate to a survival instinct 'laid down in our genes'.[42] According to Lythgoe, when you make a good decision based on resourcefulness, your brains generate 'a few chemicals, giving you a buzz, a little rush', as a 'reward for getting it right'. This encourages us 'to remember a good move or ingenious act, just in case we might need it in the future to help our survival strategy'. What Wentworth finds in the everyday practices that he photographs, Lythgoe suggested, is this very 'buzz' or 'rush'. Wentworth agreed with him, and suggested that this sounds 'as near a metaphor for an orgasm' as he has ever heard. This would seem to add an evolutionary spin to the pleasures and perils of *bricolage* recast as a metaphor for survival itself.

The issue of agency certainly lay at the heart of surrealism and its definitions of automatism in particular. Automatism is defined by Breton in 'The Automatic Message' as a passive stance, an attempt to 'grasp involuntary verbal representation and fix it on the page without imposing on it any kind of qualitative judgement'.[43] In the same text, Breton cites a 1910 article from *The Occult Review* which argues that any act, whether it is to write or 'to toss one's hair back', can become 'habitual, and therefore outside of the thinker's control'.[44] This seems to outline a grey area of automatism in which the unconscious seems to be closely linked to habits, reflexes, and even natural instincts such as 'to satisfy an appetite'.

As Laurent Jenny has pointed out, Breton's emphasis on a 'passive automatism' posed a challenge for surrealism in as much as it could not easily be reconciled with a revolutionary programme. In order to be politically and socially viable, automatism had to become 'active', it had to emerge 'from solipsism, recognising itself as a symbolic manipulation, engaging collective values'.[45] If Dalí was the main protagonist of the shift towards 'active automatism' through the development of his 'paranoiac-critical method', Jenny suggests that Roger Caillois also played a role in developing the 'collective values' involved in symbols emerging from automatism. With Caillois, for example, the dread felt by the surrealists towards the praying mantis who consumes her mate during and after copulation was cast as a universal fear rather than an individual phobia. According to Caillois, the example of the praying mantis demonstrates that men's 'fear of being devoured by a woman' is in fact a 'vestigial residue, in one species, of behavioural patterns observed in many others', which fully justifies any castration anxiety.[46]

If this 'vestigial residue' seems to brings us back to the world of instincts and survival, the other component of Caillois's discussion of the mantis in the pages of *Minotaure* complicates the picture substantially. For the other feature of the mantis according to Caillois is its mimetic ability to merge with its background. Where this is usually described as the animal's 'ruse' to escape from its predators, however, Caillois proposes that in fact 'alongside the instinct of self-preservation that somehow attracts beings towards life, there proves to be a very widespread *instinct d'abandon* attracting them toward a kind of diminished existence'.[47] This, as Steven Harris has explained, allowed the mantis to become an 'emblem of automatism' itself: not only can the mantis be both active (it consumes its partner) and passive (it is consumed by space), but its mimetic tendency allows it to stand for an automatism 'pushed to its most radical point',[48] the point at which the identification with what is outside the subject results in the complete loss of self, rather than the construction of an identity.

In their celebration of the *bricoleur*'s survival strategies, Certeau's theory of everyday life and Wentworth's photographs lack the anxiety that accompanied the blows that surrealism first dealt to the unified, centralised subject. The reason for this, in my opinion, is that Certeau and Wentworth consider the micro-narratives of agency to be inseparable from the meta-narratives of activities and processes that take place *beyond* individual death and life drives. They focus on what Certeau describes as 'modes of operation or schemata of action', rather than 'the subjects who are their authors or vehicles'.[49] This is why Wentworth can explain that 'exactly the same forces are at work in the West as those in the Third World, which generate shelters built of Coke cans, papered with old copies of *Life* magazine' (MD, p. 22); and why Certeau's 'practices of everyday life' range from the ruses developed by Latin American indigenous populations forced to live under their European colonisers' rule, to the ways in which North African immigrants inhabit French council housing. The agents of these processes, according to them, are constantly being redefined by specific circumstances. Like Perec's written traces, Certeau's tactics do not occur in a void: ruses always draw on a 'practical', 'mobile' memory 'nourished by a multitude of events'.[50] It is at the moment in which 'the lightning flash of this memory illuminates the *occasion*' that the personal and the collective are brought together, and that individual agency temporarily emerges from the murky field of reflexes, habits, traditions and survival instincts through which it is constituted.[51] The 'occasion' is the site of Certeau's tactical ruses, and of Wentworth's 'ripostes to formalism', and 'idiosyncratic responses and solutions'. It is in the occasion that the previously mentioned 'key-glove' falling from above takes on its 'inevitable' meaning in a form of impersonal objective chance; that the praying mantis, like the fish and plants mentioned by Certeau, stages its disappearing act, and a 'sheeplike subversion' is somehow possible.

Unlike the surrealists, or analysts of everyday life such as Walter Benjamin or Henri Lefebvre, Certeau does not believe that there are any privileged spaces that would give us a glimpse of a potential future. Indeed, the everyday always harbours what Blanchot called 'the corrosive force of human anonymity', which constantly threatens individual agency with dissolution in a general indeterminacy and irresponsibility – a collective equivalent, perhaps, of the praying mantis's *instinct d'abandon*. If this premise makes it impossible for Wentworth and Certeau to invest any gesture of resistance with the promise of revolution and transformation, it also forces them to develop an innovative methodology to study these changing, elusive practices that exist at the fleeting junction between agents and specific circumstances.

Ben Highmore has argued that 'the relations between tactical and strategic forms of everyday life' in Certeau's writings 'are being imagined as *something like* the relationship between the unconscious and the conscious "modes" in Freudian psychoanalysis'.[52] This methodological approach firstly allows Certeau to cast the tactics of everyday life as permeating all spheres of the strategic order, in the same way as the unconscious escapes through our conscious barriers with everyday slips of the tongue and other psychopathologies of everyday life. The two spheres – of conscious and unconscious, of tactics and strategies – are seen to inhabit a common space, that of the everyday. Secondly, Certeau can claim that tactics are constantly censured and repressed by strategies, in the same way as the conscious seeks to contain unconscious drives. What emerges, then, is the need to develop a set of tools – like those of psychoanalysis – to draw out the suppressed practices of what could be called a 'collective', 'cultural' unconscious. For if tactics are like the unconscious, the usual strategic taxonomies used to study everyday life replicate the mechanisms of censorship and defence and only serve to contain them further.

'The challenge then of de Certeau's work is to provide an archival practice that allows such "tactical" material to proliferate, a practice that can "listen" to the everyday and hear there the tales of repressed activity.'[53] This analysis by Highmore could also apply to Wentworth's photographs. Both Wentworth and Certeau can be seen as creating a 'science of singularity': 'a science of the relationship that links everyday pursuits to particular circumstances'.[54] This is of course what psychoanalysis also tries to do, as each case study presents an intrinsically personal experience to be analysed with a range of tools. Where Certeau privileged interviews and oral history as the sites where a repressed 'cultural unconscious' could surface, Wentworth turns to an amateur type of photography which can let these gestures 'speak for themselves', without the mediation of a 'strategic' discourse of interpretation and without, I would add, transfiguration. Within these potentially endless archival collections, both projects focus as much on lacunae and absences as on the facts themselves. Just as Wentworth's photographs are haunted by absent bodies, Certeau explained that both tools and proverbs provide '*imprints of acts* or of enunciation processes'.[55] Wentworth himself is aware of the limitations of the archival process, as he exclaims: 'I am still amazed at how much information can drop off in a photograph ... as if the world is resisting' (MD, p. 23). Conversely, with the optical unconscious, the photograph also captures objects that were not originally noticed by the photographer. As William Talbot noticed early on, close examination of a photograph can disclose 'a multitude of minute details, which were previously unobserved and unsuspected'.[56]

The everyday, as Michael Sheringham's excellent study has demonstrated, has repeatedly been cast as the 'unobserved' and overlooked, which is simultaneously 'resistant to codification' and 'dependent on forms of attention that grasp it as a totality that only exists modally, at the level of practice or usage'.[57] Philosophers and artists have developed tools to address the opaque stubbornness of everyday life, its fundamental indeterminacy. Dalí and Brassaï's *Involuntary Sculptures* certainly present a new 'mode of attention' by combining the technique of the close-up – an established means of bringing to light previously 'invisible' objects – with Dalí's tongue-in-cheek explanatory captions. Rather than testifying to biographical obsessions, the performative processes embodied by each 'sculpture' evoke collective everyday behaviours, but the deliberate defamiliarisation that accompanies the close-up stamps these anonymous acts with the authors' intentions, thus isolating them from the temporality and intersubjectivity typical of the everyday. The obdurate materiality of reality is hinted at in the sculptural properties of the objects as traces or residues, and in Dalí's supposedly explanatory captions, which in their parody of scientific, sociological and art historical vocabularies suggest an awareness of the self-defeating project of reading the everyday through existing forms of knowledge.

Wentworth offers another type of attention, as he explains:

> We become accustomed to natural partners – the door and its doormat. When their positions are disrupted something fundamental happens. The displaced doormat has a new identity, a shift of an inch or two changes it from passive to active. Such adjustments invigorate tired and overlooked relationships, as the contradiction, humour and absurdity of the new alliance presents itself (MD, p. 23).

While the 'contradiction, humour and absurdity' that Wentworth highlights can also be found in the *Involuntary Sculptures*, amateur photography allowed him to explore a new form of mediation of the everyday, highlighting its temporal and intersubjective dimension. Neither bent on profit nor on artistic pride, the amateur photographer, as Stallabrass explains, finds pleasure precisely in the erasure of his or her personal investment in the photographed object – like automatism, it is an actively passive stance, a voluntary renunciation of control. Photography was able to frame the automatism of the world in general – as its 'optical unconscious' reveals even the smallest gestures that are inscribed in our bodies, a 'cultural unconscious' or 'practical memory' at the crossroads of intent and reflex. But amateur photography is what allows the involuntary to seep through the interstices of the voluntary gaze of productivity, surveillance and autonomous art. Unsurprisingly, Wentworth has defined his very activity of photographing as a kind of automatism: his photographs, he says, are 'meaningless thoughts, a kind of intake'; he likens their relation to his sculptural work 'to the relationship between … appetite and food'.[58]

If there is a language of objects and a formal vocabulary of everyday gestures and actions, it can only be grasped 'at the level of practice or usage', as Sheringham put it, in its *modes* of operation. This is where new definitions of sculpture as performance echo Certeau's definition of the everyday, as Serra's quote reminds us: 'It's how we do what we do that confers meaning on what we've done.' As Wentworth tries to capture his involuntary sculptures as they are being produced, in the form of singular yet transient arrangements, barely legible among the chattering profusion of signs and objects which surround them, and teetering on the verge of disappearance, he immerses his photographs in the very rhythms and patterns of everyday experience, and lets them speak of its endless variations and creative ambiguity.

Notes

1 See Richard Wentworth, 'Making Do and Getting By', *Artscribe*, 14 (September 1978), pp. 21–3 (hereafter cited in the text as MD); Michael Archer and Jenni Lomax (dirs), *Making Do and Getting By*, videotape (London, 1985). See also *Richard Wentworth/ Eugène Atget: Faux Amis* (London, 2001).

2 Transcript of Richard Wentworth's talk at the Manchester Museum, April 2005, published in *Papers of Surrealism* 4 (Winter 2005), www.surrealismcentre.ac.uk/ papersofsurrealism, pp. 1–26 (Hereafter referred to as C).

3 The exhibition was *Thinking Aloud*, a national touring exhibition (London, 1998). For a discussion of the debates surrounding the inclusion of the *Involuntary Sculptures* in *Minotaure*, see Chapter 1 in this volume.

4 I will not be developing these comparisons in this text, although they will be included in a book-length study provisionally entitled *Almost Nothing: Precariousness in Art since the 1960s*. I would include in this grouping practices by Gabriel Orozco, Francis Alÿs, Thomas Hirschhorn, and the duo Peter Fischli and David Weiss. Orozco's work is discussed by Margaret Iversen in Chapter 9.

5 Richard Wentworth, 'Losing Battles: A Conversation between Richard Wentworth and Stuart Morgan, May 1984', in *Richard Wentworth* (London, 1984), p. 13.

6 Richard Serra, 'Interview with Liza Béar', *Avalanche* (Summer 1973), quoted by Benjamin H.D. Buchloh, 'Process sculpture and Film in the Work of Richard Serra (1978)', in Hal Foster with Gordon Hughes (eds), *Richard Serra* (Cambridge, MA, and London, 2000), p. 16.

7 Rosalind Krauss, 'The Photographic Conditions of Surrealism', *October*, 19 (Winter 1981), p. 31.

8 Walter Benjamin, 'A Small History of Photography' [1931], in *One-Way Street*, trans. E. Jephcott and K. Shorter (London, 1979), p. 243. Samantha Lackey also refers to Benjamin's 'optical unconscious' in Chapter 3 of this volume.

9 Krauss, 'The Photographic Conditions of Surrealism', p. 31.

10 Ian Walker, *City Gorged with Dreams: Surrealism and Documentary Photography in Interwar Paris* (Manchester and New York, 2002).

11 Julian Stallabrass, *Gargantua: Manufactured Mass Culture* (London and New York, 1996), p. 23.

12 Salvador Dalí, 'De la beauté terrifiante et comestible de l'architecture Modern'style', *Minotaure*, 3–4 (1933), p. 72. Unless otherwise specified, all translations are mine.

13 Ibid., p. 74.

14 Walker, *City Gorged with Dreams*, p. 12.

15 Wentworth, 'Making Do and Getting By'.

16 Jeff Wall, '"Marks of Indifference": Aspects of Photography in, or as, Conceptual Art' [1995], in Douglas Fogle (ed.), *The Last Picture Show: Artists using Photography, 1960–82* (Minneapolis, 2003), pp. 32–44.

17 Ibid., p. 35.

18 Ibid., p. 37.

19 Ibid., p. 43.

20 Walter Benjamin, 'The Author as Producer' [1934], trans. P. Demez, in Brian Wallis (ed.), *Art after Modernism: Rethinking Representation* (New York, 1984), p. 304.

21 Wentworth, text message to the author, 22 April 2005.

22 Wentworth, 'Losing Battles', p. 14.

23 Krauss, 'The Photographic Conditions of Surrealism', p. 31.

24 Dalí, 'De la beauté terrifiante', p. 74.

25 Sigmund Freud, *The Psychopathology of Everyday Life* [1901], trans. J. Strachey, vol. 6 (London, 1960), p. 211.

26 André Breton, *L'Amour fou* (Paris, 1937), pp. 47–57. For more about the 'slipper-spoon', see Chapter 2 in this volume; on the importance of the found object for Breton, see Chapters 8 and 9.

27 Breton, *L'Amour fou*, p. 54.

28 Hal Foster, *Compulsive Beauty* (London and Cambridge, MA, 1993), pp. 42–5.

29 Wentworth, 'Losing Battles', p. 15.

30 'There's a hell of a lot of resistance to gravity [in *Making Do and Getting By*], and I think my work has a lot to do with gravity.' Richard Wentworth, quoted by Kevin Henry, 'Parallel Universes: Making Do and Getting By + Thoughtless Acts' (2007), www.core77.com/reactor/03.07_parallel.asp (accessed: 10 July 2009).

31 Georges Perec, *Espèces d'espaces* [1974] (Paris, 2000), p. 24.

32 Maurice Blanchot, *L'Entretien infini* (Paris, 1969), p. 361. Translation by Michael Sheringham in *Everyday Life: Theories and Practices from Surrealism to the Present* (Oxford, 2006), p. 20.

33 Michel de Certeau, *L'Invention du quotidien, vol. 1: Arts de faire* [1980], new edition edited by Luce Giard (Paris, 1990), p. 64.

34 Ibid., p. xxxvii.

35 Ibid., p. xxxviii.

36 Ibid., pp. xlvi–xlviii and pp. 59–63.

37 See Robin Kelsey, 'Photography, Chance, and *The Pencil of Nature*', in Kelsey and Blake Stimson (eds), *The Meaning of Photography* (Williamstown, MA, and New Haven, 2008), pp. 15–33.

38 Certeau, *L'Invention du quotidien*, p. liii.

39 Ibid., p. 293.

40 Stuart Horodner, 'The Language of Stuff: An Interview with Richard Wentworth', *Sculpture*, 20(3) (April 2001), p. 19.

41 Certeau, *L'Invention du quotidien*, p. 65.

42 Richard Wentworth and Mark Lythgoe, 'The Prehistoric Smile', in *Richard Wentworth*, (London, 2004), p. 47. All subsequent quotations in the paragraph are from this passage.

43 André Breton, 'Le Message automatique', *Minotaure*, 3–4 (1933), in *What is Surrealism? Selected Writings*, ed. and trans. F. Rosemont in (New York, 1978), p. 107.

44 Ibid., p. 103.

45 Laurent Jenny, 'From Breton to Dali: the Adventures of Automatism', trans. T. Trezise, *October*, 51 (Winter 1989), p. 109.

46 Roger Caillois, 'La Mante religieuse', *Minotaure*, 5 (1934), trans. C. Frank and C. Naish in *The Edge of Surrealism: A Roger Caillois Reader*, ed. Claudine Frank (Durham, NC, and London, 2003), p. 81.

47 Caillois, 'Mimétisme et psychasthénie légendaire', *Minotaure*, 7 (1935), in *The Edge of Surrealism*, p. 102.

48 Steven Harris, 'Beware of Domestic Objects: Vocation and Equivocation in 1936', *Art History*, 24(5) (November 2001), p. 750.

49 Certeau, *L'Invention du quotidien*, p. xxxvi.

50 Ibid., p. 125.

51 Ibid., p. 125.

52 Ben Highmore, *Everyday Life and Cultural Theory: An Introduction* (London and New York, 2002), p. 164.

53 Ibid., p. 165.

54 'Preface to the English Translation', in Michel de Certeau, *The Practice of Everyday Life*, trans. S.F. Rendall (Berkeley, Los Angeles and London, 1984), p. ix.

55 Certeau, *L'Invention du quotidien*, p. 39.

56 William Henry Fox Talbot, *The Pencil of Nature* (1844), quoted by Kelsey, 'Photography, Chance and *The Pencil of Nature*', p. 21.

57 Sheringham, *Everyday Life*, p. 363.

58 'The Caledonian Road: a Talk by Richard Wentworth' in *Richard Wentworth*, (Freiburg, 1997), p. 36.

6

In Formation: On Terry Fox's *Children's Tapes*

Carrie Lambert-Beatty

1.

In the 1967 book *How Children Think*, American educator John Holt tells a story that illustrates the model of education he and other writers popularised during the educational reform movement of the later 1960s and 1970s.[1] At the time the story takes place, Holt was developing new materials for mathematics classes, and had gotten in the habit of sitting at the back of classrooms to work out his ideas with cardboard models. This day, he was making cubes. He did nothing special to get the attention of the six-year-olds in the class, but one by one they began to come by to ask what he was doing. 'Oh, just making something', he'd say. Curiosity piqued, the children soon asked to make boxes of their own. 'Off they went', Holt writes:

> By watching me, or each other, or by thinking, or by trial and error, they all figured out that to make a rectangular box with an open top you had to cut out a piece in the shape of a heavy cross. At first these shapes were very crude, the sides not carefully measured, if at all, and the corners not square. But children have a great deal of what might be called a sense of workmanship. When they are not bribed or bullied they want to do whatever they are doing better than they did it before. So they began to make their boxes more carefully, trying to figure out how to cut them so that the sides would join evenly along the edges, and so that the top of the box would be smooth. Nobody asked me for advice. Now and then someone would watch me doing it for a while, and that was all. Then they went back to work.[2]

Holt's book is now a classic, having helped to set off a wave of alternative pedagogical thinking and practice. His story of the six-year-olds and their boxes demonstrates some of the movement's major precepts: that children are generally eager to learn; that they learn best by themselves, and will do so as long as they are interested; and that children have far more patience and ability than adults have come to expect of them. It also posited that this potential was beaten out of them by the practices of administered education: testing, standardised curricula, and the behaviourist model signalled in Holt's phrase 'bribed and bullied'. As he reports, even his box-makers did not get to continue exploring the relations between two and three-dimensional shapes:

> The first-grade teacher, naturally, felt she had to get through her curriculum, and get those children ready for second grade. So they were not able to spend enough time making boxes to explore and develop some of the mathematical possibilities that lie in such work – making boxes of exact dimensions, making boxes to hold certain quantities of wooden cubes, making boxes of shapes other than rectangular, and so on.[3]

This episode has obvious relevance, over four decades later, for those of us concerned about public education in post-Bush America (where education funding was tied to standardised test scores under the law called 'No Child Left Behind'). But to many readers of this volume, the boxes constructed by Holt and his pupils will resonate with art-historical rather than pedagogical discourse. If photographed bread and pocket litter could become, under Brassaï's surrealist lens, 'involuntary sculptures' in 1933 (Figure I.1), what Holt describes might be a kind of 'involuntary minimalism' for 1967. For six-year-olds and their teachers were not the only ones taking open boxes seriously that year. Smack-dab in the heart of minimalism's ascendance – the art world and its journals were all liberally strewn with plinths, blocks, and cubes – 1967 was the very year Sol LeWitt began the series of investigations into open cubes that led to works such as *Three-Part Variations on Three Different Kinds of Cubes* (1967–71) and the permutations of *Incomplete Open Cubes* of 1974 (Figure 6.1).

Holt had no connection to LeWitt, to my knowledge, nor to the world of contemporary art. And so bringing them together would seem a ludicrous exercise. What, besides a shape, do children's cardboard constructions have to do with minimal or conceptual art? While for the children, the making of an open cube was a hands-on exercise, LeWitt's *Variations on Three Different Kinds of Cubes* and *Incomplete Open Cubes* were a quasi-industrial, outsourced process. Where they produced a rich array of box types, he gave himself strict formal limitations. In fact, the regularity of his phalanx of distinct but homogeneous boxes might make a good emblem for the social and educational standardisation that Holt bemoans when he describes the first-grade teacher trying to get her students through the required curriculum at all costs.

On the other hand, the children in Holt's class were not making personal riffs on the cube, but trying to achieve a regular one. And as the critic Rosalind Krauss would point out in 1977, LeWitt was not illustrating some abstract ideal of cube-ness, still less rationality and cognition; he was churning out, with a babbling repetitiveness she likens to 'the speech of children or of the very old', something that could have been far more efficiently expressed in verbal or mathematical language.[4] LeWitt's specifically irrational sculpture freed the multiplicity of forms condensed in such abstractions. He spilled them into the space and time of physical, phenomenal encounter, where they reveal unseen cubbies, changing angles, and shifting shadows as a viewer moves about around them. LeWitt was being sarcastic about the labels like 'minimalism' and 'primary structures' applied to his art when he wrote, also in 1967, that 'maybe the mini-artist is a very small person, say under five feet tall. If so, much good work will

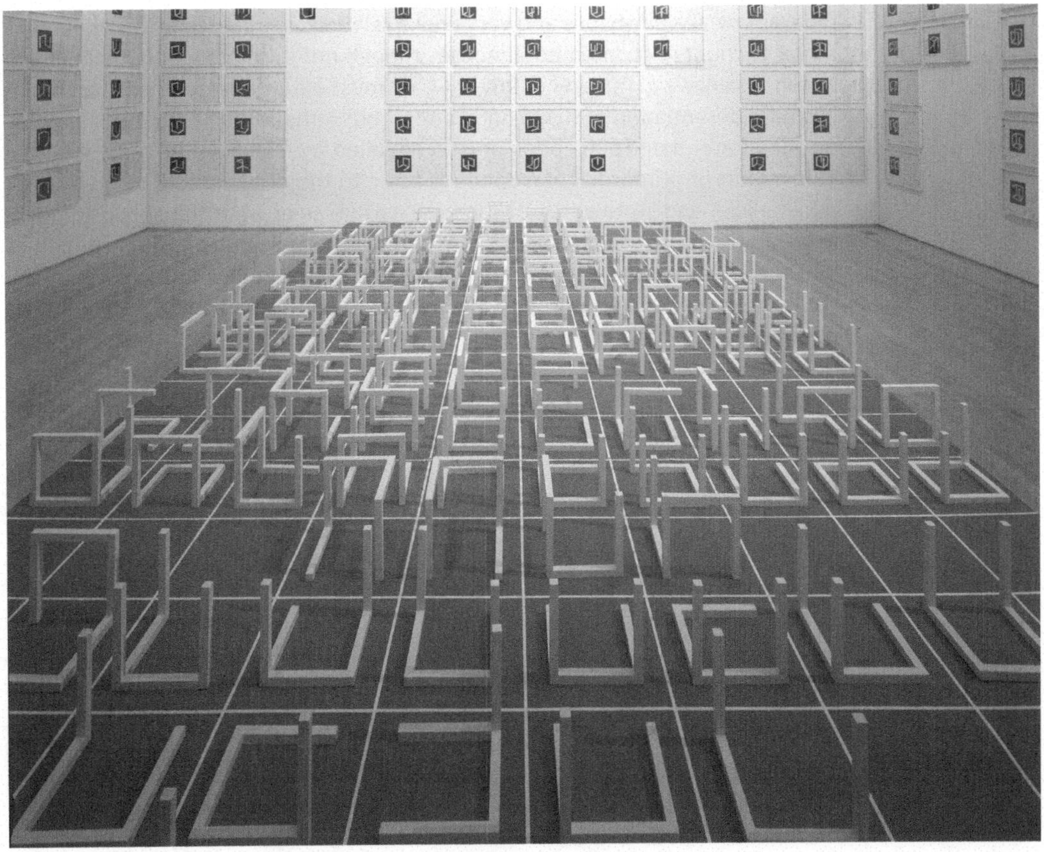

6.1 Sol LeWitt, *Incomplete Open Cubes*, gelatin silver prints, and drawings on paper, painted wood structures, 1974, sculptures: 20.3 × 20.3 × 20.3 cm, framed works: 66 × 35.6 cm, base: 30.5 × 304.8 × 548.6 cm. San Francisco Museum of Modern Art, Accessions Committee Fund: gift of Emily L. Carroll and Thomas Weisel, Jean and James E. Douglas, Jr., Susan and Robert Green, Evelyn Haas, Mimi and Peter Haas, Eve and Harvey Masonek, Elaine McKeon, the Modern Art Council, Phyllis and Stuart G. Moldaw, Christine and Michael Murray, Danielle and Brooks Walker Jr., and Phyllis Wattis. Photo: Ben Blackwell © The LeWitt Estate/Artists Rights Society (ARS), New York

be found in the primary schools (primary school primary structures).'[5] But in a sense, LeWitt's aesthetic insight of 1967 is an inverted form of Holt's educational one. Holt let children loose to discover an abstract principle through observation and experience; LeWitt unleashed perceptual experience so that adults might *un*learn the abstract principles they think they know.

This is to understand LeWitt's work through a version of what is generally called the phenomenological account of minimalism, an argument most strongly associated with Krauss, who articulated it in her criticism of the 1960s and 1970s. Writers in this vein have shown how Maurice Merleau-Ponty's evocations of a pre-rational, non-gestalt perception, of the kind we understand babies to have, explain this art's way of suspending ingrained habits of mind. To our trained eyes, an L-shape is an L-shape no matter which way it is turned. But Robert Morris's version asks us to recognise as perceptual truth what an infant would experience instead: that supposedly identical objects, differently oriented, have entirely different *perceived* shapes and very unlike relations to us as embodied beings in a real encounter. (Contemporaneously, though not in reference to minimal art, Anton Ehrenzweig argued in 1967 that art must be understood not in terms of gestalt differentiation of shape and pattern, but rather of the scattered attention and undifferentiated perception of what he called 'the child's vision of the world'.)[6] This notion of primordial perception is basic to the dominant interpretation of minimalism, and so to some of the best narratives of what happened to art in its wake (Hal Foster's *Return of the Real*, for instance, opens with a vignette in which the author and a conceptual artist friend are 'taken to school by a six-year old', as her skipping around a wood-beam-and-mirror sculpture reveals its phenomenological workings, and captures in a way their learned discourse could not the models of space, spectatorship, time, and art in the decades following the minimalist moment).[7] And so it seems worthwhile to consider a curious case study from that just-post-minimal period, a single series of quasi-sculptures that we might understand as asking this: if the adult subject of minimalism perceives like a primordial child, what happens to the category of sculpture – and to the axes of play and perception, production and consumption, duration and expectation that determined it – when the ideal viewer of the art work is a child, an American child, of a particular historical moment? Like the bank-teller's folded bus ticket immortalised by Brassaï, Holt's open cubes can be understood as art only if displaced into artistic discursive and institutional contexts. But such a link between education and art, pedagogy and post-minimalism – along with all the questions such a tendentious connection raises – was in fact provided in 1974. It shapes a singular project by the Californian artist Terry Fox, whose video work of the mid 1970s asks us to rethink the unfolding legacy of involuntary sculpture – its links between sculpture and image, documentation and chance – under the later-twentieth-century pressures of mass media, particularly television, and from the peculiar angle that is a child's-eye-view.

2.

In 1974, David Ross, then curator of video at the Everson Museum in Syracuse, New York, offered a solo show to the San Francisco-based artist Terry Fox.[8] Thirty years old, Fox was known for his contributions to Bay Area conceptualism and the emerging genre of body art. He didn't even own a video camera. For several months, however, he had been playing with a small set of ordinary household objects: spoon, fork, bowl, candles and matches, water and bits of cloth. On his mind as he worked out their interacting properties was his five-year-old son, and the boy's television habit. The programmes he watched disgusted Fox enough to prompt him to imagine something better. So he asked Ross to send him some blank tapes, borrowed a Sony Portapak, hung a 1,500-watt bulb over his worktable, and in a week and a half in March 1974 produced 34 videos to send to Syracuse for his show.[9] He called the material the *Children's Tapes*.[10]

Each of the *Tapes*, which range from 50 seconds to 17 minutes in length, is a piece of unedited, real-time footage. Adjustments of zoom and focus are the only special effects. Static, the sound of objects gently touching each other

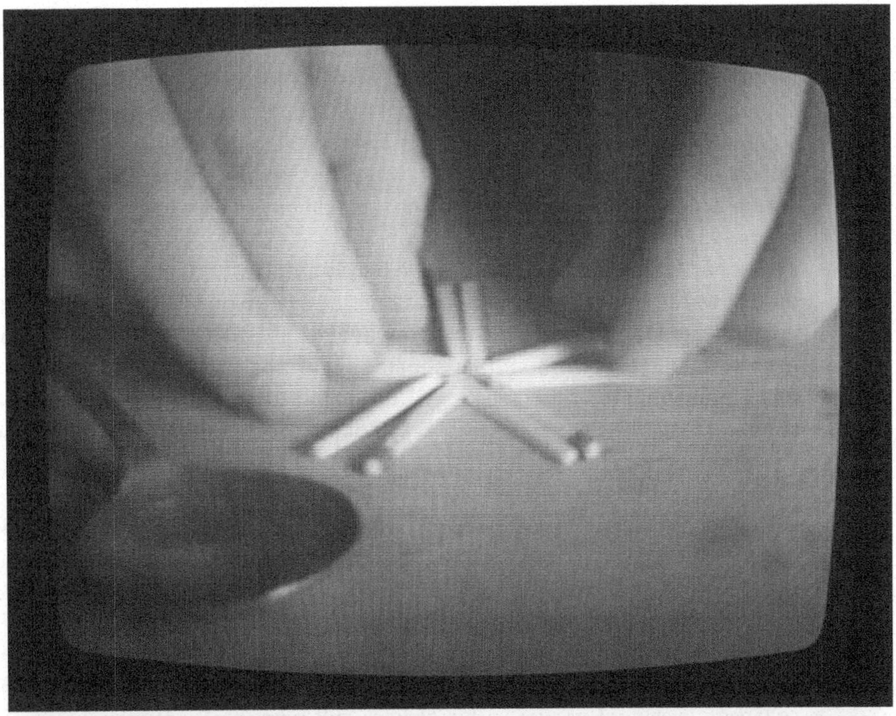

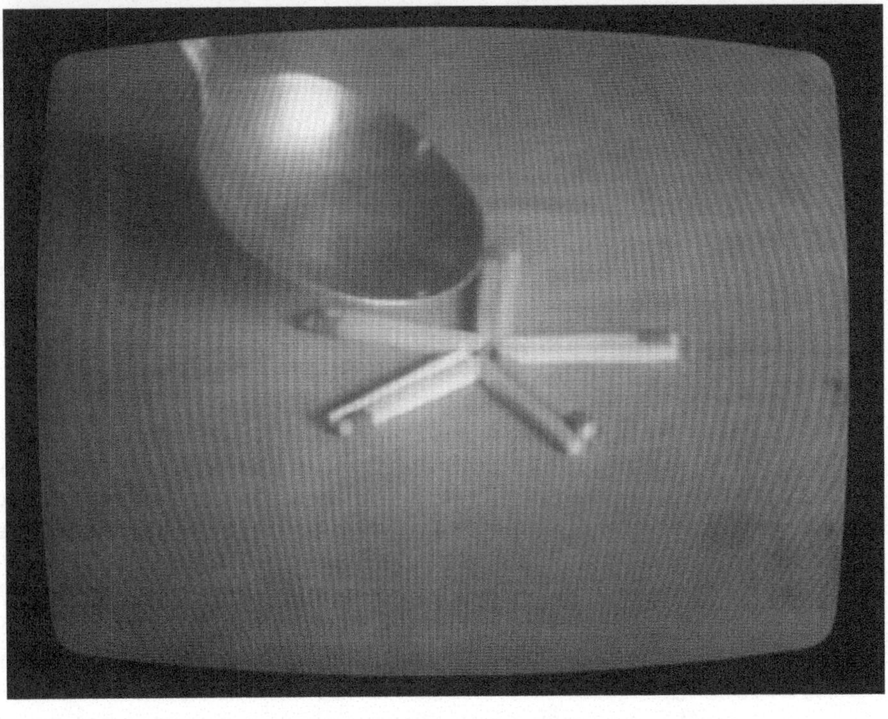

6.2 and 6.3 **Terry Fox, *The Children's Tapes*, video stills, 1974 © Estate of Terry Fox**

or the table, and very occasionally an inaudible background voice or bit of street noise, are the only audio accompaniment. In each tape, the camera frames a tiny plot of tabletop; in each, Fox's hands enter to manipulate some combination of small, ordinary objects. In each – through the murky grey soup in which so much early video is awash – we watch the artist establish a tabletop tableau with his kitchen-drawer props: a carefully arranged sculptural set-up which unfolds, in each case, into a small physical and phenomenological drama.

One tape, for example, opens with a tightly cropped shot of a spoon holding a drop of water, resting on the tabletop alongside a few wooden matchsticks. Hands enter the image and take up each of the five matches in turn, carefully snapping each at its midpoint without fully separating the two halves. Painstakingly, with many adjustments and corrections, the fingers then configure the tiny bent sticks, arranging them splintered break-point to splintered break-point, until they form a neat, five-pointed asterisk (Figure 6.2). The hands, now off screen, then take up the spoon. Carefully, tremblingly, its drop of water is poured onto the matchstick formation (Figure 6.3). Like synchronised swimmers, the broken matches then begin to *move*: gliding in unison, the wooden asterisk swells under the pressures of gravity and surface tension until it is transformed into an open-centred, five-pointed star (Figures 6.4, 6.5).

Each of the tapes is as painfully slow, as halting, and as humble as this. And each is as miraculous. In one, a candle is lit at both ends and watched until it collapses in a pool of wax, a bit of wick still persistently aflame. In another, capillary action draws water through a bit of cloth, slowly transferring the liquid from a bowl to a spoon lying beside it. In one of the most memorable, a piece of ice is placed atop a strip of cloth resting in the bowl of a spoon, itself carefully balanced, see-saw style, on a fork bent to serve as its fulcrum. Over three minutes the viewer of the tape literally watches ice melt. Approaching a cliché for dull spectatorial experience – it is not so different from watching paint dry – the tableau gradually becomes riveting, however, as one realises that the melting ice is wetting the strip of cloth, and that as the water spreads toward the ends of the strip it is shifting the centre of gravity of the whole apparatus. The spoon begins to jerk and tilt wildly on its forked support, and one watches in rapt anticipation, guessing what is going to happen but waiting to have the intuition confirmed – as it is when the spoon finally tilts a millimetre too far and the whole arrangement collapses into an abject heap.

A work like this fits nicely into many of the themes art historians like to use when teaching art of the 1960s and 1970s. Its intentionally modest, even humble aesthetic makes it a late entry in what amounts to an international cult of the quotidian in this period, from the Judson Dance Theater to Arte Povera. No tool or technique related to fine art enters the *Children's Tapes*, aside from a pen, which Fox inverts to use as a pivot point for another gravity-defying cutlery construction. The silverware is cheap enough to bend, the piece of cloth is rough-edged and nondescript. The candles are the type sometimes labelled 'utility'. Yet with these ordinary domestic wares, Fox produced perceptual dramas every bit as intense as the massive ones being staged in galleries around this time.

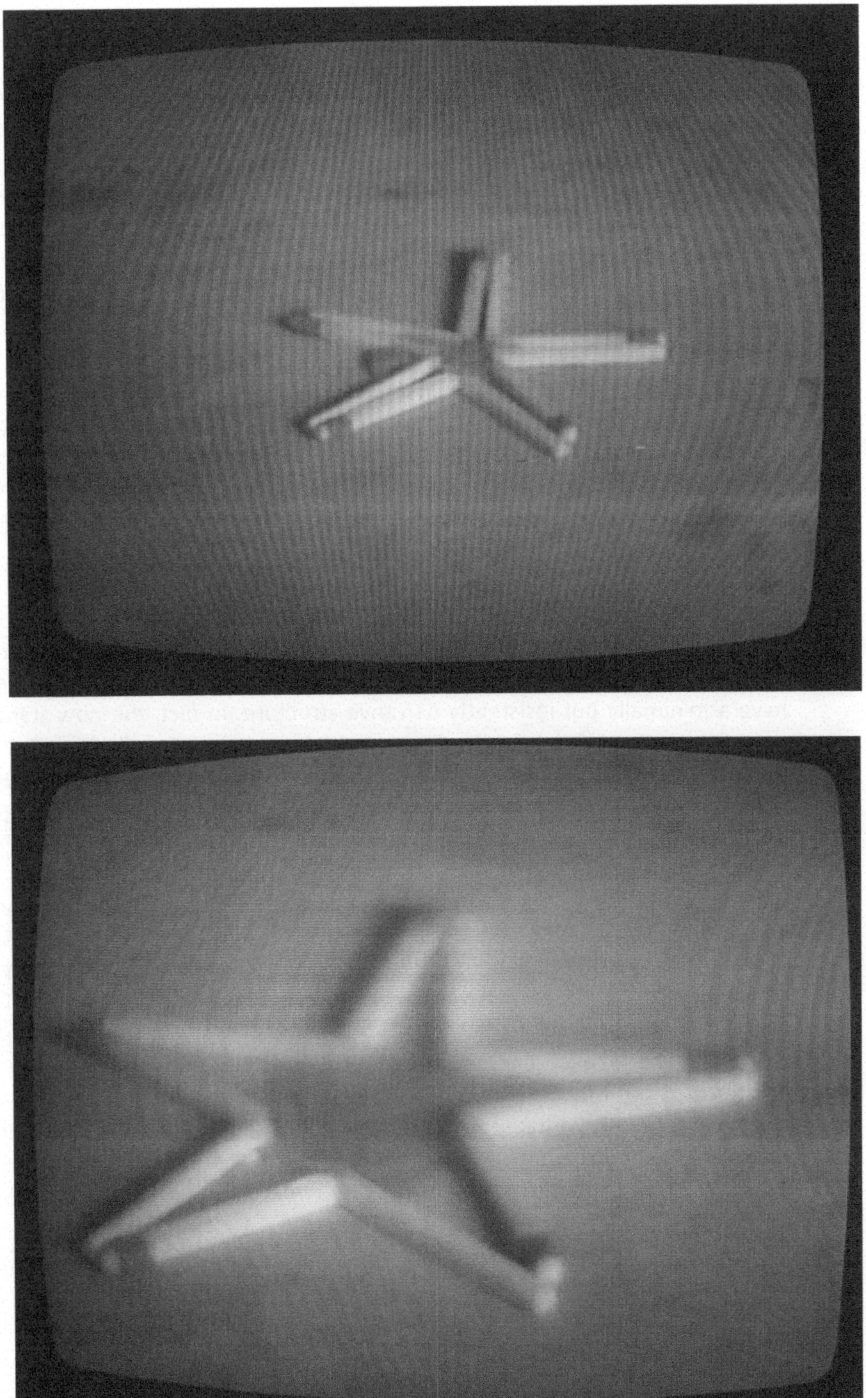

6.4 and 6.5 Terry Fox, ***The Children's Tapes***, **video stills, 1974 © Estate of Terry Fox**

3.

Though they don't move, Richard Serra's *Prop* sculptures of the late 1960s are perpetually falling, the parts suspended only because they are toppling against one another in a calibrated way (Figure 5.3). To be physically in the space of these objects is to feel a certain tingle of bodily awareness, to weigh the size and mass of the potentially unstable behemoths against one's own flesh and bone, and it is understandable that they have been considered threatening as well as vitalising (in order to be shown recently they have had to be roped off or invisibly secured to the wall). To this aesthetic, the scenarios in the *Children's Tapes* might be understood as a gentle, West Coast rejoinder. For, without requiring special reinforcement of the gallery floor, without imperilling anyone's life or limb, without spending more than the cost of a blank video tape, and certainly without risking accusation of hubris or machismo, Fox created one-ounce props that are, like Serra's larger ones, time-based suspensions. Like his, they are constructions that re-imagine sculpture as a contingent and situational thing, less a built object than a balance of forces. And they, too, produce bated-breath phenomenal drama.

Of course, it would be specious to argue that the drama in each is the same. For one thing, while both works function in duration, only Fox's ever comes to a close. The whole point of the Serra works is to endlessly defer the denouement that Fox delivers. With beginnings, middles, and ends, Fox's videos have a minimally but insistently narrative structure. In fact, the now-standard compilation of the *Children's Tapes* ends with an anticipation-satisfying flourish: a trap made of a pot lid, edge propped on a vertical matchstick, is with a tug on a piece of string brought slamming down, trapping a hapless fly and ending *The Children's Tapes* with a literal sense of closure.[11]

By comparison with Serra's suspensions, then, Fox's mini-narratives can seem quite conservative, in the sense that they proffer in their rudimentary way the satisfactions of conventional narrative form which Serra's perpetual suspensions – and so many other artworks of the period – rigorously avoid. Alternatively, however, Fox's works can also be experienced as surprisingly generous for a rigorous durational artwork of the 1970s; or as an unnoted link to then-emerging developments in experimental film, where narrative, foreclosed under the strictures of both minimalism and structuralist film-making, was coming back with a vengeance.[12] Perhaps most provocatively, however, they can be considered an alternative to some of the assumptions underlying not only work like Serra's props but the postmodern criticism and theory developed in their wake.

4.

If Fox's prop pieces offer just the kind of closure Serra's withhold, this is not because Fox couldn't deal with suspense. His very first sculptures, made in 1968 and unfortunately never photographed, were stacks of cobblestones: simple towers of one stone atop another, tall enough to sway but balanced enough to remain standing. Here, again, is a modest version of similar, but industrially scaled

American works of the same moment (such as Serra's aptly named *Skullcracker* series of 1969). Yet in their own way, the delicate cobblestone towers were, if anything, more threatening than Serra's crane-stacked slabs of steel, insofar as their physical suspense was underwritten by the political and generational tension of a particular time and place. For Fox's towers were made in Paris, of cobblestones that he, a long-haired 25-year-old, had driven there from Germany in the trunk of a car, along with a container of gasoline ... in May 1968.[13]

With less political edge, but a similar sensitivity to site, Fox returned to tension as a simultaneously sculptural and psycho-social force in 1987, in an installation at the Capp Street Project in San Francisco consisting of 11 constructions called *Instruments to be Played by the Movement of the Earth*. A metal funnel of dried peas positioned over a steel wok; mallets resting on a drum; a lead ball suspended just in front of a crystal disk: each carefully poised configuration of objects was designed to make a noise, but each would only sound if an earthquake were to shake the gallery. As it happened, there was no tremor that month in famously quake-prone San Francisco, but that was really beside the point. Despite the title, these were instruments played primarily by the mind of the beholder. It is almost impossible not to imagine the sound these objects would make if they vibrated, collided, or fell – just as once one of the *Children's Tapes* configurations is set in place it is impossible not to anticipate what will happen to its delicate equilibrium. In this case, however, the imagined banging and breaking and crashing sounds were site-specific, bringing to the surface San Franciscans' always-present awareness of the possibility of devastating natural disaster.

In its own less frightening register, this is precisely the kind of imaginative work – the work of anticipation – that the *Children's Tapes* provoke in their viewers. David Antin described one of the *Tapes* in 1975: 'It takes you how long to figure out that the ice cube will melt? That the cloth will absorb the water. That the balance will be upset. But which way? You watch as though waiting for an explosion. It comes and you feel relieved. It has the form of drama.'[14] The reason for this drama – the reason why, unlike the cobblestone stacks, or the San Francisco *Instruments*, or Serra's works, the *Children's Tapes* actually reward expectation by performing the anticipated action – has to do with the nature of the viewer they presume. Hal Foster has pointed out that while minimalist art was unlike previous modernism in centring on the physical, literal role and action of the beholder in real space and time, that beholder was always a generalised subject, physically situated, but not located in terms of class, gender, or other social categories. The viewer of the *Children's Tapes* is post-minimalist: a specific as opposed to a neutral, generalised subject. For as the title suggests, the presumed viewer of this work – the subject position any viewer inhabits in watching it – is a child, and one who is historically situated. The viewer of the *Children's Tapes* is a child of the televisual regime.

5.

Another way in which Fox's mini-'prop pieces' are unlike Serra's is that their phenomenological effects are completely dependent on the video medium.

The physicality and immediacy on which Serra's sculptures are premised is produced in the *Children's Tapes* only by the camera's ability to frame and zoom. This near-paradox is simultaneously what makes them a part of an art-historical trajectory out of minimalism *and* what makes them socially relevant. For like much early video, the *Children's Tapes* exploit a particular tension between the minimalist priority on situational experience and a televisual way of knowing – which it turns out may be inseparable from it. For in historical perspective, it seems evident that the emphasis on the immediate and the situated in minimalism and related art is the flip side of a growing period awareness of (and anxiety about) the conditions of life in an era of spectacle. In 1990 Rosalind Krauss reflected on the minimalist art she championed so influentially in the 1960s and 1970s, realising that there was something almost therapeutic – her word is 'compensatory' – about minimalism's phenomenological immediacy.[15] That is, to be situated in real space and time, aware of the seamless co-constitution of subject and object, is to get reassuring relief from the postmodern condition that renders so much of the rest of our existence an exercise in mediation. Perhaps no work demonstrates better than *The Children's Tapes* – a *video* intended to allow children the experience 'of relating to something real'[16] – the central contradiction of this condition: the desire to return to the world of materiality and embodiment and the need to acknowledge the prevalence of mass-mediated modes of attention, learning, and knowing. For the video-dependent dramas of mass, energy, and gravity which Fox constructed and taped suggest that in 1974 a child had to be led to an appreciation of material physicality through the apparatus of spectacle.

The significance of the video medium to these works is also what places Fox's video-sculpture in the legacy of the similarly miniature, intricate, mundane, and serial 'involuntary sculptures'. In the *Children's Tapes* we have something like the images Brassaï might have made, had he been able to film the bus-rider's hand in his pocket, tearing that ticket half-through and rolling its two sections into horn-like tubes. In fact, Fox's arrangements do evoke a certain kind of absent-minded fiddling, the kind of play with matches or cutlery one might grow absorbed in while conversing over the remnants of a meal. But their careful execution is anything but involuntary. Rather, what they share with the surrealist precedent is that to obtain their import they had to be submitted to the special kind of attention that is the focused lens.

Rosalind Krauss argued years ago that the key to the *Minotaure* layout – and to much of surrealism itself as an artistic movement – lay in the photographic framing of the smears of toothpaste or rolled-up bits of paper, which rendered them not only sculptural, but semiotic. The seemingly realist medium of photography, she argues, which normally wants to open onto the world as it is, also clips these little bits of worldly material from reality's continuum, constituting them as traces, as *signs*.[17] Something similar could be said of the videographic framing of Fox's tableaux, for as objects of thought the *Tapes* oscillate wildly between the sign-like and the world-like. On the one hand they offer up a new appreciation of physical properties of matter and energy; heat, gravity, mass. On the other hand they do so only because of the way they are staged for the camera and presented to view.

Moreover, the extended duration of each tiny transformation and the repetition of the cast of characters – spoon, candle, water, flame – make it almost impossible not to read them metaphorically. Here the distance from Serra's work is absolute. For however mundane the objects in the videos, their imagery evokes rituals of church and synagogue, narratives of baptism, death, and redemption. One flame sacrifices itself to light another; another nearly flickers out only to be reborn; and again and again the corporeal and material – often the implements of eating – are momentarily and magically transformed.[18] Or rather, *consubstantiated*: a term taken from Protestant doctrinal debates and brought to bear on the tapes by Fox himself, who noted rather opaquely in 1974 that they 'involve the subject of consubstantiation'.[19] This term names the idea that in the Eucharist the bread and wine do not become Christ's body and blood, as in Catholic belief, nor merely represent them, but that the four coexist in that moment. 'Consubstantiation' names the near-paradoxes of the *Children's Tapes*: the concurrence in their strange, modest form of the obdurately physical and the blatantly symbolic, of the material and the imagistic. This artwork manifests an imagination in which the categories of the physical and the representational are not opposed.

6.

The Children's Tapes were made at night. This is because Fox waited to begin working until his son had gone to bed, so that in the morning he could surprise him with another instalment of the video experiments. When edited versions of the tape were shown at the Everson Museum, he made sure to have Syracuse schoolchildren come to the exhibit on field trips. Fox screened the tapes for the children of friends like conceptual artist Tom Marioni, and that same year, made five separate excursions to kindergartens around San Francisco, during which he borrowed monitors in order to show his tapes to the gathered children.[20] In other words, the work's title is to be taken seriously: this may have been video art at the medium's cutting edge, and post-minimalist artistic intervention on a high order, but it was also art for kids.

When I have shown the *Children's Tapes* to my much older students, some 30 years later, they find it funny that anyone would think a five-year-old would watch these murky, nearly silent images, with their slow, sometimes fumbling, real-time actions. What Fox reports encountering in the mid 1970s, however, is that greatest of challenges to the idea that children have shorter attention spans than adults: *'Play it again!'*[21] This insistence on children's patience and capacity for durational attention is one axis of the critique of mainstream television implicit in the *Children's Tapes* – one confirmed by recent research which finds a significant correlation between hours of television watched by very young children and attention-deficit problems later, as if it actually robs children of their attentive capacities.[22] Other research confirms Fox's anecdotal experience: a study from 2002 shows that given a choice, young children actually prefer slower-paced shows with longer segments and less action.[23] This finding was such a blow to conventional wisdom on children's television that it has actually caused *Sesame*

Street, the most celebrated of educational programmes – and one of the lasting legacies of late-1960s social optimism – to adjust its format. However, *Sesame Street* had received similar critique long before the 2002 study. A 1975 book called *Sesame Street Revisited* focused a series of criticisms that had begun to emerge, questioning the programme's lauded educational value and faulting it for accepting the idea that images had to be bright, high-volume, and fast-paced to keep children's attention.[24] Among the most common complaints was that though it was shown on public television without advertising, the format of *Sesame Street* – stories broken up by short, unrelated scenes – was structurally identical to commercial television. Famously, Mary Winn in *The Plug-In Drug* suggested that what *Sesame Street* really educated children in was how to watch commercial television. However laudable its makers' intentions, it was a starter drug for information addicts; the marijuana of the mediascape.[25]

Winn famously described a 'television trance' witnessed in children watching television, for which she mustered empirical studies of viewers' respiration rates and pupil dilation. A rosier view of the television-absorbed child, however, had been put forth in 1964 by Marshall McLuhan, for whom television offered perceptual training not in passivity, but rather in absorption and *involvement*. This divergence in Winn and McLuhan's views can be situated in the context of Jonathan Crary's landmark study of the emergence of scientific and artistic attention-discourse in the nineteenth century.[26] Crary's research counters the view, most famously articulated by Walter Benjamin, that the experiences typical of the modern age are shock, fragmentation, and above all, distraction. Distraction, rather, is revealed to be one extreme of a continuum of attentive states defined, problematised, enforced, and evaded in the later nineteenth century, when a pervasive discourse on attention wound its way through Euro-American culture. When it comes to intense, focused attentiveness, Crary stresses its dual nature – necessary for productive labour and normative socialisation in modern economies on the one hand, and proximate to potentially liberatory and non-utilitarian experiences like reverie, self-hypnosis, and trance on the other. Winn and McLuhan's views of the TV-watching child rotate around a similar dichotomy (though likely Winn would deny the liberatory aspect of the TV-trance, and McLuhan its utilitarianism). Crary's subject is the rise of modernity's 'regime of attention' and, as I have argued elsewhere, the 1960s–1970s is another key moment in that regime's history, as evidenced in period psychology (relatively little discussed during the heyday of behaviourism, the questions of capacity for attention returned in the new cognitive science of this period); in elements of the counterculture (mind-altering substances, psychedelic music and imagery, meditation, and mysticism); and in the period's visual art, particularly the time-based mediums of performance and video.[27]

McLuhan described children brought up with television this way: 'They pore, they probe, they slow down and involve themselves in depth.' His was a view of television premised on black-and-white, very low-resolution mid-century television broadcasts, the visual poverty of which he thought acted, like a populist form of the blanks and discontinuities in modernist poetry, to increase the viewer's interpretive and imaginative effort. 'The [low-definition] TV image requires each instant that we "close" the spaces in the mesh by a convulsive sensuous participation that is profoundly kinetic and tactile.'[28] Whether McLuhan was empirically correct about television as a medium that promotes this kind of participatory, multi-sensory involvement is less interesting than the way his vision of young television-watchers' attentional structure describes the kind of spectatorship much early video art aimed to achieve. For technical as well as aesthetic reasons, it generally featured low-contrast, low-resolution black-and-white images played on small monitors. Terry Fox's *Children's Tapes* exemplify this 'artists' television' – as video art was still sometimes called in the mid 1970s – which resembled McLuhan's mid-century TV more than it did commercial broadcasts of its own time.

Perhaps it is only coincidental that McLuhan described participatory televisual attention with the adjective 'convulsive', beloved of the surrealists. The relationship between sculpture, attention, and mediation that took one important form in the surrealist category of involuntary sculpture does have an echo in Fox's McLuhan-like experiments. The photographically found objects of the *Involuntary Sculptures* perform – and cause the viewer to perform – a special kind of attentiveness. Katherine Conley has described them this way:

> Shot in such tight close-up and enlarged, with an almost irrationally lavish attention, these objects are literally transformed by their framing into more than the ephemera that they are – bread to be eaten; rolled bits of paper to be thrown out with the garbage – having outlived their usefulness as signs of minor economic transactions. What is more, rarely would a person, particularly an adult, see these objects in such an intimate way. And that intimacy, that spectral sense, is part of what makes these 'sculptures' surrealist, because, like surrealist 'found' objects, they seem almost animate and organic.[29]

The involuntary sculptures are super-mundane: attentional bridges between the everyday and the fantasmatic, or even the metaphysical, as Aragon suggests in his discussion of pre-adult perception: 'Children sometimes fix their attention on an object to the point where their concentration makes it grow larger, grow so much that it completely occupies their visual field, assumes a metaphysical aspect and loses all relation to its purpose.' Aragon likened this to another mediatic model, that of the cinema, where 'objects that were a few moments ago sticks of furniture or books of cloakroom tickets are transformed to the point where they take on menacing or enigmatic meanings'.[30] This parallel vision from the earlier twentieth century helps us to locate the second axis of Fox's implicit critique of the media of his day. Instead of visualising children's imagination as departing from the everyday world, as in the unnatural creatures and gravity-defying antics of TV cartoons and puppetry, he modelled imagination as the creative transformation of everyday objects: as the marvel *of* the mundane, the metaphysics of the physical.[31]

7.

Did Fox fear that children were losing the ability to enact such miracles, their attention warped and displaced by commercial television? Did he want to create, not mini-minimalists, but small surrealists? Perhaps. But if the *Children's Tapes* are vehicles of surrealist attentiveness, they are also 1970s pedagogical instruments. If on the one hand they 'restrict the field of vision so as to intensify expression', as Aragon writes of shots of everyday objects in cinema, they also do so to intensify *education*. They do not seem much like a typical schoolroom offering, of course – they do not explain what capillary action is, they just show it working. But this is precisely the kind of teaching progressive educators like John Holt, associated with 'learner-centred' and 'discovery' learning, were then advocating: demonstrations, like an adult making his or her own cardboard boxes in the back of the room, that engage children's natural curiosity about how things work.[32] This movement's constant theme was that very young children are far more patient, dexterous, and self-motivated, have greater capacity for concentration, and are better able to solve problems than most adults realise – and that when they are allowed to deploy freely this native ability to learn, they learn more, better, and more happily.

In fact, Holt sounds like he is suggesting projects for Terry Fox when he muses that since what really interests kids are the things adults deal with, 'maybe certain ordinary household objects would be good presents for small children; an eggbeater, a saucepan, a flashlight'. And Fox sounds like an adult version of Holt's students when he explains that he did not know the scientific principles behind *The Children's Tapes*; rather, he learned physics in the making of them.[33] If the *Tapes* thus are an act of learning as well as an act of teaching, it seems relevant that, as the sometimes lurching zooms and imperfect focus suggest, they were the first videotapes Fox had filmed, so that at the level of the medium they also involved a trial-and-error process of self-education.

The critical alternative to television provided here is also a model of art making, which is in turn a model of learning inscribed in a period educational philosophy. And together, this constellation complicates the prevalent vision in art criticism and history of the period's cultural investments. Just as, in Crary's terms, the videos are poised on the threshold between liberatory and productive attentiveness, Fox's project links on the one hand to critiques of the already-formed subject of humanist philosophy, and on the other to a culture of cognitive development – one dedicated to the continual building of self-sufficiency and understanding; to the formation of the self.

8.

In the world of the *Children's Tapes*, we are very small. We peer from a position barely higher than the tabletop. We watch a pair of enormous adult hands manipulate objects both commonplace and fascinating. We are patient, inquisitive, and active, making meaning rather than accepting it; we are trusted to decide what physical principles we want to ask about, or which symbolic meanings we want to pursue. We are products of the intellectual shift toward the readers rather than producers of texts, the viewers, rather than the makers of art, and we are the embodiment of the idealism of our parents' generation.

For it is worth noting that as Michael Rossman, one of the leaders of the 1960s Free Speech movement, remarked – in the same year Fox made his *Children's Tapes* – the educational reform movement of the 1970s was the direct product of student-activism in the 1960s.[34] That this might be the case was already suggested in 1969, when Louis Althusser, in his famous essay on ideology, singled out the educational system as the dominant and primary vehicle for the reproduction of the capitalist system: 'no other ideological State apparatus has the obligatory (and not least, free) audience of the totality of the children in the capitalist social formation, eight hours a day for five or six days out of seven'.[35] Accordingly, alternative educational practice was one of the sites where some of the best ideals of the 1960s – participatory democracy, localism, egalitarianism, utopianism – took root.

In the world of the *Children's Tapes*, however, we are not only the beneficiaries of these principles – we are also television addicts. Holt mused in 1967: 'It makes me think how much children must have learned from watching other people do real work, in the days when a child could see people doing real work. It is not so easy to manage this now' – now, one imagines, because of the specialisation of labour and separation of work and home; but also because of the image-viewing that replaces observation of people.[36] The child of the *Children's Tapes* is not the physically situated, materially involved viewer of minimalist and other 1960s art – or rather, it *is* that viewer, with its dialectics revealed. For the *Children's Tapes* are built on the 1970s paradox of a subject who learns by doing in a society of watching. The drive of the tapes is to pull together these two terms, doing and watching, experience and mediation. They propose their consubstantiation. Fox had two stated hopes for his work: on the one hand, that they might give children new ways to watch: an attitude 'of wonderment ... of contemplation'. And on the other the hope, however faint, that 'maybe they would want to do some of what they saw'.

He reported that they did.[37]

Notes

1 John Holt, *How Children Learn* (New York, 1967).

2 Ibid., pp. 139–40.

3 Ibid.

4 Rosalind E. Krauss, 'LeWitt in Progress', in *The Originality of the Avant-Garde and Other Modernist Myths* (Cambridge, MA, 1985), pp. 244–58, p. 253.

5 Sol LeWitt, 'Paragraphs on Conceptual Art', *Artforum* (June 1967).

6 He was referring to the perception of an infant or very young child, to which he likened the 'syncretic vision' that interested him. See Anton Ehrenzweig, 'The Child's Vision of the World', chapter 1 in *The Hidden Order of Art: A Study in the Psychology of Artistic Imagination* (Berkeley, 1967).

7 Hal Foster, *The Return of the Real: The Avant-Garde at the End of the Century* (Cambridge, MA, 1996), p. ix.

8 While he is better-known in Europe, in the United States Fox (b. 1943) remains quite obscure. In the 1970s this was certainly not the case. In that decade alone, the San Francisco-based artist was included in two Whitney biennials, Documenta 5 and 6, a São Paulo Biennial, a number of the early travelling exhibitions of video art, and group shows at SFMOMA and at museums in Buenos Aires, Medellín, and Montreal. He had almost two dozen solo shows or invited performances at galleries and museums, including Reese Palley in San Francisco and New York, Ileana Sonnabend in Paris, the University Art Museum, Berkeley, the Long Beach Museum of Art, and the Kitchen in New York. In addition to the feature articles in *Avalanche*, *Domus*, and *Arts*, his work was discussed in at least 20 articles in the art press, including landmark essays on performance and video by Cindy Nemser, David Antin, and David Ross. Part of the reason for his relative obscurity in the US today is that in 1980 Fox moved to Europe, where he lived (in Italy, Belgium, and Germany) until his death in 2008.

9 There is some discrepancy as to whether the video camera was borrowed or was his own. In an interview a few years before his death (interview with the author, 28 September 2004), Fox said that he had just received an NEA grant and used it to buy the Portapak to make these tapes. But in a 1974 interview (Willoughby Sharp and Liz Bear, 'Terry Fox ... Children's Videotapes', *Avalanche* [December 1974]), he talks at some length about the process of making the tapes, and about how he wishes he owned a camera. When I pressed him on this, he repeated the 2004 version of events, but posited that perhaps he had not yet received the cheque from the NEA. So it seems likely that while he knew he would be buying it, he had to borrow the camera in March, and still didn't own it when the conversation with Bear and Sharp took place.

10 The 34 original tapes now circulate as a 30-minute compilation of 12 of the original tapes – Fox says the compilation includes only the shortest of the episodes (interview with the author, 28 September 2004). The original masters were lost sometime in the 1970s; Fox says that this happened after he sent them to Howard Wise in New York for his then new project, Electronic Arts Intermix. EAI, which continues to be the distributor for the *Children's Tapes*, has no knowledge of the lost tapes. The compilation can be purchased or rented from EAI (www.eai.org).

11 No flies were harmed in the making of the *Children's Tapes*, I am assured. Terry Fox, interview with the author, 28 September 2004.

12 In the 'New Talkies' of Yvonne Rainer or Marguerite Duras, for example. I have been helped in thinking about this aspect of Fox's piece by conversations with Austin Guest and Branden Joseph.

13 The action guaranteed him a long ordeal of interrogations at the French border, but eventually he was allowed to continue into embattled Paris. 'I Wanted to Have My Mood Affect Their Looks', interview by Willoughby Sharp, *Avalanche* (Winter 1971), reprinted in Terry Fox, *Ocular Language: 30 Years of Writing and Speaking about Art*, ed. Eva Schmidt (Cologne, 2000), p. 41. Fox's affiliations were more with hippie culture than the period's explicitly political movements. Years later, Fox told me that he had been involved in confrontations with police during the altercations of May 68, getting beaten by Parisian police, throwing cobblestones, and breaking windows, but he claimed no substantive involvement with the students or workers. He experienced the uprisings as an exciting if frightening period in which ordinary rules and consequences were ignored. 'CLB: All the normal rules were suspended. TF: Everything was suspended'. Telephone interview with the author, 28 September 2004.

14 David Antin, 'Video: The Distinctive Features of the Medium', in John G. Hanhardt (ed.), *Video Culture: A Critical Investigation* (New York, 1986), p. 164.

15 Rosalind Krauss, 'The Cultural Logic of the Late Capitalist Museum', *October*, 54 (Fall 1990).

16 Liz Bear, Willoughby Sharp and Terry Fox, 'Terry Fox ... Children's Videotapes', *Avalanche* (December 1974), p. 33.

17 Rosalind Krauss, 'The Photographic Conditions of Surrealism', *October*, 19 (Winter 1981), pp. 3–34.

18 Fox explained that there were originally 34 tapes because this is the number of turns in the paving-stone labyrinth at Chartres Cathedral, to which he felt a strong connection when he first visited it in 1972. The labyrinth has 11 rings, and in 1972, the year a final operation cured his Hodgkin's lymphoma, he had just come out of an 11-year cycle of health and sickness. Much of his early work dealt obliquely or specifically with his illness, and evoked a tension, dramatised also in the *Children's Tapes*, between the physicality of the body and the immateriality of consciousness, which he traced to experiences of enforced isolation and motionlessness during the many hospitalisations and procedures he had to undergo. The metaphorical representations of death, near-death, and rebirth that the *Children's Tapes* allow (but do not insist on) link the video project to his experience of life-threatening illness. See 'Comments on some works and performances, 1968–81', in Terry Fox, *Ocular Language*, p. 127. The relation between his work and his experience of illness is discussed in most of his early interviews.

19 Terry Fox, 'Children's Tapes', *Arts*, 49(4) (December 1974), pp. 54–8.

20 Antin, 'Video: The Distinctive Features', p. 164.

21 Interview with the author. David Ross remembers children (as well as adults) enjoying the tapes in the Everson exhibition. Ross, email to the author, 23 September 2004.

22 Dimitri A. Christakis, Frederick J. Zimmerman and David L. DiGiuseppe, Carolyn A. McCarty, 'Early Television Exposure and Subsequent Attentional Problems in Children', *Pediatrics*, 113(4) (April 2004).

23 Julie Salamon, 'Children's TV Catches Up with How Kids Watch', *New York Times* (9 June 2002).

24 Thomas D. Cook, Hilary Appleton, Ross F. Conner, Gary Tamkin and Stephen J. Weber, *'Sesame Street' Revisited* (New York, 1975).

25 Mary Winn, *The Plug-In Drug* (New York, 1977).

26 Jonathan Crary, *Suspensions of Perception: Attention, Spectacle, and Modern Culture* (Cambridge, MA, 1999).

27 Carrie Lambert-Beatty, 'Pay Attention: 1960s Art Performance and the Economy of Spectatorship', lecture at University of California, Berkeley, 19 October 2002, and Harvard University, April 2004.

28 Marshall McLuhan, *Understanding Media: The Extensions of Man* [1964] (Cambridge, MA, 1994), p. 314.

29 Katharine Conley, 'Modernist Primitivism in 1933: Brassaï's "Involuntary Sculptures" in *Minotaure*', *Modernism/modernity*, 10(1) (2003), pp. 127–40, p. 135.

30 Louis Aragon, 'On Décor' [1918], in Richard Abel (ed.), *French Film Theory and Criticism: A History/Anthology, 1907–1939*, vol. 1 (Princeton, 1993), p. 166. For a discussion of Aragon's text in relation to the use of the close-up among the historical avant-garde, see Chapter 3 in this volume.

31 'When anyone does anything for kids, they go into this phony artificial childlike world of make-believe. But I don't think kids really want that until it's too late. Then they want it because that's all they usually get ...'. Fox interviewed in Liz Bear and Willoughby Sharp, 'Terry Fox ... Children's Videotapes', *Avalanche* (December 1974), p. 33.

32 See Wayne Jennings and Joe Nathan, 'Startling/Disturbing Research on School Program Effectiveness', *Phi Delta Kappan* (March, 1977); *Innovations in Education for the Seventies: Selected Readings*, ed. Julia E. de Carlo and Constant A. Madon (New York, 1973); Herbert R. Kohl, *The Open Classroom: A Practical Guide to a New Way of Teaching* (New York, 1969); John Holt, *How Children Learn* (New York, 1967). This was not an American phenomenon. For the British open education movement see Gary Easthope, *Community, Hierarchy and Open Education* (London, 1975); David Nyberg (ed.), *The Philosophy of Open Education* (London, 1975); John Sharp, *Open School: The Experience of 1964–70 at Wyndham School, Egremont, Cumberland* (London, 1973).

33 Telephone interview with the author, 28 September 2004.

34 Michael Rossman, 'Looking Back at the Free Speech Movement', *California Monthly* (December, 1974), reprinted at http://mrossman.org/fsm/lookingback(1974).html (accessed: 20 January 2011).

35 Louis Althusser, 'Ideology and Ideological State Apparatuses', in *Lenin and Philosophy and Other Essays*, trans. B. Brewster (New York and London, 1971), p. 156. Available online at www.marx2mao.net/Other/LPOE70NB.html (accessed: 11 January 2011).

36 By the 1970s 'real work' often consisted precisely of image-watching – as in the monitoring of radar screens, equipment indicators, or computer operations: durational, attentive exercises for which the *Children's Tapes* could be considered training tools. See Lev Manovich, 'The Labor of Perception', *Telepolis: magazine der netzkultur* (15 June 1996) www.heise.de/tp/english/inhalt/co/2036/1.html (accessed: 11 January 2011). For a more general critical theory of spectatorship as labour in a post-industrial economic order, see Jonathan Beller, *The Cinematic Mode of Production: Attention Economy and the Society of the Spectacle* (New England, 2006).

37 Interview, 28 September 2004. To encourage this bridge from watching taped experiments to performing physical ones, when he showed the tapes at kindergartens in the 1970s, Fox sometimes set up simultaneous 'live' versions of the video-taped experiments in front of the monitor.

7

Documents, Dreams and Fantasies: Passages through the Involuntary from Photography to Sculpture in the Work of Mike Kelley

John C. Welchman

The work of the Detroit-born, Los Angeles-based artist Mike Kelley has long been associated with pioneering work in performance, painting, drawing, sculpture and video; and, above all perhaps, with the extraordinary confluence of these generic singularities in the social and synaesthetic profusion of what is probably his magnum opus to date, *Day Is Done* (first seen as a video/sculptural installation at the Gagosian Gallery in New York in 2005; but present still as a feature-length film on DVD and as a CD 'sound track'). I want to argue here, however, that it is Kelley's dissident, unpredictable and somewhat intermittent work in various forms of photography that stands at the centre of his practice, where it acts as a kind of archaeological horizon for the conceptual disputes and negative dialectics around which much of his career has developed. In addition to several parallel functions, photography in these conditions serves as a reservoir, or platform of potentials, for the production of work that eventuates in alliance with other material formats, giving rise to a range of both purposed and unpredictable reconfigurations. But what Kelley brings into being on the prompt of various photographic considerations is not a pure function of 'involuntary' production. This strand of his work arises, rather, from sustained engagement with the operation of certain more or less involuntary categories of experience that include the reflex capacity of the camera to 'take'; the emergence – both spontaneous and more mediated – of repressed ideas or emotions; and the institutional and ideological structuring of Kelley's education and artistic formation, notably his encounters with formalised systems of art pedagogy, production and display – in universities, art schools, galleries, museums, as well as in his encounters with a litany of art world 'assumptions'.

For Kelley, various formations of involuntary experience, and – crucially – the processes associated with them, serve as a kind of administrative hub from which his main preoccupations are creatively dispersed. While several of these experiences are specific to the field of photography, and will be discussed in what follows, others arise from, or are released by, the artist's work in and across other material practices. Most, however, are the product of the pressures exerted as subjects are caught up in and pass through macro-institutional discourses including the family, religion or socioeconomic stratification.[1] Kelley's work with stuffed toys, Afghan throws, blankets and soft clothing, which he commenced in the later 1980s, for example, is activated by discrepancies between the various economies of value – economic, emotional, temporal – that coursed through these objects before they were compositionally and affectively re-routed by the artist. The cornucopian assemblage of handmade stuffed animals and Afghans that makes up *More Love Hours Than Can Ever Be Repaid* (1987) offers a direct address to one of the involuntary pressures exerted by the production of 'family values', focused here on what Kelley describes as 'the hidden burden of the gift'. Prompted by the relative absence of formal or monetary locations for the craft object, which is thus stranded outside a 'normative' exchange system, Kelley retrains the signifying terrain of these objects onto a psychological economy predicated on 'mysterious worth', intractable 'guilt', and 'emotional usury'.[2]

Kelley's specific engagement with the photograph has two main points of commencement. The first arose as the artist developed his 'general working methodology in the late 1970s and early 80s'. As attested in the statement accompanying his photo series 'The Poetry of Form' (1985/1996), Kelley's mobilisation of a founding substrate of photographic material is often animated by strategies of appropriation or unintentional reorganisation. The artist would search through various, generally popular cultural, sources in order to select, 'somewhat randomly, a limited number of word or image pairings' which he would use as the basis to 'research associated topics'. This process:

> yielded a vast amount of disconnected information that I would then attempt to organize mythopoetically into what, on the surface at least, resembled a coherent belief system. As part of this process, I shot many photographs out of library books. Sometimes these photos were used as source materials for the black and white image/text paintings that I produced during this period; sometimes they were incorporated as slide projections within my performances; and at other times they were used as illustrations for published texts (some of the cave photos from 'The Poetry of Form' series were, for example, in my book *Plato's Cave, Rothko's Chapel, Lincoln's Profile*). Less often, I would exhibit selected photographs as finished artworks. The rarity of this presentational method didn't stem from any prejudice against photography; I simply did not have the financial resources to have photos printed at that time.[3]

Kelley's typically candid account of his working procedures and of the role played by photography within them emphasises two modes of commitment. The first is to the archival assemblage of images, often photographs, based on an intriguing combination of the relatively random contingencies of happenstance and personal preference, on the one hand, and what we can term an involuntary seriality (such as that established for images of cave formations), on the other. The second offers to open up this involuntary constituency by re-conjugating the images according to what Kelley terms 'mythopoetic' or otherwise 'coherent belief systems'. Somewhat like the third level of semiotic reference established for the advertising photograph in Roland Barthes's well-known discussion,[4] this second operation resets the primary or denotative signification of various involuntary points of origin into an ideologically recoded connotative matrix governed by one or another form of symbolic systematicity.

The second moment of commencement for Kelley's use – and abuse – of photography arrives in a more specific form in the mid 1970s with his earliest real-time performances. Unlike the more deliberate deployment of documentary photography by conceptual, land and performance artists during the previous decade, in which the camera was brought into calculated apposition with a live event or served to make visible a conceptual gesture, Kelley was largely uninterested in the formal documentation of his performances with either still or videotaped images, and on many occasions actively prohibited it. This resistance seems in part the product of Kelley's early consecration of real-time performance and in part the consequence of a general antipathy towards the production of iconically specific, potentially commodifiable remainders, supplements to an event that might end up substituting for it and taking it over.[5] But it is also a function, I want to suggest, of a thoroughgoing suspicion of the documentary pretentions of the camera, especially when not controlled by Kelley himself.

Yet, as Kelley's work entered into various forms of creative dialogue with the materials present on stage or *in situ* during his performances, particularly with the emergent categories of performative and sound-producing objects (such as *Spirit Voices*, 1978) and black and white image-text paintings, a new signifying space was generated for photography, giving rise to a genre referred to by the artist as 'set-up photos'. These include *One-eyed King* (1981), which responds to the leitmotif of the winking figure in *Meditation on a Can of Vernors* (1981); and *Neoclassical Soap Box*, conceived at around the same time for the same project. Intended as in-studio sketches, the 'set-ups' mobilised props and adjacent materials in recombinant arrangements that solicited an aesthetic of interchangeability or modular becoming at odds with the finality of the photographic print. As no performance stills exist for *Meditation on a Can of Vernors*, these images function in a parallel scenographic space, drained of the action and speech that offers, in the end, our only mode of access to the ethos of an undocumented – and thus lost – live event. Like the performance itself, they are detours or precipitations of the 'broken symmetry' that fuels Kelley's meditation. One of the first manifestations of Kelley's skewering of photography on a misbegotten axis aligned between truth and fiction, document and imaginative projection, these images already portend the dissipation of photographic accountancy as the demonstrative logic of the medium is first blurred by speculative, serial association and then tainted with falsehood and blankness.

Kelley's first sustained exercise in photography, achieved a few years earlier, comes at these issues from another side. *The Poltergeist* (1979) (Figure 7.1) is a seven-part black and white photographic work, made alongside an investigation into the same theme by David Askevold, one of his instructors at the California Institute of the Arts, whom Kelley had befriended.[6] The circumambient texts (which, like the drawing sections, are rendered photographically) and much of the associated statement written by Kelley about the project are lifted from the voluminous literature on the subject of the destructive spirit and its emanations – located by Kelley at the allegorical centre of a humorous exercise in the production of palpable falsehood and patent simulation. But the piece is much more than a squib launched against occultist credulity or manipulative spoof. It was conceived by both artists, first of all, as a retort in kind to the strategic primacy of the documentary photographic style in the then-dominant conceptual art movement and the often belaboured seriousness of much post-conceptual work

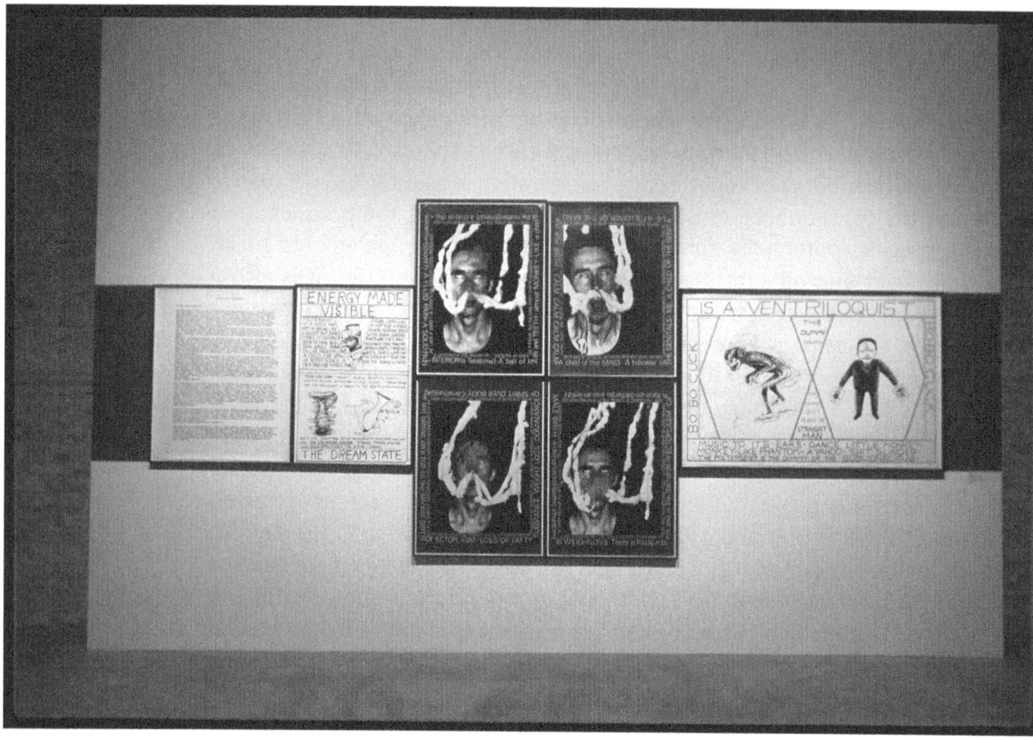

7.1 Mike Kelley, *The Poltergeist*, framed photographic prints, 1979. Seven parts: two photographs, 40 × 27.5 inches, 40 × 62.5 inches; text photograph, 40 × 33 inches; four photographs, 40 × 30 inches each. Photo: Roberto Marossi. Courtesy Mike Kelley Studio

using image and text. At the same time, Kelley, in particular, was interested in poltergeist imagery as a cipher for adolescent sexualities and their mythologising representations. The explosive eruption of matter – heat, vapour, steam, ectoplasm – from inside a body, venting unstoppably through its pores and orifices, offers a counterpoint to psychoanalytic theories of sublimation; for unlike the repressive smothering of desire or fantasy, possessed bodies are subject to material overflow as the operative energies coursing through them are 'made visible'.

As with much of Kelley's thinking in general, and on photography in particular, the subjects represented in *The Poltergeist* have a reflexive relation to the medium that engenders them. The technical precipitations, shifts and final chemical 'fixing' of the photographic image based on exposure to light offer Kelley a ready-made arena for the exploration of viscous or gelatinous matter. The spewing of ectoplasm is thus paired both conceptually and materially with images of other bodily *ejecta*, especially the money shot that became the staple of pornographic photography during the artist's college years.[7] These interests culminate in Kelley's essay on 'The Aesthetics of Ufology' in which he reflects on the undifferentiated and transcendental 'formlessness' of light itself – the qualities of which, like water, but 'unlike slime's earthy weightiness', are apprehended, he suggests, as 'both unitary and actively kinetic'. 'This is why', Kelley continues, light:

> has found such favor in religious imagery in the form of the halo, and why fixed heavenly bodies, despite their ambiguous nature and qualities, are not fear-inducing.

In 'documentary' photographs of UFOs this elevated status is threatened and light is imbued with terrifying, negative connotations. For, despite eyewitness accounts that describe 'flying saucers' as tangible technical apparatuses, they have rarely been photographed as such. Of the innumerable photographs purporting to document flying saucers collected by the government agency Project Blue Book, very few reveal any recognizable form. Often, they show only spots of light floating in the sky. It is not the fact that these photographs image what could be potentially dangerous technologies in the service of unknown beings that makes them terrifying, it is their impenetrable quality. These photographs 'picture' that which cannot be seen – or known. They do so by employing the sign of the formless: the blob.[8]

Here we encounter another of the hermeneutically entropic delivery systems for which Kelley is famous. For one of the final destinies of his interest in photography routes it through the iconographies of goo and excreta only to return the technology to the place from which it originated in the general formlessness of light.

Kelley's *Untitled (Dust Balls)*, a series of thirteen, silver-gelatin prints made in 1994,[9] offers a way-station in this journey of formless becoming (Figure 7.2). The images derived from pieces of fluff harvested from the lint trap of Kelley's laundry-room dryer which he broke into tiny lumps and then shot 'against a reflective surface so that they wouldn't have any ground ... I wanted them to look like they were floating ... I printed them that way too'.[10] Kelley's aim was to generate 'an ethereal, floating quality' so that viewers would be unable not only to decode the iconography of what they were looking at, but would also have no sense of scale. Made for the same exhibition at the Rosamund Felsen Gallery, Los Angeles, that featured his suspended sculptural object *Silver Ball* (1994) – 'this big, lumpy, silvery-colored thing ... very physical ... a very particular size and weight' – the dust ball images are thus situated in one of the closest appositions between sculpture and photography in Kelley's career – pivoting on the different valences of 'silver' they both share. The tin foil ball itself was something of a cross between an errant asteroid and a UFO, while its hollow interior 'looked like a cave', Kelley notes, and was 'lit with lights, like they do in tourist caves'. Multiple speakers connected to boom boxes were buried in the foil, producing several channels of droning voices uttering 'meaningless things' (actually the cut-up text, 'Light and Color, Mostly', mixed with electronic and organ drones) which 'caused the whole thing to buzz'. In *The Poetry of Form* (discussed below) (Figure 7.3), Kelley will switch again from one mode of subterranean imagery – supplied by a sculptural object with sonic correlates – to another – brokered this time by photography and written language.

Both objects and photographs in the Felsen show are subject to forms of blurred or decontextualised presentation that at the same time preserve a residuum of dimensionally oriented signifying effects, as intimations of volume and space are infiltrated into the gap between them. The Felsen exhibition also featured egg-shaped paintings made with shiny enamel paint applied directly onto metal surfaces, with imagery taken from science fiction aliens transformed into biomorphic abstractions. Kelley brings together, here, his interests in Ufology, biomorphism and what he terms 'highish tech', at the same time offering a volatile 'mixture of body-loathing, tech fetishism (and technophobia).' The

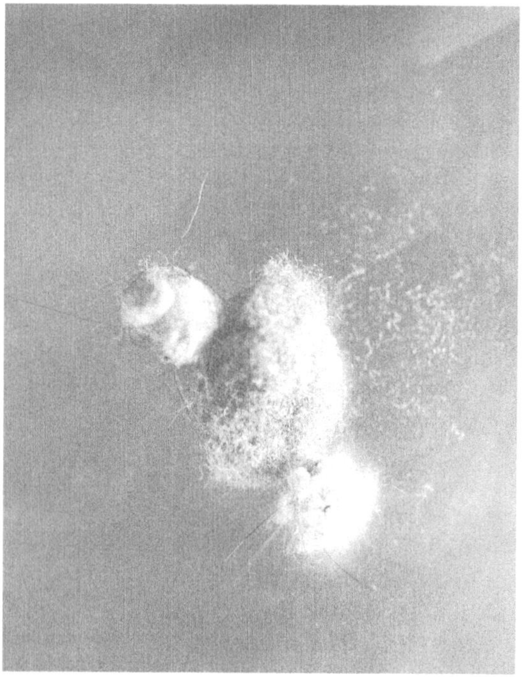

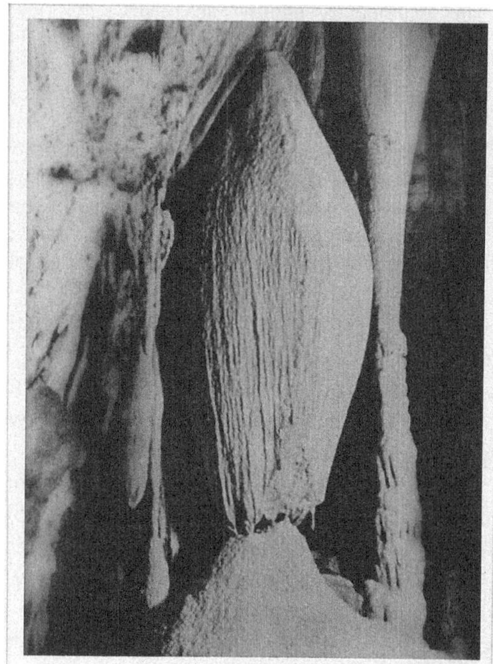

7.2 Mike Kelley, *Untitled (Dust Balls) #11*, black and white photograph on museum board, 31 × 22.5 inches, 1994. Edition of 5. Courtesy Mike Kelley Studio

7.3 Mike Kelley, *Niobe's Tear (from The Poetry of Form: Part of an Ongoing Attempt to Develop an Auteur Theory of Naming)*, gelatin silver print, title text on mat, 16 × 12 inches, 1985/1996. Edition of 5. Courtesy Mike Kelley Studio

synaesthetic cacophony that results is underwritten by the kind of descriptions in the UFO literature that interested Kelley the most: those that 'propose connections between light, sound, color and physical effects'.

If, then, the assemblage mapped out by ectoplasm, sperm, dust and finally floating spots of light represents a set of limit-terms for Kelley's triangulation of subjects on the threshold of formal dissolution, we can identify a number of dialogues with modifications of these conditions established elsewhere in his earlier work. One of these takes up with photography and form, another with photography and deformation; brief consideration of both will help us to track another trajectory for the photographic that leads away from the abstractions of mass and surface towards the Kelleyean interrogation of place and history.

The first of these projects is *The Poetry of Form*: *Part of an Ongoing Attempt to Develop an Auteur Theory of Naming* (1996), a publication comprising 34 black and white photographs of cave formations, shot from various books while he was at work on *Plato's Cave* in 1984 and 1985 (Figure 7.3). These photographs served multiple purposes: some appeared as illustrations in Kelley's book *Plato's Cave, Rothko's Chapel, Lincoln's Profile*, for example, and Kelley recalls showing the whole series as a slide show in a public lecture. As the subtitle indicates, however, the artist was mainly interested here in the picturesque associative nomenclature inherited from the books, postcards and cave pamphlets he had researched or collected. The caves and their characteristic accretive formations had already been named by an unknowable collective of amateur spelunkers and photographers, guides, gatekeepers, book and postcard publishers, or by consensus from folkloric inheritance. Each of the names clearly reaches for a projective reconstruction of the cave element it 'describes' in the form of phrase-based similes. In the titled images collected in *The Poetry of Form* there are four main registers within which these similarities are developed. The first is based on various kinds of animal analogy, whether to real creatures, or to mythological beasts such as *The Sphinx*. A second refers to human characters, whether derived from popular or everyday culture (*Mutt and Jeff*, *The Backyard Gossip*); mythology (*Niobe's Tear*); body parts or their actions (*The Pointing Hand*, *The Eternal Kiss*); or body coverings (*The Bridal Veil*). The most popular register in this sample, thirdly, is predicated on architectural reference. Several of these names are trans-temporal (such as *The Temple of the Sun II*); while others are orientalising (*The Black Pagoda*); ritual or religious (*The Totem Pole*, *The Hall of The Sabbath*); aristocratic (*The Queen's Chamber*), Native American (*The Papoose Room*); or refer to miniatures (*The Doll's Theater*). Fourthly, two of the names designate specific objects (*The Parachute*) or landscape elements (*The Frozen Cascade*).

Kelley's technique of re-photography in *The Poetry of Form* was quite different from the modes of appropriation dominant in the mid-1980s New York art world. He viewed the ensemble of photographs as 'recontextualisations' or 'mythic insertions' and aligned them more with what Guy Debord and the Situationists termed *détournement* than with the re-photography of Richard Prince or Sherrie Levine. The photos were printed in soft focus, thus offering 'romantic' connotations, and two of the negatives in the series were manipulated with the addition of black spots to efface any signs of human presence.

As often in Kelley's work, an assemblage of images of one particular motif – here the cave – becomes the launching pad for the release of often circuitous and involuntary series of metaphorical mediations riffing, inferentially, on its structures and socio-aesthetic implications. *The Poetry of Form* offers an especially rich recombinant scene for the unfolding of these passages and elisions. Beginning with some of the broadest axes in the general map of his career – drawing or painting, on the one hand, and photography on the other; using colour on the one side, and black and white on the other – Kelley points to the presence of certain structural and educational determinations or blockages that informed his training, competence and choices. His commitment to black and white (both acrylic paintings and photography), for example, was in part mandated by his relation to the post-minimalist and conceptualist milieus in which he found himself at Cal Arts and in Los Angeles in the mid -and-later 1970s, and his avoidance of colour by the overweening impact of his earlier formal training and the ubiquity of what he refers to as 'typical' 'abstract formalist composition in the [Hans] Hofmann manner' – perpetrated by the archpriest of his educational abuse.

A second early photo-based project, *Reconstructed History* (1989), points us in another direction, but finally arrives at a similar set of questions. This limited edition artist's book contains 61 photographs and illustrations selected from a much larger group that Kelley found in used and yard-sale books on American history that he then graffitied. The embossed cover of *Reconstructed History*, with crest and scholastic 'Lamp of Knowledge', mimics the look of a High School Yearbook or coffee table historical tome, and features a clear dust-jacket defaced with morbid adolescent doodles. The book's interior design, on the other hand, resembles a high-end photography book, with protective barrier sheets between each isolated image. Kelley's introduction was printed, in script, on faux parchment, emulating 'Colonial' design. Its style, tone and range of references – even the original graphic layout using a pseudo-historical typeface – are all duplicitous. The images in the book are not 'found' but made, and the voice of the text deliberately stilted. The result is an elaborate hoax, one of the more vivid of Kelley's many efforts to perform, write and represent through fictitious adopted personae. Examples of this dissimulation include 'The Gateway to Freedom' (Figure 7.4), which skewers that emblematic personification of the city, the Statue of Liberty by adding a breast, as well as pubic and underarm hair, to a common photograph; and 'With Malice Toward None, With Charity For All', a well-known photograph of a formally attired Abraham Lincoln on which the artist has appended a swastika, boils and pointed teeth.

The photographs in *Reconstructed History* negotiate a series of thoroughgoing disputes in which photography is a vainglorious first term whose alliances with truth and history are ruinously undone. Referred to in Kelley's text as 'confused and gruesome' the symbolic orders of patriotic history are, it claims, predicated only on various 'passions fired by the flesh' – 'murder, war, the struggle for power, the desire for wealth, and the disruption of social order'. The 'historical specificity' of the photograph is, then, in each case foreclosed to 'convey' another array of what Kelley terms 'general American values'. The scurrilous marks added to the photos are the product of a general 'childish resentment' which issues in a desire to sully, vandalise or otherwise 'render inoperable' the superficial 'pictures of health' they supposedly summon up. The 'besmirchment' (*sic*) thus let loose is fuelled by sexuality 'in its most culturally unacceptable expressions, such as homosexuality, pedophilia, and bestiality', by 'scatological' 'bodily functions', and by various 'crimes against the family'.[11]

By attributing the photographic defacements of *Reconstructed History* to ordinary 'grade school children', 'normal young people', Kelley notes, 'who would no doubt consider themselves patriotic Americans and conservative heterosexuals',[12] the elaborate spoof engineered by the artist threatens to dissolve its own logic. The graffitied photographs become tokens of a perverse form of health as they mark the process of becoming-adult in children who wholesomely refuse the common taboos of social repression, thus proving themselves worthy as future civic leaders. The intricately ridiculous circuitry that renders such a conclusion possible is a mark of Kelley's relentless satirical drive. Predicated on ceaseless exchange and boomeranging recurrence, Kelley's molten generic categories – aesthetic, social and historical – defeat the putatively immobile parameters of truth and falsehood, and the very notion of a noble past and rationally predictable future.

Photography itself is subject to a special form of deconsecration in the service of Kelley's parodic revisionism. Its special contact zone with evidence and documentary veracity is unceremoniously unravelled by the artist's relentless exposure of the temporising relativity of what it quite literally brings to light. So as photography is accorded a key role in a succession of projects following on from *The Poltergeist*, *The Poetry of Form* and *Reconstructed History*, the artist subjects the medium's fundamental premises, ranging from its material constituency to its signifying economies, to confounding volleys of bait and switch. This is most literal, perhaps, in the installation *An Architecture Composed of the Paintings of Richard Powers and Francis Picabia*, made with Paul McCarthy in 1997, which took the form of a maze-like structure set with large-scale reproductions of work by Powers and Picabia rendered by a Los Angeles sign painter. While the exhibition itself had no formal photographic components, it was predicated on 'the breaking down of cultural categories – that a commercial artist such as Powers began to use traditionally avant-garde pictorial tropes in the context of popular art, and that, around the same time, an avant-garde artist like Picabia began to make paintings copied from photographs found in popular girlie magazines'. 'In a sense', Kelley noted, 'our installation addressed a specific point in American art history when the distinction between so-called "high" and "low" art was still in place, but entering a period of categorical crisis.' Photography, in the form of soft-core pornographic images, is a pretext, here, for the scrambling of values and conditions across the strata of high and low art.

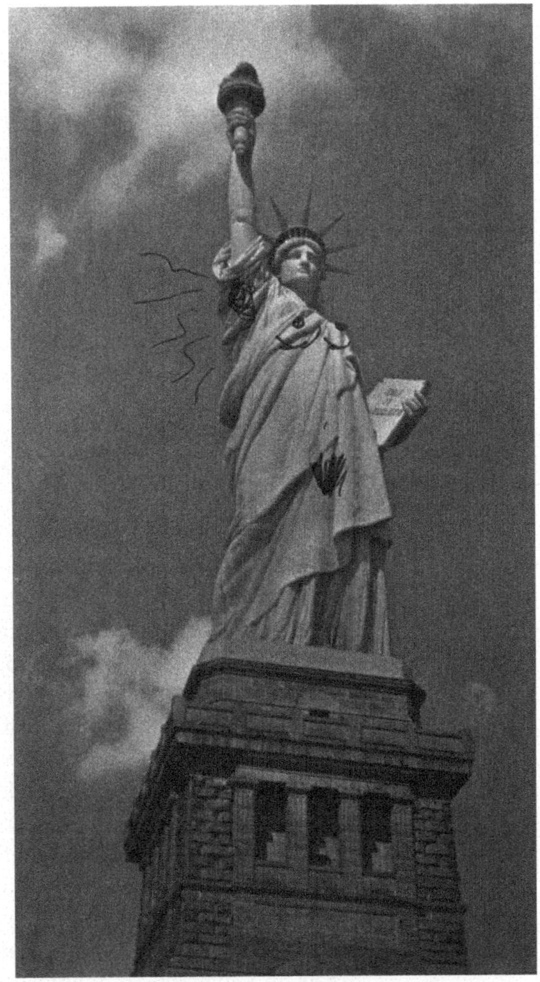

7.4 Mike Kelley, *The Gateway to Freedom*, black and white photograph, 8 × 10 inches, 1989. Courtesy Mike Kelley Studio

But the centrefold is not the only popular cultural denomination of the photographic with which Kelley's work creatively absconds. His highly charged 'protest poster', *A Stopgap Measure* (1999), for example, takes as its starting point one of the more extreme forms of photographic 'taking' – by the news photographer as stalker – but returns to the questions of sexuality, repressed desire and voyeurism on which it is generally based. Kelley's millennial essay in social satire is a modest proposal – with allegorical accoutrements – that offers, quite literally, to perform a '69' on the 'fantasy-figures' of celebrity culture, harvesting their vanity and allure to feed and thus dissipate the repressions of a 'sex-starved' general citizenry. *A Stopgap Measure* delivers on the implications of the relentless drive by stalkerazzi to capture telephoto-enabled, candid photographic images of celebrities, offering to solve the health care crisis by making stars sexually available for public use as a therapy for mass repression and sexual dysfunction. The reflex public lust for salacious gossip and prurient celebrity images is fed-back into an uncanny, therapeutic nightmare for the rich and famous – which has a second involuntary outcome as a facetious solution to one of the gravest social issues in the US.

If *An Architecture Composed of the Paintings of Richard Powers and Francis Picabia* and *A Stopgap Measure* engage the photographic in its more dramatic or contentious forms, which precipitate involuntary effects as a kind of energetic ricochet, another strand of Kelley's work reverses these terms by commencing with forms of photography that offer pretexts for something neutral, given or socially established. *We communicate Only through Our Shared Dismissal of the Pre-Linguistic: Fourteen Analyses* (1995), for example, takes the form of a series of colour photographs that document paintings made under Kelley's tutelage by kindergarten students while he was an undergraduate art student at the University of Michigan in the early 1970s. Building quite deliberately on the hermeneutic dysfunction we have already encountered in *Reconstructed History*, Kelley used photography in the form of Ektachrome prints (made more than two decades later) to offer a neutral form of material stability for the series of painted or drawn images that he then subjected to plausibly outlandish analyses based on extensive readings in child art analysis and art therapy.

We Communicate takes on the very predicates of the involuntary, which in this case arise from two sets of cultural 'givens': on the one hand, the series of purportedly expressive children's drawings (which, it is supposed, arise 'spontaneously' and 'characterologically' from the young subjects who make them); on the other, the analytical paradigms of child psychology which transform the paintings into supposedly unpremeditated testimony. The flatness and neutrality of the photograph is the catalyst through which both the materials of the paintings and the theoretical apparatus that occasions their interpretation are forced to pass. As in the wider culture, photography becomes a levelling device that generates a fine-grained evenness or social flatness. The concomitant ubiquity of photographic imagery is a kind of camouflage that disguises and then collides the apparently antithetical postulates which fire up the piece. First it serves to massage the textural and other physical traits of the pictorial originals so that their surfaces can be trawled for symbolic depth; and, second, it conjures a disparate sequence of children's paintings into an archival assemblage which can be subjected to generalised analysis. All this converges – satirically and disruptively – in the very nature of the purportedly involuntary actions on which the project is predicated: the assumption by child psychology that such images grant access to the phobias, traumas and fantasies of the subjects who paint them. By questioning the etiquettes of the *decoding* processes that attempt to secure this assumption, Kelley is challenging some of the fundamental points of connection between will and reflex, consciousness and unconsciousness; and, finally, refusing to draw a line between what might be voluntary and involuntary.

While photographic neutrality is something of a pretext in *We Communicate*, Kelley subsequently produced a remarkable sequence of multi- and inter-media installations in which the signifying work of the photograph is subject to a beguiling array (and combination) of cancellations and subtractions and of fantasies and projections. The simultaneous under- and over-coding of photographic material that arises from these conjunctions and their relation to the generation of work in other media, including sculpture, is most clearly evident in the grouping of photographs, sculpture and archival apparatus in *Black Out*, made for *Artists Take on Detroit: Projects for the Tricentennial* (2001).[13] Here Kelley adopts the subject-position of the anthropologist, conducting his version of field research along the Detroit River, during which he visited most of the islands in the Detroit area (where he was born, and lived through his college years). As attested by photographs such as *Butter Colored Vision of the Land O' Lakes Girl, Peche Island* (2001), one aim of this project was to generate pseudo-documentary images replete with the projected exoticism and personal fantasies associated with these locales, including simulated, faux-primitivising photographs of the Indian Maiden pictured on the Land O'Lakes butter pack (a privileged subject from Kelley's boyhood sexual imagination). These images are part of a wider conceptual spectrum, long of interest to Kelley, in which photography is brought alongside the social compulsion to see and record objects, beings or situations which are implausible or whose very existence is contested – such as the 'Bigfoot' monster or UFOs. Referring to another, black and white, photograph of the Indian Maiden, Kelley addresses this connection explicitly, noting that it 'mimics the famed "Bigfoot" photo – with the figure in the distance, obscured by foliage'.[14]

This form of fantasised mimicry is aligned, however, on just one of several photographic axes that come together in *Black Out*. Another is constituted, in part at least, by the happenstance of technical malfunction. The eight, horizontal-aspect, gelatine-silver photographic prints in the *Black Out (Detroit River)* series (2001) were intended as more straightforward documentary images of the shoreline of the river viewed from the boat in which Kelley was travelling; but a camera or processing error meant that all but thin slivers of the resultant photographs came out black. In a typically resourceful gesture, this unique instance of blankness coming to Kelley, rather than the other way round, was creatively rehabilitated by the artist, and the images became central to the project (eventually providing its title). 'I realised that the camera error was providential', Kelley notes. 'For, these black, empty areas perfectly represent the "missing time", the blocked-out trauma described in repressed memory syndrome literature.'[15] The blackness that dominates these would-be locative photographs offers a degree zero for the absence and nullity that governs a crucial aspect of this medium: it acts as a cipher for the provisional nature of memory and an indicator for the blindside of the documentary idiom.

Kelley commenced work in 1998 on a third axis in the complex and recursive interrogation of photographic signification taken on in *Black Out* when he undertook a research project in the archives of the local newspaper of the Detroit suburb where he was raised, the *Wayne/Westland Eagle*. Using the time-frame of 1968–72, that is, from the period when he 'first developed an interest in fine art to when [he] left home', Kelley took some 150 photographs of articles and their accompanying photographs which represented in some manner what he described as 'local culture', along with 'vestiges of surrounding material to provide an overall cultural context'. Kelley understood the concept that focuses this inquiry according to a 'broad' definition, 'including overtly aesthetic examples, like arts and crafts shows and music concerts, as well as civic events such as parades and holiday spectacles'. In addition 'local culture' 'also includes what could be construed as "counter-cultural" activities, like vandalism and drug activity'. He also added to the investigation of his formative milieu a medium-specific quotient by printing all of the images three times, using different paper stocks, which he correlated with the production of different effects: 'One paper', he noted, 'produces a very high contrast image, giving the photograph a documentary look; another is warmer in tone and more in line with the tradition of "art photography"; while the last variety is a sepia tone paper that gives the image a "nostalgic" feeling.' In the completed work, *Local Culture Pictorial Guide, 1968–72 (Wayne/Westland Eagle)* (see Figure 7.5), the photographs were, finally, 'grouped according to different associational systems, and mounted on double-sided 4 × 8 feet vertical panels, which may be pulled, like drawers, out of two display cabinets'.[16]

Local Culture Pictorial Guide and its relation to the other parts of *Black Out* represent probably the most ambitious attempt in Kelley's oeuvre to think through the social, cultural and aesthetic valances of photography, and to align both these process and their results with other forms of material eventuation. Commencing with a quasi-sociological investigation that matches the pseudo-anthropology of his river expedition three years later, Kelley interleaved an archival research methodology with a series of appropriational shots or re-rephotographic takes – which are governed by the conceptual limit-term of 'local culture'. In a sense *Local Culture Pictorial Guide* looks back to some of the strategies pioneered by conceptual artists, notably in Joseph Kosuth's *Second Investigation* (1969) in which both national and local newspapers were infiltrated by various thesaurus headings and sub-categories purchased as advertising space,[17] or, later, by Sarah Charlesworth's *Modern History* series (1977 – *c.*2003) which took the form of black and white photographic prints made from masked newspaper pages, often front pages, from around the world, reproduced in their original scale, each addressing either a particular international headline event (such as the Red Brigade's announcement of the assassination of Italian Prime Minister Aldo Moro, 20 April 1978), or different text and image formats of the same paper (for example, *Herald Tribune, September 1977*).[18]

But Kelley's engagement with the newspaper is different in several aspects. First, if Charlesworth's project is decidedly international and national, and Kosuth works at the intersection of the national and the regional, Kelley's emphasis is defiantly local: to the extent, in fact, that the artist uses a local medium to produce a barometer of the particular intersection of locality with cultural production we could term it *meta-local*. Secondly, Kelley's project attempts to run deeper by taking a much larger sample (around 150 items), as opposed to the series of fortnightly or monthly date or issue-specific pages and roughly the same number of publication-specific photos deployed by Charlesworth, or the small clusters of half-a-dozen or so regional and national newspapers in Britain, New York and elsewhere 'occupied' in the various geographical instalments of Kosuth's investigation. While, like Charlesworth, Kelley is interested in assaying the structure and effects of editorial decision-making, and the social dynamics of topic and issue selections, his 'coverage' here – as with the floor pieces of the *Arena* series – is 'blanket'. If the paradigm of what counts as culture has been defined by Kelley himself somewhat arbitrarily, he nevertheless endeavours to find and re-photograph each and every instance of it within the chronological brackets that he also laid down (the very period, beginning in 1968–69, it turns out, that saw Kosuth move from his *First* to the *Second Investigation*).

This leads to the third constitutional difference between these projects: in apparent contradistinction to Kosuth and Charlesworth, the primary predicate of *Local Culture Pictorial Guide* is a form of crypto-autobiography as the image-based guide that results offers a field of visual evidence for the types of neighbourhood and suburban culture in which the artist was enmeshed at a crucial moment of his formation. Kelley also cross-hatched the format of the newspaper with his own biography in the 15 black and white photo-texts of *Timeless/Authorless* (1995), which deployed simulated newspaper front pages with mastheads relating to cities that had specific pertinence to Kelley's upbringing and art career. As I argue elsewhere, however, one of the characteristic misunderstandings of conceptual art, both in its heyday and among second- and third-generation practitioners, has been the tendency to count out almost every form of relation between the work and the subject-positions or geographic locations of the artist. In fact, one of the more significant contributions of the *Second Investigation* lies precisely in the sardonic commentary it offers about the various milieus of the conceptual movement (from Manhattan to Coventry – where several of the Art and Language group worked or lived; from Antwerp to Vancouver).[19] This said, it is surely as rare for the earlier conceptual artists to make explicit references to their social selfhood as it is for Kelley to refrain from doing so.

The primary datum with which Kelley works here, then, is the 'given' of his own educational and social experience. In this condition what is involuntary is the opposite of a reflex or semantic twitch occasioned by a specific trigger. It is instead an amorphous arena of dilute, deferred, perhaps unconscious – yet (or hence) often unpredictable – determinations: the sum of all that was somehow done to the subject against or loosely in spite of (his) will. The heartland of Kelley's understanding of the involuntary must be routed through the small-town values that nurtured him, where it clearly merges from time to time with the conceptual vernacular of Americana itself. The material in this zone ranges from dysfunctional nurture, to institutional indoctrination and abuse, real or imagined, but it also includes moments of passion, intrigue and erratic conviction, including the 'juvenile "aesthetic" events' and their corollary images (such as the one taken from the *Westland Eagle*, April 23, 1969), somewhat facetiously assembled in 'Some Aesthetic Highpoints' (1991).[20]

Many issues are raised by the autobiographical constituencies of Kelley's work, but what concerns us here is one particular routing system through which the photographic substrates of involuntary contextualisation are reconvened in sculptural form. The fourth and fifth parts of *Black Out*, which we have not yet discussed, furnish some of the most consequential of these physical realisations. One takes up, however, with the sculptural only as it is mediated through the photographic, at the same time crossing it quite directly with the question of Kelley's art education. In 2001 the artist took a series of photographs of the sculpture garden at the Ann Arbor home of Gerome Kamrowski, his former teacher in the art department of the University of Michigan. But as with the *Black Out (Detroit River)* series another accidental technical malfunction intervened during the developing process. As Kelley puts it: 'I found that the entire roll was covered with inexplicable chainlink-shaped, white wave patterns, especially evident on a strip of underexposed frames of film. I have printed four of these frames as one image in a long horizontal photograph titled *Psychic Waveforms (Gerome Kamrowski's Sculpture Garden, Ann Arbor, MI).*' Multiple strands of involuntary activity are woven together here: launched by the happenstance of Kelley's pedagogical experience, the objects in the sculpture garden are made visible by a technical error, which the artist has transformed into an opportunistic commentary on two aspects of a possible history of the involuntary in Kamrowski's work – its connection with the surrealist movement (one of the epicentres of the cultivation of automatic aesthetic effects); and its relation to another *cause célèbre* of the involuntary, what Kelley refers to as the 'direct effect of psychic activity on photographic film'.[21]

It is in the fifth component of *Black Out*, however, that the pressures of the involuntary become most palpable – the more so as this work, *John Glenn Memorial Detroit River Reclamation Project (Including the Pictorial Guide, 1968–72 [Wayne/Westland Eagle])* (Figure 7.5), houses and digests the newspaper image-texts present in its subtitle. The material basis of the piece was furnished by the involuntary assemblage in a pre-WWII dumpsite on one of the small islands in the Detroit River of a multitude of metallic, vitreous and ceramic fragments. Kelley had originally intended to use these found elements to make a biomorphic or blob-like sculptural form, cementing the units together with black, silicon rubber 'like the absent "memory-zones" in the river photos', in a manner that resembled the Canadian tradition of memory ware.[22] Prompted by a chain of personal memories and associations. Kelley instead resolved to use the dredged debris to coat the surface of a statue of the astronaut and (future) senator, John Glenn, modelled on one made according to the textured stylisation of mid-century modernism situated in the library of his high school (which was actually named after Glenn). Typically, Kelley also factors in several other levels of reference: to the 'clinker'-like constituency of the astronaut-turned-vampire in the science fiction film *First Man into Space* (dir. Robert Day, 1959); to the heroic scale of socialist realism; and to colourised photography, represented here by the presence of several large photos – of the original Glenn statue, of a 'carving of the mythical Bigfoot from the Redwoods area of northern California', and of the sites of the scattered debris on two Detroit River islands. The anti-naturalistic, 'spotty colorisation' of one pair of photographs and the ambient fragmentation of the other mimics the tessera-like formatting of the statue and attests to the foundation of all memory and its attendant images in chopped and broken forms. *John Glenn Memorial* is completed by a series of low, ramp-like structures used to display materials left over from the fabrication of the sculpture, and organised as a walkway punctuated by a pair of cabinets at each end which house the *Local Culture Pictorial Guide*.

The final element of *Black Out* is another sculptural series, *Lingam and Yoni*, named for the Hindu terms for the male and female principles. Made from soil samples collected on the islands, the lingam or phallic component of each work rises to a height dictated by the amount of clean soil in each sample; while the dimensions of the yoni basins were proportional to the amount of stone and detritus 'arranged in a naturalistic recreation of the groundcover of

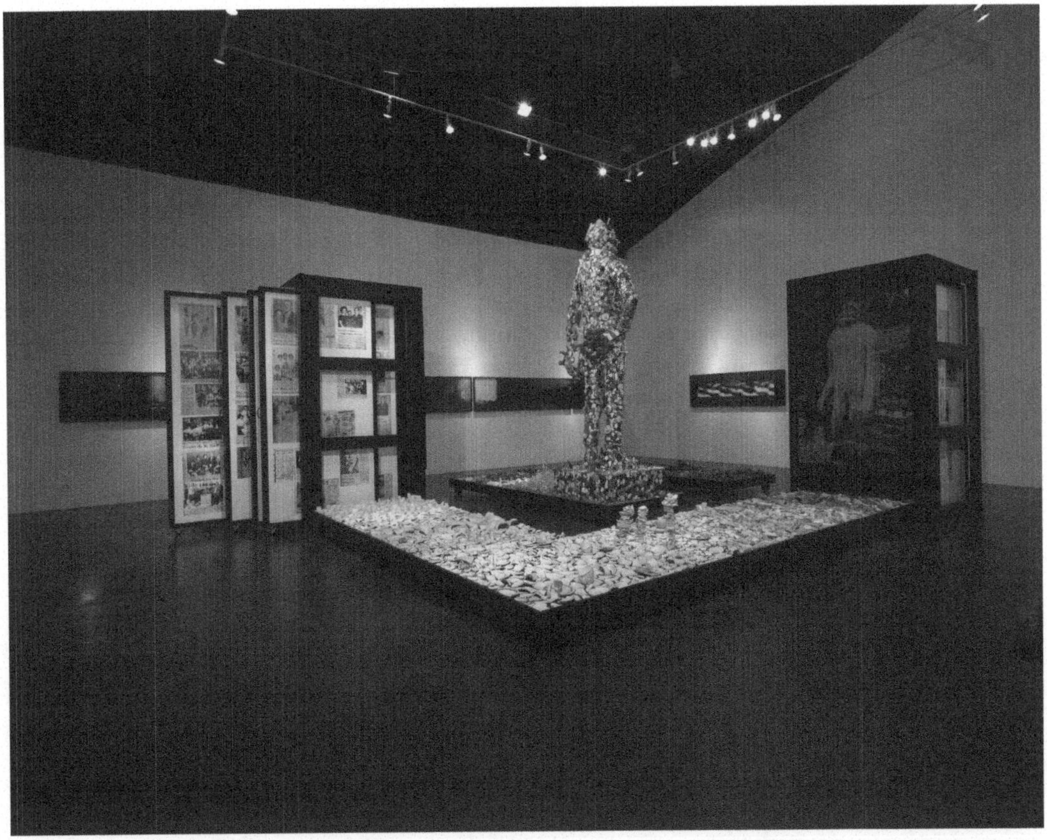

7.5 Mike Kelley, *John Glenn Memorial Detroit River Reclamation Project (Including the Local Culture Pictorial Guide, 1968–1972, Wayne/Westland Eagle)*, mixed media installation, 137 × 216 × 249 inches, 2001. Photo: Fredrik Nilsen. Courtesy Mike Kelley Studio

the island from which it was collected'. To the pressures of the involuntary as apprehended though historical accumulation, contextual determination and the happenstances of nurture, Kelley now adds a three-dimensional surrogate for the involuntary play of sexual fantasy: 'I chose to sculpt the island soil into the forms of the lingam and yoni to emphasize the sexual fantasy nature of my original desire to explore the islands of the Detroit River.'[23] The tongue-in-cheek, cross-cultural allegorisation of *Lingam and Yoni* skews the drive for locality with the universalising protocols of psycho-sexual generalisation. In the end they deliver us back to the unstable circuits of desire and projection that gave rise to the voyeuristic sightings of the Indian Maiden, with which *Black Out* commenced.

The cabbalistic figures composed photographically and sculpturally by Kelley from the arrangement of memory, history, accident and desire almost know no end. Central to this investigation was *Educational Complex* (1995), a project founded on the tessellation of blanknesses that form the partial un-recall of Kelley's memory of the educational institutions he attended, from kindergarten to Cal Arts, from youth to university – which he assembled as an architectural model. Kelley compared the 'missing time' of the black areas in the photographs of *Black Out* to the 'unfinished sections' of unremembered spaces in that model, and created another three installations inspired by *Education Complex*. *A Continuous Screening of Bob Clark's Film* Porky's *(1981), the Soundtrack of*

Which Has Been Replaced with Morton Subotnick's Electronic Composition The Wild Bull *(1968), and Presented in the Secret Sub-Basement of the Gymnasium Locker Room* (2002) was composed of the two-dimensional leftovers from the construction of the *Educational Complex* arranged in an enterable sculpture that includes various floor plans, architectural sketches, and working drawings used to produce the *Educational Complex*. These were mounted onto wooden panels, arranged into a structure resembling a section of office work cubicles; and overwritten by annotations hurled back against the institutional structures that bore Kelley into adulthood. The major terms in the long title of this piece – the frat-house film *Porky's*, Morton Subotnick's modernist score, and the sub-basement of the gym locker room, were all appropriated from 'notes made on some of the school floor plans describing "recovered memories" of events that took place within the various "repressed" spaces'.[24] By using the paradigm structures of the modern workplace, Kelley transforms the photographs, annotated copies, blueprints and other archival materials into a continuous array of office notes and pin-ups, creating an oddball study zone for the uncanny recombinant scene of his own institutional formation.

A Continuous Screening relates in turn to another large-scale sculpture, *Double Contour with Side Bars* (first presented at the Hussenot Gallery in Paris in 2000), which was constructed from the three-dimensional scraps left over from the *Educational Complex*, as well as those from the sculpture *Framed and Frame* (1999). What we encounter here are quasi-fictive miniaturised spaces, made from modelling materials cast off from the inaugural process of structuring in three dimensions the loose diagrammatic jottings of Kelley's faulty memory ... which grew dimmer and dimmer the further it reached back. All this of course speaks eloquently, though in art world tongues, to Michel Foucault's concern to examine the subjective and social formations of the institution not from the top down, but from the bottom up.

These disquisitions on the social and subjective economies of the photographic image, and its reflexive sequestration by other genres and discourses, reach a giddy climax in *Day Is Done: Extracurricular Activity Projective Reconstruction #2–32* (2004–2005) (Figure 7.6). The two conditions announced in the title, the draining away of light and the dawn of a leisure time in which various 'extracurricular activities' transpire, join with a third that animates and defines them, the multiple 'projective reconstructions'. Together they constitute the three key dimensions of this work: a metaphoric temporality that commences with the sunset; a substrate of actions and an event horizon conducted in downtime; and a phantasmatic reconstitution produced at the interface of some sort of photographically engendered documentary information and imaginative extrapolation. But the carnivalesque profusion of *Day Is Done* was launched, almost perversely, by an animating force that turns like a motor in reverse, fuelled by a battery running backwards.[25]

The absent scenes of social formation in the 1995 *Educational Complex* become in *Day Is Done* the organising principle for a more generalised regimen of repressed memories, a dream-book of traumatic episodes transacted in the über-institutional space that frames the exhibition. Kelley has engineered a panorama of repressed episodes precipitated by an iconic assemblage of

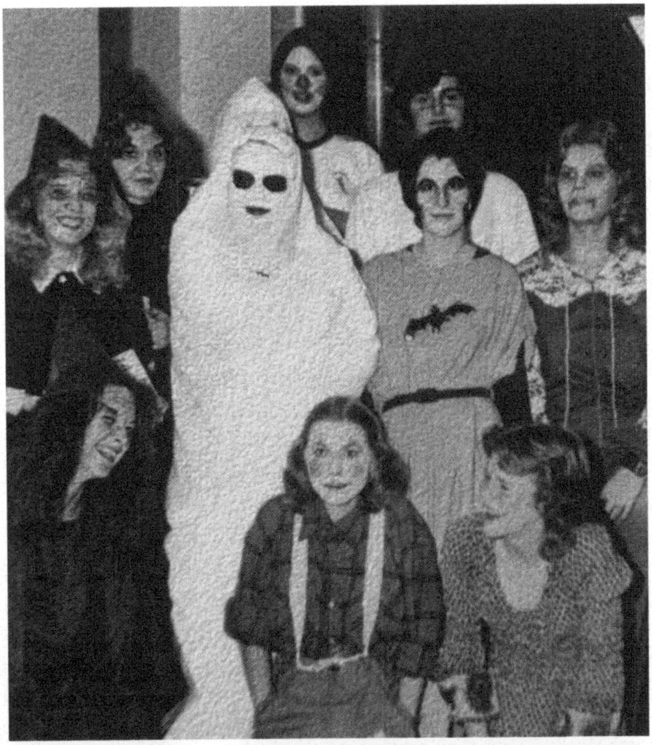

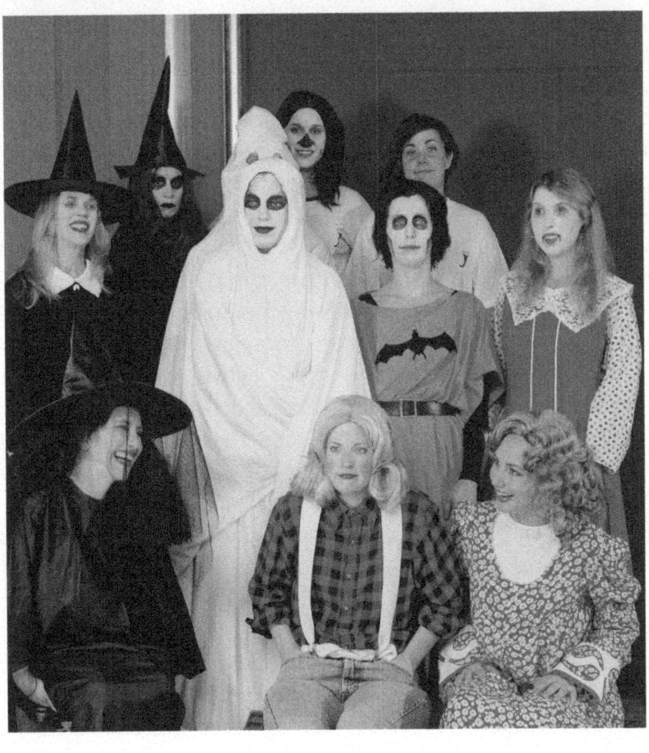

7.6 Mike Kelley, *Extracurricular Activity Projective Reconstruction #10 (Group Portrait)*, chromogenic print and black and white Piezo print on rag paper, 73.5 × 37.5 inches, 2004–2005. Edition of 5. Courtesy Mike Kelley Studio

yearbook photographs, representing different types of generic activity – religious, motivational, costume, equestrian and so on – which he wilfully recalls into art. But he kick-starts the tumult of *Day Is Done* with what amounts to a gigantic evacuation, a de-*mise-en scène*, in which the subject-matter is always already available but at the same time eventuates as pure projection – a paradox caught up at the heart of the testimonial histories of Repressed Memory Syndrome that offer another point of commencement.

Founded thus on surprising absence and retreat, it comes as a further shock to realise that each section of one of the most generically hybrid, episodically layered and plurally allusive works of recent times is formed from a single, focused point of origin. The objects that corral the whirligig of types and situations almost manically unfolded from them are photographs sourced from among the hundreds of categorised images from high school yearbooks that Kelley has hoarded over the years. For Kelley, however, the yearbook has blossomed cinematically from its anodyne social functions into an archive for the recovery of missing time – traumatic, repressed, abandoned.

The series of carefully selected grainy yearbook pictures act like Freudian dream-texts, but – once more – in reverse. Already seemingly supplied with many of the quotients of the dream-work described by Freud in the sixth chapter of *The Interpretation of Dreams* – object displacements, self-revelatory poses, intimations of the grotesque, erratic juxtapositions of bodies and objects, prurient peer dynamics, and so on – they are, in themselves, precisely *not* the product of dream or fantasy, but found images snipped from the quotidian world of ritualised postures. Instead of arriving as a consequence of delirious dreaming, personal history or familial repressions, the unconscious activities that animate the photos are a complexly inaccessible product of the social unconscious of regional Americana. Kelley has taken on this image repertoire with a reformulated touch of the terrifying precision attributed to the mutating objects unveiled by Salvador Dalí in his theory and practice of critical paranoia. Like his, they are images that feed interpretation back onto their appropriators.

A slew of misrepresentations streams from images that are deeply embedded in the ritual forms their protagonists enact. *Day Is Done* thrives in the space between the found, the plausible and the fantasised. It throws into question the opposition between the restorative – a situation in which the artist acts like a detective to engineer the closest possible visual and performative fit with the character or type – and the utterly fictive. Mixing the predicative and the freeform, the imaginary and the reconstructive, the exhibition stakes out an intensely fertile middle ground between these terms and in the process administers a surprising jolt to the category of the art work. By layering artistic fantasy over the formal remainders of social misunderstanding and blending both with Kelley's characteristic structural clarity, *Day Is Done* invents a new set of creatively unstable relations between objects and projections.

One of Kelley's achievements here is a kind of tumultuous obverse – and scintillating retort – to that round of 're-photographic' practice that so gripped the art world from the late 1970s through the 1980s. Both Kelley and Sherrie Levine, for example, begin with a photograph, one ultra-vernacular, the other 'high' or 'fine'. But while Levine's gestures of singular appropriation thrive almost exclusively on the critical context that underwrites their reception – recycling it through questions of originality, authorship and the copy which viewers and critics extend – Kelley subjects his found photographs to social and formal extrapolation, overloading them with a giddy combination of faux-logical implications and situational projection. Levine inters the photograph in the coffin of its authorship; Kelley resurrects its anonymous protagonists into a voracious afterlife of apocryphal dimensions.

Notes

This essay was written before Mike's tragic passing in January 2012. We had discussed the idea of an essay on his work in photography in the late 1990s, but I was unable to commence it until a decade later. Mike read a first draft in the early summer of 2010 and we met in July that year to discuss further. The final version presented here benefited from the typically generous and always forthright comments that I have been fortunate enough to receive from the artist numerous times over the years, beginning with my first attempts to reckon with his work in the mid 1980s. I still cannot believe that I can never again send my thoughts over to Mike and that they will never again be leavened, chastised and surprised by his unique and richly creative intelligence.

1 For more on the relation of Kelley's work to theories of institutionalisation and the art world movement known as Institutional Critique, see my 'L'arte e le institutione: Riempire (e cancellare) dei vuoti', in Stefano Chiodi (ed.), *Le funzioni del museo: Arte, museo, pubblico nella contemporaneità* (Florence, 2009), pp. 12–37; and 'God, Family, Fun, and Friends: Mike Kelley in Conversation with John C. Welchman', in Welchman (ed.), *Institutional Critique and After* (Zurich, 2006), pp. 337–66.

2 Mike Kelley, 'In The Image of Man', statement for The Carnegie International 1991, Carnegie Museum of Art, Pittsburgh; in Mike Kelley, *Minor Histories: Statements, Conversations, Proposals*, ed. John C. Welchman (Cambridge, MA, 2004), pp. 50–54; see also my 'Survey: The Mike Kelleys' in *Mike Kelley* (London, 1999), pp. 62–4.

3 Mike Kelley, 'The Poetry of Form' [1995], in *Minor Histories*, p. 96.

4 Roland Barthes, 'Rhetoric of the Image' [1964], in *Image, Music Text*, ed. and trans. Stephen Heath (New York, 1977). See also, in the same volume, 'The Photographic Message' and 'The Third Meaning'.

5 For a discussion of the fraught relations between the ephemeral artwork and its documentation, see Martha Buskirk's essay on Allan Kaprow, in Chapter 4 of this volume.

6 See Mike Kelley's statement on *The Poltergeist* (1979) in *Minor Histories*, pp. 252–7.

7 See Jane Mills, *The Money Shot: Cinema, Sin and Censorship* (New South Wales, 2001) and Linda Williams, *Hard Core: Power, Pleasure and the 'Frenzy of the Visible'* (Berkeley, 1999), especially p. 101.

8 Mike Kelley, 'The Aesthetics of Ufology' [1997/2002], in *Minor Histories*, p. 403.

9 The *Dust Ball* photographs were shown at Metro Pictures Gallery, New York in an exhibition titled *Mike Kelley: 13 New Untitled Black and White Photographs*, 3 December to 22 December 1994, and also at the Rosamund Felsen Gallery in Los Angeles.

10 My discussion of *Untitled (Dust Balls)* is based on an interview with Kelley at the artist's studio, 10 July 2010; all citations from the artist are from this source.

11 Mike Kelley, 'Introduction to *Reconstructed History*' [1990], in *Minor Histories*, pp. 28–31; *With Malice toward None* is reproduced on p. 29.

12 Kelley, 'Introduction to *Reconstructed History*', in *Minor Histories*, p. 31.

13 Curated by MaryAnn Wilkinson and Rebecca Hart, the exhibition was shown at the Detroit Institute of Arts in 2001.

14 Mike Kelley, 'Black Out' [2001], in *Minor Histories*, p. 159.

15 Ibid., p. 159.

16 All quotations in the paragraph are from ibid., p. 158.

17 I discuss this important, but rather overlooked, project, in 'Ideas Being Given: Joseph Kosuth's Media and Public Projects from the *Second Investigation* (1969) to 2006', lecture delivered at 'Die Aktualität der Conceptual Art', Kunsthistorisches Institut der Rheinischen Friedrich-Wilhelms-Universität Bonn and Kunstmuseum Bonn (6 and 7 July 2007); publication in progress.

18 See Sarah Charlesworth, 'Unwriting: Notes on Modern History', in *Sarah Charlesworth: Modern History (Second Reading)* (Edinburgh, 1979).

19 See note 17, above.

20 See Mike Kelley, 'Some Aesthetic Highpoints' [1991], in *Minor Histories*, pp. 40–48; citation from Kelley's introduction to the reprint, p. 40.

21 Kelley, 'Black Out', in *Minor Histories*, p. 160.

22 Ibid., p. 160.

23 Ibid., p. 161.

24 Ibid.

25 This discussion of *Day Is Done* draws on my essay 'Fête Accompli', for Mike Kelley, *Day Is Done* (New York, 2006; New Haven and London, 2007).

8

Chance/Lens (Subversive Translation)

Simon Baker

> Surrealism is *mutism*: if it spoke it would cease to be what it wanted to be, but if it failed to speak it could only lead itself to misunderstanding. (Georges Bataille)[1]

Inventive and influential curatorial gambits at the turn of the twenty-first century, exemplified by the exhibitions *L'Informe: mode d'emploi* (Pompidou Centre, Paris, 1996) and *Surrealism: Desire Unbound* (Tate Modern, London, 2001) have linked the notions of surrealism's avant-garde postures and activities with both post-war and contemporary art, emphasising the elasticity of the term 'surrealism' and suggesting a proliferation of ways in which it can be seen to have had an impact.[2] It seems only natural that this expanded field should include both the legacies of surrealist practice, in visual and literary cultures, and the legacies of theoretical debates that garnered much of their weight from the ballast that surrealism provides. It also seems clear that the legacy of the journal *October*, both in terms of its making available new translations, and from the influential theoretical perspectives offered (primarily) by Rosalind Krauss and Hal Foster, has had the side-effect of legitimising certain kinds of surrealisms at the expense of others. This is an argument that has been put forward very effectively by David Hopkins in relation to the work of Matthew Barney.[3] But even those contemporary artists, like Thomas Hirschhorn or Mike Kelley, who have been steeped in the radical chic offered by Georges Bataille, would probably still balk at the idea of being associated in any way with Magritte, soft clocks, or a visual grammar of truncated female body parts. The concern of one contemporary artist contacted by this author is perhaps symptomatic: 'You *do know* I have nothing to do with surrealism, don't you?' And similarly, in a 2003 interview for *Papers of Surrealism*, Jake Chapman is very careful to differentiate between the surrealist co-ordinates with whom he identifies, like Sade, Nietzsche and Freud, and actual surrealists, whom, he suggests, should have been shot for crimes committed in the name of idealism.[4] The Chapman brothers, it is worth mentioning, openly acknowledge their employment of obvious surrealist techniques such as the 'exquisite corpse' but do not accept that this means buying into the aims associated with the movement.[5]

A similar argument might be made for the 'automatic writing' at the heart of Pierre Bismuth's series of 2004–2005 works 'Following the right hand of' actresses (Marlene Dietrich, Rita Hayworth, Liz Taylor) in famous films (*The Blue Angel, You'll Never Get Rich, Suddenly Last Summer*):[6] the apparently automatic results represent an obsessive retracing of movement, revealing or realising an overlooked trajectory rather than, as it might appear, creating an 'original' graphic work in the surrealist mould. The complexity of the example that Bismuth offers is evident in the compound nature of these works, which resolve rather than highlight the conflict of interest between means and ends. It could therefore be argued that at the start of the twenty-first century, surrealism is truly, to borrow a surrealist expression, 'd'abord et toujours' (first and always), but not necessarily in the forms that its founders and adherents imagined. This essay will argue that it is the radical possibilities offered by surrealist theories of process that continue to offer a way forward for the current generation of artists, long after the embarrassing stigma of misogynistic imagery and political idealism have been consigned to history books.

This is the context into which I would like to introduce the work of contemporary American sculptor Melissa McGill: in terms not only of a very specific legacy of surrealist practice, but also of the textual mythology of that practice. McGill, who works and exhibits primarily in the United States, has risen in prominence in Europe following an initial 2003 exhibition of work in Louise Neri's influential series *Inside the White Cube* in London.[7] McGill subsequently had a solo exhibition in Bologna in 2004, curated by Germano Celant, and had works selected by Marina Warner for the impressive 2005 exhibition *Only Make Believe: Ways of Playing*.[8] Taken together, the works exhibited in these shows form the basic subject matter for this essay, with a particular focus on the sculptures, wall-mounted work, and photographs that were shown together at White Cube (Figure 8.1). It was through my discussions with the artist at the time of this exhibition (and subsequently) that it became clear that the process through which these works were produced had much in common with one of the most fascinating surrealist origin stories: the one where André Breton and Alberto Giacometti are supposed to have 'found' objects by searching in a flea market.[9] Surrealism is full of equivalent parables, seductive half-truths offered up for inspection and dissection. There is another of Breton's memories, recounted to great effect by Hal Foster, in which the soon-to-be surrealist encounters a shell-shocked soldier traumatised into the belief that the Great War was a fake, elaborately staged to fool him, 'with the wounded made up cosmetically and the dead on loan from medical schools'.[10] These surrealist episodes can be described as 'origin stories' because they share the didactic logic of the explanatory myths of many complex systems of thought and belief. Just as the poetic imagination of the shell-shocked soldier speaks volumes about the paucity of reality for Breton (and hence Foster), the idea that Giacometti could only finish a sculpture through the intervention of an object found with Breton has always seemed too good (and too useful) to be true. This is not to say that it is not, but that surely it is the significance that Breton attaches to this process that animates the object, contextualising it, before dropping it, all moodily lit, in front of Man Ray's camera lens (Figure 8.2). McGill, as I will show, engages both with the intervention of chance (*hasard*) and the lens (*objectif*) within the sculptural process, thereby realising something implicit in Breton's mythology of the found object that is never openly admitted.

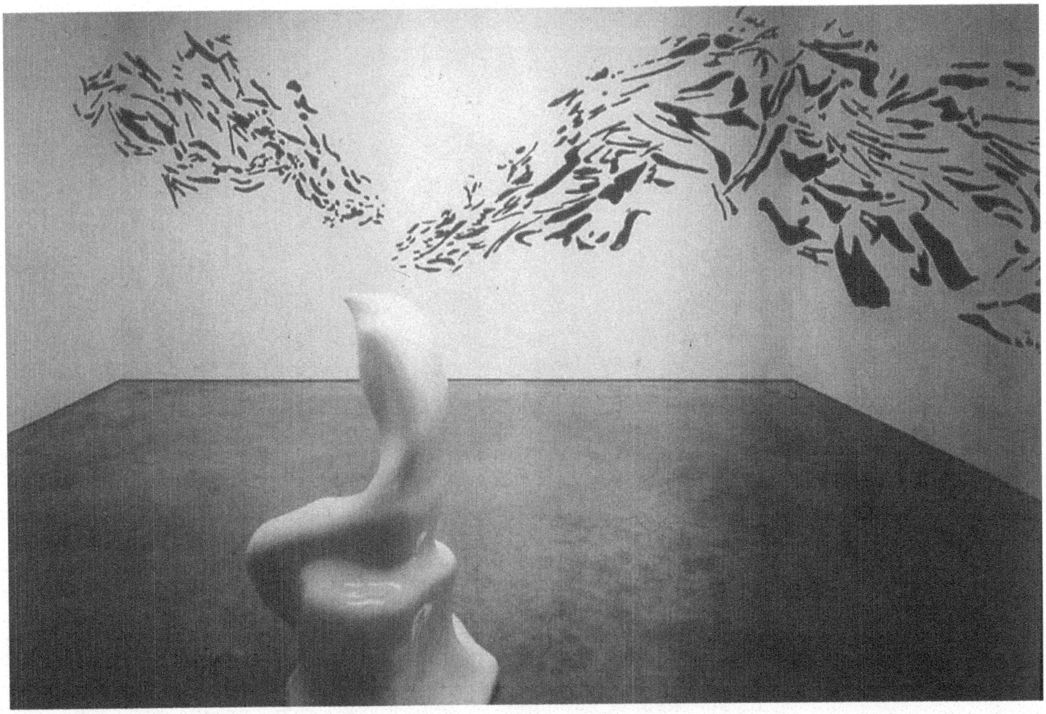

8.1 Installation shot of Melissa McGill's *Inside the White Cube* exhibition, White Cube, London, 6 May – 1 June 2003; *Untitled*, porcelain (foreground), 2002, and *Shadow of Ecstasy* (rear left on wall), 2003. Courtesy the artist

Describing the Giacometti episode (which is supposed to have taken place in 1934) as an origin story for the found object requires an acknowledgement that Breton's interest in such surrealist objects dates back into the 1920s, giving rise to both textual and physical manifestations. There is, for example, the well-known and well-fetishised bronze glove reproduced with the memorable caption 'also a woman's glove' in his 1928 book *Nadja*.[11] Here, the object is offered as the material residue of a narrative about a woman who visits the surrealist 'centrale' (a research bureau) and is asked to leave behind one of her 'remarkable sky-blue gloves'.[12] The image in *Nadja* is of the alternative that she offers in its place, 'a bronze one she happened to possess ... also a woman's glove, the wrist folded over, the fingers flat' that Breton (apparently) 'can never resist picking up'.[13]

This example from *Nadja* epitomises Breton's mythology of the object, as it is crafted into, and by, the text that it is supposed to have generated. In Breton's imagination, the complicity of the object is intrinsic to its effectiveness. But the involuntary nature of the associations that Breton claims for the object is underpinned as well as undermined by his insistence on the visual remainder, that is to say, by the striking availability of the image on the page. It is not just a story about a pair of gloves, one cloth, and one bronze, but a semiotic game put in play by the image that, when reproduced in grainy black and white, is able to stand for either (or both). For Breton, perhaps it is a surrealist object first and then, also, a woman's glove.

Breton's key theoretical texts on the object date from 1934 to 1936, by no means coincidentally a period of crisis and consolidation for surrealist thought, encompassing the rise and fall of the revolutionary group Contre-Attaque,

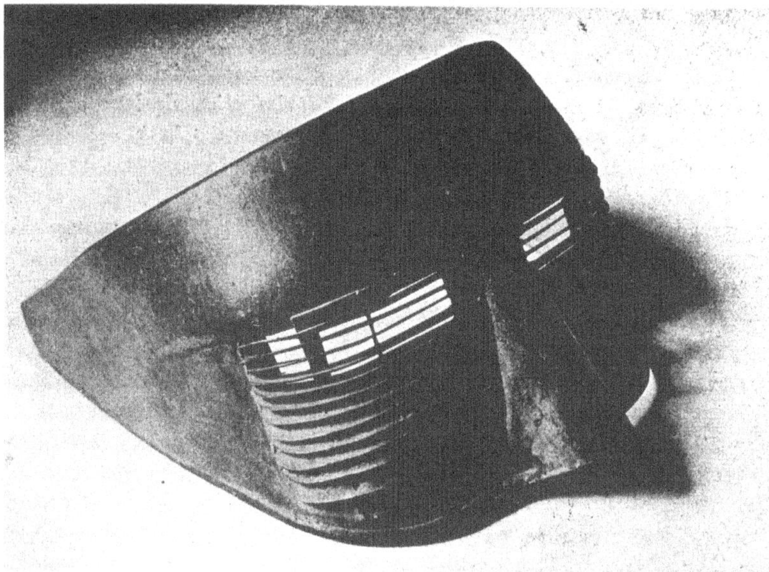

PHOTO MAN RAY

d'abord retenus. Bien que le caractère remarquablement définitif de cet objet semblât échapper au marchand qui nous pressait de l'acheter en suggérant de le peindre d'une couleur vive et de le faire monter en lanterne, Giacometti, pourtant très détaché en général de toute idée de possession à propos de telles choses, le reposa à regret, parut chemin faisant concevoir des craintes sur sa destination prochaine, finalement revint sur ses pas pour l'acquérir. A quelques boutiques de là, un choix presque aussi électif se porta pour moi sur une grande cuiller en bois, d'exécution paysanne, mais assez belle, me sembla-t-il, assez hardie de forme, dont le manche, lorsqu'elle reposait sur sa partie convexe, s'élevait de la hauteur d'un petit soulier faisant corps avec elle. Je l'emportai aussitôt.

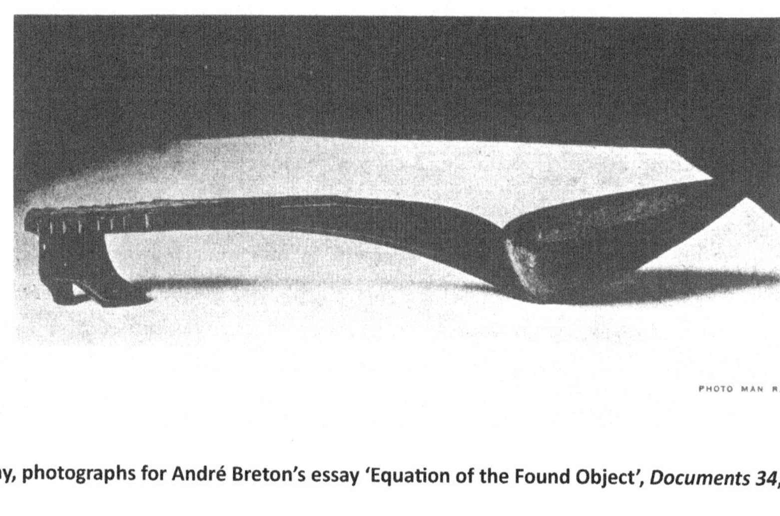

PHOTO MAN RAY

8.2 Man Ray, photographs for André Breton's essay 'Equation of the Found Object', *Documents 34*, 1934

in which he worked with Georges Bataille for the first time.[14] 'Situation of the Surrealist Object' was given as a lecture in Prague in March 1935.[15] His essay 'The Crisis of the Object' accompanied the 1936 exhibition of surrealist objects and a special edition of *Cahiers d'art* in the same year.

The best-known Breton text, however, most accessible without (and outside) surrealism, is the third section of the 1937 book *L'Amour fou* (*Mad Love*). It is, for example, this mannered and polished presentation of the found object that is highlighted by Alex Potts in his authoritative book *The Sculptural Imagination*.[16] *Mad Love* includes a Dora Maar photograph of what Breton describes as Giacometti's 'statue', *Hands Holding the Void (Invisible Object)*, and two photographs of found objects taken by Man Ray (Figure 8.2). Although completed in this form in 1936, it consists principally of a text originally entitled 'Equation of the Found Object', which appeared with the same illustrations two years earlier, in the Belgian surrealist journal *Documents 34*.[17] The 1934 'equation of the found object' however, assumed its place in a complex network of political associations, so Breton's text, the Dora Maar and the Man Ray photographs appear alongside revolutionary calls to action in the present, as well references to historical revolt in the figures of Sade and Gracchus Babeuf.[18] This context, I would argue, draws Breton's text into a series of responses to calls for direct action, entrenching the idea of faithful adherence to surrealist practices defined as appropriate by Breton in the *Second Manifesto of Surrealism*. It might also, it is tempting to suggest, have stood as a rebuttal to scathing political critiques of aesthetic flea-marketeering such as that offered by Ilya Ehrenburg's in his 1933 book *My Paris*. It is almost certainly the surrealists who, he says, come to the flea market 'to satisfy a secret passion ... in love with the loveliness of indigence'.[19]

In addition to the first 1934 draft of what would become the established account of the found object in *Mad Love*, Breton also contributed what appears to be a visual coda to the text later in *Documents 34*: a murky (and un-attributed) photograph of an assemblage combining virtuoso serviette-folding with arcane instructions entitled 'Communication relative au hasard objectif' (Communication Pertaining to Objective Chance).[20] What, at first glance might appear to be a rather droll warning about the effect of too much starch in the diet, should instead be regarded as a carefully contrived *tableau mordant*, complete with Dalí-esque slices of half-eaten bread. However, despite its unequivocal claim of relevance to the principle to which its title refers, Breton's communication could not have been expected to last, and it seems subsequently to have slipped away from the term that it apparently represents.[21]

It is worth remembering, however, that by the time Breton revisited the concept of 'objective chance' for the publication of *Mad Love*, it had become central to the surrealist movement as he then saw it. What is most obvious in the book (as the use of its title for the groundbreaking 1986 exhibition *L'Amour fou: Photography and Surrealism* suggests) is the reconfiguring of the role of the photographic image.[22] It is certainly *not* by chance that *Mad Love* contains work by Brassaï and Henri Cartier-Bresson, in addition to the expected contributions by Man Ray (which Breton had reproduced with previously published texts). Breton's use of Brassaï in particular stands as a reclamation of the discursive possibilities of the medium exploited in previous surrealist publications but long-since recuperated by the mainstream media. Brassaï's photographs of Paris at night, for example (like similar work produced by André Kertész and Germaine Krull) were published in a wide range of contexts in France in the early 1930s, culminating with Brassaï's 1932 book *Paris by Night*.[23] The difference effected by this avowedly non-surrealist context provides an illuminating foil for Breton's choice of illustrations in *Mad Love*. Ian Walker recounts another of Breton's origin stories which binds Brassaï's photograph of the Tour Saint-Jacques into the logic of objective chance: in this instance, Breton asks Brassaï to produce a photograph of the medieval anomaly for the section of *Mad Love* also published as an essay called 'The Night of the Sunflower', only to find that Brassaï had independently and serendipitously already taken the very photograph that Breton desired of the tower, 'beneath its ghostly veil of scaffolding'.[24]

In *Mad Love* Breton returned to his own 1934 text on the found object with a renewed sense of purpose, in terms of the poetic role of the photographic image, but he could also demonstrate the utility of the medium. Between 1934 and 1936, the objects reproduced at the heart of Breton's text had been recognised from Man Ray's photographs. The mask that, according to Breton, was responsible for the angular visage of Giacometti's 'statue' was resituated in its proper historical moment through the reminiscences of Joë Bousquet, who had seen the mask in *Documents 34* and written Breton a letter describing its specific wartime use.[25] In this way, the object 'found,' photographed, and published, subsequently 'found' yet another alternative narrative; what Breton called its 'evil role'.[26] The object's complex and ever changing afterlife, rather than making it somehow 'disagreeable', fulfilled Breton's wish that it continue to multiply in significance, drawing its various viewers, through time, into a complicit web. The role of spectatorship in this process is crucial:

> I recently learned that while Giacometti and I were examining this object, we had been *seen without seeing them* by two people who had just, a few seconds before, been handling the mask: one of these people, whom I lost sight of years ago, is none other than the person to whom the last pages of *Nadja* are addressed, and who is designated by the letter X in *Les Vases Communicants*, the other being her friend. Although she was intrigued by the mask, she had put it down as I had.

A little further on, Breton continues: 'an encounter so precisely based upon such an object, led me to think that in this moment it becomes the precipitate of the "death instinct" ...'.[27]

As this short extract from *Mad Love* demonstrates, the found object only *gradually* comes to symbolise the death instinct as it circulates within the surrealist crowd. Or perhaps it would be more accurate to say, in the surrealist library, as the spectators present when they are found are conflated with and through Breton's own surrealist texts. It is also striking that the mask, which would clearly inhibit vision, is framed in the text by the phrases 'been seen without seeing them' and 'whom I lost sight of'. Within this process of the accumulation of significance, Breton confesses, such objects 'measure their strength on me, blow by blow'.[28]

It is evident from this brief sketch of Breton's account of the found object that a key attribute was its ability to multiply the potential for representation within a carefully ordered and retrospectively rehearsed viewing context. For this process to work, everyday objects must retain the ability to surprise and disturb without associative elaboration (that is to say, in advance of umbrella-and-sewing-machine style juxtapositions). There is, however, a clause in this apparent democratisation of the sculptural marvellous that Breton refers to as 'circumstantial magic', namely that it is the perceptual regime into which the object is introduced that dignifies its 'found' status. And this is precisely where photography comes into play: 'circumstantial magic' is, after all, the title given by Breton to one of Brassaï's close-up photographs of a sprouting potato.[29]

This effect can be contrasted with the logic at work in Jacques-André Boiffard's photographs of monuments for Robert Desnos's 1930 *Documents* essay 'Pygmalion and the Sphinx'.[30] Despite being aimed squarely at their targets, Boiffard's shots of statues like Charles Antoine Coysevox's Louis XIV effectively rob the objects of their monumental function, cancelling them out and drawing attention instead to their pedestals (the magic of disappearance rather than the 'circumstantial magic' of the close-up).[31] It could, however, be argued that despite the materialist opposition of the authors of *Documents* to mainstream surrealism, Boiffard anticipates precisely subsequent masterpieces of photographic *de-materialisation* like Brassaï's better-known *Marshal Ney in the Fog* and *Tour Saint-Jacques* published in *Minotaure* (the latter reselected for *Mad Love*). In fact, all Breton's found objects (from masks to medieval edifices) are imbued with a superlative aesthetic quality in spite of nods towards their banal heritages. This change in register (an involuntary manifestation of significant form) is perhaps apparent in the installations for the exhibitions of surrealist objects (with their glass-cased faux empiricism), but it is overwhelming in the photographs that not only record, but actually *produce* found objects for Breton's texts, preserving their found status intact in perpetuity. It is here that we find the crux of the argument about involuntary sculpture, which lies neither in the operation of chance, nor the sculptural process, but in the mediation of vision. As Breton himself argues in 'Situation of the Surrealist Object': 'By fully mechanizing the plastic mode of representation, photography must deal it the decisive blow.'[32]

Coming back to the photographs that accompany Breton's original discussion of the found object (Man Ray's mask and 'slipper-spoon'), the idea of the 'touch' of photography (a restraining of its ability to deal blows) becomes a powerful one. It makes Man Ray a *de facto* fourth handler, following Breton and Giacometti even as they followed the un-named woman in the flea market in feeling their way around the strange contours of the metal mask. And despite Breton's fear that for Giacometti 'any feminine intervention was likely to be harmful', it was Dora Maar who added the finishing touch to the sculptor's 'invisible object', permitting the smooth passage of the 'personage féminin' into a narrative where women were usually designated by an 'X'. If we return to *Documents 34* and Breton's 'Communication relative au hasard objectif', *objective chance*, can also, but not by chance, be read as *chance lens*. The camera, with only the lightest of touches, cuts a glass in two with the blade of a knife. It is, I would suggest, the intervention of the camera that dramatises the role of the spectator in the production of the found object, revealing this decisive touch.[33]

Melissa McGill works with pre-existing images and objects to reveal what could be called 'found space' through a process that moves from found objects, through the camera's lens, to sculptural form: an involuntary revitalisation of Breton's origin story. It is significant to note in this context that McGill worked for many years as a picture editor, and has compiled an archive of 'found' photographs which, although never exhibited alongside her work, form a visual context for her sculptural processes. A recent exhibition catalogue reproduced a selection of these images which include classical figures, fragments of sculpture and Chinese manuscripts.[34] I would suggest that the role of this archive is analogous to the wall of Breton's study, petrified in its glass case in the Pompidou Centre, which tells us everything we need to know about how Breton mediated objects that we only ever experience in their mediated form. Like McGill's archive, it is far from being merely a record of choices, or revelatory source for inspiration or formal content. For McGill, it is the process of selectively and critically reading her own photographic archive that is critical to her sculptural practice, in which the photograph always already presents an assisted found object, if only through the dramatisation of light and shadow evident in Man Ray's work for Breton, or Boiffard's disappearing Louis XIV.

It would be true to say that McGill's wall-mounted work, *Shadow of Ecstasy* depends for its form on Bernini's baroque sculpture *The Ecstasy of St Theresa* (see Figure 8.1). But it is not enough to point out this derivative relationship, to seek to resolve the original work through the refracting lens of its descendant. The final work, the shadow, has the most fragile of relationships to the object that lends its form, a relationship that admits and insists upon the camera's presence. It would be more accurate to say that *Shadow of Ecstasy* is based not on Bernini's sculpture, but on a specific photograph of the three-dimensional original. To produce her 'shadows', McGill projects a slide of this already mediated image onto the studio wall, stretching and/or reversing the projection, producing the kind of hugely distorted and flattened Bernini familiar to any art history student taking a slide test. McGill not only accepts and works with this distortion, but accentuates the manipulative potential of the camera lens as it collapses depth and shadow into dark flat patches. The misleading shapes produced by the projection are then duplicated in a shiny black rubber, producing a series of new forms that represent both darkness and depth as interchangeable equivalents. Multiplied and installed on the gallery wall, these cast rubber shadows offer their own responses to light, both individually and collectively, as the viewer moves within the space of the work. In places, the arrangements of shiny black forms double, as they in turn catch the light reflected across the corners of the rooms around which they spread. This complex play of reflections is as evident in photographs of the finished work as the shadows in the photographic projection on which it was based.

The accidental or involuntary aspect of the way in which the camera misleadingly captures light, suggesting shadow as form, is key to another series of works in which McGill employs photographs of a three-dimensional sculpture: this time Bernini's *Apollo and Daphne*. In this case, the medium is liquid rubber, dripped and poured onto a paper surface on which the image is projected, in an attempt to account for the areas of shadow with a substance that, unlike the carefully cast patches of the *Shadow of Ecstasy*, is almost impossible to control. The resulting work is a frantic, black and white account of what are, in fact, only slight differences in shades of grey, sometimes subtle shadows cast on stone, sometimes the spaces in between sculpted forms. The absurdity of attempting to capture a sculpture in the round, through a medium which, even in colour, insistently reduces form to black and white is revealed: the camera inadvertently produces a new work every time.

Both McGill's *Shadow of Ecstasy* and the rubber drawing based on *Apollo and Daphne* demonstrate an attitude to the photograph and the use of the camera within a process that relates closely to the way that both Man Ray and Dora Maar activate Breton's mythology of the found object. But McGill has also produced a series of works that follow directly in the footsteps of the original flea market search, returning to, and insisting upon, the potential for *trouvailles* to reveal secrets. It is this series of sculptures and photographs that I would suggest offer the most compelling legacy of the mythology of the surrealist object.

A set of small photographs, produced in collaboration with the photographer Ellis Michael Quinn, introduced McGill's large scale untitled porcelain 'personages' at the White Cube exhibition (Figure 8.3). A crowd of smiling, colourful figurines, brilliantly lit and uncannily close: coy pixies, blushing urchins, diminutive oriental figures, a metallic-shirted accordion player with a tiny head. Without the aesthetic gloss of professional photography, the ensemble could have suggested any selection of unfashionable collectables: like a grandmother's overcrowded cabinet of miniature china shoes. But these merry figurines, sought out in junk-shops and markets, and redeemed for the artist by the camera, are intimately connected with the larger porcelain forms that they introduce in the gallery space.

The result of the process by which these little ornamental crimes were mass-produced means that within each tiny figure is an un-looked for, unheeded space, which McGill 'finds', reveals and reconstitutes. So at the moment that it was photographed, the tiny, disproportionate accordion player already contained the form of the porcelain sculpture many times its size. In practical terms, the process by which one gives birth to the other is logical but complex, and anything but involuntary. First, a silicone cast of the interior is made, the liberation of which entails the destruction of the coloured figurine, leaving a small rubber form, which accounts precisely for the inner space of the lost object. The moment that the figurine is smashed is the first time that this new form will ever have been seen, leaving the photograph of the original with a strangely mournful relationship to the final sculpture. This found shape is then used to produce a mould from which any number of identical forms can be cast, either in rubber or porcelain. In the case of the White Cube exhibition, the moulds used were magnified to many times their original scale – human-size rather than figurine-size – and were cast and fired by the artist at the Kohler porcelain factory in Wisconsin (see Figure 8.1).[35]

What interests me about the finished works is not just the found status of the spaces that the finished personages represent, but the circular relationship between the photograph of the lost original figurine and the finished porcelain

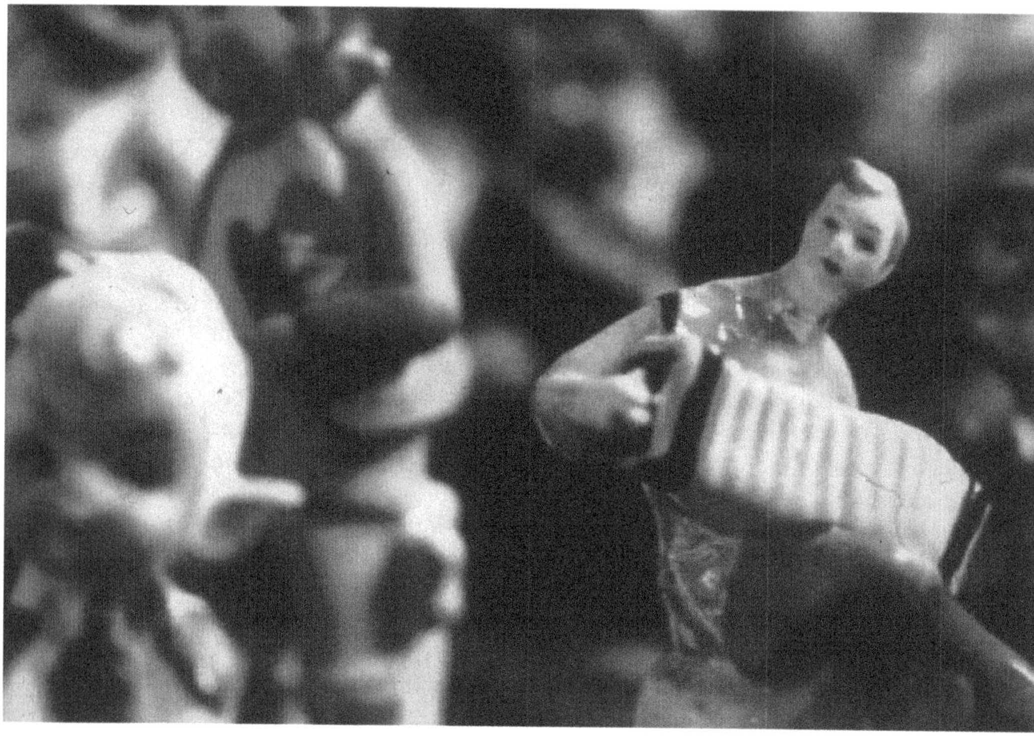

8.3 Melissa McGill and Ellis Michael Quinn, *Untitled*, C-print, 2000. Courtesy the artist

sculpture which, when exhibited together, cannot help but suggest an umbilical link. In the course of its production and subsequent reception, the finished work turns against and opposes its progenitor, through its form, scale, colour and surface. These descriptive differences are key to the antinomies of abstraction and legibility. Through what can accurately be called a *process* of abstraction, an easily recognisable figure offers something disarmingly unlike itself. In these terms, abstraction, rather than operating in opposition to figuration, is confirmed as that which figuration produces under pressure. The accordion player is readily legible, while its sculptural counterpart resists rather than refuses the idea of the body in a series of counterpoints.

The contradiction in scale is the most immediately obvious; after all, the porcelain personage is many times larger than the original space from which it was drawn. It is, as I have pointed out, a very deliberate move to scale the object in relation to the viewer rather than the figurine; that is to say, to its destination rather than its origin. This difference is reinforced by the transformation in colour and tone from kitsch exuberance to neutral monochrome. However, given that it is the internal logic of the original figurine that is relevant here, what occurs is less of a rejection of colour than a reversal of surfaces. The surface usually left unfinished, facing the void inside the object, is reversed and accorded the fine polish normally reserved for exteriors. A further feature of the porcelain personage is that it too was cast and contains its own internal space, suggesting far more than just an anamorphic similarity but a narrative of infinite regression; an endless series of found spaces.

Elsewhere in McGill's earlier work, the found spaces are cast in rubber and porcelain to the same scale as the original objects and like their forebears they too are displayed and photographed in groups (Figure 8.4). These group photographs are compelling in that they treat the forms as figures in the absence of the attributes necessary to confirm them as such, raising the question of whether these objects individually or cumulatively suggest the human form. In this way, the found, cast interiors of absent others retain a collective identity, primarily suggested by their scale, but then confirmed by a gentle gradient from near-complete figure to unidentifiable abstraction. The effect is a kind of involuntary figuration where the result of the original casting process leaves an alternative figure with an accidental pathos every bit as ludicrous and tragic as that of the original figurines.

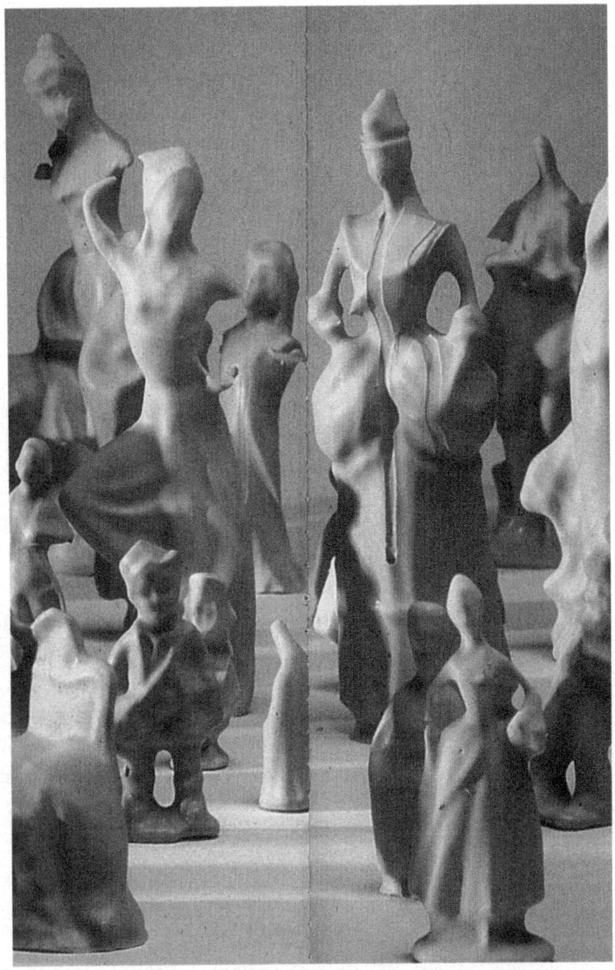

8.4 Melissa McGill, *Untitled*, porcelain, 2000. Courtesy the artist

Despite the series of oppositional aspects of the relationship between form and space there remains the material continuity: the porcelain itself, transformed, made unlike itself, uncomfortable with its own skin. Porcelain could be said to have its own significance, from fragile, and thus precious, commercial collectibles to industrial-strength, mass-produced toilets and bath tubs. *Fountain*, Marcel Duchamp's most famous porcelain 'sculpture' offers an inviting point of reference for McGill's work, which returns to the source material of the original readymade to redirect the found object in the direction of found space. *Fountain*, however, like McGill's accordion player, was only the beginning of a process of abstractions from an original object to a finished sculptural form. Duchamp's *Fountain*, the result of the simplest act of appropriation, was subsequently complicated by the intervention of Alfred Stieglitz. In the light and shadow of an ordinary urinal, as it lay on its porcelain back, Stieglitz photographed the miraculous outline of the Madonna, her intimate plumbing crudely denoted by the shadow cast in a pipe hole.[36]

In McGill's work, the camera, and the decisive touch that it brings, are so deeply implicated in the production of sculptural form that photography persistently haunts the finished work. The spaces found and realised as objects, whose surfaces were never meant to see the light of day, remain subject to the insistent companionship of the lens. Some of the most striking examples of McGill's work can be found where the play of forms accommodates and accentuates this interdependence. For Breton, the found object offered the solution to a sculptural problem, made visible to the viewer through photography. Here, the found object is an enigma, for which photography is the resolution, made visible to the viewer through sculptural form.

Notes

1 The author would like to thank Jay Joplin and White Cube for permission to republish, in an expanded form, material that originally appeared as the short text 'Hands Holding the Void' in the catalogue to the series of exhibitions *Antipodes: Inside the White Cube*, edited by Louise Neri and published in 2003. Thanks also go to Anna Dezeuze and Julia Kelly for the opportunity to present this material at the 'Involuntary Sculpture' conference. Finally, sincere thanks to Melissa McGill for the honest and generous discussions, without which this essay would not have been possible.

Georges Bataille, 'Surrealism', in *The Absence of Myth: Writings on Surrealism*, trans. and introduction Michael Richardson (London and New York: 1994), p. 56.

2 I would also draw attention, in this context, to the establishment in 2002 of a research centre for the study of 'Surrealism and Its Legacies' (a collaboration between the Universities of Essex, Manchester and the Tate galleries in the United Kingdom) directed by Dawn Ades, David Lomas and Jennifer Mundy (at Essex, Manchester and the Tate respectively). See www.surrealismcentre.ac.uk/ (accessed: 18 January 2011).

3 In fact Hopkins traces Barney's work through both dada and surrealism. See the catalogue for his 2006 exhibition at the Fruitmarket Gallery in Edinburgh, *Dada's Boys* (New Haven and London, 2006).

4 'Jake Chapman on Bataille, an interview with Simon Baker', *Papers of Surrealism*, 1 (Winter 2003), www.surrealismcentre.ac.uk/papersofsurrealism/journal1/index.htm (accessed: 18 January 2011).

5 Examples of the Chapmans' exquisite corpse drawings can be seen in the following sources: Jake and Dinos Chapman, *Hell* (London, 2003), pp. 127–37; Jake and Dinos Chapman, *Like a Dog Returns to its Vomit* (London, 2005), pp. 12–27.

6 *Pierre Bismuth*, trans. Susan Pickford (Paris, 2005), pp. 52–5,110–11 and 137.

7 The catalogue for the series was published as Louise Neri (ed.), *Antipodes: Inside the White Cube* (London, 2003). McGill's work is reproduced on pp. 130–41 and p. 166.

8 Marina Warner, *Only Make Believe: Ways of Playing* (Compton Verney, 2005). McGill was exhibited alongside Hans Bellmer, and her work is reproduced in the catalogue pp. 64–5.

9 André Breton, *Mad Love*, trans. M.A. Caws (Lincoln and London, 1987), pp. 25–38.

10 Hal Foster, *Compulsive Beauty* (Cambridge, MA, and London, 1993), p. xi.

11 André Breton, *Nadja*, trans. R. Howard (New York, 1960), plate 16, p. 57.

12 Breton, *Nadja*, pp. 55–6. On the role of the 'centrale' in generating surrealist objects, see Julia Kelly, 'The Bureau of Surrealist Research' in Therese Lichtenstein (ed.), *Twilight Visions: Surrealism and Paris* (Berkeley and Los Angeles, 2009), pp. 79–101.

13 Breton, *Nadja*, p. 56.

14 For an in-depth account of Contre-Attaque and its relation to the production of surrealist objects see Steven Harris, 'Coup d'oeil', *Oxford Art Journal*, 24(1) (2004), pp. 89–112; chapter 5 of his book, *Surrealist Art and Thought in the 1930s: Art, Politics and the Psyche* (Cambridge, 2004), pp. 178–218; and also Simon Baker, '*Psychologie des Foules*: Surrealism and the Impossible Object', in Brandon Taylor and Fiona Russell (eds), *Sculpture and Psychoanalysis* (Aldershot, 2006).

15 This lecture by André Breton is available in translation as 'Surrealist Situation of the Object', in Pontus Hulten (ed.), *The Surrealists Look at Art*, trans. M. Palmer and N. Cole (Venice, CA, 1990), pp. 159–88.

16 Alex Potts, *The Sculptural Imagination* (New Haven and London, 2000), pp. 117–24.

17 *Documents 34: Intervention Surréaliste* was published in Brussels in 1934 by E.L.T. Mesens and is no relation to the journal *Documents* published between 1929–31 in Paris by Georges Bataille, Michel Leiris and others. It is available in facsimile as *L'Arc* 37, Paris, n.d.

18 The journal begins with 'L'Action Immédiate' signed by the Belgian surrealist group but also has statements in favour of general strike and unity of action signed by the French surrealists. Many of the contributions are political in nature including Maurice Heine's 'Hommage' to Sade, a complex essay by René Crevel, 'Tandis que la Pointolle se Vulcanise la Baudruche' and Louis Scutenaire's 'La Justice Immanente' with its collage 'hommage à Babeuf'.

19 Ilya Ehrenburg, *My Paris* [1933], trans. O. Ready (Paris, 2005).

20 Ibid., p. 78.

21 This work by Breton seems to have attracted relatively little attention in discussions of the idea of objective chance, despite the fact that it is published in the same place as the first version of what would become perhaps his most important account of the concept.

22 Rosalind Krauss and Jane Livingston, *L'Amour Fou: Photography and Surrealism* (Washington D.C., New York and London, 1985).

23 Brassaï, *Paris de Nuit* (Paris, 1932), republished as *Paris by Night*, trans. S. Gilbert (Boston, London and New York, 1993).

24 Ian Walker, *City Gorged with Dreams: Surrealism and Documentary Photography in Interwar Paris* (Manchester, 2002), p. 149.

25 Breton, *Mad Love*, pp. 37–8, '2nd P.S. (1936)'.

26 Ibid., p. 38.

27 Ibid., p. 38.

28 Ibid., p. 38.

29 André Breton, 'La beauté sera convulsive', *Minotaure*, 1(5) (Paris, 1934), pp. 8–16.

30 Robert Desnos, 'Pygmalion et le Sphinx', *Documents*, 1 (1930), pp. 33–40.

31 Dawn Ades draws attention to this effect in her essay 'Photography and the Surrealist Text' in Krauss and Livingston (eds), *L'Amour Fou*, pp. 164–5. I discuss these images

in greater detail in 'Surrealism in the Bronze Age: statuephobia and the efficacy of metaphorical iconoclasm' in Stacy Boldrick and Richard Clay (eds), *Iconoclasm: Contested Objects, Contested Terms* (Aldershot, 2007), pp. 189–214.

32 Breton, 'Situation of the Surrealist Object', in *The Surrealists Look at Art*, p. 179.

33 In another context but also with respect to the relationship between photography and surrealist spectatorship, Rosalind Krauss has suggested that 'the [surrealist] condition of vision produces images', in *L'Amour Fou*, p. 25.

34 Neri (ed.), *Antipodes*, pp. 132–4.

35 Ibid., p. 166.

36 Alfred Stieglitz's photograph accompanies Louise Norton's essay 'The Buddha of the Bathroom' in *The Blind Man* 2 (May 1917). (This issue also contained Duchamp's 'defence' of his work, 'The Richard Mutt Case'.) See Francis Naumann, *Making Mischief: Dada Invades New York* (New York, 1997), pp. 89–91 and the catalogue *DADA* (Paris, 2005), pp. 192–3.

9

INVOLUNTARY PHOTOGRAPHY

Margaret Iversen

In 'The Surrealist Situation of the Object' (1935), André Breton called on poets and painters to incorporate in their work the 'precision of sensible forms'. This call was prompted by his Hegelian analysis of the problem of the visual arts in the post-romantic period when material things had proven inadequate to the task of conveying thought. Although poetry was deemed to be better suited to the task, it ran the risk of becoming introspective and abstract. To counter this, Breton urged that poetry should dialectically include its other: 'In the measure that poetry tends in time to predominate over the other arts, Hegel's magnificent analysis revealed that it increasingly manifests, *contradictorily*, the need to attain ... the precision of sensible forms.'[1] The surrealist poet is therefore obliged to go wandering in the world of devalued, accidental, heterogeneous things, epitomised by the flea market, dispersing himself amongst them and gathering them in. In the 1930s, Breton himself demonstrated this practice beautifully with his invention of the *poème-objet* – an assemblage of text punctuated by small *objets trouvés*.

In the same text, Breton offered a dialectical analysis of the situation of painting in a world where photography has taken over the mimetic function of representation. Painting is forced to retreat to the domain of inner perception, but this does not imply that painting detaches itself from external reality, for, as Breton insisted, there is no such thing as 'spontaneous generation' in mental reality any more than in physical reality.[2] Rather, '[t]he creations of the Surrealist painters that seem most free can naturally come into being only through their return to "visual residues" stemming from perception of the outside world'.[3] These 'residues' are visual impressions that have attracted constellations of formerly dissociated thoughts, giving them an unusual density and opacity. In other words, painting depends on the psychic trace of a chance encounter. Breton's conception of objective chance governing the encounter with the found object is indebted to his reading of Freud's *Beyond the Pleasure Principle*.[4] This is particularly evident in one of Breton's key formulations: 'Chance would be the form taken by external reality as it traces a path (*se fraie un chemin*) in the human unconscious.'[5] Margaret Cohen has pointed out that the verb Breton employs, *frayer*, is used by the French translator of *Beyond the Pleasure Principle* to render Freud's term *Bahnung* (facilitation), which has to do with laying down a permanent trace of an excitation.[6] Traumatic events bypass what Freud refers to as the protective crust of consciousness, leaving behind an indelible trace. Chance encounters touch on that raw nerve. Clearly, the 'found object' is not conceived, by Breton, as an ordinary empirical object, but rather as something more like an object of desire or one that precipitates a traumatic encounter. Such objects can only be approached obliquely, accidentally, involuntarily. Breton mobilised Freud on dreams and on trauma in order to give the Hegelian dialectic a more materialist texture; for him, the mind must be furnished with impressions, traces of the real, in the same measure as the world is penetrated by thought – it being understood that '*only the perception of the outside world had permitted the involuntary acquisition of the materials which mental representation is called up to use*'.[7]

In an important early essay, 'Introduction to the Discourse on the Paucity of Reality' (1924), Breton railed against the impoverishment of reality imposed by clichéd ordinary language and stale poetic tropes. He aimed to extend and amplify reality with a kind of literature that would be both imaginative and verifiable. To this end, he proposed fabricating and putting into circulation objects met with in dreams. He described one of his own dream encounters: in the open-air market near Saint-Malo, he found a book with a spine made out of a wooden gnome whose white beard was cut in the Assyrian fashion.[8] Breton does not tell us anything about the probable circumstances of his life that produced this bearded dream-book, but it puts me in mind of Freud's 'Dream of the Botanical Monograph' which was seeded by the visual residues left by a book he had chanced to see in a shop window.[9] Unlike Breton's, however, the book in Freud's dream is a case of an ordinary object being seized upon by the unconscious where it sprouts many tendrils of associations. Another case is the story told by Breton about Giacometti's sculpture, *Invisible Object* (1934), which had an indifferent face until he found a metal mask in a flea market (see Figure 8.2). Breton notes that before this lucky find 'there was lacking any reference to the real, something to lean on in the world of tangible objects'.[10] But the mask is far more than just tangible, for it turns out to have provoked in Giacometti latent anxieties about death. These examples illustrate the twin poles of a reciprocal movement practised by the surrealists, both to objectify the subjective and to subjectify the objective. Breton looks forward to the moment when poetic creations take on this tangible quality provided by the found object so that they may effect a 'peculiar shifting of the boundaries of the so-called real'.[11]

Photography would seem to have a special place marked out in this project of putting into circulation phantasmatic, yet precise and sensible forms. It is worth pointing out in this connection that anonymous photographs were amongst the objects found by chance by the surrealists, which, as Dawn Ades notes, were garnered from their hunting grounds in the street, junk shops and markets, popular and scientific magazines and elsewhere.[12] Breton's most direct statement on the matter compares it with automatic writing: 'The invention of photography has delivered a mortal blow to the old forms of expression, painting as well as poetry for which automatic writing, appearing at the end of the nineteenth century, is the true photography of thought.'[13] In short, photography is to vision as automatic writing is to thought. This formula makes it clear that the automatism of photography is valued as a way of by-passing consciousness, of short-circuiting intentionality and rationality. Even though sophisticated cameras are designed to produce predictable pictures in the hands of a skilled photographer, the automaticity of the process lends itself to unintended happy (or unhappy) accidents and even the most skilled photographers value this. As Walker Evans so eloquently put it, the camera excels at 'reflecting swift chance, disarray, wonder, and experiment'.[14]

How can photography be construed as involuntary? I want to argue that there is a link between the indexical character of the photograph and its involuntariness. Indexicality is often mobilised in the discourses of photography as though it functioned as a guarantor of mimetic verisimilitude, but this is based on a misunderstanding. In Charles Sanders Pierce's typology, the index is classified on the basis of its mode of inscription, that is, the close, sometimes causal, connection between the sign vehicle and the object. In his scheme, it is the icon that signifies by virtue of resemblance, and so photography is classed as a hybrid type of sign, part index, part icon, but it is presumably capable of emphasising either aspect.[15] In his 'Ontology of the Photograph', André Bazin exaggerates the bond between indexical image and object to the point of identification, yet he also makes a crucial point: 'No matter how fuzzy, distorted, or discolored, no matter how lacking in documentary value the image may be, it shares, by virtue of the process of its becoming, the being of the model of which it is the reproduction; it *is* the model.'[16] The slippage in this passage from fuzzy image to identity is clearly unjustified. Nevertheless, Bazin's remarks about the fuzzy image points to the fact that indexicality is a non-mimetic mode of representation – a point that I think has been insufficiently registered.

Man Ray's exploration of what he called the rayograph is an exemplary case of a type of photography that takes advantage of the *aniconic-indexical* aspect of the medium at the same time as it fosters an involuntary procedure. In 'Notes on the Index' (1977), Rosalind Krauss observes that the rayograph 'forces the issue of the photograph's existence as an index'. She describes the images resulting from putting objects directly onto light sensitive paper as the 'ghostly traces of departed objects';[17] Man Ray himself put it beautifully in terms that recall Breton's 'visual residues'. He called the rayograph 'a residue of an experience ... recalling the event more or less clearly, like the undisturbed ashes of an object consumed by flames'.[18] Although the rayograph may be classed as a studio trick, it is one that dispenses with the traditional craft of photography and involves a good deal of chance. Man Ray's more experimental photography might be understood as aiming at the 'the look of chance'. If one can take Man Ray's word for it, the techniques of solarisation and the rayograph were discovered by chance. The doubly exposed portrait of *La Marquise Casati* (1922) was, he claims, also an accident. In 'Photography is not an Art', Man Ray listed what he considered his 10 best photographs. Topping the list is 'an accidental snap-shot of a shadow between two other carefully posed pictures of a girl in a bathing suit'.[19] A photographer of great technical mastery, Man Ray could quip that he had learned 'to produce accidents at will'.[20] In an article on Man Ray, Susan Laxton observed that 'the Dada subject in the darkroom was no more than a conduit for the passive transcription of the irrationally white shadows of temporary assemblages'.[21] In my view, photography was one of the many techniques the surrealists used to circumvent intentionality, allowing the agency of chance to bring about the unexpected.[22] As with André Masson's automatic drawings, Max Ernst's *frottages* or the *Involuntary Sculptures* photographed by Brassaï (Figure I.1), the image precedes the idea or, better, the process precedes the image. This is perhaps why Breton believed that the 'blindness' of the camera gave it access to unconscious material normally only accessible to automatism and dream.[23] Ann Banfield has discussed this aspect of the medium, noting that 'what the photograph is sensible of can be outside the ego, a thought unthought, unintended, involuntary and without meaning'.[24]

Indexicality is a persistent theme in Rosalind Krauss's work. Her 'Notes on the Index', Parts I and II, are extended meditations on the theme. Part I is about Duchamp, and particularly his *Tu m'* which is said to present a 'panorama of the index'.[25] The article is also about the rise of photography in the 1970s. Part II concerns some installation work of the 1970s, in particular work displayed in P.S. 1 in 1976. Krauss argues that the index's evocation of 'sheer physical presence' short-circuits 'the more highly articulated languages of aesthetic conventions'. For her, the indexical sign, including the photograph, 'heralds a disruption of the autonomy of the sign. A meaninglessness surrounds it which can only be filled by the addition of a text.'[26] Its regressive aspect, 'its reduction of the conventional sign to the trace', is compensated for by the inclusion of a supplemental text. Of course, this might also serve to characterise the situation of surrealist photography, much of which was originally embedded in the pages of magazines or books. Yet, instead of opposing the mute photograph and compensatory text, my argument suggests that the surrealists regarded both writing and photography as hypersensitive recording instruments. This is more obviously the case with photography for, as Man Ray declared, 'photography is not limited to the role as copyist. It is a marvelous explorer of the aspects that our retina never records.'[27] Similarly, within the surrealist practice of automatic writing, the disturbances of language catalogued by Freud (slips, substitutions, memory blanks) all register the activity of the unconscious.

Barthes's *Camera Lucida* (1980) revived interest in the indexical and involuntary aspects of the photographic medium, in particular through his discussion of what he calls the *punctum* – an accidental detail in the photograph 'which rises from the scene, shoots out like an arrow, and pierces' him.[28] But why, particularly, do only photographs have *puncta*? It must surely have something to do with the combined indexicality and involuntariness of the medium. Michael Fried has drawn attention to the lack of intentionality that is productive of Barthes's *punctum*:

> The *punctum*, we might say, is *seen* by Barthes but not because it has been *shown* to him by the photographer, for whom it does not exist; as Barthes recognizes, 'it occurs [only] in the field of the photographed thing', which is to say that it is a pure artifact of the photographic event – 'the photographer could not *not* photograph the partial object at the same time as the total object' is how Barthes phrases it – or, perhaps more precisely, it is an artifact of the encounter between the product of that event and one particular spectator or beholder, in the present case, Roland Barthes.[29]

The *punctum* is closely related to the found object; it, too, is something found as if by chance. The *as if* is important here, because it is finally some desire or lack in the beholder that the object answers. In *The Four Fundamental Concepts of Psychoanalysis*, Jacques Lacan refers to the *sujet troué* (the subject full of holes), inventing a complementary term for *objet trouvé*. In just the same way, there is no *punctum* without desire. The passivity and surprise of encountering the *punctum* is owing to the fact that desire is unconscious.[30] In other words, the automatism of the camera mimics the automatism of the subject, giving access to an unexpected *sur*reality that cuts through the banality of the average photographic image. 'By the mark of *something* the photograph is no longer "anything whatever"', Barthes wrote.[31]

In the late 1970s, the theories of Walter Benjamin, Gilles Deleuze and Jean Baudrillard were mobilised, mostly in the pages of *October*, to advance the idea of photography as the paradigmatic simulacrum, the copy without an original, circulating as pure sign-image. The point of this, as Krauss put it in 'Reinventing the Medium' (1999), was to mimic the condition of non-art, such as the commodity or advertising, 'in order to critique the unexamined pretensions of high art', including notions of originality and autonomy.[32] In keeping with this project, art practices that foregrounded photography's simulacral quality, such as Sherrie Levine's appropriations or Cindy Sherman's *Film Stills*, were championed. After *Camera Lucida*, critics and artists shifted their ground. Hal Foster, for example, proposed his interpretation of Warhol's photo silk screens as both simulacral and as indexically touched by the real.[33] Sherman's later work probed disgusting substances and abject scenarios and, incidentally, made explicit reference to the surrealist photography of Hans Bellmer.

In an article called 'The Index and the Uncanny', Laura Mulvey implicitly supports this idea of the dialectical relationship between the simulacral and the indexical when she suggests that the current revival of interest in the indexicality of the photograph is related to the development of digital photographic technologies.[34] Digitalisation dis-indexes the photograph: there is no prior existent, no moment of exposure, no split temporality of the now of the image and the then of the event. The virtual, constructed, digital image brings back into focus the issue of indexicality. The ubiquity of the simulacrum in the age of visual culture calls, contradictorily, for the object. Breton's call for 'the precision of sensible forms' finds a response in the work of some contemporary artists where the photograph and the found object are pitched against the ubiquity of the simulacrum.

Christian Boltanski

Christian Boltanski very self-consciously plays on the distinction between the simulacral readymade and the found object.[35] His strategy is to use the connotations that attach to both, mixing and destabilising them. All commentators characterise the work as crossed by contradiction, ambivalence or paradox. Abigail Solomon-Godeau, for instance, points to his incompatible identifications with both Joseph Beuys, the self-styled shaman and Andy Warhol, the self-styled machine.[36] Didier Semin analyses his work in terms of tension between the Duchampian readymade and the relic, and describes his self-presentation as an oscillation between messiah and conman.[37] These observations help to capture something of the troubling ambivalence at the heart of Boltanski's work. A typical Boltanski piece is a curious hybrid, taking the form of a pseudo-relic, a fraudulent fragment or trace of a simulated past. In 1969, he produced his first book called *Research and Presentation of Everything That Remains of My Childhood, 1944–50*. Photographic documents of a lock of hair and a swatch of jumper are presented as if they were precious souvenirs of youth, but everything is fabricated. As if to underscore this aspect of fabrication, a year later he produced *Attempts to Reconstruct Objects That Belonged to Christian Boltanski between 1948 and 1954*, which consists of plasticine models of toys, blankets, cloths and ink bottles displayed in tin drawers. Instead of piecing together fragments of a past, these simulations effectively obstruct memory, insinuating themselves in its place. Barthes said something very similar about the nature of most photographs – they serve only to weaken the living memory. Boltanski invests these objects with a phony aura – and, as a consequence, he effectively mutually contaminates both the auratic relic and the mass-produced ready-made. The series of *Reference Vitrines* (Figure 9.1) supposedly bring together autobiographical mementoes from the artist's life.

For the series of installations called *Inventories* (1973–79), Boltanski instructed gallery curators to display the possessions of a recently deceased, anonymous person. Photographic documents of the items were made for the book of the exhibition which resemble surrealist photographs of found objects. In fact, only one of the displays, in Baden-Baden, was based on the possessions of a dead person. *Inventory of Objects that Belonged to a Resident of Oxford* (1973) was based on the possessions of a young man studying abroad for a year. Nevertheless, these objects wrenched from any context of everyday use still carry an emotional charge. They are not just a collection of random items of consumption, but rather 'personal effects' that seem to betray something about the life of their absent owner. Of course, this may be an illusion, but certainly our relation to them is quite different from our stance in relation to pop art. This is partly owing to the fact that the used or second-hand object bears a patina of age that takes it out of the realm of pure consumption. The found object is rarely new. And when such objects are presented as the orphaned possessions of a dead person, they become empty husks that signify absence or death. Boltanski gives them a relic-like character with an isolated, centred photographic presentation, but their everyday banality keeps them in constant danger of sliding back into 'anything whatever'.

The combination of the patina of age and the theme of death are put to powerful use in the series of installations that combine connotations of a chapel with some infernal bureaucracy (Figure 9.2). Found photographs such as the group photo taken in 1931 of the children of the Jewish Gymnasium in Vienna (*Lycée Chasse* [1986–87]) are re-photographed, enlarged and cropped. The blurring of the nth generation copy gives the photograph a weaker hold on the object, depleting its indexicality, but, precisely because of that weak

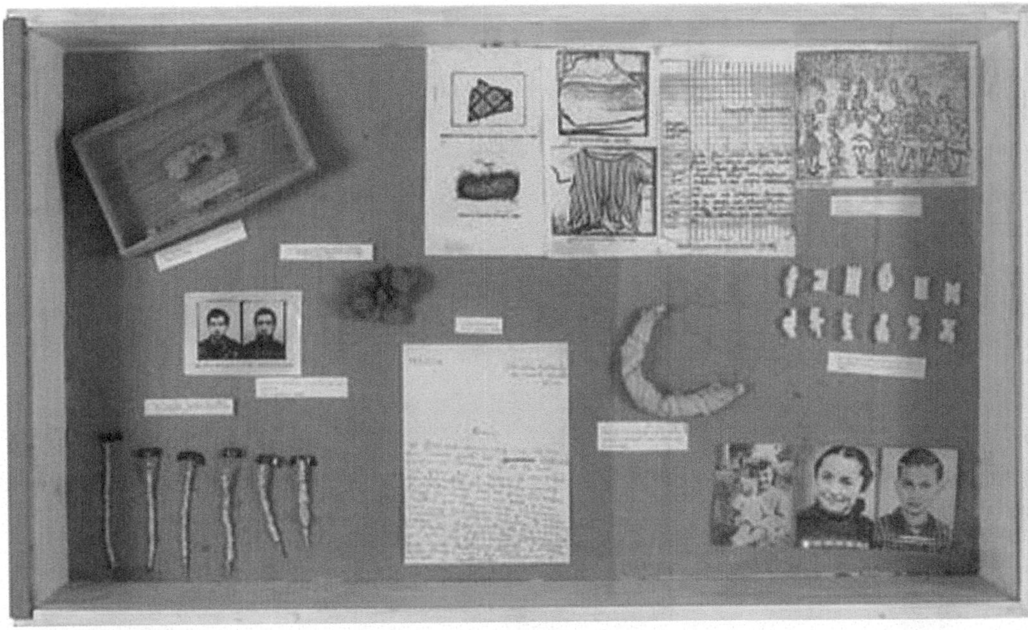

9.1 Christian Boltanski, *Vitrine de réference*, white painted wood, playdough, ball of dirt, Xerox, black and white photographs, sugar cubes, trap, hand written letter, Gillette razor blade mounted on wood, 120 × 70 × 15 cm, 1972. Courtesy the artist and Marian Goodman Gallery, New York/Paris

hold, it also has a stronger emotional charge. The blurred image recalls Bazin's 'fuzzy' photographic index. The ubiquitous biscuit tins in these installations are also given an accelerated patina of rust. Boltanski's blurring signifies ageing, transience, a slipping into the past and falling from memory, causing us to cling all the more to this seemingly last, fragile trace. Comparisons could be made with Gerhard Richter's painterly blurring; in his case, too, space of memory is shadowy. Solomon-Godeau contends that Boltanski's blurring generalises the portrait face and thereby traduces the singular identity and particular historical circumstances of the person.[38] I think, however, that their anonymity, or better, the tension between their anonymity and singularity is central to Boltanski's work and related to his avowed interest in the way a subject becomes an object, which bears on both Boltanski's themes of the Holocaust and the nature of photography.

I wonder if *Camera Lucida*, published in 1980, gave permission, as it were, for Boltanski's turn to a less sceptical understanding of photography as index of the traumatic real. Certainly, in the mid 1980s when he began to take the Holocaust as an explicit theme, the aspect of his early work that had to do with simulation or false evidence or mislabelling is less evident. But even in those later works that do not explicitly evoke the mass-extermination of the Jews, the traumatic-real side of photography is foregrounded. Boltanski did a series called *Lost Property* which displayed just that. In New York, 3,000 items lost on trains bound for Grand Central Station were shown. In 1994, items lost on the Glasgow tramway were exhibited. The invitation reproduced one of the photographic documents for the accompanying book – a photo of an isolated single glove. The glove is no doubt a reference to the photograph of a bronze glove in Breton's *Nadja*, but Boltanski attaches a darker connotation to it. Because the glove is separated from both

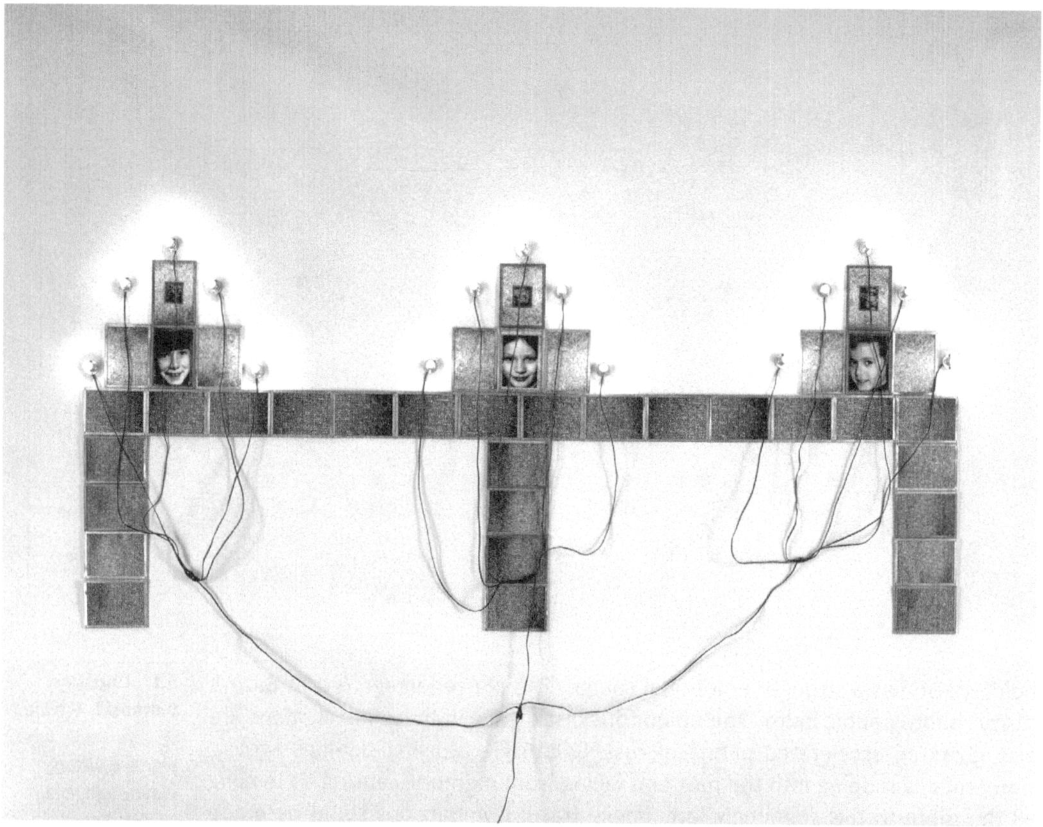

9.2 Christian Boltanski, *Monument*, black and white photographs, colour photographs, colour collage and light, 114.9 × 280 × 7 cm, 1986. Courtesy the artist and Marian Goodman Gallery, New York/Paris

its pair and its owner, because the photograph is separated from its referent, it invokes death. In an interview with Tamar Garb, Boltanski made this clear, noting that in his work 'there is a direct relationship between a piece of clothing, a photo and a dead body, in that someone once existed but is no longer there'.[39]

Gabriel Orozco

Benjamin Buchloh has written about the sculpture of the Mexican artist, Gabriel Orozco, in terms of an indexical art practice resisting the simulacrum. We desire 'silent objects', he says, in order to restore the 'opacity of the signifier', and, he continues: 'Typical of the desire to establish an opaque, irreducible and indivisible material experience with artistic means is the recurrence of the indexical procedure, an operation that claims the material trace as strictly non-transcendable, as a pure material causality.'[40] Orozco's problem is to respond to this need without being relegated to the position of primitive other or negating the specificity of his Mexican cultural formation. Buchloh's analysis of *My Hands Are My Heart* (1990) illustrates how the artist manages this. Orozco squeezed a lump of brick clay in his hands, making a negative imprint of his fingers.

The resulting heart-shaped object simultaneously makes reference to late-1960s casts of body parts such as Bruce Nauman's and to a specifically Latin American iconography of the heart. The connotational weight of *My Hands Are My Heart* springs not only from the associations mentioned by Buchloh, but also its suggestion of some insect or prehistoric fossil. It is simultaneously intimate and strange, like Rachel Whiteread's casts. It has the ambivalent status of both a mute index and a charged symbol.

Buchloh does not connect Orozco's practice to the surrealist object, but this can easily be done. The 1936 *Surrealist Exhibition of Objects* brought together a bewildering range of items including natural objects, interpreted natural objects, incorporated natural objects, found objects, perturbed objects (a glass found after a volcano), readymade objects (Duchamp's *Bottle Rack*), American objects, Oceanic objects, mathematical objects and surrealist objects, including Meret Oppenheim's fur-lined tea cup. This heterogeneous collection of objects exhibited on shelves and so allowing the objects to communicate with each other, was mimicked in Orozco's installations where objects, studies and scale models are arranged on tables. This is what Orozco has to say about this form of display:

> They are a bit like relics but I did my best to put them in such a way as not to look like a museum display and more like an organic world that was working, that you could mentally play ... I think the interaction happens in the mind of the spectator when one makes all the connections between the drawings and the pieces here and there and the photograph on the wall ... It's a platform for an action.[41]

An artist, says Orozco, needs more than an idea; the idea needs to be developed, 'it then becomes something complex that you can't really understand'.[42] It then becomes, I would add, an object that is encountered – that is to say, only experienced retrospectively.

Orozco often takes photographs of small sculpture-like objects. He claims a lack of interest in pictorial composition, using the camera in as neutral a way as possible. He tends to fix on found traces, rather than found objects – accidental marks, the effects of sun and rain. This accords with his quasi-ethical attitude of receptiveness or vulnerability, perfectly figured in his work, *Yielding Stone* (1992), a ball of plasticine that has been rolled through the street picking up marks and debris (Figure 9.3). His work conveys a spontaneous, involuntary aspect and an attraction to ephemeral configurations of 'low' materials. The artist executes a mini-performance, as in *Extension of Reflection* (a kind of Zen drawing made with rain water for ink and bicycle wheels for a brush) (Figure 9.4) or *Melted Popsicle* (1993), a diminutive homage to Robert Smithson's glue pour, but it is the trace left behind that Orozco records. He favours a slight temporal displacement. Or, as he himself has written: 'I photograph what has already happened. I photograph the wake of the past.'[43] Working amongst the involuntary, found and the fabricated object, Orozco is intent on giving his work what Breton called 'circumstantial magic' ('circumstantial' meaning the opposite of magical, that is, factual, non-essential, everyday).

The *Sculptures Involontaires* photographed in close-up by Brassaï are themselves carefully posed, some raised off the ground on a piece of glass, and

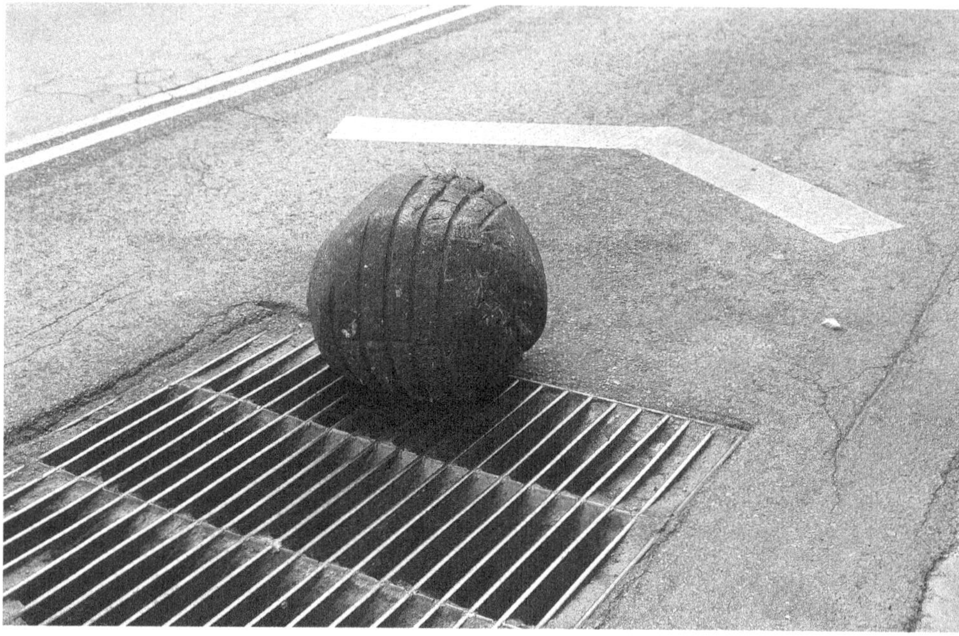

9.3 Gabriel Orozco, *Yielding Stone*, plasticine, 35.6 × 43.2 × 43.2 cm, 1992
Courtesy of the artist and Marian Goodman Gallery, New York

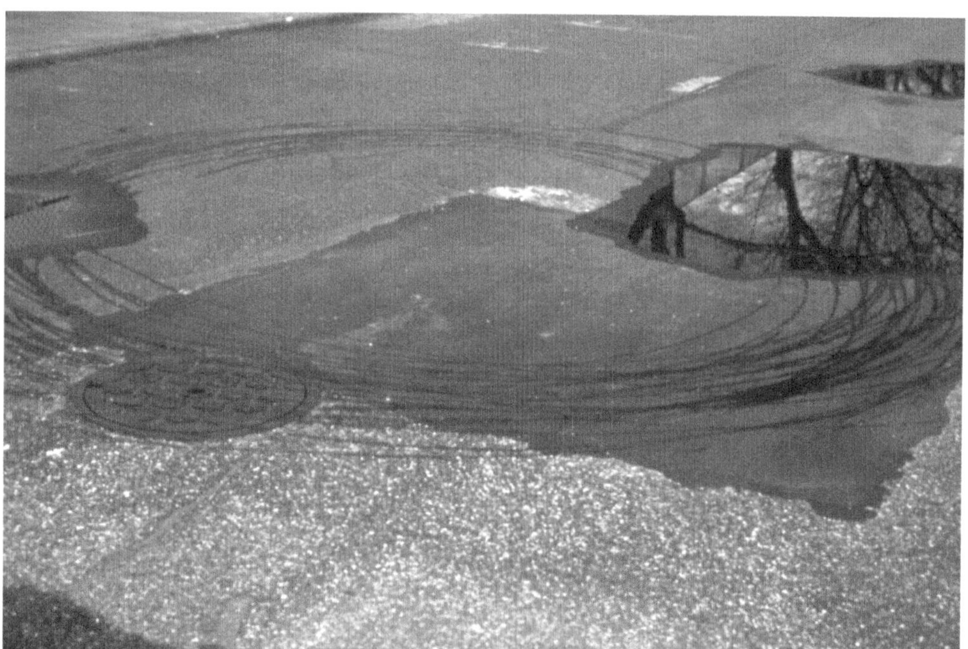

9.4 Gabriel Orozco, *Extension of Reflection*, chromogenic colour print, 40.6 × 50.8 cm, 1992
Courtesy of the artist and Marian Goodman Gallery, New York

lit with a raking light. They are thus taken out of circulation from the everyday world and made to float uncannily in a space without scale or dimension. Breton called for artists and poets to incorporate in their work the precision of sensible forms, yet he also demanded that they be detached from the domain of perception-consciousness. These photographed objects, and the others I have discussed, thus inhabit a space at once real and phantasmatic.

Notes

1 André Breton, 'The Surrealist Situation of the Object', in *Manifestoes of Surrealism*, trans. R. Seaver and H.R. Lane (Ann Arbor, 1972), pp. 259–60. See also Breton, 'The Crisis of the Object' [1936], in *Surrealism and Painting*, trans. S. Watson Taylor (Boston, 2002), pp. 275–80. The part Salvador Dalí played in Breton's turn to the object is crucial but too complicated to take up in this context. See Haim Finkelstein, *Surrealism and the Crisis of the Object* (Ann Arbor, 1979).

2 Breton, 'The Surrealist Situation of the Object', p. 273.

3 Breton uses the phrase 'visual residues', suggestive of Freud's 'day's residues' in *The Interpretation of Dreams*, on more than one occasion. Ibid., p. 273.

4 Sigmund Freud, *Beyond the Pleasure Principle: The Standard Edition of the Complete Psychological Works of Sigmund Freud*, vol. 17 (London, 1955), pp. 1–64. See my book on the artistic and theoretical legacy of this essay: Margaret Iversen, *Beyond Pleasure: Freud, Lacan, Barthes* (Pennsylvania, 2007).

5 André Breton, *Mad Love*, trans. M.A. Caws (Lincoln and London, 1987), p. 25; *L'Amour fou* (Paris, 1937).

6 Margaret Cohen, *Profane Illumination: Walter Benjamin and the Paris of Surrealist Revolution* (Berkeley and Los Angeles, 1993), p. 138.

7 Breton, 'The Surrealist Situation of the Object', p. 277 (my emphasis). It is necessary to stress this point since some of Breton's statements about painting 'referring to a purely internal model' can be easily misinterpreted. See 'Surrealism and Painting' [1928], in *Surrealism and Painting*, p. 4.

8 André Breton, 'Introduction to the Discourse on the Paucity of Reality', trans. R. Sieburth and J. Gordon, *October*, 69 (Summer 1994), pp. 133–44. From Breton, *Point du Jour* (Paris, 1970), pp. 141–2.

9 Sigmund Freud, 'Dream of the Botanical Monograph', in *The Interpretation of Dreams: The Standard Edition*, vol. 5 (London, 1953), p. 169ff. This dream appears in the section 'Recent and Indifferent Material in Dreams'.

10 Breton, *Mad Love*, p. 30. For another discussion of this episode, see Chapter 8 in this volume, above.

11 Breton, 'Introduction to the Discourse on the Paucity of Reality', pp. 133–44.

12 Dawn Ades, 'Photography and the Surrealist Text', in Rosalind Krauss and Jane Livingston (eds), *L'Amour fou: Photography and Surrealism* (London, 1986), p. 155.

13 'Max Ernst', *The Lost Steps*, trans. M. Polizzotti (Lincoln Nebraska, 1996), p. 60; André Breton, *Les Pas perdus* (Paris, 1924), p. 101.

14 Walker Evans, 'The Reappearance of Photography' [1931], in Alan Trachtenberg (ed.), *Classic Essays in Photography* (New Haven, 1980), p. 185.

15 Charles Sanders Peirce, 'Icon, Index, Symbol', in *Collected Papers: vol. 2: Elements of Logic* (Cambridge, MA, 1960), p. 159ff, and 'Logic as Semiotic: The Theory of Signs', in Justus Buchler (ed.), *The Philosophy of Peirce* (New York, 1940), pp. 98–119.

16 André Bazin, 'The Ontology of the Photographic Image', in *What is Cinema?* vol. 1 (Berkeley and Los Angeles, 1967), p. 14.

17 Rosalind Krauss, 'Notes on the Index: Seventies Art in America', *October*, 3 (Spring 1977), p. 75.

18 Man Ray, 'The Age of Light', in Trachtenberg, (ed.), *Classic Essays on Photography*, p. 167.

19 Man Ray, 'Photography Is Not an Art', in Lucy Lippard (ed.), *Surrealists on Art* (Englewood Cliffs, NJ, 1970).

20 Neil Baldwin, *Man Ray: American Artist* (New York, 1988), p. 158.

21 Susan Laxton, 'Flou: Rayographs and the Dada Automatic', *October*, 127 (Winter 2009), p. 44.

22 See Margaret Iversen (ed.), *Chance* (London and Cambridge, MA, 2010).

23 Breton, *Les Pas perdus* (1924), p. 101; *The Lost Steps*, p. 60.

24 Ann Banfield, '*L'imparfait de l'objectif*: The Imperfect of the Object Glass', *Camera Obscura*, 24 (September 1990), p. 85.

25 Krauss, 'Notes on the Index', p. 70.

26 Ibid., pp. 81 and 77. See also Rosalind Krauss, 'Notes on the Index: Seventies Art in America, Part 2', *October*, 4 (Autumn 1977), p. 70.

27 Man Ray, 'Deceiving Appearances', in Christopher Phillips (ed.), *Photography in the Modern Era* (New York, 1989), p. 12.

28 Roland Barthes, *Camera Lucida: Reflections on Photography*, trans. R. Howard (New York, 1981), p. 26. *La Chambre claire: Note sur la photographie* (Paris, 1980).

29 Michael Fried, 'Barthes's *Punctum*', *Critical Inquiry*, 31(3) (Spring 2005), p. 546.

30 For an account of the Lacanian background to *Camera Lucida*, see Iversen, 'What is a Photograph?', *Art History*, 16(4) (1993), pp. 450–63. Also in Iversen, *Beyond Pleasure*.

31 Barthes, *Camera Lucida*, p. 49.

32 Rosalind Krauss, 'Reinventing the Medium', *Critical Inquiry*, 25 (Winter 1999), p. 295.

33 Hal Foster, 'The Return of the Real', in *The Return of the Real* (Cambridge, MA, 1996), p. 134. See also Foster, 'Death in America', *October*, 75 (Winter 1996), pp. 37–60.

34 Laura Mulvey, 'The Index and the Uncanny', in Carolyn Gill (ed.), *Time and the Image* (Manchester, 2001).

35 On this subject, see my 'Readymade, Found Object, Photograph', *Art Journal*, 63(2) (Summer 2004), pp. 44–57.

36 Abigail Solomon-Godeau, 'Mourning or Melancholia: Christian Boltanski's *Missing House*', *Oxford Art Journal*, 12(2) (1998), pp. 1–20.

37 Didier Semin, 'From the *Impossible Life* to the *Exemplary Life*', in D. Semin (et al.), *Christian Boltanski* (London, 1997), p. 19.

38 Abigail Solomon-Godeau, 'Mourning or Melancholia', p. 11.

39 'Tamar Garb in conversation with Christian Boltanski', in Semin, *Christian Boltanski*, p. 19.

40 Benjamin H.D. Buchloh, 'Refuse and Refuge', in M. Catherine de Zegher (ed.), *Gabriel Orozco* (Kortrijk, 1993), p. 43.

41 Jean-Pierre Criqui (et al.), *Gabriel Orozco, Trabajo 1992–2000* (Cologne, 2004), p. xxv. See Briony Fer, 'Crazy about Saturn' (Interview with Gabriel Orozco), and Benjamin Buchloh, 'Sculpture as Recollection', in *Gabriel Orozco* (London and Mexico City, 2006).

42 Criqui (et al.), *Gabriel Orozco*, p. lxxvii.

43 Gabriel Orozco, *Photogravity* (Philadelphia, 1999), p. 163. Benjamin H.D. Buchloh writes that the temporal dialectic in Orozco's photographs lies 'between the not yet and the nevermore'. He also touches on the nerve of my argument when he refers to conceptual artists' interest in photography's 'capacities to collect and represent information on the subject's modalities of spatial and temporal experience'. See his 'Cosmic Reification: Gabriel Orozco's Photographs', *Gabriel Orozco* (London, 2004), pp. 86, 76. See also the catalogue, *Gabriel Orozco: Photographs* (Washington, D.C. and Göttingen, 2004).

Bibliography

Abel, Richard (ed.), *French Film Theory and Criticism: A History/Anthology, 1907–1939*, vol. 1 (Princeton: Princeton University Press, 1993).

Abstraction–Création 1931–36 (Münster: Westfälisches Landesmuseum für Kunst und Kulturgeschichte and Paris: Musée d'art moderne de la ville de Paris, 1978).

Ades, Dawn, 'Between Dada and Surrealism: Painting in the *Mouvement flou*', in Terry Ann R. Neff (ed.), *In the Mind's Eye: Dada and Surrealism* (New York: Abbeville Press, 1985), pp. 23–41.

Ades, Dawn, *Dalí* (London: Thames and Hudson, 1995).

Ades, Dawn and Simon Baker, *Close-Up: Proximity and Defamiliarisation in Art, Film and Photography* (Edinburgh: Fruitmarket Gallery, 2008).

Affron, Matthew, 'Léger's Modernism: Subjects and Objects', in Carolyn Lanchner (ed.), *Fernand Léger* (New York: Museum of Modern Art, 1998).

Allan Kaprow (Pasadena: Pasadena Art Museum, 1967).

Alley, Ronald, *Paule Vézelay* (London: Tate Gallery 1983).

Alloway, Lawrence, *Topics in American Art since 1945* (New York: Norton & Co., 1975).

Alloway, Lawrence (et al.), *New Forms – New Media 1* (New York: Martha Jackson Gallery, 1960).

Althusser, Louis, 'Ideology and Ideological State Apparatuses', in *Lenin and Philosophy and Other Essays*, trans. B. Brewster (New York and London, 1971), p. 127–188.

André Breton, 42, rue Fontaine, Calmels Cohen Book Catalogue (Paris, 2003).

Andreotti, Margherita, *The Early Sculpture of Jean Arp* (Ann Arbor: UMI Research Press, 1989).

Aragon, Louis, 'Du décor', *Le Film*, 131 (16 September 1918), pp. 8–10.

Aragon, Louis, 'L'Ombre de l'inventeur', *La Révolution surréaliste*, 1(1) (1924), pp. 22–4.

Aragon, Louis, 'Introduction à 1930', *La Révolution surréaliste*, 12 (December 1929), pp. 57–64.

Aragon, Louis, 'La Peinture au défi' [1930], in *Les Collages* (Paris: Hermann, 1980).

Aron, Robert, 'Films de révolte', *La Revue du cinéma*, 5 (15 November 1929), pp. 41–5.

Arp, Hans, 'A propos de l'art abstrait', *Cahiers d'art*, 6 (7–8) (1931), pp. 357–58.

Arp, Hans, 'Looking', in James Thrall Soby (ed.), *Arp*, trans. Ralph Manheim (New York: The Museum of Modern Art, 1958), pp. 12–16.

Arp, Hans, *Jours effeuillés: Poèmes, essais, souvenirs 1920–65*, ed. Marcel Jean (Paris: Gallimard, 1966).

Arp, Hans, 'Dadaland' [1938], trans. Ralph Manheim, in Lucy R. Lippard (ed.), *Dadas on Art* (Englewood Cliffs, NJ: Prentice Hall, 1971).

Arp, Hans, *Arp on Arp: Poems, Essays, Memories*, ed. Marcel Jean, trans. Joachim Neugroschel (New York: The Viking Press, 1972).

Bachelard, Gaston, *Water and Dreams: An Essay on the Imagination of Matter* [1942], trans. Edith R. Farrell (Dallas: The Dallas Institute of Humanities and Culture, 1983).

Baker, Simon, 'Jake Chapman on Bataille: An interview with Simon Baker', *Papers of Surrealism*, 1 (Winter 2003), www.surrealismcentre.ac.uk/papersofsurrealism/journal1/index.htm.
Baker, Simon, '*Psychologie des Foules*: Surrealism and the Impossible Object', in Brandon Taylor and Fiona Russell (eds), *Sculpture and Psychoanalysis* (Aldershot: Ashgate, 2006), pp. 33–52.
Baker, Simon, *Surrealism, History and Revolution* (Oxford: Peter Lang, 2007).
Baker, Simon, 'Surrealism in the Bronze Age: Statuephobia and the Efficacy of Metaphorical Iconoclasm', in Stacy Boldrick and Richard Clay (eds), *Iconoclasm: Contested Objects, Contested Terms* (Aldershot: Ashgate, 2007), pp. 189–214.
Balázs, Béla, *Theory of the Film (Character and Growth of a New Art)*, trans. D. Dobson (New York: Dover Publications 1970).
Baldwin, Neil, *Man Ray: American Artist* (New York: Da Capo Press, 1988).
Balfour, Henry, *The Evolution of Decorative Art* (London: Rivington, Percival & Co., 1893).
Banfield, Ann, '*L'imparfait de l'objectif*: The Imperfect of the Object Glass', *Camera Obscura*, 24 (September 1990), pp. 64–87.
Barthes, Roland, *Image Music Text*, ed. and trans. Stephen Heath (New York: Hill and Wang, 1977).
Barthes, Roland, *Camera Lucida: Reflections on Photography*, trans. Richard Howard (New York: Hill and Wang, 1981).
Bataille, Georges, *The Absence of Myth: Writings on Surrealism*, trans. and introduced by Michael Richardson (London and New York: Verso, 1994).
Bazin, André, *What is Cinema?* (Berkeley and Los Angeles: University of California Press, 1967).
Beller, Jonathan, *The Cinematic Mode of Production: Attention Economy and the Society of the Spectacle* (Lebanon, NH: University Press of New England, 2006).
Benjamin, Walter, 'The Author as Producer' [1934], trans. P. Demez, in Brian Wallis (ed.), *Art after Modernism: Rethinking Representation* (New York: The Museum of Contemporary Art, 1984), pp. 297–309.
Benjamin, Walter, 'The Work of Art in the Age of Mechanical Reproduction' [1936], in W. Benjamin, *Illuminations* [1955], ed. Hannah Arendt, trans. Harry Zohn (New York: Schocken Books, 1969), pp. 217–51.
Benjamin, Walter, 'The Work of Art in the Age of Its Reproducibility' [1936], in Howard Eiland and Michael W. Jennings (eds), *Walter Benjamin: Selected Writings Volume 3: 1935–1938* (Cambridge, MA. and London: The Belknap Press of Harvard University Press, 2002).
Benjamin, Walter, 'On Some Motifs in Baudelaire' in *Illuminations* (London, 1973), trans. H. Zohn, pp. 155–200; first published in *Zeitschrift für Sozialforschung*, 8(1–2) (1939).
Benjamin, Walter, *One-Way Street and Other Writings*, trans. E. Jephcott and K. Shorter (London: New Left Books, 1979).
Billeter, Erika (ed.), *Skulptur im Licht der Fotografie: Von Bayard bis Mapplethorpe* (Duisburg: Wilhelm Lehmbruck Museum, 1997).
Blanchot, Maurice, *L'Entretien infini* (Paris: Gallimard, 1969).
Bois, Yve-Alain (et al.), *Gabriel Orozco* (London, Thames and Hudson, 2006).
Bois, Yve-Alain (ed.), *Gabriel Orozco* (Cambridge, MA: MIT Press, 2009).
Brassaï, *Paris de Nuit* (Paris, 1932), republished as *Paris by Night*, trans. S. Gilbert (Boston, London and New York, 1993).
Brassaï, 'Du mur des cavernes au mur d'usine', *Minotaure*, 3–4 (December 1933), pp. 26–30.
Brassaï, *Proust in the Power of Photography* [1997], trans. R. Howard (Chicago: University of Chicago Press, 2001).
Breton, André, 'Introduction to the Discourse on the Paucity of Reality' [1924], trans. R. Sieburth and J. Gordon, *October*, 69 (Summer 1994), pp. 133–44.
Breton, André, *Les Pas perdus* (Paris: Gallimard, 1924).
Breton, André, *Nadja* [1928], trans. Richard Howard (New York: Grove Press, 1960).
Breton, André, 'Il y aura une fois', *Le Surréalisme au service de la révolution*, 1 (July 1930), pp. 2–4.

Breton, André, 'Le Message automatique', *Minotaure*, 3–4 (1933), in *What is Surrealism? Selected Writings*, ed. and trans. F. Rosemont (New York: Monad, 1978), pp. 97–109.

Breton, André, 'La Beauté sera convulsive', *Minotaure*, 1(5) (1934), pp. 9–16.

Breton, André, 'Surrealist Situation of the Object' [1935], in Pontus Hulten (ed.), *The Surrealists Look at Art*, trans. M. Palmer and N. Cole (Venice, CA: Lapis Press, 1990), pp. 159–88.

Breton, André, 'Crisis of the Object' [1936], trans. Lucy R. Lippard, in L.R. Lippard (ed.), *Surrealists on Art* (Englewood Cliffs, NJ: Prentice Hall, 1970).

Breton, André, *L'Amour fou* (Paris: Gallimard, 1937).

Breton, André, *Mad Love* [1937], trans. Mary Ann Caws (Lincoln and London: University of Nebraska Press, 1987).

Breton, André, 'Seconde Arche' [1947], in *Oeuvres complètes*, vol. 3, ed. Marguerite Bonnet and Etienne-Alain Hubert (Paris: Gallimard, 1999).

Breton, André, *Conversations: The Autobiography of Surrealism* [1952] (New York: Paragon, 1993).

Breton, André, *Manifestoes of Surrealism* [1962], trans. R. Seaver and H.R. Lane (Ann Arbor: University of Michigan Press, 1972).

Breton, André, *Surrealism and Painting* [1965], trans. Simon Watson Taylor (Boston: MFA Publications, 2002).

Breton, André, *Oeuvres complètes*, ed. Marguerite Bonnet (Paris: Gallimard, 1992).

Buchloh, Benjamin H.D., 'Refuse and Refuge', in M. Catherine de Zegher (ed.), *Gabriel Orozco* (Kortrijk, 1993), pp. 38–51.

Buchloh, Benjamin H.D. and Judith F. Rodenbeck, *Experiments in the Everyday: Allan Kaprow and Robert Watts: Events, Objects, Documents* (New York: Miriam & Ira D. Wallach Art Gallery, 2000).

Buskirk, Martha, *The Contingent Object of Contemporary Art* (Cambridge, MA: MIT Press, 2003).

Cahun, Claude, *Les Paris sont ouverts* [1934], in François Leperlier (ed.), *Ecrits* (Paris: Jean-Michel Place, 2002).

Cahun, Claude, 'Prenez garde aux objets domestiques', *Cahiers d'art*, 11 (1936), pp. 45–8.

Caillois, Roger, 'Le Décor surréaliste de la vie', *Documents 33*, 5 (August 1933), pp. 16–17.

Caillois, Roger, *The Edge of Surrealism: A Roger Caillois Reader*, ed. Claudine Frank (Durham and London: Duke University Press, 2003).

Certeau, Michel de, *L'Invention du quotidien, vol. 1: Arts de faire* [1980], ed. Luce Giard (Paris: Gallimard, 1990).

Certeau, Michel de, *The Practice of Everyday Life*, trans. S.F. Rendall (Berkeley, Los Angeles and London: University of California, 1984).

Cohen, Margaret, *Profane Illumination: Walter Benjamin and the Paris of Surrealist Revolution* (Berkeley and Los Angeles: University of California Press, 1993).

Conley, Katharine, 'Modernism Primitivism in 1933: Brassaï's "Involuntary Sculptures" in *Minotaure*', *Modernism/modernity*, 10(1) (2003), pp. 127–40.

Costello, Diarmuid and Margaret Iversen (eds), *Photography After Conceptual Art* (Oxford: Wiley-Blackwell, 2010).

Crary, Jonathan, *Suspensions of Perception: Attention, Spectacle, and Modern Culture* (Cambridge, MA: MIT Press, 1999).

Crevel, René, *L'Esprit contre la raison et autres écrits surréalistes* (Paris: Société nouvelle des Éditions Pauvert, 1986).

Criqui, Jean-Pierre (et al.), *Gabriel Orozco, Trabajo 1992–2000* (Cologne: Verlag der Buchhandlung Walther König, 2004).

DADA (Paris: Pompidou Centre, 2005).

Dalí, Salvador, 'Objets surréalistes', *Le Surréalisme au service de la révolution*, 3 (December 1931), pp. 16–17.

Dalí, Salvador, 'The Object as Revealed in Surrealist Experiment' [1932], in Lucy R. Lippard (ed.), *Surrealists on Art* (Englewood Cliffs, NJ: Prentice Hall, 1970), pp. 87–96.

Dalí, Salvador, 'De la beauté terrifiante et comestible, de l'architecture Modern'style', *Minotaure*, 1 (3–4) (December 1933), pp. 69–76.
Dalí, Salvador, 'Le Phénomène de l'extase', *Minotaure*, 1 (3–4) (December 1933), pp. 76–7.
Dalí, Salvador, 'Lettre à André Breton' [1933], in *Oui 2: L'Archangélisme scientifique*, ed. Robert Descharnes (Paris: Denoël, 1971), pp. 17–18.
Dalí, Salvador, *La Conquête de l'irrationnel* (Paris: Éditions surréalistes, 1935).
Desnos, Robert, 'Pygmalion et le Sphinx', *Documents*, 1 (1930), pp. 33–40.
Dezeuze, Anna (ed.), *The 'Do-it-yourself' Artwork: Participation from Fluxus to New Media* (Manchester: Manchester University Press, 2010).
Doesburg, Theo van, 'Comments on the Basis of Concrete Painting' [1930], trans. Joost Baljeu, in J. Baljeu, *Theo van Doesburg* (New York: Macmillan, 1974), pp. 181–2.
Duchamp, Marcel, *Notes* (Paris: Flammarion, 1999).
Ehrenburg, Ilya, *My Paris* [1933], trans. O. Ready (Paris: Éditions 7L, 2005).
Ehrenzweig, Anton, 'The Child's Vision of the World', in *The Hidden Order of Art: A Study in the Psychology of Artistic Imagination* (Berkeley, 1967).
Eluard, Paul, *Poésie involontaire et poésie intentionnelle* (Paris: Seghers, 1942).
Eluard, Paul, *Letters to Gala*, trans. Jesse Browner (New York: Paragon House, 1989).
Endt, Marion, *Nature and the Marvellous in Surrealism and Contemporary Art*, PhD thesis (Manchester: University of Manchester, 2009).
Epstein, Jean, 'Grossissement', *Bonjour Cinéma* (Paris, 1921), pp. 93–108.
Epstein, Jean, 'The Cinema Continues', in Richard Abel (ed.), *French Film Theory and Criticism, vol. 2: 1929–1939* (New Jersey, 1988), pp. 63–68.
Fer, Briony, 'Surrealism, Myth and Psychoanalysis', in B. Fer, David Batchelor and Paul Wood, *Realism, Rationalism, Surrealism: Art between the Wars* (New Haven and London: Yale University Press, 1993), Chapter 3.
Fer, Briony, *On Abstract Art* (New Haven and London: Yale University Press, 1997).
Finkelstein, Haim, *Surrealism and the Crisis of the Object* (Ann Arbor: UMI Research Press, 1979).
Fogle, Douglas (ed.), *The Last Picture Show: Artists Using Photography, 1960–82* (Minneapolis: Walker Art Center, 2003).
Foster, Hal, *Compulsive Beauty* (Cambridge, MA: MIT Press, 1993).
Foster, Hal, *The Return of the Real: The Avant-Garde at the End of the Century* (Cambridge, MA: MIT Press, 1996).
Foster, Hal, and Gordon Hughes (eds), *Richard Serra* (Cambridge, MA, and London: MIT Press, 2000).
Fox, Terry, 'Children's Tapes', *Arts*, 49(4) (December 1974), pp. 54–8.
Fox, Terry, Liza Bear and Willoughby Sharp, 'Terry Fox: Children's Videotapes', *Avalanche Newspaper* (December 1974), pp. 32–3.
Fox, Terry, *Ocular Language: 30 Years of Writing and Speaking About Art*, ed. Eva Schmidt (Cologne: Salon Verlag, 2000).
Frank, Claudine (ed.), *The Edge of Surrealism: A Roger Caillois Reader* (Durham, NC, and London: Duke University Press, 2003).
Fraser, Andrea, 'How to Provide an Artistic Service: An Introduction' [1994], in Zoya Kocur and Simon Leung (eds), *Theory in Contemporary Art since 1985* (Malden, MA: Blackwell Publishing, 2005), pp. 69–75.
Freud, Sigmund, *The Interpretation of Dreams* [1900–1901], in *The Standard Edition of the Complete Psychological Works of Sigmund Freud*, trans. J. Strachey, vols 4 and 5 (London: Hogarth Press, 1953).
Freud, Sigmund, *The Psychopathology of Everyday Life* [1901], in *The Standard Edition*, vol. 6 (London: Hogarth Press, 1960).
Freud, Sigmund, *Beyond the Pleasure Principle* [1920], in *The Standard Edition*, vol. 18 (London: Hogarth Press, 1955).
Fried, Michael, 'Barthes's *Punctum*', *Critical Inquiry*, 31(3) (Spring 2005), p. 539–74.

Friedberg, Anne, *Window Shopping and the Postmodern* (Berkeley: University of California Press, 1994).

Frizot, Michel, and Dominique Païni (eds), *Sculpter Photographier/Photographie Sculpture* (Paris: Éditions du Louvre, 1993).

Gell, Alfred, 'The Technology of Enchantment and the Enchantment of Technology', in Jeremy Coote and Anthony Shelton (eds), *Anthropology, Art and Aesthetics* (Oxford: Oxford University Press, 1992), pp. 40–67.

Gell, Alfred, *Art and Agency* (Oxford: Clarendon Press, 1998).

Giacometti, Alberto, 'Objets mobiles et muets', *Le Surréalisme au service de la révolution*, 3 (December 1931), pp. 18–19.

Giacometti, Alberto, 'Je ne puis parler *qu'indirectement* de mes sculptures', *Minotaure*, 1(3–4) (December 1933), pp. 18–19.

Giacometti, Alberto, *Ecrits* (Paris: Hermann, 1995).

Giedion-Welcker, Carola, 'The World of Forms and Phantoms in Arp's Work', *Quadrum*, 11 (1961), pp. 188–90.

Grant, Kim, *Surrealism and the Visual Arts: Theory and Reception* (Cambridge: Cambridge University Press, 2005).

Green, Christopher, *Léger and the Avant-Garde* (New Haven and London: Yale University Press, 1975).

Grigson, Geoffrey, *The Arts To-Day* (London: Bodley Head, 1935).

Guigon, Emmanuel, Hans van der Werf, and Mariet Willinge (eds), *L'Aubette ou la couleur dans l'architecture: Une Oeuvre de Hans Arp, Sophie Taeuber-Arp, Theo van Doesburg* (Strasbourg: Musées de Strasbourg/Association Theo van Doesburg, 2006).

Gunning, Tom, 'The Cinema of Attractions: Early Film, Its Spectator and the Avant-Garde' [1986], in Thomas Elsaesser (ed.), *Early Cinema: Space – Frame – Narrative* (London: British Film Institute, 1999), pp. 56–62.

Gunning, Tom, 'An Aesthetics of Astonishment: Early Film and the (In)Credulous Spectator' [1989], in Linda Williams (ed.), *Viewing Positions: Ways of Seeing Film* (New Brunswick: Rutgers University Press, 1995), pp. 114–33.

Gunning, Tom, '"Now You See It, Now You Don't": The Temporality of the Cinema of Attractions', *The Velvet Light Trap*, 32 (Fall 1993), pp. 3–12.

Gurney, Edmund, Frederic W.H. Myers and Frederick Podmore, *Phantasms of the Living*, vol. 1 (London: Trübner, 1886).

Haddon, Alfred, *Evolution in Art: As Illustrated by the Life-Histories of Designs* (London: Walter Scott, 1895).

Hammond, Paul (ed.), *The Shadow & Its Shadow* (San Francisco: City Lights Books, 2000).

Hancock, Jane, 'Arp's Chance Collages', in Stephen C. Foster (ed.), *Dada/Dimensions* (Ann Arbor: UMI Research Press, 1985), pp. 47–82.

Hancock, J. and Poley, S. (eds), *Arp 1886–1966* (Cambridge: Cambridge University Press, 1987).

Hanhardt, John G. (ed.), *Video Culture: A Critical Investigation* (New York: Peregrine Smith Books, 1986).

Hapgood, Susan, *Neo-Dada: Redefining Art, 1958–62* (New York: American Federation for the Arts, 1994).

Harris, Steven, 'Beware of Domestic Objects: Vocation and Equivocation in 1936', *Art History*, 24(5) (November 2001), pp. 725–57.

Harris, Steven, 'Coup d'oeil', *Oxford Art Journal*, 24(1) (2004), pp. 89–112.

Harris, Steven, *Surrealist Art and Thought in the 1930s: Art, Politics, and the Psyche* (Cambridge: Cambridge University Press, 2004).

Haskell, Barbara, *Blam! The Explosion of Pop, Minimalism, and Performance, 1958–64* (New York: Whitney Museum of American Art, 1984).

Heartney, Eleanor, 'Report from Sydney: The Expanded Readymade', *Art in America*, 78 (September 1990), pp. 91.

Highmore, Ben, *Everyday Life and Cultural Theory: An Introduction* (London and New York: Routledge, 2002).

Holly, Michael Ann, *Past Looking: Historical Imagination and the Rhetoric of the Image* (Ithaca: Cornell University Press, 1996).

Holt, John, *How Children Learn* (New York: Pitman, 1967).

Holt, Nancy (ed.), *The Writings of Robert Smithson* (New York: New York University Press, 1979).

Hopkins, David, *Dada's Boys* (New Haven and London: Yale University Press, 2006).

Horodner, Stuart, 'The Language of Stuff: An Interview with Richard Wentworth', *Sculpture*, 20(3) (April 2001), http://www.sculpture.org/documents/scmag01/april01/went/went.shtml.

Huelsenbeck, Richard, *Memoirs of a Dada Drummer* [1957], ed. Hans J. Kleinschmidt, trans. Joachim Neugroschel (New York: The Viking Press, 1974).

Ingold, Tim, 'On Weaving a Basket' [2000], in Fiona Candlin and Raiford Guins (eds), *The Object Reader* (London: Routledge, 2008), pp. 80–91.

Iversen, Margaret, 'Readymade, Found Object, Photograph', *Art Journal*, 63(2) (Summer 2004), pp. 44–57.

Iversen, Margaret, *Beyond Pleasure: Freud, Lacan and Barthes* (Pennsylvania: Penn State University Press, 2007).

Iversen, Margaret (ed.), *Chance* (Cambridge, MA: MIT Press and London: Whitechapel Gallery, 2010).

Jenny, Laurent, 'From Breton to Dalí: the Adventures of Automatism', trans. T. Trezise, *October*, 51 (Winter 1989), pp. 105–14.

Johnson, Geraldine (ed.), *Sculpture and Photography: Envisioning the Third Dimension* (Cambridge: Cambridge University Press, 1998).

Jones, Amelia, *Irrational Modernism: A Neurasthenic History of New York Dada* (Cambridge, MA: MIT Press, 2004).

Kaprow, Allan, *Assemblage, Environments and Happenings* (New York: Harry N. Abrams, 1966).

Kaprow, Allan, *Essays on the Blurring of Art and Life*, ed. Jeff Kelley (Berkeley and Los Angeles: University of California Press, 1993).

Kelley, Jeff, *Childsplay: The Art of Allan Kaprow* (Berkeley and Los Angeles: University of California Press, 2004).

Kelly, Julia, 'The Unfamiliar Figure: Henry Moore in French Periodicals in the 1930s', in Jane Beckett and Fiona Russell (eds), *Henry Moore: Critical Essays* (Aldershot: Ashgate, 2003), pp. 43–65.

Kelly, Julia, *Art, Ethnography and the Life of Objects, Paris c.1925–35* (Manchester: Manchester University Press, 2007).

Kelly, Julia, 'The Bureau of Surrealist Research', in Therese Lichtenstein (ed.), *Twilight Visions: Surrealism and Paris* (Berkeley and Los Angeles: University of California Press, 2009), pp. 79–101.

Kelley, Mike, *Minor Histories: Statements, Conversations, Proposals*, ed. John C. Welchman (Cambridge, MA: MIT Press), 2004.

Kelsey, Robin, and Blake Stimson (eds), *The Meaning of Photography* (Williamstown, MA: Clark Institute and New Haven: Yale University Press, 2008).

Klemm, Christian, *Alberto Giacometti* (New York: The Museum of Modern Art and Zurich: Kunsthaus Zurich, 2001).

Kolbowski, Silvia, 'an inadequate history of conceptual art', *October*, 92 (Spring 2000), pp. 53–70.

Kovács, Stephen, *From Enchantment to Rage: The Story of Surrealist Cinema* (Princeton: Princeton University Press, 1980).

Kracauer, Siegfried, *From Caligari to Hitler: A Psychological History of the German Film* (Princeton: Princeton University Press, 1947).

Krauss, Rosalind, 'Notes on the Index: Seventies Art in America', *October*, 3 (Spring 1977), pp. 68–81.

Krauss, Rosalind, 'The Photographic Conditions of Surrealism', *October*, 19 (Winter 1981), pp. 3–34.

Krauss, Rosalind, *The Originality of the Avant-Garde and Other Modernist Myths* (Cambridge, MA: MIT Press, 1985).

Krauss, Rosalind, 'The Cultural Logic of the Late Capitalist Museum', *October*, 54 (Fall 1990), pp. 3–17.

Krauss, Rosalind, 'Reinventing the Medium', *Critical Inquiry*, 25 (Winter 1999), pp. 289–305.

Krauss, Rosalind and Jane Livingston, *L'Amour fou: Photography and Surrealism* (Washington D.C.: Corcoran Gallery of Art and New York and London: Abbeville Press, 1985).

Kubler, George, *The Shape of Time: Remarks on the History of Things* (New Haven: Yale University Press, 1962).

Kubler, George, 'Style and the Representation of Historical Time', *Aspen*, 5+6 (1967), section 3.

Lambert-Beatty, Carrie, 'More or Less Minimalism: Performance and Visual Art in the 1960s', in *A Minimal Future? Art as Object 1958–68* (Los Angeles: Museum of Contemporary Art, 2004).

Laxton, Susan, 'Flou: Rayographs and the Dada Automatic', *October*, 127 (Winter 2009), pp. 25–48.

Lee, Pamela M., *Chronophobia: On Time in the Art of the 1960s* (Cambridge, MA,: MIT Press, 2004).

Léger, Fernand, 'Mechanical Ballet', *The Little Review* (Autumn/Winter 1924–5), pp. 42–4.

Léger, Fernand, *Functions of Painting*, ed. Edward F. Fry and trans. A. Anderson (London: Thames and Hudson, 1973).

Leiris, Michel, *Pierres pour un Alberto Giacometti* (Paris: L'Echoppe, 1991).

Lepecki, André, 'Redoing 18 Happenings in 6 Parts', in *Allan Kaprow – 18 Happenings in 6 Parts – 9/10/11 November 2006* (Göttingen: Steidl, 2007), pp. 45–50.

LeWitt, Sol, 'Paragraphs on Conceptual Art', *Artforum* 5 (10) (June 1967), pp. 79–83.

Liébault, Auguste, *Du sommeil et des états analogues considérés au point de vue de l'action du moral sur le physique* (Paris: Masson, 1866).

Liébault, Auguste, *Le sommeil provoqué et les états analogues* (Paris: O. Doin, 1889).

Lippard, Lucy (ed.), *Surrealists on Art* (Englewood Cliffs, NJ: Prentice Hall, 1970).

Lippard, Lucy, *Six Years: The Dematerialization of the Art Object from 1966 to 1972* (London: Studio Vista, 1973).

Malraux, André, *Museum without Walls*, trans. S. Gilbert and F. Price (Garden City, NY: Doubleday, 1967).

Malt, Johanna, *Obscure Objects of Desire: Surrealism, Fetishism and Politics* (Oxford: Oxford University Press, 2004).

Man Ray: Directeur de mauvais movies (Paris: Pompidou Centre, 1998).

Manovich, Lev, 'The Labor of Perception', *Telepolis: magazine der netzkultur* (June 15 1996) www.heise.de/tp/english/inhalt/co/2036/1.html.

Max Ernst: Sculptures, maisons et paysages (Paris: Pompidou Centre, 1998).

McAllester Jones, Mary, *Gaston Bachelard: Subversive Humanist* (Madison: The University of Wisconsin Press, 1991).

McEvilley, Thomas, *Sculpture in the Age of Doubt* (New York: Allworth Press, 1999).

McLuhan, Marshall, *Understanding Media: The Extensions of Man* [1964] (Cambridge, MA: MIT Press, 1994).

Meyer-Hermann, Eva, Andew Perchuk and Stephanie Rosenthal (eds), *Allan Kaprow: Art as Life* (Los Angeles: Getty Publications, 2008).

Mike Kelley: 13 New Untitled Black and White Photographs (New York: Metro Pictures Gallery, 1994).

Mills, Jane, *The Money Shot: Cinema, Sin and Censorship* (New South Wales: Pluto Press, 2001).

Molesworth, Helen (ed.), *Part Object Part Sculpture* (Columbus, OH: Wexner Art Center, 2005).

Moritz, William, 'Americans in Paris: Man Ray and Dudley Murphy', in Jan-Christopher Horak (ed.), *Lovers of Cinema: The First American Film Avant-Garde 1919–45* (Madison, WI: University of Wisconsin Press, 1995), pp. 118–36.

Mowry, Robert D., *Worlds within Worlds: The Richard Rosenblum Collection of Chinese Scholars' Rocks* (Cambridge, MA: Harvard University Art Museums, 1997).

Mulvey, Laura, 'The Index and the Uncanny', in Carolyn Gill (ed.), *Time and the Image* (Manchester: Manchester University Press, 2001), pp. 139–48.
Mundy, Jennifer, *Biomorphism*, PhD thesis (London: Courtauld Institute of Art, 1986).
Mundy, Jennifer, 'Comment on England', in Chris Stephens (ed.), *Henry Moore* (London, 2009), pp. 22–37.
Münsterberg, Hugo, *The Photoplay: A Psychological Study* [New York, 1916] (New York: Dover, 1970).
Nash, Paul, 'Foreword', *Catalogue of Paintings and Sculpture by Paule Vézelay* (London: Lefevre Galleries, 1936).
Naumann, Francis, *Making Mischief: Dada Invades New York* (New York: Harry N. Abrams, 1997).
Neri, Louise (ed.), *Antipodes: Inside the White Cube* (London: White Cube, 2003).
Nixon, Mignon, 'On the Couch', *October*, 113 (Summer 2005), pp. 39–76.
O'Doherty, Brian, 'Art: 3 Displays Run Gamut of Styles', *New York Times* (6 June 1961), p. 43.
O'Doherty, Brian, 'The Gallery as Gesture', in Reesa Greenberg, Bruce W. Ferguson, and Sandy Nairne (eds), *Thinking about Exhibitions* (London: Routledge, 1996), pp. 321–40.
Objects of Contemplation: Natural sculptures from the Qing Dynasty (Leeds: Henry Moore Institute, 2009).
Orozco, Gabriel, *Photogravity* (Philadelphia: Philadelphia Museum of Art, 1999).
Partens, Alexander, 'Dada Art', in Richard Huelsenbeck (ed.), *Dada Almanac* [1920], eds Malcolm Green and Alastair Brotchie (London: Atlas Press, 1993).
Paule Vézelay Retrospective (London: England & Co, 2000).
Peirce, Charles Sanders, 'Logic as Semiotic: The Theory of Signs', in Justus Buchler (ed.), *The Philosophy of Peirce* (New York: Dover, 1940), pp. 98–119.
Peirce, Charles Sanders, 'Icon, Index, Symbol', in *Collected Papers: vol. 2: Elements of Logic* (Cambridge, MA: Harvard University Press, 1960).
Perec, Georges, *Espèces d'espaces* [1974] (Paris: Galilée, 2000).
Phillips, Christopher (ed.), *Photography in the Modern Era* (New York: Aperture, 1989).
Pietz, William, 'The Problem of the Fetish, Part I', *Res*, 9 (Spring 1985), pp. 5–17.
Potts, Alex, *The Sculptural Imagination* (New Haven and London: Yale University Press, 2000).
Pudovkin, Vsevolod I., *Film Technique and Film Acting*, ed. and trans. Ivor Montague (London: Vision Press, 1958).
Ray, Man, 'L'Age de la lumière', *Minotaure*, 1 (3–4) (December 1933), pp. 39–40.
Read, Peter and Julia Kelly (eds), *Giacometti: Critical Essays* (Farnham: Ashgate, 2009).
Regards sur Minotaure: La Revue à tête de bête (Geneva: Musée d'art et d'histoire, 1987).
Reiss, Julie H., *From Margin to Center: The Spaces of Installation Art* (Cambridge, MA: MIT Press, 1999).
Reynaud Paligot, Carole, *Parcours politique des surréalistes 1919–69* (Paris: Éditions du CNRS, 1995).
Reynolds, Ann, *Robert Smithson: Learning from New Jersey and Elsewhere* (Cambridge, MA: MIT Press, 2003).
Richter, Hans, *Dada, Art and Anti-Art* (London: Thames and Hudson, 1965).
Rosenzweig, Phyllis (ed.), *Gabriel Orozco: Photographs* (Göttingen: Steidl Publishers and Washington D.C.: Hirshhorn Museum and Sculpture Garden, 2004).
Rubin, William, *Dada and Surrealist Art* (New York: Harry N. Abrams, 1969).
Salmon, André, 'Apologue du petit poisson de fer blanc', *La jeune sculpture française* (Paris: Albert Messein, 1919), pp. 8–19.
Sanouillet, Michel and Elmer Peterson (eds), *The Writings of Marcel Duchamp* (New York: Da Capo Press, 1989).
Sayag, Alain, and Annick Lionel-Marie (eds), *Brassaï: The Monograph* (Boston: Little, Brown & Co., 2000).
Schimmel, Paul, *Out of Actions: Between Performance and the Object, 1949–79* (Los Angeles: Museum of Contemporary Art and London: Thames and Hudson, 1998).

Schimmel, Paul, 'Intentionality and Performance-Based Art', in Miguel Angel Corzo (ed.), *Mortality Immortality? The Legacy of 20th-Century Art* (Los Angeles: Getty Publications, 1999), pp. 135–40.

Schneider, Pierre, 'Arp Speaks for the Laws of Chance', *ARTnews*, 57 (November 1958), pp. 50–51.

Semin, Didier (et al.), *Christian Boltanski* (London: Phaidon, 1997).

Seuphor, Michel, 'L'Art nouveau et le surréalisme', *Abstraction création art non figuratif*, 1 (1932), p. 11.

Sheringham, Michael, *Everyday Life: Theories and Practices from Surrealism to the Present* (Oxford: Oxford University Press, 2006).

Smithson, Robert, *The Writings of Robert Smithson*, ed. Nancy Holt (New York: New York University Press, 1979).

Solomon-Godeau, Abigail, 'Mourning or Melancholia: Christian Boltanski's *Missing House*', *Oxford Art Journal*, 12(2) (1998), pp. 1–20.

Sontag, Susan, 'The Aesthetics of Silence', *Aspen*, 5+6 (1967), section 3.

Stallabrass, Julian, *Gargantua: Manufactured Mass Culture* (London and New York: Verso, 1996).

Stauffacher, Frank (ed.), *Art in Cinema* (New York: Arno Press, 1968).

Tériade, E., 'Emancipation de la peinture', *Minotaure*, 1 (3–4) (December 1933), pp. 9–20.

Trachtenberg, Alan (ed.), *Classic Essays in Photography* (New Haven: Leete's Island Books, 1980).

Turvey, Malcolm, 'Jean Epstein's Cinema of Immanence: The Rehabilitation of the Corporeal Eye', *October*, 83 (Winter 1998), pp. 25–50.

Tzara, Tristan, 'Marcel Janco', *Dada* 1 [July 1917] (Paris: Jean-Michel Place 1981), pp. 39–41.

Tzara, Tristan, 'Essai sur la situation de la poésie', *Le Surréalisme au service de la révolution*, 4 (December 1931), pp. 15–23.

Tzara, Tristan, 'D'un certain automatisme du goût', *Minotaure*, 1 (3–4) (December 1933), pp. 81–4.

Valéry, Paul, 'The Screen', in *The Collected Works of Paul Valéry, vol. 2: Poems in the Rough*, ed. Jackson Matthews and trans. H. Corke (London: Routledge & Kegan Paul, 1969).

Walker, Ian, *City Gorged with Dreams: Surrealism and Documentary Photography in Interwar Paris* (Manchester and New York: Manchester University Press, 2002).

Warner, Marina, *Only Make Believe: Ways of Playing* (Compton Verney Art Gallery, 2005).

Watts, Harriet, 'Arp, Kandinsky, and the Legacy of Jakob Böhme', in *The Spiritual in Art: Abstract Painting 1890–1985* (Los Angeles: Los Angeles County Museum of Art and New York: Abbeville Press, 1986), pp. 239–55.

Welchman, John C., 'Survey: The Mike Kelleys', in *Mike Kelley* (London: Phaidon, 1999), pp. 42–93.

Welchman, John C., 'God, Family, Fun, and Friends: Mike Kelley in Conversation with John C. Welchman', in J.C. Welchman (ed.), *Institutional Critique and After* (Zurich: JRP/Ringier, 2006), pp. 337–66.

Welchman, John C., 'Fête Accompli', in Mike Kelley, *Day is Done* (New Haven and London: Yale University Press, 2007).

Wentworth, Richard, 'Making Do and Getting By', *Artscribe*, 14 (September 1978), pp. 21–3.

Wentworth, Richard, 'Losing Battles: A Conversation between Richard Wentworth and Stuart Morgan, May 1984', in *Richard Wentworth* (London: Lisson Gallery, 1984), pp. 13–19.

Wentworth, Richard, 'In Conversation with Anna Dezeuze', *Papers of Surrealism* 4 (Winter 2005), www.surrealismcentre.ac.uk/papersofsurrealism/journal4/.

Wentworth, Richard (et al.), *Richard Wentworth* (London: Tate Publishing, 2004).

Williams, Linda, *Hard Core: Power, Pleasure and the 'Frenzy of the Visible'* (Berkeley: University of California Press, 1999).

Wilson, Sarah, *Paule Vézelay/Hans Arp: The Enchantments of Purity* (Leeds: Henry Moore Institute, 1995).

Wood, Jon, *Close Encounters: The Sculptor's Studio in the Age of the Camera* (Leeds: Henry Moore Institute, 2001).

Wood, Jon, David Hulks and Alex Potts (eds), *The Modern Sculpture Reader* (Leeds: Henry Moore Institute, 2007).

Zervos, Christian, 'Quelques notes sur les sculptures de Giacometti', *Cahiers d'art*, 7 (1932), pp. 337–42.

INDEX

In general, French titles are listed in their English translations
Contributor names are only listed for references to previously published work cited by other authors
Pages including illustrations are in **bold**

abstract art, abstraction 18, 22–4, 26–7, 29–30, 64, 85, 120–21, 141–3, 166–7, 171; *see also* biomorphic, minimalism, concrete, form
accident, accidental 7, 44, 46–7, 149, 151, 164, 171–4, 179
Ades, Dawn 5, 61, 172
agency 9, 111–2, 174
Alloway, Lawrence 7
Althusser, Louis 133
amateur photography, *see* photography
anthropology, *see* Balfour, Henry; Gell, Alfred; Ingold, Tim
anthropomorphic, anthropomorphism 44, 46–7, 49
Antin, David 127
Aragon, Louis 18, 42, 54, 65–6, 71, 131–2
Arp, Hans 13, 15, 19, 22–30, 40–41, 46, 49, 51–2
  Bell and Navels 51
  Head with Annoying Objects 25, **26**, 29
  Human Concretion 27, **28**
  Navel and Two Thoughts 23, 25, **27**, 29
artisan, artisanal 39, 50, 100; *see also* craft, labour
Askevold, David 139
assemblage 18, 22, 39–40, 83, 85–6, 138, 142–3, 146, 150, 152, 161, 171, 174
attention, attentive 3, 5, 9, 22, 60–69, 72–3, 113–4, 119, 122, 128–132; *see also* distraction
Aron, Robert 64
aura 3, 9, 20, 22, 176
automatic, automatism 1, 5–6, 13, 15–19, 22, 26, 31n8, 33n28, 40, 42–4, 46–8, 52, 54, 60–63, 99, 101–102, 104, 111–2, 114, 150, 157–8, 172–5
  automatic drawing 174
  automatic sculpture 43–4, 46, 101
  automatic writing 5–6, 16–17, 22, 43, 102, 104, 157, 172, 174

Baker, Simon 5, 61
balance 7, 46, 108, 124, 126–7
Balázs, Béla 66
Balfour, Henry 44, 46–9
Barney, Matthew 157
Barthes, Roland 4, 6, 90, 93, 138, 174–6
  Camera Lucida 174–6
  'Death of the Author' 90, 93
Bataille, Georges 61, 157, 161
Bazin, André 173, 177
Bellmer, Hans 168n8, 175
Benjamin, Walter 4, 20–22, 65, 71, 102, 105, 112, 130, 175
Bismuth, Pierre 157–8
biomorphic, biomorphism 46–7, 49, 51–2, 141, 150
Blanchot, Maurice 109, 112
Boiffard, Jacques-André 61, 104, 163–4
Boltanski, Christian 6, 175–8
  Inventories 176
  Lost Property 177
  Monument **178**
  Reference Vitrines 176, **177**
Bourgeois, Louise 5, 8
Brancusi, Constantin 4, 14–15, 26–8
Brassaï, 1, **2**, 3, 5, 8–9, 14–16, 31n7, 32n12, 40, 50, 61, 99, 102, 105–106, 109, 114, 120, 122, 128, 161–3, 174, 179
  Paris by Night 162

photographs for *Mad Love* 161–3
and Dalí, Salvador, *Involuntary Sculptures*, see *Involuntary Sculptures*
Breton, André 5, 9, 15–19, 28–9, 30n3, 33n28, 39–40, 42–4, 46–9, 54, 61–3, 104, 107, 111, 158–9, 161–5, 168, 171–5, 177, 179, 181
Nadja 5, 43, 104, 159, 162, 177
Mad Love 43, 107, 161–3
bricolage, *bricoler*, *bricoleur* 109–12; *see also* fiddling
Buchloh, Benjamin 8, 178–9
Buñuel, Luis 61, 64
and Salvador Dalí, *Un Chien andalou* 61

Caillois, Roger 19, 111–2
Cartier-Bresson, Henri 161
Certeau, Michel de 100, 109–14
chance 1, 24, 42, 44, 47, 62, 93, 107, 112, 122, 158, 161–3, 171–5; *see also* accident, encounter (chance)
objective 107, 112, 158, 161–3, 171
Chapman, Jake and Dinos 157
child, children 5, 9, 22, 28, 42, 66, 119–22, 127–33, 144, 146, 176; *see also* play
children's education 119–22, 130, 132–3, 137, 143, 149, 151
close-up 1, 5, 60–61, 65–9, 71–2, 102, 114, 131, 163, 179
conceptual art, conceptualism 6–7, 78, 80–81, 88, 90–92, 94, 104, 120, 122, 128, 139, 143, 148–9, 183n4; *see also* photography (conceptual)
concrete, concrete art, concretion 17–18, 22–30, 47, 101, 104
Conley, Katharine 13, 15, 32n12, 131
contingency, contingent 1, 7, 41, 91–2, 126, 138
contraptions 40–42
craft 16–17, 19, 26, 30, 54, 138, 173; *see also* artisan, labour
Crary, Jonathan 130, 132

dada 18, 23–4, 26, 29, 40–42, 59–60, 64, 69, 173
Dalí, Salvador 1, 3–5, 14–19, 23, 26, 29, 31n8, 31n9, 32n16, 39, 43, 54, 61, 99–100, 104, 106, 109, 111, 114, 154, 161; *see also* Luis Buñuel, *Involuntary Sculptures*
critical-paranoiac theory 111, 154
'De la beauté comestible de l'architecture modern 'style' 16, 19, 31n8, 31n9, 32n16, 32n18, 33n28, 104
Lobster Telephone 4
Phénomène de l'extase, Le 16, 31n8, 31n9, 32n15, 32n16
death 4, 6, 30, 63, 68, 86, 91, 107–8, 112, 129, 135n18, 158, 162, 172, 176, 178
dematerialisation 4, 6–7, 163; *see also* materiality
demi-sommeil 9, 63; *see also* dreams
desire 6–9, 44, 72, 81, 104, 106–7, 140, 144–5, 151, 172, 175
détournement 110, 143
display 62, 68, 72, 77, 137, 148, 176, 179
distraction 3, 9, 22, 30, 61–5, 67–8, 71, 130; *see also* attention, fiddling
document, documentation, documentary 1, 3–4, 6–7, 77–8, 81, 83–4, 86, 91, 94, 104, 122, 139, 141, 144, 146–8, 152, 173, 176–7; *see also* photography (documentary)
Doesburg, Theo van 23–4
drama, dramatic, dramatisation, dramatise 3, 7, 46, 91, 102, 105, 124, 126–8, 146, 163–4; *see also* narrative
dream 17, 25–6, 29, 39, 42, 61, 64–5, 68, 84, 152, 154, 172, 174; *see also demi-sommeil*, reverie
Duchamp, Marcel 5, 8, 24, 29, 41–2, 47, 70, 78, 89–91, 93, 167, 174, 176, 179
Bicycle Wheel 41
Bottle Rack 179
'Creative Act, The' 90, 93
Dust Breeding 8
Fountain 167
inframince 8
readymades 5, 8, 47, 78, 90, 93, 167, 176, 179
Rotoreliefs 42, 70
Tu m' 174
and Man Ray, *Anemic Cinema* 70

Eluard, Paul 9, 14–16, 31n6, 31n9, 31no10, 99
encounter 5, 9, 15, 17, 19, 25, 28, 63, 81, 99, 107, 110, 120, 122, 162, 171–2, 174–5, 179
chance encounter 5, 19, 171–2
Ehrenzweig, Anton 122
Epstein, Jean 67–8
Ernst, Max 17, 29, 47, 174
Evans, Walker 173
experience 5, 9, 20, 27, 43, 62–5, 68–73, 78, 80–81, 84–5, 93–4, 104, 113–4, 121, 124, 128, 130, 133, 137, 164, 173, 178–9

experiment, experimental 4, 6, 9, 14, 39, 42, 65, 70–71, 82, 126, 129, 131, 173
  experimental film 9, 126
  experimental photography 4, 173
  experimental psychology 63

falling 59, 107–8, 126; *see also* balance, gravity
fantasm, fantasmatic, *see* phantasm, phantasmatic
fantasy 4, 7, 137, 140, 145–7, 151, 154; *see also* phantasm
fear 6, 111, 140
Fer, Briony 8, 16, 29–30
fetish, fetishism 4, 7, 141, 159
fiddling 1, 50–51, 54, 107, 109–10, 128; *see also bricolage*, distraction
flea market 40, 43, 48, 107–8, 158, 161, 163, 165, 171–2
Fogle, Douglas 6–8
form 1, 3, 8, 16–19, 22, 24–7, 29–30, 39, 41–4, 46–9, 51–4, 87, 94, 108, 120, 138, 140–143, 150, 164–8, 171–2, 175, 181; *see also* formless, transformation
formless, formlessness 8, 17, 140–142, 157
Foster, Hal 30, 107, 122, 127, 157–8, 175
Foucault, Michel 152
found object, *objet trouvé*, *trouvaille* 5–6, 39–40, 43–4, 46–50, 52–4, 61, 69, 94, 99, 104–7, 110, 131, 158–68, 171–2, 175–6, 179
  'mask' **160**, 162–3, 172; *see also* Man Ray
  'slipper spoon' 43, 48–9, 107, **160**, 163; *see also* Man Ray
found photograph 7, 104, 145, 154–5, 164, 176
Fox, Terry 6–7, 122–33
  Children's Tapes 6–7, 122, **123**, 124, **125**, 126–9, 131–3
Freud, Sigmund 16, 62–3, 106, 113, 154, 157, 171–2, 174
  Psychopathology of Everyday Life 16, 106
Freytag-Loringhoven, Elsa von 41

Gell, Alfred 47, 54
Giacometti, Alberto, 3, 5, 14–15, 19–20, 22, 25, 28–9, 32n13, 39, 41–3, 47–54, 82, 158–9, 161–3, 172
  Caress 49
  Disagreeable Object 19, **21**, 22, 28, 48–9
  Hands Holding the Void (Invisible Object) 161, 163, 172
  Point to the Eye 42, 50
  Suspended Ball 41–3, 51
  Vide Poche 49, **50**, 54
Graham, Dan 6, 104
gravity 101, 108, 124, 128, 131; *see also* balance, falling
growth 3, 22, 24, 27, 29–30, 46–7, 54, 66, 82, 85, 131
Gunning, Tom 62, 70

happenings 77–8, 81–6
haptic 16, 19–22, 25–8; *see also* tactile
Harris, Steven 75n31, 112, 169n14
hasard objectif, see chance (objective)
Highmore, Ben 113
Hirschhorn, Thomas 115n4, 157
Holt, John 119–22, 132–3

index, indexical 59, 173–179; *see also* signs
informe, *see* formless
inframince, *see* Duchamp, Marcel
Ingold, Tim 46
instinct 9, 24, 111–2, 162; *see also* reflex
intentional, intentionality 43, 173–4
involuntary 1, 3, 6, 9, 40–41, 47, 54, 111, 114, 120, 122, 128, 137–8, 143, 145–6, 149–51, 159, 163–4, 167, 171–4, 179; *see also* accident, automatism, instinct, *Involuntary Sculptures*, reflex
Involuntary Sculptures, *Sculptures involontaires* 1, **2**, 5–9, 13–18, 30, 31n8, 31n9, 33n28, 40, 50, 61, 99–102, 104–6, 108, 114, 120, 122, 128, 131, 174, 179

Janco, Marcel 41
Jenny, Laurent 43, 111

Kandinsky, Wassily 15, 23–4, 35n43
Kaprow, Allan 7, 77–95
  18 Happenings in 6 Parts 78, 83
  Yard 79, **80**, 81–7, **88**, **89**, 91–4
Kelley, Mike 5–7, 9, 137–155, 157
  Black Out 146–51
  Day is Done 137, 152, **153**, 154
  Dust Balls **141**, 142
  Educational Complex 151–2
  John Glenn Memorial Detroit River Reclamation Project 150, **151**
  Local Culture Pictorial Guide 147–50
  Poetry of Form, The 138, 141, **142**, 143–4
  Poltergeist, The 139, **140**, 144
  Reconstructed History 143–4, **145**, 146
Kelly, Julia 34n36, 169n12
Kelsey, Robin 110
  and Stimson, Blake 6
Kolbowski, Silvia 80–81

Kracauer, Siegfried 68
Krauss, Rosalind 5, 19, 62, 102, 106, 109, 120–1, 128, 157, 173–5
Kubler, George 90–91

labour 1, 16–17, 19, 32n13, 71, 130, 133
  division of 16, 19
  manual 19, 71
Lacan, Jacques 15, 175
Laurens, Henri 3, 14–15, 19
Laxton, Susan 173
Le Corbusier 16
leftover, sculpture as 8; *see also* relics, residue
Léger, Fernand 60, 69–73
  Ballet mécanique 60, 69, **70**, 71–3
Leiris, Michel 31n10, 47
Levine, Sherrie 143, 154–5, 175
LeWitt, Sol 92, 120, **121**
Lipchitz, Jacques 3, 14, 19
Lippard, Lucy 7
loss 46, 107, 112

Maar, Dora 161, 163, 165
McCarthy, Paul 77, 145
McEvilley, Thomas 4
McGill, Melissa 6, 158–9, 164–8
  Inside the White Cube 158, **159**
  Shadow of Ecstasy **159**, 164-5
  Untitled ('personages') 165, **166**
  Untitled (porcelain figures) **167**
McLuhan, Marshall 130–31
magic 9, 43, 48, 129; *see also* spiritualism, transformation
  'circumstantial magic' 163, 179
Maillol, Aristide 3, 14–5, 19
Malraux, André 4, 84, 91
Man Ray 15, 29, 32n12, 32n16, 40, 59–73, 158, 161–5, 173–4; *see also* Duchamp, Marcel
  Aeneas Carrying his Father **45**, 46
  Moving Sculpture 3
  Rayographs 59, 61, 173
  Return to Reason (*Le Retour à la raison*) 59, **60**, 61, 64, 73
  'slipper spoon' 43, **160**, 163
  Woman Holding Giacometti's Objet Désagréable 20, **21**
mannequin 40, 72
marvellous 5, 65, 72, 102, 105, 107, 131, 163, 174; *see also* wonder
Masson, André 29, 31n10, 51, 174
materiality 4, 7, 51, 59, 114, 128
maternal imagery 28–9
memory 9, 47, 68, 80–81, 91, 111–2, 114, 150–52, 154, 174, 176–7
  Repressed Memory Syndrome 147, 154
  screen memory 81
Merleau-Ponty, Maurice 121
minimalism, minimalist 8, 86–7, 104–5, 120–2, 126–8, 132–3
Minotaure 1, **2**, 13–15, 19, 23, 31n4, **45**, 46, 99, 112, 163
modernism, modernist 6, 13–14, 16, 23, 39, 77, 82, 127, 130, 150, 152
Molesworth, Helen 7–8
Moore, Henry 22, 46, 49, 100
Morris, Robert 25, 121
Mulvey, Laura 62, 175
Münsterberg, Hugo 67–8
myth 46, 138, 140, 143, 150, 158–9, 165; *see also* tale, narrative, symbolic

Namuth, Hans **83**, 85
narrative 6, 46, 62, 64, 69, 94, 105, 112, 126, 129, 159, 162–3; *see also* drama, tale
natural objects 5, 43–4, 46–7, 49, 179
Nauman, Bruce 78, 179
Nixon, Mignon 81

objectification 9, 15, 18–19, 22, 67, 172; *see also* reification
objective chance, *hasard objectif*; *see* chance
objet trouvé, *see* found object
O'Doherty, Brian 80, 82, 89
Oldenburg, Claes 82–4, 86, 94
Oppenheim, Meret 4, 179
Orozco, Gabriel 6–8, 78, 115n4, 178–80
  Extension of Reflection 179, **180**
  Yielding Stone 179, **180**

parodic, parody 104, 114, 144
Perec, Georges 109, 112
perform, performance, performative 7, 79–80, 87, 90–92, 94, 101, 109, 114, 127, 130–31, 137–9, 144–5, 156, 179
phantasm, phantasmatic 9, 63–4, 131, 152, 172, 181; *see also* fantasy
phenomenological, phenomenology 121–2, 124, 127–8; *see also* Merleau-Ponty, Maurice
photography
  amateur 7, 102, 104–5, 113–4
  conceptual, photoconceptualism 6–7, 104–5
  documentary 6, 102, 105, 138–9, 141, 147–8; *see also* document
  found, *see* found photograph

simulacral, *see* simulacral
surrealist 4–5, 62, 102, 109, 174–6
and appropriation 138, 143, 148, 154, 175
and technical accidents 7, 149, 173
Picabia, Francis 70, 145–6
Pierce, Charles Sanders 173
play 19, 22, 54, 122, 128, 158
games 42, 48, 50
parlour tricks 42
toys 42, 50, 137, 176
political, politics 8, 13–14, 17, 22, 71, 110–11, 127, 134n13, 158, 161; *see also* revolution
Pollock, Jackson 77–8, 83–5
post-minimalism, post-minimalist 122, 127, 129, 143; *see also* process art
Potts, Alex 161
process art 6–7, 101, 108; *see also* post-minimalism
Proust, Marcel 9
Pudovkin, Vsevolod 66

readymade, *see* Duchamp, Marcel
reflex 111–2, 114, 137, 145–6, 149; *see also* instinct
reification 8, 29–30; *see also* objectification
relic 80, 176, 179; *see also* leftover, residue
representation, representational 4–5, 61, 68, 72, 105, 111, 129, 140, 162–3, 171–3
residue 16, 90, 94, 109, 111, 114, 159, 171–3; *see also* leftover, relic
reverie 25–6, 84, 130; *see also* dream
revolution, revolutionary 13–14, 17, 111, 113, 159, 161,
Révolution surréaliste, La 3, 40, 42, 104
rocks and stones 1, 4, 23, 25, 29, 40, 42–4, 46–7, 49, 53–4, 126, 150, 179
Rodin, Auguste 4
Ruscha, Ed 105

Schimmel, Paul 87, 92–4
sculpture
as leftover *see* leftover
automatic *see* automatic
involuntary *see Involuntary Sculptures*
surrealist 3, 13, 15, 20, 29–30, 40
Sculptures involontaires, see *Involuntary Sculptures*
Serra, Richard 6, 101–2, **103**, 108, 114, 126–9
Sheringham, Michael 113–4
Sherman, Cindy 175
sign, signifier 6, 16–18, 102, 106, 109, 114, 128, 173–8; *see also* index, representation, symbolic
simulacral, simulacrum 6, 175, 178
skill 16, 19, 49, 110, 173; *see also* artisan, craft, labour
Smithson, Robert 6, 90–91, 93–4, 104, 179
Solomon-Godeau, Abigail 175, 177
Sontag, Susan 89–90
spectacle, spectacular 44, 46–8, 62–3, 68, 77, 81, 102, 128
spiritual 24, 44
spiritualist, spiritualism 60, 63
Stieglitz, Alfred 167
Surréalisme au service de la revolution, Le 14, **20**, 42
surrealism
surrealist film 64
Surrealist Exhibition of Objects 161, 179
surrealist object 3–5, 8, 16, 18–19, 22, 25, 29, 39–43, 48–9, 54, 159, 161, 163, 165, 179; *see also* found object, natural object, readymade
surrealist photography, *see* photography
surrealist sculpture, *see Involuntary Sculptures*, sculpture
symbolic, symbolical, symbolism 4, 8, 15, 18, 22, 40, 42–3, 48, 105, 111, 128, 132, 138, 144, 146, 162, 179; *see also* myth

tactile, touch 8–9, 20–22, 28, 40–41, 48–9, 51, 54, 131, 163; *see also* haptic
Talbot, William Henry Fox 3, 110, 113
tale 9, 48, 113; *see also* found object, myth, narrative
Tatlin, Vladimir 41
television 122, 129–133
Tériade 13–14, 16, 23
touch, *see* tactile
trance 63, 130
transformation, transformative 46, 48–9, 64, 66, 68, 71, 77, 87, 92, 105, 124, 129, 131, 141, 166–7; *see also* form, formless, growth
trauma, traumatic 46, 146–7, 152, 154, 158, 172, 177
trouvaille, *see* found object
Tzara, Tristan 16, 18–19, 22–3, 40–41, 59

uncanny 5, 30, 41, 107, 145, 152, 175
unconscious 5–6, 8–9, 14, 16–17, 19, 26, 29–30, 44, 62–5, 67–8, 81, 102, 106, 111, 113–4, 146, 149, 154, 171–2, 174–5
collective 9, 113

Vézelay, Paule 39, 51, **52**, 53–4

Boat and Fruit, 51
Garden **53**, 54

Walker, Ian 32n12, 102, 104, 162
Wall, Jeff 104–5
Wentworth, Richard 6–7, 99–114
Making Do, Getting By 6–7, 99, **100**, **101**, 102, 104–105, 107, **108**, 109–14
wonder, wonderment 104, 133, 173; *see also* marvellous

For Product Safety Concerns and Information please contact our EU representative GPSR@taylorandfrancis.com Taylor & Francis Verlag GmbH, Kaufingerstraße 24, 80331 München, Germany

Printed and bound by CPI Group (UK) Ltd, Croydon, CR0 4YY
16/10/2025
01977775-0018

Books and Periodicals in Brazil 1768-1930
A Transatlantic Perspective

LEGENDA

LEGENDA, founded in 1995 by the European Humanities Research Centre of the University of Oxford, is now a joint imprint of the Modern Humanities Research Association and Routledge. Titles range from medieval texts to contemporary cinema and form a widely comparative view of the modern humanities, including works on Arabic, Catalan, English, French, German, Greek, Italian, Portuguese, Russian, Spanish, and Yiddish literature. An Editorial Board of distinguished academic specialists works in collaboration with leading scholarly bodies such as the Society for French Studies, the British Comparative Literature Association and the Association of Hispanists of Great Britain & Ireland.

MHRA

The Modern Humanities Research Association (MHRA) encourages and promotes advanced study and research in the field of the modern humanities, especially modern European languages and literature, including English, and also cinema. It also aims to break down the barriers between scholars working in different disciplines and to maintain the unity of humanistic scholarship in the face of increasing specialization. The Association fulfils this purpose primarily through the publication of journals, bibliographies, monographs and other aids to research.

Routledge
Taylor & Francis Group
LONDON AND NEW YORK

Routledge is a global publisher of academic books, journals and online resources in the humanities and social sciences. Founded in 1836, it has published many of the greatest thinkers and scholars of the last hundred years, including Adorno, Einstein, Russell, Popper, Wittgenstein, Jung, Bohm, Hayek, McLuhan, Marcuse and Sartre. Today Routledge is one of the world's leading academic publishers in the Humanities and Social Sciences. It publishes thousands of books and journals each year, serving scholars, instructors, and professional communities worldwide.

www.routledge.com

STUDIES IN HISPANIC AND LUSOPHONE CULTURES

Studies in Hispanic and Lusophone Cultures are selected and edited by the Association of Hispanists of Great Britain & Ireland. The series seeks to publish the best new research in all areas of the literature, thought, history, culture, film, and languages of Spain, Spanish America, and the Portuguese-speaking world.

The Association of Hispanists of Great Britain & Ireland is a professional association which represents a very diverse discipline, in terms of both geographical coverage and objects of study. Its website showcases new work by members, and publicises jobs, conferences and grants in the field.

www.legendabooks.com/series/shlc

STUDIES IN HISPANIC AND LUSOPHONE CULTURES

1. *Unamuno's Theory of the Novel*, by C. A. Longhurst
2. *Pessoa's Geometry of the Abyss: Modernity and the* Book of Disquiet, by Paulo de Medeiros
3. *Artifice and Invention in the Spanish Golden Age*, edited by Stephen Boyd and Terence O'Reilly
4. *The Latin American Short Story at its Limits: Fragmentation, Hybridity and Intermediality*, by Lucy Bell
5. *Spanish New York Narratives 1898–1936: Modernisation, Otherness and Nation*, by David Miranda-Barreiro
6. *The Art of Ana Clavel: Ghosts, Urinals, Dolls, Shadows and Outlaw Desires*, by Jane Elizabeth Lavery
7. *Alejo Carpentier and the Musical Text*, by Katia Chornik
8. *Britain, Spain and the Treaty of Utrecht 1713-2013*, edited by Trevor J. Dadson and J. H. Elliott
9. *Books and Periodicals in Brazil 1768-1930: A Transatlantic Perspective*, edited by Ana Cláudia Suriani da Silva and Sandra Guardini Vasconcelos
10. *Lisbon Revisited: Urban Masculinities in Twentieth-Century Portuguese Fiction*, by Rhian Atkin
11. *Urban Space, Identity and Postmodernity in 1980s Spain: Rethinking the Movida*, by Maite Usoz de la Fuente

Books and Periodicals in Brazil 1768–1930

A Transatlantic Perspective

EDITED BY ANA CLÁUDIA SURIANI DA SILVA AND
SANDRA GUARDINI VASCONCELOS

Routledge
Taylor & Francis Group
LONDON AND NEW YORK
2014

First published 2014 by Modern Humanities Research Association and Routledge

2 Park Square, Milton Park, Abingdon, Oxfordshire OX14 4RN
52 Vanderbilt Avenue, New York, NY 10017

Routledge is an imprint of the Taylor & Francis Group, an informa business

First issued in paperback 2020

ISBN 978-1-909662-32-2 (hbk)
ISBN 978-0-367-59962-1 (pbk)

CONTENTS

Acknowledgements ix

Notes on the Contributors x

Introduction I
Ana Cláudia Suriani da Silva and Sandra Guardini Vasconcelos

1 Reading in Colonial Brazil 13
Márcia Abreu

2 Booksellers in Rio de Janeiro: The Book Trade and Circulation of Ideas from 1808 to 1831 35
Lucia Maria Bastos Pereira das Neves and Tania Maria Tavares Bessone da Cruz Ferreira

3 Seditious Books and Ideas of Revolution in Brazil (1830–71) 52
Marisa Midori Deaecto and Lincoln Secco

4 Migratory Literary Forms: British Novels in Nineteenth-Century Brazil 68
Sandra Guardini Vasconcelos

5 The Library that Disappeared: The Rio de Janeiro British Subscription Library 87
Nelson Schapochnik

6 The History of a Pseudo-Dumas Novel: *The Hand of the Dead* 118
Paulo Motta Oliveira

7 *Revista Nacional e Estrangeira* (1839–40): A Foreign or a Brazilian Magazine? 133
Maria Eulália Ramicelli

8 The Role of the Press in the Incorporation of Brazil into the Paris Fashion System 148
Ana Cláudia Suriani da Silva

9 The Brazilian and the French *Bas de Page* 163
Lúcia Granja

10 How to Be a Professional Writer in Nineteenth-Century Brazil 176
Marisa Lajolo and Regina Zilberman

11 Print Technologies, World News and Narrative Form in Machado de Assis 199
Jussara Menezes Quadros

12 The Brazilian Book Market in Portugal in the Second Half of the Nineteenth Century and the Paradigm Change in Luso-Brazilian Cultural Relations 215
Patrícia de Jesus Palma

13 Popular Editions and Best-sellers at the End of the Nineteenth Century in Brazil 230
Alessandra El Far

14 The Brazilian Publishing Industry at the Beginning of the Twentieth Century: The Path of Monteiro Lobato 245
Cilza Bignotto and Milena Ribeiro Martins

Bibliography 261

Index 275

ACKNOWLEDGEMENTS

❖

The editors and authors gratefully acknowledge the National Council for Scientific and Technological Development (CNPq), the Coordination for the Improvement of Higher Education Personnel (CAPES), the São Paulo Research Foundation (FAPESP), the Research Commission of the Faculty of Education of the University of São Paulo (USP), the Rio de Janeiro Research Foundation (FAPERJ), the Hermès Fellowship Programme and the Cultural History Centre of the New University of Lisbon for sponsoring the research that generated some chapters of this book and their translation into English. We would also like to thank the Graduate Programme in English Language and Literature, USP, for contributing towards its publication.

We are very grateful to Carl Good, David Hardisty, Frank Hanson, James Gentry, Inpokulis Traduções and Mônica Saddy Martins for translating, and John Gledson, Madeleine Brook and the graduate students of the Master Program in Translation, University of Surrey, 2012–13, especially Alex Gardiner, Alison Le Douarec, Anna Sutton and Kate Ogden, for proofreading the chapters.

A.C.S. & S.G.V., July 2014

NOTES ON THE CONTRIBUTORS

Alessandra El Far is Lecturer in Anthropology at the Federal University of São Paulo (Unifesp, campus Guarulhos) and has done research on the history of the popular book in Brazil. She is the author of *A encenação da imortalidade* (2000), *Páginas de sensação* (2004) and *O livro e a leitura no Brasil* (2006).

Ana Cláudia Suriani da Silva is Lecturer in Brazilian Studies at University College London. She is the author of *Machado de Assis's Philosopher or Dog?: From Serial to Book Form* (2010) and has edited *Linha reta e linha curva: edição crítica e genética de um conto de Machado de Assis* (2003) and the bilingual edition of Victor Hénaux's *De l'amour des femmes pour les sots/Queda que as mulheres têm para os tolos* (2008). She has published articles and book chapters on the works of Machado de Assis, Artur Azevedo, Joseph Conrad and on the relationship between literature, the press and fashion.

Cilza Bignotto is Lecturer in Brazilian Literature at the Federal University of Ouro Preto (UFOP). She has written several articles on Monteiro Lobato's practices as a publisher in twentieth-century Brazil. Her book *Novas perspectivas sobre as práticas editoriais de Monteiro Lobato (1918–1925)* is to be published in 2014.

Jussara Menezes Quadros (PhD in Literary Theory, UNICAMP, Brazil), has worked as Lecturer at Princeton University and now teaches Brazilian Literature and Literary Theory at the Federal University of the State of Rio de Janeiro (Unirio). She has written several articles on Brazilian Literature in relation to book publishing and the practices of the press in the nineteenth century. Her book *Impressões românticas: gêneros literários e cultura impressa no Brasil no século XIX* will be published in 2014.

Lincoln Secco is Reader in History at the University of São Paulo (USP). He has published articles and books on the political and cultural history of Brazil and Portugal. His most recent book is *História do PT* (2013).

Lucia Maria Bastos Pereira das Neves is Professor of Modern History at the State University of Rio de Janeiro (UERJ) and holds research grants from the National Council for Scientific and Technological Development (CNPq) and the Rio de Janeiro Research Foundation (FAPERJ). Her area of research is Political History and History of the Book and Reading. She is the author of *O Império do Brasil* (1999); *Corcundas e constitucionais: a cultura política da Independência, 1820–1822* (2003), *Napoleão Bonaparte: imaginário e política em Portugal, c.1808–1810* (2008) and she has edited, among others books, *Retratos do setecentos e do oitocentos* (2009). Neves has also published her research in peer-reviewed journals and multi-authored books in Brazil, Portugal, Spain and France.

Lúcia Granja is Lecturer in Brazilian Literature at the São Paulo State University (Unesp, Campus São José do Rio Preto). She has published on Machado de Assis's *crônicas* and on the relationship between literature and the press. She has co-edited Machado de Assis's *Notas semanais* with John Gledson (2009), Machado de Assis's *Comentários da semana* (2008), and *Machado de Assis: ensaios da crítica contemporânea* (2008). She is the author of *Machado de Assis, escritor em formação: à roda dos jornais* (2000). He current research project on Brazilian literature published by Baptiste-Louis Garnier is affiliated to the international research project 'The Transatlantic Circulation of Printed Matter: The Globalization of Culture in the Nineteenth Century'.

Márcia Abreu is Reader in Literature at the University of Campinas (UNICAMP), Department of Literary Theory. She has authored *Histórias de cordéis e folhetos* (1999), *Os caminhos dos livros* (2003), *Cultura letrada: literatura e leitura* (2006) and edited some volumes on book history, including *Leitura, história e história da leitura* (2000), *Cultura letrada no Brasil: objetos e práticas*, with Nelson Schapochnik (2005), *Trajetórias do romance: circulação, leitura e escrita nos séculos XVIII e XIX* (2008), and *Impresso no Brasil: duzentos anos de livros brasileiros*, with Anibal Bragança (2010).

Maria Eulália Ramicelli is Lecturer in British and American Literature at the Federal University of Santa Maria (UFSM), Brazil. She has published on the circulation of British fiction in Brazil in the nineteenth century. She is the author of *Narrativas itinerantes: aspectos franco-britânicos da ficção brasileira, em periódicos da primeira metade do século XIX* (2009).

Marisa Lajolo is Professor of Brazilian Literature at the State University of Campinas (Unicamp) and also teaches literature at the Universidade Presbiteriana Mackenzie. She has published many books and articles, including *Do mundo da leitura para a leitura do mundo* (6th edn, 2010). Her latest book is *O poeta do exílio*, a biography of the Brazilian romantic poet Gonçalves Dias (FTD). She co-edited *Monteiro Lobato livro a livro (obra infantil)*, which won a Jabuti Prize in 2009. Her current research focuses on children's literature and the history of reading in Brazil.

Marisa Midori Deaecto is Lecturer in Book History at the School of Communication and Arts, University of São Paulo (ECA, USP) and is the author of *O Império dos livros: instituições e práticas de leituras na São Paulo oitocentista* (2011), which won the National Library Foundation's Sérgio Buarque de Holanda Prize in 2011, and the Jabuti Prize in 2012. She has also published many articles on print culture. Her blog can be found at <http://bibliomania-divercidades.blogspot.com.br/>.

Milena Ribeiro Martins is Lecturer in Brazilian Literature and Literary Theory at Federal University of Paraná (UFPR), Brazil. She has published articles on Monteiro Lobato's works, on book history and on the teaching of literature. Her present research deals with Lobato's view of the United States of America, fictionally represented in the book *América* (1932).

Nelson Schapochnik is a historian and Lecturer in History at the Faculty of Education, University of São Paulo (USP). He is the author of *João do Rio: um dândi na Cafelândia* (2004), *A hora futurista que passou e outros escritos* (2006), and co-author of *História da vida privada no Brasil* (volume 3, 1998) and he has published essays on Cultural History in Brazilian, French and Spanish journals. He is also member of the Advisory Board of *Portuguese Literary & Cultural Studies* (U.Mass Dartmouth) and *Tempo* (UFF).

Paulo Motta Oliveira is Reader in Portuguese Literature at the University of São Paulo (USP) and is the author of many articles and book chapters on nineteenth- and twentieth-century Portuguese literature, comparative literature and literary history. He co-authored *Literatura, história e política em Portugal, 1820–1856* (2007) and is the editor of *Travessias: D. João VI e o mundo lusófono* (2013), *Figurações do oitocentos* (2008) and *Literatura portuguesa: história, memória e perspectivas* (2007). His current research project focuses on the rise of the Portuguese novel.

Patrícia de Jesus Palma is doing a PhD in Portuguese Studies at the School of Humanities and Social Sciences, New University of Lisbon. Her area of research is Book History and Textual Criticism, more specifically literary culture in peripheral areas (Algarve: 1772–1910). The project received the award of a PhD grant from the Foundation for Science and Technology (FCT). Her master's dissertation, *A produção literária impressa no Algarve durante os séculos XIX e XX*, is on typographical and literary activities in the Algarve in the nineteenth and twentieth centuries.

Regina Zilberman is Reader in Portuguese Literature at Federal University of Rio Grande do Sul (UFRGS). She has published books on children's literature (*A literatura infantil na escola* (1987) and *Como e porque ler a literatura infantil brasileira* (2005), among others), reading practices (*A leitura e o ensino da literature* (1988) and *Fim do livro, fim dos leitores?* (2001)) and on the history of reading in Brazil, with Marisa Lajolo.

Sandra Guardini Vasconcelos is Professor of English and Comparative Literature at the University of São Paulo (USP). She has carried out postdoctoral studies at the University of Cambridge, and has been Visiting Research Associate at the Centre for Brazilian Studies, University of Oxford, and Visiting Professor at the University of Manchester. She has published on the eighteenth- and nineteenth-century English novel, on comparative literature (England–Brazil) and is the author of *Puras misturas: estórias em Guimarães Rosa* (1997), *Dez lições sobre o romance inglês do século XVIII* (2002), *A formação do romance ingles: ensaios teóricos* (2007). She holds a CNPq grant for her present research.

Tania Maria Tavares Bessone da Cruz Ferreira is Professor of History at the State University of Rio de Janeiro (UERJ). She has published on Brazilian cultural and book history, including the book chapters 'A biblioteca de Rui Barbosa: origens e preservação', in *Livros e impressos: retratos do setecentos e do oitocentos* (EdUERJ, 2009), 'As origens da resenha no Brasil: as experiências de *O Patriota*', in *Repensando o Brasil do oitocentos: cidadania, política e liberdade* (Civilização Brasileira, 2009), and co-edited *Literatura, história e política em Portugal (1820–1856)* (EdUERJ, 2007). She is a senior researcher at the National Council for Scientific and Technological Development (CNPq) and the Rio de Janeiro Research Foundation (FAPERJ), and an honorary fellow of the Brazilian Historic and Geographic Institute (IHGB).

INTRODUCTION

Ana Cláudia Suriani da Silva and Sandra Guardini Vasconcelos

'The nation cannot read'

In a *crônica* dated 15 August 1876[1], Machado de Assis, bringing to mind the recent publication of the 1872 General Census of the Empire, had a certain Mr Figure comment that '[t]he nation cannot read. There are only 30% of individuals living in this country who can read, of which 9% cannot read handwriting, while 70% remain in a state of complete ignorance'.[2] If in Machado's pen the prosopopoeia is far from surprising, his reader is bound to ask himself why the chronicler has in fact resorted to the results of the survey to colour his remark about the Constitution, thus putting side by side the two ideas, that is, the high levels of illiteracy in the country, which the figures brought to the foreground and made visible, and the body of norms and principles which rule civil rights and the organization of the State. The man who wrote this *crônica* was not yet the great Machado of the most famous and mature novels like *Memórias Póstumas de Brás Cubas* [*Posthumous Memoirs of Bras Cubas*], only to come out in 1881; however, he was the writer who had already published two novels (*Ressurreição* [*Resurrection*], 1872 and *A Mão e a Luva* [*The Hand and the Glove*], 1874) and had for almost two decades had a very active participation in the public sphere as a chronicler and journalist.

Beyond the mere statistical data, or the complaint of a writer aware of the limited reading public which was after all that which he addressed here, on bringing together the realm of the law and that of the letters, Machado put a finger on one of the sore points that characterized the process of modernization of Brazilian society, brought forth by the removal of the Portuguese Royal family to Rio de Janeiro in 1808 and by the Independence of the country in 1822. A few lines before, the narrator of the *crônica* had stated: 'I like figures, because they do not allow half measures or metaphors. They call things by their name, sometimes an ugly one [...]'.[3] Absolute master in the art of disguise that he was, however, or perhaps sure that his reader would be able to interpret the numbers, he avoids 'calling things by their name' and seems to judge that it was enough to leave a suggestion hanging in the air. He thus passes on to his audience the task of interpreting and, if the latter wishes, naming what the chronicler refuses to evince. The closeness barely touched on by Machado between civil rights and the world of letters can take us a long way if we want to interrogate some of the mechanisms of exclusion that shaped Brazilian society in the nineteenth century and determined the specificities of our literary system, an exclusion that the numbers of the Census mentioned in the *crônica* flaunt in their raw and crude nature. It was the first time that the social conditions of the young Brazilian nation were being translated into numbers. The 1872 Census encompassed almost the entire nation, leaving out only 181,583 inhabitants from 32 districts, which had been unable to meet the deadlines. As a matter of fact, illiteracy levels were even more alarming than the picture drawn by Machado, since according to the survey 7,290,294 (82%) out of the 8,854,774 inhabitants over the age of five could not read at all.[4]

When the Portuguese Royal Family disembarked in Rio de Janeiro in 1808, fleeing Napoleon's imminent invasion of Portugal and the threat to the Portuguese monarchy, the colony boasted 2,400,000 inhabitants in its territory, of which one million were slaves and 800,000 were Indians. Rio, as we know, was a modest colonial town of approximately 60,000 people, described as a chaotic, badly planned, dirty and stinking place — 'a black and mixed town in two thirds of its population' — that would experience new routines with the arrival of the Court and soon witness rapid changes in the urban landscape.[5] With the help of a French mission, specially commissioned by Dom João VI to plan buildings and urban equipment, a new town came into existence, with the creation of a Botanical Garden, a National Library, a Military Academy and a School of Medicine. Thus, while the precarious urban milieu of the first years was altered and modernized by constructions and urban interventions, out of the encounter between the colonial elite, which would Europeanize its habits, and the Portuguese and immigrants of other nationalities who had recently arrived, new practices and day-to-day forms of sociability would arise.

With the Portuguese Prince Regent's decision to flee to his Brazilian colony during the Napoleonic invasion and to open its ports to foreign trade, the colony was also suddenly and rapidly integrated into the literary marketplace, thanks to the diligent and interested efforts of merchants on both sides of the Atlantic. Throughout the colonial period, censorship had been very strict and the Portuguese authorities had kept close control over the circulation of books, even though there is evidence that they were available and that novels could be found in private collections or for sale, having been smuggled into the country to circumvent official bans on them.[6] Without its own press, with books needing the approval of censors before distribution, and with a small number of booksellers, the country — even after the opening of its ports — depended on illegal trade, carried out by the British, the French, and the Dutch, and on a small publishing industry of books in Portuguese which supplied its small consumer market from London and Paris.[7]However, with the foundation of the *Impressão Régia* [Royal Press] in 1808, the suspension of censorship in 1821, and the growing number of booksellers and bookshops in Rio de Janeiro, this picture started to change. Gradually, these literate circles began to introduce and offer cultural equipment and goods on the 'fluminense' market.[8] Measures like the foundation of newspapers and magazines, and the opening of reading rooms counted on the active engagement of foreigners such as the Portuguese Zeferino Vito de Meireles, founder of *Diario do Rio de Janeiro* in 1821, the Frenchman Pierre Plancher, founder of *Jornal do Commercio* in 1827, the Germans who created the Gesellschaft Germania (1821), the British of the Rio de Janeiro British Subscription Library (1826), and the Portuguese of the Real Gabinete

Português de Leitura [Royal Portuguese Circulating Library] (1837). They were all initiatives which enabled the circulation of books and printed matter, making reading more accessible, even if to a small number of literate people.[9] This is the paradox that will run through the nineteenth century — the increasing availability of reading materials in contrast with the pervading exclusion of vast swathes of people from the world of letters. Although the 1824 Constitution had promised to offer 'free primary instruction to all citizens', in 1867 only 10% of the school-age population was enrolled at elementary schools, while in 1879 the end of the ban on school enrolment for slaves was still under debate. The living conditions of free workers, that is, the non-black poor, former slaves and mulattoes, whose subsistence came from labour, were not strikingly different. Their lives, as suggests Antonio Candido in his reading of the novel *Memórias de um sargento de milícias* [*Memoirs of a Militia Sergeant*], oscillated between the spheres of order and disorder.[10] Nothing was farther from the notions of bourgeois individualism and economic liberalism prevailing in nineteenth-century Europe than the patrimonialism, clientelism, and slave labour that structured Brazilian society at the time.[11] In so far as individualism and citizenship are notions that cannot be dissociated in the bourgeois order, there could be no social and political recognition of the individual in a society whose mode of production was based on slavery and where there was, therefore, no exercise of civil rights by the majority of the population, alienated, among other things, from the access to public education. The process of modernization in Brazil thus obeyed a principle according to which progressive moments corresponded to and perpetuated regressive ones. In other words, backwardness was the other, complementary, face of progress. In this context of exclusion, in which reading and writing practices were rights and privileges of race, gender, and class, one needs to relativize ideas about their universality. No one challenges that there were readers. Not only were reading sessions around the hearth common, but contemporary newspapers often published advertisements placed by readers interested in buying new and second-hand novels, trying to recover borrowed or stolen books, or to return lost books to their owners. In spite of the implementation of reading practices and the institutionalization of spaces devoted to the production and diffusion of printed artefacts, however, the expansion of culture and of Rio as a lettered city in nineteenth-century Brazil remained within the bounds and limits imposed by the socioeconomic reality of the country.[12]

This was the backcloth and cultural environment in which flourished, developed and circulated the books, novels and periodicals that the booksellers and circulating libraries made available at the Court, mainly after the suspension of censorship in 1821. Publicizing their merchandise in catalogues or in newspapers, they offered potential readers a varied repertoire in which Britain and France appeared as the main sources of titles and authors. The obvious presence of European novels at the heart of the intellectual and artistic life of nineteenth-century Brazil also had an undeniable role in the making of the Brazilian novel.

Opening a Business in Rio

The existence of a growing readership and book market, even before the notion of Brazilian literature came into being and despite the discouraging results of the 1872 census, is confirmed by the growing presence of European novels, periodicals, booksellers and publishers in Brazil after 1808. The circulation of books in general, and of European novels in particular, between 1808 and 1821 was fostered by the establishment of French and Portuguese bookshops in the new seat of the Portuguese Empire.[13] As Leila Algranti makes clear, this was a period when several publishing houses of French origin which had been established in Portugal since the previous century 'began to open up branches in Brazil and send their representatives to take part in the book trade'.[14] At this stage, this was not a specialized activity, 'and there were dealers who among various types of hardware and luxury items also sold books'.[15]There were also French traders who came to Brazil after 1815 either to escape from the Restoration of the Monarchy or in search of better living conditions, and set up different kinds of business that included selling books.[16] The suspension of censorship in 1821 stimulated the book trade even more significantly, and became a landmark in the process of expansion of printed culture throughout the country.

The development of book publishing in Europe in the nineteenth century helps not only draw a pattern of the expansion of this international business, but also explain Brazil's participation in this market and the impact of the circulation of European printed matter — British, French, Portuguese and the well-known Belgian counterfeit editions — in Brazil in that period. The effects of this expansion, however, only started to be felt at the beginning of the 1830s, when the nation began to enjoy the benefits of having become politically independent. From the 1840s onwards, a number of circumstances made it easier for printed matter to spread around countries in Europe, and they included the innovations, improvements and greater speed in transport by land (railways) and sea (steamships), banking transactions,[17] postal services, printing techniques and forms of production and distribution as well as an increase in readership thanks to greater literacy. In addition, the legal regulation of international bookstores (which began to include reciprocal legal rights, laws of copyright and bilateral agreements between editors) gave rise to the setting-up of sales networks which allowed professionals to make contact and forge close links by means of a permanent official bookseller. The exporter of printed matter often ended up opening a proper branch office abroad by using a member of his own family as an intermediary, as was the case with B. L. Garnier in Rio de Janeiro in 1844.[18]Apart from this, we know, for example, that as soon as the ports were opened in 1808 'a large number of British arrived. By August, there were between 150 and 200 traders or commercial agents in Brazil'.[19]

It was also in the nineteenth century that 'contexts of reception' were organized, with the establishment of new reading sites, which gradually became widespread and took on different shapes.[20] By the 1820s, shops that lent and sold books were opened and were soon followed by the foundation of membership and circulating libraries similar to those in Britain and France. These shops and libraries helped spread the circulation of the books sent by European book dealers to Brazil. This is how Gesellschaft Germania, Rio de Janeiro British Subscription Library, Real Gabinete Português de Leitura, and Bibliotheca Fluminense (1847) came into existence. These institutions started operating as important spaces of sociability, and thus encouraged the expansion of literate culture, while providing entertainment, information and instruction to their members and users.[21] This process, which began in the Imperial Court, soon extended to the provinces, with the diffusion of a multifaceted network consisting of public and membership libraries, as well as other popular institutions.

In spite of the unfavourable social, political and economic circumstances that prevented the universalization of literacy and access to books and periodicals, to which Machado's *crônica* gives testimony, the gradual growth and improvement of material conditions for their circulation is an undeniable fact.

This Book

Although much has been published on the circulation of printed matter, publishers, reading practices in Brazil and on the relations between Brazil and Europe in the field of Book History, very little of this output is known in the English-speaking world because it is usually written either in Portuguese or in French. There is a plethora of materials — theses, books, articles and special issues of journals — on this extensive subject that, unfortunately, fails to reach the number of readers that it should, outside the academic circles where the actual research was conducted.[22] In addition, although many findings are already available online, it is only more recently that some of these projects have been published in English.[23] As a result, with the exception of Lawrence Hallewell's *Books in Brazil* (1982), there have been no recent publications in English devoted exclusively to this subject.

The publication in English of a book which reveals the state-of-the-art research in Book History in Brazil will, we hope, stimulate a growing interest in this subject area outside Franco-Brazilian circles, and allow comparisons between research work of a transnational kind in the world of print culture between different European countries and Brazil, and the rest of the world.

Books and Periodicals in Brazil 1768–1930: A Transatlantic Perspective brings together a collection of original articles on the transnational relations between Brazil and European countries, especially Britain and France, in the domain of literature and print culture from the beginning of the nineteenth century. This covers the time when there were restrictions on printing in Brazil, and Portugal strictly controlled which books were sent to the colony, through the period when a transnational printing industry and book market flourished after 1822, to the shift of hegemony in the printing business from foreign to Brazilian control at the end of the nineteenth century.

In the opening chapter, Márcia Abreu challenges the general belief that there was little interest in reading books in colonial Brazil. She outlines the kinds of books that were sent most often to Rio de Janeiro and seeks to disprove the allegation that the American continent suffered from cultural penury in the colonial period, while also providing some possible explanations for the supposed lack of interest in reading. During the whole of the eighteenth and part of the nineteenth century the Portuguese crown tried hard to control the book trade between Europe and their colonies in America, fearing that the circulation of ideas could stir up feelings against the monarchy or the Catholic Church or even suggest subversive ideas and lead to immoral behaviour. It imposed restrictions by compiling detailed registers of the books sent to America — through legal means. Abreu lays stress on the preferences of readers, by using the lists of books sent officially to Brazil as her source.

In Chapter 2, Lúcia Maria Bastos Pereira das Neves and Tania Maria Tavares Bessone da Cruz Ferreira investigate the book trade and circulation of ideas in Rio de Janeiro from 1808 to 1831. In the main newspapers published in the town, such as the *Gazeta do Rio de Janeiro*, the *Diario do Rio de Janeiro* and the *Jornal do Commercio*, one finds advertisements for books, as well as booksellers who, having settled in the tropics, had shops in the new Court. An investigation of documents such as the licences issued by Mesa do Desembargo do Paço [Board of the Appellate Court] which were an essential requirement for the booksellers before their books could be released through the Rio Customs Clearance, or the catalogues they produced, makes it clear that there was a flourishing book trade in Rio de Janeiro. This involved specialized booksellers or dealers in French and Portuguese books and a few from Britain. Names frequently mentioned in these documents, like those of João Roberto Bourgeois, Paul Martin, Bompard, Mandillo, Pierre Constant Dalbin, Francisco Luiz Saturnino da Veiga, Henrique Miller, Evaristo da Veiga, and Pierre Plancher, among others, may account for the wide range of works in circulation. Thus, their chapter analyses how books, booksellers and printers that are characterized by their great diversity require an approach involving historical research of the Brazilian cultural practices in the first decades of the nineteenth century. It also confirms how, through this book trade, the ideas that circulated in Brazil (originating from European countries, particularly Portugal and France) were conveyed both in their original version, by being published in the language in which the text was written, and in translation.

Since the 1980s there have been many studies that have sought to understand how the ideas of the French Revolution resonated in the political emancipation movement in Brazil. Apart from investigations on the cultural and ideological matrices of Inconfidência Mineira [the Minas Conspiracy] and Conjuração Bahiana [Revolt of the Tailors], ideas of revolution, from the mildest to the most powerful, also kindled other rebellions like those in the Brazilian states of Rio de Janeiro and Pernambuco, reaching a climax in the uprisings that broke out in the Northeast in 1817. In Chapter 3, Marisa Midori Deaecto and Lincoln Secco explore the role of print culture in disseminating revolutionary ideas. Instead of relying on inventories of private libraries, they draw on booksellers' catalogues, books and newspaper advertisements, together with French editions about the Revolution translated into Portuguese, to investigate the different influences of the revolutionary ideology and its multiple re-readings by the Brazilian intellectual community between two landmarks in the history of the French liberal revolutions, 1848 and 1871.

The following three chapters look into the rapid integration of the recently liberated Brazil with the European literary book markets. In Chapter 4, Sandra Guardini Vasconcelos argues that the novel was a sign of modernity in a country that had only recently been freed from colonial rule. Her main interest lies in discussing the crucial theoretical issue of how narrative forms become acclimatized to different historical contexts. In the light of the international circulation of British novels in the nineteenth century and Brazil's participation in the literary market in the first half of that century, Vasconcelos discusses how foreign narrative themes and techniques found their way into Brazil and to what extent they were appropriated by Brazilian novelists. Her corpus comprises hundreds of titles by more than one hundred different novelists, which maps out the transatlantic diffusion of these narrative paradigms. These can be compiled to form a 'literary geography' of the genre, in the system adopted by Franco Moretti in his *Atlas of the European Novel*.[24]

In Chapter 5, Nelson Schapochnik makes the first attempt to reconstruct the history of the Rio de Janeiro British Subscription Library, founded in 1826 by British immigrants. His source material consists of periodicals published in nineteenth-century Rio de Janeiro (*Jornal do Commercio*, *Almanack Laemmert*), travel books, the rules and regulations of the library and the three catalogues of the Subscription Library, published in 1842, 1864, and 1882 respectively. The Rio de Janeiro British Subscription Library was a space for sociability, and provided both instruction and leisure for its users. Moreover, it was part of a network of institutions representing the cultural practices of the British community in the imperial court, such as the British Episcopal Church, the British Burial Ground and the British Benevolent Fund. As such, it helped strengthen ties between its members to establish their identity, provided them with an aura of distinction and encouraged male sociability. The presence of significant novels in the library's catalogue seems to have stimulated the imagination of many readers, such as James W. Wells (1873), who after a brief stay in Rio de Janeiro embarked on a 3000 mile journey through the interior of Brazil.

In Chapter 6, Paulo Motta Oliveira analyses the editorial history of *The Hand of Death*, a sequel to the *Count of Mount Cristo*, published by a Portuguese writer, Alfredo Hogan, and examines its circulation in Portugal, Spain and Brazil. From the nineteenth century until today, this book has been usually attributed to Alexandre Dumas, and Alfredo Hogan was never credited in any of these editions. In his chapter, Oliveira shows that *The Hand of Death* was published in a large number of editions in Catholic countries but was almost unknown in others — like Britain, USA and France. He also explores the particular history of these editions in Portugal and Brazil, given that Hogan wrote several revised versions.

Chapters 7 to 9 focus on Brazilian periodicals. Newspapers and magazines constituted a means of updating and modernizing the Brazilian social and cultural context in the nineteenth century. Modernization was regarded as an urgent social requirement as it was believed it would lay down the basic intellectual and social conditions that would allow a politically independent Brazil to integrate with the international socio-economic and cultural system. Each chapter focuses on one aspect of the close ties between Brazil and Europe in the production and readership of periodicals. In Chapter 7, Maria Eulália Ramicelli explores the adoption of French and British models in the creation of the Brazilian periodical *Revista Nacional e Estrangeira*, which, among its many interests, addressed the question of the formation of a sovereign Brazilian State. According to Ramicelli, the importance of the periodical press was particularly felt during the period of the Brazilian Regency (1831–40), when the country was on the brink of territorial disintegration and Portuguese recolonization. It was in this context that the launching of the *Revista Nacional e Estrangeira* (May 1839–December 1840) was planned by three men of letters who also belonged to the official administration of the central government in Rio de Janeiro: João Manuel Pereira da Silva, Josino do Nascimento Silva, and Pedro d'Alcântara Bellegarde. In putting forward ideas to allow well-informed decisions to be made about the structure of the Brazilian State, they made use of foreign collaborators, since there was a belief that the Brazilian intellectual milieu lacked the capacity to build a distinctive Brazilian cultural and social system all by itself. While the French *Revue Britannique* (1825–1901) was declared to be a model, it was in fact the direct source of a large number of fictional and non-fictional texts published in the Brazilian periodical. By taking account of the circumstances in which the *Revista Nacional e Estrangeira* was produced, Ramicelli discusses the collection of foreign texts that were translated and published in its pages so as to determine what they meant for Brazilian intellectuals. Moreover, as both the *Revista Nacional e Estrangeira* and the *Revue Britannique* are little known to French and Brazilian researchers, this chapter will also seek to retrieve neglected or unknown literary sources.

In Chapter 8, we move on to another sector of the printing industry: the fashion press. Ana Cláudia Suriani da Silva investigates the role of the press in the inclusion of Brazil in the Paris fashion system by making a survey of the periodicals with fashion content that circulated in Rio de Janeiro throughout the nineteenth century. In the first part of her chapter she examines how Paris became the empire of fashion and the means by which Rio de Janeiro was incorporated in the Paris fashion system. In the second part, she presents a survey of Brazilian periodicals with fashion content that circulated in Rio de Janeiro in the nineteenth century and the main characteristics of the Brazilian fashion magazine, showing that they were from their birth a hybrid, multicultural product, combining local and imported visual and textual content.

In Chapter 9, Lúcia Granja is concerned with tracing the development of a particular journalistic genre in Brazil, the *crônica*, which derives from the French *bas de page* and *fait divers*. The *bas de page* (*rodapé*, in Portuguese) was the space, separated off by a horizontal line, at the bottom of the page in many nineteenth-century newspapers. Granja investigates the adjustments made to texts originally published in the *bas de page* of French periodicals so that they could be published in translation in Brazilian newspapers: these comprised the publication criteria, plot changes, and the creation of new characters, which were carried out when the texts were revised in order to be published in Brazil.

Chapters 10 to 14 deal with the role of authors, new technology and the implementation of copyright laws, in a fast growing and increasingly international market for books and newspapers in Brazil at the end of the nineteenth century. As mentioned above, Brazil only acquired its first printing press in 1808, quite late compared with other Western or Latin American countries. Only when the Portuguese Crown, needing to escape Napoleon, transferred the Portuguese government to Rio de Janeiro was the colony allowed to have its own printing facilities. During the nineteenth century, a steady development of literary output, along with the parallel growth of the book trade, led authors to fight for legislation to establish authorship rights and the payment of advances against royalties. Thus in Chapter 10 Marisa Lajolo and Regina Zilberman reconstruct the history of copyright in Brazil from the first political campaigns, to the collective movements for the establishment of the first Brazilian copyright laws in 1898.

In Chapter 11, Jussara Meneses Quadros, in her turn, discusses Machado de Assis's critical view of the increased speed of news dissemination brought about by new forms of technology, such as the transatlantic cable, improvements in lithographic reproduction and photography. From the time he made his debut in the press in 1855 up to the turn of the century, Machado de Assis was not only a regular contributor to the daily and weekly papers, but also a privileged witness of the technological advances of the new media. From 1876 onwards, the effects of the invention of the telephone began to be felt, while the transatlantic cables of the Western and Brazilian Telegraphic Company increased their transmission and provided faster access to world news. Machado de Assis's *crônicas* of the 1860s often describe the annoying delays that resulted from news being sent by packet boats, whereas closer to the end of the century he adopted an opposite attitude to speed. Increased access to world news widened the scope of his journalism, but it paradoxically coincided with the novelist's resorting to fictional memoirs. According to Quadros, in his work Machado de Assis argues against the acceleration of time resulting from this new technology, and against the prevailing ideology of progress. His *crônicas* and novels from the end of the nineteenth century contemplate historical events through a retrospective and oblique gaze, mediated by complex and often competing acts of interpretation.

In Chapter 12, we cross the Atlantic to see what the Brazilian book market in Portugal was like. Marked as it was by a system based on imports, it was very significant moment when the country acquired the ability to export literature. Patrícia de Jesus Palma focuses on the time when Brazilian authors started to gain recognition abroad and their works were first being published and becoming known in Portugal. Palma investigates the Brazilian book market in Portugal by studying the catalogues of booksellers and publishers in the nineteenth century, and is thus able to identify the exact time when Brazilian literature began to be understood, marketed and recognized as independent from Portuguese literature.

The last two chapters of the book focus on the consolidation of literature in Portuguese as a major market at the end of the nineteenth century. In Chapter 13, Alessandra El Far deals with popular editions and best-sellers. According to El Far, by the end of the nineteenth century, Rio de Janeiro bookstores were advertising 'books for the common folk' to a growing market of readers. In the columns of newspapers it was easy to find a wide range of low-priced volumes with eye-catching titles, advertised as novels, children's books, short stories, almanacs, and cookery books, among others, which together made up the world of popular literature in Brazil. Some of these titles, which showed clear signs of a strong European influence, sold thousands of copies in only a few weeks, and became a successful publishing phenomenon. This was especially the case with 'sensational narratives' and 'novels for men only'. The 'sensational narratives' described adventures that were full of passion, blood and mystery, and were thus capable of stirring emotions unknown in the routine of everyday life. In contrast, the 'novels for men only' were forbidden to women, and introduced the public to pornographic plots full of love encounters and erotic pleasures. These books were responsible for the creation of a new publishing dynamic in Brazil aimed at attracting the attention of a wider public. From the perspective of publishers, who were always searching for promising business, the 'best book' was the one projected to sell the most.

Finally, in the last chapter Cilza Bignotto and Milena Ribeiro Martins investigate the role played by Monteiro Lobato, one of the most important Brazilian publishers at the beginning of the twentieth century, through his periodical *Revista do Brasil* and his editorial enterprises. *Revista do Brasil* became a means of advertising publications for Monteiro Lobato's publishing house and, at the same time, a space for discussion on the direction that should be taken by the publishing market in Brazil. The issues that were discussed included the professionalization of writers, the need to expand readership, the growing convergence (as an aspiration and politico-cultural objective) of Brazilian and other Latin American publishing markets, the relations between cinema and literature, and between literature and illustrations. At a time when the Brazilian publishing market was gathering momentum, Monteiro Lobato was not only a successful editor, but was also able to attract academics who discussed issues related to the publishing market and how it could flourish. Martins and Bignotto analyse the main ideas of these men of letters as reflected in private and public documents (letters and articles) as a means of increasing our knowledge of the Brazilian publishing market in the early twentieth century.

With this collection of essays, we hope therefore to fill the gap and offer the English-language reader a variegated panorama which is intended to shorten the distance that the Atlantic has imposed between us. It is also an attempt to investigate one generally neglected aspect of the relations that Brazil and Europe entertained in the past. As Christopher Hill once suggested, 'History has to be rewritten in every generation, because although the past does not change the present does; each generation asks new questions of the past, and finds new areas of sympathy as it re-lives different aspects of the experiences of its predecessors'.[25]

Notes to the Introduction

1. We have maintained the term *crônica* in Portuguese. The *crônica* is a hybrid form of expression halfway between literature and journalism. It is often translated as 'chronicle'. See for example *Divergent Modernities: Culture and Politics in Nineteenth-Century Latin America*, trans. by John D. Blanco (Durham, NC: Duke University Press Books, 2001), p. 71, where Julio Ramos calls Martí's *crônicas* 'chronicles'. For more on the *crônica*, see Chapters 9 and 11 of this book, by Lúcia Granja and Jussara Menezes Quadros respectively. A longer definition of the *crônica* is to be found in Chapter 9.
2. Machado de Assis, 'História de Quinze Dias', in *Revista Brasileira*, 15 August 1876, and in *Obra Completa*, 4 vols (Rio de Janeiro: Nova Aguilar, 1986), III, 345.
3. Ibid, p. 344.
4. See Alceu Ravanello Ferraro, 'Analfabetismo e níveis de letramento no Brasil: o que dizem os censos?', *Educ. Soc.* [online], 23.81 (2002), 21–47 <http://www.scielo.br/pdf/es/v23n81/13930.pdf> [accessed 10 July 2012]; also Mario Marcos Sampaio Rodarte and José Maria dos Santos Júnior, 'A estrutura ocupacional revisitada: uma proposta de correção dos dados do Recenseamento Geral do Império de 1872', XVI Encontro Nacional de Estudos Populacionais, Caxambu, MG, Brazil, 29 September–3 October 2008 <http://www.abep.nepo.unicamp.br/encontro2008/docsPDF/ABEP2008_1854.pdf> [10 July 2012].
5. Jurandir Malerba, *A corte no exílio: civilização e poder no Brasil às vésperas da Independência (1808 a 1821)* (São Paulo: Companhia das Letras, 2000), p. 126.
6. See Chapter 1 in this book by Márcia Abreu and also her *Os caminhos dos livros* (Campinas: ALB/Mercado de Letras; São Paulo: FAPESP, 2003). Luiz Carlos Villalta has examined private collections and postmortem inventories in his work. See his 'O que se fala e o que se lê: língua, instrução e leitura', in *História da vida privada no Brasil*, ed. by Laura de Mello e Souza, 3 vols (São Paulo: Companhia das Letras, 1997), I, 331–85.
7. Rubens Borba de Moraes points out that Jonathan Swift's *Gulliver's Travels* (1726) and Laurence Sterne's *Sentimental Journey* (1768) could only be read by special licence because they had been included in the list of books forbidden by the Real Mesa Censória [Royal Board of Censorship]. See his *Livros e bibliotecas no Brasil colonial* (Rio de Janeiro: LTC, 1979), p. 56. See also Chapter 1 of this book, by Márcia Abreu.
8. In the nineteenth century the demonym for the city of Rio de Janeiro was 'fluminense', taken from the Latin word *flumen*, meaning 'river'. Nowadays, it is 'carioca', from the indigenous Tupi language meaning 'white man's house'; 'fluminense' is more often taken today as the demonym for the whole state of Rio de Janeiro.
9. 'In the year 1839, the backward and unwholesome town of Rio de Janeiro, had a population of around three hundred thousand people, a great part of which were slaves, whose numbers grew constantly due to the clandestine traffic, forbidden and repressed only *for the English to see*, as people said at the time. The natural beauties flaunted by the town did not conceal its deficiencies, among which stood out the lack of hygiene and the precariousness of transports.' See R. Magalhães Júnior, *Machado de Assis: vida e obra*, 4 vols (Rio de Janeiro: Editora Record, 2008), I, 11.
10. Manuel Antonio de Almeida, *Memoirs of a Militia Sergeant*, trans. by Ronald W. Sousa (New York: Oxford University Press, 2000). See Antonio Candido's 'Dialectic of Malandroism', in *On Literature and Society*, trans., ed. and intro. by Howard S. Becker (Princeton, NJ: Princeton University Press, 1995), p. 79–103.
11. Patrimonialism is a concept which derives from Max Weber and is used in Brazilian social thought to refer to the treatment of the *res publica* by the authorities as if it were private, leading to the lack of distinction between the public and the private spheres. Clientelism has been defined as a set of actions based on the give-and-take principle, with the practice allowing both clients and patrons to gain advantage from the other's support. Richard Graham, 'Clientelismo na cultura política brasileira: toma lá dá cá', Braudel Center Papers, 15 (1997) <http://pt.braudel.org.br/publicacoes/braudel-papers/downloads/portugues/bp15_pt.pdf> [accessed 28 March 2014].

12. 'Lettered city' is borrowed from Angel Rama, *The Lettered City*, trans. by John Charles Chasteen (Durham, NC: Duke University Press, 2006). For more on reading practices and the institutionalization of spaces devoted to the production and diffusion of printed artefacts, see Chapter 5, by Nelson Schapochnik, and his article 'Contextos de leitura no Rio de Janeiro do século XIX: salões, gabinetes literários e bibliotecas', in *Imagens da cidade, séculos XIX e XX*, ed. by Stella Bresciani (São Paulo: ANPUH-SP/Marco Zero/FAPESP, 1994), pp. 147–62 (pp. 147–48).
13. Maria Beatriz Nizza da Silva, 'Livro e sociedade no Rio de Janeiro (1808–1821)', *Revista de História*, vol. 46.94 (April–June 1973), 441–57; Lúcia Maria Bastos Pereira das Neves, 'Comércio de livros e censura de idéias: a actividade dos livreiros franceses no Brasil e a vigilância da Mesa do Desembargo do Paço (1795–1822)', *Ler História*, 23 (1992), 61–78; Leila Mezan Algranti, 'Censura e comércio de livros no período de permanência da corte portuguesa no Rio de Janeiro (1808–1821)', *Revista Portuguesa de História*, 23.1 (1999), 631–63.
14. Leila Mezan Algranti, 'Política, religião e moralidade: a censura de livros no Brasil de D. João VI (1808–1821)', in *Minorias silenciadas: história da censura no Brasil*, ed. by Maria Luiza Tucci Carneiro (São Paulo, EDUSP/ Imprensa Oficial do Estado/ FAPESP, 2002), pp. 111–12.
15. Lúcia Maria Bastos Pereira das Neves, 'Comércio de livros e censura de idéias', p. 64.
16. See Tânia Bessone da C. Ferreira e Lúcia Maria Bastos P. das Neves, 'Livreiros franceses no Rio de Janeiro, 1808–1823', *História hoje: balanço e perspectivas*, IV Encontro Regional da ANPUH-RJ (Rio de Janeiro: Associação Nacional dos Professores Universitários de História, 1990), pp. 190–202.
17. The testimony of foreign businessmen in Rio de Janeiro in the period 1810–20 provides evidence of the delay in the delivery of products and customs clearance, as well as the lack of adequate port facilities. See Herbert Heaton, 'A Merchant Adventurer in Brazil, 1808–1818', *The Journal of Economic History*, 6.1 (May 1946), 1–23.
18. See Frédéric Barbier, 'Le Commerce international de la librairie française au XIXe siècle (1815–1913)', *Revue d'histoire moderne et contemporaine*, 28 (January–March 1981), pp. 94–117.
19. Rory Miller, *Britain and Latin America in the Nineteenth and Twentieth Centuries* (London and New York: Longman, 1993), p. 42. Herbert Heaton: 'By the end of 1808 at least five million dollars' worth of British goods had been sent to Brazil. With them or ahead of them went British merchants or commission agents by the score. In September it was possible to get sixty-two British firms in Rio to sign a petition; and, since they described themselves as comprising "a very large majority of the respectable merchants resident here," it seems safe to assume that if we added the minority and the nonrespectables we should reach a total of a hundred British traders in Rio alone', in 'A Merchant Adventurer in Brazil, 1808–1818', p. 6.
20. Dominick LaCapra, 'History and the Novel', in *History and Criticism* (Ithaca, NY: Cornell University Press, 1985), pp. 115–34.
21. See Nelson Schapochnik, 'Os jardins das delícias: gabinetes literários, bibliotecas e figurações da leitura na corte imperial' (unpublished doctoral thesis, Universidade de São Paulo, 1999).
22. While some of the specialists have contributed to this collection, we could also mention a few others, like Luiz Carlos Villalta, Aníbal Bragança, Circe Bittencourt Fernandes, Tânia Regina de Luca, Gabriela Pellegrino Soares, Eliana de Freitas Dutra, Fábio Franzini, Júlio Pimentel Pinto, and Giselle Martins Venâncio.
23. See, for example, the outputs of the research projects 'Memória de Leitura', 'Caminhos do romance no Brasil' and 'A circulação transatlântica dos impressos: a globalização da cultura no século XIX', respectively 'Memory of Reading Practices' <www.unicamp.br/iel/memoria>; 'The Ways of the Novel' <www.caminhosdoromance.iel.unicamp.br>; and 'The Transatlantic Circulation of Printed Matter: The Globalization of Culture in the Nineteenth Century' <http://www.circulacaodosimpressos.iel.unicamp.br/index.php?cd=&lang=en> [accessed 27 March 2014].
24. Franco Moretti, *Atlas of the European Novel, 1800–1900* (London: Verso, 1998).
25. Christopher Hill, *The World Turned Upside Down* (London: Penguin, 1991), p. 15.

CHAPTER 1

Reading in Colonial Brazil[1]

Márcia Abreu

Contrary to what is often assumed, the Portuguese colony in America did not ignore the use and appeal of books. Works of all kinds, of all periods, of all origins arrived in Rio de Janeiro, spreading widely the titles in circulation — at least, this is what one perceives when looking at the documentation produced by the censorial boards established in Portugal and Rio de Janeiro between the middle of the eighteenth century and the beginning of the nineteenth.[2] The Portuguese crown, intending to keep control over the thoughts and wishes of its subjects, tried to examine all written material circulating in its domains, demanding from those who intended to transport books that they fill in authorization requests to be submitted to the appropriate censorial board.[3]

This strict control on books and documents, although disastrous for the spread of ideas, favoured the thorough recording of works entering Brazil through legal channels and therefore, allows us to know what was being purchased, and presumably read, in the colony. Until 1807, the only possibility of legal acquisition and transport of books and documents for those who lived in Brazil was to import them from Portugal, which involved making an authorization request to the Portuguese censorial board. After the transfer of the crown to Rio de Janeiro in 1808, new forms of contact with books were opened up, though constantly supervised by censorial boards. From 1808 on, it was possible to acquire books printed in Brazil by the Impressão Régia [Royal Press], or to import them from other places besides Portugal, after obtaining an authorization from the Mesa do Desembargo do Paço — an institution seated in Rio de Janeiro, with powers similar to those of its Portuguese counterpart. Even after the control system was thus duplicated, the volume of requests submitted to the censorial board in Lisbon remained high.[4]

The inhabitants of Rio de Janeiro were among the most avid — or the most controlled — readers in Portugal and its domains. Although they read many religious and professional texts, they enjoyed the contact with the belles-lettres and had marked preferences. Before the transfer of the crown, the books most regularly shipped were as shown in Table 1.1.

Of a total of 519 titles sent to Rio de Janeiro, the most requested had thirty-eight requisitions, whereas there were 312 titles for which there was only one requisition — on average, fewer than three requisitions for each title. Since the authorization requests do not mention the number of copies, it is possible that, for each requisition

	Title	Quantity
1	*Les Aventures de Télémaque*, François de Salignac de la Mothe-Fénelon	38
2	*Night Thoughts on Life Death and Immortality*, Edward Young	24
3	*Selecta Latini Sermonis exemplaria e scriptoribus probatissimis*, Pierre Chompré	22
4	*Histoire de Gil Blas de Santillane*, Alain René Lesage	21
5	*Le Voyageur François ou la connoissance de l'ancien et du nouveau monde*, Joseph de Laporte	19
6	*Meditations and Contemplations*, James Hervey	18
	The Paradise Lost, John Milton	18
7	*Caroline de Lichtfield*, J. I. P. de Bottens Baroness Isabelle de Montolieu	15
	El Ingenioso Hidalgo Don Quixote de la Mancha, Miguel de Cervantes	15
	História do Imperador Carlos Magno e dos doze pares de França, Anonymous	15
	Lances da Ventura acasos da desgraça e heroísmos da virtude, D. Felix Moreno de Monroy y Ros	15
	Rimas, Manuel Maria Barbosa du Bocage	15
8	*Viagens de Altina nas cidades mais cultas da Europa e nas principais povoações dos Balinos, povos desconhecidos de todo o mundo*, Luís Caetano de Campos	13
9	*Delli viaggi di Enrico Wanton alle terre incognite Australi ed al paese delle scimie, né quali si apiegono il carattere, li costumi, le scienze e la polizia di quegli straordinari abitanti*, Zaccaria Seriman	12
	O Feliz independente do mundo e da fortuna, ou arte de viver contente em quaisquer trabalhos da vida, Father Theodoro de Almeida	12
10	*Fables*, Aesop	11
	Obras, Luís de Camões	11
	Rimas, João Xavier de Mattos	11

TABLE 1.1. The most requested belles-lettres titles in requisitions sent to Rio de Janeiro, and kept in the archives of the Real Mesa Censória [Royal Censorship Board], relating to the period between 1769 and 1807[5]

of *Les Aventures de Télémaque*, for instance, hundreds of copies had been sent — a hypothesis that becomes stronger in light of the fact that nineteen of the shipments which included Fénelon's book were signed by booksellers. However, as the documentation does not give information about quantities sent, it is not possible to go beyond suppositions.

The impression that the number of requisitions for each book is very small lessens when one considers the number of copies circulating. In mid-eighteenth-century France, most books had an edition of less than one thousand copies. Rousseau's *La Nouvelle Héloïse*, an unquestionable best-seller in eighteenth-century France, had an edition slightly higher than four thousand.[6] In Britain, at the same time, few books sold more than ten thousand copies. None of those successes was written by renowned authors; on the contrary, they were somewhat sensationalist news and religious pamphlets.[7] Likewise, in the United States, at the end of the eighteenth century, a novel had a regular edition of one thousand.[8] In Portugal, editions did not exceed one thousand either. *O Uraguay* [The Uruguay], published in 1769, supported by the most powerful Portuguese minister, the Marquis of Pombal, had a first edition of 1,036 copies, a considerable amount for that time.[9]

Allowing, then, for the small number of requests, one nevertheless sees some recurring patterns. The absolute predominance of foreign texts is striking. Of the eighteen works considered, only six were originally written in Portuguese. However, there is no absolute predominance in the source language: there are six texts originally written in French, three in English, one in Spanish, one in Greek, one in Italian. Latin, the language of culture until the eighteenth century, appears only to a limited extent, since the *Selecta Latini* — an anthology of excerpts taken from the Latin classics — has been organized and written in French (except, as it is evident, for the excerpts copied from Latin authors).

The presence of Latin culture was significant in Rio de Janeiro, although not concentrated on particular titles, which prevented Latin texts from being among the most demanded. Between 1769 and 1807, there are 190 requests for Latin works; however, the title in greatest demand — *Cartas de Ovídio* [*Ovid's Letters*] — was requested only nine times. There follow Phaedrus's *Fábulas* [*Fables*] (also with nine requisitions); Cicero's *Orações* [*Orations*] (eight); Horace's *Odes* and Ovid's *ad usum*[10] (seven); Horace's *ad usum*, Cicero's *Epístolas* [*Epistles*], Virgil's *ad usum*, and Cicero's *Obrigações* [*On Obligations*] (each with six requisitions).[11] Curiously, the most requested among the Latin texts was mentioned, in all requisitions, in Portuguese, which allows us to imagine that, even when Latin authors were being demanded, Portuguese was the language of contact with the text. In this case, the nine requesters would have had in mind the book *Cartas de Ovídio, chamadas heroides, expurgadas de toda a obscenidade e traduzidas em rima vulgar: com as suas respostas, escriptas umas pelo mesmo Ovidio, outras por Sabino e Sidronio e a maior parte dellas pelo traductor; e um epílogo no fim de cada uma, em que se mostra a doutrina que d'ellas se pode tirar, etc.*, translated by Miguel do Couto Guerreiro, and published in Lisbon in 1789.[12] At least one of them made clear that he was looking for 'Ovid's letters by Miguel do Couto Guerreiro'.[13] In this case, what was read was a version 'purged of all obscenity', with the addition of Sabinus's and Sidronius's texts, and expanded by the translator, responsible for the 'major part' of replies to the letters.

Likewise, all those who requested *ad usum* versions of Latin texts were exposed to didactic versions revised and amended by editors. To designate the educational purpose of books, they employed expressions such as *ad usum delphini* (for the use of the Dauphin — i.e. the heir to the throne), *ad usum studiosae juventutis* (for the use of studious youth), *ad usum scholarum* (for pedagogical use), *ad christianae juventutis usum* (for use of Christian youth), or simply *ad usum*. The sanction of this expression to name didactic works made some requests for authorization indicate, for instance, 'Cornelius Nepos *ad usum*', although there was no publication with this title. Undoubtedly, the requester just wanted to show his wish to send to Brazil a simplified and didactic version of Cornelius Nepos's writings.

Thus, even though 66% of the books most often sent to Rio de Janeiro were written in a foreign language, it is not necessary to assume that the native readers were polyglot. All books under high demand had already been translated into Portuguese in the eighteenth century.[14] The Portuguese publishing world hence seems quite active, able to offer translations of the most successful books. One of the most demanded books in this period, Milton's *Paradise Lost*, was translated in

1789 by Father José Amaro da Silva, who, in the Prologue, extols the importance of translations:

> I believe this suggestion, which occurred to me when translating this Poet, will be well accepted. It is fair that this Nation should have in its Language all that others have, because not only must the Sages read, but all others, for them either to be sage or to acquire learning. In the Nation in which even the dregs of Society can read, that is the one where customs are better, the Motherland is loved, Religion more observed, and Sovereigns obeyed and held in more esteem. Ignorance, and absence of study, are the source from which flow disorder, arrogance, despotism, disobedience, and even superstition and irreligion.[15]

The priest's enthusiasm for translations and the power of reading seems to have been shared by those who addressed the Portuguese censorial board, since most requisitions that display complete bibliographies make explicit that translations were being shipped. Even when there was no choice of a Portuguese translation, a translation was read, since books written in English, Spanish, Italian, or Greek were mentioned on the lists in their French or Portuguese versions, and never in the original language. While it is possible to understand the preference for these languages as opposed to English or Italian — thinly spread as international languages in the period — the case of *Don Quixote* is perplexing, since it has never been requested in Spanish, but always in French or Portuguese.

The profitable business of translation made rival versions in the same language proliferate. Sometimes, this multiplication was due to the editor's desire to provide readers with a better text, as it seems to have been the case of the bookseller and editor Rolland, who, having published a translation of *Paul et Virginie*, by Jacques-Henri Bernardin de Saint-Pierre, decided to look for a new translator at the moment of reissuing it. This is what one sees in a note written by his cousin, Estevão Semiond, to a translator:

> telling me that his [Rolland's] edition of 'Paul and Virginia' is almost over and that you had told him, once, about a better translation you had made, and since he has to reprint it, he would like to do something worthy of 'const.' [constitutional?] times [...] instead of the old one, we will print yours, in which the public finds more benefit, reading pure Portuguese and not Frenchified [the word was crossed out] Portuguese, as in the other. This way, you would benefit the public and favour my cousin.[16]

In other instances, the success of a book attracted different translators, as it happened, for example, with *Les Aventures de Télémaque*, the object of several different translations in the eighteenth century.[17] In each new edition or reissue, translators would praise their own work and point out the faults of others.[18] A merry-go-round of translations was described in a preface to a Portuguese edition of *Les Aventures de Télémaque* by José da Fonseca, who 'touched up and corrected' the edition of Fénelon's work:

> For a long time I have wished to offer my fellow countrymen a new edition of Telemachus, revised and corrected by myself. Today, finally, my wish is fulfilled with this work presented to the public. As I talked, in Paris, to the inimitable Francisco Manuel, I heard from him that the translation circulating

> in Portugal under the name of Captain Manuel de Sousa owes much to our Poet [i.e. Francisco Manuel], a close friend of the said captain. 'I (Francisco Manuel's words) translated, with the original in my hands, walking around my room, and Manuel de Sousa wrote what I dictated to him: afterwards, he touched up the version at home; so we worked until completing it.'
>
> Indeed, only Francisco Manuel (then in his home country, and with his mind full of classical terms and phrases) could spread such an abundance of good language in this book, a real *treasure of the Portuguese language*: but the great celerity with which that translation was made (perhaps at the bookseller's urging) has not allowed these two distinguished sages to purge it of many terms, vulgar and incongruous with the subject; of endless repetitions; and, besides, to give sentences that harmonious finish required by the poetic prose of the original. This was the task, which I faced despite the difficulties, whose execution was offered to me; of which I will say nothing: it falls to the scholar to evaluate it, comparing this work of mine with the version I used, printed in Lisbon in the year of 1776.[19]

This curious system of translation involved three people, who played a number of different roles, not only as translator, but as copyist, proofreader and adapter. The freedom given to translators at that time allowed them to interfere in the plot, adding, amending, or removing whole passages. Some would go even further. In 1765, José Manoel Ribeiro Pereira translated Fénelon's book into Portuguese for the first time, and thought the story 'lacked a finishing touch', because it did not give an account of the hero's marriage. He did not hesitate and wrote the *Aventuras finaes de Telemaco*, narrating what, in his opinion, it was lacking.

The number of translations and editions in the same period is evidence of this book's success, which made important booksellers and editors, such as Rolland, Reycend and Bertrand, want different editions in their catalogues.[20] The public at times expressed an inclination for one version or another. Thus, in 1799, Jozé Antonio da Silva requested 'Telemachus in verse',[21] a strange request at first sight, since the original was written in prose. However, Jozé Antonio da Silva could choose among the several adaptations available: *Il Telemaco in ottava rima*, by Flamino Scarselli, Rome, 1747; *Aventuras de Telémaco. Traduzido em verso portugues*, by Joaquim José Caetano Pereira e Sousa, Lisbon, 1768; *Le Télémaque mis en vers*, published by Nicolas Buget, Weimar, 1797. Had he waited for some years, he could have read Charles Burdett's English verses in *Telemachus versified*, published in London in 1820.[22]

Among the works originally written in Portuguese, it is surprising that the greatest demand was for Bocage's writings and the novel *Lances da Ventura*, followed by *Viagens de Altina* and *O Feliz Independente do mundo e da fortuna*. The works by Luís de Camões, now considered the most important Portuguese writer, seem to have aroused less interest than novels quite forgotten today, and the same can be said of João Xavier de Mattos's poetry — influenced, precisely, by Camões's verses. The perception of the readers' interest for the work of the Portuguese poet is slightly altered when we consider the six requests for *Os Lusíadas*. The poet had the same bad luck among readers in Porto, where his *Obras* were sent only five times, his *Rimas*, three times, and *Os Lusíadas*, twice.[23]

Authors and books subsequently integrated in Portuguese literary histories seem to have had even less penetration in Rio de Janeiro than Camões: *Crônica do Imperador*

	Title	Quantity
1	*Les Aventures de Télémaque*, François de Salignac de la Mothe-Fénelon	65
2	*Les Mille et Une Nuits*, by Antoine Galland	55
	Selecta Latini Sermonis exemplaria e scriptoribus probatissimis, Pierre Chompré	55
3	*Histoire de Gil Blas de Santillane*, Alain René Lesage	50
4	*Magazin d'enfants*, Pauline de Montmorin, Mme Leprince de Beaumont	46
5	*História do Imperador Carlos Magno e dos doze pares de França*, Anonymous	41
6	*Obras*, Manuel Maria Barbosa du Bocage	39
7	*O Feliz independente do mundo e da fortuna, ou arte de viver contente em quaisquer trabalhos da vida*, Father Theodoro de Almeida	37
	Lances da Ventura, acasos da desgraça e heroísmos da virtude, D. Felix Moreno de Monroy y Ros	37
8	*Le Buffon de la jeunesse*, P. Blanchard / Matheus José da Costa	34
9	Horace *ad usum*	30
10	*Marilia de Dirceu*, Thomas Antonio Gonzaga	28
	O Piolho Viajante, António Manuel Policarpo da Silva	28

Table 1.2. The most requested belles-lettres titles in requisitions sent to Rio de Janeiro, and kept in the archives of the Real Mesa Censória [Royal Censorship Board], related to the period between 1808 and 1826.[25]

Clarimundo, by João de Barros, was requested six times; *Obras*, by Sá de Miranda, four; *Obras poeticas*, by Domingos dos Reis Quita, four; *Odes pindáricas*, by António Diniz da Cruz e Silva, three; *Menina e Moça*, by Bernardim Ribeiro, three. There is not even a single requisition for some of Gil Vicente's works, for example. Texts considered important for the constitution of Brazilian literature, such as *Marília de Dirceu*, by Tomás Antônio Gonzaga, and *Caramuru*, by Santa Rita Durão, had eight and four requisitions, respectively. On the other hand, there are ten requisitions for a book written by a Brazilian completely forgotten today: *Aventuras de Diófanes*, by Theresa Margarida da Silva e Horta.[24]

After the royal family transfer to Brazil, bookselling gathered momentum, which resulted, until 1826, in eight hundred titles being sent to Rio de Janeiro. The increasing number of books in circulation resulted in even greater dispersion, since 56% of them (487 titles) were sent only once. Other tendencies remained steady, as we can see from the list of the preferred books in Table 1.2.

There is a clear continuity in readers' preferences: 44% of the works of the first period continue to be imported often, notably *Les Aventures de Télémaque*, ranking first. Fénelon fulfilled the contemporary writer's impossible dream: to be at the top of the best-sellers list for more than one hundred years, not only in his own country, but also in lands as distant, at that time, as Brazil.[26] The case of *Les Aventures de Télémaque* is not the only one — it is followed by books such as *Histoire de Gil Blas de Santillane* and *Obras* by Luis de Camões — revealing stability in taste unknown today.[27] If interest in those works has remained the same since their release, others seem to have been 'discovered' late, as with the case of the first French edition of *Les Mille et une nuits* (1704), which had not attracted any attention until 1815, when it began to be shipped several times a year.[28] The other books, although not as long-lived as these, are not exactly a novelty: all were written in the eighteenth century or before. Not even the translations into Portuguese were recent, since all of them had been made in the eighteenth century, except for *One Thousand and One Nights*, translated into Portuguese in 1801 (which perhaps helps to explain why it was relatively forgotten during the eighteenth century). An exception, remarkable at a time when the pace of change was slow, is the book *O Piolho Viajante*, published for the first time in 1802, and promptly incorporated into the universe of favourites.[29]

Marília de Dirceu offers an interesting phenomenon. If the information in the documents submitted to the Portuguese censorial board is true, the first eight years of the publication went unnoticed by the inhabitants of Rio de Janeiro. It had been published for the first time in 1792, but only in 1800 did this book begin to be shipped to Rio de Janeiro. In the same period, according to Hallewell, it had four editions in Lisbon, one of which sold two thousand copies in only six months.[30] In Brazil, *Marília de Dirceu* does not seem to have been well-known in the eighteenth century, since only eight requisitions were registered until 1807 — even though the volume of books shipped may have been relatively high, considering that all licence requests were made by booksellers.[31] Maybe this low demand can be explained by fear caused by the proximity of the persecution of the 'Inconfidentes'[32]. Between 1808 and 1826, though, interest in the book increased significantly, and the predominance of merchants in the shipping of copies to the colony remained — twenty-five requisitions are signed by people related to trading, prominent among them João Gomes de Oliveira, responsible for nine requisitions, followed by Rolland, with six. The large-scale importation of this book is even more remarkable when we recall that it was also printed by Impressão Régia in Rio de Janeiro, in 1810[33] (and therefore, it was not strictly necessary to import it).[34] This book was successful not only in Brazil, for, according to Innocencio da Silva, 'except for Camões, no other Portuguese in this century won the honour of such popularity!',[35] — referring to the fact that *Marília de Dirceu* had fifteen editions in the first half of the nineteenth century.

If, in number of editions, Camões outdid Gonzaga, the same was not true concerning the reading preference of Rio de Janeiro inhabitants. However, this situation would change, if we added to the twenty-seven requisitions for Camões's *Obras*, the twenty-four requests for *Os Lusíadas* — whose demand was four times as great after the arrival of the royal family. It is possible that the court wished to keep in touch with its homeland reading these books and others originally written in Portugal.

Nevertheless, Portuguese does not prevail as the predominant source language, a position taken by French (46% of the most requested books were written in this language, as against 30% in Portuguese). Interest in books written in languages other than Portuguese may be explained, in part, by the considerable growth in the presence of foreigners in Rio de Janeiro, following the opening of the ports. It may be for this reason that there was an increase in requisitions for works in the original language, even when Portuguese translations of them were available. The little Babel in which Rio de Janeiro was transformed can be seen in requisitions for *Les Aventures de Télémaque*, requested as 'The Adventures of Telemachus in French and Spanish', 'The Adventures of Telemachus in English and Spanish', 'Telemachus in English and French' — referring, probably, to the multilingual editions of the book[36] — besides conventional requisitions, such as 'Fénelon, Aventures de Télémaque, Paris, 1799', 'Adventures of Telemachus', 'Telemachus in Portuguese'.

Although English versions of texts originally written in other languages began to be requested from then on, British authors diappeared from the list of the most requested — requisitions for *Night Thoughts*, *Meditations and Contemplations* and *The Paradise Lost* decreased to 14, 13, and 11, respectively. Daniel Defoe's *The Life and Strange Surprizing Adventures of Robinson Crusoe of York, Mariner* reached the top of the list among the English books, with eighteen requisitions between 1808 and 1826. Just as there were those who preferred reading *Les Aventures de Télémaque* in English, there were those who requested 'Aventures de Robinson Crusoe, Paris, 1799'. The Portuguese translator and his editor seem to have made the same choice, for they explained that *Vida e aventuras admiráveis de Robinson Crusoé, que contêm a sua tornada à sua ilha, as suas novas viagens e as suas reflexões* was 'translated from the French by Henrique Leitão de Sousa Mascarenhas', in Lisbon, 1785.[37]

Besides these changes in the nationality of books and the languages in which they were requested, there appear a growing number of Latin authors among the most requested. If, until 1807, Latin culture was represented only by a school anthology — *Selecta Latina*, by Pierre Chompré — from 1808 on, there was also interest in the didactic version of Horace's works, which had thirty requisitions. A fundamental aspect of the scholastic culture of the eighteenth century and of the beginning of the nineteenth centred on the study of classical authors and texts of antiquity, a knowledge of which was considered essential to the educational process. Under the general heading of Letters was sheltered the learning of Latin and Greek grammar, Poetics, and Rhetoric, together with the knowledge of History and Geography. A written and oral command of Latin and familiarity with classical culture were the objectives of these initial studies, which should prepare students for the complete reading of the original works.

Despite the supposition, at that time, that the classical authors corresponded to the apex of the art of writing, their presence in Rio de Janeiro was timid and fundamentally associated to didactic texts, anthologies, and abridged versions. Classical works in versions *ad usum delphini* stood out in number of titles and requisitions. A great success in Europe during the eighteenth and nineteenth centuries, these publications were organized according to principles very close to those structuring the *Selecta Latina*: abstract, selection of excerpts, presentation of explanatory notes, and adaptations to suppress licentious passages or those considered difficult. In the Portuguese editions, the titles of these books do not contain the expression *ad usum*, they are given names that can make one suppose they are unabridged versions of the works of Greek and Latin authors. However, the requesters of authorizations for shipping books to Brazil made clear that they were interested in precisely this kind of edition. As explicit were some Portuguese bookbinders, who engraved, only on the spine of books, the name of the classical author followed by *ad usum*, leaving the whole title out. With an eye to customers, the catalogue of Impressão Régia in Lisbon dismissed doubts on the products it used to sell, making clear the difference between the *ad usum* or *in usum* versions and the others. The catalogue tells apart, for example, two editions of Cicero's works: 'Ciceronis Opera omnia cum delectu commentariorum in usum delphini, edit. a Josepho Oliveto. Genevae, 1743' and 'Ciceronis Opera, quae supersunt omnia ad fidem aptimarum editionum diligenter expressa. Glaguae 1749'.[38] Most of the works advertised in Portugal was printed abroad; the reason appears at the beginning of the catalogue, a 'Notice to the Public':

> Those who want some Books of those that are printed in Foreign Countries will be able, with extreme swiftness and convenience, to obtain them, handing in signed requests to Francisco de Paula da Arrabida, Administrator of the shop of Impressão Regia at Praça do Commercio, who has established correspondence with Italy, France, Holland, Germany, and England, and with all diligence will fulfil the orders made to him.

Something brought together those who lived in Rio de Janeiro and those who lived in Portugal: both should resort to imports and submit to the control of censorial boards to have in their hands the books they were interested in.

The transfer of the crown to Brazil and the resulting opening of ports may have made the acquisition of imported books easier. There are records of requisitions for 1,190 different titles (totalling 1,956 editions). The interest of those who addressed the Mesa do Desembargo do Paço, established in Rio de Janeiro, was quite distinct from the interest of those who addressed the Portuguese censorial board, as we see in Table 1.3.

Books like *Les Aventures de Télémaque*, *Histoire de Gil Blas de Santillane* and *Don Quixote de la Mancha* seem to have attained unquestionable success all over the

	Title	Quantity
1	*Les Aventures de Télémaque*, François de Salignac de la Mothe-Fénelon	38
2	*Fables de La Fontaine*, Jean de La Fontaine	28
	Voyage de La Pérouse au tour du Monde, L. A. Milet Mureau	28
3	*Histoire de Gil Blas de Santillane*, Alain René Lesage	17
	Jerusalem liberata, Torquato Tasso	17
4	*Oeuvres*, Racine	16
5	*Oeuvres*, Molière	14
	Voyage du Jeune Anacharsis en Grèce, Jean-Jacques Barthélemy	14
6	*Oeuvres*, Corneille	13
7	*El Ingenioso Hidalgo Don Quixote de la Mancha*, Miguel de Cervantes	12
	The Life and Strange Surprizing Adventures of Robinson Crusoe, Daniel Defoe	12
	Oeuvres, Boileau	12
	Oeuvres, Alain René Lesage	12
	Paul et Virginie, Jacques-Henri Bernardin de Saint-Pierre	12
8	*Oeuvres*, Prevost	11
9	*Le poeme sur la Religion*, Racine	9
	Opera, Virgil	9
10	*Oeuvres*, Gresset	8
	La Henriade, Voltaire	8
	Tales of Fashionable life, Maria Edgeworth	8

Table 1.3. The most requested belles-lettres titles in requisitions submitted to the Desembargo do Paço in Rio de Janeiro between 1808 and 1821.[39]

world, arriving in Brazil from either Portugal or other European countries. Despite these repetitions, the list based on entries inspected by Mesa do Desembargo do Paço in Rio de Janeiro shows important novelties, maybe because of the different circumstances in which it was made.

Whereas, in the first period, of the 205 requisitions submitted to the Portuguese censorial board, 116 were signed by booksellers or merchants and, in the second period, of the 357 requisitions, 226 were under the responsibility of merchants, here, of the eighty-four requests, only thirty were submitted by merchants.[40] That is, if in book shipments from Portugal to Rio de Janeiro more than half were made by merchants, in the case of Desembargo do Paço most requests were made by individuals. Besides, the merchants who addressed the censorial board did not persist in this business — at least not in this way — since seven of them made it only once. Carlos Durand, who in his requests introduces himself as a 'French merchant running a store of fabrics and books in this city', was the one who addressed the censorial board more often for clearing books; however, he did not do it more than five times. Thus, it is possible to suppose that the great part of books cleared at the Rio de Janeiro customs belonged to ordinary people, who had requested them in Europe or transported them in their luggage. It is also likely that some of the foreigners who came to the city after the crown transfer brought books for 'their own use', as some declared.

This would help to explain the astonishing dispersion of titles and the low frequency with which they entered the city. The censorial board passed requests for clearing 1,190 different titles, of which 924 were requested just once in fourteen years. Moreover, the fact that those books arrived in Brazil from different parts of the world — and not only from Portugal anymore — can also have contributed to this situation, as well as the records of printed material in domestic transit between Brazilian ports.

In any case, dispersion was greater and concentration was smaller. Apart from less frequent repetitions, the quantity of requisitions by title is low, even considering only the most requested. Therefore, Gresset's *Oeuvres*, Voltaire's *La Henriade*, and Miss Edgeworth's *Tales of Fashionable life* entered Rio de Janeiro eight times in fourteen years, although they rank tenth.

Thus, though this list and the one in Table 1.2 refer to the same city and, practically, to the same period, they are quite distinct. Works that are among the favourites in the documents of the censorial board in Rio de Janeiro had aroused little interest in those who submitted authorization requests for shipping books from Lisbon. For instance, *Voyage de La Pérouse autour du Monde* was not even recorded in the Lisbon archives, whereas *Jerusalem liberata* was mentioned once. There were records of some of Racine's works: four requisitions for *Oeuvres* and four for the poem *La Religion*, three requisitions for the tragedy *Athalie*, two for *Théâtre*, and one for *Phèdre*. Molière was not a big draw either; he was requested only five times. *Voyage du Jeune Anacharsis en Grèce* was requested twice, and the same for Corneille's *Oeuvres*. As for Boileau's *Oeuvres* and Voltaire's *La Henriade*, they were mentioned in four requests. Lesage's, Prévost's and Gresset's *Oeuvres* were not even requested, and the idea of reading Miss Edgeworth's work did not occur to anyone.

The predominance of French authors increases greatly among the most requested — 75% of works were written in French whereas 10% are of English origin, with the rest being 5% of Italian authors, 5% of Spanish, and 5% of Latin. The prevalence of French authors is visible also in the making of requests, since titles were recorded primarily in this language, even though there were translations available or the source language of the text was different. Torquato Tasso's work is not mentioned in Italian, for instance, but as *Jerusalem délivrée*. Besides, there is no book of Portuguese origin among the most shipped, although there is a significant number of Portuguese requesters among those responsible for the requisitions. Therefore, these works seem more intended for the foreigners in Rio de Janeiro than for the natives or for the court and its followers.

It is also impressive that this is the list in which there is the highest number of authors who are household names today, with emphasis on writers of the *grand siècle* — Racine, Corneille, Boileau, and Molière — who comprise the pantheon of great authors together with Voltaire, Tasso, Cervantes, and Virgil. The two other lists, made out of Lisbon documents, are much less orthodox. Although they contain well-known titles (as *Don Quixote*, *Paradise Lost*, *Marília de Dirceu*, Camões's and Bocage's *Obras*), authors less respected by literary critics have a strong presence, such as Young, Hervey, Lesage, Galland, Fénelon, and Mattos. Most of the works are texts excluded from the established tradition and completely ignored today — *Le Voyageur François*, *História do Imperador Carlos Magno*, *Caroline de Lichtfield*, *Lances da Ventura*, *Viagens de Altina*, *O Feliz independente*, *Delli viaggi di Enrico Wanton*, *O Piolho Viajante*. Together with them are works such as *Selecta Latini*, Aesop's *Fables*, and Horace *ad usum*, discredited due to their school use more than for the authors or texts involved. Twice as discredited are *Magasin d'enfants* and *Buffon de la jeunesse* (see Table 1.2), since, besides being fictional narratives whose purpose was moralization and education, they had children and youth as their target group.

Magasin d'enfants was always mentioned in Portuguese — as *Thesouros de meninas*; once again, the inhabitants of Rio de Janeiro preferred a translation. The full title of this book synthesizes its objectives and contents:

> The young misses magazine: containing dialogues between a governess and several young ladies of quality, her scholars. In which each lady is made to speak according to her particular genius, temper, and inclination: their several faults are pointed out, and the easy way to mend them, as well as to think, and speak, and act properly; no less care being taken to form their hearts to goodness, than to enlighten their understandings with useful knowledge. A short and clear abridgement is also given of sacred and profane history, and some lessons in geography. The useful is blended throughout with the agreeable, the whole being interspersed with proper reflections and moral tales.[41]

Translated in 1774 by Joaquim Ignácio de Frias, this work seems to have fulfilled the translator's wishes, who warns in the 'Prologue' that the book 'must be the first to be given to a boy or girl, so much so that it is for the learning of reading and writing', attracting the public on both sides of the Atlantic. Its objectives were not restricted to the acquisition of literacy, since the true purpose of reading was to make boys leave school 'still tender in years, old in virtue, and free from those damages with which Parents, Nurses, and Schoolmasters disorganize their brains.'[42] He supposes that narratives in which a Preceptor and some girls participate would accomplish this purpose. Within this narrative framework, Biblical stories are told, such as Adam and Eve's, or fiction, such as *The Beauty and the Beast*, which, besides allowing to instil notions of moral, virtue and religion, would make possible to teach school subject matters as 'the four cardinal points', 'the butterfly and its metamorphoses', 'notions of geography', etc.

The book's success all over the world made the author carry on with a series of *Magasins*, at the same time as the publication of translated *Thesouros* continued.[43] The *Thesouros*'s popularity produced an interesting editorial event with the publication of *Thesouro de meninos, resumo de historia natural, para uso da mocidade de ambos os sexos, e instrucção das pessoas, que desejão ter noções da Historia dos tres Reinos da Natureza.*[44] According to the 1813 edition, by the Impressão Régia of Lisbon, it is an 'elementary work, compiled and arranged by Pedro Blanchard, translated from French, and offered to the Portuguese Youth by Matheus José da Costa, Beneficiary and Master of Ceremonies of the Holy Patriarchal Church of Lisbon'. Deciding who is really responsible for the text is a difficult task, but the 'Translator's Preface' warns that he has not followed closely the original, where he found several mistakes.[45] He even changed the title: 'as all this work is intended to educate the Youth, I did not hesitate to give it the title *Thesouro de Meninos*, instead of *Buffon da Mocidade* [Buffon of youth], the one given by its Author'.[46] A third person takes part in the composition of the text, Doctor Felix de Avellar Brotero, who took charge of amending the excerpts where there were inaccuracies — 'of which were many', warns the translator. The result of this triple authorship is a narrative in which the 'Head of a Family' instructs four young people in cosmography, mineralogy, botany, and zoology, within a narrative framework that takes them to excursions, observations of nature, and conversations, with plenty of advice on the 'duties of Morality, Virtue and Civility'.

The interest in children's books is not exhausted by these two titles, since there are a further nineteen requisitions submitted to the Portuguese censorial board between 1808 and 1826, requiring authorization for shipping 'Livros dos meninos' ['Books for children']. The lack of more precise information prevents us from learning which publication is meant, since it was possible to obtain the following: *Livro para meninos, no qual se propoem hum methodo facil para os ensinar a ler: com huma breve historia da creação do mundo, e outra dos animaes, ambas adornadas com figuras, etc.*, by Manoel Dias de Souza,[47] the *Livro de educação de meninos ou ideas geraes e definição das cousas que devem saber*, translated from French by Luis Pedro Le-Cor,[48] or the *Livro dos meninos, ou idéas geraes, e definições das cousas, que os meninos devem saber*, translated by João Rosado de Villalobos.[49]

Although the requests submitted to Mesa do Desembargo do Paço do not mention *Thesouros*, the presence of children's books is significant, with a large number of original titles mentioned in authorization requests submitted to the censorial board. A whole series of *Magasins* arrived in Rio de Janeiro: *Magazin des adolescentes, pour servir de suite au Magazin des Enfants* (six requisitions), *Instructions pour les jeunes dames, qui entrent dans le Monde, se marient, &c. pour servir de suite au Magazin des Adolescentes* (four requisitions) and *Magasin des enfants* (four requisitions), all by Mme de Beaumont.[50]

Besides these books, another twenty-six of a similar nature entered Rio de Janeiro, according to the inspection carried out by the censorial board, which records as follows:

> *'Morale en action', 'Biographie de geunes [sic] gens — three', 'Children's books A B C', 'Contes a mes jeunes amis — six', 'Enciclopedia da Infancia', 'Ensayo de meninos', 'Estudes de demoiselles', 'Three — Etrennes a mon fille', 'Three — Galerie des enfans' [sic], 'Juvenile Games', 'L'ami des enfants', 'Three — Le Cabinet des enfants', 'Les contes de fées', 'Nine Le garçon sans souci', 'Three Le livre des Enfans [sic] Laborieux', 'Three Le loisir de l'enfant', 'Les enfans [sic] (contes)', 'Les enfants célèbres', 'Three — Les escoliers en Vacance', 'Three Les nuits enfantines', 'Two Marmontel, memoires d'un Père a ses enfants', 'Le menthor des enfants', 'Meus meninos', 'Nine — Modellos das meninas', 'Three Musée de la Jeunesse', 'Mytologie de la jeunesse', 'Passatempo da Mocidade'.*[51]

European specialists in children's literature, like André Bay, consider that, from the eighteenth century on, it 'rapidly becomes the property of all children of the world, at least of the world of the white'.[52] The number and variety of titles listed show that children living in Rio de Janeiro — sometimes not so white — already knew the children's literature produced in Europe in the beginning of the nineteenth century. The transfer of the crown to Rio de Janeiro, as well as the permission for foreigners to enter the country, probably caused an increase in the number of children and hence in the number of parents interested in giving their children a bookish and belletristic education. This is what one can suppose considering the significant rise in the number and variety of children's, youth, and didactic titles when compared to those available before 1808.[53]

Children's interest — or rather that of their parents — in books made the Impressão Régia load its printing presses, in 1818, with *Leitura para os meninos, contendo huma collecção de Historias Moraes relativas aos defeitos ordinarios ás idades tenras, e hum dialogo sobre a Geografia, Chronologia, Historia de Portugal, e Historia Natural*, by José Saturnino da Costa Pereira.[54] This book seems to have pleased the public, for it was reissued in 1821, 1822 and 1824.

If the works mentioned above are explicitly for children and youth, other titles in high demand were part of the children's and youth list as well. In some cases, they are books produced for adults, but adopted by younger readers, such as *Robinson Crusoe* and *Don Quixote de la Mancha*. In other instances, it is just the opposite: books produced for children catch the interest of mature readers. This is what happens, for example, with *Les Aventures de Télémaque*; although it cannot be considered a book read only by children, it seems to have been aimed in the first place at Louis XIV's young son. The legend says that Fénelon, having difficulties in disciplining and instructing the heir to the throne, conceived the idea of taking Ulysses' son as the hero of a narrative which could arouse the interest of his pupil and to inform him about the Greek world at the same time. The similarities in the situation of the protagonist and the reader should favour identification and stimulate the restless pupil's interest.

If we are to believe Fénelon, the book was not intended to be printed, having reached the printing press only 'because of the infidelity of a copyist'.[55] As soon as it was published, it achieved immediate success, surpassing the didactic moralizing limits within which it was conceived, and becoming a practically mandatory reading for the nobility, who saw in the text a concealed irony towards the court and the sovereign, identifying real people under the mask of different characters. Although this supposed equivalence between fiction and reality was advantageous for the book's success, which it enjoyed almost immediately in most European countries, nothing could have been more disastrous for the author's fortune than arousing Louis XIV's wrath.

Thus, in its conception, *Les Aventures de Télémaque* is a work *ad usum delphini*, as well as the versions of the Greek and Latin classics. In this case, however, there is an important novelty, for it is not the adaptation of a known work, but rather it shapes material from history, geography, mythology and poetry according to the formula of a successful genre: the novel. Though undervalued at that time as a lesser genre, for not following the principles of Poetics or Rhetoric, the novel was, among the belletristic writings, the one that aroused the most interest among readers.[56] In Rio de Janeiro, novels were not only mentioned in most requisitions, but also ranked highly on lists of the most prized books. It is enough to observe that Fénelon's work had been an unquestionable bestseller in the city since at least 1769. Others entered and left the readers' preferences without shaking the supremacy of the genre: in the first period, 55% of works on the list of favourites are novels; in the second, considering shipments controlled by the Portuguese censorial board, novels make up 58% of the most requested. Although the concentration of classics in requests examined by Mesa do Desembargo do Paço in Rio de Janeiro was higher than those found in the Portuguese documents, the presence of novels is also quite significant — 45% of the most shipped works belong to this genre.[57] Therefore, the widespread reading of novels at the end of the eighteenth century and the beginning of the nineteenth is undeniable, a tendency recognized in European countries and, as we can see, as strong in Brazil.

Besides imported novels, there were also those produced by the first printing house established in Rio de Janeiro. Even if the printing presses at Impressão Régia [Royal Printing Press] were occupied primarily with government documents and panegyric and circumstantial booklets, there was space for novels, though in a modest way. However, this activity was hardly in tune with the public's preference — at least with that expressed in imports. Only on rare occasions did the Impressão Régia in Rio de Janeiro produce books that were in demand from abroad, producing works such as *Paulo e Virginia: Historia fundada em factos*, in 1811, or *O Diabo Coxo, verdades sonhadas e novellas da outra vida traduzidas a esta*, in 1810.[58] More often the printing house invested in titles unknown or rarely seen on the market, as *A boa mãi* and *As duas desafortunadas*.[59]

In addition to novels, however, the Impressão Régia dedicated itself also to publishing works even more 'popular' in character and even less regarded as aesthetic productions, such as the pamphlets *Historia da Donzella Theodora* and *História verdadeira da princeza Magalona*[60] — examples of the Portuguese chapbooks quite regularly shipped to Brazil. If a dim view was taken of novels, as trivial and of no real interest, it is easy to imagine what was thought of those booklets, produced from adaptations intended to win great numbers of readers. Their presence in Rio de Janeiro, together with novels, didactic books and children's books, is perhaps one of the keys to understand the widespread discourse about the lack of reading habits in the country.

In the eighteenth and nineteenth centuries — as today! — the problem does not seem to be a lack of interest in reading, but, rather, of interest in a particular kind of reading. Whereas the established tradition valued the classics of antiquity, as well as more recent writings which mimicked them, only the school versions of adapted, abridged and annotated Latin texts were being read in Rio de Janeiro; whereas Greco-Latin culture was believed to contain and express the highest artistic production, modern novels and children's stories were being read. That books taken as a model were not the most read is not a reason for astonishment, either in colonial Brazil or old Europe, where the books read in Rio de Janeiro with so much interest came from — and where they must have been bestsellers as well, considering their successive editions. However, what may be strange is the fact that, in Rio de Janeiro, there were not (or at least not in significant numbers) craftsmen, workers, literate servants, small merchants, who belong to the segments said to be responsible for spreading the reading of novels and other lesser readings. It is more likely that the economic elite was reading them, since it is difficult to imagine slaves and poor free people involved with authorization requests to import books.

Thus, interest in 'popular' editions must have been expressed by the people with the resources to take upon themselves, and pay for, the legal procedures for importing them, or else they were buying them from booksellers and merchants established in the city. Therefore, they would have the money and time available to dedicate to reading — which identifies the handling of books as a possible activity, primarily, for the economic elite. On examining the list of favourite books, one sees that financial status and cultural insertion are not equivalent, that is, the rich were not interested only in books written by great authors and well appraised by the intellectual elite.

Professors, intellectuals and other authorities in the world of letters certainly were shocked (and still are) at the readers' choices, imagining, perhaps, that reading novels and reading nothing were equivalent attitudes (or even that the second hypothesis was preferable to the first). The discourse about the lack of culture in Brazil in the colonial times cannot be sustained in the face of the data provided by the documentation of that period. Taking that into account, it is difficult to complain about the absence of books, since it shows that, in Brazil, people used to read everything — but, above all, what was considered 'low literature'. Which, for some, is still a reason for complaint.

Notes to Chapter 1

1. Research conducted with the support of CNPq. An earlier version of this text was published in Portuguese in the journal *Remate de Males* (Campinas: Unicamp, 2002), 131–63.
2. The *corpus* analysed in this paper is composed of documents produced by the Real Mesa Censória [Royal Censorship Board], the Comissão Geral para o Exame e a Censura dos Livros [General Committee for the Examination and Censorship of Books], the Santo Ofício [Holy office], and the Desembargo do Paço [The Appellate Court] (both in Lisbon and Rio de Janeiro). The period considered begins in 1768 (constitution of the Real Mesa Censória, by order of the Marquis of Pombal) and continues up to 1826 (when Portugal recognized Brazil's independence). The institutions in charge of controlling the circulation of books and documents change from time to time, though with no significant changes in the nature of the documents submitted to appraisal. The documents preserved in the Arquivos Nacionais da Torre do Tombo [Torre do Tombo National Archives] in Lisbon, containing requests for shipping books to Brazil between 1769 and 1826 ('Catálogo para Exame dos Livros para Sairem do Reino com Destino ao Brasil' [Catalogue for the Examination of Books to be sent from the Kingdom to Brazil]), are gathered under the name 'Real Mesa Censória' [Royal Censorship Board]. The authorization requests for books to enter the Brazilian ports produced between 1808 and 1822 are preserved by the Arquivo Nacional [National Archive] in Rio de Janeiro, in the archives of Mesa do Desembargo do Paço (Licenses). In the analysis of the documents, I have focused only on authorization requests for shipping belles-lettres books to Rio de Janeiro. I gratefully acknowledge the collaboration of Cilza Carla Bignoto in data transcription and Valéria Florenzano in tabulation.
3. I analysed the requests to ship books to Rio de Janeiro in *O caminho dos livros* (Campinas: Mercado de Letras/ALB/FAPESP, 2003).
4. See Chapter 2 of this book for more on Mesa do Desembargo do Paço.
5. According to 'Catálogos: exame dos livros para saída do reino', destination: Rio de Janeiro, boxes 153–54, Real Mesa Censória [Royal Censorship Board], Arquivos Nacionais da Torre do Tombo [Torre do Tombo National Archives], Lisbon (from now on RMC — ANTT). In this table — and the following — titles are as they appear in the original publication. In the licence requests works are referred to in different ways and in different languages, especially Portuguese.

   Some of these works have eighteenth- and nineteenth-century English translations. The following titles are neither the only ones nor the first editions. The list below is a sample of the presence in the Anglophone editorial world of the favourite books by Rio de Janeiro readers.

   Fénelon, *The Adventures of Telemachus the Son of Ulysses* (London: Printed for A. and J. Churchil, 1700), part I (in five parts); Le Sage, *The History and Adventures of Gil Blas of Santillane* (London: Printed for Jacob Tonson, 1732), in three volumes; Montolieu, *Caroline of Litchfield: a Novel* (New York: Richard Scott, 1815); Cervantes, *The History of the Valorous and Wittie Knight-Errant, Don-Quixote of the Mancha*, translated [by Thomas Shelton] out of the Spanish (London: William Stansby, for Ed. Blount and W. Barret, 1612); *The Life & Death of Charles the Great, King of France and Emperor of Germany*, by Samuel Clarke (London: Printed for William Miller, 1665); *Æesop's fables* (London: Printed and sold in Aldermary Church Yard, Bow Lane, London, [1775?]); Camões, *Works* (London: B. Quaritch, 1880–84).

   It was not possible to find English translations of the following titles; the following translations of the titles are mine: *Selecta Latini Sermonis exemplaria e scriptoribus probatissimis* [Selected examples of Latin Language from excellent writers/authors]; *Le Voyageur François ou la connoissance de l'ancien et du nouveau monde* [The French traveller or the knowledge of the old and the new world]; *Lances da ventura* [Episodes of Fate], by Monroy y Ros; *Rimas* [Rimes], by Bocage; *Viagens de Altina* [The Travels of Altina], by Campos; *Delli viaggi di Enrico Wanton alle terre Australi* [The Travels of Henry Wanton], by Seriman; *O Feliz independente do mundo e da fortuna* [The Happy Man, Independent of the World and the Fortune], by Almeida; and *Rimas* [Rimes], by João Xavier de Mattos.
6. Didier Masseau, *L'Invention de l'intellectuel dans l'Europe du XVIII siècle* (Paris: PUF, 1994), p. 46.
7. Ian Watt, *The Rise of the Novel* (London: Chatto and Windus, 1957). Brazilian edition, *A ascensão do romance* (São Paulo: Companhia das Letras, 1990), p. 46.

8. Cathy N. Davidson, 'The Life and Times of *Charlotte Temple*: The Biography of a Book', in *Reading in America: Literature and Social History*, ed. by Cathy N. Davidson (London and Baltimore, MD: Johns Hopkins University Press, 1989), pp. 157–79 (p. 159).
9. Ivan Teixeira, *Mecenato pombalino* (São Paulo: FAPESP/EDUSP, 1999), p. 412.
10. *Ad usum* is a Latin expression initially coined to name the edition of classical texts organized by Bossuet and Huet, 'for the Dauphin's use', that is, for the son of Louis XIV.
11. The presence of Greek books is even smaller — there are only thirty-one requisitions.
12. Translation of the title: *Letters to Ovid, called Heroides, exempt from any obscenity and translated in the vernacular: with replies, some written by the very Ovid, some by Sabino and Sidronio and the great majority by the translator; and an epilogue at the end of each letter, in which their doctrine is explained, etc.*
13. Manoel Jozé Pereira de Campos, in a requisition of 1800, 'Catálogos: exame dos livros para saída do reino', destination: Rio de Janeiro, box 153, RMC — ANTT.
14. A. Gonçalves Rodrigues, *A novelística estrangeira em versão portuguesa no período pré-romântico* (Coimbra: n.pub., 1951); and A. Gonçalves Rodrigues, *A tradução em Portugal* (Lisbon: Imprensa Nacional–Casa da Moeda, 1992) vol. I: *1495–1834*.
15. J. Milton, *Paraiso perdido, poema heróico de..*, traduzido em vulgar pelo Padre José Amaro da Silva, presbitero Vimaranense. Com o Paraiso Restaurado, Poema do mesmo Author; Notas Historicas, Mythologicas, &c. de M. Racine; e as Observações de M. Addisson sobre o Paraiso Perdido (Lisbon: Na Typographia Rollandiana, 1789). Com licença da Real Meza da Comissão Geral sobre o Exame, e Censura dos Livros. P. V. [With permission of Royal Board of the General Commission for the Examination and Censorship of Books].
16. Francisco da Gama Caeiro, *Livros e livreiros franceses em Lisboa nos fins de setecentos e no primeiro quartel do século XIX* (Separata do boletim Bibliográfico da Universidade de Coimbra, vol. 35, 1980), Comments in the text by Caeiro.
17. 1. *Aventuras de Telemaco, filho de Ulysses; traduzido do original francez na lingua portugueza por* José Manuel Ribeiro Pereira [*Adventures of Telemachus, the Son of Ulysses; translated from French into Portuguese by...*], 2 vols (Lisbon, 1765). *Aventuras finaes de Telemaco, filho de Ulysses, novamente compostas pelo bacharel* Joseph Manoel Ribeiro Pereira [*The Final Adventures of Telemachus, newly written by the bachelor...*]. (Lisbon, 1765). *Segunda edição correta e emendada pelo mesmo traductor da primeira edição d'estas Aventuras* [*Second edition revised and amended by the same translator of the first edition of these Adventures*], translation by José Manuel Ribeiro Pereira, 2 vols (Lisbon, 1784). Reissue of *Aventuras finaes* [*Final Adventures*] (Lisbon, 1785).
 2. *Aventuras de Telémaco. Traduzido em verso portugues* [*Adventures of Telemachus. Translated in verse into Portuguese*], by Joaquim José Caetano Pereira e Sousa, 2 vols (Lisbon, 1768). Reissued in Lisbon, 1787, in 2 volumes. New edition as *Aventuras de Telemaco, traduzidas em verso portuguez, a que se ajuntam algumas notas mythologicas e allegoricas para inteligencia do poema. Dedicadas ao Ser. Principe do Brasil* [*Adventures of Telemachus in Portuguese verse, to which some mitological and allegorical notes were added to the understanding of the poem*], 2 vols (Lisbon, 1788).
 3. *O Telémaco* [*The Telemachus*], translated by Captain Manoel de Sousa (Lisbon, 1770, 2 vols). Reissued as *O Telemaco de Mr. Francisco de Salignac de la Motte Fenelon, etc traduzido* [*The Telemachus by Mr. Francisco de Salignac de la Motte Fenelon, etc translated*], 2 vols (Lisbon, 1776). New reissues in Lisbon, in 1785 and 1825.
 4. *Aventuras de Telemaco, filho de Ulysses... Com hum discurso sobre a Poesia Epica e Excelencia do Poema de Telemaco e notas geograficas e mythologicas.* [*The Adventures of Telemachus, son of Ulysses... With a discourse on Epic Poetry and the Excellence of Telemachus' Poem, and geographic and mythological notes*], no indication of translator (Lisbon, 1785).
18. Concerning the several Portuguese translations and editions of Fenelon's book, see Fernando Alves Cristóvão, 'Presença de Fénelon no espaço literário luso-brasileiro: subsídios para um estudo' (Paris: Fondation Calouste Gulbenkian, Centre Culturel Portugais, 1983), pp. 135–50.
19. *Aventuras de Telemaco, filho de Ulysses*, por Francisco Salignac de la Mothe Fenelon, traducção do Capitão Manuel de Sousa, e de Francisco Manuel do Nascimento, retocada e correcta por José da Fonseca [*The Adventures of Telemachus,* son of Ulysses, by Francisco Salignac de la Mothe Fenelon, translated by Capitan Manuel de Sousa and Francisco Manuel do Nascimento, retouched and corrected by José da Fonseca] (Paris: na Livraria Europea de Baudry, 1842). The first edition is from 1837.

20. *'Aventuras de Telemaco, filho de Ulysses* por M. Fénélon, traduzidas do francez em portuguez: com um discurso sobre a poesia épica e excellencia do poema Telemaco; e muitas notas geográficas, e mythologicas para intelligencia do mesmo poema: edição executada com caracteres novos e adornada com o retrato do mesmo Fénélon, Lisboa, 1785', in Francisco Jozé Freire, *Livros impressos por Francisco Rolland, Impressor-Livreiro em Lisboa, no Largo do Loreto.* Bound together with *Secretario Portuguez, ou methodo de escrever cartas* (Lisbon: Typografia Rollandiana, 1801). *'Aventuras de Telemaco,* traduzidas de Francez, em 8. 3 tomos. Nova edição correcta, e emendada, os dois primeiros tomos vendem se separados', in *Catalogo dos livros portuguezes, impressos á custa de João Baptista Reycend e Companhia,* mercadores de livros, no largo do Calhariz, na esquina da Bica grande em Lisboa, que se achão de venda na sua loja. Undated catalogue circulating in 1784. *'Aventuras de Telemaco,* com Notas, em 8', in *Livros impressos por Francisco Rolland, Impressor-Livreiro em Lisboa.* Bound together with *Fábulas de Esopo* (Lisbon: Typografia Rollandiana, 1791). *'Aventuras de Telemaco* traduzidas do Francez de M. Fénélon, pelo Capitão Manoel de Sousa, em 8. 2 vol. 1770' — Advertised for sale, in 1791, in the catalogue of Widow Bertrand's Bookstore.
21. 'Catálogos: exame dos livros para saída do reino', destination: Rio de Janeiro, box 153, RMC — ANTT.
22. Translation of titles into English: *Il Telemaco in ottava rima* [*Telemachus in octava rima*]; *Aventuras de Telémaco. Traduzido em verso portugues* [*The Adventures of Telemachus. Translated into Portuguese verse*]; *Le Télémaque mis en vers* [*Telemachus in verse*];
23. English translations: *The Lusiad: or, The Discovery of India: An Epic Poem* (London: G. Bell, 1877), ed. by Edward Richmond Hodges, trans. by William Julius Mickle. *Works* (London, B. Quaritch, 1880–84).
24. It was not possible to find English translations of the following books: *Chronicle of the Emperor Clarimundo*, João de Barros; *Works of Sá de Miranda*; *Poetic works*, Quita; *Odes*, Cruz e Silva; *Marília of Dirceu*, Gonzaga; *The Caramuru*, Durão, *Adventures of Diofanes*, Horta. There is a recent translation of Ribeiro's book: Bernardim Ribeiro, *Maiden and Modest: A Renaissance Pastoral Romance*, trans. by Gregory Rabassa (Dartmouth, MA: Tagus Press at UMass Dartmouth, 2012).
25. According to 'Catálogos: exame dos livros para saída do reino', destination: Rio de Janeiro, boxes 154, 155, 156, RMC — ANTT.

Some of these works have eighteenth- and nineteenth-century English translations (in addition to the previously mentioned): *Arabian nights entertainments Consisting of one thousand and one stories*: told by the Sultaness of the Indies. Translated into French from the Arabian MSS, by M. Galland and now done into English from the last Paris edition (London: Printed for W. Taylor, W. Chetwood, and S. Chapman, 1721–22); Mrs Le Prince de Beaumont, *The young ladies magazine: or dialogues between a discreet governess and several young ladies of the first rank under her education* (London: Printed for J. Nourse, at the Lamb, opposite Catherine-Street, in the Strand, 1760); Blanchard, *The youth's treasure, or, A treatise on morality, virtue, and politeness: enlivened with anecdotes and examples* (London: Darton and Harvey, 1804).

It was not possible to find English translations of the following titles: *Obras* [Works], Bocage; *Marília de Dirceu* [Marília of Dirceu], Gonzaga; *O Piolho Viajante*, Silva [The Travels of a louse].
26. *Les Aventures de Télémaque* was published in Paris in 1699.
27. *Histoire de Gil Blas* was first published in 1715; Camões's *Obras Completas* [*Complete Works*] was published for the first time in 1720.
28. Until 1807, *As Mil e uma noites* [*One Thousand and One Nights*] had been shipped only six times. Curiously, one of the books written to imitate it, *Les Mille et un quart-d'heure. Contes Tartares* [*One Thousand and one quarter of an hour. Tartar stories*] (published in Paris in 1715, and translated into Portuguese as *Divertimento de um quarto de hora*, by P. João Silverio de Lima, in 1782), aroused more interest, and was shipped nine times.
29. *O Piolho Viajante, cujas viagens são divididas em mil e uma carapuças* was published, anonymously, in weekly brochures, until the seventy-two *carapuças* [*caps*, as in 'if the cap fits, wear it', since each chapter corresponds to a story that can fit some readers] which compose it were completed. Released in 1802, it was sent to Rio de Janeiro, for the first time, in the following year, at Simão Taddeo Pereira's request. In 1821, the brochures were bound in volumes, whose authorship is

attributed to António Manuel Policarpo da Silva. Editions in volumes: 1821, 1837, 1846 and 1857.

30. Laurence Hallewell, *O livro no Brasil* (São Paulo: EDUSP, 1985), p. 23 [English edition: *Books in Brazil*, (London and Metuchen, NJ: The Scarecrow Press, 1982)]. The publishing history of *Marília de Dirceu* is quite complex in these first years, including apocryphal editions and the diffusion of poems of uncertain authorship. See the preface prepared by M. Rodrigues Lapa for the edition *Marília de Dirceu e mais poesias* [*Marília de Dirceu and other poems*], Tomás Antônio Gonzaga (Lisbon: Livraria Sá da Costa, 1937).
31. Books were shipped by: Viuva Bertram e Filhos and Francisco Rolland (in 1800); Paulo Martins and, again, Francisco Rolland and Viuva Bertram e Filhos (1802); Simão Taddeo Pereira (twice in 1803); Paulo Martins e Filhos (1807).
32. *Inconfidentes* were the participants of *Inconfidência Mineira*, a political movement against the Portuguese crown, which occurred in Minas Gerais between 1785 and 1789. Tomás Antônio Gonzaga took part in it, and was arrested on 21 May 1789. He remained in prison until 23 May 1792, when he was deported to Mozambique to serve a ten-year banishment sentence.
33. *Marilia de Dirceo*. Por T. A .G. Nova edição (Rio de Janeiro. Na Impressão Regia). Com licença de S. A. R. 1810. 3 partes [With permission of His Royal Highness].
34. Authors born in Brazil did not have the same fortune. Santa Rita Durão was in low demand, with four requisitions for *Caramuru* (three in 1819 and one in 1815). Theresa Margarida da Silva e Horta did not succeed either. Her *Aventuras de Diófanes* decreased from ten requisitions in the first period to only four. *O Uraguay*, by José Basilio da Gama, which had not been requested before, although it had been published in 1769, was sent twice (in 1816 and 1819).
35. Innocencio Francisco da Silva, *Diccionario Bibliographico Portuguez* (Lisbon: Imprensa Nacional, 1858).
36. In the nineteenth century, there were editions which contained Fénelon's text in many languages. This is the case, for example, in *Essai d'un Télémaque polyglotte, ou les Aventures du Fils d'Ulysse en langue française, grecque moderne, arménienne, italienne, espagnole, portugaise, anglaise, allemande, hollandaise, russe, polonaise, illyrienne, avec une traduction en vers grecs et latins* [*Essay of a multilingual Telemachus, or The Adventures of the Son of Ulysses in French, modern Greek, Armenian, Italian, Spanish, Portuguese, English, German, Dutch, Russian, Polish, Illyrian, with a translation into Greek and Latin*] (Paris: Fleury-Lécluse, 1812).
37. Translation into English: *The life and marvellous adventures of Robinson Crusoe, containing its return to his island, his new journeys and his thoughts.*
38. *Catálogo de livros que se vendem por seus justos preços na loge da Impressão Régia* sita na Praça do Commercio em abril de 1772. Lisboa. Com licença da Real Mesa Censória. My emphasis. Translation of titles into English: Complete works of Cicero with selected comments for student use; Works of Cicero, all existing works carefully presented according the authority of excellent editors.
39. According to documentation preserved by Mesa do Desembargo do Paço — Licenses — boxes 168, 169 (AN-RJ).

    Some of these works have eighteenth- and nineteenth-century English translations (in addition to the previously mentioned): La Fontaine, Jean de. *Fables and tales from La Fontaine.* (In French and English. Now first translated. To which is prefix'd, the author's life. London: Printed for A. Bettsworth [*sic*] and C. Hitch, and C. Davis, 1734); La Pérouse, Jean-François de Galaup; Mureau, L M A Milet de; Lesseps, Jean-Baptiste-Barthélemy. *The voyage of La Pérouse round the world, in the years 1785, 1786, 1787, and 1788, with the nautical tables.* (London: Printed for John Stockdale, 1798); Tasso, Torquato. *Jerusalem delivered; an heroic poem* (translated from the Italian of Torquato Tasso, by John Hoole. London: Printed for J. Dodsley, in Pall-Mall; And T. Davies, in Russel-Street, Covent-Garden, 1772); Racine, Louis. *Dramatic works of J. Racine.* (Accompanied with explanatory notes and critical remarks. London, J. Souter, 1834); Moliere. *The works of Moliere* (Glasgow: Printed by Robert Urie, and sold by John Gilmour, 1751); Barthélemy, *Travels of Anacharsis the Younger in Greece during the middle of the fourth century before the Christian æra.* (Translated from the French. In seven volumes, and an eighth in quarto, containing maps, plans, views, and coins. London: Printed for G. G. and J. Robinson; and L. White, Dublin, 1793–94); Corneille, P. *The Works of Corneille* (Edited by H. E. Huntington.

London: Rivingtons, 1887); *The works of Monsieur Boileau Despreaux.* (Made English from the last Paris edition. To which is prefix'd, his life, written to Joseph Addison, Esq; by Mr. Des-Maizeaux. With some account of this translation, by N. Rowe, Esq. London. Printed for E. Curll, 1714); Le Sage. *Works of Le Sage* (London, J. C. Nimmo and Bain, 1881); Saint-Pierre, *Paul and Virginie,* (London: 1788); Racine. *Religion: a poem* (London: Printed by W. Strahan and sold by J. Hodges, London Bridge, J. Newbery, St. Paul's Church-yard, W. Owen, Temple-bar, A. Strahan, Cornhill, and Wilson and Durham in the Strand, 1754); *The works of Virgil* (Edinburgh: Printed for Alexander Donaldson; No. 48, St. Paul's Church-Yard, London ; and at Pope's Head, Edinburgh, 1777); Voltaire, *The Henriade: An Epic Poem, in Ten Cantos* (Translated from the French of Voltaire, Into English Rhyme, with Large Historical and Critical Notes. Burton and Company, 1797). It was not possible to find English translations of *Oeuvres* [works] de Prévost e de Gresset.

40. Twenty-three booksellers and merchants shipped books between Portugal and Rio de Janeiro until 1807. The same amount (but not necessarily the same people) was involved in shipments from Portugal to Rio de Janeiro after the royal family transfer. Between 1808 and 1822, sixteen merchants made thirty clearances at the Mesa do Desembargo do Paço.
41. *The young misses magazine* Printed for William Young, bookseller and stationer, no. 52 South Second Street, Philadelphia, 1800. The Portuguese translation in entitled: *Thesouro de Meninas...* Composto na lingua francesa por Madama Leprince de Beaumont, traduzido na lingua portugueza, e offerecido a Ill.ma e Exc.ma Senhora D. Leonor Ernestina Dhaum, marqueza de Pombal por Joaquim Ignacio de Frias. Nova Edição, Adornada com oito estampas [*The young misses Treasure...* Composed in French by Madame Leprince de Beaumont, translated into Portuguese and offered to Mrs. Leonor Ernestina Dhaum, Marquess of Pombal by Joaquim Ignacio de Frias. New Edtion. Adorned with eight illustrations], Rio de Janeiro, Typographia de J. J. Barroso e Comp, 1838. The Portuguese translator as well as the English one were literal in their translation of the French title: *Magasin d'enfants, ou dialogues d'une sage gouvernante avec ses élèves de la première distinction, dans lesquels ont fait penser, parler, agir, les jeunes gens suivant le génie, le tempérament et les inclinations d'un chacun. On y représente les défauts de leur âge, l'on y montre de quelle manière on peut les corriger, on s'applique autant à leur former le cœur qu'à leur éclairer l'esprit. On y donne un abrégé de l'Histoire Sacrée, de la Fable, de la géographie, etc. le tout rempli de réflexions utiles et de Contes Moraux, pour les amuser agréablement, et écrit d'un style simple et proportionné à la tendresse de leurs âmes*, whose first edition is from 1757.
42. 'Prologo do Traductor', *op. cit.*, p. XI.
43. At the same time, these were shipped to Rio de Janeiro: *Thesouro de adultos* [*Adults' treasure*] (three requisitions), *Thesouro de adultas* [*Female adults' treasure*] (five requisitions), *Thesouro dos Prudentes* [*Treasure of prudent people*] (one requisition), *Thesouro da Paciência nas chagas de Jesus Cristo* [*Treasure of Patience on Jesus' wounds*] (eight requisitions). The Desembargo do Paço passed five requisitions for *Morale en action* [Morality in action], translated into Portuguese as *Thesouro da mocidade portugueza ou a moral em acção. Escolha de factos memoraveis, e anecdotas interessantes* [*Treasure of the Portuguese youth or moral in action. A selection of memorable facts and interesting anecdotes*].
44. Translation into English: *Boys' treasure, summary of natural history, for the use of young people of both sexes, and for instructing those who wish to acquire knowledge about the History of the three kingdoms of Nature.*
45. *Le Buffon de la jeunesse*, P. Blanchard (1801). English translation: P. Blanchar, *The youth's treasure, or, A treatise on morality, virtue, and politeness: enlivened with anecdotes and examples* (London: Darton and Harvey, 1804).
46. *Thesouro de meninos, resumo de historia natural, para uso da mocidade de ambos os sexos, e instrucção das pessoas, que desejão ter noções da Historia dos tres Reinos da Natureza.* Obra elementar, compilada, e ordenada por Pedro Blanchard, Traduzida do Francez, e offerecida á Mocidade Portugueza, por Matheus José da Costa, Beneficiado, e Mestre de Cerimonias da Santa Igreja Patriarcal de Lisboa, 6 Tomos [*Boys' treasure, summary of natural history, for the use of young people of both sexes, and for instructing those who wish to acquire knowledge about the History of the three kingdoms of Nature.* Elementary work, compiled and organized by Pedro Blanchard, translated from French and offered to the Portuguese Youth, by Matheus José da Costa, Beneficiary and Master of Ceremonies of the Saint Patriarchal Church of Lisbon, 6 tomes] (Lisbon: na Impressão Régia,

1813), p. XVIII. In tome III, the role of translator/adapter is reinforced: 'Traduzida do Francez, com muitas correcções e artigos novos. Offerecida, a sua Alteza o Principe Real do Reino Unido de Portugal, e do Brazil, e Algarves; Duque de Bragança, o Senhor D. Pedro de Alcantara por Matheus José da Costa' [Translated from French, with many corrections and new articles. Offered to Your Highness Royal Prince of the United Kingdom of Portugal and Algarves; Duke of Bragança, Lord D. Pedro de Alcantara by Matheus José da Costa'].

47. Dias de Souza, Manoel, *Livro para meninos, no qual se propoem hum methodo facil para os ensinar a ler: com huma breve historia da creação do mundo, e outra dos animaes, ambas adornadas com figuras, etc.*, (Coimbra, 1799). Translation of title into English: *Book for Boys, which proposes an easy method to teach them to read: with a brief history of the creation of the world, and of other animals, both adorned with figures, etc.*.

48. Le-Cor, Luis Pedro. *Livro de educação de meninos ou ideas geraes e definição das cousas que devem saber...* traduzido da lingua franceza na portugueza por... [*Book for the education of children or general ideas and the definition of things that they should know, translated from French into Portuguese by...*] (Lisbon: na Officina de Joseph da Costa Coimbra, 1746).

49. João Rosado de Villalobos, *Livro dos meninos, ou idéas geraes, e definições das cousas, que os meninos devem saber,* tradução do francez por... Nova edição [*Children books or general ideas and the definition of things that they should know, translated from French by...*New edition (Lisbon: Typ. Rollandiana, 1824).

50. Translation into English: The adolescent magazine, in continuation of The young misses magazine; Instructions for young ladies on their entering into life, their duties in the married-state, and towards their children; The young misses magazine.

51. Quoted as they appear in the requests. Translation into English: 'Morality in action', 'Biography of young people', 'Tales to my young friends', 'Children's Encyclopaedia', 'Children's Essay', 'Young ladies Studies', 'Presents for my daughter', 'Children's gallery', 'The children's friend', 'The children's cabinet', 'Fairy tales', 'The worry-free boy', 'The book of laborious children', 'Child's Recreation', 'Children (tales)', 'Famous children', 'School children on vacation', 'Children's nights', 'Marmontel, Memories of a father to his children', 'Children's mentor', 'My boys', 'Girls models', 'Youth Museum', 'Mythology for youth', 'Pastime for the young'.

52. André Bay, 'La littérature enfantine', in *Histoire des littératures*, Encyclopédie de la Pléiade (Paris: Gallimard, 1967), tome III, p. 1608.

53. About children's literature in Brazil, see: Marisa Lajolo and Regina Zilberman, *Literatura infantil brasileira: história & histórias* (São Paulo: Ática, 1985), and *Um Brasil para crianças: para conhecer a literatura infantil brasileira: histórias autores e textos* (São Paulo: Global Editora, 1986).

54. Translation of title into English: *Reading for children, containing a collection of moral stories related to faults of the young ages, and a dialogue about Geography, Chronology, History of Portugal, and Natural History.*

55. *Apud*: Laffont-Bompiani, *Dictionnaire des Oeuvres de tous les temps et tous les pays*, 4th edn (Paris: Société d'Édition de Dictionnaires et Encyclopédies, 1962).

56. A preference for novels was also perceived by Irving A. Leonard in his study 'Favorite fiction', in which he considers books read in the sixteenth century by the Spanish conquerors and their descendants. Just as in Brazil, theological, moral and religious writings were the most shipped to America, but, among the belles-lettres works, 'the novel in its multiple manifestations, the picaresque, the pastoral and, of course, the adventurous and sentimental romances of chivalry, enjoyed immense popularity'. Irving A. Leonard, *Books of the Brave: Being an Account of Books and of Men in the Spanish Conquest and Settlement of the Sixteenth-Century New World* (Berkeley, Los Angeles, and Oxford: University of California Press, 1992), p. 106.

57. In this period, there is no stability in the designation of fictional prose texts, called novel, novelette, short story, story, adventure etc. Fictional prose shipped between 1769 and 1807: *Les Aventures de Télémaque*; *Histoire de Gil Blas de Santillane*; *Le Voyageur François*; *Caroline de Litchfield*; *El Ingenioso Hidalgo Don Quixote de la Mancha*; *História do Imperador Carlos Magno*; *Lances da Ventura*; *Viagens de Altina*; *Delli viaggi di Enrico Wanton*; *O Feliz independente do mundo e da fortuna*. Shipped between 1808 and 1826: *Les Aventures de Télémaque*; *Les Mille et Une Nuits*; *Histoire de Gil Blas*; *Magazin d'enfants*; *História do Imperador Carlos Magno*; *O Feliz independente*; *Lances da Ventura*; *Thesouro de Meninos*; *O Piolho Viajante*; *Voyage de La Perouse*; *Voyage du Jeune Anacharsis en Grèce*;

El Ingenioso Hidalgo Don Quixote de la Mancha; *Robinson Crusoe*; Lesage's *Oeuvres*; *Paul et Virginie*; Prévost's *Oeuvres*; *Scènes de la vie du grand monde*.

58. Saint-Pierre, *Paulo e Virginia: Historia fundada em factos* (Rio de Janeiro: Impressão Régia, 1811). Lesage. *O Diabo Coxo, verdades sonhadas e novellas da outra vida traduzidas a esta* (Rio de Janeiro: Impressão Régia, 1810). Translation of tiles into English respectively: *Paul and Virginia, a story based on facts*; and *The Lame Devil, dreamed truths and novels of the other life translated into this one*.
59. *A boa mãi*. Novella: traduzida do francez (Rio de Janeiro: na Impressão Regia), 1815. *As duas desafortunadas*. Novella: traduzida do francez (Rio de Janeiro: na Impressão Regia, 1815). Under permission. Translation of titles into English respectively: *The good mother. Novel translated from French*; and *The two unfortunate ladies. Novel translated from French*.
60. *Historia da Donzella Theodora, em que se trata da sua grande formosura, e sabedoria*. Traduzida do Castelhano em Portuguez. Por Carlos Ferreira Lisbonense (Rio de Janeiro: na Impressão Regia, 1815). Under permission. *História verdadeira da princeza Magalona, filha delrei de Napoles, e do nobre, e valeroso cavalleiro Pierres Pedro de Provença, e dos muitos trabalhos, e adversidades que passárão, sendo sempre constantes na fé, e virtudes; e como depois reinarão, e acabárão a sua vida virtuosamente no serviço de Deus* (Rio de Janeiro: na Impressão Regia), 1815. Translation of titles into English respectively: *The Story of Maiden Theodora, in which her great beauty and wisdom are addressed*; and *True story of the Princess Magalona, daughter of the king of Naples, and of the noble and brave knight Pierres Pedro of Provences, and of the many tasks and difficult situations, being always constant in faith, and virtue, and of as they will later reign, and eventually end their virtuosly your life in God's service*].

CHAPTER 2

Booksellers in Rio de Janeiro: The Book Trade and Circulation of Ideas from 1808 to 1831

Lucia Maria Bastos Pereira das Neves and
Tania Maria Tavares Bessone da Cruz Ferreira

NEWS ITEM

The following interesting works are forthcoming: *Memória histórica da invasão dos franceses em Portugal no ano de 1807. Observações sobre o comércio franco do Brasil.*[1]

This was the first advertisement about books that appeared in the *Gazeta do Rio de Janeiro*, the first and only newspaper that existed in Brazil in September 1808. The arrival of the Portuguese Court in January of that year had ushered in a new political situation and required the constitution of a cultivated and illustrious society to surround it. With this objective, the Impressão Régia [Royal Press] was founded by royal decree on 13 May 1808. It was responsible for the publication of newspapers and many works of a scientific and literary character, as well as official documents. From that time on, the book trade and the establishment of book stores began to flourish in Rio de Janeiro.

For many years, the prevailing view of historiographers was that there was no space for a book trade in Rio de Janeiro. This is what is stated in records of the period, whether they are written by librarians or travellers. For example, Luís Joaquim dos Santos Marrocos, the royal librarian, stated in a letter to his father in 1813 that there was 'little business in books' since there were only two booksellers in Rio de Janeiro, both of whom were French and, therefore, 'scoundrels'. The traveller Theodor von Leithold (1771–1826) in turn declared in 1819 that there were no bookshops but only print dealers in Brazil.[2] However, a closer scrutiny of the existing sources shows that even before 1808 there was in fact a thriving book market in Rio de Janeiro.[3]

In the light of this, this chapter seeks to analyse the book trade that flourished in Rio de Janeiro between 1808 and 1831 by examining the advertisements in periodicals such as *Gazeta do Rio de Janeiro*, *Diario do Rio de Janeiro*, and *Jornal do Commercio*. The Mesa do Desembargo do Paço granted licences to bookshops and private concerns so that they could retrieve their books from the Customs House of Rio. Licences were also given to bookstores based in Lisbon, with the aim of sending books to the main towns and cities of Brazil, and the catalogues were produced and printed by 'book people'.[4] In the same way, this chapter seeks to show that books, bookstores, and printing houses can present diverse avenues for historical research, resulting in a novel approach to the cultural and political practices of the early 1800s, as well as making it possible to determine how new ideas originating in European countries, particularly Portugal and France, became widespread in the Court. This view is predicated on the assumption that the history of books can be equated with investigating the meaning of messages conveyed by the written word, since books can turn into a privileged means 'of entering into a dialogue with the past, of creation and innovation'.[5]

The Book Trade

In 1795, a French bookseller established in Lisbon, Jean Reycend, sought permission from the board of censors to send books to Rio de Janeiro, in particular, the complete collection of the periodical *Mercúrio Histórico*, various comedies, tragedies, dramatic farces, and papers recently printed in Lisbon.[6] In the same period, a correspondence took place between the house of Francisco Rolland and Captain Antônio Luís Fernandes, a wholesale contractor in the main square of Rio de Janeiro, which has been analysed by Gama Caieiro. This letter exchange attempted to persuade the bookseller of his business opportunities, 'since if he wanted to send an assortment of books on his own account, [...] he will never cease to do good business and I am sure he will never regret it'. He added that it was religious books that sold most copies — missals, breviaries, and books of hours — although 'books out of the ordinary' also attracted a lot of attention, which suggests that Brazilian society was also finding new interests.[7]

Thus, although the *Almanaque do Rio de Janeiro de 1799* suggested that there were only two bookstores in the capital of Portuguese America,[8] the Court, and all the cultured people that accompanied it when it arrived in Brazil, found that there was an active book trade and that this was diversified through the trade's supply channels in the city. On the one hand, advertisements in the *Gazeta do Rio de Janeiro* announced sales in 'bookshops', 'bookstores', and 'shops owned by book traders'.[9] These were strictly speaking bookshops that were almost entirely devoted to selling printed works. It was still quite common for these bookshops to sell other goods, although these were related to books. Thus there were advertisements for the sale of musical notation paper, writing parchment, ink, lined books suitable for Portuguese or English book-keeping, foreign playing cards, prints, and designs. For example, J. G. Guimarães, a bookseller established in Rua do Sabão, announced that he had been sent a large amount of different papers from London on the ship *Geni*, such as stationery paper from Bath which could serve to register important documents. It was also possible to find liturgical vestments and other objects to celebrate Mass, as was advertised by 'Livreiro Francisco Luiz Saturnino Veiga, in Rua do Ouvidor'.[10]

Another space for the book trade, perhaps the most common one, was within more diversified merchandise categories, such as luxury items, perfumes, or even more exotic goods. Pierre Constant Dalbin announced at the end of his own book catalogue that in 'the same house' the following materials were for sale:

> Paper — Wallpaper to line houses of any quality.
> Perfumes — Bath — Hair-oil — Transparent soap — Soap from Paris — Eau-de-Cologne [...]
> Fashion items — Satin ribbons — [...] — Silk stockings — Ties — Ladies' jackets — branches, wreaths and bouquets of flowers.[11]

In turn, in 1818, Imbert de Nagis, a French businessman, placed an advertisement in the *Gazeta do Rio de Janeiro* for the sale in his shop of a large assortment of Portuguese, French, and English books, together with furniture, crystal, china, pianos, and the popular *Rub Antisyphilitique*, an ointment for men with venereal disease.[12]

Auctions of books, carried out by various traders or private individuals, constituted another privileged means of marketing these books. On 22 September 1815, William Lennox, an English trader, hosted 'in his big hall in Alfândega and Candelária streets, an auction of a large collection of books in various languages, French prints, a magic and phantasmagoric lantern, some exotic apparatuses for making tea, a complete telescope [...]'.[13] There were even private auctions, which, according to Nizza da Silva, could have been a strategy to allow some shop owners to obtain a higher price for their goods. In the *Gazeta do Rio de Janeiro* in 1817, a public servant — an official from the Secretary of State for Business in Brazil — auctioned a collection of law books and Portuguese, French, and English classics, as well as some leaflets. The auction took place on consecutive days until all the books were sold.[14]

It was still common for some houses, such as pharmacies and religious establishments, to sell specialist books. Thus, advertisements in the *Gazeta do Rio de Janeiro* demonstrate that the pharmacies which, as a general rule, 'were places where remedies and medicines were sold', also advertised the sale of works such as *Análise química das águas férreas de Bom Jardim* or *Reflexões sobre o método iatraléptico, ou modo de administrar os remédios pelo sistema cutâneo.*[15] All these titles could be found in the pharmacy of José Vicente da Rosa.[16]

In the case of religious works such as missals, Marian hours, bibles, and doctrinal pamphlets, the religious institutions took charge of this business and these products could be found in the doorways of the Hospício de N. Sra. do Patrocínio in Rua das Marrecas. Thus prayer-books were effectively sold in specialized bookstores.[17]

Another way that the book trade operated was through private dealers, who often worked as sellers of Portuguese publications in Rio de Janeiro or even sought subscribers for works printed in Lisbon.[18] Thus in 1817 Luís Joaquim dos Santos Marrocos handled the subscriptions for the *Coleção dos Retratos e Elogios dos Varões e Damas Portugueses com memórias históricas de suas Vidas*, already published in facsimile in Lisbon.[19] He arranged for the subscription to be offered in three bookstores — those of Francisco Saturnino da Veiga, Silva Porto, and Manuel Mandillo — which he deemed to be the best known and most frequented; there was also a sheet subscription which was entrusted to the priest Joaquim Dâmaso (1777–1833), the curator of the Royal Library.[20]

It was also possible to sell books at the author's home, as it is mentioned in *Gazeta do Rio de Janeiro*: 'This has come to light: *Novo e infalível método de substituir o leme de qualquer navio no alto mar, com uma estampa* by the naval captain André Jacob. This is for sale in the shop of Manoel Mandillo, [...] and at the author's house [...]'.[21]

Since there were so many channels for the sale of books, it was evidently a profitable business. There is further evidence to support this statement. In the first place, it is significant that the newspapers were full of advertisements about publications.[22] Surprisingly, in the period 1808–12, the number of advertisements for books proved to be higher than for any other merchandise. In 1810, for example, of a total of seventy-five advertisements, thirty-three were related to the sale of books or prints, 44% of the total figure, while there were only eleven advertisements for the sale of furniture, two for textile goods, and one for slaves. On average, in the period 1808–22, 14.99% of the advertisements published in the *Gazeta do Rio de Janeiro* were for the sale of books and other printed material, while for furniture, slaves, and textiles, the figures were 20%, 15.94%, and less than 2% respectively.[23]

Newspapers like *O Patriota*, published in the Court in the period 1813–14, also included books that had been published in Rio de Janeiro. There were works which covered areas such as chemistry, mathematics, agriculture, literature, history and the arts, and these were disseminated in a way that made them available for sale.[24] In addition, the *Diario do Rio de Janeiro* of June 1821 stated that 'all and every kind of advertisement or private news is published free of charge'.[25]

Another periodical in which advertisements for books, bookstores, and auctions of books could be found was *Jornal do Commercio*, founded in 1827 and, despite many changes of proprietors and editorial characteristics, still published today. At first, the newspaper belonged to a bookshop and the French typographer, Pierre Plancher. He held auctions for his works and those of others in the central square, and made the *Jornal do Commercio* an important vehicle for the book trade, both in the retail and wholesale sector.[26]

Although this analysis is restricted to the area of Rio de Janeiro, all this activity in the book trade, accompanied by intense publicity, suggests the presence in that period of a public capable of purchasing and even reading these books, although the readership was probably confined to an intellectual elite.

The number of bookshops and booksellers in the Court was much higher than is indicated by previously known data. Through advertisements in the *Gazeta do Rio de Janeiro* and documents from the Mesa do Desembargo do Paço, four booksellers can be identified in 1808: Francisco Luís Saturnino da Veiga (1771–1841) (Rua do Ouvidor), Manuel Jorge da Silva (Rua do Rosário), Paulo Martin (1779–1823/24?), and João Roberto Bourgeois (1754–1814) (Rua da Quitanda). In 1809, Manoel Mandillo had a shop in front of Capela dos Terceiros de Nossa Senhora do Carmo. From that time on, the number of establishments increased considerably. Before 1822, several specialist booksellers could be identified, such as Manoel Joaquim da Silva Porto (Rua da Quitanda), José Antonio da Silva (Rua Direita), Jerônimo G. Guimarães (Rua do Sabão), Francisco Nicolau Mandillo (Rua da Quitanda), João Baptista dos Santos (Rua da Cadeia), Joaquim Antonio de Oliveira (Rua da Quitanda), and Antonio Joaquim da Silva Garcez (Rua dos Pescadores).[27] There were also the *Diario* shop, the *Anais Fluminenses* typographic store, and the Impressão Régia. Many names can be added to those that appeared in the advertisements, and not only those of booksellers. In comparison, according to data supplied by Hallewell, in Buenos Aires there were only five bookshops in the same period (in 1826) and none at all in Chile. It should be pointed out that until 1820, according to the Chilean writer Subercaseaux, in Santiago there was only one official typographer and one private one, Esteban Valles.[28]

After the growth experienced in Brazil under the government of D. João (1808–21) and during the reign of Pedro I (1822–31), the book trade went through a degree of stabilization, expanding again in the reign of Pedro II (1840–89). Some bookshops closed but others sprang up, such as that of Jean Baptiste Bompard (1797–1890), in Rua dos Pescadores, which replaced Paulo Martin's bookshop, and that of Evaristo da Veiga (1799–1837) and his brother, who acquired Silva Porto's bookshop, and that of Pierre Plancher (1779–1844).

The increase of publications and sales that occurred during the first decades of the nineteenth century in Rio de Janeiro benefited from the fact that several typographic workshops were established. Until 1821, the only press of an official nature was the Impressão Régia. The first private typographer appeared in Bahia in 1811, a business expansion for a bookstore owned by the Portuguese trader, Manuel Antônio da Silva Serva (?–1819). Between 1821 and 1822, nine typography workshops emerged. The Impressão Régia was not able to keep up with the volume of written productions now requiring printed publication. Due to the popularity of the liberal and constitutional ideas stemming from the liberal Revolution in Portugal in 1820 and the accompanying political debates about Brazilian independence, a number of private typography workshops began to spring up in Rio. These were responsible for many of the works on current affairs and also for the publication of periodicals. The first private typography workshop to have permission to operate in 1821 was the 'Nova Oficina Tipográfica' [New Typography Workshop], whose owner, José de Cristo Moreira, formed a partnership with the bookseller Antonio Joaquim da Silva Garcez in 1821 to open Moreira & Garcez Typography as well. Thus by 1822 there were six typography workshops in the city. This also led to the consolidation of the book market, as books were now not only imported, but also began to be printed in Brazil. The art of typography continued to expand in the years following Brazilian independence: by the beginning of the 1830s there were around twelve typographers in Rio. One significant name is that of the above-mentioned Plancher, who arrived in Rio de Janeiro in 1824 and set up a publishing house in the premises of a small typography workshop in Rua dos Ourives, which later moved to Rua do Ouvidor. As early as May 1824 Plancher was granted the title Imperial Printer and his firm was called the Plancher Imperial Typography, on account of his friendship with the young emperor, Pedro I. His printing press was employed to issue an edition of the 1824 Constitution.[29]

Those Who Deal with Books[30]

Between 1808 and 1831, there was a sharp increase in the number of people who 'deal with books'. If we take as an example the specialist bookstores and their proprietors, a typology can be formed of their country of origin: those of French descent, those from Portugal, and those born in Portuguese America.

João Roberto Bourgeois and Paulo Martin were the first booksellers established in Rio de Janeiro. Although regarded as Portuguese, they were of French descent and had for a long time monopolized 'the business of bookstores', not only in Portugal, but also in Spain and some cities in Italy.[31] According to the passport records of João Roberto Bourgeois — '28 years old, of average height, with a long face, white and brown eyes, and chestnut hair' — he was Portuguese and had been in Brazil since at least 1782.[32] In 1799, his sister came to live with him in Rio de Janeiro, where he was 'established with a Trading House'.[33] Therefore one of the bookstores that existed in the city in 1799 and was registered in the *Almanaque* belonged without doubt to Bourgeois. As well as having a wide range of contacts in Brazil, Bourgeois maintained links with Simão Tadeu Ferreira in Lisbon, a well-known Portuguese printer who sent books to Rio de Janeiro and other provinces. Bourgeois also held the post of 'Administrador das Cartas de Jogar' [Administrator of Playing Cards Factory]. The cards were sold in the city of Rio de Janeiro in 1802. According to Santos Marrocos, Bourgeois died suddenly, early in 1814.[34]

At the beginning of the nineteenth century, another name emerged in the book trade: Paulo Agostinho Martin, who became one of the most famous booksellers in Rio de Janeiro owing to his activities as an editor from the early 1800s to 1823. He was the son of a French family who came from La Salle in the valley of Briançon, the common origin of the other French booksellers who settled in Lisbon and set up business in the 1780s.[35]

However, Paulo Martin's migration to Rio de Janeiro did not go smoothly. In 1799, the Portuguese traders requested the Board of Trade in Lisbon not to issue a passport to Paulo Martin's and Francisco Rolland's sons, to prevent them from settling in any country in the American continent. These French traders had already caused considerable harm to Portuguese interests and now wanted to expand their business by 'attempting to set up two trading houses for the sale of books in Rio de Janeiro, under the pretext that their sons had been born in the kingdom and could thus be regarded as naturalized citizens'. They were warned of the existence of decrees that forbade foreigners to open up trading houses in Brazil, 'above all in the area of books which at this time are a very dangerous commodity'. The accused replied by stating that they were doing nothing illegal since their descendants could be regarded as Portuguese by virtue of having been born in the kingdom and were thus entitled to set up any kind of business overseas. They also gave an assurance that they had no intention of establishing their children in the book trade since they were going to learn 'business in general'.[36] Despite this, on his request for a passport dated October 1799, Paulo Augusto Martin stated that he intended to work as a clerk for José [*sic*] Roberto Bourgeois, 'businessman' and resident of Rio. José Roberto Bourgeois was no less than João Roberto Bourgeois, who devoted himself solely to the book trade.[37] On 22 October 1799, the Prince Regent authorized the issuing of a passport to Paulo Agostinho Martin, 'aged 20, of average height for his age, long face, dark eyes and chestnut hair, on account of being Portuguese, and who is going to be a clerk in a trading house of that city'.[38]

It has not been possible to determine the date on which Paulo Martin began his personal activities as a bookseller in Rio de Janeiro. However, from its first issue (10 September 1808) onward, the *Gazeta do Rio de Janeiro* stated that acquisitions and subscriptions could be made 'in the shop of Paulo Martin Filho, book merchant in Rua da Quitanda'.[39] In 1811, the *Almanaque* of the city confirmed his position as *Gazeta do Rio de Janeiro*'s official sales representative, among the list of the administrative staff and employees. As well as several advertisements that appeared in the *Gazeta do Rio de Janeiro* and *Diario do Rio de Janeiro*, there are a few extant catalogues that give a good idea of the works that could be found for sale in the shop and of the pamphlets and books printed by him. The activities of Paulo Martin as editor are also recorded in the requests to the Desembargo do Paço to print the book *Notícia histórica da vida e das obras de José Hayden* in 1819, which to some extent suggests the degree of interest in classical music that could be found in court circles. The historian Rubens Borba de Moraes states that he was probably the first editor in Brazil. This bookseller published many novels, stories, funeral speeches, and poems that were printed by the Impressão Régia, such as *O Diabo Coxo* (1707) by Lesage, considered the first novella printed in Brazil.[40] In 1817, Paulo Martin was awarded the Insignia of the Order of Christ in recognition of his services to the Crown and his achievements in the book trade.[41]

Martin died in Rio de Janeiro, probably at the end of 1823 or beginning of 1824, although there is no documentary evidence to show the exact day of his death. However, an announcement in *Diario do Rio de Janeiro* on 17 April 1824 gives a definitive account of his demise:

> J. B. Bompard, resident in Rua dos Pescadores, nº 14, and Mr. Paulo Martins' executor begs everybody who had any works or papers for sale in his shop to come and look for their goods as soon as possible.

Jean-Baptiste Bompard was Paulo Martin's cousin. He was born in Briançon in 1797 and arrived in Rio de Janeiro from Lisbon in December 1818. He spent his first years in Rio in a shop. After Martin's death, Jean-Baptiste successfully continued the commercial activities of selling the books, cartographic products, and publications of Paulo Martin. According to Hallewell, he became 'the main Court bookseller' from 1824, when he took over the bookshop, until 1827, the year he gave up his activities and returned to France.[42]

During these years, Bompard continued to distribute books, periodicals, pamphlets, and political essays printed in different languages and countries, as can be seen both in the advertisements that appeared in *Diario do Rio de Janeiro* and in the Catalogue for 1825, an index of the 4305 titles held by his bookshop.[43] Bompard decided to leave Brazil in 1827 and sold his bookshop to another well-known bookseller — Evaristo da Veiga.

Finally, among the group of Frenchmen, the name that stands out is Pierre René François de la Noé, more commonly known as Pierre Plancher. He arrived in Rio de Janeiro in 1824, fleeing the political struggles in France in the period of the Restoration and was a known supporter of Napoleon Bonaparte. His decision to go to Brazil was not simply fortuitous, since the prospects for the book trade there were auspicious and the tradition of sending professional booksellers there had been going on for several decades. He quickly became established in the city with a bookstore and typography workshop, at first selling a large stock of books on constitutional issues and later translating and publishing them in Portuguese.[44]

Among the group of Portuguese origin, Francisco Saturnino Veiga, Manuel Joaquim da Silva Porto, and Manuel Mandillo should be highlighted. The first, Saturnino da Veiga, was Portuguese by birth and probably arrived in Rio de Janeiro in 1784, when he became a Latin teacher.[45] In the early 1800s, he began his activities as a bookseller and was thus a contemporary of Bourgeois and Paulo Martin. His first advertisement appeared in the *Gazeta do Rio de Janeiro* in October 1808. Although he described himself as a bookseller, he advertised other products too:

> If anyone has some houses for sale, either two-storeyed houses or bungalows situated in or below Rua dos Ourives, with enough land, they should go to the Shop of Francisco Luiz Saturnino Veiga in Rua do Ouvidor, which is entrusted with buying them.[46]

In 1809 Saturnino da Veiga was already advertising the sale of books, and in 1813 he informed the public that he was moving his shop to another address: 'it will be moved from Rua do Ouvidor to Rua da Alfândega'.[47] Whether he was importing books from France and sending others to other places such as Angola and India, or selling new publications in Rio de Janeiro, Saturnino Veiga was a man of some prestige in the Court, because in 1817 he gave a donation of as much as 100 *contos* (100 million *réis*) to the Crown, to quell the revolt in Pernambuco.[48]

Manuel Mandillo's advertisements appeared as early as 1809. He held the title of Master Bookseller of the Royal Household, which he obtained in December 1810. The title gave him the right each month to a number of dwellings that were recorded in the *Livro da Matrícula dos Moradores* [Registration Book of Residents] of the Royal Household.[49] He resided opposite the Capela dos Terceiros de N. S. do Carmo, or more precisely in Rua Direita. In 1814, according to an advertisement in the *Gazeta do Rio de Janeiro*, he was linked to José Borges de Pinho, who had a glass shop. Although he announced that his books would be sold in this establishment, with 'discounts', he continued to print advertisements giving directions to his old address until 1820. He marketed works that arrived from the state of Bahia, some of them printed in the typography workshop of Silva Serva and others sent from Lisbon and Porto 'at very reasonable prices', while still offering to carry out orders of this kind from both cities.[50]

Finally, Manuel Joaquim da Silva Porto stands out in this group. He was of Portuguese descent and a native of Porto, the city of his surname, as inferred by Innocencio, and became a bookseller, typographer, and author.[51] According to the records of the *Real Junta do Comércio, Agricultura, Fábricas e Navegação* [Royal Chamber of Commerce, Agriculture, Manufacturing, and Navigation], he was in Brazil from 1811. By 1812, he was already established and owned 'a shop for merchandising books'.[52] As a dealer, he formed a series of relationships with other people, in particular Silva Serva in Bahia, becoming one of the most important booksellers of the Court throughout the kingdom of Brazil at the beginning of the reign of Pedro I (1822–31). Many of his contemporaries opined that his bookshop was one of the most frequented in the city. He expanded his business in 1815 when he associated himself with Pedro Antonio de Campos Bello, who owned a paper store. Their partnership became known as Campos Bello e Porto and they started to sell books as well, but the partnership was dissolved in March 1822.[53]

In mid-1821, Silva Porto requested a licence to set up a typography workshop in Rio de Janeiro, because the dilatoriness of the Royal Typography meant it was unable to complete half of its printing commissions. He thus believed that his typography workshop could be turned into a 'useful establishment' for the Court. A licence was granted in March 1822, and Silva Porto became the first bookseller in Rio de Janeiro to have his own typography workshop: the Silva Porto and Co. Workshop.[54] The workshop probably remained active until 1825, the date of Porto's last publications, while his bookshop was bought in October 1823.[55] After this, all traces of Silva Porto begin to disappear. In 1827, *O Almanaque Plancher* no longer featured the name of his establishment. On 3 March 1828, a notice was placed in the *Intendência Geral da Polícia da Corte* [Quartermaster-General's Office of the Court Police] stating that 'Manuel Joaquim da Silva Porto, a native of Porto, Brazilian subject, aged 40' had left for the city of Bahia.[56] According to the lexicographer Francisco Inocêncio, Silva Porto left Brazil in 1835. Years later it was still possible to find a translation of three works by Silva Porto — *A gastronomia ou prazeres da mesa*, *Enciclopédia industrial*, and *Methodo facil de escripturar os livros* — the last being dated 1854. However, these were published in Porto, which supports the hypothesis that Silva Porto had returned to Portugal and settled down again in his native city.[57]

Of the group of businessmen born in Brazil, the careers of the Veiga brothers — Evaristo and João Pedro — should be highlighted. Both worked as clerks in their father's bookshop. When their father remarried in 1823, they took advantage of the inheritance they received from their father and entered the book trade by buying the bookshop that belonged to Manuel Joaquim da Silva Porto. In 1827, Evaristo bought Bompard's bookshop and João Pedro continued his business dealings on his own.

There is no evidence of anyone of British origin among the specialist booksellers in Rio de Janeiro. However, there were British traders who marketed books, together with other merchandise by their firms. Thus, Henry Miller, an English trader who had been settled in Rio de Janeiro since 1809 at the latest, was still conducting business in 1827 in Rua dos Pescadores, according to data in *Almanaque do Rio de Janeiro*. He submitted a request to the Desembargo do Paço for a licence that would allow ninety-five book titles consisting of 896 copies to be admitted in Brazil, which certainly suggests they were a part of his business. The titles were all written in Portuguese and included *Poemas* by Milton (1608–1674), as well as *História dos Poetas Ingleses*, *Instruções na Língua Inglesa*, and *Epístolas* by John Wolcott (1738–1819), *Odes Pastorais* by Robert Bloomfield (1766–1823), and *Poemas para guardar a saúde* by John Armstrong (1709–1779). The latter was *The Art of Preserving Health — a Poem* by John Armstrong, M. D., originally published in London in 1744.[58]

The Spread of Ideas and Historical Trends

In the first years of the nineteenth century, books, printing presses, and bookstores were caught up in the march of historic events and can be understood as a part of the many facets that make up historical progress. During this period, books became essential tools for the transmission of knowledge and political ideas, leading to the formation of a new public arena.[59] They also acted as cultural intermediaries between Brazil and the world on the other side of the Atlantic.

The works sold by the booksellers accompanied the political processes of the government of D. João in Brazil (1808–21) and later the reign of Pedro I (1822–31). Certain periods were significant: the Napoleonic wars, the advent of liberal ideas in 1821, the independence movement in 1822, and the abdication of Emperor Pedro I in 1831. Hence, the advertisements of these booksellers concerned the sale of works related to these events.

As the Napoleonic wars marched on, and under the influence of the fear of *the abominable French principles*,[60] particularly between 1808 and 1815, several advertisements appeared in the *Gazeta do Rio de Janeiro* about the sale of books, essays, and pamphlets written against Napoleon Bonaparte and the French Empire, and they also included panegyrics about the prince D. João, the British military leaders, and the restoration of Portugal. There were also texts of a historical nature on the French invasions, written in the form of memoirs.[61]

Several advertisements published by Bourgeois, Paulo Martin, and Saturnino da Veiga include references to 'new works' already printed in Portugal and some reprinted in Rio de Janeiro. Paulo Martin stands out not only for his numerous advertisements in the *Gazeta do Rio de Janeiro* for works of this kind, but also because he printed them at his own expense, as is made clear in the first *Catálogo das obras impressas, que se acham à venda em sua loja* [*Catalogue of printed works that can be found for sale in his shop*]. The catalogue was published together with *O Plutarco Revolucionário*, a work translated from English that contains the life of Empress Josephine and other members of Napoleon's family. The entries in this catalogue demonstrate that the bookseller-editor mostly published successful political pamphlets in that period: twenty-four out of thirty-six titles. Many had first been published in Lisbon and were re-edited in Rio de Janeiro, proof of a text's success and only a small financial risk to the publisher.[62]

The advent of constitutional ideas propagated by the Regeneração Vintista [Regeneration of the 1820s] in Portugal, which rapidly spread to Brazil at the beginning of 1821, led to the publication of topical literature that brought history and politics together, and introduced a new vocabulary and new ideas. Language became politicized and part of public life, transforming old into new concepts. This became a key interpretation for reconstructing processes that took place over a long period of time, such as the construction of the Brazilian Empire itself.[63]

Against this context, two booksellers — Paulo Martin and Silva Porto — held key positions: the former through the sale of such 'modern works'[64]; the latter through the role that the bookshops and typography workshops played in the formation of a new public arena for discussion.

Paulo Martin brought out two catalogues in 1821 and 1822, considered to be the first that an editor-bookseller had produced in separate copies. The catalogues were advertised in the *Gazeta* and *Diario do Rio de Janeiro* and consisted of a simple sheet of paper that could be pinned to a wall or sent round by slave boys, in the same way that other goods were sold. In general, the lists consisted of a series of political pamphlets called 'constitutional leaflets' by the bookseller and showed a clear concern to explain to the citizens the real importance of the constitutional system and the fundamental aspects of the liberal political vocabulary.

As well as selling these constitutional leaflets, Manoel Joaquim da Silva Porto also carried out other professional and political activities, including that of a writer, bookseller, and editor of liberal periodicals. After June 1822, in order to bring his work in the bookshop into line with current political events, he began to use his own typography to advertise and print articles that raised the possibility of the separation of Brazil from the old metropolis.[65]

Pierre Plancher was also a prominent figure during the reign of Pedro I (1822–31) on account of his publication of a large number of constitutional works that were originally written in French, especially the works of Benjamin Constant. Plancher published several periodicals, which demonstrates their importance as a means for conveying ideas. He also published the *Almanaque Plancher*, a simple catalogue that provided useful information about means of transport, merchandise, and calendars, and also the very popular *Folhinhas de Algibeira e de Porta* [*Pocket and Door Books*]. These were a kind of pocket calendar with the dates of the year. Plancher was also responsible for introducing lithography into Brazil.

Another important means of spreading ideas on both sides of the Atlantic was the records of requests for exporting books from Lisbon to Brazil, or more precisely, to certain provinces with works addressed to the Amazon region, Pernambuco, or Bahia, as well as Rio de Janeiro.[66] The orders to the booksellers based in Lisbon are wide-ranging and include legal books, dictionaries, compilations of laws, and works in Latin, together with novellas, poetry books, novels, catechisms, and primers. All this activity is evidence of the close ties that existed with the bookshops in Lisbon.[67]

In this way, these bookstores and typography workshops maintained a brisk business between Rio de Janeiro and the other provinces, as well as Lisbon and some countries in Europe and Africa. In the notices of the newspapers, these booksellers and printers excelled in writing advertisements for works sold on the other side of the Atlantic and sought to give an impression of being both informative and business-like. Thus, by means of licences granted by the Mesa do Desembargo do Paço, it is clear that Bourgeois was a dealer of great importance between 1809 and 1811, since his network of contacts stretched from the squares of Lisbon to Porto, Luanda, and London, and in Brazil to São Paulo, Santos, and Porto Alegre.

Analysis of the advertisements, catalogues, and licences provides evidence that Paulo Martin sold works that originated from Lisbon and were sent by his father and later by his brothers. They were works of a scientific nature, such as publications by the Academy of Sciences in Lisbon, technical books about the manufacture and whitening of cotton wool, books on business and economics, legal treaties and compilations of laws, among others. The bookseller also aimed to offer readers novels and other general literature, such as *Werther* by Goethe, the works of Bocage, and a 'large assortment of poetry books', as well as novellas, a new genre that particularly appealed to the female public, works such as *História de dois amantes*, *Paulo e Virgínia*, and *A filósofa por amor*, among others.[68] He also advertised examples of *Spelling Books*, 'suitable for young people to learn English', which sold for 1600 *réis*.[69]

In the catalogues of Pierre Plancher, amongst the largest of the period, there were lists of works in French, Portuguese, and English, which were essential for the dissemination of European proposals concerning the legal system, laws, and the making of new constitutions.[70] Works written in French predominated in the catalogue, although some were originally written in another language, such as English.[71] *A Coleção de Leis e Decretos do Império do Brasil* featured prominently in the catalogue and was dedicated to the Legislative Assembly; it was preceded by a preface and concluded with an alphabetical index, and was written by 'A Brazilian'. Benjamin Constant (1767–1830) was a constant presence with his *Collection Complete des Ouvrages publiés sur le gouvernement représentatif de la Constitution de la France* (1818), *Cours de Politique Constitutionnelle* (1818/20), and *Histoire des Cent jours en forme de lettres* (1820). These works depict the political beliefs of Pierre Plancher, and they helped him have a decisive influence on burgeoning public opinion in Brazil.[72]

Thus, the catalogues, which represented another essential tool for exchanging ideas between European countries and Brazil, supplied books to a more sophisticated public by showing lists of the wide range of books in stock. These were written not only in Portuguese but also in other languages such as French, English, Spanish, German, Latin, and Greek, and included books of religion, grammar, sciences, literature, biographies and history.

In addition, analysis of these catalogues allows the changes in the genres of published works to be traced and provides evidence of a tension between tradition and novelty. If for a long time religious works, including books on theology, predominated in the sales list of the booksellers and continued to be the 'classics' for most people in society, in the first years of the 1800s, other genres were gradually emerging that were linked to scientific innovations and the arts. From the perspective of the Iberian Enlightenment, there was a more significant offer of books focusing on scientific development in the kingdom of Brazil, with special attention being given to works adopted in the first higher education institutions — the Royal Military Academy, the Naval College, and the School of Surgeons in Rio de Janeiro.

Conclusion

There is no doubt that the world of books, printing presses, and booksellers began to be important to the reading public in Portuguese America and then to the Brazilian Empire. Thus it should be stressed that, although there is a lack of concrete data available for the period in question, it is evident that there was a much more significant 'consumer' public for books than has been recognized by traditional historiography. This becomes even more apparent when account is taken of the existence of specialist bookshops, as well as the competition in business, the volume of advertisements for bookshops, and the presence of catalogues, as outlined in this chapter. The role and importance of these booksellers as dealers is becoming more evident too, including their links to other branches of the book trade — paper and engraving shops, as well as the processes of printing books and typography.

In addition, the book trade evidently represented a profitable undertaking, as shown in the case of Paulo Martin, whose family traditionally belonged to the book trade both in Portugal and in Brazil. In his will (dated September 1813), Paulo Martin senior showed that he was in possession of a relatively large estate for the period. His possessions included a shop in Lisbon and another in Rio de Janeiro, where for some time he maintained two sons, and a splendid house with a small farm in Benfica, Portugal, and assets that amounted to the equivalent of 70,000 *cruzados*, not including his stock of books in the two shops.[73]

Another example is the family of Saturnino Veiga. His sons, João Pedro and Evaristo, entered the book trade later, and Evaristo separated from his brother and acquired Bompard's bookshop at quite a high price — eleven *contos de réis*, which at that time was the equivalent of about £1420.[74] The fact that the two sons were established in the same line of business as the father is highly suggestive that, at that time, the book trade was a profitable undertaking.[75]

It should be stressed that with the advent of the constitutionalist movement and the freedom of the press, from 1820 onwards, bookshops and typographies began to engage in other activities. They became public arenas that allowed politics to supplant the traditional institutional space of power — the Court — and become truly public.

Finally attention should be drawn to the fact that bookshops, printers, and printed works in the period in question led to the formation of new political languages which revealed a close relationship with the political events of the country. This enabled debates to take place on the basis of the ideas that had arisen from reading the material that had been disseminated in Brazil and opened up a path for the advent of a new kind of liberalism in the Empire.

Notes to Chapter 2

1. *Historical memoir of the invasion of Portugal by the French in 1807. Observations about French trade with Brazil.* In *Gazeta do Rio de Janeiro*, no. 1 (10 September 1808).
2. Luís Joaquim dos Santos Marrocos, *Cartas do Rio de Janeiro, 1811–1821* (Lisbon: Biblioteca Nacional de Portugal, 2008), p. 218; Theodor von Leithold and Ludwig von Rango, *O Rio de Janeiro visto por dois prussianos em 1819*, ed. and trans. by Joaquim de Sousa Leão Filho (São Paulo: Companhia Editora Nacional, 1966), p. 48. There is some testimony by other travellers that contradicts this information, for example, Spix and Martius, who refer to the existence of four bookstores. Johann Baptiste von Spix and Karl Friedrich Philipp von Martius, *Viagem pelo Brasil (1817–1820)*, pref. Mário Guimarães Ferri, trans. by Lúcia Furquim Lahmeyer, notes by Basílio de Magalhães, 3 vols (São Paulo: Editora da Universidade de São Paulo, 1981).
3. See Chapter 1 by Márcia Abreu for titles of books that circulated in Brazil before 1808, which were found in listings of the Appellate Court and Customs House of Rio. In recent years, several authors have shared this opinion and adopted a new approach to the history of books in Brazil, including: Maria Beatriz Nizza da Silva, *Cultura no Brasil colônia* (Petrópolis: Vozes, 1981); Laurence Hallewell, *O livro no Brasil*, 2nd edn, revised and expanded (São Paulo: EDUSP, 2005); Lucia Maria Bastos P. Neves, 'Comércio de livros e censura de ideias: a atividade dos livreiros franceses no Brasil e a vigilância da Mesa do Desembargo do Paço (1795–1822)', *Ler História* (Lisbon), 23 (1993), 61–78; Luiz Carlos Villalta, 'Bibliothèques privées et pratiques de lecture au Brésil colonial', in *Naissance du Brésil moderne (1500–1808)*, ed. by K. M. de Queirós Mattoso et al. (Paris: Presses de l'Université de Paris-Sorbonne, 1998), pp. 319–36; Tania Maria Bessone, *Palácios de destinos cruzados: bibliotecas, homens e livros no Rio de Janeiro, 1870–1920* (Rio de Janeiro:

Arquivo Nacional, 1999); Márcia Abreu, *Os caminhos dos livros* (Campinas: Mercado de Letras/ ALB/FAPESP, 2003); Aníbal Bragança, 'Uma introdução à História editorial brasileira', *Cultura: revista de história e teoria das ideias*, n.s. (UNL, Lisbon), 14.20 (2002), 57–83 (pp. 70–73).

4. In Portuguese: 'Gentes do livro'. For this expression, see Diogo Ramada Curto, Manuela Domingos et al., *As gentes do livro: Lisboa século XVIII* (Lisbon: Biblioteca Nacional, 2007).
5. Christian Jacob, 'Préface', Marc Baratin & Christian Jacob, *Le Pouvoir des bibliothèques. La Mémoire des livres en Occident* (Paris: Albin Michel, 1996), p. 11.
6. National Archive of Torre do Tombo (IAN/TT). Real Mesa Censória [Royal Censorship Board]. Examination of the books that are leaving the kingdom and are destined for Rio de Janeiro, Caixa 153, Lisbon, 9 November 1795.
7. Private correspondence of booksellers in São Paulo in the eighteenth century (1791). Microfilm of the private archive of Francisco da Gama Caeiro. Library of the Faculty of Education, University of São Paulo. See F. da Gama Caeiro, 'Livros e livreiros franceses em Lisboa, nos fins de setecentos e no primeiro quartel do século XIX', in *Dispersos*, 2 vols (Lisbon: Imprensa Nacional — Casa da Moeda, 2000), pp. 133–56.
8. Transcript in *Revista do Instituto Histórico e Geográfico Brasileiro*, 21:156 (January–March 1858).
9. In Portuguese, 'loja de livros', 'loja do livreiro', and 'loja do mercador de livros'. For these expressions, see *Gazeta do Rio de Janeiro*, no. 5 (17 January 1810), no. 7 (5 October 1808), and no. 10 (15 October 1808), respectively.
10. *Gazeta do Rio de Janeiro*, no. 8 (27 January 1821) and no. 7 (5 October 1808).
11. *Catálogo de Livros portugueses que se achão na venda em casa de P. C. Dalbin e Ca.* (Rio de Janeiro: [n.pub.], 1820).
12. *Gazeta do Rio de Janeiro*, no. 25 (28 March 1818). The 'big Rub Antisyphilitique' was a remedy against syphilis that was used until the end of the nineteenth century. It was based on syrup of sarsaparilla, senna honey, sugar, and other ingredients. Cf. Boyveau-Laffecteur, *Observations sur l'histoire et les effets du rob anti-syphilitique* (Paris: Chez l'Auteur, 1810).
13. Guilherme Lennox was born in London at the end of the eighteenth century and probably arrived in Brazil in 1812. He established himself in Rio de Janeiro as a trader, married a Portuguese woman, and died in the same city. For the advertisement, see *Gazeta do Rio de Janeiro*, no. 73 (13 September 1815).
14. *Gazeta do Rio de Janeiro*, no. 40 (17 May 1817). See Maria Beatriz Nizza da Silva, *A Gazeta do Rio de Janeiro (1808–1822): cultura e sociedade* (Rio de Janeiro: EdUERJ, 2007), p. 189.
15. Translation: *A Chemical Analysis of the Pure Water of Bom Jardim* or *Reflections on the Iatraleptic Method* or *the Way of Administering Remedies Through a Cutaneous System.*
16. For the meaning of "Botica", see Antonio de Moraes Silva, *Diccionario da lingua portuguesa*, 2nd edn (Lisbon: Tip. de M. P. de Lacerdina, 1813), vol. 1 (facsimile: Rio de Janeiro, 1922), p. 295. For the advertisements, see *Gazeta do Rio de Janeiro*, no. 21 (13 March 1819) and no. 6 (19 January 1820). For details of this sale, see also Maria Beatriz Nizza da Silva, *A Gazeta do Rio de Janeiro (1808–1822)*, p. 188.
17. *Gazeta do Rio de Janeiro*, no. 28 (7 April 1821). For the announcement of the bookstores that were entrusted with the sale of religious works, see *Gazeta*, no. 80 (4 October 1817).
18. The subscribers did more than just enrol their names: they supported the publication before it took place. In that period, the word 'stamp' was used instead of 'print'.
19. Translation: *A Collection of Portraits and Eulogies of Portuguese Gentlemen and Ladies with Historical Accounts of their Lives.*
20. See Luís Joaquim dos Santos Marrocos, *Cartas do Rio*, pp. 352–55. This collection was not published in Rio de Janeiro. What had already been published by Impressão Régia in Brazil (1816 and 1818) was *Collecção de Retratos de todos os homens que adquirirão nome pelo gênio, talentos, virtudes etc, desde o princípio do mundo até os nossos dias* [*Collection of Portraits of Men who became Renowned for their Genius, Talent, Virtues, etc. from the Beginning of the World until Today*]. The names of the shops are transcribed in *Gazeta do Rio de Janeiro*, no. 37 (7 May 1817).
21. *Gazeta do Rio de Janeiro*, no. 100 (13 December 1817). Translation: *A New and Infallible Method of Replacing the Rudder of a Ship on the High Seas with an Engraving.*
22. A summarized inventory based on one out of every five copies was selected from the *Gazeta do Rio de Janeiro*, which at first published two issues every week. This increased to three after July 1821.

23. Advertisement in *Gazeta do Rio de Janeiro (1808–22).*
24. *O Patriota. Jornal literário, político, mercantil.* See *Iluminismo e Império no Brasil: O Patriota (1813–1814)*, ed. by Lorelai Kury (Rio de Janeiro: Fiocruz, 2007). It includes a digitized CD-ROM for the whole period, as well as the *Índice histórico* [Historical Index].
25. *Plano para o estabelecimento de hum util e curiozo Diario nesta Cidade* (Rio de Janeiro: Typ. Real, 1821).
26. Advertisements of auctions and books are found in the issues of *Jornal do Commercio* published on 27 October 1827 and 21 December 1827, as well as 6 January 1828, 17 February 1828, 20 February 1828, 24 February 1828, and 8 January 1829, 11 March 1829, 24 April 1829, and 6 June 1829.
27. It was not possible to find data on the births and deaths of all the booksellers mentioned here, although research covering this period and extending through to the present was conducted in the Biographical Collection of Documents at the National Library of Rio de Janeiro, in the Mesa do Desembargo do Paço, and the Register of Foreigners in the National Archives.
28. See Laurence Hallewell, *O Livro no Brasil: sua história*, pp. 108 and 120. In 'Subsídios para a história das livrarias', Marcello de Ipanema and Cybelle de Ipanema state that in April 1821 there were sixteen bookshops, among which were names such as João Roberto Bourgeois, who died in 1813, and others who no longer appeared in the advertisement of the *Gazeta do Rio de Janeiro* and *Diario do Rio de Janeiro* newspapers. See by the same authors, 'Subsídios para a história das livrarias', *Revista do Livro*, 11[32] (1968), 23–31. See also Bernardo Subercaseux, *Historia del libro en Chile (Alma y Cuerpo)* (Santiago: Editorial LOM, 2000), p. 34.
29. Lucia Maria Bastos P. Neves, 'Tipografias', in *Dicionário da história da colonização portuguesa no Brasil*, ed. by M. Beatriz Nizza da Silva (Lisbon: Verbo, 1994), pp. 788–91; Martha Abreu, 'Tipografias', in *Dicionário do Brasil Imperial*, ed. by Ronaldo Vainfas (Rio de Janeiro: Objetiva, 2002), pp. 697–98; Laurence Hallewell, *O livro no Brasil*, pp. 120–21 and 141–42. On Plancher, see Marco Morel, *As transformações dos espaços públicos: imprensa, atores políticos e sociabilidades na cidade Imperial (1820–1840)* (São Paulo: Hucitec, 2005), pp. 23–25.
30. 'Those who deal with books' is how book dealers were referred to in coeval texts. It is the meaning of bookseller at that time, according to Antonio de Moraes Silva, *Diccionario da lingua portuguesa*, vol. 2, p. 232.
31. Fernando Guedes, *Os livreiros franceses em Portugal no século XVIII: tentativa de compreensão de um fenómeno migratório e mais alguma história* (Lisbon: Academia Portuguesa da História, 1998), p. 23.
32. 'Almanaque do Rio de Janeiro para o ano de 1799', *Revista do Instituto Histórico e Geográfico Brasileiro*, 21: 156 (January–March 1858). Arquivo Histórico Ultramarino (A. H. U.), Codex 805, Passports 1782–1787, fl. 12v.
33. A. H. U. Codex 807, Passports 1791–1798, fl. 127, and Codex 808, Passports 1798–1806, fl. 68. The citation was found in the latter Codex.
34. A. H. U. Office of Viceroy of the State of Brazil. Box 205, Document no. 14408. 30 September 1802. L. Joaquim dos Santos Marrocos, *Cartas do Rio*, p. 250.
35. See Diogo Ramada Curto, Manuela Domingos et al., *As gentes do livro: Lisboa século XVIII*, pp. 163–64. According to Fernando Guedes, Paulo Martin settled in Lisbon in 1778. Cf. *Os livreiros franceses em Portugal no século XVIII*, pp. 60–80.
36. IAN/TT. Board of Trade, Book 132 — Register of Queries, 1799–1801, f. 32–33. The decision of the Board of Trade went in favour of the two booksellers.
37. A. H. U. Overseas Council. Box 176. Document no. 12952.
38. A. H. U. Codex 808, Passports 1798–1806, fl. 54. With regard to the son of Rolland, there are no references to indicate the date of his arrival in Brazil.
39. Although called Paulo Agostinho Martin, he signed himself as Paulo Martin Filho, at least until 1821, when he published in the *Gazeta do Rio de Janeiro*, no. 18 (3 March 1821): 'Paulo Martin Filho, trader in the square, declares that from the 17th instance of this month and year he will sign himself Paulo Martin and no longer Paulo Martin Filho'.
40. 'Almanaque do Rio de Janeiro para o ano de 1811', *Revista do Instituto Histórico e Geográfico Brasileiro*, 282: 230 (January–March 1969). *Notícia de algumas obras modernas e constitucionais chegadas modernamente à loja de Paulo Martin, rua da Quitanda nº 33* (Rio de Janeiro: Typografia Nacional, [1821]). For the printing of works, see The National Archives — Rio de Janeiro (AN-RJ). Mesa

do Desembargo do Paço, Box 171, 3, Document no. 39, 1819. See Rubens Borba de Moraes, *O bibliófilo aprendiz*, 3rd edn (Brasília: Briquet de Lemos; Rio de Janeiro: Casa da Palavra, 1998), pp. 191–92.

41. National Library–Rio de Janeiro (BN-RJ). Manuscripts Dept. 14, 3, 12. The Honours List (1816–1819).
42. Laurence Hallewell, *O livro no Brasil*, p. 122.
43. BN-RJ, Manuscripts Dept., 14,1,15.
44. Laurence Hallewell, *O livro no Brasil*, pp. 66–67. See also Marco Morel, *As transformações dos espaços públicos*.
45. Octávio Tarquínio de Sousa, *Evaristo da Veiga* (Belo Horizonte: Itatiaia; São Paulo: Editora da Universidade de São Paulo, 1988), p. 25.
46. *Gazeta do Rio de Janeiro*, no. 117 (25 October 1809).
47. *Gazeta do Rio de Janeiro*, no. 69 (28 August 1813).
48. AN-RJ. Mesa do Desembargo do Paço, Box 169, Document no. 109, 1817. The request for India and Angola was made in the name of João Pedro da Veiga e Barros, son of Saturnino Veiga, who already worked in his bookshop. Márcia Abreu noted the request and stated that the large number of titles did not leave any doubt that João Pedro da Veiga e Barros marketed books, although without identifying himself as the son of Saturnino Veiga. See Márcia Abreu, 'Os lugares dos livros: o comércio livreiro no Rio de Janeiro Joanino', in *História do livro e da leitura*, special issue of *Floema*, 5A (October 2009), 7–30 (p. 14).
49. BN-RJ. Manuscripts Dept., Collection of Biographical Documents C-0933,031 n°001.
50. *Gazeta do Rio de Janeiro*, no. 52 (29 June 1814). For the sale of books from abroad, see *Gazeta*, no. 49 (18 June 1814). *Gazeta*, no. 87 (28 October 1820).
51. Francisco Inoccencio da Silva, *Diccionario bibliographico portuguez*, vol. VI (Lisbon: Imp. Nacional, 1861), p. 22.
52. AN-RJ. Codex 171. v. 1. Chamber of Commerce. Register of Traders. Manuel Joaquim da Silva Porto, f. 84, 27 June 1811, and Code 137, General Register of Awards, v. 16, f. 176 e v. 21, f. 190.
53. Laurence Hallewell, *O livro no Brasil*, p. 108. For an in-depth study of Silva Porto, see Cybelle de Ipanema and Marcello de Ipanema, *Silva Porto: livreiro na Corte de D. João — Editor da Independência* (Rio de Janeiro: Capivara, 2007).
54. On the early years of the Silva Porto and Co. Workshop, see *A Malagueta*, no. 11 (March 1822), a newspaper printed in the typography of Silva Porto.
55. See advertisements in the *Diario do Rio de Janeiro*.
56. AN-RJ. Codex 422. Quarter-Master General of the Police. Book 7, fl.181.
57. Francisco Inoccencio da Silva, *Diccionario bibliographico portuguez*, vol. XVI, p. 235.
58. AN-RJ, Mesa do Desembargo do Paço, Box 169, Packet 2, Document no. 72, 1809–1818. 'Almanaque do Rio de Janeiro para o ano de 1827', *Revista do Instituto Histórico e Geográfico Brasileiro*, 300:193 (July–September1973). For the poem, see J. Armstrong, *The Art of preserving Health: a Poem* (London: A. Millard, 1744).
59. On public spaces, see F.-X. Guerra, Annick Lempérière et al., *Los espacios públicos en Iberoamérica: ambigüedades y problemas. Siglo XVIII–XIX* (Mexico: FCE, 1998); Jürgen Habermas, *The Structural Transformation of the Public Sphere: An Inquiry into a Category of Bourgeois Society* (Cambridge, MA: MIT Press, 1989); Marco Morel, *As transformações dos espaços públicos*, Lúcia Maria Bastos P. Neves, *Acervo*, 8.1–2 (1995), 123–38.
60. 'Abominable French principles' (*abomináveis princípios franceses*) is a coeval expression that appears in the rulings given by the censors of books at that time.
61. Nuno Daupiás d'Alcochete, 'Les Pamphlets portugais anti-napoléoniens', *Arquivos do Centro Cultural Português*, 11 (1977), 7–16; Lucia Maria Bastos P. Neves, *Napoleão Bonaparte: imaginário e política em Portugal* (São Paulo: Alameda, 2008).
62. 'Catálogo dos Folhetos impressos à custa de Paulo Martin, filho, que se achão na sua loja da rua da Quitanda n° 33', in *O Plutarco Revolucionário na parte que contem as vidas de Madama Buonaparte e outros desta família* (Rio de Janeiro: Imprensa Real, 1808). For a transcription of the catalogue, see Maria Beatriz Nizza da Silva, *Cultura no Brasil colônia*, pp. 147–48. The book was translated as *The Revolutionary Plutarch, exhibiting the most Distinguished Characters, Literary, Military and Political,*

in the Recent Annals of the French Revolution. The Greatest Part from the Original Information of a Gentlemen Resident at Paris (London: John Murray, 1804).

63. J. G. A. Pocock, *Virtue, Commerce, and History* (Cambridge: Cambridge University Press, 1988); R. Koselleck, *Futures Past: On the Semantics of Historical Time* (Cambridge, MA: MIT Press, 1985). For an analysis of the political leaflets, see Raymundo Faoro's introduction in his book, *O debate político no processo da independência* (Rio de Janeiro: Federal Council of Culture, 1973), pp. 5–24; Maria Beatriz Nizza da Silva, *Movimento constitucional e separatismo no Brasil, 1821–1823* (Lisbon: Livros Horizonte, 1988); Lúcia Maria Bastos P. Neves, *Corcundas e constitucionais: a cultura política da Independência do Brasil (1820–1822)* (Rio de Janeiro: Revan/Faperj, 2003).

64. *Notícia de algumas obras modernas e constitucionais chegadas modernamente à loja de Paulo Martin, rua da Quitanda nº. 33* (Rio de Janeiro: Imp. Nacional, [1821]).

65. Cf. Octávio Tarquínio de Sousa, *Fatos e personagens em torno de um regime* (Belo Horizonte: Itatiaia; São Paulo: EDUSP, 1988), p. 145.

66. IAN/TT, Mesa do Desembargo do Paço, Department of the Court, the Extremadura region and islands, 1827–1831, Maço 872, Document no. 13, Request for Licence by Borel & Borel Bros. to send books to Brazil, Lisbon, 2 April 1829, 12 November 1829, 5 December 1829, 12 February 1830, and 13 August 1830. Also see Maço no. 872, Document no. 10, Request by Borel & Borel Bros. to send books to Brazil, Lisbon, 22 September 1830.

67. Cf. Diogo Ramada Curto, Manuela Domingos et al., *As gentes do livro*, pp. 29–34.

68. *História de dois amantes ou o templo de Jatab*, trans. and adapted by J. P. S. A new edition (Rio de Janeiro: Impressão Régia, 1811); Bernardin de Saint-Pierre, *Paulo e Virgínia: história fundada em factos*, translated into the vernacular, new edition (Rio de Janeiro: Impressão Régia, 1811); *A filósofa por amor, ou cartas de dois amantes apaixonados e virtuosos*, translated from Spanish, new edition (Rio de Janeiro: Impressão Régia, 1811).

69. *Gazeta do Rio de Janeiro*, no. 43 (29 May 1813). This probably refers to G. Fulton and G. Knight, *A Pronouncing Spelling Book: with Select Lessons in Prose and Verse* (Edinburgh: Peter Hill, 1813), which in 1813 had reached a fifth edition.

70. The catalogue has thirty-six titles in English, including Alexander Pope (1688–1744): *The Works of Alexander Pope*; John Milton (1608–1674); W. Blackstone (1723–1780): *Commentaries on the Laws of England*; James Harvey (1714–1758): *Meditations and Contemplations*, and *The Dictionary of the Portuguese and English Languages*. There were also works by French authors advertised in English, such as *Ruins* by Volney (Constantin-François de Chasseboeuf, Comte de Volney, 1757–1820), *The Ruins or a Survey of the Revolutions of Empires*.

71. For example, the works of Thomas R. Malthus (1766–1834), *Principes d'économie politique*; all works by J. Bentham (1748–1832); J. Price (1735–1813); and Lord Clarendon (1609–1674).

72. BN-RJ *Extrait du Catalogue de Librairie de Pierre Plancher-Seignot* (Imprimeur-Libraire de Sa Majesté L'Empereur, Rue D'Ouvidor, no. 95, n.d.), microfilmed.

73. The will was drawn up a few days before Paulo Martin died. IAN//TT. General Register of Wills, book 366, ff. 220–21^{v}. Transcribed in Diogo R. Curto, Manuela Domingos et al., *As gentes do livro*, pp. 635–38.

74. Nathaniel H. Leef, *Subdesenvolvimento e desenvolvimento no Brasil: estrutura e mudança econômica, 1822–1947* (Rio de Janeiro: Expressão e Cultura, 1991), Table 6 of 'Anexo Estatístico' [Statistical Appendix].

75. For the relationship between books and business, cf. Jean-Yves Mollier, *L'Argent et les Lettres. Histoire du capitalisme d'édition, 1880–1920* (Paris: Fayard, 1988).

CHAPTER 3

Seditious Books and Ideas of Revolution in Brazil (1830–71)

Marisa Midori Deaecto and Lincoln Secco

Introduction

After the French Revolution of 1789, the ideas, names of authors, and books from France began to reach Brazil more frequently. For example, we know that at the beginning of the nineteenth century, the Court of Rio de Janeiro was supplied with 12,000 copies of the French Constitution by the bookseller Diogo Borel. Moreover, there were other political figures with personal libraries, such as Agostinho Gomes (one of those involved in the sedition in Bahia in 1798), who often obtained banned French books.[1]

However, it was only after the Napoleonic invasion of southern Europe and the transfer of the Portuguese court to Brazil that what can strictly be regarded as the commercial history of Brazil got underway, through the judicial ruling of 28 January 1808. This opened the ports to the so-called 'friendly nations' and put an end to the Colonial Pact. Brazil developed into the de facto seat of the Empire. On 18 June 1814, the Prince Regent D. João signed a decree authorizing a cultural exchange with France that strengthened the ties between the two nations.

At this time, French culture was synonymous with civilization, as was its merchandise. According to Joseph Arthur, Count of Gobineau (1816–1882), in 1869, Brazilians passionately longed to live in Paris. The 'Paulista' poet Álvares de Azevedo (1831–1852), the rebellious reader and follower of Byron (1788–1824) and Goethe (1749–1832), wrote his first verses in French. As will be demonstrated below from his correspondence, he ordered his books from French importers based in Rio de Janeiro. By the end of the nineteenth century, French had become the most important foreign language in the Faculty of Law of São Paulo. Of the 1820 works consulted in its library in 1898, 473 were in Portuguese and 240 in French, with only two in Italian and two in Greek.[2] In summary, this was the cultural pattern which gave Franco-Brazilian commercial relations a *sui generis* nature that was not enjoyed by any other of Brazil's trading partners.

The preference for French works was not a feature confined to Brazilian intellectuals. There was a great expansion of publishing in France in the post-revolutionary period and French literary works spread everywhere, or at least to that fraction of the world that surrounded the powerful field of the 'City of Light', which, according to Franco Venturi, reflected a 'geography of Enlightenment'.[3] For example, German readers claimed that their country had published the original version of *L'Ancien Régime et la Révolution*,[4] yet the important publisher Brockhaus had ordered the metal plates of the book from Calmann-Lévy in 1856.[5]

France was at the centre of civilization in a spiritual sense. Gérard de Nerval (1808–1855) referred to Austria as the 'China of Europe', with its powerful despotic regime.[6] He felt like a solitary civilized country in a Viennese theatre because it sat alongside Hungarians, Bohemians, Greeks, Turks and Romanians.[7] This same distancing of the French from other cultures and fashions can be observed among the travellers who visited the towns and cities of Brazil throughout the nineteenth century. What the French had in common in their dealings with other people, among other factors, was an attitude of superiority to the local population. In 1818, Auguste de Saint-Hilaire (1779–1853) found in the slurred speech of the people of São Paulo a symptom of laziness — a feature the French traveller could not condone, although he had shown a great liking for the town and its inhabitants. Indolence and laziness were interpreted by the naturalist as a sign of the origins of the inhabitants who were the 'descendants of Indian-European half-castes [and] had retained all the carefree spirit of the indigenous race; recent immigrants quickly adopted these customs too'.[8]

The issue of laziness was a topical question in the town and was dealt with in a humorous way in the 1879 edition of the *Almanach Litterario de São Paulo*, where the differences were listed between provincial laziness in the case of the 'Paulistas' and a cosmopolitan type of laziness that was typified by the French:

> Parisian laziness is found in everyday activities; it despises business so that the mind has the leisure to indulge in the trivialities of the newspaper and the gossip of the café. It prefers to vegetate rather than being employed in a job and vegetating means getting up at ten o'clock, wasting time over dressing up in a careless way, strolling about without a purpose, finding out about whatever is new, and then asking a question or suggesting a change without wanting to be bothered. The speed of fleeting impressions dispenses with the need for reflection, which is avoided. The lazy Brazilian rises with the sun. He doesn't dress up because he doesn't take off his clothes; he keeps on his undergarments and smokes in the doorway that he never leaves except to lie down on a hammock. If you ask him where someone lives, such as his neighbour, he has no idea. Speaking wearies him as much as thinking.[9]

And at the end of this long meditation, he concludes that 'both are as useless as each other'.[10]

It should be noted that the cultural dependence of Brazilian intellectuals on France made the main Brazilian urban centres (which were few and far between) less distant in material terms from the European countries than had been the case in the previous century. The report on development issued by the United Nations in 2000 revealed that the disparity in income between the richest and poorest countries was in the order of 3:1 in 1820, while at the end of the twentieth century it had widened to 80:1.[11]

Similarly, the French and Brazilians drew closer to each other as a result of living together on a more regular basis, in so far as the French foreigners travelled more widely beyond their national soil and many put down roots in Brazil. In view of this, it must be recognized, as emphasized above, that Brazilian intellectuals had a close affinity with French culture. Without ignoring issues of material life, which affect the world of merchandise and fashion that pervade everyday life, this investigation is mainly confined to the plane of political ideas. This involves activities that are governed by a set of ideas, which, in a given situation, turn into the blueprints for revolution. The premise here is that, in Brazil, French ideas and activities took on various forms which allowed sketches of liberal projects to be drawn, but which also gave signs of strong anti-revolutionary attitudes among the local political class. This is evident in 1830, 1848, and 1871, when events in France reverberated in the national political environment and were reflected in the different shades of opinion.

Two French Revolutions (1830–48)

In July 1830 a revolution broke out that brought down the Bourbon dynasty, but rather than installing a republic, it ushered in a new monarchy as a form of compromise: the *juste milieu*.[12] The French example made some of the other European monarchies the target of criticism. However, it was evident that liberal intellectuals were unsure which political system was best suited to the situation. The case of the Brazilian Emperor left no room for doubt. According to Oliveira Martins, D. Pedro I (1798–1834) wanted to be another George Washington (1732–1799) without, however, ceasing to be a monarch. Dom Pedro I believed 'freedom was a present and not a recognition of public rights'.[13]

Attempts at reform by Brazilian liberals, who were inspired by reading of events in France, were no different. The French yearbook for 1830, which was picked up by chance in a São Paulo second-hand bookstore, stated the following:

> Les nouvelles de la Révolution de Juillet, qui arrivèrent au milieu de cette fermentation de passions et de haines, à Rio de Janeiro, à Bahia, à Pernambouc et jusque dans les Mines de Geraes, y réveillèrent les idées de république et de confédération qui s'étaient manifestées lors de la première déclaration de l'indépendance brésilienne. L'empereur alarmé des progrès de l'esprit révolutionnaire essaya vainement d'en comprimer l'essor.[14]
>
> [The news of the July Revolution, which reached Rio de Janeiro, Bahia, Pernambuco, and even Minas Gerais in the midst of a world of feverish passions and hatred, aroused ideas of a republic and federation which are expressed in a way that goes beyond the first declaration of Brazilian independence. The Emperor, alarmed by this revolutionary spirit, tried in vain to restrain this development.]

In São Paulo there was a delay in the arrival of the news of the 1830 July Revolution, which only became known in October.[15] The students of the Academy of Law were elated with the good news and expressed their strong support for triumphant liberalism. Their noisy demonstration led the Justice of the Peace, Candido Japyassu, to order an official inquiry, a development which stirred up the local wits even more. In *O Observador Constitucional*, a magazine produced by the Italian Libero Badaró (1798–1830), the Justice of the Peace was not spared any outspoken criticism.

The Municipal Chamber also protested against Japyassu and sent an official letter to the Vice-President of São Paulo, in which it was claimed that there was danger of a 'rebellion' erupting if the order was carried out. Finally, it was decided that an inquiry was not justified on the grounds that 'the tyrannical government, which had borne down so heavily on France, had been overthrown'.[16]

This official letter referred to the extraordinary session of 8 October in which the councillor Gomide complained about Japyassu in the following terms: '[...] being the Justice of the Peace of this Legal Department and conducting an indeterminate inquiry of non-existent facts, the only pretext for them being that peaceful citizens were clearly visible in their windows on the night of the 5th instant, expressing their joy at the latest news from France'.[17]

The demonstrations of the students who sympathized with French liberalism were the first in a series of incidents that led to a direct confrontation between the supporters of liberalism and the defenders of absolutism orchestrated by D. Pedro in São Paulo. These conflicts culminated in the assassination of the Italian journalist Libero Badaró on the night of 20 November 1830.

Libero Badaró had won the hearts of the 'paulistanos' with his eloquent prose and ideas that were advanced for his time. Inspired by nationalism and liberalism, he had founded the magazine *O Observador Constitucional* in October 1829.[18] In addition to discussing the everyday problems of the town and national politics, his articles were sharply critical of some of the constitutional authorities and the periodical made constant references to the political situation in France. This can be found in the second number of *O Observador Constitucional* on 26 October 1829, concerning the news of the rise of the conservative cabinet of Polignac, where he lays out his criticism of the conservative policies of Charles X (1757–1836).

The magazine attracted correspondence from the interior of the province, as well as including miscellaneous features and advertisements. In an impeccable prose style, the paper censured the collaboration of prominent 'paulista' personalities and the students at the Academy of Law in São Paulo, which at the time was frequented by people older than the students who enrolled in later years. The first phase of this magazine was characterized by its daring outspokenness.

The criticism made of the authorities was that they were real 'abusers of freedom of the press', an expression that often appeared in the magazines of that time, at least among those who followed the liberal principles at the end of the First Reign (1822–31). In commenting on these protests, the journalist stated that freedom of the press is 'the soul of any government that is founded on rights and not on force'.[19] This phrase illustrates the sharpness of Badaró's mind, because he not only links freedom to the corporate rights of journalists and even public opinion, but also to a new system of government that is not based on the arbitrary decisions of a single person but on the will of the people. Liberal dogma permeated the minds of the people of that epoch. Libero Badaró acquired notoriety and became the target of reactionary conservatism as a result of his revolutionary ideas and eloquent prose. His death had a profound effect on the public and accelerated the political measures that were taken during the Second Reign, as was noted by some of his contemporaries, including the British businessman, John Armitage (1807–1856).[20]

The crisis of the First Reign should be understood as the outcome of a movement in opposition to absolutist regimes that began with the French Revolution and was being radically reshaped in the mid-1830s. The era of liberal politics experienced comings and goings, and advances and retreats which were at times consolidated by Jacobin terror and at other times by the Thermidorian reaction. To a certain extent, the French Empire regulated and completed the work of 1789, as the Restoration (1815–30) caused a new crisis that had to be dealt with in a moderate way, that is, by establishing a liberal monarchy that could be seen to be bourgeois.

This suggests that the political career of D. Pedro I should not be analysed as an isolated phenomenon, but understood within a movement of radical change with deep roots in the Europe of 1789 and 1830. It has been shown how the *orléanista* revolution of July 1830 reverberated forcefully in São Paulo. Together with these external pressures, there were others that were gathering momentum within the national political scene: economic instability (reflected in the increasing devaluation of the currency), parliamentary opposition, and dissidents in the armed forces. In addition there was a series of local incidents that gathered strength and became a national movement, leading to the abdication of D. Pedro I on the night of 7 April 1831, in a similar manner to the assassination of the journalist, Libero Badaró, in São Paulo. The murder of Badaró added to the hostility that the Brazilian Emperor experienced during his visit to Vila Rica (now Ouro Preto), Minas Gerais, in the mid-1830s, and the 'Noite das Garrafadas' in the Court.

D. Pedro I was viewed in Brazil as the Emperor who had succumbed to absolutist temptations. He returned to Portugal after his abdication, where he became D. Pedro IV, the military head of the Portuguese Liberal Revolution (with the support of other European countries including France). This part of the biography of the former Emperor of Brazil and King of Portugal is relatively unknown even to the Brazilian reader, despite the fact that it was thanks to his political and military leadership that Portugal was able to carry out its bourgeois revolution and achieve a liberal victory in 1834 — the year of D. Pedro IV's death.

The Reader in a Time of Transition and Revolutions

What did romantic authors in São Paulo read in the mid-nineteenth century? Álvares de Azevedo provides a good example. He was an unusual poet, narrator, and dramatist.[21] Nothing could be more disheartening to a cosmopolitan and urban spirit like that of Álvares de Azevedo than the town of São Paulo in the first half of the nineteenth century. But no other place in the world could have served him better as a source of inspiration or allowed the development of his ideas and imagination, than that old community of students, even though the town lacked any kind of material comfort and civil society. The poet gives a glimpse of this in his letters.[22]

Álvares de Azevedo was ahead of his time. One biographer has claimed that he was a liar. If his life had not run 'smoothly and serenely like a country stream', he would not have had a spirit that was so tormented and rebellious because this, the biographer reminds us, 'expressed itself in a time of transition and revolutions'.[23] Although he had not actually experienced the tempestuous waves of revolutions that had intoxicated part of the Old World, he was nevertheless inspired by the sources that lay behind the authors of that era. His personality was the outcome of his nonconformity, an attitude that he adopted in everyday situations. It was typical of the life of a student restricted to the provincial communal life of the town of São Paulo in the first half of the nineteenth century.[24]

This anxiety is expressed in various ways in the letters and it is worth highlighting the repetitive and impatient orders of articles from the Court even when his financial means were limited, as is testified by his frequent references to his allowance and the need to earn more money. The orders for merchandise which could not be found for sale in São Paulo even stretched the resources of the postal services of that time, which only operated from the town once a week, to the despair of the poet who often required greater speed in the delivery of the items he had requested. These consisted of buckles for his trousers, suspenders, glass for his lamp, a dozen pairs of shoulder pads, a waistcoat, gloves, a dress coat, a daguerreotype, as well as musical scores, periodicals, and books.

In a letter dated 11 June 1851, Azevedo ordered some musical scores:

> I move on to make an order as clearly as it is possible to make a request. It is an order for 3 or 4 musical scores that are the most modern and most in fashion. My request is for the order to be dispatched by post this month since it is a present for someone having a birthday at the beginning of the month of July. It can be safely sent by post.[25]

The books filled the time of the poet in the hours devoted to studies and in interludes of pure enjoyment. He proved to be up to date with the most recent publications of the era because São Paulo followed the news that was printed in the Fluminense magazines, which were sent to the Court every week.

In a letter addressed to his mother dated 7 June (probably of 1848), the poet added the following postscript:

> I still haven't received the orders — so far — by the arrival of the post — I am anxiously waiting for the Girondinos which you said in a previous promise that you would be able to send me as a present — I hope that the promise of a portrait will be fulfilled and that when you receive it you won't exchange it for others ... from Nhãnhã and — (perhaps if I have a wicked tongue, I'll say it) — yours.[26]

The 'Girondinos' he mentions must be the eight octavo volumes of the first edition of *L'Histoire des girondins* by Alphonse de Lamartine (1790–1869), the first edition of which came out in 1847, in other words, only a year before Azevedo had reiterated, not without some impatience, the request he made to his mother. A year later, on 7 July 1849, he made a new request and showed that he had not only kept abreast of the editions that had appeared in France, but also that he was very interested in French political historiography:

> As for me I also want to make two orders — a copy of *Démocratie en France* by Guizot — and *Raphael* by Lamartine, which are advertised in the newspapers, one for 200 rs. and the other for 800.[27]

As the letter shows, Álvares de Azevedo wrote the title of the work by Guizot in French. However, at that time there was a translation of *Démocratie en France* in Portuguese, which was published in the same year, 1849. The publication of the work in Portuguese was carried out by an admirer of Guizot (1787–1874), a Brazilian who lived in Paris, but who unfortunately did not wish to be identified. In his announcement of the volume, José Lucio Correia explained the publication in Paris of the Portuguese edition as follows:

> To Brazilians
> I cannot help being seriously affected by the news of the recent disastrous events in Pernambuco that have stirred up my patriotism. [...]
> The dissemination of this book will be a powerful means of combatting the harmful passions that are united in acting against society in areas where it is inviolable and more saintly [...].[28]

The edition is supplemented with a facsimile of the manuscript written by Guizot, in which he gives his approval of — and for political reasons, even encourages — the translation of his book:

> I have no objection, Sir, to your plan to translate my last book about democracy in France. On the contrary, it will give me great satisfaction if it can serve the cause of truth and social order even outside my country. I only ask that you kindly send me a copy of your translation when it sees the light of day [...]. Guizot. Bomptou, 21 January 1849.

Returning to the announcement, Correia concluded by saying that 'the purity of intention and important reasons for the project are an insufficient excuse for taking such a bold measure'.[29]

Álvares de Azevedo relentlessly pursued every possible avenue to obtain the original edition of the translation referred to above. He was able to obtain the French edition without difficulty — according to the notice in the bookstore of Serafim José Alves, this and other works by Guizot were for sale in Rio de Janeiro. The notice not only advertised the sale of *A democracia na França*, an unusual book devoted to political projects, but also other works by Guizot:

> Serafim José Alves Bookstore — There is a large number of copies of this book in stock and others by the same author. Substantial discounts for bulk purchases. Typography. Binding. Rua Sete de Setembro, 83.[30]

It is very likely that Álvares de Azevedo was sent the books that he ordered in his letter of 7 July 1849, including the copy of Guizot, because in a letter addressed to his mother on 14 October 1849 he wrote:

> If I have sometimes left my book *Direito das Gentes* [*The Rights of Man*] unopened on the table, together with my special favourites — *Reddée* and *Ortolan* — it is not just to read romances instead. There is a study which has superseded them in No.1 position — and written in my own language — My romances are a bit lacking in taste compared with the works of Antony, Raphael, and Consuelo.[31]

In the same letter, the author acknowledges receipt of the law books, a fact which bears witness to his interest in the subjects studied at the Faculty, as well as his evident liking for literature in general.

The comments made by Azevedo in his letters show the student's recognition of the efforts made by his parents, in particular his mother, to cater for the needs of their child and also at times show the annoyance he feels at delays in the shipments. Álvares de Azevedo is also fully aware of the difficulty and costs that certain bibliographical requests will cause his parents. In the last consignment recorded in the correspondence he writes:

> I greatly appreciate the receipt of my books on civil law — and would like to express my gratitude for the trouble you have taken in sending them from Portugal — the effort has been well worthwhile given the fact that they have been put to good use.[32]

The interest the author had in political works is not surprising since he had been inspired by the inflammatory speeches of the time to found the academic society *Ensaio Filosófico*. The end of the 1840s was marked by political fervour in Brazil, as well as in some European countries, and the conservative reaction against it, which set in after the French Revolution, as is made clear in the preface to the translation of the work by Guizot. Guizot, who had fought bravely against the Restoration in his early life, by the beginning of the 1830s was now guided in the direction of reactionary conservatism.

It is also not surprising to see the interest of Azevedo in Lamartine and the extensive knowledge that the Brazilian poet had of his principal works.[33] It is true that Álvares de Azevedo showed himself to be a lover of literature and books; he knew everything and cited everybody, which led Brito Broca to express doubts about the origins of his quotations.[34] Lamartine never ceased to be quoted by Azevedo because he was one of those universally popular personalities, for it was through his writing that 'the men of the Revolution' were brought to life again, as was noted by Alexis de Tocqueville (1805–1859) in his *Lembranças de 1848*.[35]

For reasons that still need to be explored in greater depth in studies of political history in Brazil, it can only be stated that it was the same volumes that gave rise to 'all the memories' and recollections of the 'men of the first revolution' that had crossed the ocean with notable success. This is in striking contrast with France, where these works were part of a climate of crisis in the years preceding the revolutionary wave of 1848 and which resulted in the bankruptcy of many companies.[36] Moreover, the copies of French works had a greater influence on the world of letters than their actions, a fact that led Álvares de Azevedo to declare to his father his 'theory [...] that nothing caused revulsion', in a letter dated 3 July 1850.[37] This correspondence presents valuable evidence of the range of books that aroused the interest of the young student at the Academy of Law in São Paulo and perhaps that of the whole generation that would one day fill key political positions in the country.

Furthermore, the revolution of 1848 was in tune with the political environment of Brazil, at least in the world of readers, which can be described as a socialist interregnum. The works read by Álvares de Azevedo demonstrate that among the students and teachers there were readers concerned with the facts of the French Revolution and the liberal ideas that would transfer to Brazil.

Many of these ideas were influenced by Auguste Comte (1798–1857), ex-secretary to the utopian socialist Saint Simon and the eclectic Victor Cousin (1792–1867).

The utopian activities of the French engineer, Vauthier, also played a key role in Pernambuco, a subject that has been studied by Gilberto Freyre.[38] The periodical *O Globo* borrowed the Parisian homonym *sansimoniano*. The expression *fourierismo* featured even more prominently. A Phalanstery was established in Brazil beside the Peninsular do Saí in Santa Catarina, and another in Palmital. According to a study conducted by Adelaide Gonçalves, in July 1841 the Chamber of Deputies agreed to grant a loan of sixty-four *contos de réis* [sixty-four million *réis*] to support the setting up of this project.[39]

In 1844, the journalist Antônio Pedro de Figueiredo wrote an informative piece for the magazine *O Progresso* about the League of the Just, of which Friedrich Engels was a member.

The same year (1844) saw the publication of *O Socialista da Província do Rio de Janeiro*.[40] Soon the magazine began to include examples of what would become modern socialism. In the editorial of the first number of *O Socialista*, M. G. de S. Rego explained the meaning of the term as referring to:

> Every kind of improvement that can be rendered to society at a provincial, national or global level, whether in the moral or material sphere, in what can naturally be distributed in the human domain throughout the world. Hence, since the socialist is concerned with practical agronomy, social economics, 'Jacotist' didactics, domestic medical treatment, and preventive healthcare, and above all, scientific exploration, it is enough to say that its goal is to teach people to love one another.[41]

The correspondence between the movements continued in the Spring of the People. The end of the 1840s brought the final revolutionary spasm of the epoch — the prolongation of the regency rebellions in the interminable period of the Second Reign (1840–1889), where the 'coastal rebellion' embodied vaguely socialist ideas and was influenced by the European revolutions of 1848. At least this was what the conservatives imputed to it, as is illustrated by a São Paulo magazine that refers to 'socialist ideas and the barbaric practices of the coastal movement' and to the 'plundering of the rich classes by the rebellious poor'.[42] It is abundantly clear that the term 'socialism' was already being used by the upper class as a subtle weapon to attack the lower class. The echoes of the European revolutions also reached Portugal, which already had a generation of intellectuals influenced by the ideas of Fourier (1772–1837) and Proudhon (1809–1865).[43]

The first book about socialism published in Brazil was by General Abreu e Lima, and it came out in the 1850s, although it questionable whether the concept could be related to the radical ideas that occupied the minds of Europeans.[44]

1871: A New Situation?

Although the years following 1848 were described by Álvares de Azevedo as having the liberal tinge of the second generation of post-French Revolution authors, who tended towards an exasperated form of conservatism, there was nothing rebellious in the interest that young academics had in the events that took place in France in 1871. These were other times and a long way from those experienced by Álvares de

Azevedo in São Paulo. In this period, the student Joaquim Nabuco (1849–1910) had a good impression of the intellectual and political 'paulistano', which he expressed in the following words:

> In the first years that I spent in São Paulo doing my first year course at the Academy, I could not give up being a liberal student [...]. However, my ideas were mixed up and all my feelings were confused. I was eager to obtain new impressions and had my first encounter with the famous authors, renowned books, and unrestrained ideas. Everything that was dazzling, original, and harmonious seduced and captivated me in the same way. The excitement of making new discoveries, the flowering of the spirit: all these kinds of difficulty were spontaneously suppressed like ephemeral roses.[45]

The events in France did not pass unnoticed by the academic world. Interest in literature was perhaps greater than that in politics in those early years. This continued until the space for politics grew among older people — as it became established in Nabuco's memories and was then born in the world of books and French letters. And it became tangible on the occasion of his first visit to Paris, when he came into contact with people and ideas that he had come to know through the intermediary agency of books.

In his memoirs, Joaquim Nabuco shows an unusual awareness of the role of the bookseller as a mediator of reading:

> I don't know to whom I owe the good fortune of having discovered the work of Bagehot or if I found it by chance among the new items of the Lailhacar bookstore in Recife. If I knew who put me in touch with this great English thinker, I would thank him for the relations I have had with this writer in 1869.[46]

In this period, the presence of bookshops, and of one bookshop in particular, made it possible to head for the 'French meridian', especially because in the second half of the nineteenth century, Brazilian bookstores followed the editorial policies *d'outre-mer* more closely — hence the importance of De Lailhacar in Recife and of his partner in São Paulo, the bookseller Anatole Louis Garraux.

The role played by the Garraux bookshop, as it was known, is revealed in several sections of the catalogues produced by the store. With regard to political works, in 1872, the bookshop inaugurated a bibliographical section that was completely innovative because it abandoned the standards of librarianship that were employed at that time: 'Works concerning the political and historical events of France, (1870–1872). The fall of the Empire, the War, the Commune etc.'.[47] Fifty-five titles were assembled in this section, all of them in French, with prices that ranged from 1$000 [one thousand *réis*], in the case of pamphlets or brochures (which circulated in France for a few centimes, or one franc at most), to 16$000 [sixteen thousand *réis*] for books about the Franco-Prussian War, the high price of which was very possibly due to the costs of preparing the maps that were enclosed in the volumes. It should be noted that the prices which Álvares de Azevedo referred to (books at $800 or $900 [eight hundred or nine hundred *réis*]) no longer existed.

Whether or not as a result of the bibliographical additions, another phenomenon that survived the inclement conditions was dilettantism. The scholar Joaquim

Nabuco confessed that his youth had been pervaded with the pleasures of travelling and that for much of the time books established a close bond for him. In his case in particular, he had taken advantage of all the resources and goods that were available to someone of his generation. This was how he summarized the years of his youth:

> During those ten years I've referred to, all I was curious about was going on journeys, discovering the character of different countries, reading new books, going to the theatre, and finding out about society.[48]

However, he did not only live to enjoy literature, and following the year 1871 many people became more concerned about political issues elsewhere. On 20 June 1871, Machado Freire Pereira da Silva, the representative of Pernambuco in the Chamber of Deputies, applauded the victory of the 'cause of civilization in the capital of France'.[49] The possibility that Brazil would become a place for refugees or *communards* was debated in parliament, as well as what should be done about those who might be discovered by chance in the country, having entered the country clandestinely. The deputy from Bahia, João José de Oliveira Junqueira, declared that he was content because communism and socialism had not conquered the 'capital of the civilized world' (Paris), and he asked for the Parisian revolutionaries to be regarded as common criminals so that they could be repatriated.[50] In fact, the deputies warmed to a request made by Jules Favre that was aimed at every country that had diplomatic relations with France. In response to this, almost all the Brazilian deputies united against the 'criminals of Paris'. Only the deputy from Piauí, in the north-east of Brazil, Antonio Coelho Rodrigues, adopted an equivocal position, but not on account of any sympathy with the *communards* but rather as a reprisal for the lack of support that Brazil had received from most countries during the War of the Triple Alliance against Paraguay.[51]

One speech that revealed the ambiguity of Brazilian liberalism, however radical it might appear to be in certain contexts, was that of the senator José Inácio Silveira da Mota from the province of Goiás, in the hinterland of the country. He began by saying that there were no communists in that house but that the Commune in Paris had been brought about by the personal, dictatorial, and corrupt style of government of Napoleon III. Following this, he stated that he understood why European governments had taken cautious measures and only declared that he was against the proposal of the government in meeting the request of Jules Favre because he thought that it was impossible that those 'incendiaries in the Commune of Paris would ever come to Brazil'.[52] Silveira da Mota was a reformist, abolitionist, and republican.

The final vote sanctioned the conservative proposal and the government request was approved. In reality, the Brazilian congress was not in conflict with the interests of the French government, although the attitude of Louis Adolphe Thiers (1797–1877) was understandable in the light of his objective — to crush a socialist workers' movement. In the case of Brazil, there was neither a workers' movement nor socialism, but only a large number of slaves without any rights. Thus even with regard to the most retrograde form of French liberalism, the Brazilian deputies expressed a strictly conservative view.

In contrast with the past, the French Third Republic was born out of the ruins of a revolution and was not its product. Its conservative features are evident. The ideologue Thiers, who was responsible for carrying out the massacre of Paris, was the celebrated liberal author of the *História da Revolução*, in the wake of Guizot and so many others. Part of the liberal concept survived in subsequent approaches, but on the whole it was replaced by a new historiographical debate, which featured positivism, socialism, and the patriotism of the Third Republic.

A New 'Revolutionary'

The historiography of the French Revolution entered a new phase with the founding of the Third Republic. A new dawn was ushered in by the following events: the marking of 14 July as an official holiday on the calendar, the positivist interpretation of Hippolyte Taine (1828–1893), the debate about this with François Victor Alphonse Aulard (1849–1928), the socialist readings of Jean Jaurès (1859–1914), the conservative readings of Augustin Cochin (1876–1916), and, much later, the ideas about insurrection of Albert Mathiez (1874–1932). These were much more wide-ranging than what had been consolidated at the beginning of the Restoration and made sacrosanct after 1830 through Thiers and Guizot. But the left-wing readers only came to Brazil after 1930 with the publication of the work by Mathiez, *História da Revolução Francesa*.[53]

'Liberal-Conservative' readings predominated in Brazil towards the end of the nineteenth century. The works of Guizot and Thiers can still be found in Brazilian second-hand bookshops until today. In 1877, for example, the second edition of the *História Completa da Revolução Franceza desde 1789 até 1815* [*The Complete history of the French revolution in the period 1789–1815*] was published. In fact it is only a summary of the work by Thiers. Curiously, the second volume came with an introduction that was intended to be a 'summary of the History of France from the beginning of the Monarchy' written by 'a Brazilian'. It has not been possible to establish the name of this 'Brazilian'. There is no note about this in the dictionary of Innocêncio F. da Silva or that of Sacramento Blake.[54]

In one copy, the former owner wrote in pencil beside the inscription: '"a Brazilian": Visconde do Porto Seguro, or perhaps, Francisco Adolfo de Varnhagen'.[55] However, no attribution of the translation to Varnhagen could be made because no reference to this text can be found in his bibliography.

The 'Brazilian' mentioned in the *História Completa da Revolução Franceza desde 1789 até 1815* is not the author since he lived before the translator and organizer of the work. The author of this text is Felix Bodin. However, the preface written by the translator is more curious than the summary itself. He analysed the French Revolution in the form of a drama in which the monarchies and the ideas opposed to them played the key roles. While sharing the idea of history as a lesson for the benefit of the present and future, the compiler promises to make a comparison between the French and English Revolutions. However, the English Revolution was left for another volume to be published later. Although the book in question was advertised as a summary of the work by Thiers, it also made use of the works by François Auguste Marie Mignet (1796–1884) and Mme de Staël (1766–1817). The Brazilian translator thus proved to have affinities with a particular liberal school of the Revolution.

Finally, he laid stress on the pedagogical aspects of the work:

> Today enlightened and free people can regard the French Revolution as the commemoration of the burdens of a great nation, which sought to bring to mankind the Magna Carta and all its freedoms. Thus the service that we seek to render to our fellow citizens is to popularize the knowledge of the French Revolution for our fellow citizens who belong to the those social classes that are still not in a position to study the French historians.[56]

Conclusion

This chapter has examined the extent to which books and French culture exerted a real influence on Brazilian political practices. Brazilian politicians read and declaimed French poetry about freedom while they were studying at the Academy of Law in São Paulo or carrying out their public duties in the capitals of the provinces. However, when they returned to the manor houses on their farms, they were reminded of their rural and conservative roots. They were liberal slave owners.

These nineteenth-century Brazilians took part in promoting the individualism of the citizen without citizenship and thus fostered the illusion of an illusion or the ideology of an ideology. In reality, this was concerned with an ideology because it concealed private interests beneath the cover of universality. But at the same time, the ideology was exposed as showing a denial of its universal assumptions about justice. These problems were raised by Vicente Licínio Cardoso when he noted that we would import from Europe 'attitudes, gestures, top hats, and overcoats, the name of an orator and his own discourse. But nobody sees what lies behind [...]'.[57] In other words, the oratory and ideas are present, but not their material supports, industry, contracts etc.

In many of his articles, Libero Badaró wrote about freedom or different kinds of freedom, a word that in both its singular and plural form in Portuguese sums up European history in a long-term perspective (i.e. from the eleventh century to the twentieth century). This is what can be seen in this French example where the movement of ideas and books has a direct bearing on the politics of the State:

> At the beginning of his reign, Louis XVI wanted to gauge public opinion with regard to everyday business. So he secretly entrusted a bookseller to allow him to lay out all the pamphlets about public businesses in a small safe for which only he had the key, so they would be exposed to the light of day. For a certain time everything went well, but the minister, who was not concerned about whether the king knew how things were going, went to arrest the bookseller and imprisoned him in the Bastille. When the king found the box was empty, he ordered someone to call the bookseller, whom he had come to admire a great deal, only to be told that he had been imprisoned by order of the S. M. The king ordered him to be freed, but the minister was not dismissed.[58]

This article refers to the History of France and the subversive role of books and the press. There is no denying the revolutionary role of the printed press, whether it be in the anxious minds of the readers or in institutions. It was precisely because books can be regarded as both material and spiritual goods of a high value that the dominant classes in Brazil did everything to ensure they were only a luxury item and would be restricted to a small *coterie* who could enjoy them without being excessively excited by them.

Notes to Chapter 3

1. Marianne Reisewitz, 'Dom Fernando José de Portugal e Castro: prática ilustrada metropolitana na colônia (1788–1801)' (unpublished master's thesis, FFLCH, USP, 2001).
2. *O Estado de São Paulo*, 7 September 1898.
3. 'Are local variations not more important than common features? If we look closer at the picture, and scrutinise in more detail the situation in Spain, Italy, Vienna, Berlin and Paris, it must at least be concluded that the ties that bind these and other similar features, are stronger and more variegated than what appears to be the case at first glance. It is clear that the circulation of ideas was more widespread than could have been suspected and that the hopes and expectations moved in the same direction and effectively accompanied what emerged from the "Europe of the Enlightenment" ', Franco Venturi, 'The Chronology and Geography of the Enlightenment', in *Utopia e reforma no Iluminismo*, trans. by Modesto Florenzano (São Paulo: EdUSC, 2003), p. 222. English edition: Franco Venturi, *Utopia and Reform in the Enlightenment* (Cambridge: Cambridge University Press, 1971).
4. Alexis de Tocqueville, *L'Ancien Régime et la Révolution* (Paris: Calmann-Lévy, 1856).
5. Jean-Yves Mollier, *L'Argent et les Lettres. Histoire du capitalisme d'édition* (1880–1920) (Paris: Fayard, 1988), p. 94.
6. Gérard de Nerval, *Voyage en Orient* (Paris: Club des libraires de France, 1955), p. 55.
7. Ibid., p. 38.
8. Auguste de Saint-Hilaire, *Viagem à província de São Paulo e resumo das viagens ao Brasil, província Cisplatina e missões do Paraguai*, trans. by Rubens Borba de Moraes, 2nd edn (São Paulo: Martins, 1945), p. 199.
9. *Almanach Litterario de São Paulo para o anno de 1879*, published by José Maria Lisboa, 4th series (São Paulo: Typographia da Província, 1878), p. 92.
10. Ibid.
11. Nicolau Sevcenko, *A corrida para o século XXI: no loop da montanha-russa* (São Paulo: Companhia das Letras, 2001), p. 43.
12. The *juste milieu* was installed in 1830 and was a regime characterized by compromise because it supposedly put an end to the class struggle (according to Guizot). The period of openness in 1830 was to be one of balance after the excesses of the French Revolution and the Restoration, which is clearly signalled in the statement of Lafayette, quoted earlier in this article.
13. Oliveira Martins, *Portugal contemporâneo* (Lisbon: Guimarães Editores, 1952), p. 46.
14. C. L. Lesur, *Annuaire Historique Universel pour 1830* (Paris: Thoisnier-Desplaces, Libraire, November 1832), p. 772.
15. The presence of works about the French Revolution was a striking feature in the inventory of the library of José da Costa Carvalho (1796–1860), the founder of the first 'Paulista' journal, *O Farol Paulistano*, and a partner of Libero Badaró in the 'anti-absolutist' propaganda that was spread through the city among the teachers and young students at the Academy of Law. Cf. Marisa Midori Deaecto, 'Os primórdios da imprensa paulista: Costa Carvalho and Farol Paulistano (1827–1831)', *Revista de História Regional*, 12 (2008), pp. 29–50.
16. 'Official letter of the Chamber to his Excellency the Vice-President of this province and its Council', São Paulo, 8 October 1830', *Registro Geral da Câmara*, vol. 20 (São Paulo, 1832), p. 481.
17. *Atas da Câmara Municipal de São Paulo*, 8 October 1830.

18. It should be noted that the title of the magazine shows close relations were maintained with the French press, which was subject to censorship in the period of the Restoration (1815–30). Publications defending constitutional monarchy and liberalism were suppressed in the towns and cities of *Hexagon*, as is well attested by Stendhal (1783–1842): 'At this point the Justice of Peace, who had a large number of children, passed several sentences which appeared unjust; they were all directed against those inhabitants who read *Le Constitutionnel*', Stendhal, *Le Rouge et le Noir*, ed. by Henri Martineau (Paris: Garnier, 1950), p. 24.
19. Nicoláo Duarte e Silva, *Libero Badaró (1830–1930)* (São Paulo: Edição do Autor, 1931), pp. 568–75.
20. John Armitage, *History of Brazil from the Arrival of the Braganza Family in 1808, to the Abdication of Don Pedro the First in 1831*, 2 vols (London: Smith, Elder and Co., 1836).
21. Décio de Almeida Prado, *História concisa do teatro brasileiro* (São Paulo: EdUSP, 2003), p. 51.
22. The troubling relationship the poet had with the town has been noted in several studies of São Paulo in the 1830s, when a perception of it began to emerge as a city in contrast with that of a small town, or in other words, between the kinds of urban life that were superimposed on the colonial customs. See Azevedo Amaral, 'Álvares de Azevedo, o único brasileiro romântico', *Revista Nova*, 1 (1922), 2–28 (p. 3); Richard Morse, *Formação histórica de São Paulo* (São Paulo: Difel, 2001), pp. 121–30.
23. Vicente de Azevedo, *A vida de Álvares de Azevedo* (São Paulo: Revista dos Tribunais, 1931), pp. 170–71.
24. 'On the Chapter *relações minhas em S. Paulo* — I must tell you that Dr Pacheco came to visit me and I paid him a visit — but I didn't find him at home. The only house where I sometimes go is that of Dr Claudio, who has visited me and treated me very well — in a way that has really delighted me — I haven't gone to the other houses, which I don't regret because it would only have taken me to people who never visit me, and this saved me the trouble of breaking my feet on the soft pavements of São Paulo by paying visits. When, in speaking about Dr Claudio, I say the only house, don't understand this to mean that I haven't paid a visit to D. Maria do Rodrigo, D. Anna Vicencia, and even Gomide — This last house has a cross on the door because it is not one of the best or most praiseworthy — on the contrary it casts a blemish on the reputation of those young ladies who still go out to balls etc!! — Ad.s — gives her blessing to f.°. Manoel Ant.o'. As regards the high society lady, it is clearly stated in our correspondence: 'Don't think I'm exaggerating when I say that the girl who is otherwise the most beautiful and perfect statue in the whole of Belisaria (Mineira) is someone stupid and who says things like: — "We don't know how to dance 'cos...", and despite her beauty she is only a statue and without any life — as the sonnet of Octaviano says.' *Cartas de Álvares de Azevedo* (São Paulo: Academia Paulista de Letras, 1976), p. 73 and p. 106.
25. *Cartas de Álvares de Azevedo*, p. 190.
26. *Cartas de Álvares de Azevedo*, p. 82.
27. *Cartas de Álvares de Azevedo*, p. 114.
28. F. Guizot, *A democracia na França*, trans. by *** (Paris: Typ. de E. Thurnot et Cie., 1849).
29. F. Guizot, *A democracia na França*, trans. by ***, p. VIII. The author refers to the act of sedition that took place in the assault of Recife in 1848. It deals with the 'coastal' movement, which led to a crisis in the liberal party in power at the time. See Caio Prado Jr., *Evolução política do Brasil e outros estudos*, 3rd edn (São Paulo: Brasiliense, 1961), pp. 79–80.
30. *Etiqueta*, in Guizot, *A democracia na França*.
31. According to Vicente de Azevedo, 'Théodore Ortolan, the author of *Règles Internationales de la Diplomatie de la Mer [International Rules for the Diplomacy of the Sea]*, 2 vols (Paris, 1844) is a book that has a deservedly high reputation. *Reddée* has been forgotten and cannot be compared with *Ortolan*. When the dates of the letter and the edition of *Ortolan* are compared, it is remarkable how much Álvares de Azevedo had his finger on the pulse! Added to this is the fact that International Law was not a subject included in the law course. Even the chair of Roman Law was only created during the educational reforms of 1854', Vicente de Azevedo, *Álvares de Azevedo*, pp. 142–43.
32. Ibid., p. 131.
33. Twenty years later, the works of Lamartine were advertised in the *Catálogo* of A. L. Garraux in

1872, in an extensive list of books costing between 2$000 and 30$000 [two thousand and thirty thousand *réis*]. The cheapest were in the field of literature and the most expensive in history. In this period, the volume of *Raphaël*, which according to Álvares de Azevedo originally came out at $800 [eight hundred *réis*], now cost 2$000 [two thousand *réis*]. A *Histoire des Girondins* was first sold at 16$000 [sixteen thousand *réis*], in an edition in six quarto volumes.

34. Brito Broca, 'O que liam os românticos', *Revista do livro*, 4 (1959), 163–72.
35. Alexis de Tocqueville, *Souvenirs* (Paris: Gallimard, 2004).
36. Jean-Yves Mollier, *L'Argent et les Lettres*, pp. 104–05.
37. *Cartas de Álvares de Azevedo*, p. 164.
38. Gilberto Freyre, *Um engenheiro francês no Brasil*, 2nd edn, 2 vols (Rio de Janeiro: José Olympio, 1960) [1st edn, 1940].
39. Adelaide Gonçalves, 'Comunidades utópicas e os primeiros sinais de socialismo no Brasil', *E-topia: Revista Electrônica de Estudos sobre a Utopia* 2 (2004) <http://ler.letras.up.pt/uploads/ficheiros/artigo10561.pdf> [accessed 21 March 2014].
40. See Ivone Gallo, 'O Brasil e o socialismo do século XIX: fourieristas no Saí', in *Franceses no Brasil (séculos XIX–XX)*, ed. by Tania Regina de Luca and Laurent Vidal (São Paulo: Fundação Editora Unesp, 2009), pp. 147–60.
41. *O Socialista da Província do Rio de Janeiro*, no. 1 (1 August 1845).
42. *Aurora Paulistana*, 5 April 1852.
43. Joel Serrão, *Liberalismo, socialismo, republicanismo*, 2nd edn (Lisbon: Livros Horizonte, 1979).
44. José Ignacio de Abreu e Lima, *Socialismo* (Recife: Typographia Universal, 1855).
45. Joaquim Nabuco, *Minha Formação* (São Paulo: Instituto Progresso Editorial, 1947), p. 15. This is from the first edition of his complete works. The volume *Minha formação* was completed by the author in 1900.
46. Ibid., p. 19.
47. *Catálogo da Livraria Garraux*, 1872, pp. 33–36.
48. Joaquim Nabuco, *Minha formação*, p. 151.
49. J. N. Tavares, *Marx, o socialismo e o Brasil* (Rio de Janeiro: Civilização Brasileira, 1983), p. 100.
50. Ibid., p. 101.
51. Ibid., p. 102.
52. Ibid., p. 104.
53. Mathiez, *História da Revolução Francesa* (São Paulo: Atena, n.d.).
54. Inocencio Francisco da Silva, *Diccionario Bibliographico Portugues*, 26 vols (Lisbon: Imprensa Nacional, 1923); Augusto Victorino Alves Sacramento Blake, *Diccionario bibliographico brazileiro*, 7 vols (Rio de Janeiro: Typographia Nacional; Conselho Nacional de Cultura, 1970).
55. The copies were found in two Paulista second-hand bookstores, one in São Paulo and one in the town of Bauru. The copy found in Bauru includes the registration of the purchaser, followed by the year: 1944. The other copy had an annotation dated at the end of the nineteenth century. The copy found in the middle of the State of São Paulo has the registration of the owner who acquired it in 1944 in the town of Avaré.
56. *História Completa da Revolução Franceza desde 1789 a 1815 e precedido por um resumo da História da França por um brazileiro* (Rio de Janeiro: Laemmert, 1877), p. VIII.
57. *apud* D. Menezes, *O Brasil no pensamento moderno* (Rio de Janeiro: INEP, 1957), p. 140.
58. Libero Badaró, 'Liberdade de Imprensa', *Revista do Instituto Histórico e Geográfico de São Paulo*, 28 (1930), 24–82.

CHAPTER 4

Migratory Literary Forms: British Novels in Nineteenth-Century Brazil[1]

Sandra Guardini Vasconcelos

> In sum, foreign debt is as inevitable in Brazilian letters as it is in any other field, and is not simply an easily dispensable part of the work in which it appears, but a complex feature of it.
>
> ROBERTO SCHWARZ[2]

It has long been a commonplace among Brazilian literary historians and critics that French novels and novelists played a central role in the development and consolidation of the Brazilian novel during the nineteenth century. The received view has been that French novels were the predominant — almost exclusive — model available to Brazilian writers, and much of the evidence to date confirms the idea that the influence of these materials was pervasive, and included not only canonical works, but also popular fiction in French, as Antonio Candido makes clear in *Formação da Literatura Brasileira*:

> [...] translated books belonged, in the main, to what is today considered third-rate literature; but frequently they were cherished novelties, just like the good works. Thus, side by side with George Sand, Merimée, Chateaubriand, Balzac, Goethe, Irving, Dumas, Vigny, stood Paul de Kock, Eugène Sue, Scribe, Soulié, Berthet, Souvestre, Féval, as well as others whose names do not mean anything today: Bard, Gonzalès, Rabou, Chevalier, David, etc. They were French, in the vast majority, revealing in their titles the genre we call feuilleton. Who knows which and how many of these by-products influenced the making of our novel? Sometimes, they may have had more relevance than the important books on which we prefer to fix our attention.[3]

However, the question of the influence of less canonical literature and literature in French translations can be explored further. This essay takes up this challenge and argues that British novels also made a significant and hitherto unrecognized contribution to the formation of the Brazilian novel as a genre during this period. Alternative sources of information — such as newspapers, catalogues and literary periodicals — make it clear that although France always functioned as an intermediary in the literary marketplace, Britain brought to Brazil much more than a regular supply of merchandise and manufactured goods, such as the chinaware, glass, pots and pans, cutlery or tools found on the shelves of shops and warehouses in Rio de Janeiro in the nineteenth century. Not only were hardware and utensils

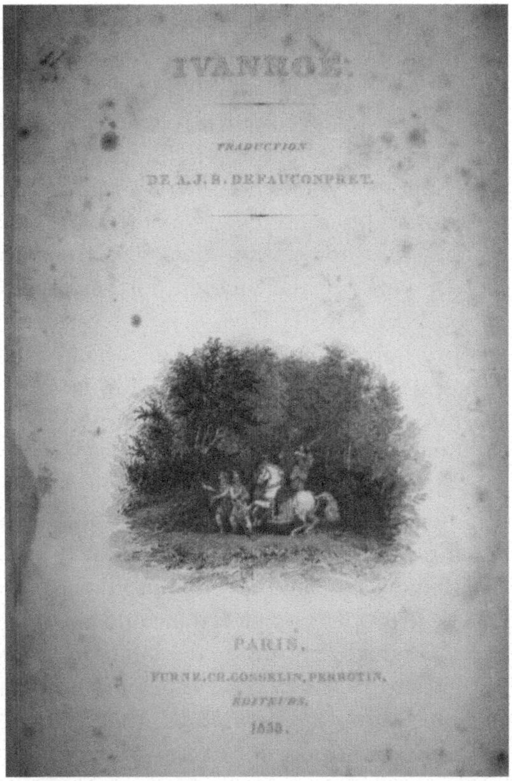

Fig. 4.1. Title page of an imported French translation of Sir Walter Scott's *Ivanhoe*

from Britain available to the inhabitants of the still small and provincial Brazilian capital, but books and periodicals in general, and novels in particular, also found their way into the country, accompanying the introduction of new habits of consumption, new fashions, and a certain refinement of manners that even today is attributed to the British influence on everyday life in Rio de Janeiro after 1808. The supply of British novels, sparse though it was at first, increased when bookshops and circulating libraries were opened. These novels often arrived in Rio de Janeiro's harbour via Lisbon, in Portuguese translation, or via Paris, translated into French, and circulated themes, narrative procedures and techniques that had already become standard in fiction produced in Europe.

In addition to reconstructing the history of the circulation of British novels in Brazil, this essay works to substantiate Roberto Schwarz's claim that '[t]he novel had existed in Brazil before there were any Brazilian novelists',[4] and explores the ways in which British narrative models were appropriated by the first Brazilian prose fiction writers. It does not, however, discuss the prominent role played by translation and by Portuguese and French translators in this process. Neither does it touch upon the issue of reading practices; although scholarship can establish which books were available on library shelves, it is nearly impossible to ascertain whether or how they were read.

Nonetheless, the history of the circulation of literary materials during this period and the appropriation of narrative techniques and processes drawn directly or indirectly from British literature makes it clear that the unitary model of French influence is flawed and incomplete. From beneath the fragmentary references, misspellings, French titles and anonymity — frequent in the advertisements and catalogues that publicized these works — a more variegated picture of the conditions governing the development of the genre in Brazil begins to emerge.[5] This picture encompasses a collection of eighteenth- and nineteenth-century novels, written by both famous and lesser-known novelists.[6] The collection of British novels present in Brazil is highly representative of the history of the European edition and publishing market; the subscription and circulating libraries in Rio de Janeiro had on their shelves works of the most important publishers and booksellers in Europe. Their presence in Rio de Janeiro is not surprising, since the most famous nineteenth-century publishers, such as Aillaud and Hachette in Paris, Routledge and Bentley in London, and Bernhard Tauchnitz in Leipzig, were businessmen who had a keen eye on the market and employed agents globally. Nor was this export trade insubstantial. The *Revue Britannique*[7] for March 1840 reports a shipment of books valued at 230,000 francs sent from France to Brazil for the year 1838 (with another shipment worth 60,000 francs sent to Cuba in the same year), while sales of Belgian piracies amounted to 16,000 francs for Brazil and 112,000 francs for Mexico in 1837.[8]

Although beyond the scope of Franco Moretti's *Atlas of the European Novel* (1998), Brazil, if properly explored, would no doubt complete the literary routes that he draws for Europe in his discussion of narrative markets operating around the middle of the century. As in most European countries, so in Brazil 'the majority of novels are, quite simply, *foreign books*', that is, French and British novels, which 'become models to be imitated'.[9] Less clear, from the examination of individual collections, is what he defines as the 'overpowering presence of the canon', an anachronistically problematic concept when used with reference to the nineteenth century, and one which can only be applied with the benefit of hindsight. In addition, the apparently peaceful coexistence of major and minor novelists on the shelves of Brazilian circulating libraries equally refutes any notion of the predominance of canonical works.

Nevertheless, this common literary repertoire seems to reinforce Moretti's argument in favour of the hegemonic role of what he calls the 'Anglo-French core' over a literary world-system.[10] Moretti contends that, 'in cultures that belong to the periphery of the literary system (which means: almost all cultures, inside and outside Europe), the modern novel first arises not as an autonomous development but as a compromise between a Western formal influence (usually French or English) and local materials.'[11] There can be no doubt that, to a certain extent, this model applies to Brazil. Yet one would need to relativize Moretti's use of the term 'compromise' to define the 'encounter of Western forms and local reality' in order not to ignore the importance of particularities and contexts.[12] A very strong critical tradition in Brazil argues for treating texts individually, since artistic elaboration is always rooted in real processes, and their explanatory power is embedded in the literary form itself. As Schwarz insists, 'there is no simple consequence to be drawn from such a dualism [between European model and Brazilian reality]; in a culturally dependent country like ours, its presence is inevitable, and its results can be either good or bad. Each case must be judged on an individual basis. Literature is not a matter of rational judgment; but of imaginative form'.[13]

Crossing the Oceans

'Traduit de l'anglais': this is how most eighteenth-century British novels got to France, after having taken Britain by storm and becoming fashionable with common readers. Crossing the English Channel, however, was simply the first leg in a long journey to foreign lands and audiences. If *Pamela, or Virtue Rewarded*, published by Samuel Richardson in 1740, became a model imitated by countless British novelists, its impact on the European continent was undoubtedly almost as great. Translated into French by the Abbé Prévost in 1742, this story of a heroine who resists all attempts at seduction by her master, but who ends up marrying him and climbing socially as a reward for her chastity, was enthusiastically received, thanks to Richardson's clever combination of realism and morally uplifting narrative. As he made clear, his main goal in his novels was to amuse and edify ('instruction without entertainment [...] would have but few readers'), and his work not only inspired many other novels of the period, but also inculcated models of behaviour for marriageable young ladies.[14] Pamela, then, becomes a kind of 'civilizing' heroine, who came to inhabit the pages of novels across the English Channel, as well as in Britain, and left indelible marks on the imaginary of novelists abroad. In its wake came hundreds of other novels which, both in Britain and France, filled the leisure hours of female readers, their privileged public, and helped consolidate the new genre.

From its birth, the novel had been described as a bastardized and popular genre that was seen by many as disreputable reading, the pastime of the idle, or, even more dangerously, as a corrupter of manners. Yet the positive reception that the works of the founding fathers of the British novel had in France, mainly between 1740 and 1760, was only the starting point for a dynamic process of exchange between the two countries, prompting a French critic and historian to define the eighteenth century as the century of the novel.[15]

Never an especially affordable pastime, since sale prices were not particularly low, in Britain novels found an excellent source of publicity and dissemination in the circulating libraries, which became a crucial factor in the development of the habit of reading and in the genre's popularity. Things were not much different in France. After the first *cabinet de lecture* opened in Paris in 1767, French readers' taste for the novel was fed by the same stories of adventure, crime and passion.[16] In fact, a comparison between the list of British novels translated into French and the catalogue of the publisher Pigoreau reveals an intriguing coincidence of titles and authors.[17] Pigoreau also provides clues to deduce what parameters may have guided the translation of these novels into French. After all, meeting public demand took precedence over fidelity and respect to the original, since the modern concept of authorship, with strict controls over intellectual property, had yet to develop:

> The lively and quick Frenchman does not read a novel but to amuse himself for a few minutes; he wants to be led to the conclusion by the shortest route. The phlegmatic Englishman loves to stop at the details, and does not want to reach the dénouement before strolling about the long circuits of a labyrinth.[18]

It was, therefore, in the temperament of the reader that Pigoreau located the main differences between British and French novels, thus defining the guidelines that should govern the translator's process of adaptation. Pigoreau must have known what he was talking about, since he was one of the main publishers and booksellers in Paris and an important purveyor of novels to the circulating libraries.[19]

The booksellers and the circulating libraries were responsible, in Brazil as in Europe, for the diffusion and circulation of novels, playing as central a role as those in Britain and France as shapers and mediators of taste.[20] If, in the 1820s, the shops adjacent to the daily newspapers sold and rented books, in the 1830s, entrepreneurs founded libraries and circulating libraries similar to those in Britain and France as commercial ventures to make packages of novels sent from the metropolis available in the provinces. It would have been the 'remainders', or the surplus editions for the French circulating libraries — as well as the '*bestsellers*' already translated into Portuguese — that ended up with Lisbon and Rio de Janeiro as their destination.[21] The expression 'translated from the French', which appears in a great number of novels that circulated in Brazil, is frequently a false clue, hiding the British origin of the novel, and may have served as a kind of cachet, to make these books easier to sell and rent; according to Laurence Hallewell, there was in Brazil 'an exceptional receptivity towards the ornaments of French culture', which were seen as modern and progressive, French being also the language of elite culture and society.[22]Moreover, the bitterness of Anglo-Brazilian relations, mainly over the slave trade and what was considered to be the British government's undue interference in local matters, may have contributed to this preference for things French. Symbols of civilization and refinement, French cultural products had the extra advantage of not being associated with imperialist politics or diplomatic imbroglios, in contrast with those from Great Britain.

An examination of Pigoreau's *Petite bibliographie biographico-romancière* and of Harold Streeter's *The Eighteenth-century English Novel in French Translation* testifies to the British origin of many of the novels 'translated from the French' which were listed in the catalogues of circulating libraries in Rio de Janeiro.[23] A comparison of the bibliographical information available, which includes the translator's name or initials, shows that often the edition that came to Brazil, or served as the source text for the translation into Portuguese, was identical to the editions that appeared in French circulating libraries. This is the case, for example, of *L'Italien, ou le confessional des pénitents noirs* (1830) by Ann Radcliffe or *Alberto, ou o Deserto de Strathnavern* (1827) by Mrs Helme.[24] Thus, as Marlyse Meyer has pointed out, the forms of the novel which came to Brazil were always British, though their mediation was French.[25]

Between 1808 and 1822, during the Viceroyalty, the books published by the *Impressão Régia* show a predominance of works translated from French and a considerable amount of sentimental stories and 'moral tales'. Likewise, the 1815 'Catalogue of Manuel Inácio da Silva Alvarenga's Books' records *Gil Blas*, *Aventures de Telemaque*, Prosper Jolyot de Crébillon's *Oeuvres* (1802), and Denis Diderot's *Jacques le fataliste* (1778; 1796), all of them French works.

Similarly, the *Gazeta do Rio de Janeiro*, from its foundation on 10 September 1808

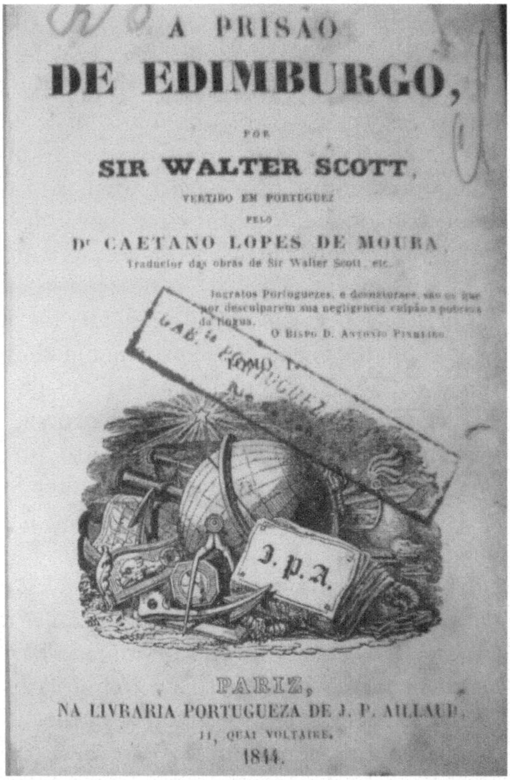

Fig. 4.2. Sir Walter Scott comes to Portuguese via French

until it ceased circulating on 22 June 1822, published in its section 'Loja da Gazeta' lists of works available, for example, at the shop of Paulo Martin, Filho, a bookseller established at 34 Rua da Quitanda. While they give evidence of the regular supply of foreign works to the reading public in Rio de Janeiro, these advertisements announced several 'very modern and entertaining novels': some were of anonymous authorship; some were old and well-known books like Alain René Lesage's *Diabo Coxo,*[26] Jacques-Henri Bernardin de Saint-Pierre's *Paulo e Virgínia* and *A Choupana Índia, Mil e Huma* [*sic*] *Noites*, François-René de Chateaubriand's *Atala, ou Amores de Dois Selvagens*, and Jean-François Marmontel's *Belizario.* Others, however, were British fiction: Mrs Helme's *Luiza, ou o Cazal* [*sic*] *no Bosque* (21 September 1816), Jonathan Swift's *Viagens de Guliver* (15 March 1817), Daniel Defoe's *Vida e Aventuras Admiráveis de Robinson Crusoe* (9 April 1817), Henry Fielding's *Tom Jones, ou O Engeitado* [*sic*] (10 May 1817), the anonymous *Vida de Arnaldo Zulig* (4 July 1818), and Samuel Richardson's *Historia da Infeliz Clarissa Harlowe* in 8 volumes (8 March 1820).[27] Everything seems to indicate that these are the first British fictional works to have circulated in Brazil.

It is also worthwhile noting the advertisements for the arrival in 1809 of *Cartas de Maria Wollstonecraft, relativas à Suécia e Dinamarca, com uma notícia de sua vida por Francisco Xavier Baeta* and, in the year 1819, of *Carta escrita pela senhora de ***, residente em Constantinopla* [illegible] *em que trata das mulheres turcas, do seu modo de viver, divertimentos, vestidos, maneira de tratar os maridos, etc.*, which must certainly be one of Lady Mary Wortley Montagu's 'Turkish Embassy Letters', which appeared in 1763. But it is Mary Wollstonecraft who merits a brief mention in one of Brazil's earliest novels, Joaquim Manuel de Macedo's *A Moreninha* (1844). Amidst a lively dispute between two of the young male characters about courtship and women's hearts, the British writer is invoked as a vindicator of the rights of women that the female protagonist may have known and read. The reference may not say much about women readers at the time, but it does inject a note of verisimilitude, as well as demonstrating that Macedo was well informed about what kind of writer she had been.[28]

The *Jornal do Commercio*, founded by Pierre Plancher in Rio in 1827, also adopted the systematic practice of announcing the sales of its novels. British novels continued to figure in supply lists in the pharmacies and bookshops that had now become part of the landscape of the town. But these works were to be found not only in the imperial capital; Gilberto Freyre notes that it was possible to find Portuguese translations of Defoe, Walter Scott and Ann Radcliffe in the interior of the country, as well.[29] Since reading habits and practices were rarely recorded during the nineteenth century, it is difficult to tell why these novelists were chosen and how these novels were used. However, it is not off the mark to claim that what was offered to the small Brazilian reading public was what was in vogue or commercially successful in London and Paris.

British novels could also be found at the Rio de Janeiro British Subscription Library, which had a good supply of the latest European works.[30] The British had established this venue in 1826 to serve the resident British community. This is where most of the novels could be found in their original English-language version, though editions in English also appear in the catalogues of the Gabinete Português de Leitura do Rio de Janeiro (founded in 1837) and of the Biblioteca Fluminense (founded in 1847). Most novels in these catalogues, however, had already been translated into Portuguese from their French versions.

The French bookshops which, from the 1820s, clustered around the Rua do Ouvidor, the centre of elegant life in the town, also ensured the sale and rental of novels to a tiny literate population, for whom novel reading became a part of the pattern of good manners to be followed and imitated.[31] The truth is that the packages of British novels that did arrive in Rio de Janeiro in the first three decades of the nineteenth century almost always came from Paris or Lisbon, translated from the French. The flow may have been slow at first, due to the two-month voyage separating Europe from Brazil, but after 1850, with steamships, Liverpool was only twenty-eight days away from Rio de Janeiro, ensuring that the flow not only remained constant, but even intensified. As the century progressed, advances in the means of transport, changes in the economics of publishing and in banking, and, above all, the interest of readers were crucial factors to guarantee that these novels were available not only in the collections of libraries and circulating libraries, but surely also on their shelves throughout this period.

The Burden of the Novel

Perceived as 'light reading', in the words of journalist Quirino dos Santos, owner of the *Gazeta de Campinas*, or 'tenth-rate novels', in the words of another newspaperman, these books left strong impressions on the imaginary of Brazilian novelists. José de Alencar was among those who believed that reading this type of novel had contributed to 'imprint on my spirit the moulds of this literary structure'.[32] These were the novels which crossed the oceans, carrying within them some recurring themes — marriage, private and domestic life, the usurpation of rights and inheritance — all of them imbued with strong and exaggerated emotions, expressed, most of the time, in ornate, high-sounding language, a characteristic of the era. Similarly, the different genres of the novel (domestic, sentimental, Gothic, of manners, of doctrine, historical) current in eighteenth- and nineteenth-century Britain also circulated in Brazil, offering ideas to the country's first fiction writers. Following the useful distinction between *novel* and *romance* made by Clara Reeve in her *The Progress of Romance* (1785), the romance repertoire can be said to be present to a high degree in this initial period of novelistic production. Uncontrollable passion, seduction, kidnapping, betrayal, terrible villains, disrepute, last-minute revelations, absence of half-tone, lack of causal link between events, stereotyped characters (extremely good or extremely evil), etc., all crop up repeatedly in these works.

Some texts, however, began to lay more emphasis on verisimilitude and plausibility, presenting more life-like language and scenes and bringing the story closer to the life of common people, which is typically the novel's primary concern. It seems that because of the embourgeoisement of manners and the changing role of women in Brazilian society, the novel flourished to the detriment of the romance, although the latter never completely disappeared from the work of romantic novelists. In its initial stages, Brazilian fiction also suffered from an overall generic indefinition, with texts referred to as novels, short stories or novellas regardless of their length or formal characteristics. The use of the genre as 'an instrument for the discovery and interpretation of the country',[33] however, would soon make realism predominate, with only a residual recourse to the romance.

The process of the formation and consolidation of the novel took about a hundred years in Britain, if Daniel Defoe's *Robinson Crusoe* (1719) is taken as its point of departure and Walter Scott's works as its culmination. In Brazil, this timeline was compressed, since the nature of the country's cultural relations with Europe and the simultaneous availability of novels produced across a longer period of time in Britain and France gave Brazilian novelists a much wider range of models from which to draw. Thus, the works by the founders of the British novel in the previous century — Daniel Defoe, Samuel Richardson, Henry Fielding, Tobias Smollett and Laurence Sterne — were on offer at the same time as those by the great nineteenth-century novelists.

Practically all sub-genres current in Britain were available in Brazil: in addition to Richardson's domestic and sentimental novel, Horace Walpole's and Ann Radcliffe's Gothic, Fanny Burney's novel of manners, William Godwin's novel of doctrine,

Samuel Johnson's Oriental fantasy *Rasselas* (1759), and William Beckford's *Vathek* (1786), works by writers such as Edward Bulwer-Lytton and William Harrison Ainsworth could also be obtained. A survey of the British novels in circulation also attests to the presence of women novelists who had become well known and widely read in Britain throughout the eighteenth century: Fanny Burney, Elizabeth Inchbald and Sophia Lee among them, together with those uncovered by Marlyse Meyer — Elizabeth Helme, author of *Sinclair das Ilhas* [*St Clair of the Isles, or the Outlaws of Barra*] (1803), and Regina Maria Roche, author of *Amanda e Oscar* [*The Children of the Abbey*] (1796).[34] There was also a considerable number of anonymous works and of novelists generally associated with the 'popular novel', that is, works whose literary quality was limited and which were destined to feed the novel market and to meet the demands of the reading public in Britain and France.

The seclusion of Brazilian women, their limited education, and the circumscribed world in which they lived made them a privileged public as far as the consumption of *feuilletons* and popular novels was concerned, a situation very similar to that of British women in the eighteenth century. Confined to the domestic sphere and within the borders of the patriarchal family, Brazilian women of status were denied access to the open world of the streets, where only prostitutes and slaves could roam unaccompanied. Familial and social control over their lives also constrained their access to education and a professional life. Motherhood, home and family were the only occupations in which they could engage, and marriage was the only means for them to ascend socially or to maintain their status, and was always a matter of familial concern and interest. With the gradual introduction of bourgeois habits and values in Brazilian society, mainly during the second half of the nineteenth century, women became responsible for the family and the education of their children. Handed over from the authority of their fathers to that of their husbands, young women had very little room for intellectual development, and their main accomplishments included playing an instrument (usually the piano), embroidery, and, if they were literate, reading.

Given the scarcity of available data, it is difficult to make generalizations about reading habits. However, judging from the number of circulating libraries established in several regions of the country, mainly in the second half of the nineteenth century, it appears that the activity of reading novels became more widespread. A study by Ana Luiza Martins records the presence of almost twenty circulating libraries in the state of São Paulo alone, scattered across the province.[35] Her survey confirms the predominance of the genre, especially *feuilletons*, and the massive presence of foreign authors in translation, among them Scott and Dickens. This expansion was certainly an object of concern, which may explain Júlia Lopes de Almeida's complaint at the end of the nineteenth century about the pernicious effects that reading novels might have on women. She warned women against 'detrimental, unwholesome novels, filled with romantic adventures and dangerous heroes', while recommending works of a morally uplifting nature.[36] Almeida undoubtedly echoes the authoritative voices of the medical and psychological theorists, writers of advice manuals, reviewers, periodical journalists, and educators who had laboriously attempted to control women's reading throughout the nineteenth century in Britain, worried as they were about the imaginative fulfilment of desire or the affective power which reading might entail. Rather than celebrating its beneficial potential, essayists and reviewers often speculated about the dangers of novel-reading, its corrupting and morally debilitating action, mainly to women.[37]

To a certain extent, Horace's maxim *Omne tulit punctum qui miscuit utile dulci*, touchstone of the eighteenth-century British novel, also crossed the Atlantic to Brazil.[38]Surprisingly, however, it appeared more often in response to demand on the part of the critics than as an essential component of Brazilian novels themselves. In some critical texts, this demand is explicit, and fiction is expected to fulfil an edifying function, thus contributing to the development of virtue and good habits. For the novelist Antonio Gonçalves Teixeira e Sousa, '[t]he aim [...] of the novelist is (if the background of his work is fabulous) almost always to present the beauty of nature, to delight and moralize'.[39] The 'first manifestations of fiction in Bahia' also had, according to David Salles, a moralizing goal and valued example, moral correction, and the edification of good principles.[40] Published in periodicals that were intended to spread civilizing habits and introduce new European works, these short fictional exercises set in motion the usual Romantic machinery (villainy, incest, coincidences, surprises, seduction, last-minute revelations) in order to tell a story that set good moral examples of behaviour and condemned vice.

Fearful of the nefarious effects that novel-reading could have over young ladies, the genre's first critics hastened to insist that writers pay attention to morality and virtue. Such is the case of Dutra e Mello's criticism of *A Moreninha* (1844), published in *Minerva Brasiliense* on 15 October 1844, and also of the article published in *Guanabara* in 1855 about *Vicentina* (1853), both novels by Joaquim Manuel de Macedo:

> The novel has a modern origin; it came to substitute the romances and stories that so delighted our parents [...] Through it one can moralize and instruct the people [...] If the theatre was justly called the school of manners, the novel is moral in action. But in order for it to bring the benefits we have just admired, it must follow the rules that belong to it; it must be like a beehive of tasty honey and not a cup of deleterious poison. The people in their candid simplicity seek through it to *instruct* while *entertaining* themselves.[41](My italics)

In this comment, J. C. Fernandes Pinheiro simply echoes the opinion, common among British critics and reviewers, that the novel only justified its existence by its capacity for moral instruction, as an instrument of reform intended to instil a rising social class with appropriate patterns of behaviour. In a new society like the Brazilian one, it is not difficult to understand why some also expected the novel to fulfil its mission as an instigator or reformer of customs. The gradual re-Europeanization of Rio de Janeiro during Dom João VI's reign, exemplifying the need to introduce more 'refined' habits, brought about substantial changes in men's and women's ways of living. It altered customs dating from colonial times and made available to the emerging political, economic and social elite better education, cultural products and equipment (theatres, libraries, books and bookshops, printing shops), as well as the latest improvements of European civilization. As mentioned earlier, with the establishment of the Portuguese Court in Rio de Janeiro and, later, with the town made into the seat of the First Empire, there was investment in urbanization and a campaign to polish manners and normalize conduct. There was, therefore, a clear intent on the part of the elite to 'civilize' the people and build a national culture. Literature played a central role in this civilizing march and in the process of building a national consciousness through literary periodicals, newspapers, and the prose fiction that was beginning to be produced locally. Novel-writing became part of this cultural movement, though it was late in coming.[42] It is easy therefore to understand the interest that European novels generated among intellectuals, journalists and writers at the time.

There was also the need to justify the new genre's lack of theoretical nobility which, according to Antonio Candido, made seventeenth-century French men of letters — and, I would add, eighteenth-century British novelists as well — avail themselves of the artifice of the 'sweet remedy' (the *utile et dulci*) to overcome the perception that fiction was inferior to tragedy and epic. Because it arrived in Brazil as a genre that had already established itself in Europe, the novel did not have to struggle so hard to gain acceptance, and Brazilian novelists could quickly move on to other materials and topics, such as the everyday life of the common people. Indeed, when compared to its British counterpart, the Brazilian novel did not take long to rid itself of the blemish of being a minor and bastardized form.[43]Likewise, the genre had fewer problems embracing mimesis and the 'free play of creative fantasy', since it was directly engaged in the task of mapping out the country, its history, geography, topography and people on the one hand, and of raising a national consciousness on the other, while still looking to British and French models for guidance.[44]

As Marlyse Meyer comments, 'the fictions imagined by eighteenth-century ladies and spinsters lulled Brazilian nineteenth-century imaginations' — an observation which seems valid for writers and readers alike.[45]In her exemplary study of the *feuilleton*, Meyer shows not only the remarkable penetration of the '*romance-folhetim*' (counterpart of the popular British novels) in Brazil in the nineteenth century, but also its later ramifications in melodrama and soap operas. The formula is not at all different from the one found in popular British fiction: kidnapping, treachery, dishonour, virtue in distress, terrible villains, seduced and abandoned heroines, all combined with the realistic painting of scenes of everyday life, the valorization of domestic space, and the new role of women in the bourgeois family.

In Brazil, as in Britain, the interest in novels and romances may very well have been related to other types of changes also taking place in Brazilian society. As Nelson Werneck Sodré points out, writing about the 1860s:

> If the great majority of the public was constituted by marriageable young ladies and students, and the privileged literary theme must be, exactly because of that, marriage, a little blended with the old love motif, the press and literature, closely connected then, were bound to be led to meet this demand. Women began to free themselves, little by little, from colonial confinement and submitted themselves to the patterns of European fashion, appearing in the drawing rooms and a little on the streets.[46]

Borrowings

One of the most visible effects of what Candido calls the novel's 'state of ashamed shyness' — that is, its permanent need for self-justification — was that this also found expression among Brazilians. This explains the various artifices employed by the country's first writers of fiction aiming, on the one hand, to respond to the moralizing appeal and, on the other, to lend a certain air of truthfulness to their accounts. The assurance of authenticity was an efficient tool for convincing readers that the hours they dedicated to reading fiction were not a waste. The many attestations of veracity and the strategies used in the search of verisimilitude often seem formulaic (a mere imitation of similar claims in British novels), since by this time the suspicion against fiction had considerably diminished. In fact, there was not that much condemnation of fiction in Brazil except from very conservative quarters and the Church, and the novel there had the clear purpose of developing and stimulating a patriotic spirit and spreading knowledge about the country. However, it is not very difficult to come across some of the tricks commonly found in eighteenth-century novels, or even in nineteenth-century ones for that matter, like the recourse to old manuscripts, employed by Walpole, for instance, and as is the case of 'Olaya e Júlio, ou a Periquita':

> As a matter of fact, at bedtime, my guest trusted me with a quite voluminous manuscript, which I devoured during the night and of which, with its owner's permission, I took a copy. I cannot publish it in its entirety, it being too long; but I presume that the summary I have made of it will be worthy of my readers' attention.[47]

In José de Alencar's *Lucíola* (1862), Paulo's letters are the raw material out of which the novel is composed, employing roughly the same device as *Pamela*. There, Richardson presents himself as the editor of a correspondence that has its 'foundation both in *Truth* and *Nature*' and that was entrusted to him so that, once made public, it could become exemplary. Moreover, the recurring references to the novel's commitment to truth cannot be overlooked, as is the case in *Os Dois Amores* (1848) by Joaquim Manuel de Macedo:

> '[...] do you think novels are lies? [...]'
> 'I am sure about that.'
> 'You are very misinformed in that matter, D. Celina; novels are always founded on truth; the novelist's hardest task consists in misrepresenting that truth in such a way that his contemporaries cannot give the characters acting in it their true names.'[48]

Similarly, Manuel Antonio de Almeida's narrator apologises to the reader for the repetitions he is obliged to incur: 'It is most unfortunate for those of us who write these lines to fall prey to the monotony of nearly always repeating the same scenes with minor changes: however, we are obliged to be faithful to the times whose customs we are attempting to depict.'[49] In Alencar's *Senhora* (1875) once again, the prologue claims that the 'story is true; and the narrative comes from a person who was a confidant(e), in circumstances I am unaware of, to the main actors of this curious drama'.

A common practice among these well-known novelists, these attestations to the truth of their narrative were, even more understandably, also invoked in the works of their predecessors as they rehearsed their first steps in fiction writing. 'A Perjura', a novella published in 1838 in *O Gabinete de Leitura*, contains the epigraph '*All is true*' and also employs as its strategy a letter that one Eugênio had sent to the narrator. The letter contains the story that the latter now retells and serves as an illustration of a discussion they had had about perjury and remorse. In it, Eugênio recounts a narrative he heard from an old lady while he was on his way to a trial in Cabo Frio. This story concerns her granddaughter Henriquetta, who has been exemplarily punished for relinquishing Eduardo, the man she had promised to marry, and for letting herself be seduced by the rakish Domingos, whose lover she has become. Fate has it that Eduardo perishes trying to save her from an accident with her carriage. Henriquetta, consumed by remorse, is overcome by hallucinations and madness and eventually dies. The moral implications of the narrative and of the character's behaviour are obvious, though not a word of condemnation is uttered.

In another story, 'A Ressurreição de Amor (Crônica Rio-grandense)', published in four parts in the *Jornal do Commercio* between 23 and 27 February 1839, an atmosphere of mystery and terror predominates, conventions most certainly borrowed from the Gothic novel, as popular on this as on the other side of the Atlantic. Its distraught protagonist Francisco violates the tomb of his beloved only to discover that she is still alive, in the best tradition of the genre. Using hyperbolic language, the narrator wastes no opportunity to praise the natural beauties of his province, while he tells a tale of horror and death. With long descriptions of the natural landscape, the anonymous author struggles to establish some causal relationship between setting and plot, producing a formal fracture between the Brazilian scenery and the story of love and madness very much in the fashion of European melodrama — a narrative of thwarted love stemming from the social differences between the aristocratic Francisco, the governor's brother, and Amália, a rich but plebeian young lady.

The examples above show that early Brazilian writers of fiction not only capitalized on these artifices and arguments to persuade their readers, but also lavishly recycled the repertoire of situations, norms of behaviour, and characters borrowed from European novelistic paradigms. The moralizing mission and the reform of manners, though not always explicitly proclaimed, reveal themselves in the choice of intrigue and dénouement, with the punishment of vice and the reward of virtue, at the same time that extravagant plots, unhappy love, mystery and terror, revenge and seduction constitute the dainty dish served in slices to readers, male and female.

However, a disjuncture between form and content is nearly always evident. Attempts to provide 'local colour' through descriptions of Brazilian landscape end up making these texts out of sync with their European-shaped plots. Brazilian authors of the period were not unaware of this contradiction and its implicit rejection of realism. Thus Paula Brito, in the preface to 'O Enjeitado' (published in the 'Folhetim' section of *Jornal do Commercio*, on 28 and 29 May 1839), claims that he wishes to discard the conventions of the Gothic, leaving aside castles, feudal lords, dungeons and the supernatural in favour of 'simple narratives' and contemporary stories. He states that he is interested in recounting the lived experience of his era, rather than fantastical stories rooted in the past:

> When the books sent to us from old Europe are but remembrances of ancient ages; when after the Goths, Vandals, and feudal lords have annoyed us, today we are only presented with Vandals, Goths, and feudal feats; when, after so many sermons against the crusades, Walter Scott and other pens, if not of the same stature, then at least of superior fame, had as many sermons in their favour, [when] our imaginations are fired with the heroes of Palestine, it will be hard to believe that we appear before the public with such naive narratives; but we, whose life is recent, whose history is contemporary, whose annals are not yet concealed in the dust of old books buried at the bottom of libraries, we tell only what we see or hear, lending it only a few garments.[50]

Ironically, what follows is the narrative of the misfortunes of the lovers Emília and Júlio, both of them haunted by the mysterious origins of the young man. The bourgeois drawing room where they find themselves — very similar to hundreds of European ones — is the stage for a conversation in lofty language in which the habitual sentimental and moral clichés can be distinctly heard, without anything that might betray the Brazilian character of the story.

However, the recourse to scene and the delineation of conflict, which sound very promising in comparison with other contemporary narratives, soon give way to a long narrative summary, where the narrator takes on the responsibility of uncovering his protagonists' past. The effort to explain to his readers his characters' motivation is evident, but, in order to propel the action forward, the use of coincidences seems inevitable, and it is Emília's mother who providentially unveils the secret of Júlio's birth. In a flashback, now reporting the mother's narrative, the narrator leaves behind the bourgeois drawing room for a prosperous sugar plantation, where 'there were hundreds of slaves' and whose owner 'was feared by all who approached him for any reason'. Brazilians are at last on truly national grounds and recognize the patriarch who 'treats everybody as if they were his slaves', above all his daughters, 'whose will is never consulted'. If adultery and illegitimacy are common themes in European models, the authoritarianism, tyranny and violence in this section of the narrative are genuinely Brazilian. This juxtaposition interests Brazilian writers and readers exactly because it exposes the author's difficulties in confronting his materials. Nothing is satisfactorily tied together, from a formal point of view, although the effort to achieve some level of resolution is clear.

Narrative Paradigms

In *Formação da literatura brasileira*, Candido points to two main narrative structures, thus establishing a fundamental distinction between novels that explore the subjective layers of characters' inner lives, in the manner of Feodor Dostoyevsky and Joaquim Maria Machado de Assis, and those which deal with life as a series of related actions, where all the emphasis lies on the scene and event, and what matters is the 'larger movement of social life', as in Manuel Antonio de Almeida's work.[51] Candido thus sums up the two main paradigms that had structured plots since at least the time of Richardson and Fielding in 1740s Britain and which were closely imitated by their followers on both sides of the English Channel.

The clash between social and economic position, on one side, and virtue and the laws of the heart, on the other — which, according to Candido, is already delineated in Alencar's *A Viuvinha* (1857) and would become the central conflict in *Senhora* — seems like the transposition, to a Brazilian social milieu, of the pattern created by Richardson's *Pamela* and taken to extremes in *Clarissa*. It is not a coincidence that Alencar, in a letter to D. Paula de Almeida, declares, 'There are two ways of studying the soul: one is dramatic, similar to Shakespeare's; the other, philosophic, as in Balzac. The novelist has both at his disposal; but he should, whenever possible, choose the former, and make his characters reveal themselves in the course of action'.[52] In his comments about this method of composition, Richardson employs exactly the same arguments, which Alencar may not have read directly, but which he may have learned from the novels that he had encountered when young and which had been written by followers of the author of *Pamela* and *Clarissa*, as he testifies in 'Como e porque sou romancista'.

Also fruitful are the relations that can be established between Fielding's novelistic method, expressed in his prefaces and introductory chapters, and Almeida's *Memórias de um sargento de milícias*, in spite of the significant differences in perspective between the two novelists. Employing wit and humour, Fielding aims to set an example, which he does by advocating goodness and innocence; in the case of the Brazilian novelist, however, his criticism of the 'sad moral state of our society' (which is how his narrator describes his social milieu) is more adequately inscribed in the framework of the chronicle of manners. In both cases, however, what predominates is the logic of the event, the absence of soul-searching conflicts, and the narrator's distance in relation to that which he chronicles, characterized by a certain ironic — and at the same time playful — stance in the treatment of his material.

From 'Amélia', the short treatise on virtue by Emílio Adet, to *A Moreninha*, fiction had come a long way, not so much in chronological terms, but from the point of view of what had been learned and incorporated, thanks to the availability and accessibility of foreign models. It would fall to Alencar and Machado de Assis, Brazil's first two great novelists, to resolve and overcome the impasses and formal mismatches that had characterized the work of their predecessors. Despite their limitations, those earlier writers were essential participants in the process of acclimatizing the European bourgeois novel to Brazilian soil. Their first attempts, even if clumsy, paved the way for the more challenging and mature formal solutions found in Alencar and Machado. Of course, the acclimatization of the novel in Brazil took on a very particular shape: it became a powerful instrument in the hands of the first fiction writers, deeply engaged in the mission to construct a nation and a national consciousness. In their as yet inexperienced hands, this mission translated itself into blanket praise for what they conceived to be the most Brazilian of all subjects — its nature and its people. Later, with *O Guarani* (1875) and *Iracema* (1871), two of his Indianist novels, Alencar shaped his own imaginary version of a national literature and a hybrid cultural identity.

As noted earlier, the aura of inferiority surrounding the novel in the face of classical forms like the tragedy and the epic meant that novelists were forced to defend themselves for choosing it as their means of expression. Criticism also seems to have been guided by its demand that novelists offer readers 'the image of virtue [...] and the abhorrence of vice', as A. F. Dutra e Mello proclaims in his study of *A Moreninha*, in *Minerva Brasiliense*, in which he actually quotes Horace's precept. Exemplifying that contrast would be the noble mission of a genre that came into the world a bastard, according to many of these critics.

Yet critics did not restrict themselves to the desire for edification, having also addressed a few formal problems and offered some pointers for novelists with little experience in the new genre. They demanded fidelity to the real because of the genre's investment in domestic settings and everyday life. Nonetheless, they failed to realize that, deep down, didactic and moralizing purposes and fidelity to the real might be contradictory demands. As Alencar perceptively remarks in his foreword to *Asas de um anjo* (1858), written in response to accusations of immorality made against his comic play:

> I do not consider reality, or rather, artlessness, the reproduction of nature and of social life in the novel or in comedy, a school or a system; but the only element of literature: its soul. [...] I agree, as has been said, that at times, repulsive scenes are copied from nature and from life that decency, taste and delicacy cannot tolerate. But then the error lies not in the literature but in the writer; it is not art that renounces beauty; it is the artist who does not know how to give his picture those divine touches that gild the thickest darkness of corruption and destitution.[53]

Almost one hundred and fifty years after Crusoe stepped forward in a short preface to address his readers and justify the story they were about to read, one can still hear the echoes of similar conceptions, critiques, defences and arguments that were part and parcel of the history of the novel in Britain and France and made the period of its rise one of the richest in its history, both in Brazil and on the other side of the Atlantic.

Notes to Chapter 4

1. This essay presents the preliminary results of a research project still in progress and sponsored by two Brazilian funding bodies, FAPESP and CNPq.
2. Roberto Schwarz 'The Importing of the Novel to Brazil and its Contradictions in the Work of Alencar', in *Misplaced Ideas: Essays on Brazilian Culture*, trans. by John Gledson (London: Verso, 1992), pp. 41–77 (p. 50).
3. Antonio Candido, *Formação da literatura brasileira (momentos decisivos)*, 4th edn, 2 vols (São Paulo: Livraria Martins Editora, 1971), II, 121–22. All translations from Portuguese are mine, unless otherwise stated.
4. Schwarz, *Misplaced Ideas*, p. 41.
5. The catalogues include books covering different subjects and novels in several languages, with the exception of that of the Rio de Janeiro British Subscription Library, which only lists works in English: *Catálogo de Algumas Obras que Se Vendem na Loja de Paulo Martin (Vindas neste Ültimo Navio de Lisboa)* (Rio de Janeiro: Tip. Nacional, 1822); *Catálogo da Biblioteca do Gabinete Português de Leitura do Maranhão* (Maranhão: Tip. do Frias, 1867); *Catálogo da Biblioteca Municipal do Rio de Janeiro* (Rio de Janeiro: Tip. Central de Brown A. Evaristo, 1878); *Catálogo da Livraria de B. J. Garnier*, no. 23 (Rio de Janeiro: Tip. de Pinheiro; Paris: Tip. de Simon e Cia., 1865); *Catálogo dos Livros da Biblioteca Fluminense* (Rio de Janeiro: Tip. Thevenet SC., 1866); *Catálogo dos Livros do Gabinete Português de Leitura no Rio de Janeiro* (Rio de Janeiro: Tip. Americana de L. P. da Costa, 1844); *Catálogo dos Livros do Gabinete de Leitura da Cidade do Rio Grande de São Pedro do Sul*

(Rio Grande: Typographia do Cruzeiro do Sul de José Vieira Braga, 1864); *Catálogo de Livros Portugueses que Se Acham à Venda na Loja de Mongie* (Rio de Janeiro: n.pub., n.d.); *Catálogo das Obras Existentes no Gabinete Português de Leitura da Bahia* (Bahia: Tip. de Tourinho SC., 1868); *Catálogo Supplementar dos Livros do Gabinete Português de Leitura no Rio de Janeiro* (Rio de Janeiro: Tip. Perseverança, 1868); *Catalogue of the Rio de Janeiro Subscription Library* (London: Smith, Elder & Co., 1842); *Primeiro Suplemento ao Catálogo dos Livros da Biblioteca Fluminense* (Rio de Janeiro: Tipografia do Arquivo Médico Brasileiro, 1849). See also B. F. Ramiz Galvão, *Catálogo do Gabinete Português de Leitura do Rio de Janeiro*, 2 vols (Rio de Janeiro, 1906–07).

6. The collection comprises a wide range of titles and novelists, including works in English, French, and Portuguese. A considerable number of them can still be found in the Real Gabinete Português de Leitura in Rio de Janeiro.
7. See Chapter 8, by Maria Eulália Ramicelli, for more information about the *Revue Britannique*.
8. 'De la situation actuelle de la librairie et particulièrement des contrefaçons de la librairie française dans le nord de l'Europe', in *Revue Britannique*, 4th series, 26 (March 1840), 52–97. A table with comparative values can be found on p. 80.
9. Franco Moretti, *Atlas of the European Novel, 1800–1900* (London: Verso, 1998), p. 187. See esp. Chapter 3, 'Narrative Markets, ca.1850'.
10. Moretti, 'Conjectures on World Literature', *New Left Review*, 1 (Jan–Feb 2000), 54–68, and 'More Conjectures', *New Left Review*, 20 (Mar–April 2003), 73–81.
11. Moretti, 'Conjectures', p. 58.
12. Moretti, 'Conjectures', p. 62. 'Compromise' in its correlated meanings of 'mutual agreement', 'arrangement', 'adjustment', and 'accommodation' hardly describes what results from this encounter.
13. Schwarz, *Misplaced Ideas*, p. 46.
14. Letter to Lady Echlin, 22 September 1755, in *The Correspondence of Samuel Richardson*, ed. by Anna Laetitia Barbauld, 6 vols (London: Richard Phillips, 1804), iv, 59–60. The full quotation reads: '[...] but [I] am afraid instruction without entertainment (were I capable of giving the best) would have but few readers. Instruction, Madam, is the pill; amusement is the gilding.'
15. See Georges May, *Le Dilemme du roman du XVIIIe. siècle. Étude sur les rapports du roman et de la critique (1715–1767)* (Paris: PUF, 1963), p. 163.
16. See Françoise Parent-Lardeur, *Lire à Paris au temps de Balzac. Les Cabinets de lecture à Paris, 1815–1830*, 2nd edn (Paris: Éditions de l'École des Hautes Études en Sciences Sociales, 1999), p. 10.
17. A. N. Pigoreau, *Petite bibliographie biographico-romancière, ou Dictionnaire des romanciers tans anciens que modernes, tant nationaux qu'étrangers; avec un mot sur chacun d'eux et la notice des romans qu'ils ont donné, soit comme auteurs, soit comme traducteurs, précédé d'un catalogue des meilleurs romans publiés depuis plusieurs années, et suivi de tableaux propres à en faire connaître les différents genres et à diriger dans le choix des ouvrages qui doivent faire la base d'un cabinet de lecture* (Paris: Pigoreau Libraire, 1821–28, including supplements).
18. Ibid., 5th Supplement, February 1823, p. 18.
19. Marlyse Meyer, *Folhetim: uma história* (São Paulo: Companhia das Letras, 1996), p. 34. See also n. 28, pp. 49–50. Other French circulating library catalogues also confirm Pigoreau's prominent role in the business. Though Pigoreau is not directly mentioned in Balzac's *Illusions Perdues* (1835–43), critics generally agree that he is the model for Doguereau, the bookseller to whom Lucien de Rubempré offers his work for publication. See Pierre Citron's introduction to Honoré de Balzac, *La Comédie Humaine*, 12 vols (Paris: Gallimard, 1979), v, 54–58.
20. Nelson Schapochnik records the existence of Cremière's circulating library, on Rua da Alfândega, and those of Mongie, Dujardin and Mad Breton, on Rua do Ouvidor. See 'Contextos de leitura no Rio de Janeiro do século XIX: salões, gabinetes literários e bibliotecas' in *Imagens da cidade: séculos XIX e XX*, ed. by Stella Bresciani (São Paulo: ANPUH/Marco Zero/FAPESP, 1993), pp. 147–62.
21. 'Remainders' is a term used to refer to unsold stocks bought at reduced prices from the original publisher.
22. Laurence Hallewell, *O livro no Brasil (sua história)* (São Paulo: T. A. Queiroz/EDUSP, 1985), p. 117. France always served as a kind of role model as far as cultural artefacts and products were concerned.

23. See Harold Streeter, *The Eighteenth-Century English Novel in French Translation: A Bibliographical Study* (New York: Institute of French Studies, 1963).
24. Respectively *The Italian, or the Confessional of the Black Penitents* (1797) and *Albert, or the Wilds of Strathnavern* (1799).
25. See Marlyse Meyer, 'O que é, ou quem foi *Sinclair das Ilhas*?', *Revista do Instituto de Estudos Brasileiros*, 14 (1973), 37–63.
26. Translation of *Le Diable Boiteux* (1707) and the first novel published by Impressão Régia, in 1810, according to Rubens Borba de Moraes, in *Livros e bibliotecas no Brasil colonial* (Rio de Janeiro: LTC, 1979), p. 120.
27. Respectively *Paul et Virginie* (1788) and *La Chaumière Indienne* (1791); *A Thousand and One Nights*; *Atala* (1801); *Belisaire* (1767); *Louisa, or the Cottage on the Moor* (1789); *Gulliver's Travels* (1726); *The Life and Surprising Adventures of Robinson Crusoe* (1719); *The History of Tom Jones, A Foundling* (1749); *Life of Arnold Zulig* (1790); *Clarissa, or the History of a Young Lady* (1747–48). The information in parentheses in the body of the essay above refers to the dates when the novels were first advertised in the newspaper. From 1801, there is evidence of license requests made to the Portuguese board of censorship for the shipment of the French versions of Defoe's and Richardson's novels: *Aventures de Robinson Crusoe* (Paris, 1799); *Histoire de Clarisse* (Venice, 1788); *Histoire de Grandisson* (Amsterdam, 1777). For the circulation of books in the colonial period, see Abreu, pp. 95–97.
28. Joaquim Manuel de Macedo (1820–1882) was a doctor and man of letters. See *A moreninha* (1844; São Paulo: Ática, 1995), p. 69.
29. Gilberto Freyre, *Ingleses no Brasil: aspectos da influência britânica sobre a vida, a paisagem e a cultura do Brasil*, 3rd edn (Rio de Janeiro: Topbooks, 2000), p. 43. Both Freyre and Hallewell note that in 1832 the Tipografia Pinheiro, Faria e Cia. published, in Olinda, the novel *A Caverna da Morte*, but both wrongly attribute it to Ann Radcliffe. It must be the anonymous *The Cavern of Death: A Moral Tale* (1794).
30. See also Nelson Schapochnik's chapter about the Rio de Janeiro British Subscription Library.
31. Bookshops belonging to Villeneuve, Didot, Mongie, Crémière, Garnier, Plancher and Dujardin were all situated in this area.
32. José de Alencar (1829–1877), novelist and politician, played a central role in the consolidation of the novel in Brazil. His testimony about the importance of foreign novels to his own formation as a novelist can be found in 'Como e porque sou romancista', in *Obra Completa*, 4 vols (Rio de Janeiro: José Aguilar, 1965), I. Marlyse Meyer records references to Mrs Helme's *Sinclair das Ilhas* not only in Alencar, but also in Machado de Assis and Guimarães Rosa. See her 'O que é, ou quem foi *Sinclair das Ilhas*?'.
33. Candido, *Formação*, p. 109.
34. See the state-of-the-art listing of novels at <http://www.unicamp.br/iel/memoria/Ensaios/index.htm>. There was also the overwhelmingly popular Charles Dickens and the omnipresent Walter Scott, whose appeal has yet to be explained.
35. Ana Luiza Martins, *Gabinetes de leitura da província de São Paulo: a pluralidade de um espaço esquecido (1847–1890)* (São Paulo: FFLCH/USP, 1990). See also 'As leituras às vésperas da República', in Suplemento de Cultura, *O Estado de São Paulo* 7 (no. 486), 18 November 1989, pp. 4–6.
36. Júlia Lopes de Almeida, *Livro das Noivas*, 2nd edn (Rio de Janeiro: Francisco Alves, 1896), p. 36.
37. For a discussion of reading during this period, see Kate Flint, *The Woman Reader, 1837–1914* (Oxford: Clarendon Press, 1995) and Patrick Brantlinger, *The Reading Lesson: The Threat of Mass Literacy in Nineteenth-Century British Fiction* (Bloomington: Indiana University Press, 1998).
38. A. F. Dutra e Mello, 'A Moreninha', *Minerva Brasiliense*, 1–2, II.24 (15 October 1844), p. 747. Line 344 of Horace's *Ars Poetica* continues in line 344 with the words *lectorem delectando pariterque monendo*. The passage translates as: 'He has won every vote who has blended profit and pleasure / at once delighting and instructing the reader'. See Horace, *Satires, Epistles and Ars Poetica*, trans. and ed. by H. R. Fairclough (Cambridge, MA: Harvard University Press, 1970), p. 479.
39. Antonio Gonçalves Teixeira e Sousa, Introduction to *Gonzaga, ou a Conjuração de Tiradentes*, 2 vols (Rio de Janeiro: Typographia de Teixeira & Co., 1848–51).
40. See *Primeiras manifestações da ficção na Bahia*, ed. by David Salles (São Paulo: Cultrix-INL-MEC, 1979).

41. *Guanabara: Revista Mensal, Artistica, Scientifica e Litteraria*, vol. 3.1 (1 March 1855), pp. 17–20.
42. Teixeira e Sousa's *O Filho do Pescador* (1843) is considered to be the first Brazilian novel.
43. See Antonio Candido, 'Timidez do romance', in *Educação pela noite e outros ensaios* (São Paulo: Ed. Ática, 1987), pp. 82–99.
44. Candido, 'Timidez do romance', p. 88.
45. Marlyse Meyer, 'Mulheres romancistas inglesas do século XVIII e romance brasileiro', in *Caminhos do imaginário no Brasil* (São Paulo: EDUSP, 1993), pp. 47–72.
46. Nelson Werneck Sodré, *História da imprensa no Brasil* (Rio de Janeiro: Civilização Brasileira, 1966), pp. 227–28.
47. *O Beija-Flor*, 4 (1830), 112–13. Marlyse Meyer calls this a 'Franco-Brazilian' novel and attributes its authorship to Charles Auguste Taunay.
48. Joaquim Manuel de Macedo, *Os Dois Amores* [1848] (São Paulo: W. M. Jackson Inc., Editores, 1950), XII.
49. Manuel Antonio de Almeida (1830 — 1855) wrote only one novel, *Memórias de um sargento de milícias* (1854), which became one of the most important texts in the history of the Brazilian novel.
50. See *Os precursores do conto no Brasil*, ed. by Barbosa Lima Sobrinho (Rio de Janeiro: Editora Civilização Brasileira, 1960), p. 197. It is interesting to note that the narrator indirectly shows that he is a reader of Gothic novels.
51. Candido, *Formação*, II, 215–16.
52. José de Alencar, 'Carta a D. Paula de Almeida', in *Obra Completa*, I, 1212.
53. José de Alencar, *Obra Completa*, I, 922.

CHAPTER 5

The Library that Disappeared: The Rio de Janeiro British Subscription Library[1]

Nelson Schapochnik

Seventy years after the Portuguese court was moved to its colony in Brazil in a major operation that involved the British navy and Lord Strangford, the writer Machado de Assis wrote a column in the newspaper *O Cruzeiro*, in which he commented on a confectioner's book of recipes. With a gentle irony displaying the hallmarks of Sterne, he ingeniously made use of this event to compare the practices of domestic science (as seen in the preparation of coconut candy and quince jam) to the changes in eating habits introduced by the British who resided in Rio de Janeiro:

> Now, what was our situation like ten or fifteen years ago? Ten or fifteen years ago, an alien body crept into our eating habits — raw steak. This anglicism is only tolerable to people like Oxford students who alternate their studies with regattas and clutch their oars with the same hands with which they browse Hesiod. These anglicisms show that, as well as not being able to adjust to our Fluminense way of life, they feel a repugnance for our customs and traditions. Despite this, raw steak has become part of the eating habits of this country; raw steak *for ever*, that is the motto of this generation.
>
> [...] Most people are prepared to meet the urgent demands of their stomach with a sandwich, which is no less foreign than a raw steak and just as revolting; or else they are content with a potato croquette which is equally high class and foreign; and the decadence and death of traditional sweets now seems inevitable.[2]

Presenting this in the form of 'confectionological literature' seems to adopt quite a clever approach because, while seemingly banal and commonplace, it suggests to the reader a different attitude toward aspects of anglicisms in culture. This is because, as well as having a linguistic and culinary effect on the city, the expansion of traders and the increased variety of their merchandise led to the introduction of a new pattern of consumption that affected many aspects of everyday life such as clothing, transport and accommodation, among other things. This social upheaval also involved the establishment of new cultural institutions and practices. The Rio de Janeiro British Subscription Library was one of these new spaces for 'sociability' and interaction, and it helped forge a certain identity among the British community by means of a literary culture.

Trade and Sociability in the Book World

The establishment of the British Subscription Library followed the pattern evident in other foreign communities that settled in Rio de Janeiro in the first decades of the nineteenth century. In promoting a community life where literary culture was sacrosanct, these institutions helped to lessen the feeling of being in exile and at the same time provided information, knowledge and pleasure to their members.

It should be noted that these earlier developments included the founding of foreign institutions with their origins in Prussia, Rhineland, Austria, Holland, Denmark and Switzerland, which represented the native countries of the remaining mercenaries and military officers from the regiments of the King's battalion, diplomats, traders eager to make a fortune, and artisans from small provincial centres who were seeking to escape poverty. In 1821, the *Gesellschaft Germania* [German Society] was founded in Rio de Janeiro. By frequenting the German Society, its members could strengthen their bonds of identity, support a kind of brotherhood of sociability, and even, via their association, have a certain degree of distinction bestowed upon them. The internal organization of this institution reflected a desire to search for a space that could provide a feeling of conviviality and leisure time, characterized by nocturnal meetings motivated variously by a desire to kill time in the card rooms and billiard halls or perhaps to share a 'schnapps' and cigar with the readers of newspapers, magazines, and books that were available in the library.[3]

The traders, craftsmen, civil servants and military officers from the British legation in the imperial court were instilled with a communal and Protestant culture which reinforced their reading habits and also led to the founding of a 'reading-room'.[4] According to the testimony of Ernest Ebel, in 1824 the Sala de Leitura Birnie, located in Rua Direita, was already in use. This consisted of a library that was maintained by subscriptions, largely from members of the British community:

> You can find almost all the English daily newspapers there, two French papers, the *Correspondent* of Hamburg — these papers are all sent over in batches which the English fairly regularly bring from Europe every month; in this way, we can keep abreast with everything that is going on in the world.[5]

Those who frequented Sala Birnie found that it provided them with a close link with 'everything that is going on in the world', and allowed them to obtain information every month on different perspectives on the fluctuations in international exchange, international trade, conflicts between liberalism and the restored forces of the *Ancien Régime*, and so on. No other data about this communal organization of the British in Rio de Janeiro have been located. However, this undertaking may have been the precursor of another institution, which involved a certain amount of daring, whether through setting up an agency with more subscribers, or through the inflow of a greater amount of funds — and also by the size of the collection that was gathered there.

According to the minutes written in an old, leather-bound notebook, a meeting took place on Tuesday, 1 August 1826, at which 150 British citizens in Rio de

Janeiro gathered together in the premises of the Hotel Imperial. The purpose of this meeting, which soon became a large gathering, was to organize the creation of an institution destined to be the Rio de Janeiro British Subscription Library. The concise document sets out in clear terms a short statute on how the society should be run, with the objective of 'obtaining the most popular works in English for the benefit of the subscribers'. Furthermore, in this document, Article 8 stipulated that 'all the works purchased by the institution will be written in English'.[6]

Reading this statute reveals similarities between the institution and the so-called 'voluntary societies' studied by R. J. Morris in the context of training British urban elites. Morris underlines the fact that despite the wide range of subjects ('from poverty relief, medical aid, moral reform, public order, education and thrift to the diffusion of science and culture and organization of leisure'), as well as the associations' nature and size, and number of members, these associations include an institutional feature that he called 'subscriber democracy'.[7] The voluntarist logic that governed the community feeling of the Rio de Janeiro British Subscription Library members was also based on this procedure, since Article 6 of its brief statute declared that those interested in becoming members should be able to afford 'the sum of 12$000 *réis* [twelve thousand *réis*] as an admission fee to form a fund for the immediate purchase of books and other expenses relating to the formation of the institution and also to pay a stipulated rate of 12$000 *réis* [twelve thousand *réis*] for the annual subscription'.[8]

The adoption of this organizing principle had a special effect on the reading room. Originally conceived as a formal institution that provided a particular kind of regulated leisure, this space for sociability was distinguished by its commercial, public, and unrestricted character similar to a café or club in terms of the rituals pertaining to appearance, dress code, the hierarchies of respect, and the conventions expected in aristocratic drawing-rooms.[9] These meetings were mediated by the financial subscriptions required from each subscriber and adopted a linguistic protocol that both excluded people and gave them an identity. They allowed their members to take part in meetings and late gatherings while also ensuring that they could have access to the books available in the library. However, this membership soon turned into a misogynist circle that could alleviate the feeling of isolation and transitoriness experienced by the subscribers.

It should be emphasized that the organization of the library fulfilled a purpose that was distinct from that of the institutions that formed the social entities and clubs set up by the British community in Rio de Janeiro. While the British Subscription Library attempted to introduce a kind of leisure activity that would ensure access to scientific culture and the national literary scene, the British Benevolent Fund sought to satisfy the need for social support by means of philanthropy. In its turn, the freedom of worship enshrined in the Treaty of 1810 allowed the construction of a British Episcopal Church, which was established in Rua dos Barbonos. The Treaty also lifted the restrictions on the burial of foreigners who did not profess the Catholic religion, resulting in the establishment of the *Cemitério dos Ingleses* [English Cemetery], which was financed by the British Burial Ground Fund and was situated in Praia da Gamboa.

A strong argument for the organization of this voluntary library can be found in the comments made by the Reverend C. S. Stewart about the everyday activities of foreigners in the city of Rio de Janeiro. He refers to the primacy of the world of work in leisure activities, the oddity of the customs of the people, the disorderly use of public space, and the lack of places that allow meetings to be held — all of which give rise to incisive notes expressed in the following terms:

> Mr. Dick Cunningham tells me he never can get a game, and laments the unsociable character of Rio society and their aversion to all kinds of exercise, which strikes him after ten years' life in India, as much as, and more practically, than it does me. And Rio Brazilians do not seem to meet any more than the English foreigner: there is no Park, nor Prado, nor Prater, no open-air or even covered place of meeting in the whole city or suburbs, and there are very few private reunions or parties of any size. There is not even one decent café or restaurant with seats in the streets or open air, as there are in every town in Southern or Central Europe. The people seem to live only for business — and to do none.[10]

In the light of this desolate situation recorded by Stewart on the kind of leisure activities available in Fluminense society, it is easier to understand the attraction for British citizens of participation in the general meetings in the reading room. Thus it will not come as a surprise that many of the matters raised in the inaugural meeting were left to be resolved by a future directorship at a more opportune time. These subjects included the following: the choice of books, a suitable pattern for book-binding, the appointment of the librarian and the agents responsible for the acquisition of the books, the most convenient place for operating a library and having a reading room, the formatting of the catalogue, the measures necessary to obtain tax exemption for books, the proposed lending period and the imposition of fines.

Later, when it had undergone a number of revisions that were discussed at the meetings of the institution, a short statute laid down the main guidelines to ensure the survival of the association in its initial stages. About two weeks after its foundation, the management board deliberated about what kind of reading material should be offered to the subscribers. Although no official policy has been recorded, the decision was made to begin the list with periodicals and magazines under subscription; they then added that these would soon be at the disposal of the subscribers. This list included the following: *Edinburgh Review*, *London Quarterly Review*, *New Monthly Magazine*, *Blackwood's Magazine*, *Edinburgh Monthly*, *Westminster Review*, *Magazine of Ireland*, *Dumfries Magazine*, *Ackermann's Repository*, *Literary Gazette*, *Kaleidoscope*, *Pamphleteer*, *Edinburgh Journal of Science*, *Philosophical Journal*, *Scientific Review*, *The Oriental Herald*.[11]

Although library funds were initially restricted to purchasing periodicals, by the end of the 1820s the range of listed items impressed the missionary Robert Walsh. In an enthusiastic note, he recorded the success of the undertaking in the following terms:

> They have lately established a circulating library, well supplied with all the recent publications in Europe, and also a newspaper [the *Rio Herald*], which I believe is now discontinued.[12]

The book containing the minutes of the meetings shows that there were two distinct features of the internal hierarchy of the institution. The first of these was the vertical structure of its executive board, which included at least three key positions: the president, the secretary, and the treasurer. These posts were established at the founding meeting and an area of responsibility was set out for each position. Apart from hierarchical and operational distinctions, they all had something in common that underlines the voluntary character of the association: none of the active members who comprised the executive board was remunerated.

Attention should be paid to the fact that, as a rule, the honorary position of president of the institution was that of a figurehead and involved opening the normal sessions or reading the minutes that had been prepared in advance by the secretary. This notwithstanding, he had the 'casting vote' when this was necessary. Although the applicant for the post of president was always ratified by the electoral process, it was not uncommon for the position to be filled by the person of highest status in the community. It should be stressed that, in the same way as similar institutions founded in Great Britain in this period, the British Subscription Library was planned to attain its objectives without having to rely on government aid.[13] This explains the absence of members of the diplomatic corps or any representative of the judiciary. In particular regard to the post of president, this was generally occupied by wealthy businessmen or leading figures in the *Igreja Episcopal Britânica* [British Church Fund], the *Cemitério dos Ingleses* [English Cemetery], run by the British Burial Ground Fund, and the *Sociedade Inglesa de Beneficência* [British Benevolent Fund].

The secretary had more onerous duties and, to a great extent, it was he who ensured that the institution was run smoothly. The full range of his responsibilities can be illustrated by the fact that he was mandated to conduct negotiations with the owner of the Exchange Hotel for a lease concerning the rent at a rate of 600$000 [six hundred thousand *réis*] per annum. The expenses included the facilities of the British Subscription Library, examining and contracting typography to prepare the library catalogue, 'which could not be printed in the city for less than 100$000 *réis* [one hundred thousand *réis*]', contracting agents in the London bookshops to dispatch the titles requested by the associations, and handling and transferring the assets of those members who were in debt to the institution.[14] It was also the responsibility of the secretary to arrange for necessary information to be published in the Rio press so as to ensure the smooth running of the association, as is made clear in the announcements reproduced below:

> Notice is hereby given that the Half-Yearly Subscriptions to the Rio de Janeiro British Subscription Library are now due, and if not paid on or before 15th Inst. fines will be incurred according to the Regulations. Samuel Norris, Secretary.[15]

> The proprietors of the British Subscription Library are requested to attend the General Meeting, to be held at the rooms, on Monday 19th Inst. at 11 o'clock, a.m. Rio, 16 January 1857, R. Francis, Secretary.[16]

> A general meeting will be held at the Library, Saturday the 30th Inst. at 4p.m., for the purpose of receiving the report at the Committer [*sic*], and taking into consideration the code of laws lately drawn up. Rio de Janeiro, 15 September 1864, Robert W. Garret, Secretary.[17]

The treasurer was responsible for the book-keeping and a range of accounting activities that included managing the revenue from the subscriptions (receipt of entrance fees, annuities, and fines) and the commitment to pay the expenses necessary to maintain the association (rent, gas bills, payments to suppliers, and municipal taxes), as well as preparing the balance sheet and the financial report that was issued at the annual general meetings. Although it did not form a part of the directorship of the club, the post of librarian was filled by different members, and the job involved checking the books were kept in order on the bookshelves, controlling the flow of books being borrowed and returned, and making sure that the required degree of decorum and silence was maintained in the reading room.

The second hierarchical feature, which was more horizontal, was implemented some years before at the British Subscription Library and brought about a distinction between two categories of members: 'proprietors' and 'non-proprietors'. The first group had to bear the cost of an entrance fee of 20$000 *réis* [twenty thousand *réis*], which was used to compile and add to the collection and for the normal expenses of the association, as well as an annual fee of 12$000 *réis* [twelve thousand *réis*]. The financial contribution gave the 'proprietor' the right to exercise his vote in the general meeting, which enabled him to intervene in decisions, make recommendations, and even stand as a candidate for the governing board. In the second group, the six-monthly subscription was reduced from 14$000 to 12$000 *réis* [fourteen thousand to twelve thousand *réis*], and as a result, its voting power was revoked. This meant that the 'non-proprietor' could only enjoy the lending services of the library and the use of the reading room. Although accepted by most of the members, this arrangement stirred up a 'heated debate'.[18]

Since the sole purpose of the *Minute Book* was to record the minutes of the meetings and assemblies held in the period 1826–34, it was necessary to search through the advertisements published in the *Almanack Laemmert* (and later in the pages of the *Jornal do Commercio*) for information that would allow us to retrieve the names of the governing board. It should be noted that although the statutes of the British Subscription Library expected annual changes in the people who filled the different posts of the board of governors, Table 5.1 shows a certain tendency to keep on some of the members, and even to add to their responsibilities.

Despite the fact that there are lacunae and that this prevents speculation about the size of the inner circle of members, Table 5.1 opens up a number of avenues for understanding the socio-professional position of the members of the British Subscription Library. Among those who assumed the presidency, the clergy of the British Episcopal Church stand out, together with 'foreign traders', as they are designated in the list of names in the *Almanack Laemmert*. In the other posts, the hegemonic presence of traders is repeated in the information supplied by the same almanac. Under this general heading, the following 'foreign traders' appear (Adam Hogg, Vibert, Diogo MacGrowther, Andrew Muir, W. Morrisy, Charles Schwind Jr, Joseph Forest Fry, Richard Francis, J. U. Naylor, Henry Miller), 'trading agents' (John Moore), 'business agencies and commissions' (Albert Tootal), 'consignment of foreign wares' (E. W. May), 'imports and exports' (William Ford), 'dealer in merchandise' (Geo. E. Cox), and 'manufacture, storage, and shops for roasted coffee'

Year	President	Treasurer	Secretary
1826	Stewart Ruthven McKay		
1831		Adam Hogg	Robinson
1832	Vibert	Southam	Robinson
1842	Vibert	Southam	Jordan Crewse
1846			Samuel Norris
1850			S. M. Waddington
1851	Frederick Benjamin	Thomas J. Tovey	Henry Whittle
1852	Diogo MacGrowther	Henry Chrisholm	William Morrissy
1853–55	F. Morphew	F. Morphew	George L. Hall
1856	Rev. George Graham	Rev. George Graham	Henry Miller
1857	Richard Francis	Richard Francis	Henry Miller
1858–59	Rev. George Graham	Rev. George Graham	Richard Francis
1860–62	Henry Miller	Henry Miller	W. P. Campbell
1863	Joseph Fry	William C. Carré	Thomaz Fred. Tove
1864–65	J. U. Naylor	Collin Mckenzie	R. W. Garret
1866	William Ford	Collin McKenzie	R. W. Garret
1867	William Wilson	M. Carroll	Marine T. W. Chandler
1868–69	A. Whittle	Rob. Duncan	E. Stewart
1870–71	Rev. George Henry Preston	Albert Tootal	R. W. Garret
1872	Rev. George Henry Preston	Charles Schwind Jr	R. W. Garret
1874–75	E. W. May	Andrew Muir	R. W. Garret
1876	Andrew Muir	–	R. L. Hyde
1877–80	Andrew Muir	H. R. Brodie	R. L. Hyde
1881–82	Andrew Muir	Andrew Paterson	R. L. Hyde
1883–84	–	Alfred F. Youle	James S. Benest
1885–88	Rev. F. Young	Edward J. Smart	Geoffrey E. Cox

Table 5.1. British Subscription Library Directorship (1826–88)
Data taken from *Minute Book* (1826–1832), vol. 1;
Jornal do Commercio (1842 and 1846); *Almanack Laemmert* (1846–88)

(Alfred F. Youle). It should be emphasized that the areas of responsibility of these board members were not confined to commercial activities. It was not uncommon for some of them to act as guarantors of loans and suppliers of credit, or to mingle with members of the Portuguese-Brazilian community to finance other economic ventures (such as exports of coffee, navigation companies and insurance companies), or even be involved in introducing facilities into the urban infrastructure. In this case, it is significant that one member, John Moore, also appears on the almanac list identified as a 'banker', and that the institution accepted on its governing board the presence of an administrator (Colin McKenzie) and an engineer (James S. Benest) from Rio de Janeiro City Improvements Company Limited.

While admission to the club would confer prestige and recognition on the members of the lowest class of the British community, at the same time there was a need to seek financial support to ensure the maintenance for the undertaking — that is, the need to attract new members and subscriptions encouraged the adoption of company employers as a strategy for filling the governing board. As a result, some of the posts were occupied by illustrious figures or those whose reputations had been firmly established through positions they had held or activities they had carried out in other voluntary and professional societies. The application of this procedure is evident in the case of members of the clergy who held positions on the Board and who, in a tacit way, were employed by other directors who may or may not have simultaneously held positions and responsibilities in the British Burial Ground (Henry Miller), the British Church Fund (Charles Schwind Jr), the British Amateur Athletic Association (H. R. Brodie and Geoffrey E. Cox), and the *Associação Comercial do Rio de Janeiro* [Rio de Janeiro Commercial Association] (Albert Tootal).

Without a doubt, the donations not only helped in the acquisition of new works for the collection or for maintaining and purchasing items designed for the comfort of the members, but also served as a strategy of self-promotion. In this case, the qualities and acts of generosity displayed led to the donor being endowed with an aura of dignity, and through his good example he could act as an inspiration for other members of the British community to make the same gesture and emulate what he had done. The closing down of commercial activities in Rio de Janeiro and the return of the British to their home country represented a significant occasion when this image of benevolence was publicly acknowledged, as can be seen in this news item published in *The Anglo-Brazilian Times*:

> The British Library here has received, through Messrs. John Moore and Co., and from Mr. Colin McKenzie, on his retirement from Rio, a donation of 100$000 *réis* [one hundred thousand *réis*]. While thus marking his appreciation and kind remembrance of an institution which is so great to our English-speaking population here, Mr. McKenzie has, at the same time indicated how other old members of the British Library might gracefully and advantageously assist so valuable an institution. The Library is thoroughly self-supporting but additional support would enable its supplies of current literature to be increased and thus make it more attractive and more useful to a resident population cut off here from many of the social and intellectual amusements enjoyed at home.[19]

In the same way that the lacunae in the documents belonging to the institution prevent us from estimating or even inferring the number of members, it is not possible to understand the reason for the institution constantly changing sites, or even to know if it chose its own site. Throughout its journey through different kinds of buildings (commercial halls, hotel rooms, and residential dwellings), it was clear that, from time to time, all the objects and furniture comprising bookshelves, books, tables, chairs, ornaments and other items that ensured the comfort of the members and subscribers were moved to new premises that were not always large enough for all the furniture.

As a means of providing an insight into these removals, Table 5.2 provides the addresses that appeared in the advertisements published in *Almanach Laemmert* and in the *Rio News*.

Aside from the periods 1851–53, 1863–66, and 1874–77, all the other leases lasted for a period of five years or more. Thus, just as it is possible to see a regular period

Period	Address
1826–32	Largo do Paço, 14
1844–50	R. das Violas. 38
1851	R. da Quitanda, 143
1852–53	R. do Sabão, 3 (2nd floor)
1854–62	R. Direita, 48 (2nd floor)
1863–66	R. Direita, 44
1867–72	R. da Quitanda, 157
1874–77	R. de São Pedro, 55
1878–87	R. do Ouvidor, 48 (2nd floor)
1887–92	R. dos Ourives, 35 (1st floor)

TABLE 5.2. British Subscription Library addresses as given in the advertisements published in *Almanach Laemmert* and in the *Rio News*.

Period	Timetable
1844 – 51	9 a.m. to 8 p.m.
1852	10 a.m. to 6 p.m.
1853 – 55	9 a.m. to 12 a.m.
1856 – 62	9 a.m. to12 a.m., 2p.m. to 5p.m.
1863 – 66	6 a.m. to 10 p.m.
1867 – 69	9 a.m. to 9 p.m.
1870	8:30 a.m. to 12 a.m., 3 p.m. to 6p.m.
1871 – 75	8:30 a.m. to 11 a.m., 2 p.m. to 6 p.m.
1876 – 84	2 p.m. to 6p.m. (weekdays) 1 p.m. to 5 p.m. (Saturdays)
1885 – 88	12 a.m. to 6 p.m. (weekday) and 1 p.m. to 5 p.m. (Saturdays)
1889 – 92	12 a.m. to 6 p.m.

TABLE 5.3. British Subscription Library opening hours

between the changes of the institution, probably as a result of contracts, it is also clear that all the locations listed are situated around the centre of the city, in an area that includes the customs house, business district, sugar mills, wholesale stores and various shops. In this way, despite repeated moves, the site of the membership library was generally found close to different workplaces.

From the advertisements published in *Almanack Laemmert*, it is possible to work out the timetable that the institution followed, as Table 5.3 shows.

It is notable that it was only in the periods 1844–52 and 1863–69 that the institution made its facilities available to members after 6 pm. The restriction of opening hours largely to match those of commerce and public administration seems to indicate that the library did not engage employees to carry out the relevant functions, but depended on volunteers drawn from the membership or the governing body. It may be added that the option of operating by way of morning and afternoon sessions might indicate a deliberate strategy for saving on lighting costs, by making the best use of available daylight. Finally, the fact that a large number of members of the British Subscription Library were dealers and owners of trading houses that presumably granted them a degree of freedom in frequenting the premises of the club and withdrawing books during business hours should not be underrated.[20]

The traveller Robert Elwes raised quite a plausible suggestion when he reflected on the restricted periods during which the library operated. In his view, 'there is not much society for a stranger in Rio de Janeiro, for the English residents mix but little with the natives [...]. Another drawback is that the English live chiefly in the country, at a distance of four or five miles, and leave town after business hours and ride home'.[21] Again, the question of the lack of interaction or sentimentality between the members of the British community, caused by their obsession with work, is combined with valuable information about the fact that this group prefers to live in zones that are far from the centre and raise a family in the tropics, the style of life that they identify with countryside dwellings. This decision to seek places with a milder climate, owing to the altitude and the existence of the shade from vegetation, is also supported by the opinions of hygienists who found that contagious diseases were more likely to spread from the miasmic mangrove swamps that were located in the part of the city with the lowest altitudes.

As has already been shown, the kind of sociability that emerged from the facilities of the British Subscription Library contrasted with the orality and musical soirées of the drawing-rooms of Brazilian aristocracy. Its private and non-profitmaking character distinguished it from the well-known conviviality of the cafés, although the habit of smoking and drinking while reading a paper was not forbidden. The kind of social practices that evolved there showed close ties with recreational societies (music, clubs and literary societies). The group of subscribers was undoubtedly not uniform, and there were probably sharp differences of opinion about politics and religion as well as of social status. Nonetheless, they shared a space for socializing, which was eventually endowed with legitimacy, as it was rooted in the spread of a literary culture. Moreover, the members were stimulated to hold discussions and debates and encouraged to read books, magazines, and newspapers, which offered features for broadening knowledge and values. In this way, processes of differentiation were established among the members, which helped forge an awareness of themselves as an urban middle class.

These different degrees of contrast and similarity between the circles and the associations frequented by the British community in the city of Rio de Janeiro did not evolve at a constant rate or with increasing intensity, but varied in accordance with social conventions and the degree of their commitments. Eventually, the process ceased, as recorded by a merchant who lived in Rio de Janeiro in the 1840s, and who, returning in the mid-1870s, found extensive alterations to the spaces that some of the members of the British community had frequented:

> When I lived here in the years 1848 and 1849, there was much sociability — amongst the English residents at all events — but this appears to have quietly died out, and even ceremonial visits are now rarely exchanged. The only society worthy of the name existing in Rio is that associated with the diplomatic circle, which is of course more or less exclusive in its character. I must nevertheless notice one institution in which I found a great change for the better. I mean the English Church. A good deal of money has been spent in connection with this edifice, entirely raised by private subscriptions, and certainly it has been

well spent. The recess built for the communion table is very pretty, and the organ is well placed, in a line with the body of the church. There is a good choir, the whole arrangements being very complete, and the service efficiently performed. The Rev. Mr. Preston is chaplain.[22]

In whatever manner, whether as a result of having a social base that was suitable for holding events or through its symbolic role in the most extensive group of members of the British community established in Rio de Janeiro, the British Subscription Library was recommended as a space for the assemblies and meetings of other clubs and celebrations. This is revealed in the news about the gatherings published in the Fluminense press:

> Notice is hereby given that a general meeting will be held at the British Library on Thursday 24th Inst. at 4.30 p.m. for the purpose of electing new members, and transacting other business connected with the Rio British Cricket Club. By order of the Committee, William S. King, Secretary.[23]

> The British Residents are hereby invited to attend a Meeting to be held this day at 11 o'clock, at the Rooms of the British Subscription Library, for the purpose of considering a form of welcome to be given to His Royal Highness Prince Alfred, Duke of Edinburgh, expected shortly to arrive at this Port. Rio de Janeiro, 3 July 1867.[24]

> The Annual General Meeting of the British Benevolent Society will be held at the British Subscription Library on Saturday, 26th Inst., at 1 p.m., when the yearly Report and Statements of Accounts will be presented and the Committee elected for the ensuing twelve months. The attendance of Subscribers is particularly requested.[25]

Approaches to the Collection Using Catalogues

In accordance with its statutory provisions, the purpose of the British Subscription Library was to promote the practice of reading, and to achieve this it was necessary to provide the members with access to a wide range of printed material. The initial decision was to seek subscriptions to newspapers and magazines that summarized and combined wide fields of knowledge, and added controversial articles about current political issues.

In the same meeting that decided what kind of periodicals would be ordered by the institution, the subscribers who were present drew up some guidelines that helped to form the collection. The first of these concerned the large amount of financial resources that would be spent on acquiring textual artefacts and thus a monthly fund of twelve pounds was established. Following this, it was agreed that this amount would be made available to the London agents, Smith & Elder, who became responsible for the purchase and dispatch of periodicals and books. The exclusive rights obtained by the London agents was based on the respectability they had obtained in the book market, together with their experience in publishing and, equally important, the fact that they offered a small discount.[26] Finally, it was agreed that in the case of 'popular works', they would be sent in batches of 'two, three or four collections, one of which had uniform binding and the others with a paperback cover'.[27] This last decision implies that an index was supplied on the kinds of distribution and use of the collection; that is, the bound collections had to remain on the bookshelves of the institution, although in the case of the other collections — according to the standard guidelines — subscribers who wished to consult them in the reading room could access them.

Unfortunately, the minutes of the British Subscription Library have a large lacuna which prevents us from knowing how the new works were obtained (whether by donation or by acquisition), or the precise number of members, or even the agreements and disagreements between the subscribers and the governing board about their wishes and suggestions. However, it was possible to determine that, at certain times, the assets of the association benefited from the acquisition of the library in the Clube do Livro that existed in the city, and also from sporadic donations.[28]

As Christian Jacob points out, 'L'accumulation des livres n'est pas une mécanique sans conséquences [the accumulation of books is not a mechanism without consequences], but follows the criteria of choice and selection that, even when not explicitly witnessed in the whole library, makes the library a 'lieu de la mémoire' [place of memory]. As a result, far from being a neutral space 'où se déposent les strates des inscriptions laissées par les générations passées' [where the strata of lists left by past generations are clearly laid out], they represent a stage for negotiations between 'les limites et les fonctions de la tradition, les frontières du dicible, du lisible et du pensable, la continuité des généalogies et des écoles, la nature cumulative des champs du savoir ou leurs fractures internes et leurs refondations' [the limits and effects of traditions, the frontiers of the sayable, readable and thinkable, the continuation of genealogies and schools, the cumulative nature of fields of knowledge or their internal fractures and reconstructions].[29]

Since the directorship had benefited from the increase in the number of members and the opportunity to add to the collection, and as there was a need to control the way the books were lent out, it complied with the decision reached at the general meeting held on 30 July 1841, when it was decided to publish the first *Catalogue of the Rio de Janeiro British Subscription Library*, under the auspices of the London agents Smith & Elder.

Published in 1842, this catalogue shows the existence of a complex collection made up of 2100 works grouped in eleven distinct categories: the first category — '*Religious Literature*, covering works on Religious History and the Church, Theology, Controversial issues, Mythology, Moral issues, Missionary work etc.'; the second category — '*Classical Literature and Philosophy*, including works about Politics, Natural History, Sciences and Arts, critical and professional works etc.'; the third category — '*Historical literature*, General History (Ancient and Modern)'; the fourth — '*Biographical Literature*, Personal history, Autobiography, Correspondence etc.'; the fifth — '*Travel*, covering works about the manners and customs of the kingdom and descriptions of the outside world'; the sixth — '*Poetry* , and dramatic literature, including all works in verse'; the seventh — '*Works of fiction*, covering works in prose, Novels, Short stories etc.'; the eighth — '*Miscellaneous*, including serialized publications works about games etc.'; the ninth — '*Reference books*, which cannot be

Category	No. titles	%
Works of fiction	555	26.42
Travel	428	20.38
Biographical literature	331	15.76
Classical literature and philosophy	286	13.61
Historical literature	146	6.95
Poetry	139	6.61
Religious literature	85	4.04
Miscellaneous	69	3.28
Reference books	36	1.71
Periodicals	15	0.71
Journals	10	0.47

TABLE 5.4. ***British Subscription Library Catalogue (1842)***
Source: *Catalogue of the Rio de Janeiro British Subscription Library.*

lent out'; and, finally, the list of 'Magazines' and other 'Journals'.[30] Table 5.4 shows in a more detailed way the range of books listed in the catalogue.

Regrettably, the catalogue strictly adheres to the guidelines sent by the commission of the British Subscription Library, which prescribes the use of alphabetical order both for the classification of the works ('to place each classification into alphabetical order'), and the need for spaces below each alphabetical entry to allow new entries ('to leave between each letter a sufficient number of blanks for the insertion of new works').[31] The adoption of this system makes it very complicated to assess the list, since the category of the work was not included. Neither are descriptive features shown (the place of publication, the name of the editor, the name of the translator, or the number of the edition), which could help interpret the practices of the directors in forming the collection, the presence of 'cultural' translations, or even the acquisition of pirated editions. It also seems wise to warn that this catalogue provides an unorthodox scheme of attribution, since many of the works are listed in a particular category or order that is very different from the standard pattern adopted in bibliographical classifications. This shows a flexibility that is partly the outcome of a constant reorganization of the order of subjects, but also of idiosyncrasies deriving from intellectual traditions, personal characteristics, and the failures of individuals to complete their task.

Before commenting on the results shown above, it should be made clear that the use of the expression 'literature' to describe the vast range of classifications covered by the catalogue shows some traces of the radical reorganization of the way discourses were formed towards the end of the eighteenth century. As Terry Eagleton points out, until that period the concept of literature was pluralized and included philosophy, history, essays, poems and letters, and conformed to certain patterns of 'belles-lettres'. The modern sense of the word 'literature' was an invention of the eighteenth century and was based on the 'creative imagination' as 'an image of non-alienated labour'. This is converted into an alternative ideology to rationalism and empiricism, and 'its task is to transform society in the name of those energies and values which art embodies'.[32]

The high proportion of 'works of fiction' in the collection of the British Subscription Library is not surprising since it corresponds to the same pattern observed in other membership libraries established in Rio de Janeiro in the same period.[33] Under the term 'works of fiction' can be found a wide range of works in prose, and it is possible to distinguish between the 'tale', 'romantic story', and the 'novel', which account for a total number of 555 or 26.42% of fiction. Although it has not always been possible to identify the author of the work mentioned, it can be clearly stated that this list largely comprises titles published by British and American writers from the second half of the eighteenth century and the first decades of the nineteenth century. This does not exclude the presence of works derived from other traditions such as *Corina*, *Don Quixote*, *Gil Blas*, *Wilhelm Meister*, *Marmontel's Moral Tales*, *The Sorrows of Werter*, or even anthologies of foreign authors translated into English. With regard to the latter, it is worth highlighting *Polish Tales* and the series of *German Novelists*, *Italian Novelists*, and *Spanish Novelists*, compiled by Roscoe.

Different kinds of narratives could be found in the category entitled 'Travel', which made up 428 works or 20.38% of the catalogue; some referred to the ordinary writing of diaries and correspondence including investigations and descriptions of landscapes and customs of a greatly varying breadth and scale, from the municipal, regional, and national level to the new and distant possessions in Africa and Asia. By means of these reports the symbolic aspects of the empire can be explored, and the appearance of representations of the 'other' and the image the Europeans had of themselves form a rich inventory.

Among the kinds of books represented by 'philosophic literature and the classics' and 'historical literature' there is common ground, since they feature works about political oratory, philosophical treatises, and accounts of war and revolutions, which, when combined, make up 432 titles, representing 20.56% of the collection.

In the category called 'Biographical Literature', exemplified by a profusion of 'memoirs', 'lives of...', 'conversations', 'reminiscences', and 'portraits', there were 331 titles, corresponding to 15.76% of the collection in the institution. The curiosity aroused by biographies among nineteenth-century readers resulted from their similarity 'both to novels and to moral speeches but, in contrast to the former, they claimed to be telling the truth and unlike the latter, they strengthened the message not with vague prejudices but with real examples'.[34] These works provided a wide range of past and present models of conduct or examples of virtuous behaviour in the political and moral sphere, based on the lives of aristocrats or middle-class people, military, religious, and political figures, and traders, lords, ladies, and commoners who were notable for some exceptional deed.

The existence of a class devoted to 'poetry', as distinct from 'works of fiction', is understandable enough, especially because it combines works of poetry, *stricto sensu*, but it also includes dramatic works. Although this only represents 6.61% of the entire collection, or 139 works, this category shows the strength of a tradition that attributes to two genres the highest place in the field of belles-lettres. When arranged alphabetically by title or by the name of the author, there are works from other schools or standpoints with a few representatives from other 'imagined communities' foreign to the British (or American) milieu, such as translations of Goethe's *Faust*, Le Gros's *Fables and Tales*, Schiller's *Don Carlos*, or Tasso's *Jerusalem*.

Although in quantitative terms the number of works listed in the category 'religious literature' was insignificant and included 85 titles (4.04%), it covered the variety of beliefs and religious controversies in the British community (which included Anglicans, Catholics, Methodists, and dissenters), while at the same time also providing accounts of the missionary activities in various parts of the Empire. Here attention should be drawn to the presence of some works that show an attempt to understand the alternative religious practices of people subjected to imperial or colonial rule, from the translation of the *Koran* by Sale, to the *Doctrines and History of Buddhism* by Upham, and *Moslems in India* by Meer Hassan Ali.

The section called 'Miscellaneous' combined a wide range of works, in particular the collection of the *Library of Entertaining Knowledge*, *Family Library* and *Lardners's Cabinet Cyclopaedia*, and many titles that were duplicated in the 'periodicals' section, as was the case with *Blackwood's Magazine* (1817–18, 1828–39), *Chamber's Edinburgh Journal* (1831–40), *Edinburgh Review* (1827–39), *Mechanics Magazine* (1831–39), *Metropolitan Magazine* (1831–39), *Mirror* (1830–34), *New Monthly Magazine* (1821–39), *North American Review* (1830–39), *Quarterly Review* (1827–40), *United Service Journal* (1829–39), and the *Westminster Review* (1824–39). The emergence of these publications was closely linked to the rise of new readers represented by different strata of the lower-middle class, urban workers, women, and children.[35] The 'miscellaneous' formula was originally adopted in the third edition of the *Encyclopaedia Britannica*, completed in 1797, and represented 'an eminently editorial strategy based on projected estimates of the reading habits of the general public which was increasingly merged with systems for the organization of knowledge conceived by societies of cultured people or by the particular steps taken by writers'.[36]

By employing the procedure of rewriting texts, selecting excerpts, and using collage, the editors of these periodicals managed to include various subjects in the same issue. These ranged from useful information about everyday activities (business, exchange, international politics, journeys of vessels) to excerpts from articles with information about scientific knowledge expressed in a simple language, to entertainment features (charades, cookery recipes, and fashion designs), or even popular fiction and stories.

Finally, it is worth drawing attention to the fact that the institution maintained the subscription of four weekly periodicals (*The Age*, *Atlas*, *Examiner*, *Weekly Dispatch*), three newspapers that came out three times a week (*The English Chronicle*, *Evening Mail*, *London Mercantile Journal*), and three other daily newspapers (*The Courier*, *Standard*, and the *Jornal do Commercio*).

The diverse material and the extent to which the collection of the library was kept up to date was commented on by the American missionaries Kidder and Fletcher who, with considerable subtlety, highlighted the specific features of some of the standard reading habits that could be found in the city around 1850, in the following terms:

> While the student at Rio may find in the national library nearly all that he can desire in the field of ancient literature, he may also easily gain access to more modern works in the subscription-libraries.

> The English, the German and the Portuguese residents have severally established such libraries for their respective use. That of the English is somewhat extensive and valuable.[37]

In the 1860s the Director of the British Subscription Library was compelled to redraft the statutes and submit them to the Council of State for their approval. The reason for this change was the scandalous demise of limited partnerships, which had been all the rage at the end of the 1850s following the euphoria of the 'prosperous times'. In the extraordinary meeting arranged by the Board of Directors and held on 29 June 1863, a number of alterations were agreed upon. These included, in particular, an increase in the annual subscription rate which rose to 30$000 *réis* [thirty thousand *réis*], through the introduction of a new article that established the need for a quorum of a half plus one for a general meeting to be held. Moreover, the legal regulations had to be updated in the event of the need for the dissolution of the institution. The new statute reiterated the objective of the association: 'to obtain books and any kind of political, scientific, and literary periodical, (both national and foreign)'. It also made books available for consultation and perusal in the reading room of the library and granted permission to withdraw books suitable for reading at home.[38]

We were restricted to examining the 1882 catalogue published by the typography of George Leuzinger, who was established in Rio de Janeiro. This was owing to the lack of any register recording the daily movement of books and the lending that was carried out, as well as the fact that it was impossible to search through the bookshelves of the association and examine the way the books had been arranged. When compared with the previous catalogue, the collection of the British Subscription Library jumped from 2100 to a new level of 3566 works, representing an increase of nearly 70%.

Newspapers were not included in this new catalogue nor were periodicals subscribed to by the institution. It was evident from reading the catalogue that arbitrary criteria continued to be adopted for the inclusion of works, while at the same time there was a new system for organizing and classifying works that involved reducing the number of entries and led to employing referral criteria through which the works were arranged in alphabetical order by author's surname. Another feature that remained was the way the collection strengthened its ties of cultural identity by virtue of the fact that the entire collection of books was published in English.

It should be noted that the 'reference books' section was subdivided into a number of categories: Annals (10), Biography (10), Business (76), Languages (21), Literature (16), Law (7), Politics (7), Arts and Sciences (55), and Miscellaneous (10).

It was clear that the way funds were obtained for the library strengthened the secular and recreational character of the association (see Table 5.5). This is evident when the number of theological works is compared with the other classes of books listed in the catalogue. A certain epistemological identification allows us to put the different headings 'Biography' and 'Travel books' (comprising 1238 works or 34.71% of the collection) together, such that they offer both a moral and narrative account of some of the great personalities of history and a picture of a number of

Classes of books	No. works	%
Novels	1205	33.79
Travel books	711	19.93
Biography	527	14.77
Miscellaneous	333	9.33
Classics	309	8.66
Drama and poetry	223	6.25
Reference books	212	5.94
Theology	46	1.28

Table 5.5. British Subscription Library — RJ Catalogue (1882)
Source: *British Subscription Library. Catalogue compiled under the direction of the committee* (Rio de Janeiro: G. Leuzinger & Filhos, 1882).

non-European societies. The books provide us with an image of evolving knowledge, shown from various angles and illustrated through factors such as genealogy, chronology, descriptions of conduct in politics, and the living testimony of the experiences of travellers. From the two standpoints of time and space, they offer a surreptitious argument that ultimately leads to a Eurocentric conception and justification of the terrible 'white man's burden'.

It is not surprising that there was a predilection for novels among the members of the library, and this remained the section with the largest supply of books. However, if this section is added to the headings 'Theatre and poetry' and 'Classics', the alteration in the total figure would indicate the presence of 1737 works, corresponding to 48.7% of the collection. This breakdown of the figures can allow a better understanding of the literary culture reflected in the institution and perhaps also a better understanding of the literary taste of the public.

Since my aim is to provide a more detailed understanding of the textual artefacts that comprise the literary section of the library, I will concentrate on examining three of the features mentioned above.

As mentioned above, prose fiction — in particular, novels — comprised 33.79% of the library collection and a total of 1205 books. This high percentage of novels in the library is significant, because until the end of the eighteenth century, novels were often not regarded as a respectable art form. It was only in the nineteenth century that they became more prestigious and began to be the literary expression of a triumphant bourgeois society. Moreover, as Lionel Trilling makes clear, the novel was the most effective agent of the moral imagination:

> It was never, either aesthetically or morally, a perfect form and its faults and failures can be quickly enumerated. But its greatness and practical usefulness lay in its unremitting work of involving the reader himself in the moral life, inviting him to put his own motives under examination, suggesting that reality is not as his conventional education has led him to see it. It taught us, as no other genre ever did, the extent of human variety and the value of this variety. It was the literary form to which the emotions of understanding and forgiveness were indigenous, as if by the definition of the form itself.[39]

The list below shows the authors with the most number of works available:

Charles Dickens — 35
Anthony Trollope — 29
Walter Scott — 28
William Makepeace Thackeray — 27
George Payne Rainsford James — 25
Edward Bulwer Lytton — 25
Mary Braddon — 21
Wilkie Collins — 20
George John Whyte-Melville — 19
Catherine Gore — 18
Margaret Oliphant — 18
Charles Lever — 16
William Black — 14
James Fenimore Cooper — 12
Benjamin Disraeli — 11
Henry Kingsley — 11
Capt. Marryat — 11
Eleonor F. Trollope — 11
Maria Edgeworth — 10
George Eliot — 10
Dinah Mulock — 10
Charles Reade — 10

The first factor that attracts attention in this list is that they are all English-speaking writers who come from Great Britain (bar one from the United States and one from Ireland). There is nothing strange about this in itself, as it seems to derive from the statutory provisions and it shows a linguistic and cultural affinity among the community of readers. Nonetheless, throughout the catalogue, there are clear signs of authors from other linguistic communities, less well represented, such as, the French: Jules Verne (9), Victor Hugo (6), Erckmann-Chatrain (5), Alexandre Dumas (3), Alphonse de Lamartine (2), Gabriel Ferry (1), Emile Souvestre (1); the Germans: Frederick Gerstaecker (2), Gustav Freytag (1), H. W. Hackländer (1), Ida Hahn Hahn (1); the Spanish: G. A. Sala (4) and Don T. de Trueba (1); the Italians: Garibaldi (1); the Swedes: Frederika Bremer (1); and the Danes: Hans Christian Andersen (3), all invariably translated into English.

This list of novels mainly comprises contemporary works and shows unmistakably that the list of works in the library was up to date. Obviously, this does not exclude works in the literary canon that attest to a national literature, which, to a certain extent, strengthened the imaginative bonds that linked this community. However, these were confined to the titles of famous writers like Chaucer (2), Defoe (1), Dr Johnson (1), and Sterne (1).

While this linguistic and historical record must have had a great effect on literary culture, it also strengthened the modern aspect of the institution. However, it is quite difficult to establish the extent to which there was a desire and ability among members of the association to be influenced by the new works and translations published by British (and to a very limited extent American) firms and the business interests of the agents of booksellers who were employed to carry out this service. Whatever may have been the strongest link, there is no doubt about the fact that nineteenth-century writers predominated, with the most popular works being different genres of novels. These can be categorized as follows: historical novels (Walter Scott, George Payne Rainsford James, Fenimore Cooper, Lord Lytton, Whyte-Melville), gothic novels (William Harrison Ainsworth), detective stories (Wilkie Collins, Mary Elizabeth Braddon), social problem novels (Charles Reade, Henry Kingsley), realistic novels (Elizabeth Gaskell, Charles Dickens, William Thackeray, Anthony Trollope, Benjamin Disraeli), and naturalist novels (George Eliot).

The tensions and social issues that characterized the Victorian era were portrayed in prose fiction and provided an outlet for their expression. These issues included the following: the pastoral and picturesque features associated with country life as opposed to the artificial life of society; the profound changes witnessed in urban life as a result of industrialization; class conflicts and enmity between individuals; the crises of conscience and existentialist dramas arising from disillusionment with the world; attacks on bourgeois philistinism and the oppression of women; the sexual fantasies and frustrations caused by rigid moral standards; and the emergence of a conspicuous form of consumerism that was in sharp contrast with the wretchedness of the working classes.

It was not by accident that many of these works were cast in the form of inquiries or reports — like a description or genuine imaginative reconstruction of a social milieu with its appropriate dialect — accounts of journeys that explored 'local colour' and the peculiar features of other stopping points, and the biographies of heroes or fictitious characters narrated in an epic manner. Finally, the genre of the novel did not reject methods that could have the fascination of a documentary, even though they invited the reader to use his/her imaginative faculty and converted the medium into a survey that involved great expectations and lost illusions, in which the writers and readers were simultaneously agents and spectators.

In Britain, the growth in the number of fictional works was broadly driven by a huge increase in literacy, and the emergence of a new reading public who combined features of the urban middle classes with those of the working class. Above all, there was the appearance of supporting media, especially magazines and newspapers, which were published in serialized form and at a very low price. Many of these works were later published in the form of books, some of which crossed the Atlantic, where they were offloaded on the Pharoux pier to cater for the tastes of those who frequented the English Library.[40]

A second factor that is a particular feature of this collection — when it is compared with the books in other libraries — is the large number of works written by female writers. Apart from those already mentioned, the following can be added: Mrs Henry Wood (9), Amelia Edwards (8), the Countess of Blessington (6), Mrs Opie (6), Harriet Beecher Stowe (6), Jane Austen (5), Marie Louise de la Ramée (5), Shirley Brooks (5), Mrs Marsh (5), Mrs T. F. Riddel (5), Charlotte Yonge (5), Sarah Tytler (5), Grace Aguilar (4), Mrs. Alexander (4), and a further fifty-two writers who appear with fewer than four books.

Although some of them disguised their identity under male pseudonyms (George Eliot, Currer Bell, Henry Wood) or added titles of address in the forms 'Mrs' or

'Miss', which hid their Christian names and allowed them to use their husband's surname or that of their family of origin, a host of female writers claimed a space for themselves among the great creators of literature.[41] They played an active role in the principal literary magazines published in Great Britain and, in commercial terms, were very successful. They were able to overcome the traditional low estimation of their sex, the difficulties in coping with the male superiority of some critics and writers, who saw them as a threat and affront to what had traditionally been regarded as a male preserve.[42]

Although not all of these writers were doctrinaire feminists, their works addressed the hardships and troubles experienced by women in different social classes, through moralistic plots in a romantic setting. It is not by accident that the issue of stereotyping the good woman/housewife, cases of marriage of convenience, and of female altruism were exploited in novels and detective stories. In dealing with the lives of their characters, these included detailed descriptions of cases that involved betrayal, bigamy, scandal and boredom that arose from class conflicts or clashes of temperament between the protagonists, as well as the misfortunes and failures of love affairs.

Although women were not the only readers of novels, they were treated as the main target of romantic and popular fiction. According to Martyn Lyons,

> the fact that so many readers of novels were women, seems to confirm the prevailing prejudices about the role of women and their intelligence. Novels were believed by some people to be suitable for women because they were seen as being governed by their imagination and with a limited intellectual capacity that was frivolous and emotional. Novels were the antithesis of practical and instructive literature. They made few demands on the reader and were only designed to give pleasure to people with free time on their hands.[43]

'Poetry books and plays' were responsible for 6.25% of the collection of works in the library and were represented by 223 books. The authors with the most works available were as follows:

Alfred Tennyson — 11
Edward Bulwer Lytton — 10
Henry Wadsworth Longfellow — 7
Robert Browning — 6
James Sheridan Knowles — 6
Thomas Moore — 6
Charles Mackay — 5
Schiller — 5
William Morris — 4
J. E. Reade — 4
Walter Scott — 4
Charles Algernon Swinburne — 4
Robert Southey — 4

The same time frame is found for the works of poetry as for the novels, with a predominance of nineteenth-century authors. The names that stand out are representatives of romantic poetry (Thomas Moore, Walter Scott, Southey), who alongside Coleridge (1) and Wordsworth (1), wrote in verse forms that included sonnets and lyrical ballads, often expressed in a colloquial language that was a reaction against an artificial classical style, and on subjects that included national and popular topics. The list of names cited above also included writers who broke away from accepted romantic conventions in the area of aesthetics, such as Tennyson, Longfellow, Robert Browning and Swinburne.

The catalogue also includes other poets who belong to the distinguished tradition of British culture. This made available other poets within the tradition of poetry and included John Dryden (1), Gay (1), Alexander Pope (2), Edward Young (1), Oliver Goldsmith (1), William Cowper (1), 'Ossian' (James McPherson) (1) and the contemporary poets Shelley (1), Lord Byron (1), J. Greenleaf Whittier (3), Leigh Hunt (2), and Edgar Allan Poe (1). With regard to poets in other languages, there were only two translations: Goethe (1) and Tasso (1). Finally, mention should be made of the striking absence of John Donne, William Blake and John Keats.

The plays were mixed with the books of poetry and, astonishingly, only the works of James Sheridan Knowles, an actor and dramatist who was highly regarded in the period and a leading modern author of tragedies, and the German Schiller had a large number of works in the collection. There were also works by the Elizabethan dramatists Shakespeare (1), Marlowe (1), and Beaumont and Fletcher (1), and the Restoration playwright Dryden (1).

The last section to be examined is what can be classified as 'classics', which accounted for 309 books or 8.66% of the library's collection. This section is far from representative of all the authors and works of antiquity, since those of Greek origin were confined to Plutarch, and only Pliny and Cicero featured among the writers from Rome. Moreover, it should be remembered that the existence of a category called 'Classics', which is kept separate from the 'Novels' and 'Poetry and plays' section, might be an indication of the empowerment of Foucault's concept of 'discursive formations', which were traditionally confined to the area of belles-lettres.

Nevertheless, it is an unmistakable fact that this old formula for organizing knowledge was undermined, since books of a distinct character were still kept among the 'Classics', and these included works of a surprisingly broad range and variety of forms and genres. Although most of them constituted literary works, the small sample shown below provides a glimpse of the eclecticism of this section:

Jeremy Bentham — 5
Thomas Carlyle — 5
George Combe — 4
Thomas De Quincey — 4
William Hazlitt — 4
John Ruskin — 4
Lord Henry Peter Brougham — 3
John Foster — 3

Mixed in with works on political philosophy, such as writings by Jeremy Bentham, Thomas Carlyle, and Lord Brougham, were essays on literature and social questions by Thomas De Quincey and William Hazlitt, and books on art by John Ruskin. Other important figures can also be found in the collection, including world-famous philosophers (Francis Bacon, David Hume, John Stuart Mill), an American essayist (Ralph Waldo Emerson), historians (Macaulay, H. Buckle, Robert Southey, G. H. Lewes), poets and essayists (Addison, Goldsmith, S. T. Coleridge, Charles Lamb), satirists (Swift and Thackeray), novelists and short-story writers (Sterne, Walter Scott, Edgar Allan Poe, Henry Kingsley,), publicists, pamphleteers, and political commentators (Swift, G. Canning, Burke, Macaulay), and travel writers (Thomas Ewbank, John Mawe, Richard Burton, Louis Agassiz, Charles Darwin). There were also some foreign authors in the English-speaking community, such as the French (Guizot, Montesquieu, Chateaubriand, Mme du Deffand, and T. A. D'Aubigné) and the German (Schlegel, Humboldt, and Schiller).

In the light of this heterogeneity and breadth of works, it seems reasonable to consider two alternatives when attempting to understand the 'Classics' category. On the one hand, exemplary works and authors are grouped together and these are expected to be imitated or praised as the most significant representatives of a particular genre, whether it is fictional or otherwise. On the other hand, it was a way of highlighting *first-rate* works, which, by being very well published and bound, could be proudly displayed by their possessor or reader and had to be arranged in a particular way.[44]

The inference made by Kidder and Fletcher that the library collection was updated and modernized through subscriptions and the improved seating arrangements of the reading rooms is supported by the fact that has already been made clear, that these changes were not confined to the first decades of the nineteenth century. This statement can be more widely applied and taken as a more general trend. As a space for social conviviality and to support a literate culture, the British Subscription Library continued throughout the century to add life to the British community and perhaps for some Brazilian readers, too. This is what is learnt from the laconic record of James Wells who, while walking along Rua do Ouvidor in the mid-1880s, not only described it as the 'Bond Street of Rio', but also added a short descriptive passage of 'the British subscription library, a great boon to the residents, and much appreciated by them'.[45]

Despite the difficulties in obtaining accounts of what the members read at the British Subscription Library, it is worthwhile citing another passage from James Wells (mentioned above), because it illustrates one of the possible effects of reading these books. After remaining for several weeks in the imperial court, he was entrusted with carrying out a long investigation that involved surveying the streets, barometric levelling, and writing reports about the districts so that the navigable traffic could travel from São Francisco to Tocantins. At the D. Pedro II railway station, with trains going to Barbacena, he observed the movements of the collection of wealthy farmers and traders, 'in white linen ponchos, patent leather boots, and Panama hats [...] loud of voice and redolent of garlic and tobacco', 'bilious-looking tradesmen, sallow clerks, fat Portuguese and a nondescript crowd of brown and black *matutos* (peasants)'. After making himself comfortable in one of the large seats, now covered with straw, he enters into an inner dialogue, which is later turned into a narrative of the journey:

> I sat down with a feeling of exultation as I realized that at last I was then fairly on my way for the long-desired dream of my youth — a long sojourn and travel

> in tropical wilds. I am afraid Defoe and his 'Robinson Crusoe', and Captain Mayne Reid and similar writers are largely responsible for the wild imaginings that they create in youthful minds, and that sends so many Englishmen out into the wide world, and makes our race such a roving one, and the British Empire so vast.[46]

The Critic and the Crisis

As already explained, reconstructing the institutional path and reading practices carried out within the precincts of the British Subscription Library is a task based on circumstantial evidence. This is because, apart from the *Minute Book* and the library catalogues, it was not possible to obtain anything about the everyday transactions of the institution (lists of members, receipts of payment of annuities and the purchase of books, records referring to the archives of the books and lending to household readers, reprimands, suggestions etc.). In addition, it was not possible to locate diaries or the correspondence of some of the members, which could have helped provide access, albeit of an indirect kind, to the records and show how the readers reacted to the various works available in the library.

Nonetheless, the production and circulation of periodicals to cater for the tastes of the British and American community during the 1880s allows an understanding of some of the representations of the association and its members.[47] One of the commonplaces that can be found in the scanty information about the institution is the perception of a crisis occurring in the British Subscription Library. Some very blunt comments appeared in the pages of *The Rio News* and *The Anglo-Brazilian Times* referring to the effects of amateurism in compiling the catalogue and its effects on those wishing to consult it. They also spoke of the problems of management in the association, which were characterized by the exclusive nature of its membership, together with attempts — not always effective — to overcome the apathy of the members and attract their interest in the paths followed by the institution.

Unlike the catalogue of 1842, which was prepared by Smith & Elder (the prestigious publishing house of the commercial bookstore in London), the 1882 catalogue was put together by a committee of members who took on the task voluntarily and then entrusted the Casa Leuzinger (Rio de Janeiro) for the printing. The edition of the new catalogue reflected the unmistakeable expansion of the number of books acquired and, under the eyes of the administrators, the need to ensure it was kept in order. But the existence of a catalogue also shows the importance of having a new instrument that could enable the reader to find what he was looking for. For this reason, it is worth recording that 'les manières de chercher et les moyens de découvrir, et ainsi les habitudes de lecture, tiennent non seulement à des questions de distinction et de l'ordre, mais aussi aux difficultés et aux facilités présentées par l'accumulation des livres sur les rayonnages' [the ways of seeking, and the means of discovering — and equally reading habits — depend not only on questions of distinguishing and order but also on the drawbacks and advantages of having a vast stock of books on the shelves'.[48] In view of this, the preparation of the catalogue necessarily required considerable expertise, a quality that the journalist of *The Rio News* did not find in the work carried out by those responsible. Not even the expenditure of time which could have been employed in other activities or the voluntary work of these people was enough to offset the dubious nature of the criteria used for classification or the many oversights recorded in the revision and preparation of the materials for publication. Its appraisal was incisive:

> This catalogue is not an inventory of goods which can be filed away with one's private papers; it is a public document, open to the inspection of all comers, and designed to last for many years. As published, it simply makes the committee and this whole community ridiculous. If permitted to stand, it will be a continual discredit to the library and its patrons. Those who subscribed for the work have a right to expect something well done; and we have no doubt but that they would gladly have paid double their subscriptions, if necessary, in order to have it done by an expert.[49]

The journalist argued that, although the aim envisaged for this type of work was to be at once an inventory and a search tool, the guidelines followed in preparing the catalogue were too confusing. To start with, it was a simple list of titles arranged in alphabetical order and grouped in new categories: novels, travels and voyages, history, biography, classics, theology, reference books, miscellaneous, plays and poems. There was not even a list of authors. He also underlined the fact that even when the person consulting it knew the title of the work, the chance of finding it in the pages of the catalogue could require a full review of listing, since for example, *Confessions of an English Opium Eater, The History of Crime*, and *Oliver Cromwell* were found together under the heading of 'Novels'; the *War Correspondence of the Daily News 1877–78* under that of 'Biography', *Studies in Animal Life, Lectures on Astronomy, On the Descent of Man, Court Fools, On Fortification, Physical Geography of the Sea, History of the Opera, The Anatomy of Melancholy, Proverbial Philosophy, Characteristics of Women*, and so on, under that of 'Classics', *Encyclopaedia of Rural Sports* under that of 'Reference' works or 'Sciences and arts'; and the *Royal Atlas* and *Narrativa da Liberação do Brazil* under that of 'Miscellaneous'. Still following the critical annotations of the journalist, the mistakes made in classification only constitute the beginning of a series of errors of attribution, through which the same author is given various entries: 'Charles Dickens figures under several designations of "Dickens", "C. Dickens", "Chs. Dickens", and "Charles Dickens"; Charles Lever generally figures as plain "C. Lever"; J. Fenimore Cooper as "J. F. Cooper"; Captain Burton as "Richard F. Burton", "Richard R. Burton" and "Rich.d F. Burston"; Thomas Carlyle as "T. Carlyle" and once as "W. Carlyle"; and unhappy Geo. Francis Train has his surname twisted into that of "Twain". A two-volume edition of *Martin Chuzzlewit* is credited to "Anthony Smith the Elder", while Dickens has the *Martins of Cromartin* added to his long list of works. In another place an entry entitled "Dixon's Two Queens" is credited to "Dixon Hepworth". The book is simply running over with such errors as these'. Finally, he points out a number of revision errors, which include titles that are completely different from those outlined in the list of works. Thus, an analogy can reasonably be established between the discomfort caused to the critical reader of the new catalogue and the misleading information of the institution.

A close and critical scrutiny of the crisis that was afflicting the British Subscription

Library was carried out in the form of a report that was published (unsigned) in the pages of *The Anglo-Brazilian Times* in 1883. By adopting a comparative standpoint, the essay drew attention to the valuable items of the Gabinete Português de Leitura [Portuguese Circulating Library] and the Sociedade Germânia [German Society], which, despite having a clear numerical difference in their collections (about 24,400 and 12,000 works respectively), were made up of modern books and periodicals that were sent from Germany, Great Britain, Portugal and France. The items in the British Subscription Library were already being described as consisting of 'a few thousands of volumes in most part composed of what in England are consigned to three-penny and sixpenny stalls, the classic authors chiefly conspicuous by their absence, the reading room adorned with about four English papers, a dozen monthlies and a gratuitous trade list, no new books added during the last year and none, we hear, to be received this year also'.[50]

As well as the diverse nature of the collection and the effect this could have on attracting potential readers, the critic queries the reasons for the decline of the association. Again, he contrasts it with the success of the German and Swiss communities which, although fewer in numerical terms, succeeded in establishing long-lived and stable socio-cultural institutions. 'So far as we know,' writes the journalist, 'no reports of its affairs are ever *published*, though possibly shown *en famille*, but it would seem as though the errors are being repeated in respect to it that ruined the British Club, which perished, we have always been told, of mismanagement of its finances, and cliquism.'[51]

About four weeks after the publication of the first essay, the journalist took up the subject again and offered the readers new arguments to understand the extent of the crisis of the association. Although it is lengthy, it is worth transcribing the full appraisal that was published:

> One cause of the miserable state of our British Subscription Library is the narrow area of its subscription list. As managed, the library is maintained virtually for the delectation, not of the British colony, but of the clerks of the principal British import and export houses, the subscriptions of all other persons being discouraged by a heavy discriminating charge against them, all who are not clerks, and even those among the favored class whose 'skippers' do not contribute 30$ to the library funds, having to pay two and a half times the clerkly subscription of 12$, the *privilege* of shareholders being to pay but *double*. We do not say that 12$ is too little, in fact, in view of the miserable literary pabulum supplied, we are inclined to think it far too much, but it is certain that the heavily discriminating tariff keeps away great numbers of persons who would otherwise subscribe. Moreover, there is a feeling outside that anyone connected with the retail trade or mechanics will be cold-shouldered — as a fact we believe that no one connected with either or with the telegraph office figures on the subscription list. However this may be, there is no doubt as to the dwindling of the subscriptions and to their insufficiency for even maintaining the existing books in decent condition after paying for the dozen or so periodicals which form almost the only remaining attraction to subscribers. The library question is in fact a question of existence. Under careless management and exclusiveness it has been going for many years from bad to worse. Evidently, therefore, the necessary reforms should be in the direction of

> placing all subscriptions on equality and of opening the subscription lists and reading room to every respectable person who wishes to subscribe — in a word, class should be subordinated to the general interest of the colony, which is to secure a *living* library stocked with the classics of at least English literature and kept up fairly with the times.[52]

This passage is a scathing attack and does not spare the administrators of the library for perpetuating admission procedures, which, far from strengthening reading habits and thus bringing together and maintaining this imagined community, supports the hegemony of a select group of traders and employs strategies of perpetuation and exclusion. It should also be noted that the clarity shown in the analysis of the different rates charged for the members and the other potential users (employees in the retail sector, mechanics and craftsmen, service providers and sailors) was discriminatory. It is possible to detect a review of this question through the adoption of a single rate that put the readers on an equal footing and placed the institution at the service of the whole community. Ultimately, the desire to emulate its rivals and the attempt to create a particular status quo through subscription, ended up by leading to an unexpected outcome — that is, the financial difficulties and insolvency experienced by the association.

Another symptom of the crisis at the British Subscription Library is shown in the information about an annual general meeting held at the institution. As has already been explained, the notifications sent out to the members summoning them to a meeting were characterized by conciseness — that is, they supplied precise information about the occasion and were published in the classified section of the paper, which received some kind of payment for the advertisement. However, the announcement that was published in the pages of *The Rio News* about the general meeting to be held on 5 July 1887 did not follow the usual standard procedures, as it was also accompanied by a short passage for which the writers of the newspaper were responsible. It explained the serious risks that faced the management in the following terms:

> We hear that this old institution is still in debt and badly supported. The present committee have been on duty three years and feel very much inclined to throw it up and to recommend the closing of the library and selling of the books. We trust some way may be found to avoid this backward step, and that something will be done to put the library on a better footing. It is hardly creditable to the English colony of this city that this most useful institution should be permitted to go to ruin in this manner.[53]

A few weeks after the publication of the summons to the meeting, the newspaper published a short note signed by the administrative committee announcing the bankruptcy of the library. However, despite this, it also announced that it was committed to restructuring the library and the enrolment of twenty new subscribers.[54] All this led people to believe that the inclusion of new members meant there was a new impetus, as well as further financial resources available.

About two months after this meeting was held, the directors of the British Subscription Library informed the public that the association had moved: 'the Library has been moved to new and commodious premises at nº35 Rua dos Ourives,

1st floor, and [...] the situation is most convenient for both ladies and gentlemen'.[55] This news about the change to new premises was in itself enough to arouse some suspicion about the strangeness of the costs and disturbance this would cause to the life of the association — but what could be said about the additional mention of 'ladies'? Although there is no official document in the statutes and regulations concerning the possible veto on women becoming members or using the reading room in the library, this is the first explicit reference to their presence. It is impossible to say whether this right to frequent the library was a commonplace fact or was adopted as a tactic to strengthen the institution. Certainly the kind of domestic reading provided to the subscribers suggests it was likely that there were female readers. Nonetheless, the kind of male influence exercised by the figure of the father, husband or brother represented a hidden form of control that may have been passed on to the reader.

The desire to strengthen the institution led the administrative committee of the British Subscription Library to issue an open letter to the editor of *The Rio News* on 28 October 1889, in which they stressed the need to join forces and rebuild the library. According to the directors, the first step was to recognize the state of calamity that had affected a part of the collection:

> It is not more than the truth to say that half the works of such writers as Scott, Dickens, Thackeray, Lytton, George Elliot [*sic*] and many others of the first rank among the novelists, are either missing from the Library, or are in such a state of decrepitude as renders them almost incapable of being read.[56]

The recovery of the collection depended on obtaining new subscribers and the effective collection of the overdue annuities, with the aim of obtaining the sum of 500$000 *réis* [five hundred thousand *réis*] which, according to the administrators, would be enough to cover the losses and bring the association back to normality. The committee stated that it could handle the situation with a fifth of the total budget and sought the assistance of the British and American communities, whose members could be the main beneficiaries from the upkeep of the library.

The committee's appeal was immediately supported by the editors of the newspaper. They soon published a declaration of support beneath an open letter, which was designed to encourage the Anglophone community to donate contributions to the library. With a good deal of perspicuity, they established a relationship between the change in the nature of the traders who had settled in Rio de Janeiro and the mishaps faced by the association, in the following terms:

> All of the old merchants of the English and American colonies in this city have been interested in its prosperity and have contributed for its maintenance. The result is a collection of books which is certainly a credit to the men who have been instrumental in building it up. Of late years, however, the Library has been permitted to fall into a state of decay. Books have been lost and worn out, and the funds for replacing them have not been supplied. In some part this is due to the changes which our colony has undergone. The old-fashioned merchant is no longer making Rio his home; he is leaving his Brazilian business to managers, or junior partners, all younger men and less interested in building up a library, or a club, in a place which they consider their residence for only a few brief years. Then, too, they have not the funds at their disposal that

> their predecessors had. All these features have helped to diminish the support which the Library has been accustomed to receive. The necessities of this really creditable and useful institution, however, are steadily increasing, and we trust the foregoing appeal will arouse the English-speaking residents of the city to the need of meeting at least a part of them at once.[57]

The final trump card for reversing this state of dissolution, which had lingered on for almost ten years, was the introduction of guidelines that, to a large extent, had already been laid down. By altering the rates and conditions of subscription, the managers of the library introduced changes which came close to providing equal rights of use. The new regulations stipulated that the subscriptions must be paid in advance and that it was up to the member to decide on the rate of 30$000 *réis* or 18$000 *réis* per year [thirty thousand or eighteen thousand *réis*]. The two choices provided the member with the right to take out four books and two magazines or two books and a magazine, respectively. In addition to this new measure, two other alterations were introduced with the aim of satisfying the requirements of the new members of the Anglo-American community, thus ensuring the subscriptions needed for the upkeep of the library. The first of these stated that 'employees of subscribing firms, banks, etc, admitted for payment of 12$000 *réis* [twelve thousand *réis*] annually, with the right to two works and one magazine'. The second catered for the interests of temporary residents who would be 'entitled to use the Reading Room, without the right of taking out books, for a monthly subscription, paid in advance, of 3$000 *réis* [three thousand *réis*].[58] All this leads to the conclusion that this measure had a palliative effect and ensured the upkeep of the library for a brief period.

The gradual disappearance of news, notes and references about the British Subscription Library in the Fluminense press anticipated the brutal termination of that project for accumulating books and knowledge over a period of several decades, during which it had added to the cultural lives of the Anglophone community in Rio de Janeiro by providing a great deal of pleasure and learning. Although it had once been a space of 'sociability' for the British merchants and a stage for the politics and culture of this imagined community, it finally succumbed to the pressures placed on it through a reduced number of readers and subscribers. It had followed the pattern of so many other libraries in fluctuating between a 'place of memory' to becoming a ruin and place of oblivion.

Notes to Chapter 5

1. Translation by Frank Hansen and proofreading by Alexandra Gardiner and Madeleine Brook. The translation of this chapter had the financial support of the Research Committee of the Faculty of Education, University of São Paulo.
2. Machado de Assis, 'Notas semanais', *O Cruzeiro*, 2 June 1878. Machado de Assis, *Chronicas*, 4 vols (Rio de Janeiro: W. C. Jackson, 1958), iv, 12–14.
3. On the *Gesellschaft Germânia*, see Nelson Schapochnik, *Os jardins das delícias: gabinetes de leitura e bibliotecas no Rio de Janeiro imperial* (São Paulo: FFLCH-USP, 1999) (PhD Thesis in Social History).
4. On the relationship between Protestant book culture and measures taken to found reading clubs and libraries by subscription, see Roger Chartier, 'A biblioteca entre o reunir e o dispersar', in

A aventura do livro (São Paulo: Ed.Unesp, 1998), p. 122 [*Le Livre en révolutions*. Entretiens avec Jean Lebrun (Paris: Éditions Textuel, 1970)]. In addition, for an understanding of the reading practices and the spread of printing among the Protestant community of New England, see David D. Hall, 'The Uses of Literacy in New England, 1600–1850', *Cultures of Print* (Amherst: University of Massachusetts Press, 1996), pp. 36–78.

5. Ernest Ebel, *O Rio de Janeiro e seus arredores em 1824* (São Paulo: Nacional, 1972), p. 119. Ernst Ebel, *Rio de Janeiro und seine Umgebungen im jahre 1824 in Briesen eines Rigaer's* (St Petersburg: Gedruckt bey der Kayserlichen Akademie der Wissenschaften, 1828).
6. Respectively, Article 1 and Article 8 of the 'Estatuto do British Subscription Library' (1 August 1826). *Minute Book*, vol. 1, p. 1.
7. A 'subscriber democracy' involved the following procedure: 'Money was collected from members. The funds were distributed and activities organized by a committee and officers elected by the subscribers at the annual general meeting. One subscription, one vote, was the general rule and uncontested elections the normal practice. Normally the result was ruled by an oligarchy selected from the higher status members of the society'. R. J. Morris, 'Voluntary Societies and British Urban Elites, 1780–1850: An Analysis', *The Historical Journal*, 26.1 (1983), 95–118 (p. 101). See also the important study by Maurice Agulhon, *La Cercle dans la France bourgeoise, 1810–1848. Étude d'une mutation de sociabilité* (Paris: Armand Colin, 1977).
8. Article 6 of the 'Estatuto do British Subscription Library'. *Minute Book*, vol. 1, p. 1.
9. The shaping of these spaces for sociability in accordance with the conventions of social and cultural status appears in Maurice Agulhon, *La Cercle dans le France bourgeoise, 1810–1848*. On the case of cafés, see the provocative work of José Martí Monteverde, *La poética del café* (Barcelona: Anagrama, 2007).
10. C. S. Stewart, *A Visit to the South Seas, including Notices of Brazil, Peru, Manilla, the Cape of Good Hope and St. Helena* (New York: John P. Haven, 1833), p. 75.
11. *Minute Book*, vol.1, 17 August 1826.
12. Robert Walsh, *Notices of Brazil in 1828 and 1829*, 2 vols (London: Westley, 1830), 1, 467; in Portuguese see *Notícias do Brasil, 1828–1829* (São Paulo: EdUSP; Belo Horizonte: Itatiaia, 1985), p. 198.
13. R. J. Morris, 'Voluntary Societies and British Urban Elites, 1780–1850: An Analysis', p. 96.
14. *Minute Book*, vol. 1, 11 August 1832.
15. *Jornal do Commercio*, 8 January 1846.
16. *Jornal do Commercio*, 18 January 1857.
17. *Correio Mercantil*, 15 July 1864.
18. *Minute Book*, vol. 1, 30 July 1832.
19. *The Anglo-Brazilian Times*, 9 April 1880, p. 2.
20. See fn. 18 which suggests that the annual meeting was held at 11 o'clock.
21. Robert Elwes, *A Sketcher's Tour Round the World* (London: Hurst and Blackett, 1854), p. 51.
22. Ulick Ralph Burke and Robert Staples Jr., *Business and Pleasure in Brazil* (London: Field and Tuer, n.d.), p. 41.
23. *The Anglo-Brazilian Times*, 24 August 1865, p. 4
24. *Diario do Rio de Janeiro*, 3 July 1867, p. 4.
25. *The Anglo-Brazilian Times*, 24 August 1882, p. 3.
26. The publishers Smith & Elder were responsible for the publication of works by John Ruskin, Charlotte Brontë, Thackeray, Elizabeth Gaskell, and George Eliot, among others. The co-owner George Smith was also the founder of the periodical *The Cornhill Magazine* (1859), whose editor was Thackeray, and of the evening paper *The Pall Mall Gazette* (1865). *The Oxford Companion to English Literature*, ed. by Margaret Drabble, 2nd edn (Oxford: Oxford University Press, 1996), pp. 923–24.
27. *Minute Book*, vol. 1, 17 August 1826.
28. 'Mr. Kietchen having presented to the Committee a List of Books about to be disposed of by the Rio de Janeiro Book Club with the original cost prices thereof, the Committee authorized this Gentleman to purchase the whole or part of the works in question to be obtained at a fair reduction upon the original cost'. *Minute Book*, vol. 1, 17 August 1826.
29. Christian Jacob, *Le Pouvoir des bibliothèques. La Mémoire des livres en Occident*, sous la dir. de Marc

Baratin et Christian Jacob (Paris: Albin Michel, 1996). Portuguese edition, 'Prefácio', *O poder das bibliotecas: a memória dos livros no Ocidente* (Rio de Janeiro: EdUFRJ, 2000), pp. 13 and 11.

30. 'Contents', *Catalogue of the Rio de Janeiro British Subscription Library*. s/p.
31. Guidelines laid down at the meeting on 12 October 1832.
32. Terry Eagleton, *Literary Theory* (Oxford: Basil Blackwell, 1983), p. 17; Brazilian edition *Teoria literária: uma introdução* (São Paulo: Martins Fontes, n.d.), p. 22.
33. For works of fiction found in the *Real Gabinete Português de Leitura* (the Portuguese Circulating Library, in Rio de Janeiro), see Chapter 4, by Sandra Vasconcelos.
34. Peter Gay, *The Naked Heart* (New York: W. W. Norton, 1995). Brazilian edition, *O coração desvelado* (São Paulo: Companhia das Letras, 1999), p. 178.
35. Martyn Lyons, *Histoire de la lecture dans le monde occidental* (Paris: Éditions du Seuil, 1997). Brazilian edition, 'Os novos leitores do século XIX: mulheres, crianças, operários', in *História da leitura no mundo ocidental*, ed. by Guglielmo Cavallo and Roger Chartier, 2 vols (São Paulo: Ática, 1999).
36. On the advent of the 'miscellaneous features' and the strategies adopted by the 'scientific, literary and leisure' periodicals, see Jussara Mendes Quadros, *Estereotipias: literatura e edição no Brasil da primeira metade do século XIX, 1837–1864* (Doctoral Thesis, Campinas: IEL-UNICAMP, 1993), p. 39. In her turn, Maria Eulália Ramicelli has traced the spread of some of these practices in the cultural translation of both fictional and non-fictional works in the Fluminense press. See: *Ciranda da ficção no século XIX: Blackwood's Edinburgh Magazine no Brasil* (Santa Maria: Ed.UFSM, 2009).
37. Daniel Parish Kidder and James C. Fletcher, *Brazil and the Brazilians Portrayed in Historical and Descriptive Sketches* (Philadelphia: Childs & Peterson; New York: Sheldon, Blakeman & Co., 1857), p. 259; in Portuguese *O Brasil e os brasileiros* (São Paulo: Nacional, 1941), p. 298.
38. National Archive — Conselho de Estado/Consulta Pública (cx.534 pc.2 doc.32). *Estatutos do Rio de Janeiro British Subscription Library*, 29 July 1863.
39. Lionel Trilling, 'Manner, Morals and the Novel', in *The Liberal Imagination* (New York: New York Review Books, 2008), pp. 205–22 (p. 222). Portuguese edition, 'Costumes, moral e o romance', in *Literatura e sociedade* (Rio de Janeiro: Lidador, 1965), p. 247.
40. For an analysis of the effects of these periodicals in creating a new reading public in an English setting, see Jon P. Klancher, 'From Crowd to Mass Audience', in *The Making of English Reading Audiences, 1790–1832* (Madison: Wisconsin University Press, 1985), pp. 76–97. On the role of this 'Internacional Romanceira' as a matrix for Brazilian prose fiction, see Marlyse Meyer, 'Mulheres romancistas inglesas do século XVIII e romance brasileiro', in *Caminhos do imaginário no Brasil* (São Paulo: EdUSP, 1993), pp. 47–72.
41. Several puzzling features of the catalogue's pages, which included the use of abbreviations and pseudonyms concealing the first name of the writers, were resolved by consulting the following works: *The Oxford Companion to English Literature*, ed. by Margaret Drabble, and *Dictionary of British Women Writers*, ed. by Janet Todd (London: Routledge, 1991).
42. Peter Gay, 'The Powerful Weaker Sex', in *The Cultivation of Hatred* (New York: W. W. Norton, 1993), pp. 288–352; in Portuguese, 'O poderoso sexo frágil', in *A cultura do ódio* (São Paulo: Companhia das Letras, 1995), pp. 331–56.
43. Martyn Lyons, 'Os novos leitores do século XIX: mulheres, crianças, operários', p. 171.
44. Goulemot states that: 'On lit du Gallimard, des Éditions du Minuit, différemment: ce que signifie que la réputation publique de ces maisons prépare une écoute: du sévère au raisonnable, du sérieux au rasoir, le sens est déjà donné' [We read Gallimard, Éditions de Minuit in different ways: this means that the public reputation of these publishing houses will be given a hearing: from the severely critical to the reasonable, from the serious to the tiresome, the meaning is already given]. See Jean Marie Goulemot, *Pratiques de la lecture* (Paris: Payot & Rivages 1993), p. 122; Portuguese edition, 'Da leitura como produção de sentidos', in *Práticas da leitura*, ed. by Roger Chartier (São Paulo: Estação Liberdade, 1996), p. 113.
45. James W. Wells, *Exploring and Travelling Three Thousand Miles through Brazil from Rio de Janeiro to Maranhão*, 2 vols (London: Sampson Low, Marston, Searle & Rivington, 1887), I, 14, in Portuguese, *Explorando e viajando três mil milhas através do Brasil: do Rio de Janeiro ao Maranhão*, 2 vols (Belo Horizonte: Fundação João Pinheiro, Centro de Estudos Históricos e Culturais, 1995) I, 45.

46. James W. Wells, *Exploring and Travelling Three Thousand Miles through Brazil*, 1, 39, 41; *Explorando e viajando três mil milhas através do Brasil*, p. 63.
47. *The Rio News* was published from 1873 onwards with three monthly editions and had a representative in New York. *The Anglo-Brazilian Times* was published from 1865 onwards with four monthly editions. Its proprietors were William Scully and James Scobell, and it had representatives in London.
48. David McKitterick, 'La Bibliothèque comme interaction. La Lecture et le langage de la bibliographie', in *Le Pouvoir des bibliothèques. La Mémoire des livres en Occident*, sous la dir. de Marc Baratin et Christian Jacob (Paris: Albin Michel, 1996), p. 109. Portuguese edition, 'A biblioteca como interação: a leitura e a linguagem da bibliografia', in *O poder das bibliotecas: a memória dos livros no Ocidente*, ed. by Marc Baratin and Christian Jacob (Rio de Janeiro: Ed.UFRJ, 2000), pp. 94–107 (p. 96).°
49. 'The New Catalogue', *The Rio News*, 15 April 1882, p. 3.
50. 'Library Matters', *The Anglo-Brazilian Times*, 9 February 1883, p. 2.
51. 'Library Matters', *The Anglo-Brazilian Times*, 9 February 1883, p. 2.
52. 'Library Matters', *The Anglo-Brazilian Times*, 2 March 1883, p. 2.
53. *The Rio News*, 5 July 1887, p. 4.
54. *The Rio News*, 24 July 1887, p. 5.
55. *The Rio News*, 15 September 1887, p. 1; also reprinted in the same newspaper on 5 October 1887, p. 2.
56. 'British Subscription Library. To the Editor of Rio News', *The Rio News*, 28 October 1889, p. 3.
57. *The Rio News*, 28 October 1889, p. 3.
58. *The Rio News*, 23 June 1890, p. 8.

CHAPTER 6

The History of a Pseudo-Dumas Novel: *The Hand of the Dead*[1]

Paulo Motta Oliveira

The Rise of the Novel in Portuguese: Some Preliminary Questions

In the mid-nineteenth century, Portugal, like many countries in Western Europe, was dominated by the French novel. The data on French novels border on improbability, bearing in mind that the principal best-selling book of the 1840s and 1850s was the now completely forgotten *A virgem da Polônia* [*The Virgin of Poland*] by José Rodrigues Bastos, which went through five editions in twenty years, and that one of the most successful books of the 1860s, *Amor de perdição* [*Doomed Love*] by Camilo Castelo Branco, had to wait seventeen years before it reached its fifth edition.[2] According to Gonçalves Rodrigues, in the period 1851–60, nine translations of the novels of Victor Hugo, sixteen of Emile Souvestre, thirty-two of Eugene Sue, and an astonishing total of one hundred and five of Alexandre Dumas were published.[3]

It can be assumed that if the novel rose to prominence as an essential genre of the nineteenth century, thanks to a militant or ' guerrilla' discourse, in countries that have a peripheral status in terms of the *novelistic tradition*, the militant discourse is something else and rather more resilient: it is opposed to an avalanche of original and translated works emanating from Paris. As Roberto Schwarz has pointed out:

> The novel had existed in Brazil before there were any Brazilian novelists. So when they appeared, it was natural that they should follow the European models, both good and bad, which had already become entrenched in our reading habits. An obvious observation, perhaps, but one which has many implications... [...].[4]

The same rationale can be applied to Portugal, too. There, novels had also appeared before there were any novelists; moreover, the Portuguese public was mainly used to reading this new genre in French. When Portuguese novelists finally began to appear, they had to compete with the huge amount of French work circulating in the literary market. This meant that they had to offer the public a hybrid product that catered for the tastes of readers who had a voracious appetite for Souvestre, Sue and Dumas, but that also offered something more in terms of local colour, where the public could recognize features that reflected its own image. It was only in this way, at the decisive moment of making a purchase, that they might prefer a Camilo Castelo Branco or an Alexandre Herculano to one of the famous French writers.[5]

In the work I have undertaken in the last few years on the works of Camilo Castelo Branco, and more recently on the tension that can be found between the use of imported features of French novels and the characteristics that can be called, for want of a better word, *nationalistic*, I was led to study a set of novelistic works published in the 1840s and 1850s. This was not only in the period of the rise of Camilo but also — this can be claimed with some degree of certainty, despite the lack of more comprehensive data — the rise of the novel in Portuguese.[6] One of the rare studies on the novels of this period, the dissertation 'Uma imagem do campo literário português no período romântico: contributo para a história da literatura produzida em Portugal entre 1840 e 1860' [A View of the Portuguese Literary Scene in the Romantic Period: A Contribution to the History of Literature in Portugal in the Period 1840–1860] by Luís Sobreira, made me aware of the four most widely published books in this era. Besides the book by Bastos already referred to, Sobreira presents *Eurico, o presbítero* [*Eurico, the Priest*] by Alexandre Herculano, the short story *Maria não me mates, que sou tua mãe* [*Don't Kill Me Maria, I'm Your Own Mother*] by Camilo Castelo Branco, and then the work that is the primary focus of this essay, *A mão do finado* [*The Hand of the Dead*] by Alfredo Hogan.[7]

The Editorial History of *The Hand of the Dead*

Although these four books were all undoubtedly successful, Hogan's novel had certain features that distinguished it from all the others. It is almost certain that this work was the most widely translated Portuguese novel of the nineteenth century. No other Portuguese novel of the period was so quickly and repeatedly published in other European countries and even in Latin America. By the 1850s, it had already been translated in Spain, Denmark and Italy, and then it crossed other borders and was published in Germany, Hungary, Argentina, Mexico, and of course in Brazil. Notably, several editions of each respective translation appeared in most of these countries throughout the nineteenth and twentieth centuries (see Table 6.1).

The whole editorial history of this book is shrouded in a mystery which is difficult to penetrate today and the answers to many questions in relation to that have been partial and tentative. Before a more satisfactory explanation can be given of the problems the novel raises, a brief outline of its history is required.

In 1853, a book was launched in Paris and Portugal almost at the same time; this was a sequel of the adventures of Edmond Dantès and other characters from *The Count of Monte Cristo*. In France the book contained the following information in the cover sheets of the first three volumes: 'La / Main du défunt / par F. Le Prince / Pour faire suite au roman: / Le / Comte de Monte-Christo / par / Alexandre Dumas / Paris / Chez les principaux libraires / 1853' [The Hand of the Dead by F. Le Prince. Sequel of the novel The Count of Monte Cristo by Alexandre Dumas / Paris / At major booksellers / 1853]. In the three volumes that followed, the year was changed to 1854. At the foot of the page, to the left of the year of publication, the following imprint was given: 'Typographie Universelle d'Edouard de Faria / à

Year	Country	Title	City and Publishing House	Attribution
1856	Denmark	*Dødningehaanden*		Alexandre Dumas
1856	Italy	*La Mano del Defunto*	Milan, Libreria di Dante	Le Prince
1859	Spain	*La Mano del Muerto*	Madrid, Libreria Española	Alexandre Dumas
1860	France/Mexico	*La Mano del Muerto*	Paris, Rosa y Bouret	Alexandre Dumas
1897*	Germany	*Die Totenhand*	Stuttgart	Dumas-Le Prince†
1944	Brazil	*A Mão do Finado*	São Paulo, Cultura	Alexandre Dumas
1955	Argentina	*La Mano del Muerto*	Buenos Aires, Editorial Tor	Alexandre Dumas
1964	Italy	*La Mano del Defunto*	Milan, Editoriale Lucchi	A. Le Prince
2003	Spain	*La Mano del Muerto*	Barcelona, Debate	Alexandre Dumas

Table 6.1. A selection of editions of *The Hand of the Dead* by Alfredo Hogan published in Europe and America[8]

* The year attributed in the catalogue of the National Library of France (Bibliothèque Nationale de France). † Translator: Karl Walther.

Lisbone, rue dos Calafates no. 114' [Universal Typography of Edouard de Faria / at 114, Calafates St., Lisbon]. The four volumes of the Portuguese edition appeared without the name of the author and with the following note in the cover sheet: 'The Hand of the Dead by Alexandre Dumas / Volume I / Lisbon/ Tip. Lisbonense de Aguiar Vianna / Rua d'Atalaia no. 31/185'.[9]

Thus far, no source has been examined that can explain the procedure adopted for this dual launch, but this is not the only mystery that surrounds the work. There are two further questions for which there appear to be no straightforward answers.

The first is bound up with the attribution of the work to Alfredo Hogan, an author who has been completely forgotten. Born in 1830, he published his first novel *Dois Ângelos ou Um Casamento Forçado* [*Two Ângelos or a Forced Marriage*] in 1851.[10] Although he died young, in 1865, his works are extensive: six novels and nineteen plays, as well as a twentieth, which he wrote in collaboration with another writer of importance in that period (although seldom mentioned), Júlio César Machado (1835–90). Of all his works, though, only *A mão do finado* went beyond a first edition. The sequel of *The Count of Monte Cristo* would only be attributed to him over twenty years after his death. From what it has been possible to ascertain up to now, the first critic to make this attribution — and he made it as if it were a fact already in the public domain — was Sampaio Bruno in *A geração nova* [*The New Generation*], a book first published in 1886. In a passage in which he analyses the success of what he calls 'novels of intrigue' in Portugal in the mid-nineteenth century, he states:

> The success was unbelievable and of such a kind that, since the public could not rid itself of the unforgettable impression made by the vengeance of *The Count of Monte Cristo* [...], the national imagination demanded that Alfredo Hogan sharpen his wits and continue the amazing narrative of the inexhaustible creole in *The Hand of the Dead*, which is a *tour de force*. In this book, it is shown how a disturbed but daring spirit seeks to hold the interest of an audience that

> is transported by the delights of the most marvellous storyteller that has ever appeared in the world.[11]

Following this passage, even after the publication of several editions that have attributed the work to Dumas, all literary histories and dictionaries have regarded it as having been written by Alfredo Hogan.[12]

Similarly, there do not seem to be any explanations for a second mystery. In Portuguese-speaking countries there are two versions of the book, as well as some others that emerged later and are referred to at the beginning of this text; these have been under discussion since the nineteenth century. The version originally published in 1853 is much longer and consists of fifty-seven chapters divided, as stated above, into four volumes. Of all the accessible editions which are kept either in the national libraries of Portugal and Brazil, or in the Real Gabinete Português de Leitura, Rio de Janeiro, only one reproduces that version in its entirety, that of the Crisus publishing house in Porto in the 1960s.[13] Most of the other editions, both in Brazil and Portugal, reproduce another version comprising fifty chapters and an epilogue, which has been circulating since the end of the nineteenth century. The essential difference between the two lies in the final chapters. Whereas the last volume of the 1853 edition has thirteen chapters, the more common version changes these into only four, which means that there is a particular section in the two editions that is significantly different in size: this section accounts for more than 10% of the 1853 edition and less than 5% of the other.

This discrepancy — which it has finally been possible to verify — has not been identified by any critics of the work, nor was any attempt made by them to explain when, why, and for whom the new version had been made. Conclusions on the matter continue to be elusive. However, since the two versions are very close in terms of the factors that have been explored here, the material for this essay is the second version, because this is the version more currently in use in Portuguese-speaking countries.

The editorial history of this book includes further mysteries. As early as 1853, the same year when the book was first published in France and Portugal, the novel began to be published in instalments in the Rio de Janeiro newspaper *Jornal do Commercio*, which had previously published *The Count of Monte Cristo*. Magalhães Junior, in his *O império em chinelos* [*The Empire in Slippers*], reproduces a letter that Alexandre Dumas sent to this periodical:

> Dear Editor,
>
> I have just found out that a novel going under my name and being advertised as a sequel to *Monte Cristo*, is being published in Rio de Janeiro, that is, in one of the cities of South America where I have been attempting to become well known.
>
> I have never written, and will probably never write, a sequel to this book [...]. It would thus be greatly appreciated if your magazine, which has a good deal of influence in the literary and political world [...], could issue a denial of this news item [...].
>
> Paris, 20 November 1853 — Alexandre Dumas.[14]

But Dumas's appeal fell on deaf ears, both in Brazil and the rest of the world. It can be appreciated that a book that is launched, as this was, by a successful author can be more easily sold through these means. In 1854, for example, the novel *D. Martins de Freitas*, was published, and on the title page there appeared the following: 'D. Martins de Freitas / Portuguese historical novel / by / Alexandre Dumas / Translated by / F. P. Gonçalves'.[15] The novel was obviously not by Dumas despite being attributed to him. What makes *The Hand of the Dead* a special case is that, even though it was not immediately shown as having been written by the author of *The Count of Monte Cristo*, it continues to be attributed to Dumas and is perennially included in his works, at least in some countries. One good example of this is the *Obras de Alexandre Dumas* [*Collected works of Alexandre Dumas*], published by Lello & Irmão from the 1930s onward and which includes *The Hand of the Dead.*[16] Another example, in this century came from the launch in 2003 by a publishing house in Barcelona (Debate) of a box set containing the translation of *The Hand of the Dead* and *The Count of Monte Cristo*, which can thus be obtained together. It is particularly interesting that although there are several other sequels to Dumas's book — among which the most famous is perhaps *O filho do conde de Monte Cristo* [*The Son of the Count of Monte Cristo*] by Jules Lermina — none of these have been attributed in any concerted way to the author of *The Count of Monte Cristo.*[17] This incorporation of *The Hand of the Dead* in the works of Dumas was carried out so comprehensively that in 1955, in the prologue of the Argentinian edition of the Editorial Tor, Ricardo Padilla Gutiérrez states that 'both his novel *El conde de Monte-Cristo* [*The Count of Monte Cristo*], and the present text *La mano del muerto* [*The Hand of the Dead*], are the preferred works of his genius, as he states in his *Memórias* [*Memoirs*]' — which is a complete falsehood.[18]

We must add an apparent geographical idiosyncrasy to this improper attribution. Without doubt, the book was a success outside the region of Lusitania, but it only crossed certain frontiers. No French edition of this book other than that published in Portugal has been located until recently, and, unlike several other sequels to the novel, it does not seem to have been published in English. The book by Lermina, to cite just one example, was published for the first time in 1881 and translated into English in 1884.[19]

The Count of Monte Cristo: Traces of Capital in a Secular World

These factors — the attribution to Dumas and the spread of the book in the local region — are two sides of the same coin. The question can only be understood in the light of the way that Alfredo Hogan appropriated *The Count of Monte Cristo* and ended up radically adapting it to the ideological assumptions that underlie the book.

It is not the aim here to analyse the two books more closely and so this study is confined to a specific range of factors. The following assumes a general knowledge of the outline of Dumas's novel — how the young and successful naval officer on the verge of becoming captain and marrying his beloved Mercédès, is incarcerated in the Chateau d'If, after being accused of Bonapartist sympathies and treason, on the same day that Napoleon lands on mainland France for the fleeting period of a hundred days. While in prison, Dantès gets to know the abbot Faria who, as Antonio Candido points out, supplies him with the two essential instruments needed in the modern world — money and knowledge.[20] After taking flight and seizing the treasure hidden on the Island of Monte Cristo, Dantès is in a position to take revenge on all those who have betrayed him.

It is worth noting that the Count never ceases to injure or indirectly kill innocent people — to use a term that will return later. The best example of this is the way he avenges himself on Villefort, the deputy public prosecutor who, concerned only about his own ambitions, sentenced the unfortunate naval officer to prison, later discovering that the letter that Dantès had brought from the Island of Elba was addressed to Villefort's father, an important supporter of Bonaparte.

As part of his plan for revenge, the Count of Monte Cristo ingratiates himself with Villefort's second wife by, almost accidentally, giving her valuable information about poisons. She, a passionately devoted mother, becomes the unconscious arm of the inexorable avenger. In her wish to ensure that her son Édouard will receive an inheritance he is not legally entitled to, she poisons her first husband's parents in a calculated way — first her father-in-law and then her mother-in-law. Following this, she attempts to murder Villefort's father who escapes thanks to a medicine he was taking, and finally believes she killed Valentine, her husband's daughter by her first marriage. When the cycle seems almost to be complete, Héloise de Villefort is unmasked by the family doctor, who had been telling the public prosecutor for some time that there was a poisoner in the house. She locks herself in a bedroom and, after poisoning her beloved son, kills herself. At that moment, Dantès appears, tells Villefort who he is, and the prosecutor, already suffering from other shocks, goes insane.

The death of the boy does not affect the Count. Despite all the deaths and misfortunes Monte Cristo leaves in his wake, he does ultimately find happiness again and a golden future in the arms of the young Haydée. If this occurs in the way suggested here, it is because there is no longer any hubris; no god is going to punish him for his excesses or for his arrogance.[21] This is a completely secular world. The stage for the characters is not affected by religion or human values. In this novel, the Mediterranean occupies a central position; it is the great lake from which various beliefs and religions emerge and are declared, but which remains a world in which there are no longer any gods.

This is as a book of consummate skill. Dumas knew how to construct much more than a treatise on revenge. He provided a treatise on the secular world that was devoid of gods and in which the only forces are knowledge and capital. Instead of liberty, equality, and fraternity, it is a world of inequality in which the important thing is to have money and power, or — the book makes this clear — to mingle with the people who possess them. Everything turns out well: for the Count, the friends of the Count, whether they are criminals, like the bandit Vampa, or honourable military officers, like young Morel. It is a world driven by money and influence, personal favours, and technology. Is there a clearer portrait or more patent example of the victory of capital as that offered in Dumas's novel? However, it is also a portrait of central Europe that will be altered in a radical way by Hogan's destabilizing sequel.

The Hand of the Dead: French Setting, Christian Ideology

Before turning to the plot of this work, examining an extract from the epilogue of one of the versions of the novel provides a good basis for understanding how this radical alteration occurs:

> So that he could punish the guilty, who in any other way would escape the course of human justice, God entered the soul of a man who had suffered a good deal; however, this man was full of pride and went too far by reaching the point of injuring the innocent. He was also, in his turn, punished by the hand of a criminal who was also punished, although he showed he was filled with remorse.[22]

In this extract, the first man referred to is Edmond Dantès. The second is Benedetto, who in Dumas's novel was a false prince, the fiancé of Danglars's daughter, and also — as is only established after this incident — the son of Villefort.

By giving the reader a direct explanation, the extract illustrates what underpins the construction of the novel, as well as clarifying the way that Dumas's story is appropriated here: the paths followed by Dantès and Benedetto are explained as two stages of the will of God. Thus, from the standpoint of the way *The Hand of the Dead* is constructed, the driving force behind the action both in the sequel and in *The Count of Monte Cristo* is not based on personal desire but on a higher force that governs everything. Those who, in their blind ambition, go beyond human limits and 'reach the point where they injure the innocent' are those who know that divine authority will punish them, too. And even those who are repentant — Benedetto, for example — will not go unpunished if they have behaved excessively. The path that Benedetto follows is a religious mission, a fact he is unaware of at the time of his conversion. This ends by giving a certain degree of unity and verisimilitude to a story that is comprised of disjointed and improbable incidents. The divine hand thus serves both to show the ideological perspective that is present in the novel and to impose a sense of unity on what, without it, would be a series of implausible episodes. Some of the features of the plot can illustrate this.

At the beginning of the novel, Benedetto is in prison. He is given sixty thousand francs by his mother, whom he does not know, and following this, he kills his gaoler. He is welcomed to his home after his existence becomes known, and after spending some time at the tomb of his father, he disinters his father's hand, which he keeps as a talisman, and flees to Italy. There then follow various incidents involving several characters from the original book — ranging from his mother, Madame Danglars, to the bandit Vampa — and he obtains the money needed to take his revenge on the man who disgraced his father. He is then almost shipwrecked in a storm, during which he sees the power of God. The criminal is ready to turn himself into a divine instrument and make the Count experience the consequences of hubris, an aspect that did not exist in the original novel.

The incidents that turn a boorish and penniless murderer into someone able to shake a giant like the Count of Monte Cristo can certainly only be explained if there is a greater power protecting Benedetto. It should be noted that there is a wide gulf separating the genesis of this second avenger (and the changes mentioned above) from that of the uncultured and poor sailor into the rich and ingenious Count of Monte Cristo: Dantès had to undergo a descent into infernal regions and be shown the light by Abbot Farias, who gave him a wide range of knowledge and a huge fortune so that he could undertake this journey. In the secular world and without the gods of Dumas, only an effective power — that endowed with knowledge and money — can bring about such a complete metamorphosis. The world created by Hogan is clearly delineated. In this alternative way of presenting man's relationship with divine powers, the count himself has to find new bearings. His story has to be rewritten and his personality reconstructed. At the end of the novel, robbed of his entire fortune, and suffering from the death of his wife and loss of his son, 'Edmond went to Rome where, after making a general confession of all his sins, he took holy orders, and returning to France, went back to Marseille'.[23] Now converted to the true religious faith and a penitent, it is he who hears the last confession of Mercédès on her deathbed:

> Two days later a priest was found dead beside the grave.
> The priest was Edmond Dantès.
> The grave was that of Mercédès.[24]

Hogan 'devours' Dumas's novel in an almost cannibalistic way and in continuing it, completely changes it. It is by no means an accident that most of the plot of Dumas's novel takes place in Paris, while Hogan's book is set in Rome and Venice. Dumas's book shows the secular and utilitarian values of post-revolutionary France, where there is no longer any belief in either the old or new trinity that is spread across the Mediterranean region. Could there be any better sign of this than the Pope granting absolution to a criminal in exchange for a precious emerald? Hogan, in turn, takes a contrary course. Dantès, the old Count now converted to a penitent, returns to Marseille and brings back to France the moral values of Christianity. Heaven is filled with people again and the novel ends with the renewed rise of a Christian Mediterranean.

The enormous gulf that separates this book from another work by Hogan — *Os mistérios de Lisboa* [*The Mysteries of Lisbon*] — will not be the subject of discussion here, but it is worth pointing out that this is at the very least an anticlerical work, as well as including a scene of incest that has no effect on the two brothers unconsciously involved.[25] In view of this, it can be assumed that in rewriting the history of the Count, Hogan is not adapting it to his ideological or religious beliefs — which in fact the modern reader is not in a position to know — but that he was writing for a certain image he had of the reader he sought to reach and captivate. He achieved this so successfully that he ended up by contriving to write a best-seller — and not just in Portuguese — that was published in four editions in only seven years. Indeed, the book was published in translation in all the Christian countries of Europe and the Americas. In other words, Hogan managed to offer something that appealed to the exotic taste of the public in a world that espoused Christian values but was used to reading novels that came from France. Hogan managed to provide something that the exotic taste of these regions required — an instalment in the French style with a Christian ideology.

This theory does not only explain the unequal nature of its success, its repeated publication in some countries while being ignored in others. It also accounts for the fact that the book is attributed to Dumas in several of the countries where it has been republished. If indeed the book had been written by Dumas, we could presume that after having created a superman — by continuing and improving, to a certain extent, Rodolphe in *Os Mistérios de Paris* [*The Mysteries of Paris*] — the author had repented and returned to a belief in noble Christian values. Hence attributing the work to the author of the *Conde* results in the creation of a pseudo-biography for Dumas which redeems him from the excesses and errors he has committed. His repentance will be similar to that of Hogan's Count. The author and character renounce their secular past and, after a period of wavering, adhere to the correct faith. It is understandable why the Argentinean critic cited earlier states that these are the two books of which Dumas was most fond. They constitute the path that leads from guilt to repentance.

This theory cannot be expanded here. However, a brief example taken from the preface of a Spanish edition of 2003 claims that there are those who even 'attribute it directly to an unknown Portuguese writer who takes refuge under the name of Alfredo Hogan'. This illustrates how there has been a Christian re-reading of a secular world:

> On the trail of its huge success, I imagine that *The Count of Monte Cristo*, in turn, gave rise to an industry of serials devoted to employing and making use of this narrative thread through a series of sequels [...] that do not always achieve the literary stature of the original work.

The Hand of the Dead has always been published with the subtitle *Sequel to the Count of Monte Cristo*, and the book sets out and achieves a moral re-reading of the Dumasian character which is reflected through the narrative as a kind of poetic justice in which the concept of vengeance will be confronted with the values of mercy and forgiveness.[26]

The Hand of the Dead in Portugal and Brazil

However, despite obtaining some understanding of the publishing career of this book, we are still a long way from explaining what happened to it in Brazil and Portugal. Although my concern is primarily with the nineteenth century, my research has led me into strange regions and later periods, including the middle of the twentieth century. This unusual situation should be considered briefly here.

An important point to remember when examining the different editions of Hogan's book is that the very fact that this is a book by nobody special is one reason why it has been altered over a period of time. The most common version — the one consisting of fifty chapters and an epilogue — has undergone repeated edits and adaptations. The discussion here will be confined to only two periods in this long trajectory, which may be considered the most significant — one Portuguese and the other Brazilian.

A luxury edition of the book in a hard-backed cover and with black and white illustrations was published either at the end of the nineteenth century or the beginning of the twentieth century (it has not been possible to determine the exact date). As well as attributing the book to Dumas, the cover has the following title: *O conde de Monte-Cristo. Segunda parte. A mão do finado* [*The Count of Monte Cristo. Part Two. The Hand of the Dead*].[27]

This edition radically alters the story of Benedetto so that at the end of the story the Count does not lose his entire fortune, as is the case in the version that has been the subject of analysis so far here. It also includes a new avenger who has never been an emissary of God. This radical change is explained at the end of the book in a note by the editor, Nunes Carvalho:

> We have received a lot of letters bearing testimony to their support for our decision to begin publication of *The Hand of the Dead* as a sequel to *The Count of Monte Cristo*. We must admit that most of them show a preference for *The Son of the Count of Monte Cristo*.
>
> It has not been possible for us to destroy the first sheets that have been printed and issued, but there is still time for us to make a firm decision.
>
> The first version of *The Hand of the Dead* is seething with such rancorous hatred that it is more likely to destroy Monte Cristo than complete it, and in view of this we have decided to issue a new version that corresponds more closely to the ideas of the author of *The Count of Monte Cristo*. We believe that we have succeeded in our aim.[28]

It can be seen how much freedom is taken with the novel. The story had a first version and now a second version will be made that is more suited to contemporary taste. There is even an attempt to update the book so that it suits a new kind of public that is about to experience Republicanism or perhaps was already doing so, since the Republic was proclaimed in Portugal in 1910.

There is no room here to make a careful comparison of the two editions, although this is essential to understanding the image that the editor — or rather whoever had requested the undertaking of this new version — had of the public that was going to read the work. Nor has it been possible to locate the archives of the editor (if they are still extant), as these could throw light on how this new novel was produced.

In whatever form, this work evidently shows that *The Hand of the Dead* was turned into a no-man's-land, and liable to be appropriated and altered at the whim of the editor, or according to the image he had of the public that would purchase it. That there were three editions, each with very different features and all published in Brazil in the 1950s, confirms this point.[29]

Magalhães Junior stated, in an article published in 1957:

> The most curious thing of all is that despite the protests of Alexandre Dumas, the fraud still continues to be practised today. At present, it can be found in a volume 'Faixa Preta' ['Black Stripe'] from a so-called 'Edição segredo' ['Secret Edition'], an unwieldy kind of pocket book issued by Gertrum Carneiro and circulated in abridged form, with the name Dumas, *The Hand of the Dead*.[30]

However, as explained earlier, this was not the only edition in circulation attributed to Dumas. There are two others also published in Brazil in the mid-1950s, as well as an older edition from the 1940s. Even before this, the novel had a long editorial history in Brazil, including with Editora Literária Fluminense at the end of the nineteenth century and Editora de Monteiro Lobato in 1925, which is one of the editions used in this study.[31]

What is odd about the editions of the 1950s is that they are different from each other and form three versions. The one referred to by Magalhães Júnior is the shortest and the only one not accompanied by paratexts. It forms a part of a collection called 'Edições Segredo' [Secret Editions] published by 'Faixa Preta Romances' [Black Stripe Novels] and issued by Editora Gertrum Carneiro S. A. It has the following information on the title page: 'Alexandre Dumas / The Hand of the Dead / (Abridged) / Black-stripe Novels'.[32]

The novel is less than a hundred pages long and is preceded and followed by details of other works by the editor, as well as references to national authors, foreign authors, and works by 'the same author' — *The Count of Monte Cristo* and *The Three Musketeers* — all preceded by an 'also read' instruction; at the end of the novel there is a page with a list of twenty-four other published titles with the instruction 'Cut out and send your order'. Some of the cited titles — all of them quite similar — go some way to clarifying the kind of interest that the editor thought the readers might have in *The Hand of the Dead*: *Como se fazer amar*; *Enfermidades sexuais*; *Costumes sexuais estranhos*; *A arte e a técnica do beijo*; *A felicidade sexual no casamento*; *Problemas sexuais dos solteiros*, books that were also published by Gertrum Carneiro.[33]

Another edition of the novel is related to the world of publications linked to sexuality in an even more explicit way. The edition published by Editora Cleópatra in 1956 was in a larger format than its predecessor and the novel encompassed about 150 pages. Written on the cover, together with the name of the supposed author and the title, was 'Translated by M. A. Camacho'. The book is full of paratexts. On the jacket is a text praising Fábio Lopes Matoso for his biography of Cleopatra, published in the wake of the 'film that is being shot in Hollywood with the star Elizabeth Taylor' and written by M. A. Camacho. Following this, we are given four pages of advertisements by the publishers. The first is a short passage about the translator of the book in which he states, among other things:

> The present translation of *The Hand of the Dead* [...] was undertaken by Camacho, a mature and experienced writer with a lucid and fluent style. Translating an author with the power of Dumas is a considerable undertaking [...]. You will really enjoy reading this translation [...] because the writer, Camacho, manages to convey exactly what Dumas wrote.[34]

This is followed by another text on Cleopatra, which is a sign that the editor intended to distribute books published in Brazil by Editora Universidade Limitada of Lisbon. Finally, there are references to two authors — one, Hedda Paette, an American and the other, Simone Costallat, French — whose works the editor was beginning to publish. An extract from the text of the latter is a clear illustration of the kind of public he had in mind:

> The muse of existentialism [...], a seductive writer whose books can soothe the minds of those who are on holiday or need to refresh their spirits, [...] Simone Costallat is being read [...] by serious and responsible men who relish literature that is down-to-earth and realistic.[35]

At the end of the novel, in addition to a notification that M. A. Camacho had already translated *The Count of Monte-Cristo*, there is a statement saying: 'If you like books that are down-to-earth, realistic and honest, don't fail to read what we are offering in the following pages'. This is an advertisement for the book *Menegheti*, also by Camacho, and an extract is reproduced.

It is clear that this edition of *The Hand of the Dead* is surrounded by references to works which have a sensual appeal. This was a lead that was greatly exploited by Camacho, who wrote books of adult interest, such as *A pecadora Salomé no palácio do rei Herodes* [*The Sinner Salome in the Palace of King Herod*] and *Maria Madalena: A corrupção de Jerusalém* [*Mary Magdalen: The Corruption of Jerusalem*].[36]

The third edition of the book, which was published in 1958 by Clube do Livro, seems to be designed to attract a different kind of public. Curiously, though, it replicated a strategy similar to that adopted in the earlier editions by displaying on the title page the fact that the translation was revised by Nelly Cordes. In both cases, the translation or revision of the work was attributed to people who did not undertake it, since the books were based on Portuguese versions. Despite the attribution of the work to Dumas, its modest length (around 140 pages) and its similarity to the two other editions, a number of differences can also be found. After the cover page, there is an 'explanatory note' signed by Afonso Schmidt which provides a short account — including some dialogue — about the genesis of the novel, which is attributed to Alfredo Hogan:

> The person who wrote *The Hand of the Dead* [...] was Alfredo Possolo Hogan, a humble public official in Lisbon. He wrote it between 1851 and 1852 when he was little more than twenty years old [...]. He died unknown and in poor circumstances on 16 April 1865.
>
> [...] It would be interesting to know why the literary establishment in Portugal and Brazil pretends to know nothing about the existence of this writer.[37]

In this volume there are also some explanatory notes which tell the reader what the Tagus is, where the Island of Monte Cristo lies, as well as some other information. At the end is a voucher form for new members to fill in.

From these brief clues, it is apparent that the form of this edition seems to be aimed at a different public from the other two. The information surrounding the text of the novel seems to be designed for a public that regards itself as being sophisticated and is accustomed to reading as a means of increasing knowledge. However, something else is also evident: the book is almost a simulacrum because there are few factual notes — only seven. Moreover, it is attributed to Dumas, and there is reference to an alleged reviewer of the translation. In addition, the text of Afonso Schmidt is a small fictional piece, and although the cover is in a dull shade, it is not very different from that of the book published by Gertrum Carneiro: there is a hand and a human figure, but the hand in the foreground on the cover of the Clube do Livro edition is much more bloodcurdling with its long claws.

Although it is still not possible to understand the sudden appearance, in the middle of the last century, of a work published in the previous century, written by a completely forgotten author of plays and novels, and falsely attributed to Dumas, these three editions point to some avenues for future research. From the outset, they corroborate and strengthen the notion that *The Hand of the Dead* seems to have been remodelled and recreated for over a century, while retaining some of its original character, so that it can cater to different publics with wide-ranging tastes. This study is thus of a peculiar nature insofar as, at the same time as conducting a comparative study, it allows access to the kind of image the editors had of their target audience. Perhaps the tone in Hogan's book had a quality that made it into a success in much of the world. This success allowed a peripheral country to turn itself into an exporter of a new hybrid form, and resulted in the validation and sanctioning of new attempts at adaptation for a wide range of new publics.

In addition to this, the publication dates for the most significant alterations — around the turn of the nineteenth to the twentieth century in Portugal and in the 1950s in Brazil — point to periods in history in which there was a rise in the number of new readers among the public. In Portugal, this roughly coincided with the period when a quarter of the population had become literate — thus reaching the same level that Spain (another backward country in this respect) had achieved fifty years previously.[38] In its turn, Brazil was undergoing a period of economic expansion and, it can be presumed, this was accompanied by a diversified public readership. All this is of course vague and uncertain. However, the data brought to light here permit a glimpse of the interest that Hogan's novel aroused, and offer material for further exploratory studies.

Notes to Chapter 6

1. This chapter is an expanded version of my article 'Um sucesso quase mundial: a mão do finado ou as metamorfoses de um conde', *Veredas. Revista da Associação Internacional de Lusitanistas*, 13 (2010), 7–24.
2. Camilo Castelo Branco (1825–90) is an author little known outside Portugal but of great importance in Portuguese and Brazilian literature in the nineteenth century. His works were first published at the end of the 1840s and he remained active for over forty years, his last novel being *Vulcões de Lama* [*Mud Volcanoes*] (1886). In his most productive period (1855–80) he wrote fifty novels. On this author, see Elias J. Torres Feijó: 'Camilo Castelo Branco', in *Dictionary of Literary Biography: Portuguese Writers*, ed. by Monica Rector and Fred M. Clark (Detroit, MI: Bruccoli Clark Layman, 2003), pp. 58–74.
3. A. A. Gonçalves Rodrigues, *A tradução em Portugal* (Lisbon: ISLA, 2003).
4. Roberto Schwarz, *Misplaced Ideas: Essays on Brazilian Culture*, trans. by John Gledson (London: Verso, 1992), p. 41.
5. Alexandre Herculano (1810–77) is one of the most important writers of the first half of the nineteenth century in Portugal. See Paulo Motta Oliveira, 'Alexandre Herculano', in *Dictionary of Literary Biography: Portuguese Writers*, pp. 133–42.
6. The term novel (*romance* in Portuguese) is used here because the rise of the genre seems to have occurred in the same period in Portugal and Brazil. To give just one clear sign of this, since this matter has not been explored here, it can be noted that the works regarded as the first Brazilian novels — *O filho do pescador* [*The Son of the Fisherman*] by Teixeira e Sousa and *A moreninha* [*The Brunette*] by Joaquim Manuel de Macedo — are contemporaries of the first novels by Alexandre Herculano and Almeida Garrett — *Eurico, o presbítero* [*Eurico, the Priest*] and *O arco de Sant'ana* [*The Arch of Sant'Ana*]. All these books were first published in the period 1843–45.
7. See Luís Sobreira's contribution to the history of literature in Portugal in the period 1840–60, 'Uma imagem do campo literário português no período romântico' (unpublished master's thesis, Faculty of Arts, University of Lisbon, 1998).
8. Reference is made to only some of the editions which show the rapid spread of the novel and

the continual issuing of new editions throughout the twentieth and even the twenty-first centuries.

9. Alfredo Hogan, *A mão do finado*, 4 vols (Lisbon: Lisbonense Typography of Aguiar Vianna, 1853); Alfredo Hogan [F. le Prince], *La main du défunt*, 6 vols (Paris: 1853–54). A digitized version in French can be found in Galica <http://gallica.bnf.fr/> [accessed 6 February 2014].
10. Alfredo Hogan, *Dois Ângelos ou Um Casamento Forçado* (Lisbon: Imp. de L. C. da Cunha, 1851).
11. Sampaio Bruno, *A geração nova* (Porto: Lello & Irmão, 1984), p. 31.
12. See, for example, the entries on Alfredo Hogan by Luiz Francisco Rebelo in *Dicionário do Romantismo literário português* (Lisbon: Caminho, 1997), p. 233, and in *Dicionário cronológico de autores portugueses*, 5 vols (Mem Martins: Europa-América, 1990), II, 151, ed. by Eugénio Lisboa. See also *História da literatura portuguesa*, ed. by António José Saraiva and Óscar Lopes (Porto: Porto Editora, 1982), p. 964.
13. Alfredo Hogan, *A mão do finado* (Porto: Crisos, 1960). For a survey of books found at the *Real Gabinete Português de Leitura* [Royal Portuguese Circulating Library], see Chapter 4, by Sandra Vasconcelos.
14. Dumas *apud* R. Magalhães Júnior, *O império em chinelos* (Rio de Janeiro: Civilização Brasileira, 1957), p. 189.
15. Anonymous: *D. Martins de Freitas* (Lisbon: Hermenegildo Pires Marinho, 1854).
16. On the cover of the book appears 'A. Dumas *A Mão do Finado* and on the title page 'O conde de Monte-Cristo segunda parte A mão do finado' [The Count of Monte Cristo second part — The Hand of the Dead], Alfredo Hogan, *A mão do finado* (Porto: Lello & Irmão), p. 1.
17. Jules Lermina, *Le fils de Monte-Cristo* (Paris: L. Boulanger, 1881); Jules Lermina, *The Son of Monte-Cristo* (Philadelphia: T. B. Peterson & Bros, 1884).
18. Ricardo Padilla Gutiérrez, 'Life of Alexandre Dumas père', in Alfredo Hogan, *La mano del muerto* (Buenos Aires: Editorial Tor, 1955), p. 7.
19. Jules Lermina, *The Son of Monte-Cristo* (1884).
20. Antonio Candido, *Tese e antítese* (Rio de Janeiro: Ouro sobre Azul, 1976), pp. 29–30. English edition: Antonio Candido, 'On Vengence', in *On Literature and Society*, translated, edited, and introduced by Howard Becker (Princeton, NJ: Princeton University Press, 1995), pp. 3–21.
21. Paulo Motta Oliveira, 'Dumas, Hogan, Camilo: um romance mediterrânico e seus desdobramentos', in *Portogallo e Mediterraneo. Atti del Congresso Internazionale* (Naples: Il Torcoliere, 2009), pp. 193–206.
22. Alfredo Hogan, *A mão do finado* (São Paulo: Editora Monteiro Lobato, 1925), p. 341.
23. Alfredo Hogan, *A mão do finado* (1925), p. 343.
24. Alfredo Hogan, *A mão do finado* (1925), p. 348.
25. Alfredo Hogan, *Os mistérios de Lisboa* (Lisbon: Tip. de Luiz Corrêa da Cunha, 1851).
26. Anonymous, 'Nota del editor', in Alfredo Hogan, *La mano del muerto* (Barcelona: Debate, 2003), pp. 7–8.
27. Alfredo Hogan, *A mão do finado* (Lisbon: Nunes de Carvalho, n.d.), p. 663.
28. Nunes Carvalho, 'Duas palavras do editor', in *A mão do finado* (Lisbon: Nunes de Carvalho, n.d.), p. 663.
29. Alfredo Hogan, *A mão do finado* (Rio de Janeiro: Gertrum Carneiro, n.d.); Alfredo Hogan, *A mão do finado* (São Paulo: Cleópatra, 1956); Alfredo Hogan, *A mão do finado* (São Paulo: Clube do Livro, 1958).
30. Magalhães Júnior, *O império em chinelos*, p. 189.
31. Alfredo Hogan, *A mão do finado* (Rio de Janeiro: Empresa Literária Fluminense, n.d.); Alfredo Hogan, *A mão do finado* (São Paulo: Editora Monteiro Lobato, 1925); Alfredo Hogan, *A mão do finado* (São Paulo: Edições Cultura, 1944). For more on the Monteiro Lobato publishing house, see Chapter 14, by Cilza Bignotto and Milena Martins.
32. Alfredo Hogan, *A mão do finado* (Rio de Janeiro: Gertrum Carneiro, n.d.). The 'Faixa Preta' series was aimed at an 'adult' market.
33. Translation of titles into Portuguese respectively: *How to Make Love*; *Sexual Diseases*; *Strange Sexual Practices*; *The Art and Technique of Kissing*; *Sexual Fulfilment in Marriage*; *Sexual Problems of Single People.*
34. Rute Rosinha, 'Prefácio', in Alfredo Hogan, *A mão do finado* (São Paulo: Cleópatra, 1956), p. 1.

35. Rute Rosinha, 'Prefácio', in Alfredo Hogan, *A mão do finado*, p. 4.
36. M. A. Camacho, *A pecadora Salomé no palácio do rei Herodes* (São Paulo: Cleopatra, n.d.); M. A. Camacho, *Maria Madalena: A corrupção de Jerusalém* (São Paulo: Edições Victor, n.d.).
37. Afonso Schmidt, 'Nota explicativa', Alfredo Hogan, *A mão do finado* (São Paulo: Clube do Livro, 1958), pp. 22–23.
38. Cf. António Candeias and Eduardo Simões, 'Alfabetização e escolar em Portugal no século XX: Censos Nacionais e estudos de caso', *Análise Psicológica*, 1 (1999), 163–94.

CHAPTER 7

Revista Nacional e Estrangeira (1839–40): A Foreign or a Brazilian Magazine?[1]

Maria Eulália Ramicelli

The *Revista Nacional e Estrangeira* [*National and Foreign Magazine*] is a Brazilian political and literary periodical that is now little known in Brazil. The historian Adolfo Morales de los Rios Filho refers to it in a positive light when he presents the main characteristics of the nineteenth-century Brazilian periodical press:

> From 1839 on, the Historical Institute began to publish its own magazine. In the same year the *Revista Nacional e Estrangeira* began running; the first and only one of its kind, it was published monthly, in eighty-page issues, by a group of men of letters consisting of Pedro de Alcântara de Niemeyer Bellegarde, João Manuel Pereira da Silva, and Josino do Nascimento Silva. It brought valuable and varied content, having survived until 1845.[2]

It is highly doubtful that the *Revista Nacional e Estrangeira* lasted for so long, mainly for two reasons. First, the existing collection at the National Library in Rio de Janeiro gathers together only the issues from May 1839 (the opening issue) to December 1840. Second, the magazine seems to have met the common fate of Brazilian magazines at the time, that is, it abruptly ceased publication as a result of financial and technical difficulties. However, the *Revista Nacional e Estrangeira* would have known a period of some success, as in June 1839 the directors announced that the 'benevolent welcome' received by the magazine encouraged them to increase the number of pages per issue: from sixty-four to eighty.[3]

Literary critic Hélio Lopes also speaks favourably of the *Revista Nacional e Estrangeira* when analysing the formation of a tradition of Brazilian magazines in the nineteenth century.[4] Lopes calls attention to this magazine because it brought together two men of letters who were very active in the periodical press: Josino do Nascimento Silva (1811–86) and João Manuel Pereira da Silva (1817–98).[5] Nascimento Silva had directed *O Cronista* (May 1836–April 1839), a conservative newspaper that carried on, though inadequately, the exercise of literary criticism started in the *Revista da Sociedade Filomática* (June–November 1833), a magazine produced by students of the Law School of São Paulo. As Lopes remarks, some members of this group later contributed to the *Revista Nacional e Estrangeira*: Francisco Bernardino Ribeiro (in a posthumous contribution), Firmino Rodrigues da Silva, Manuel Odorico Mendes and José Elói Otoni.[6] As for João Manuel Pereira da Silva, he was not only an important and active member of the dominant Brazilian intellectual and political group, but also one of the first and most prolific fiction writers in Brazil.

As Hélio Lopes builds an analytical panorama of the Brazilian political and literary press in the Romantic period, he points out that the *Revista Nacional e Estrangeira* was viewed positively by intellectuals at the time. José Manuel Valdez Palacios, director of *A Nova Minerva* (1845–46), affirmed that the *Revista Nacional e Estrangeira* had been one of the three 'most lengthy and important publications'.[7] In their turn, the directors of the magazine *Guanabara* (1849–56) — Manuel de Araújo Porto-Alegre, Antonio Gonçalves Dias, and Joaquim Manuel de Macedo (respectively, an important painter and two renowned writers) — saw both the *Revista Filomática* and the *Revista Nacional e Estrangeira* as followers of the ideas that had presided over the foundation of the famous *Niterói* (1836) and *Minerva Brasiliense* (1843–45).

All in all, research into the Brazilian periodical press of the first half of the nineteenth century demonstrates the influence of a very small group of men of letters who founded numerous magazines in Rio de Janeiro. For them, the creation of magazines was a means of starting the systematic production of literary criticism and of writing on political and economic issues that were considered to be of interest to the organization of the nation-state of Brazil, as the country had achieved its political independence very recently, in 1822. This same restricted intellectual milieu can also be seen in relation to other aspects of the material conditions of periodical production in Rio de Janeiro. For instance, the *Revista Nacional e Estrangeira* was published in the typography workshop of J. E. S. Cabral, the printer of two prestigious magazines: the *Minerva Brasiliense* (in its first phase) and the *Revista do Instituto Histórico e Geográfico Brasileiro*.

However, as the *Revista Nacional e Estrangeira* seems not to have been remembered for long after it ceased production, Lopes concludes that its editorial line was incongruous with the context of its production:

> Despite its promising beginnings, the *Revista Nacional e Estrangeira* was not any more fortunate than its counterparts. It was victimized by common disinterestedness. It must have been of feeble importance and circulation as there are hardly any references to it. Twenty-two years after its demise, T. de Melo [probably, José Alexandre Teixeira de Melo] was not sure if the magazine had gone further than the fourth issue. A little too narrow in its popularizing of scientific ideals, the restrictive milieu could not manage to support it any longer.[8]

According to Lopes and Rios Filho, the *Revista Nacional e Estrangeira* was of high quality and demanded much of the Brazilian reader. In fact, its fiction and lengthy articles on a variety of subjects aimed to introduce modern ideas into Brazil through the discussion of political, economic, and social issues.

In the opening article, the directors deplore the present state of the Brazilian periodical press because urgent topical issues are not given enough space or attention and, consequently, are not considered in enough depth or discussed as they should be. This situation seems particularly problematic for them because they are aware of the social importance of the periodical press as the basis for forming public opinion. Nascimento Silva, Pedro d'Alcântara Bellegarde (1807–64) and Pereira da Silva understood that the unsatisfactory state of the periodical press in Brazil was the result of two key factors. First, Brazil was in the early stage of its organization as an independent country and, therefore, was still in search of its own realities, that is, 'the great truths upon which the government should be based';[9] consequently, instability prevailed. Second, the predominance of private interests over public ones nourished 'uncertainty of principles' in a context in which the press would attack or defend ideas and personal positions without properly analysing them.[10] Bearing all these aspects in mind, the directors of the *Revista Nacional e Estrangeira* presented their aim: to help the Brazilian periodical press steer in a different direction. As they understood this task to be too demanding to be carried out all by themselves, they planned to make use of foreign contributions to their periodical:

> Because we do not trust our modest lights and acknowledge our own insufficiency, we will turn to others' writing rather than to ours, by modelling this publication on the *Revue Britannique*. Most Brazilian men of letters know this collection of articles on science and art, and this knowledge absolves us from the task of praising it.
>
> As we subscribe to a large number of periodicals, both English and French, which are published under the title of *Magazine*, we are able to satisfy our readers' wishes by translating and publishing the best of what we could find in them. Also, we have friends, whose talents we respect, who have promised to help us in our enterprise by enriching our collection with their own articles about the peculiar issues of Brazil. So, we are sure that reading the *Revista Nacional e Estrangeira* will not be fruitless.[11]

Given the lofty purposes of the *Revista Nacional e Estrangeira*, it seems that the directors of the *Guanabara* were not exaggerating when they related this magazine to influential Brazilian periodicals. One of the first publications belonging to this special group of magazines was *Niterói*, which has long been credited with having introduced Romanticism to Brazil. The two single numbers of this magazine were published in Paris in 1836 by a small group of young Brazilian men of letters who were studying in France; among them was Pereira da Silva. As the literary critic Antonio Candido points out, though *Niterói* is categorized as a literary magazine, it presented more articles on science and economics than on literature.[12] According to Candido, one important reason for this feature comes from the particular Brazilian context of the time, when

> this generation devoted to the cult of science the same fervour with which they venerated art; the idea was to build an intellectual life, in its entirety, with a view to the progress of the Enlightenment and the consequent greatness of the nation.[13]

An important difference between the *Revista Nacional e Estrangeira* and its predecessor should be noted though: this was a Brazilian magazine produced in Brazil, but made almost entirely of foreign content. In the light of this, it is important to discuss the relation between foreign ideas and national aims in the *Revista Nacional e Estrangeira*.

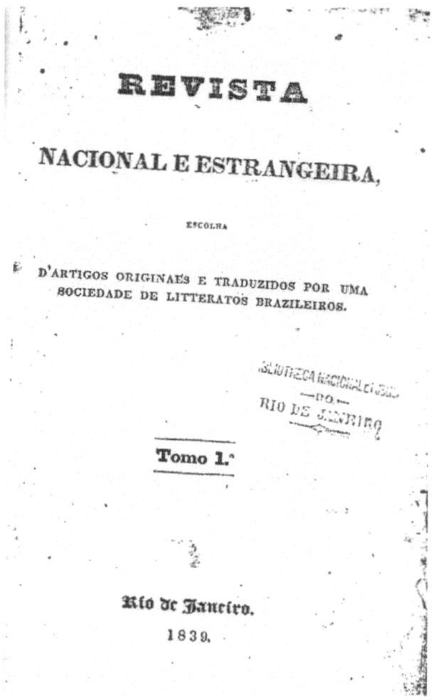
REVISTA

NACIONAL E ESTRANGEIRA,

ESCOLHA

D'ARTIGOS ORIGINAES E TRADUZIDOS POR UMA SOCIEDADE DE LITTERATOS BRAZILEIROS.

Tomo 1.°

Rio de Janeiro.

1839.

Fig. 7.1. Front page of the first issue of the *Revista Nacional e Estrangeira*, National Library of Rio de Janeiro. © National Library of Rio de Janeiro

The Foreign Content of the Revista Nacional e Estrangeira

As mentioned above, the founders and directors of the *Revista Nacional e Estrangeira* pointed to the *Revue Britannique* as a model to follow in order to produce a periodical that could contribute to in-depth reflection on serious issues in the difficult period of organizing the bureaucratic institutions and various fields of governmental activity in Brazil. In reality, the French *Revue Britannique* (1825–1901) was the chief source of most fictional and non-fictional texts published in this Brazilian magazine.

The *Revista Nacional e Estrangeira* was organized in several sections that varied from issue to issue. Two sections were constant, however: 'Variedades' [Varieties], which also included fiction, and 'Miscelânea' [Miscellany], which corresponded to 'Nouvelles de l'industrie, du commerce, de l'agriculture etc.' [News about industry, trade, agriculture, etc.], the section that closed each issue of the *Revue Britannique* by presenting short pieces of news on various topical issues.

Apart from short texts published in the sections 'Poetry' and 'Miscellany', not more than fifteen texts found in the whole *Revista Nacional e Estrangeira* are of Brazilian origin. In other words, the great majority of texts that can be found on the pages of the Brazilian magazine were reproduced from foreign periodicals. As the source is always indicated, a variety of titles can be found, such as *Architectural Magazine*, *Revista Literária*, *Revista Literária do Porto*, *Revista de Madrid*, *Journal des Débats*, *Revue du 19e Siècle* and *Courrier des États-Unis*. Browsing through the *Revista Nacional e Estrangeira* gives the impression that the variety of foreign sources is in fact much greater due to the presence of a number of titles of British periodicals, such as *Oxford Prize Essays*, *Foreign Quarterly Review*, *Edinburgh Review*, *Tait's Magazine*, *Traveller's Magazine*, *Monthly Magazine*, *Blackwood's Magazine*, *New Monthly Magazine* and *Political Primer*. However, these British titles are indicated as the original sources of fictional and non-fictional texts that the directors of and contributors to the Brazilian magazine translated from the *Revue Britannique*. Thus by keeping the same British sources that appeared in the *Revue Britannique*, and by leaving out information about the French authorship of most footnotes appended to the texts, the directors of the *Revista Nacional e Estrangeira* did not emphasize the fact that they used this French magazine as their chief source of reading material.

Free borrowing of texts was quite common at the time, both in Brazil and in Europe, as there was no international agreement about copyright laws.[14] Readers themselves were not much concerned with authorship, and in Europe they were even encouraged to send contributions to magazines. Consequently, the appropriation of somebody else's texts for publication in periodicals became a frequent practice.[15] It is then understandable that only a comparison between the *Revista Nacional e Estrangeira* and the *Revue Britannique* can reveal the full extent of the connection established between these two magazines by Nascimento Silva, Bellegarde and Pereira da Silva. That comparison shows that each issue of the *Revista Nacional e Estrangeira* brings at least one text translated from the *Revue Britannique*. In fact, several issues are almost entirely made of texts taken from this French magazine. They are: August and September 1839; January, March, June, July, September, October and November 1840. Another important aspect relates to the dates of publication of texts in both magazines. Comparison of the dates shows that this French magazine was well known to those Brazilian men of letters because the texts were translated in accordance with their editorial interests rather than in obedience to the chronological order of their publication in the *Revue Britannique*. Consequently, most foreign content of the *Revista Nacional e Estrangeira* is British-French, as the *Revue Britannique* itself was essentially comprised of translations of articles and fiction borrowed from British periodicals.

The contributors to the *Revue Britannique* (that is, the French men of letters who translated texts that fell within their respective fields of interest and activity) followed the editorial line established by one of its founders and first director, Louis-Sébastien Saulnier.[16] They adhered, more or less, to Saulnier's objective of building a critical view of the British accomplishments and social, cultural, economic and political context until the demise of the magazine. Great Britain was the undeniable leader in the international arena when the *Revue Britannique* was created and this magazine clearly demonstrates the complex relations with Great Britain established by its liberal founders at a time when Anglomania and aversion to the British Empire were two sides of the same coin, in the aftermath of the Napoleonic wars. As Nina Athanassoglou-Kallmyer remarks, in France after 1815 there was

> the ideological and social substratum of the French-British relations at the dawn of the Restoration; a changing, slippery, and insidious field, which paved the way to an ambiguous discourse characterized by admiration and rejection, attraction and repulsion, sympathy and antipathy.[17]

The *Revue Britannique* was acknowledged in Pierre Larousse's *Grand Dictionnaire Universel du XIXe Siècle* to be an important magazine for allowing the French to have deeper knowledge of the British accomplishments and acts that were influential in the international arena:

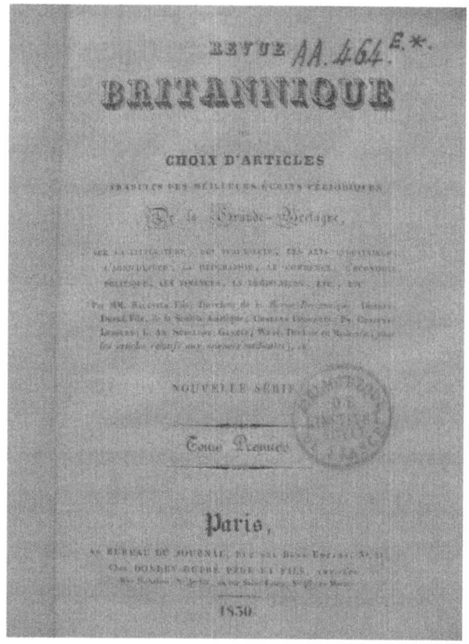

FIG. 7.2. Front page of an issue of the *Revue Britannique*, Library of the Faculty of Law, University of São Paulo © Library of the Royal Institute of France

> At the end of a period of commotion and wars, we owe to him [Saulnier] the fact that we have come better to know and understand, in France and abroad, the practice of the representative regime, the organization of manufactured work, the commercial markets, the progress of navigation, the contemporary history not only of England but also of the civilized and barbarian peoples that visit the English and American pavilions.[18]

This compliment is also covertly present in the entry on the *Revue Germanique*, a magazine modelled on the *Revue Britannique* and also published by the Dondey-Duprés firm (a father-and-son business).[19] The *Revue Germanique* is said to have failed for not having been able to present German content from a French perspective, that is, in accordance with the French character. The *Revue Germanique* would then have been essentially German rather than French.[20] By inference, then, *Revue Britannique* was successfully published all through the nineteenth century precisely because its directors and contributors knew how to handle the British context from a French perspective and reformulate it for readers in France and abroad. It is interesting to see this positive critical view of the *Revue Britannique* being expressed in the nineteenth century, as French critics rarely mention this periodical. It seems that the content of the *Revue Britannique* led French critics in general to label it — somewhat hastily — as a 'British' magazine produced in France. Such a view, which gained negative connotations in the highly centralized nationalist French context, seems to have been formed by contemporaries of the magazine, such as Charles-Augustin Sainte-Beuve, who could not accept the publication in the *Revue Britannique* of an English article, in translation, that made a virulent attack on French literature.[21]

Nonetheless, attentive reading of the *Revue Britannique* clearly shows how critical of the British context and defensive of the French one the editorial board was. In fact, this ideological position is visible in comments appended to the texts translated and adapted into French. This ideological position emerges even more strongly once account is taken of the passages inserted in the middle of the text by the French translator (these can be confirmed through comparison of the English and French versions of the text) in conjunction with the notes addressed to the readership. This reveals the strong critical position the editorial board of the *Revue Britannique* set forth about Great Britain and its achievements in the various branches of human knowledge and production, especially when British authors made negative comments on the French context. Hence Patrick Berthier argues that the real aim of the successive staff members of this magazine was to discuss the French context itself:

> the first [of the two magazines in question] is called 'britannique' not because it considered solely British intellectual production, but because its table of contents is comprised of translations of articles published in Great Britain [...] which may, therefore, concern France.[22]

Interestingly enough, this strong critical view of Great Britain running through the *Revue Britannique* was rather weakened in the translation of texts for the *Revista Nacional e Estrangeira*. In other words, French criticism of British achievements and of the social, cultural, political, and economic context is present but not emphasized in the *Revista Nacional e Estrangeira*, as it seems that Brazilians were interested in the information and ideas themselves rather than in the critical discussion or confrontation between the French and the British. Some texts are particularly significant for the discussion of the particularities of the *Revista Nacional e Estrangeira* in relation to the *Revue Britannique*, two magazines that were produced, in their respective contexts, with a view to contributing to serious reflection through the appropriation of foreign ideas.

'A conta corrente da guerra e das sedições' [The Cost of War and Sedition] was published in the September 1839 issue of the *Revista Nacional e Estrangeira*. No indication of its source is given, but the article had been published in the *Revue Britannique* in May 1831, which suggests that it was originally produced for this French magazine. The French author discusses the high cost of war and sedition, and claims that political economy is an important scientific field that helps a nation to manage its own wealth in a deliberate and gradual manner. Thus, while the author blames British greed in trade and the poor British understanding of the negative consequences of war, he laments that the French understand little of political economy. In his eyes, the recent internal turmoil (he must be referring to the popular revolution of 1830) is a sad example of how war is used in France as a means of dealing with economic difficulties. He goes on to defend the idea that, in peacetime, soldiers should do useful work for the nation in order to justify the salary they continue to receive. The author also calls for a war of principles rather than a war based on physical violence and destruction, and makes his political position clear: he is against radicalism (that is, republicanism) and is in favour of moderation. At the end of the article, he refers to the magnanimous and judicious decision of the French government to give the help requested by the Belgians to face Holland's economic interferences.

In this case, the criticism directed against Britain was retained by the Brazilian contributor. Nonetheless, in December 1839 the *Revista Nacional e Estrangeira* published an article signed by 'B' (probably Pedro d'Alcântara Bellegarde, who used to sign his texts with this initial), who refers to this French text as he discusses particular Brazilian issues that bear no relation whatsoever to the political, economic and ideological struggle between the French and the British. 'Ideias acerca da organização e conveniência de um exército permanente no Brasil' [Ideas Concerning the Organization and Convenience of a Permanent Army in Brazil] presents the Brazilian author's strong opinion in favour of maintaining a disciplined standing army. In the course of his argument, the author makes reference to the article borrowed from the *Revue Britannique* in order to argue against the notion that the army should not be employed to counter internal disorder.

A second article signed by 'B' is even more noteworthy for the role of the *Revue Britannique* as a source of progressive ideas for Brazilians. In 'Duas palavras acerca das comunicações' [Two Words about Communications], published in January 1840, B. relates the economic use of public funds to the need for developing efficient means of transportation in Brazil, with a preference for the railway system. Here, the author shows his interest in the definite improvement of Brazilian infrastructure and in the means that could facilitate human communication with a view to economic profit and the development of trade in the future. The reader of the *Revista Nacional e Estrangeira* can see that his article has connections with the translated article that follows it. The article in question here is 'Da necessidade e meios de empreenderem-se trabalhos públicos sem se aumentar os ônus aos contribuintes' [On the Need and Means of Carrying out Public Works without Increasing the Burden on Tax Payers], which was faithfully translated from the August 1831 issue of the *Revue Britannique*.[23] This text presents a much longer and substantial discussion about the different means of improving governmental action, especially in the aftermath of seditions, without lumbering the French people (that is, the French middle classes, which are the French author's real concern) with more bills to pay. The author carefully considers the cost-benefit relationship for the innovations and improvements he suggests. In fact, the contributor to the *Revue Britannique* suggests that France should follow the model set by Britain and develop its railway system, which, for him, is directly linked to the development of trade. Therefore, the advantages associated with the railway system would certainly have a positive effect on the internal French context and on France's ever-cherished leading position in the international arena. This concern with a modern type of infrastructure is highlighted by the director of the *Revista Nacional e Estrangeira*, who, in a footnote at the end of the article, warns the Brazilian reader that the reflection and discussion that he finds there are more useful to the Brazilian context than might initially be supposed.

Progressive liberal ideas are present in the *Revista Nacional e Estrangeira* both in fictional and non-fictional texts. For instance, in the August 1839 issue, Pereira da Silva published 'Associações comerciais e industriais do Rio de Janeiro' [Commercial and Industrial Associations of Rio de Janeiro], in which he also claims the need to create the political and economic conditions in Brazil that would allow the country to rise to civilization. As he goes on to say, this progressive movement implied the expansion of education and the implementation of modern infrastructure so as to level Brazil with the modern nations. He chooses not to consider the negative aspects of the capitalist *modus operandi*, as he defends this form of socio-economic organization he has identified in the leading nations. As Pereira da Silva is in favour of economic liberalism and against governmental intervention, he elects Britain and the United States as parameters to follow rather than France, whose government makes strong intervention in commercial and industrial enterprises.

The ideas defended in the French and Brazilian articles discussed above are connected to two fiction series published in the *Revista Nacional e Estrangeira*. The shortest series is called 'Contos de Mme. Marcet' [Short Stories by Mme Marcet] and was published, with no indication of its source, in the section 'Political Economy'.[24] Jane Marcet (1769–1858), a well-known nineteenth-century London popularizer of scientific and economic issues, used dialogues and tales to turn difficult subject matters into palatable reading material.[25] Her four fictional narratives published in this Brazilian magazine present a straightforward defence of the bourgeois *status quo* against the workers' attempt to discuss or change what they do not understand, namely, the capitalist mode of socio-economic organization.

Fiction was a privileged means of publicizing the bourgeois lifestyle, that is, the socio-cultural expression of the capitalist system, for it depicted human destinies that were built on and justified by this modern type of economic organization. The propagation of the bourgeois ideals in the *Revista Nacional e Estrangeira* is emphasized through the fictional series 'Diário d'um Médico' [Diary of a Physician], whose source is a renowned Scottish periodical, *Blackwood's Magazine*.[26] In reality, the eleven episodes selected from this series were directly translated from the modified French version produced by Philarète Chasles for the *Revue Britannique*. This British series originally entitled *Passages from the Diary of a Late Physician* and written by Samuel Warren, a minor fiction writer, shows domestic situations lived by bourgeois characters. Sentimentalism and moral judgment are its strongest features. It is worth noting that Chasles lightened the weight of puritan morality but retained the narrator-protagonist's essentially bourgeois attitude of looking for opportunities to ascend socially and, therefore, come closer to the upper social levels (that is, the British aristocracy and upper-middle classes) and move away, as much as possible, from the lower ones. The narratives translated for the *Revista Nacional e Estrangeira* closely follow the French version, which means to say that they present a narrator who comments on various aspects of the British socio-political context in a sharply ironical tone. In fact, Philarète Chasles made the narrator sound like a foreigner, as he strongly criticizes what he himself narrates. Thus it appears that the publication of these episodes in the *Revista Nacional e Estrangeira* had two aims: to entertain Brazilian readers (as stated in a footnote appended to the first episode by the director of this magazine) and to bring various scenes of British bourgeois life to the attention of a Brazilian audience.

For all this, it is clear that the fiction published in the *Revista Nacional e Estrangeira* had the double function of entertaining and instructing readers. The selection of fiction for publication in the *Revista Nacional e Estrangeira* would then have followed the ancient principle of *utile dulci*. This principle seems to have been valued by the directors of this magazine precisely because it implied the use of fiction to build, change, and/or defend moral values associated with the elites. It is not then a coincidence that, in July 1839, a translated article of literary criticism appeared that contained a line of argumentation clearly based on this principle. 'Juízo da Revista de Edimburgo sobre a literatura francesa contemporânea' [Appraisal of Contemporary French Literature by the *Edinburgh Review*] was originally published in the famous Scottish magazine of the title, but was translated into Portuguese from Philarète Chasles's version in the *Revue Britannique* (October 1833). It is worth noting two aspects about this article: first, Chasles, as usual, handled the text freely, by including some footnotes and passages, but leaving others out; second, this article was the subject of a broader discussion in France, as it conveyed a strong critical British view of French literature.[27]

In fact, out of the three articles of literary criticism published in the *Revista Nacional e Estrangeira*, this one is the most significant.[28] This article may have been selected because it allowed the Brazilian reader to acquire up-to-date critical knowledge of French literature, though the critical footnotes appended by Chasles were left out of the Brazilian translation. As a consequence, the clash of opinions between the British and the French was eliminated from the Brazilian version. In addition, it is likely that the pragmatic view of literature it presented, that is, the direct ideological relation between fiction and empirical reality established by the author, would have been another reason for its publication in the *Revista Nacional e Estrangeira*. In effect, the author bases his critical judgement of literature on moral pragmatism when he evaluates French writers and literary works according to what he considers to be an appropriate representation of moral values. For instance, the author strongly criticizes French writers who call themselves realist but whose works are unconvincing, because they create characters who are apparently virtuous but later reveal themselves to be criminals, or conversely characters that are taken for criminals who turn out to be virtuous. In short, the author claims that fiction writers should follow the ancient ethical-moral fictional pact that ruled the characters' destiny.

It is interesting to note that this article was openly used as a benchmark by which an anonymous Brazilian contributor criticized a narrative poem in his article 'D. Sebastião, o Encoberto, romance-poema publicado em Lisboa no ano de 1839' [D. Sebastião, the Hidden One, a Poem-Novel Published in Lisbon in the Year 1839], published in February 1840. As the Brazilian author remarks, 'our author [the author of the poem in question] was certainly struck by the illness that is a feature of French literature, which was described in an article from the *Edinburgh Review* now translated and transcribed on the pages of our periodical'.

The *Revista Nacional e Estrangeira* on the Tightrope between the Brazilian Conservative Context and Foreign Progressive Ideas

As shown above, translation was a means of appropriating foreign content in order to highlight and discuss national domestic issues on the pages of the *Revista Nacional e Estrangeira* and the *Revue Britannique*. Thus the directors of both periodicals consciously worked on a comparative basis, as they looked beyond their own country in order to search for ideas, systems, and knowledge that would improve and/or validate the position of their respective countries, both internally and externally, in accordance with their particular line of thought and editorial interests. Clearly, if Britain was the most forceful reference for those who produced the *Revue Britannique*, Britain and France were, in conjunction, the leading models for the directors of the *Revista Nacional e Estrangeira*. Consequently, these two periodicals only give the appearance of being concerned with foreign rather than national issues. However, given the differences between the French and the Brazilian contexts, what is the real value of the progressive ideas sought in the *Revue Britannique* by the creators of the *Revista Nacional e Estrangeira*?

The years 1839–40, when the *Revista Nacional e Estrangeira* was published, correspond to the end of a significant period in the history of Brazil between 1831, when Dom Pedro I abdicated the throne, and 1840, when the young D. Pedro II assumed full powers as emperor. During the Regency, the plantation owner class experienced a series of internal conflicts as they developed their status as citizens and confirmed their leading position in the political rule of the new country. Such new socio-political conditions demanded a shift in focus — from local to national — in their political, economic and social interests. This shift did not happen homogeneously or without conflict, either for this class as a whole or across Brazil. In fact, it happened more intensely for the group that had its political base in the court of Rio de Janeiro and was more economically powerful than their peers elsewhere in the country.

It was, then, during the 1830s, in Rio de Janeiro, that the new ruling class, which would establish the basis of the Brazilian state, was formed. The formation of such internal political dominance went hand in hand with the necessary adaptation of Brazil (now a politically free country in charge of its own mode of integration into the international arena) to the international economic and political context, namely, the bourgeois capitalist one. This process implied contact with liberal ideas, as clearly revealed by the founders and directors of the *Revista Nacional e Estrangeira*. They belonged to this ruling class, whose conservative members established the economic and political basis of the Second Empire. The conservative members were also responsible for the institution, defence and propagation (mainly through violent confrontation with the social groups of different provinces) of the principles of political centralization and constitutional monarchy in Brazil. Hence, from the Regency on, there was discussion of the organization and mode of operation of the National Guard, of the organization of a system of transport that could link plantations and ports more easily, and of the organization of a uniform monetary system in Brazil, among other things. These are all issues discussed in the articles published in the *Revista Nacional e Estrangeira*, most of which borrowed from the *Revue Britannique*.

In this light, the work of Ilmar Rohloff de Mattos and Maria Orlanda Pinassi is useful in the discussion of the reception of liberal ideas in the *Revista Nacional e Estrangeira*. Brazilian historian Ilmar R. Mattos analyses the conditions of the formation of the Brazilian ruling class in the nineteenth century.[29] He demonstrates how liberalism and its defence of individual private property as an unquestionable socio-economic value were received by the Brazilian ruling class. According to him, the Brazilian ruling class took liberalism as a means of validating their socio-political position, based on their right to keep their properties, that is, their land and their slaves. In this sense, modern ideas were used to justify the continuation of an old socio-economic structure. For example, there was growing pressure from the British government on Brazil to end the slavery system, pressure that, in conjunction with other forms of British interference in Brazilian affairs, contributed to rising antagonism towards Britain among Brazilians. Nevertheless, the slave traffic and system was only slowly and gradually dealt with by the Brazilian government from the 1850s on, generating high tensions within the ruling class itself. This friction between modernity and an archaic system is present in the *Revista Nacional e Estrangeira*: amid the articles and fiction that conveyed liberal ideas can also be found a fictional narrative that defends the slavery system. The narrative in question, 'O club de Southampton' [The Southampton Club], was published in July 1839 and had been taken from another French periodical, the *Revue du 19e Siècle*.

Brazilian social scientist Maria Orlanda Pinassi also throws light on the reception of liberal ideas in Brazil.[30] In her critical revision of the long established idea that *Niterói* was the first Brazilian expression of Romanticism, she remarks how the Brazilian men of letters who produced this magazine omitted the negative aspects and contradictions of capitalism in their articles. According to Pinassi, they did so in order to promote the liberal ideas that were to be the basis of new forms of socio-economic organization in Brazil. In her opinion, this omission was the unconscious result of enthusiasm deriving from their incomprehension of the socio-economic implications of capitalism, rather than an ideological intention to distort understanding of the new social, economic, and political order, which had been definitively established by the Industrial and the French Revolutions. Pinassi analyses how those young Brazilian men of letters, who produced *Niterói* far from their own country, idealized the implementation of liberal ideas in Brazil. Therefore, instead of being critical of capitalism (a criticism that was central to Romanticism), they defended it. In Pinassi's view, such defence had the status of a progressive movement, as it implied the promotion of a reformed socio-economic order and the consequent implementation of basic structural organizations that could not exist in a country whose economy was based on slavery. However, as the author points out, this modern programme did not suit the actual Brazilian social, economic, and political conditions, and was, therefore, not welcomed by the elites. Indeed, once they had returned to Brazil, those same men of letters adjusted their own progressive ideas to the conservative Brazilian milieu.

Pinassi's discussion about the omission of the negative aspects and paradoxes of capitalism and related issues in *Niterói* is of particular interest to the discussion about the production of the *Revista Nacional e Estrangeira*. It is noteworthy that this magazine included texts that were adapted by the Brazilian translator(s), who frequently eliminated parts of the text and footnotes appended by the contributor(s) to the *Revue Britannique*. As discussed above, most of these omitted passages brought critical perspectives and/or some kind of statement against the British context or against the British view of the French context in relation to the subject matter in question. This adaptation of French-British texts to the Brazilian context can also be seen both in the simplification of the sentence structure, insofar as this results in the corresponding simplification of the idea discussed in the relevant passage, and in the Brazilian translator's attempts to explain an idea more clearly to his readers.

All in all, these omissions and simplifications point to what seems to have been a frequent procedure of the Brazilian men of letters, which had the effect of weakening the level of critical discussion in the texts translated. Given the recurrence of these procedures in the *Revista Nacional e Estrangeira* and in other Brazilian periodicals at the time, it is possible to infer that the omission of negative aspects of capitalism would have been a conscious choice by the Brazilian men of letters working in Rio de Janeiro, who took into their hands the task of organizing the intellectual apparatus that was to support the formation of the Brazilian state and a sense of nationalism.

In view of the considerations presented above, it seems that the interest of the Brazilian men of letters in the *Revue Britannique* may have derived from three main related reasons. First, the importance of the British and French economic, political, and cultural contexts to Brazil in the period after independence, when there was strong rejection of Portugal, would have found an interesting expression in the *Revue Britannique* with its British-French content. Second, the sharp French criticism of the British context and achievements, as constructed in the *Revue Britannique*, would have suited the growing resentment among the Brazilian elites of British interference in Brazilian internal affairs. British interference was felt particularly keenly in relation to the pressure against the slave traffic and the slave system. Clearly, Great Britain was already experiencing a stage of capitalist production that, in the process of becoming more and more industrialized, demanded forms of financial procedures that were in conflict with societies whose economy was based on slavery. However, it is also clear that this French critical perspective of British achievements, opinions, and mode of operation did not undervalue the bourgeois ideology that finds expression in fictional and non-fictional texts borrowed from various British magazines and reviews. Third, as the *Revue Britannique* would have been well known by the Brazilian men of letters in Rio de Janeiro, as stated in the opening article of the *Revista Nacional e Estrangeira*, translating from that French magazine would have served the aim of bringing them together around a certain group of ideas and perspectives. As already mentioned, those men of letters belonged or were strongly attached to the ruling class which, by naming itself the 'good society' and 'the people', created a very exclusive domain of citizenship from which most inhabitants of Brazil were excluded.[31] In this sense, the *Revista Nacional e Estrangeira* was a magazine produced by and addressed to an exclusive group of Brazilians. As not all of them could read French, this magazine would have been functional for making 'civilizing' ideas and values accessible to them.[32]

To conclude, the translation of fiction and articles from the *Revue Britannique* for the *Revista Nacional e Estrangeira* would have been a means of gathering the Brazilian elites around liberal ideas and a bourgeois lifestyle, which, in Brazil, basically meant social deference and status. Such ideas were then made current from a particular perspective that brought together, in the Brazilian version of the texts, the French view of the British context and achievements, and the Brazilian interest in facts rather than in the problematization of these achievements. As Mattos remarks, those liberal bourgeois ideas arrived in Brazil mainly through fiction, theatre plays, and journalism.[33] Clearly, the particular Brazilian reception of the *Revue Britannique* constituted part of this process, as demonstrated in the *Revista Nacional e Estrangeira*.

Notes to Chapter 7

1. Parts of this article are drawn from different papers given at I ENAPEL (FURG/Brazil), II SIMELP (Évora University/Portugal), and the colloquium 'Le Commerce transatlantique de librairie, un des fondements de la mondialisation culturelle (France-Portugal-Brésil, XVIII–XX siècle)' (UVSQ/France; I was granted financial support by CAPES to take part in this meeting). It also presents the results of post-doctoral research developed with the financial aid of a scholarship granted by the International Hermès Fellowship Programme of the Fondation Maison des Sciences de l'Homme.
2. Adolfo Morales de los Rios Filho, *O Rio de Janeiro Imperial*, 2nd edn (Rio de Janeiro: Topbooks/ UniverCidade Editora, 2000), pp. 467–68.
3. *Revista Nacional e Estrangeira* (Rio de Janeiro: Typ. de J. E. S. Cabral, 1839–40), p. 144.
4. Hélio Lopes, *A divisão das águas: contribuição ao estudo das revistas românticas 'Minerva Brasiliense' (1843–1845) e 'Guanabara' (1849–1856)* (São Paulo: Conselho Estadual de Artes e Ciências Humanas, 1978).
5. Josino do Nascimento Silva studied at the Law School of São Paulo and occupied several offices in this field. He was the president of the provinces of Rio de Janeiro and São Paulo, a provincial and general deputy, and also a member of Emperor D. Pedro II's counsel. He was the owner of the typography workshop where periodicals such as *O Cronista* and *Gabinete de Leitura* were printed, and he was the editor of two important newspapers: *Diario do Rio de Janeiro* and *Jornal do Commercio*. As for João Manuel Pereira da Silva, he studied law in Paris. Back in Rio de Janeiro, he worked as a lawyer and held several political and bureaucratic posts, always as a conservative. Pereira da Silva founded, directed and/or contributed to a number of magazines and newspapers based in Rio de Janeiro. He was one of the founders of the Brazilian Academy of Letters and of the Men of Letters Association of Brazil. Both Josino do Nascimento Silva and João Manuel Pereira da Silva were members of several important cultural institutions in Rio de Janeiro.
6. Hélio Lopes, *A divisão das águas*, p. 30.
7. *Apud* Hélio Lopes, *A divisão das águas*, p. 40. The other two periodicals mentioned by Palacios are *Revista Trimensal do Instituto Histórico e Geográfico Brasileiro* (which still runs today) and *Minerva Brasiliense*.
8. Hélio Lopes, *A divisão das águas*, p. 31. José Alexandre Teixeira de Melo (1833–1907) was a doctor, journalist, writer, and member of the Instituto Histórico e Geográfico Brasileiro [Brazilian Historical and Geographical Institute].
9. *Revista Nacional e Estrangeira* (Rio de Janeiro: Typ. de J. E. S. Cabral, 1839–40), p. v.
10. *Revista Nacional e Estrangeira* (Rio de Janeiro: Typ. de J. E. S. Cabral, 1839–40), p. v.
11. *Revista Nacional e Estrangeira* (Rio de Janeiro: Typ. de J. E. S. Cabral, 1839–40), p. vi.
12. Antonio Candido, *Formação da literatura brasileira: momentos decisivos*, 7th edn, 2 vols (Belo Horizonte: Itatiaia, 1993), II, 12.
13. Antonio Candido, *Formação da literatura brasileira: momentos decisivos*, II, 12.
14. In 1710, with the *Statute of Anne*, England took its first steps towards creating copyright for publications, see *O preço da leitura: leis e números por detrás das letras*, ed. by Marisa Lajolo and Regina Zilberman (São Paulo: Ática, 2001), p. 40. In practice, however, during the eighteenth and most of the nineteenth century texts could be freely appropriated.
15. Robert D. Mayo, *The English Novel in the Magazines, 1740–1815. With a Catalogue of 1375 Magazine Novels and Novelettes* (London: Oxford University Press; Evanston, IL: Northwestern University Press, 1962).

16. The founders of the *Revue Britannique* were liberal French men of letters: Louis-Sébastien Saulnier (1790–1835), Jean-Michel Berton (1794–1845) and Prosper Dondey-Dupré (1794–1834).
17. Nina Athanassoglou-Kallmyer, 'Ambiguïtés britanniques. Le Peintre, le critique et Monsieur le Baron', in *Repenser la Restauration*, ed. by Jean-Yves Mollier, Martine Reid and Jean Claude Yon (Paris: Nouveau Monde Éditions, 2005), pp. 161–70 (p. 163).
18. Pierre Larousse, *Grand Dictionnaire Universel du XIXe Siècle. Français, Historique, Géographique, Mythologique, Bibliographique, Littéraire, Artistique, Scientifique etc.*, 17 vols in 34 (Geneva and Paris: Slatkine, 1982), XIII, 1130.
19. Prosper Dondey-Dupré (*fils*) was apprenticed to his father in the family's typography workshop in Paris and was in charge of the business from 1833 on. Their typography workshop was the first private one of a high standard in France. The Dondey-Duprés specialized in printing Eastern works and also published magazines such as the *Revue Britannique* and the *Revue Germanique*. See Pierre Larousse, *Grand Dictionnaire Universel du XIXe Siècle*, VI, 1092; Véronique Perrot, 'Le Cercle de la *Revue Britannique* (1825–1901): Histoire d'une revue', 2 vols (unpublished doctoral thesis, Université de Picardie Jules Verne, Faculté des Lettres, 2002), I, 554–55.
20. Pierre Larousse, *Grand Dictionnaire Universel du XIXè Siècle*, XIII, 1132.
21. Charles-Augustin Sainte-Beuve, 'Des jugements sur notre littérature contemporaine à l'étranger', *Revue des Deux Mondes*, 15 June 1836, pp. 749–56.
22. Patrick Berthier, *La Presse littéraire et dramatique au début de la Monarchie de Juillet (1830–1836)* (Villeneuve-d'Ascq: Presses universitaires du septentrion, 2001), p. 321.
23. The Brazilian translator omitted some footnotes on specific information about the French context and the relation between this and other articles previously published in the *Revue Britannique* itself.
24. The four episodes of this series were published in October and November 1839, and February 1840.
25. J. A. V. Chapple, *Science and Literature in the Nineteenth Century* (London: Macmillan, 1986), p. 6.
26. Episodes of this series were published in August, September and November 1839, and in February, March, May, June, July, August, September and October 1840.
27. Kathleen Jones, *La Revue Britannique, son histoire et son action littéraire (1825–1840)* (Paris: Librairie E. Droz, 1939), pp. 122–27.
28. The other articles are 'D. Sebastião, o Encoberto, romance-poema publicado em Lisboa no ano de 1839' [D. Sebastião, the Hidden One, a poem-novel published in Lisbon in the year 1839], a Brazilian text in the February 1840 issue; and 'Reforma da literatura na Alemanha durante o décimo sexto século' [Literary Reform in Germany in the Sixteenth Century], originally published in the *Edinburgh Review*. It was translated from the *Revue Britannique* (September 1831) for the March 1840 issue of the *Revista Nacional e Estrangeira*.
29. Ilmar Rohloff de Mattos, *O tempo saquarema: a formação do estado imperial*, 5th edn (São Paulo: Hucitec, 2004).
30. Maria Orlanda Pinassi, *Três devotos, uma fé, nenhum milagre: Nitheroy, revista brasiliense de ciências e artes* (São Paulo: Fundação Editora da UNESP, 1998).
31. This large group of excluded people comprised poor free (or freed) men and women (who were put under constant guard and control as they were considered to be dangerous and chaotic by those who called themselves 'good society') and slaves (who were legally considered to be properties of their holders).
32. In his review of the Brazilian translation of a French book about accountancy, Pereira da Silva criticizes the translator's decision of keeping many words in French when there were Brazilian readers who did not know this language. See Pereira da Silva's review of M. N. Burnier's *Elemento da contabilidade comercial* in the December 1839 issue of the *Revista Nacional e Estrangeira*.
33. Ilmar Rohloff de Mattos, *O tempo saquarema*, pp. 195–97 and 225–26.

CHAPTER 8

The Role of the Press in the Incorporation of Brazil into the Paris Fashion System

Ana Cláudia Suriani da Silva

In 1878, Joaquim Manuel de Macedo published a series of newspaper columns to give his contemporaries a picture of the urban, social and economical changes which one of the most famous streets in Rio de Janeiro, Rua do Ouvidor, had undergone from the founding of the town by Mém de Sá, in 1567, to the nineteenth century. The articles had first been published in the columns of *Jornal do Commercio* and were then assembled in a book called *Memórias da Rua do Ouvidor*. On the basis of his memories, the columnist sought to reconstruct how Rua do Ouvidor had taken part in the civilizing process brought about by influences from Europe, in particular those of Portugal, France and Britain, while taking full account of the circumstances by which the town had been turned into a privileged space for the dissemination of Paris fashion.[1] The writer noted that through the presence of shops, business men and French dressmakers from 1817 onwards

> the Queen — French fashion — had become enthroned in Rua do Ouvidor, which gave elegance, splendour and enchantment to Fluminense society and was borne out by the prestige of its shop-windows. Rua do Ouvidor entered the dazzling world of its fashion empire.[2]

This newspaper column was somewhat anecdotal in the way it treated the inclusion of Rua do Ouvidor and, by extension, the town of Rio de Janeiro, in the European, or rather, Paris fashion system of the nineteenth century. The main aim of this chapter is to examine this process, which was already under way by 1817, proceeded over the course of the century, and had become established by the time the column was written. It will concentrate on the role of periodicals — more precisely of periodicals with fashion content, in the insertion of Rio de Janeiro in the Paris fashion system. The study employs a macro-sociological analysis involving the social organization of fashion and the concept of cultural transfers, to understand the role of the printing industry in the transfer process of fashion content and concept from one place to another, and employs Rio de Janeiro and the periodical with fashion content by publishers established in Rio de Janeiro as an empirical case study.[3]

The chapter is divided into two parts. Before turning our attention to a perusal and examination of our primary sources, it is necessary, in the first part, to have a full understanding of what is meant by fashion system, to examine how Paris, in Macedo's words, had been turned into the world empire of fashion, and the means by which Rio de Janeiro was incorporated into the Paris fashion system. In the second part, a survey will be made of nineteenth-century periodicals with fashion content published, in Portuguese, by editors established in Rio de Janeiro, followed by a presentation of the main characteristics of what we consider the first successful Brazilian fashion magazine: *Correio das Modas*: jornal crítico e literário das modas, bailes, teatros, by Laemmert (1839–1840). These characteristics made of Brazilian fashion magazines a hybrid, multicultural product from its birth and are present in all main periodicals with fashion content published until the end of the nineteenth century.

Rua do Ouvidor in the Paris Fashion System

France became consolidated as a power in the fashion industry during the reign of Louis XIV (1638–1715) through the mercantilist policy of Colbert. The luxury goods business enabled the French court to maintain its prestige and power throughout Europe. By taking advantage of its cultural leadership, which it already possessed in the domain of fashion, France was able to centralize the manufacture of luxury merchandise in Paris. It also enacted sumptuary laws to limit the choice of clothes, as well as regulate imports to protect the national industry and restrict access to foreign markets. At the same time, the practices and protectionist legislation of Colbert helped boost exports which were strengthened by the trade in luxury goods. This enabled the French court to maintain its prestige and power, and resulted in French merchandise being sought after throughout Europe. Although Robespierre's principle of equality between men led to the abolition of the sumptuary laws, the French Revolution did not deprive France of its position as a benchmark for fashion throughout the world. No doubt, luxury was condemned for a time, but during the government of Napoleon (1799–1815), the trade of luxury goods and the trickle-down process of fashion prevailed again and were in force when French fashions first arrived in Brazil.

When the Portuguese Court was transferred to Brazil in 1808, the clothing trade in the new capital of the Portuguese Empire expanded, owing to an increase in the population and the opening up of the ports. At this time the Portuguese protectionist measures inspired by Colbert's practices (which were designed to curb the imports of textiles and overcome trade deficits by stimulating Portuguese factories and manufacturers) were not in force anymore, owing to the return to prosperity experienced by other Brazilian businesses and new international commitments. Even the successive pragmatic sanctions (1668, 1677, 1686, and 1698), representing decisions made by the monarchy with the legal purpose of ensuring that the use of luxury goods was restricted in accordance with a social hierarchy, were already falling into disuse or had been revoked by the beginning of the nineteenth century.[4]

However, France was not the main commercial partner with Brazil before 1808. For more than a century, the colonial town, which had been turned into the Capital of the Empire, had close commercial ties with Britain. Portugal succeeded in boosting its exports of Port wine to Britain, under the terms of the Methuen Treaty (1703), but in exchange was compelled to open up its internal market to the British woollen mills.[5] The commercial monopoly that Britain had in Brazil is confirmed by Camila Borges da Silva in her study of the history of clothing in the Portuguese Court of Brazil (1808–1821).[6] In conducting an analysis of the advertisements of *Gazeta do Rio de Janeiro* in the period from 1808 to 1821, she found that only British products were advertised in that epoch. After 1815, being aware of the appeal of the goods of its rival country, the businessmen from Britain began to advertise fans, feathers, clothes, shoes and hats made in France, as well as British merchandise. The period between the arrival of the Court and the year 1815 (the year of the defeat of Napoleon and the restoration of the monarchy in France) provided ideal conditions for the export of goods from Britain to Brazil when imports from France were prohibited. According to the researcher, this led to the British monopolizing the retail trade in Rio de Janeiro.

It is not by accident that Macedo notes the predominance of British (and Portuguese) traders in Rio until the end of the 1810s and their gradual replacement by the French:

> It's a curious fact but definitely the case and it makes me want to laugh, that the Portuguese traders who used to be in the Rua do Ouvidor have not been worried about the French invasion. However, the English (although in small numbers) have been abandoning the street so that after six years, the mighty Albion no longer has a single representative.[7]

After the final downfall of Napoleon Bonaparte and the elevation of Brazil to the status of United Kingdom of Portugal, Brazil and the Algarve, at the Congress of Vienna (1815), commercial agreements were signed with France. These also guaranteed reciprocity in the residence of French nationals in Brazil and Brazilians in France.[8] This did not only apply to a more studied group of professionals, for example, to the artists, who would later be designated by historiographers as forming the 'French Artistic Mission', and settled in Brazil on a temporary or permanent basis, either by invitation or on their own account. It also attracted to Brazil dressmakers, tailors, hairdressers and other French tradesmen linked to the fashion industry to which Macedo refers in his article.[9] We find records of these professionals in the pages of *Gazeta do Rio de Janeiro*, because they offered their services there,[10] in the fashion editorials and in the records of immigrants who settled in Rio de Janeiro after the Royal Family was transferred to Brazil. In a study of the presence of French women in Rio de Janeiro, in the period from 1816 to 1822, Lená Medeiros Menezes observes that:

> Leaving aside those who sought political refuge in Brazil or those who came here as a part of their scientific or artistic travels (or even on account of their activities as booksellers and editors), a special place should be given to those who, in current terminology, could be described as 'economic migrants'; this group has always been neglected in analyses carried out about the influence of

> French culture on cities. The emphasis here, as stated earlier, is mainly on the French dressmakers and seamstresses[11] who have been immortalized in Rua do Ouvidor, and for whom to make it to America in the Brazilian case meant, in the last analysis, fulfilling their dream of having their own business, once surpassed their Atlantic adventure.[12]

As Menezes explains, they were spinsters, widows, married women accompanied by children or other women who crossed the Atlantic to make a living in Rio de Janeiro. The presence of the Royal Family in Rio provided a 'space for new opportunities, which was able to absorb the sophistication of French "industry"' (p. 72). Menezes has recovered the names of many of these professionals: the likes of Juliana Alexandra, Joana Poyanne, Mme Chabry, Mme de Lussan, Mme Josefina Mennier, Rosa Dubois, Melanie and Virginie Durand, and Amedée Catelineau, appear in the advertisements of *Gazeta do Rio de Janeiro* or in the records of immigrants. In addition to these, is the name of Mademoiselle Dillon, Josephina Malaçon and Mme Seurat, whose services were recommended in the periodicals *Espelho Diamantino* or *Correio das Modas*. The names of male fashion professionals of French origin are also mentioned in those two periodicals: Monsieur Desmarais and Monsieur Girard, the shops of Messieurs Gary and Marcassus, Leite and the Dillon Brothers, M. Jugand, Martin and Ca., Mr. Cesar-Valais and Cia, Mr. Marcaussus.

The establishment of these professionals in Rio de Janeiro was made possible by three main factors. First, on the Brazilian side, the removal of the centre of decision-making of the Empire from Portugal to Brazil paved the way for commercial legislation which abolished the privileges of the traditional merchant classes. This gave greater freedom to the street traders and extended to women the right to take part in this kind of business.[13] Second, reciprocal agreements between Brazil and France with regard to the free circulation of French nationals in Brazil encouraged the immigration of fashion professionals to Rio de Janeiro, who catered for the interests of a growing population that was attracted by French culture. Third, on the French side, there was a sizeable number of artisans and their apprentices who were willing to migrate from France and who brought to Brazil the practices that they had carried out in their native land, dating back to Colbert's era. As Menezes stated:

> As well as being identified as a new consumer market for valuable objects produced in France, for many Frenchmen and Frenchwomen, Brazil became a distant and ideal opportunity for beginning a new life and a means of pursuing the same activities that had been carried out many years before by their ancestors.[14]

According to Menezes, the dressmaker's workshop was still the paradigm of the French economy of agricultural base. Small units comprising a master and a few employees, interlinked by an extremely hierarchized corporate body, led to the production of handicraft goods. Since the era of Colbert, this has been aimed at catering for both the home market and also consumers in other courts spread around the world.

One can see that the activities and kinds of discourses conducted both in Brazil and France brought together societies governed by the customs and features of the

'Ancien Regime' and free market practices.[15] The openness of the commercial legislation allowed commercial opportunities to a class of artisans who were controlled by a powerful hierarchical system of merchants in France.

The confirmation by Macedo that Rua do Ouvidor had finally entered the elegant world of the fashion empire implies that a group of individuals (French dressmakers and traders, as well as a section of the population of Rio de Janeiro) was carrying out collective activities, and shared similar consumption desires and views about fashion. This contributed to produce and perpetuate a belief about fashion and the culture of Paris fashion, which was maintained through continual production and reproduction.[16] Rua do Ouvidor turned into a microcosm of Paris, since its fashion system was reproduced there. This perpetuated and confirmed its dominance even though to achieve this, it was necessary to simplify and adapt it owing to the various constraints that the new nation had to undergo, the peculiarities of its society and the tropical climate.

As pointed out earlier, French fashion became dominant in Europe in the second half of the eighteenth century, during the reign of Louis XVI. Under Colbert, the government played a very important role in the development of the luxury goods industry. Moreover, the production and sale of clothes were controlled by being separated into two different institutions, while the sumptuary laws regulated the purchase of fashion in a very strict way and centred the production of fashion items on the Court. In spite of the French Revolution and wars, France succeeded in keeping its reputation as the Queen of Fashion. According to Kawamura, the concept of fashion as a system is therefore maintained by the above-mentioned interrelated institutions, organizations, groups, individuals, events or practices that form the social organization of fashion.

In the opinion of Kawamura, although not everyone agrees that fashion is an art form, it does at least follow the precepts that sociologists have postulated for the arts. Scholars such as Becker, Bourdieu and Delsaut, White and White and Wolff 1983, set out from the premise that art should be contextualized in terms of place and time, which directs the attention to the relation of the artist and artwork to extra-aesthetic considerations.[17] Kawamura states in her book on Japanese fashion designers in Paris that:

> Like art, fashion is social in character, has a social base and exists in a social context. Therefore, I align my observation also with Becker's study of art worlds (1982) in which he indicates that the making of artists is not the responsibility of one individual but a collective activity. I look at fashion organizations and institutions in relation to the people whose collective actions construct the fashion system because there is a correlation between social structures and the actions of people working collectively. It is these cooperative networks that make fashion happen and repeatedly manufacture a symbolic meaning of fashion. Fashion is a collective phenomenon which cannot be created by an individual designer, and it cannot be interpreted apart from its social context.[18]

Kawamura believes that the consolidation of the modern fashion system and of Paris as the capital of fashion, occurred at a period much later than that put forward in our study — only in 1868 — with the establishment of the Chambre Syndicale de la Couture et de la Confection pour Dames et Fillettes [Chamber of Commerce for High Fashion and the Manufacture of Clothes for Women and Girls]. This allowed fashion production to be driven and controlled by fashion designers who occupied high positions in the very hierarchical system of the fashion world. Belonging to the Chamber of Commerce gave the official fashion makers legitimacy and recognition, while at the same time, the public could feel assured that the clothes designed for it were fashionable. This was because the designers were provided with the means to produce high-quality clothing and distance themselves from the manufacturers of ready-made goods.

When Rua do Ouvidor (and by extension Rio de Janeiro and Brazil) was incorporated into the Paris fashion system, the figure of the fashion designer still did not exist. The presence in Rio de Janeiro of dressmakers, seamstresses and traders — either retailers or street sellers — of luxury goods and textiles, shows how the Paris fashion system operated in its previous phases and also, according to Kawamura, the way it became consolidated. Brazil formed a part of the Paris fashion system before it had become consolidated and, as mentioned above, before the figure of the fashion designer was recognized as someone who dictated fashion. As Kawamura and others make clear, 'prior to being institutionalized, fashion emerged out of the upper-class men and women, and thus the producer and consumer of fashion shared the same origin. Those who designed wore the clothes, and those who executed the designs remained anonymous'.[19] Fashion was a trickle-down process passing from top to bottom and driven by the principle of imitation. However, as was pointed out by Gilda de Mello e Souza, nineteenth-century society no longer erected insurmountable barriers, not even between the bourgeois and the nobility. In the nineteenth century, the possibility of communication between the groups replaced the old rigidity; or rather, the relative inflexibility of the social structure was replaced by constant mobility. Fashion played a crucial role in bringing the classes together as, according to Souza,

> it is one of the most powerful instruments of integration; it plays an important levelling function as it allows the individual to blend into the group and disappear into a larger whole which gives him support and security. And as the prevailing fashions are always those of the dominant class, the groups nearest to them are continually identifying themselves with their immediate superiors by imitating their dress.[20]

The consumers of fashion goods who were residents of Rio de Janeiro adhered to the principle of imitation, because in the Paris fashions conveyed by dressmakers and periodicals, as will be seen in what follows, they sought legitimacy by identifying themselves with the European aristocracy. By reproducing the consumption standards of the European upper classes, the Brazilian elite could materialize its desire to differentiate from the others, which included a large population of slaves. With economic growth and rising purchasing power as the century advanced, the growing middle class sought to emulate the consumption patterns of the Brazilian and European upper classes. As far as the growing middle class was concerned, Paris fashion fed their desire to climb the social ladder and attain the same level as the elite, at least in regard to appearance.[21]

The Birth of the Brazilian Fashion Magazine

As consumers, the inhabitants of Rio de Janeiro who were interested in Paris clothes and luxury goods were the driving force for the incorporation of Brazil into the Paris fashion system. This involved manpower obtained from immigration, the importing of luxury goods and textiles, the enactment of laws, the development of a commercial district in the town, as well as setting up a specialized fashion printing press.

Fashion magazines made it possible to disseminate fashion illustrations, editorials, paper patterns and descriptions of garments on a large scale and to conduct a discourse about fashion, through the incorporation, translation, adaptation and recreation of visual and textual material (either imported or local) to readers in different locations. This led to the spread of the idea of fashion as the cultural product of a city — Paris. It did not matter who signed the sketches reproduced in the engravings, who produced the engravings themselves or even the clothes manufactured on the basis of the illustrations, which might be produced by professional dressmakers or by those who intended to wear the clothes, working by hand or with a sewing-machine. Even if some dressmakers like those in Rua do Ouvidor had become well known among the customers, they were the mediators of Paris fashion in Brazil, as much as the periodicals themselves. With a design or pattern in one's hand, the same garment could be made in different places, by following the instructions of the fashion column and the written-garment.[22] Each new garment was more or less faithful to the patterns published in the magazine and adapted to the local climate, the different size of the person who would wear it and, last but not least, to the skill and creativity of the dressmaker.

Although there had been a demand since 1808 for the (re)production of fashion information and materials to a growing population both in Rio and provinces, the first periodical in Portuguese language with fashion content which we have a record of and which had a column exclusively devoted to 'Fashion' only appeared in 1827: *Espelho Diamantino*, by Pierre Plancher. As already mentioned in this book, the Brazilian periodical press was born in 1808, with the Royal Press and *Gazeta do Rio de Janeiro*, which was the official periodical of the Court of D. João. In its first two decades the press was largely political and divided between newspapers that were for or against the monarchy. From 1808 to 1827, there were huge fluctuations in the way the national press developed. The number of periodicals could rise or fall from one year to another, when new censorship measures were enforced or the political debate was broadened.[23] It was only in the 1830s that a significant number of magazines for women began to appear, both in the Court and in the provinces, among which were *O Mentor das Brasileiras* of São João Del Rey (1829), *O Espelho das Brasileiras* (1831), in Recife, and in Rio de Janeiro the above-mentioned *A Mulher do Simplício, ou a Fluminense Exaltada* (1832–46), and *Correio das Modas* (1839–40).[24] It is in the three first periodicals with fashion content published in Rio de Janeiro (*Espelho Diamantino*, *A Mulher do Simplício* and *Correio das Modas*, especially the last of these), that we can find a more systematic discussion about fashion and in the last one, for the first time, fashion illustrations from Europe.

Title	Publisher	Year of circulation
O Espelho Diamantino: Periódico de política, teatro e modas. Dedicado às senhoras brasileiras [*The Diamond Mirror*: Periodical of politics, theatre and fashion. Dedicated to the Brazilian ladies]	P. Plancher-Seignot	1827–28
A Mulher do Simplício ou A Fluminense Exaltada [*The Simplício's Wife or the Exalted Fluminense*][26]	Tipografia de Tomás B. Hunt & C., Tipografia de Lessa & Pereira, Tipografia Imparcial de F. P. Brito	1832–46
Correio das Modas: jornal crítico e literário das modas, bailes, teatros [*The Fashions Courier*: Literary and critical periodical of fashions, balls, theatres]	Tipografia Universal de Laemmert	1839–40
O Gosto: Jornal de teatros, literatura, modas, música e pintura. [*The Taste*: Periodical for theatre, literature, fashions, music, and painting]	Tipografia Imparcial de F. de P. Brito, Tipografia de Cremiere	1843
Espelho Fluminense. Novo gabinete de leitura: modas, poesias, charadas e etc. [*The Fluminense Mirror.* New reading cabinet: fashions, poems, riddles, and etc.]	Livraria Universal de E. e H. Laemmert	1843
O Martinho: Jornal de recreio que trata dos vivos e dos mortos [*Martinho*: periodical of recreation dealing with the living and the dead]	Tipografia Universal de Laemmert	1851
Novo Correio de Modas: Novelas, poesias, viagens, recordações histórias, anedotas e charadas [*New Fashions Courier*: novellas, poetry, trips, remembrances, stories, anecdotes and puzzles]	Tipografia Universal de Laemmert	1852–54
O Jornal das Senhoras. Modas, literatura, belas-artes e crítica [*The Ladies' Journal*: Fashions, literature, beaux-arts and reviews]	Tipografia Parisiense	1852–55
Recreio do Bello Sexo. Moda, literatura, belas-artes e teatro [*Entertainment for the Fair Sex.* Fashion, literature, beaux-arts and theatre]	?	1856
A Marmota [*The Woodchuck*]	Tipografia de Paula Brito	1857–61
O Espelho: Revista de literatura, modas, indústria e artes [*The Mirror*: A magazine for literature, fashions, industry and arts]	Tipografia Imparcial de Paula Brito; Tipografia Comercial de F. O. Queiroz Regadas; Tipografia Americana de José Soares de Pinho	1859–60

Revista Popular [*The Popular Magazine*]	B. L. Garnier	1859–62
A Primavera: revista semanal de literatura, modas, indústria e artes [*The Spring:* weekly magazine of literature, fashions, industry and arts]	Tipografia Popular de Azeredo Leite	1861
Semana Familiar: Jornal poético, literário, noticioso, industrial, científico, crítico, anedótico, etc., para recreio das famílias residentes no Brasil [*The Family's Week:* a journal of poetry, literature, news, industry, science, reviews, anecdotes, for the pleasure of families living in Brazil]	Rio de Janeiro: Tipografia de Fontes Irmão	1862
Jornal das Famílias [*The Family's Journal*]	B. L. Garnier	1863–78
O Pantheon: Importante jornal do importantíssimo estabelecimento de fazendas e modas – Au Pantheon – sito à rua Sete de Setembro n. 78 [*The Pantheon:* a very important newspaper of the very important fashions and fabric shop – Au Pantheon – Sete de Setembro Street, number 78]	Tipografia Acadêmica	1872–73
Illustração da Moda [*Fashion Illustration*]	? (Paris and Rio de Janeiro) Edition in Portuguese language of *Les Modes parisiennes*	1876
A Estação. Jornal ilustrado para a família [*The Season:* an illustrated journal for the family]	Lombaerts	1879–04
Archivo das Famílias: Publicação semanal consagrada ao recreio e interesses domésticos. [*The Family's Archive*: a weekly publication consecrated to entertainment and interests of the family]	Tipografia e Litografia de J. D. de Oliveir	1881–82
O Brasil Elegante: Jornal de modas das famílias brasileiras *Elegant Brazil*: fashion journal of the Brazilian families]	Tipografia Besnar D Frères	1898–04

Table 8.1. Periodicals with fashion content in Portuguese language available at the catalogue of the National Library of Rio de Janeiro, National Library of France or mentioned in studies of nineteenth-century women's magazines.[25]

Main Features of the Nineteenth-Century Brazilian Fashion Magazine

We shall see throughout this section that what we call a nineteenth-century fashion magazine was a periodical with a variety of content, visual and written, that included a fashion column and fashion illustrations. There was no periodical in Brazil in the first half of the nineteenth century dedicated exclusively to fashion — the first of this type would only appear at the turn of the century, with *O Brasil*

Elegante: Jornal de modas das famílias brasileiras, by Tipografia Besnar D. Frères (1898–1904). Furthermore, not every periodical that contained in its title the word 'fashion' published fashion content, as the inclusion of the word 'fashion' in the title of the periodical was more indicative of the editors' aspiration and a sales strategy to attract readers. The comparison between these and the periodicals that did systematically publish fashion content is crucial in distinguishing the failures from the successes of the first editorial attempts of the fashion printing industry. This allows us to reconstruct the most successful formula of periodicals intended for an audience of fashion consumers in Brazil.

After consulting the available periodicals published in Rio de Janeiro, we can conclude that it was the *Correio das Modas* that set the standard for fashion magazines that circulated in that city, displaying the main characteristics that would last until at least the end of the nineteenth century. *Correio das Modas* was published between the 5 January 1839 and 31 December 1840. In its first year of circulation, or more precisely until July 1840, it was issued on a weekly basis. In its second year of existence, as Ana Laura Donegá explains, 'its success among readers led it to begin to appear twice a week'.[27] Altogether, there were 131 numbers, of which only 79 have survived: the issues published between January and June 1840 are missing from the collection of the National Library of Rio de Janeiro.[28] On the basis of an investigation of these surviving 79 issues, we can see that the magazine maintained the same editorial policy from the first to the last number. The only change occurred when it began to be published twice a week in the second year: the weekend edition kept the same format and sections as before, while the new mid-week edition, released on Thursdays, did not contain the 'Fashion' column or the accompanying fashion patterns. Thus, 52 of the surviving 79 issues of the magazine carried the 'Fashion' section and the illustrations.

Correio das Modas was the first Rio de Janeiro fashion magazine with a column on 'Fashion' and fashion patterns that were published regularly in a significant number of issues. The two earlier magazines did not meet these criteria. *O Espelho Diamantino*, which was published fortnightly by P. Plancher-Seignot, only circulated for six months, producing fourteen issues, from 20 September 1827 to 28 April 1828, and did not to have fashion illustrations. Issues 1 and 11 are missing from the collection of the National Library, but an investigation of the twelve surviving issues confirms that there was an editorial change in the magazine from issue 7 (January, 1828) onwards, which is reflected in its content. After this date the magazine ceased to publish the 'Fashion' column, and there are only four fashion editorials in the whole collection.

Although it existed for fourteen years, *A Mulher do Simplício, or A Fluminense Exaltada*, by Paula Brito, was not published regularly, as the very frontispiece of the magazine announced: 'this magazine will appear in an indeterminate way'.[29] There were 83 issues throughout its fourteen years of circulation, which works out as an average of five per year. However, it is not possible to establish the exact frequency of publication of the periodical because we have only found the record of the publication date of the copies which are available for investigation at the National Library. At least on one occasion, there was a gap of six months between one issue and another, as recorded in the 'Fashion' column of Number 63 (23 December 1839). The 'Fashion' column, like the rest of the content of the magazine, is all in verse, one of the reasons why it was probably not published weekly or fortnightly.

Dear readers,
Virtuous beauties
Who embellish
My fatherland Rio

If you are taken aback
By my verses
I will hang on to the thread
During my song

It's already six months
That I've been away from you
But on numerous occasions
I spoke on your behalf

Of fashions which
I inquired about for you before
Today I will show
How much I have achieved[30]

The variation in the number of pages (from eight to more than twenty), the lack of a regular column on fashions, as well as its irregular appearance and lack of fashion patterns, mean that Paula Brito's periodical cannot be characterized as a fashion magazine. Nonetheless, it managed to be published for fourteen years with the same title and following the same editorial principles, which shows that it had a loyal readership. In addition to this, its long life for Brazilian standards makes it an excellent source for conducting research into the printing businesses (printing houses and stores) that enabled the production and dissemination of fashion content in Rio de Janeiro in the first half of the nineteenth century which, as a result, contributed to the inclusion of Brazil in the Paris fashion system. During its fourteen years of circulation, *A Mulher do Simplício* was printed in three different locations. To start with, the magazine was printed by the typography of Tomás B. Hunt & Co, in Rua do Sabão, and then passed to the typography of Lessa & Pereira, in Rua Detrás do Hospício. After the publication of issue number 45 of 12 December 1835, *A Mulher do Simplício* began to be printed by Paula Brito himself: 'Tipografia Imparcial' of F. P. Brito, in Praça da Constituição. The magazine was sold at least in three different places at any one time, though these changed over the years: the shops of Mr Tribuno, in Rua da Quitanda; of Baptista, in Rua da Cadeia; of Lafuente, in Rua da Cadeia; of A. e Albino, in Praça da Constituição; in the shops of Mr Severino, in Rua da Quitanda and Rua da Ajuda dos Passos, Rua do Ouvidor and also in the Imprensa Imparcial of Paula Brito. Even Laemmert, the editor of *Correio das Modas*, sold Paula Brito's magazine in the years from 1836 to 1842, or in other words, during the same period as the publication of *Correio das Modas*, apparently unconcerned about the competition.

The fashion magazine displays four main characteristics. In the first place, like all women's magazines, it can be defined as a 'feminized space',[31] in contrast with the masculine world of politics and economy, as the writer of the column for *Correio das Modas* makes clear on more than one occasion:

> While most periodicals are concerned with everyday affairs, internal and external politics, and discussing who has the last word and who does not, or who is right or wrong in the parliamentary bedlam, in what is said and done, *Correio*, goes out to its colleagues in the press and avoids the noise they make in the closet of its female readers where it always has a warm welcome. This is because *Correio* and its readers do not understand politics or anything except for what makes men amiable in society, and willingly leave these dissensions to the illustrious members of the press.[32]
>
> While the other periodicals engage in a bitter struggle to maintain the position that they adopt, one championing the good performance of the ministry and others denying it, and while they argue in the controversial field of the coming elections and strive to obtain a victory for their candidates, the *Correio das Modas*, which is fortunately free from these concerns, is discussing clothes, hats and hairstyles.[33]

Perhaps the reason why the *Espelho Diamantino* did not survive for more than fourteen issues was due exactly to the lack of a focus on strictly feminine subjects. The objectives declared in its prospectus are much too all-embracing:

> Since women form such a key part of our interests and business, they should be aware of these same commercial matters and of the principles that give rise to responsibilities and important events, so that they can form an integral part of civilization and its progress. Any intention to keep them in a state of worry and stupidity and little above domestic animals is an undertaking that is both unjust and harmful to the good of humanity and to nations that have practised it or have fallen into coarseness and moral relaxation.
>
> These truths, which are as old as the race of the children of Eve, are not unknown to any nation in Europe. There, sciences, arts and new ideas are within the grasp of the fair sex, even in their works, lessons and private periodicals. However, here they need to be replicated more than once to adapt to household customs since they still savour of the rancid nature of the moors, which remained until the time of independence as a result of colonial servility. These features still prevail in almost all classes of society and are opposed to the development of the character of a lady when the shedding of some tears, like lightning in darkness, shows a kind disposition, generous feelings, love of the country, culture and the arts and the fulfilment of all responsibilities.[34]

The first issues of *Espelho Diamantino* contained the following sections: 'Politics', 'Annals of moral virtue', 'Literature', 'Reviews of daily events in the Court', 'Fine Arts', 'Theatre', 'Fashion', 'Foreign Affairs', and 'News of the Empire'. From Number 7 onwards, as stated above, any reference to fashion was completely removed from the inside of the magazine and the following columns began to be published: 'Historical memoirs', 'News about current affairs', 'National business matters', 'Literature and theatre ', 'Serials and anecdotes'.

The second characteristic of the fashion magazine is the prominence editors gave to fashion content, especially women's fashion, since there was little variation in men's fashions.[35] In many cases, as in *Correio das Modas*, the fashion column was moved to the front page of the magazine. This enabled the development of a new journalistic genre the fashion editorial.[36] The third characteristic is that the magazine was illustrated: fashion plates reproduced from European magazines were published in almost every number. According to Ferreira, lithography had been known in Brazil as early as 1819. Since that date newspapers published advertisements alluding to this printing process.[37] The first illustrated periodical published in Rio, *Museu Universal*, is from 1837.[38] *Correio das Modas* started publication just two years later, being therefore one of the first periodicals in Brazil to publish lithography. Like the illustrations of *Museu Universal*, the imported lithography turned into a fixed and essential feature of *Correio das Modas*, and of the successful fashion magazines from then onwards. Of the fashion illustrations found in Brazilian periodicals of the second half of the century, the great majority — and possibly all of them — were reproduced from European magazines.

The inclusion of European fashion illustrations was a determining factor in ensuring that the fashion magazine was recognized as a specific type of periodical and had an international reach, because it allowed the image of the same garment to be placed in the hands of readers and subscribers of different magazines in various locations on both sides of the Atlantic. Nevertheless the nineteenth-century fashion magazine remained for more than a century text-dominant, even though the presence of visual content was growing as the century advanced. Wolbers states that:

> There was a much larger proportion of words to images. That is, the features tended to be word-heavy, with a visibly larger proportion of words to images on each page. Space in a magazine is its gold. Therefore, the editor assumed an enormous responsibility when making decisions regarding how that space was used. It took courage and vision for editors to shift away from a long-winded, text-heavy, bookish publication to the image-dominant, design-driven periodicals of today.[39]

Wolbers reached this conclusion on the basis of an examination of nineteenth-century British magazines such as *Ladies Literary Cabinet* (1819–22), *Graham's Magazine* (1826–55), *Ladies' Magazine* (1828–36), *Ladies' Repository* (1841–76) and *Peterson's Ladies' National Magazine* (1842–98). However, Wolber's analysis also applies to the fashion magazines which had both a national and international circulation and appeared in other countries such as France and Germany, as well as Brazil: *Les Journal des Dames et des Modes* (1797–1839) e *La Saison* (1868–[1902?]).[40] The fact that the text predominated over images is a characteristic of fashion magazines in the nineteenth century in general.

This, then, is the fourth characteristic of fashion magazines of the nineteenth century: the heavy predominance of text over image. They are a miscellany made up of a variety of texts and sections that range from the captions beneath the fashion illustrations (the written-garment),[41] the fashion editorial, literary texts (either translated or by national authors), and literary reviews to chronicles about the high society and local cultural life. A constant factor was the presence of serialized literature, in Brazil from *Correio das Modas* onwards, which certainly helped to consolidate the fashion magazine as an autonomous journalistic entity because it combined literature and fashion in the same periodical and thus covered two of the activities traditionally associated with both the domestic world and women — reading and needlework.[42] Added to these were the advertisements and paper patterns, which became increasingly common in the fashion magazines in the second half of the century.

The fact that European and Brazilian fashion magazines followed the same format, and the coexistence in the same magazine of imported and locally produced visual and textual contents, make them a valuable source of data for studies of cultural transfers between the two sides of the Atlantic. Even the fashion magazines published in Portuguese in the first half of the nineteenth century, such as *Correio das Modas*, consist of a multicultural and journalistic medium that is the product of artistic, graphic and intellectual processes that occur in different spaces. Like the French dressmakers, they are mediators of concepts between different cultures, with the advantage for book and print history studies of being the printed medium that enables and materializes the transfer. They were the principal means of employing print for the cultural transmission of the concept of fashion from France to Brazil.

Notes to Chapter 8

1. See for example Maria do Carmo Teixeira Rainho, *A cidade e a moda: novas pretensões, novas distinções: Rio de Janeiro, século XIX* (Brasília: Editora UNB, 2002).
2. Joaquim Manuel de Macedo, *Memórias da Rua do Ouvidor: publicações em folhetins do 'Jornal do Commercio'* (Rio de Janeiro: Tipografia Perseverança, 1878), Chapter 10, p. 151, online at <http://www.brasiliana.usp.br/bbd/handle/1918/01066400#page/5/mode/1up> [accessed 15 March 2013].
3. Yuniya Kawamura, *The Japanese Revolution in Paris Fashion* (Oxford: Berg, 2006). Michel Espagne, 'Transferts culturels et histoire du livre', in *Histoire et civilisations du livre. Revue internationale*, 5 (2009), 202–18.
4. Gabriel Almeida Antunes Rossini, 'As pragmáticas portuguesas de fins do século XVII: política fabril e manufatureira reativa', in *Saeculum. Revista de História* (João Pessoa), 22 (Jan–Jun 2010), 117–35.
5. See Rossini, 'As pragmáticas portuguesas de fins do século XVII'.
6. Camila Borges da Silva, *O símbolo indumentário: distinção e prestígio no Rio de Janeiro (1808–1821)* (Rio de Janeiro: Arquivo Geral da Cidade do Rio de Janeiro, 2010).
7. Macedo, *Memórias da Rua do Ouvidor*, pp. 154–55.
8. The full account of the agreements was published in the Rio de Janeiro daily newspaper *Gazeta de Notícias* on 17 January 1817.
9. On the French artistic mission see, for example, Lúcia Maria Bastos Pereira das Neves, 'A missão artística francesa' <http://redememoria.bn.br/2012/01/a-missao-artistica-francesa/> [accessed 23 June 2014].
10. Borges da Silva, *O símbolo indumentário*.
11. *Modista* will be translated here by 'dressmaker', *costureira* by 'seamstress'. The concept of fashion designer (*estilista* in Portuguese) did not exist in the period under consideration.
12. Lená Medeiros de Menezes, 'Francesas no Rio de Janeiro: trabalho, sonhos e ousadia (1816–1822)', *Caderno Espaço Feminino*, 12.15 (Aug–Dec 2004), 61–82 (p. 73).
13. According to Cláudia Maria das Graças Chaves, the Charter of 27 March 1810 extended to women the right to take part in this trade. Before this date, the participation of women in commercial activities had been very restricted. They only had the right to belong to the class of dealers in yarn, if they had inherited the business from a registered trader dealing in goods specifically for female use. See Cláudia Maria das Graças Chaves, 'O outro lado do Império: as disputas mercantis e os conflitos de jurisdição no Império Luso-Brasileiro', *TOPOI*, 7.12 (Jan–Jun 2006), 147–77.

14. Menezes, 'Francesas no Rio de Janeiro', p. 77.
15. See Borges da Silva, *O símbolo indumentário*; Chaves, 'O outro lado Império'; Menezes, 'Francescas no Rio de Janeiro'.
16. Yuniya Kawamura, *Fashion-ology* (Oxford: Berg Publishers, 2004), p. 39.
17. Kawumura, *Fashion-ology*, p. 33.
18. Ibid, p. 4.
19. Ibid, p. 13.
20. Gilda de Mello e Souza, *O espírito das roupas: a moda no século XIX* (São Paulo: Companhia das Letras, 1987), p. 130.
21. See Ana Cláudia Suriani da Silva, *Machado de Assis's 'Philosopher or dog?': From Serial to Book Form* (Oxford: Legenda, 2010).
22. Roland Barthes, *The Fashion System*, trans. by Matthew Ward and Richard Howard (New York: Hill and Wang, 1983).
23. According to Ipanema & Ipanema, approximately 30 periodicals were published in Rio de Janeiro in 1823; 13 in 1824; 31 in 1826, and 26 in 1827. In the years that followed, there was a steady increase in the number of periodicals published in Rio de Janeiro, which reached 52 in 1830. Marcelo Ipanema and Cybelle Ipanema, 'Imprensa na Regência: observações estatísticas e de opinião pública', *Revista do Instituto Histórico e Geográfico Brasileiro* (Rio de Janeiro), 307 (Apr–Jun 1975), 91–95 (p. 94). See also Carlos Eduardo França de Oliveira, 'Tipógrafos, redatores e leitores: aspectos da imprensa periódica no Primeiro Reinado', *Revista Brasileira de História & Ciências Sociais*, 2.3 (July 2010), <www.rbhcs.com> [accessed 10 March 2013]; and Lucia Maria Bastos Pereira das Neves, *Corcundas, constitucionais e pés-de-chumbo: a cultura política da independência, 1820–1822* (Rio de Janeiro: FAPERJ/Revan, 2003).
24. Buitoni also mentions *Jornal das Variedades* (1835); however, we did not find any record of this periodical in the catalogue of the National Library of Rio de Janeiro. On completing this study we had been unable to determine its place of publication. Dulcília Schroeder Buitoni, *Imprensa feminina* (São Paulo: Editora Ática, 1986).
25. Maria do Carmo Teixeira Rainho, *A cidade e a moda*; Dulcília Schroeder Buitoni, *Imprensa Feminina* and *Mulher de papel* (São Paulo: Edições Loyola, 1981).
26. *Simplício* is a first name. It means 'simple'. *Fluminense* means 'born in Rio de Janeiro'.
27. Ana Laura Donegá, 'Publicar ficção em meados do século XIX: um estudo das revistas femininas editadas pelos irmãos Laemmert' (unpublished MPhil dissertation, Campinas: UNICAMP, 2013), p. 48.
28. Ana Laura Donegá did not manage to locate the missing issues in other libraries either.
29. *A Mulher do Simplício*, Number 3 (10 March 1832).
30. In Portuguese: Gratas leitoras, | Belas virtuosas, | Que ornais mimosas | Meu pátrio Rio; | Se vos causa | Meu verso espanto, | Desde meu canto | Mantenho o fio. | De vós ausente | Há já seis meses, | Imensas vezes | Em vós faleis | Das modas que antes | Por vós indigo | Hoje aqui trago | Quanto alcancei.
31. Margaret Beetham, *A Magazine of Her Own?: Domesticity and Desire in the Woman's Magazine, 1800–1914* (New York: Routledge, 1996), p. 3.
32. *Correio das Modas*, n. 22, 1 June 1839.
33. *Correio das Modas*, n. 32, 18 October 1840.
34. *Espelho Diamantino*, 'Prospecto', undated [1827].
35. Margaret Beetham, *A Magazine of Her Own?*, p. 3.
36. See Ana Cláudia Suriani da Silva, 'The Genesis of the Brazilian Fashion Magazine and Fashion Editorial (1827–1851)', *Film, Fashion and Consumption* 2.3 (2013), pp. 273–85.
37. Orlando da Costa Ferreira, *Imagem e letra* (São Paulo: EdUSP, 1994), p. 323.
38. *Museu Universal. Jornal das Famílias Brasileiras* (Rio de Janeiro: Casa dos Editores J. Villeneuve e Comp, 1837–1839).
39. Marian Frances Wolbers, *Uncovering Fashion: Fashion Communications across the Media* (New York: Fairchild, 2009), p. 172.
40. On *La Saison* see Silva, *Machado de Assis's 'Philosopher or Dog?'*, especially Chapters 2 and 3.
41. See Barthes, *The Fashion System*.
42. Beetham, p. 10, and Ian Watt, *The Rise of the Novel* (London: Chatto and Windus, 1957).

CHAPTER 9

The Brazilian and the French *Bas de Page*

Lúcia Granja[1]

In the *Bas de Page* of the Newspapers

On 1 July 1836, Émile de Girardin, the proprietor of *La Presse*, published the first edition of that paper and thereby revolutionized the market, by selling it for half the customary price. This enabled the newspaper to increase the number of its subscribers and, as a result, offset the financial losses incurred by this reduction. Other strategies were also employed to expand sales and increase profits, which included keeping the back page of the paper for advertisements and introducing literature into that 'world in four pages'. However, the initiatives taken by Girardin for *La Presse* ran parallel with those of other newspapers of the period and should not be viewed as purely commercial measures.[2]

> For the first time, a newspaper proprietor put at the centre of his operations the link that he sought to forge with the public and the world of mass media which he created in this way: it was an ideological, as well as a cultural and socio-economic world where, for the first time, advertising asserted its presence and held sway.[3]

Briefly, this was the beginning of the revolution in literary journalism and meant that French prose fiction could be adapted to this kind of publication. The taste for novels, the development of journalism and the changes in readership, especially at the beginning of the second half of the eighteenth century, were, as Ian Watt has described, phenomena that were already familiar to the British public.[4]

Thus, as occurred with the English novel, the French serialized novels achieved success while also obtaining a new public, and this led to the rise of important authors like Eugène Sue and Alexandre Dumas *père*, whose novels would appear in serialized form or in complete volumes, either in French or translated, throughout most of Europe.

On the other side of the Atlantic, some new countries, in their struggle to assert their nationhood, closely followed new trends in European countries, particularly France. In Brazil it was no different, and throughout the nineteenth century the *bas de page* of the newspapers contained serialized novels, mainly translated from the pages of newspapers that had come from France. 'Why is there this success in distant shores where there are no big cities, in a formula that is bound up with a particular social period in European France?', Marlyse Meyer wondered.[5]

An answer to this question is offered in the testimony of José de Alencar (1829–1877) in *Como e porque sou romancista*: the custom of reading by the family fireside. It is there, even before the arrival of the serialized novel in Brazil, that there could already be found 'continual and repeated readings of novels and romantic stories', some from Britain although the range of books was limited: '[...] they comprised a dozen works among which the following stood out: *Amanda e Oscar*, *Saint-Clair das Ilhas*, *Celestina* and others that I don't remember'.[6] In this way 'fiction in slices', to borrow another expression from Marlyse Meyer, began to occupy an increasingly important space at the bottom of the front pages of the newspapers, sharing this site with comments on general news, reviews or the *feuilleton-variétés* or *folhetim-variedades* [critical texts], or with the first experiments concerning the texts now known as *crônicas*.[7]

Today, the Brazilian *crônica* is very often described as a 'minor genre', in the borderlines between journalism and literature. Antonio Candido called it 'the ground floor style', since it is intimate, impressionistic, familiar, and almost colloquial. As is well summarized by John Gledson, the *crônica*

> remains on the fringes of what strictly speaking is literature and it is felt [...] that there is some kind of tension or constraint surrounding it, above all a tendency to attempt to seem as respectable as possible. It is close to more prestigious genres (short stories, poetry etc.) and seeks to free itself from what seems to be its suspect journalistic origins and become something more than 'this ephemeral publication which is bought one day, and the next day is used to wrap up a pair of shoes or to cover the kitchen floor', in the words of Antonio Candido.[8]

Before reaching this format, the *crônica* was first created in the space of the *folhetim-variedades* and then underwent several adaptations. The purpose here is to raise some of the issues resulting from these alterations, and this necessarily leads to a further issue: that of the pliability of the literary forms that were created both in and for the spaces of the newspaper.

Two phenomena in particular exemplify where this flexibility acts as a constituent factor, and they are thus important for the argument here: the space of the page in the newspaper where the items are constantly being changed and assembled; and the public sphere that is outside the newspaper and where there is an interplay between the items, the readers, and the facts.[9]

The Daily Press in Brazil: The Case of *Jornal do Commercio*

One of the main daily newspapers in the nineteenth century that has survived to the present day is the *Jornal do Commercio*, founded in 1827 by bookseller, editor, and typographer, Pierre Plancher (1779–1844), a Frenchman in exile in Brazil. This newspaper took on a great importance, and was a kind of official voice during the period of the Empire (1822–89).

The *Jornal do Commercio* was so closely linked to events in the French press that from 13 October 1838 Plancher translated and published *Le capitaine Paul* by Alexandre Dumas, only a few months after the publication of the serialized version in the French paper *Le Siècle*. The *Jornal do Commercio* included some of the leading French books in serialized form in that epoch: for example, *Les mystères de Paris* by Eugène Sue, translated by Justiniano José da Rocha, and published between 1 September 1844 and 20 January 1845, which had been published in France by the *Journal des Débats* between 19 June 1842 and 15 October 1843.

In the same period, the Brazilian dramatist Martins Pena (1815–1848), also an expert in music and theatre-staging, wrote a series of articles exclusively about the opera, 'A semana lírica' [The Lyrical Week]. It should be stressed that the publication of texts of such a specialized nature was very unusual in the first half of the nineteenth century in Brazil, because social life was not regular enough to be able always to count on a 'fixed column' devoted to reviewing plays in the space in question. This means that theatrical seasons might be included in the *crônica*, but the plays were not varied enough and there was not enough material on offer to justify the publication of two or three weekly features about the performances. At all events, the seasons in the period 1846–47 offered enough promising material for Martins Pena, and the *Jornal de Commercio* covered them, as contemporary European newspapers then did. From 1852 onwards, the *Jornal do Commercio* became the first periodical to use the term *crônica* for a series of newspaper columns called 'A semana' [The Week] at the bottom of the page. In compiling this weekly *crônica*, Francisco Otaviano (1825–1889) addressed topical subjects in his articles, like almost all the Brazilian feature writers of that period who followed in his footsteps.

From the *folhetim-variedades* to the *crônica*

When account is taken of the fact that the fictional works of one of the greatest Brazilian writers, Machado de Assis (1839–1908), were originally published by several periodicals, where he also often collaborated in journalistic articles, it is clear that this is an avenue that can open up new ways of interpreting short stories and novels.[10]

When his fiction is read today, usually with the aid of supporting material in book form (and in the case of the short stories, even in general anthologies of selected texts by the authors and organizers), much critical analysis is oblivious to the possible interpretations that an awareness of the relationships between literary work and journalism could add to the scholarship on these texts.[11] The fact is that Machado de Assis created a new kind of prose fiction in and for the press, and, from the 1880s onwards, this literary work brought about a real revolution in Brazilian literature and its relationship with European models, particularly French.

Writing a weekly newspaper column was a task that posed a challenge to some of the best writers, including Machado de Assis, who began to work for the newspapers when he was still very young, and continued to do so for more than forty years, between 1859 and 1900. From the beginning of the 1860s, the writer was involved in the task of turning daily events in Brazil into *crônicas* every week and his texts also formed the origin of the genre. In the following early text by Machado de Assis (from 1859, when he was twenty), he writes at length about the genre, which provides a better understanding of this subject:

> The *crônica* was born of the newspaper, meaning that the chronicler was born of the journalist. It is this close affinity that shapes the salient features of the modern development. The chronicler is an admirable fusion of the useful and the trivial, the curious and remarkable offspring of the serious in consort with the frivolous. These two elements, poles apart, as heterogeneous as fire and water, marry perfectly in the formation of the new animal.
>
> This strange result is brought about by the striking affinity between the journalist and the chronicler. From the former there falls on the latter a serious and searching light, a calm reflection, a profound insight. As for musing and levity, it is all embodied in the chronicler himself; it's his very essence.
>
> The chronicler, in society, occupies the place the hummingbird has in the vegetable word; he hops, he swoops, he plays, he quivers, he hovers and he shakes his wings over the succulent stems, over all the vigorous saps. The whole world belongs to him; even the world of politics.[12]

These 'Aquarelas' [Watercolour Sketches] that Machado de Assis wrote for the periodical *O Espelho* in 1859 resemble some of the portraits published in the French press, pictures that represent different social types (the undesirable fellow diner, or *comensal*, the retired civil servant, the writer of serials, among others), all painted in strong colours. The chronicler 'is the observer of social life who seeks to depict the characteristics of certain kinds of people who tarnish the society in which they live'.[13] As shown in the extract cited above, the chronicler is described as a miniature version of the journalist and hence of the newspaper.

From a definition of this new 'Adam's rib', a distinction can be drawn between the journalist and the chronicler, as if the former had no bearing on the latter. However, to a large extent, this process does not occur in reverse: the journalist is described as a serious figure who reflects, observes, and has penetrating analytical powers, while the chronicler, who is more popular than the professional from whom he originates, makes a display of his light-hearted and capricious nature. He addresses all the topics of the week, including his own article, and is even prepared to enter the realm of politics, where 'the curious and unusual side of his nature consorts with frivolity'.

In France, the first *chroniques* had characteristics that were somewhat different from those that gradually emerged in Brazil, in particular with regard to form. The narrator of the first French *chroniques* made virtually no comments on politics and even less on fiction or literature, which excluded any scope for invention. As Thérenty and Vaillant point out, 1836 can be considered 'Year One of the era of mass media', owing to the considerable expansion of newspapers and their accessibility to readers.[14] The chroniclers in *La Presse* drew up an impressive list of events and retained an absolute respect for its commitment to make *facts* the reference point; it compiled a list of facts of the day before and included a wide range or hierarchy of subjects. In the case of politics, the hierarchy was the aristocracy, the daily life of the King, the royal family, the court, and only then the city. The commentaries of French essayists only included a little news and were not digressive.

In the case of the Brazilian *crônica*, it is evident that Machado de Assis's narrator linked chroniclers' activities to those of journalists and, with reference to their subjects, he notes that chroniclers 'even went as far as politics'. This remark highlights the extreme seriousness of the subject for that space. However, it should be interpreted as implying an ironic hint rather than a totally serious remark, since politics was always present in the *crônicas* that dealt with the various news items of the week. However, rather than suggesting that the journalist and chronicler were in opposition, it means that the person in opposition to the journalist was a hybrid figure combining the writer of fiction and the journalist. After all, Brazilian writers in the *crônica* section had used a different procedure for their texts compared to French journalists. In this way, the principles of the *crônica* encouraged the entry of politics into the texts, beyond the news items of the week. It is hard to imagine that the political *chroniques* of the *Revue de Deux Mondes*, for example, could have been established in this way, mixing politics and varieties, 'serious and frivolous', as Machado de Assis said.

In France, as Marie-Eve Thérenty argues, the space reserved for articles and news items on most newspapers front pages was far from providing

> a framework which freezes the current state of affairs in the world but rather imports knowledge about the world with a lightness of touch. Texts are a part of a very flexible system that allows and justifies their dissemination and in which framework, to a certain extent, solely exist so that it should be broken up in response to present circumstances.[15]

In Brazil, this flexible system seems to have been even less rigid than in France, where, as it has been shown above, the system already allowed considerable exchanges. As a result, the exchange between ideas and textual forms within the periodical was even easier, since the latter were related to less varied forms of sociability than in some European countries,[16] and the Brazilian newspapers had a more restricted scope for writing.[17]

Thus in Brazil there was a dual process — a contamination of the *crônicas* by the upper space of the page (where there was news about politics) and a commentary on this subject treated in a literary guise by the chroniclers. Consideration of the transfer and acculturation of serial writing in the newspapers brings a confrontation with the flexibilization of textual forms, which resulted in an exchange between the headings and other items that filled the space of the *crônicas*, as the section below will show.

Literary Creativity in the *Crônicas*

If Machado de Assis is taken as a general model for Brazilian writers and journalists of the mid-nineteenth century, the weekly space assigned at the bottom of the page was full of possibilities for literary creativity, and we can find there examples of rhetoric, irony, quotations from literary and cultural traditions, parody and the inclusion of short passages of fiction among the commentaries, self-referencing and other elements, all of which constitute key features. In one of his miscellaneous articles, Machado de Assis's narrator tells us what good organization should be:

> It should begin today with a funeral eulogy. I have reversed the order and kept it to the end. What mainly worried me was the transition from sadness to gaiety [...]. In the newspaper column it is a mistake to make the readers depressed and then go on to speak about cheerful or festive subjects.[18]

When considering the French political columns of the earliest period of *La Presse*, where a conventional array of subjects could be found, a self-referencing view emerges that would become as frequent as the commentaries of the Brazilian chroniclers. Why would it be a mistake to first make readers depressed and then to talk to them about cheerful things? Two hypotheses can be given to explain the reasoning behind this, which are not mutually exclusive: either the chronicler is primarily concerned with entertaining the reader (in which case he would keep the sad news to the end when he would be able to speak in a semi-casual way about the subject, as a result of the number of characters being used up in a text of a predetermined size), or the reader is confronted with a narrator who clearly represents himself as the organizer of a discourse. In this case, he shows us that the order does not matter very much since, through a rhetorical form of self-allusive commentary, he is concealing something that causes him real difficulty: making a transition between two disparate subjects.

A second example of the Brazilian *crônica*, can be added here. In some areas, Machado de Assis was preceded as a chronicler by José de Alencar, a writer of great importance for Brazilian literature, who successfully experimented with the formula of the serialized novel at the bottom of political news-sheets — *Cinco Minutos* [*Five Minutes*] (1856), *A viuvinha* [*The Little Widow*] (1857), and *O Guarani* [*The Guarani*] (1857) — and also wrote *crônicas*. From the 1860s onwards, Alencar, in contrast to Machado de Assis, continued his literary work away from the periodicals.

The following fairly well-known passage by Alencar, written a few years before Machado de Assis's text, illustrates that the writer understood very well that it would make a great difference to work on the literary part of the *crônicas*:

> However, the same didn't go well for me. I enjoyed myself of course; but that Sunday was so full of things, and in a week when I made my debut in such a brilliant way, I found such an abundance of incidents that it seriously alarmed me. I suddenly saw an interminable series of balls and *soirées*, a huge catalogue of revolutions and enough news to fill two supplements of a newspaper on the same day [...].
>
> It's a relief that I still haven't taken a lot of trouble to find out who exactly was the inventor of this monster of Horace, this new Proteus which is called *crônica* otherwise I would make use of some moments, and when I was in a bad mood, to write a biography about them, which with some annotations by certain critics that I know, I would turn this hellish subject into the purgatory where the inventor of such a disastrous idea must necessarily reside.
>
> Forcing someone to run through all the events, switching from jokes to serious subjects, from laughter and delight to the maladies and miseries of society; and to do this with the same *nonchalance* that a lady flicks through the golden pages of her album, or with all the daintiness and poise that a young blond girl hands the knave of clubs to three dozen admirers! They make the writer a kind of hummingbird fluttering in a zigzag direction and sucking, as if they are nectar from flowers, the grace, salt and spirit which he must necessarily find in the most mundane facts.[19]

As this shows, the reader is faced with a nineteenth-century 'man of letters' whose job is to draft a new text for a newspaper. Once again, it is worth noting the use of meta-language and self-referencing in the newspaper column. The chronicler has to have 'the idea of plunging into the role and being as free as space', which suggests that the nature of the column is constantly being constructed.

The 'monstrous' aspect of the newspaper column in José de Alencar's text is mainly linked to the wide range of subjects that the writer has to cover in his review of the week. However, in the extract above, it is more the profusion of subjects that is found disturbing than their nature or specific features, as in the case of politics for Machado de Assis. With Alencar, there are balls and night-time parties that occurred in the same week as revolutions, and these subjects must be balanced inside the *crônica*, as well as in the thoughts and opinions expressed by the writer himself. Developing the metaphor of Proteus, the *crônica* is a monster because the writer is still required to be inventive in his form and tone. Finally, it is the public that assesses the talent of the writer/journalist and is represented here by the reader who 'screws up the paper and flings it aside with a grimace'.[20]

Furthermore, there is another difficulty arising from the 'new Proteus', which can be found in the concern with the reading public who purchases the printed texts that are designed to please him. Alencar refers to the space on the page as being a space for compulsory entertainment, and its purpose should be to form an interesting and amusing article. However, with the means that he always had at his disposal (a pen, paper, ink), all this was undertaken rather in the style of a 'cobbler mending shoes' than in that of a refined shoemaker, as he would go on to say in the same text.[21] After all, this comparison takes a path in the opposite direction from the concept of 'industrial literature' put forward by Sainte-Beuve in his well-known article published in *Revue des Deux Mondes* (1 September 1839).

In addition to these ideas about the form and nature of the text, Alencar continues with images linking the chronicler with animals:

> And this is not everything. After the wretched chronicler, by sheer will-power, has managed to utter his last gasp and when at the expense of magic and enchantment, he has done what he can to record what is worth remembering of the times that have flown by, he finally stops thinking and lets his thoughts escape onto the page, as in a free space. He thinks he is a butterfly emerging from its chrysalis to show off its dazzling array of colours; but he is fooling himself; he is simply an ant who has created wings only then to lose them.[22]

The chronicler had been described as a graceful, swift-moving, and inventive creature, but soon he becomes abject in this relationship. From a hummingbird, he turns to a butterfly (which is the image that the chronicler has of himself), and, proceeding down the scale, he comes to compare himself to flying ants (which would be the true image of what this writer is).

These comparisons refer to the first *chroniques* of *La Presse* written on 1 July 1836, in which Frédéric Soulié compared these texts — and not the chronicler — to a butterfly. After two paragraphs, in which he makes allegorical comparisons to what would have taken place if serials had existed in antiquity, he tells us:

> But the time has passed for lovely allegorical transformations: and if it was necessary to represent the *crônicas* in a tangible form, the very thing that I dared to suggest in my lectures, it would be in the shape of a huge butterfly.

> At the back of a pen that represents the body, in the guise of wings, there are attached two strips of paper that you can read, and there you have the complete butterfly.[23]

The image of a butterfly made up of the pen that writes the column, with two strips of paper stuck to it to represent the article itself, or a flying feather that acts as a duster to sweep up the facts of the week, is not exactly the same as a creature hovering over all the subjects of the week with the aim of sucking the sap that will be used for writing the text. In any event, the image of the two butterflies (a metaphor that the Brazilian chronicler enhances as hummingbird or reduces to represent himself as a flying ant) gathers up and defines, each one in its own way, the writings at the bottom of the newspaper page. In terms of the shaping of the chronicler/*crônicas*, the images of the creator and his creations that were represented in the metaphor of the butterfly were reproduced from Soulié until they reached the South American serials twenty years later, with José de Alencar and Machado de Assis.

When considering ways to define the *crônica*, these metaphors can serve as an example of the tension that existed between facts and invention, both of them considered as nature and constraint on the prose of that kind of text: the more the columnist flutters and weakens his commitment to a theoretical reference-point, the more he overcomes the barriers of the newspaper column, which in its French version was closer to being a report and commentary; the Brazilian *crônica* followed the path of invention. The evidence suggests that this second route was chosen by José de Alencar, Machado de Assis, and practically all the other *bas de page* columnists, directing the process that leads to the singularity of the Brazilian *crônica*.

Bas de page in Brazil and in Other Countries

As shown above, in the French newspapers, in the early days of the newspaper columns, or *chroniques*, *bas de pages* were developed as articles that provided the readers with a report that was usually connected to politics and where the subjects were treated in a hierarchical way with the narrator adopting an unobtrusive stance. The subject of analysis now is the relationship between serial fiction and the development of the *crônica* in Brazil.

In the French newspapers, the serial usually occupied two *bas de page* of more or less uniform height; in Brazil, when the *Jornal do Commercio* published serial novels in translation, it adopted a dynamic of its own with regard to the use of the bottom of the page. The idea being developed here is that this spatial use provides a lot of information about the textual characteristics that the *crônicas* eventually assumed in Brazil.

There, the increase or reduction of the number of lines given to this space was frequently altered; thus there is a large amount of variation in the volume of text. For example, on 15 October 1851, *Dieu Dispose*, by Alexandre Dumas, is forty-five lines tall compared to thirty-one lines tall on 16 October 1851, as visible in the images in Figure 9.1.

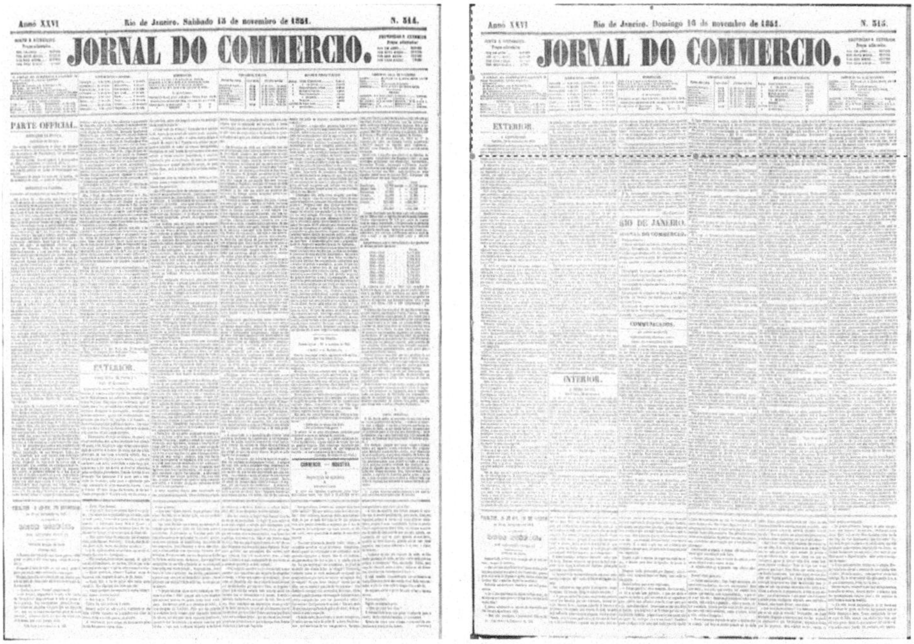

JORNAL DO COMMERCIO.

JORNAL DO COMMERCIO.

Fig. 9.1. *Jornal do Commercio*, 15 and 16 November, 1851, p. 1 — *bas de page.*
© National Library of Rio de Janeiro

On the horizontal plane, the space reserved for the serial novels in the *Jornal do Commercio* was either squeezed or enlarged for editorial and typographic reasons, or depended on the amount of political and business information that the paper had to convey, particularly that originating from the government (such as transcriptions of debates in the chambers, decrees, and all kinds of official papers). As already mentioned, the *Jornal de Commercio* operated as a kind of official newspaper for much of the period of the Brazilian Empire. Thus it was given money by the regime, which meant that its survival did not depend on subscribers. Priority was inevitably given to political and commercial news, and the serials stuck closely to this pattern.

Without doubt, the physical effect of allotting space to novels led to alterations in the way literary work was read. But what is most curious is the way that flexibility proved to be the quality that gave rise to a specific characteristic of Brazilian *crônicas*. In view of the vertical and horizontal shrinkages and enlargements, extremely variable organization is evident in the serialized novel. On some occasions, this occurred when that item followed the *crônicas*, as is illustrated by the picture in Figure 9.2.

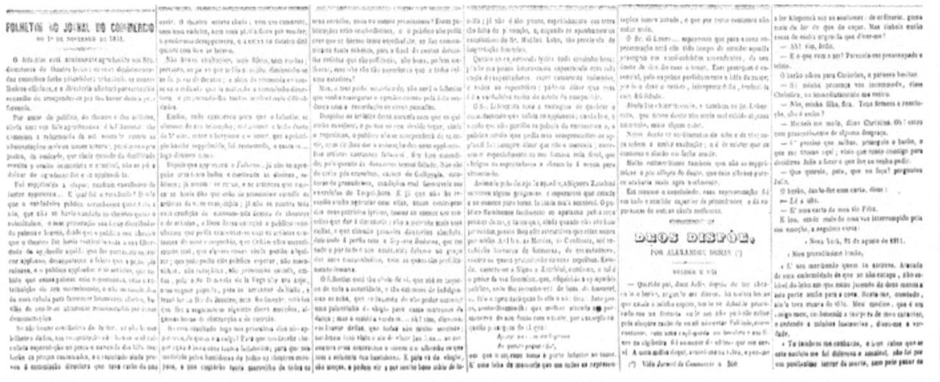
FOLHETIM DO JORNAL DO COMMERCIO
1° DE NOVEMBRO DE 1851.

DEOS DISPÕE,
POR ALEXANDRE DUMAS

Fig. 9.2. *Jornal do Commercio*, 1 November 1851, p. 1 — *bas de page*.

Admittedly this did not happen very often, but it could do so, and this shows that the space devoted to each kind of text was not strictly fixed, nor was the number of lines left to compose the *bas the page.* Thus, if there were enough topics in the *crônica*, the whole edition of the paper would be filled, but when there was a less extensive range of items, two different types of texts were put together, as on 1 November 1851 and on other occasions. At the beginning of that November, this took place in the following way: the critical column, which dealt with the lyrical theatre (i.e. the opera) with great irony, filled four and a half columns at the bottom of the first page and squeezed the novel, which continued for a column and a half of this page and the whole of the bottom of the second page. On that day, Dumas père's novels, *Le trou de l'enfer* and *Dieu dispose*, which had been appearing in the *Jornal do Commercio* for several months, broke from what had been the original cut-off point in the narrative. The *Jornal* published one and a half chapters of the serial novel (the whole of Chapter 57, 'Épouse et mère', and half of Chapter 58, ' La nuit du départ'), printing them down the penultimate column of the first page until the end of the column on the second page.

However, the full effects of a serial novel depended on the structure of its chapters. As a result, when the *Jornal do Commercio* decided to make this cut, the hiatus created between the two parts of Chapter 58 had significantly different effects on the way the novel was received. In Brazil, it completely obliterated any feeling of suspense and destroyed the effects of the passage of time, which are bound up with the state of anguish of the character, Christina, in the chapters referred to here. In the Brazilian publication, the dramatic intensity of this part of the plot, as well as the feelings of the character Christina, are weakened because of the way in which this chapter was split. As it is not especially important to the argument here, the novel's plot will not be covered in detail. Suffice to say that it is precisely in this chapter that Christina first takes stock of her husband's cowardly action. She wakes up during the night in a state of terror and discovers, to her consternation, that her husband has left for New York while she was asleep, betraying the promise he had made on the preceding evening. So, as the chapter in question was not published in its entirety, because the novel had to cede space to a theatre review in the *bas de page*, Christina wakes up on 1 November and her awareness of Júlio's departure only appears four days later on 5 November, when the newspaper continued with the publication of the novel. In this case, the *Jornal do Commercio* did not carry out the procedure of organizing the space for the text with any flexibility by varying its height (number of lines), as was commonly the case, but rather — almost going against the laws of physics — allowed two bodies to occupy the same space without really being able to share it (unless it is supposed that through this cohabitation both parts were merged and retained at the same time).

In view of this, analysis of the issues linked to the occupation of space at the *bas de page* demonstrates that having the two textual typologies share the same space can 'spoil' the effect of each, especially in the case of the serialized novel. The presence of critical columns pushed the instalment of the novel some columns forward and disrupted the way it was structured, as well as some of the effects of the reading. On the other hand, critical columns and *crônicas* modified each other by sharing the same space in the newspaper (because the same space took in, on alternate days, texts of different types), or with the possibly real sharing, as in the example above, two discursive registers — the referential (the theatre criticism) and the literary, fictional. Here is a possible motive for the intimacy with which Brazilian chroniclers moved, in their texts, between politics and anecdote, the 'useful and futile' of Machado de Assis and José de Alencar.

By Way of Conclusion

The evidence presented in this discussion suggests that *crônicas*, critical columns, and the instalments of novels, among other items, merged in the Brazilian *bas de pages*. Moreover, this was in some way bound up with the rise of the modern Brazilian *crônica*, where news, politics, analysis, commentary, and fictional works were combined in a distinct way.

Writing *crônicas* is self-referential and the narrators were constantly reflecting on the process of writing and the nature of the text that they invented every day for the periodicals. It would be difficult to find an example of a text in the whole range of Brazilian writing where the narrator positions himself discreetly. Everything takes place, both in France and in Brazil, in a similar manner. This can be illustrated on the French side by taking an example from an essay by Théophile Gautier:

> Our serialized essay is very short (the reader may find it too long) and we will need a triad on which to build a sixth column: six columns are not too many to support this transversal cross-section. It is a kind of typographic architrave which bears the weight of politics and the whole edifice of the newspaper.[24]

In this short extract, Gautier shows what the space at the bottom of the page really means, and adopts the metaphor of a building to symbolize the support of the *haut de page* [the top of the page, the space for the news] by the *bas de page*. Conceiving of it this way provides a better understanding of the power of this space at the bottom of the page and why it so naturally welcomes the self-representation of its writers/writing, as well as providing the space for the creation, invention, and communication of and between cultures.

Although the phenomena of the Brazilian and French press were similar in many aspects, the process of transferring new headings created in French newspapers resulted in radical changes when they were implemented in Brazil. This can be understood from several standpoints — sociological, literary, and discursive — and can explain the climate that prevailed when these changes occurred.

With reference to the terminology that is used to define the texts, the expressions *folhetim-variedades* and *crônica* are used almost synonymously (as far as the terms are used in Brazil) and the expression *crônicas de variedades* [columns with a range of items] can also be drawn on. However, the emphasis here has been on those described as *crônicas*, showing how they originated, to a certain extent, from a merging of different kinds of texts that filled the bottom space of Brazilian newspapers, and included political columns, miscellaneous items, critical reviews, and the serialized novels.

In *crônicas*, politics was blended with the general topics of the week, under the badge of literary creativity. The texts published in the *bas de page* in Brazil had to conform to a mild form of censorship during the years of the Empire and also had to adapt to a more limited social life, combining theatre, literature, arts, news, politics, and so on in a single weekly publication. Both in France and in Brazil, 'the men of letters were exactly the same people as the journalists',[25] but in France, from the period 1850–60 onwards, the headings, which had been severely restricted (Littérature, Premier-Paris, columns, and criticism),[26] experienced a considerable increase in range. Contemporaries of these models of journalism like Machado de Assis and José de Alencar show that in Brazil the articles that were written from a political standpoint or dealt with topical events of the week, as well as their concern with providing entertainment, combined literary inventiveness with journalism.

All this was organized in a space that belonged to the serialized novel, which had as its main objectives the provision of distraction and a leisure activity. In this way, the *crônica* brought together all these textual typologies and their respective uses of the space at the bottom of the page. In the words of Antonio Candido, 'it can even be said that from several standpoints it is a Brazilian genre, by the naturalness with which it became acclimatized here and the original way in which it has evolved'.[27] A small extra Brazilian point can be added to the words of the master: the genre also sought to reconcile contrary worlds in a peculiarly Brazilian way, a kind of *jeitinho* [knack] that reconciled things in ways that had not been imagined before.

Notes to Chapter 9

1. My thanks to Frank Hanson for the translation of this chapter, as well as to John Gledson for his helpful comments and Madeleine Brook for proofreading it.
2. As academics and historians have shown us, other magazines were launched in this period and guided by the same principles. However, although the new ideas that led to 'a newspaper revolution' had been adopted by others, like Louis Desnoyers of *Le Siècle*, the innovations were linked to the name of Girardin. See, for example, *La Querelle du roman-feuilleton. Littérature, presse et politique, un débat précurseur (1836–1848)*, ed. by Lise Dumasy (Grenoble: ELLUG, 1999), p. 6.
3. Thérenty and Vaillan (eds), *1836, l'an I de l'ère médiatique. Analyse littéraire et historique de 'La Presse' d'Émile de Girardin* (Paris: Nouveau Monde, 2001), p. 7.

4. Ian Watt, *The Rise of the Novel*, 2nd US edn (Berkeley and Los Angeles: University of California Press, 2001), pp. 35–41.
5. Marlyse Meyer, *Folhetim: uma história* (São Paulo: Companhia das Letras, 1996), p. 33.
6. Titles in English: Regina Maria Roche, *The Children of the Abbey. A Tale*, 4 vols (London: Printed for William Lane, at the Minerva-Press, 1796); Elizabeth Helme, *Saint-Clair of the Isles; or, The Outlaws of Barra. A Scottish Tradition* (London: Longman and Rees, 1803); Charlotte Smith, *Celestine* (London: printed for T. Cadell, 1791). José de Alencar, *Como e porque sou romancista*, adaptação ortográfica de Carlos de Aquino Pereira (Campinas and São Paulo: Pontes, 1990).
7. Marlyse Meyer, *Folhetim: uma história*, pp. 57–58.
8. *Conversa de burros, banhos de mar e outras crônicas exemplares*, ed. by John Gledson, Curso Breve de Literatura Brasileira, 14 (Lisbon: Livros Cotovia, 2006), p. 13.
9. Here I have adopted the definition by Jürgen Habermas, who understands *public sphere* as referring principally to 'the sphere of private people gathered together in public', see Jürgen Habermas, *L'Espace public. Archéologie de la publicité comme dimension constitutive de la société bourgeoise*, trans. by Marc B. de Launay (Paris: Payot, 2008), p. 29. It gives rise to a public readership who, owing to their new reading habits and acceptance of new publications, form a network of public communications based on the use of reason and judgement, in the heart of the private sphere. The bourgeois section of the public and public opinion thus comprise a private circle of people who, as much as the public, form relations among themselves, and conduct exchanges in the heart of this same sphere, see Habermas, *L'Espace public*, p. 39.
10. For more on Machado de Assis as a chronicler, see *Machado de Assis's 'Philosopher or Dog?': From Serial to Book Form*, by Ana Cláudia Suriani da Silva (Oxford: Legenda, 2010).
11. See Lúcia Granja, 'Antes do livro, o jornal: *Conto Alexandrino*', *Luso-Brazilian Review*, 46 (2009), 106–14.
12. Machado de Assis, 'O folhetinista', *O Espelho*, 30 October 1859. See *O Espelho*, ed. by João Roberto Faria (Campinas and São Paulo: Editora da UNICAMP, 2009), p. 56. There is also a facsimile edition of the journal: *O Espelho. Revista Semanal de Literatura, Modas, Indústria e Artes (1859–1860)*, ed. by Marco Lucchesi (Rio de Janeiro: Fundação Biblioteca Nacional, 2008).
13. Machado de Assis, *O Espelho*, p. 13.
14. Thérenty and Vaillan (eds), *1836, l'An I de l'ère médiatique*, pp. 68–69.
15. Marie-Eve Thérenty, *La Littérature au quotidien. Poétiques journalistiques au XIXe siècle* (Paris: Seuil, 2007), p. 82.
16. The idea that there were less varied social groups in Brazil can be supported by the definition of 'the worldliness of the press' as outlined by Guillaume Pinson, *Fiction du monde. De la presse mondaine à Marcel Proust* (Montreal: Presses Universitaires de Montréal, 2009). The author shows that there is a possible relationship between mass media culture (which leads to the idea of broad anonymous mediations) and sociability (which is understood here as a real form of social exchanges between individuals).
17. This refers to an idea that developed from the study of Machado de Assis's *crônicas*, but which Marie-Eve Thérenty has also applied in generalized terms to the French newspapers of the nineteenth century 'The newspaper invented [...] a complex system [...] of laying out the world with a typology that conveys as much about the world as about the writings uttered by the world', Marie-Eve Thérenty, *La Littérature au quotidien*, p. 78.
18. Machado de Assis, 'Ao Acaso', *Diario do Rio de Janeiro*, 17 July 1864, p. 1.
19. José de Alencar, 'Ao correr da pena', *Correio Mercantil*, 24 September 1854. José de Alencar, *Ao correr da pena*, ed. by João Roberto Faria (São Paulo: Martins Fontes, 2004).
20. José de Alencar, ibid.
21. José de Alencar, ibid.
22. José de Alencar, ibid.
23. Frédéric Soulié, *La Presse*, 1 July 1836, p. 1.
24. Théophile Gautier, *La Presse*, 18 June 1838, p. 1.
25. Marie-Eve Thérenty, *La Littérature au quotidien*, p. 13.
26. Marie-Eve Thérenty, *La Littérature au quotidien*, p. 16.
27. Antonio Candido, 'A vida ao rés-do-chão', in *Recortes* (São Paulo: Companhia das Letras, 1993), p. 23.

CHAPTER 10

❖

How to Be a Professional Writer in Nineteenth-Century Brazil

Marisa Lajolo and Regina Zilberman

In memory of José Mindlin, to whose generosity we are deeply indebted for allowing us to consult some of the documents mentioned in this study

Bravo! Ei-la a postos, a Literatura,
Dos autorais direitos na defesa;
E que é certa a vitória me assegura
O ardor com que se lança à heroica empresa.

[Bravo! It is ready, Literature, in defence of authors' rights.
The passion driving this heroic enterprise assures me that victory is certain.]

D. XIQUOTE (pseudonym of BASTOS TIGRE, 1882–1957)

The press in Brazil was born under the sign of denial. In 1500 the Portuguese fleet led by Pedro Álvares Cabral (*c.* 1467/68–1520) arrived at the American region assigned to Portugal in the Tordesilhas Treaty, but the newly discovered territory was not immediately occupied. The founding of São Salvador (Bahia) in 1549, São Paulo de Piratininga (São Paulo) in 1555, and São Sebastião do Rio de Janeiro (Rio de Janeiro) in 1565, marked the beginning of a mission to settle European people on American soil, probably in order to secure possession of the territory; the land was under threat from all kinds of invaders, ranging from the pirates who coveted the then highly prized trees after which Brazil was named, to the Huguenots commanded by Nicolas Durand de Villegagnon (1510–1571), who established the short-lived French Antarctic (1555–60) in the areas surrounding Guanabara Bay (Rio de Janeiro).

In this era, the Portuguese authorities forbade the existence of printing presses in its colonies, although they had been operating in Portugal since the beginning of the sixteenth century, with the entrepreneurial activities of Valentim Fernandes (14??–1518/19). It was only in Portuguese India that the press flourished as early as the sixteenth century, with the first presses landing in Goa in 1556 and in Macau in 1560, around the same time as the arrival of the printing press in Spanish American colonies: Mexico in 1539, and Peru in 1583.[1]

In Brazil the ban on printing was lifted as late as 1808, and even then only due to a combination of chance and government intervention. In 1807, when Portugal faced the threat of a French invasion by the Napoleonic troops, the Prince Regent, D. João (1767–1826), decided to transfer his court to Rio de Janeiro, where he arrived on 8 January of the following year. According to Max Fleuiss (1868–1943), shortly before embarking, the Portuguese government had been sent printing presses and typographical machinery from Britain and the crates were still in the Lisbon Customs House; it was easy to send them 'on board the frigate Medusa, one of the ships belonging to the Royal Navy Squadron' that would bring the Portuguese Court to Brazil.[2]

As the functioning of the State depended on enacting and implementing legislation, a decision was made to take advantage of the material that was originally designated for use in Lisbon, authorizing the setting up of an official Royal Press in Rio de Janeiro, which began its work on 13 May 1808, after three hundred years of the Portuguese presence in Brazil. However, it was not enough just to have the legal right to use the press and typography to print books. In the first two decades of the nineteenth century, in Brazil, the State still had a monopoly over the use of the printing press, and private companies were not allowed to set up a typography of their own.[3] There was another drawback: the publication of a work depended on a royal concession, or 'privilege', which could only be granted by the State.

The practice of dispensing printing privileges goes back to the fifteenth century, when in 1469 one was granted to Johann von Speyer (?–*c.*1477), a German typographer based in Venice, who was given permission to practice the art of printing in that Republic for five years. According to José Martínez de Souza, the granting of privileges 'prevented [another editor] from publishing [the work] during the stipulated licensing period'.[4] Artur Anselmo states that in Portugal, 'privileges to publish began to appear at the beginning of the sixteenth century and were generally granted for a period of ten years, during which time no other individual, regardless of rank or standing, could order the book to be printed or sold or brought out of the kingdom'.[5]

Three hundred years later, this model that secured the right of the State to grant privileges was maintained in Portugal and its colonies, which included Brazil during the first two decades of the nineteenth century. In other parts of Europe, however, there were several degrees of State control as a result of greater economic freedom linked to commerce and industry in countries that were no longer under the protection of an absolute monarch. In addition, there was an expansion of movements for greater recognition and remuneration of literary activities in the mid-eighteenth century, which became more manifest in the first ten years of the nineteenth century, particularly in Britain.[6]

This is not what occurred in Brazil when the use of printing presses was legalized. Two movements which, in Europe, lasted for over a century can be regarded as taking place simultaneously in Brazil, where it was necessary to adapt a traditionally illiterate culture to the world of the printing press, as well as to take action in favour of the professionalization of writers. Accordingly, it is not surprising that in the nineteenth century different ways of making the manufacture of books economically viable coexisted. In an indirect way, it determined a (substandard) degree of the professionalization — or at least of remuneration — of those who set out the text, an essential part of creating the physical book.

The trajectory of legislation in this period all over the world reflects a dual movement: privileges to publish competed for a place in the public arena with a struggle for the rights of authorship. On 12 July 1821, a Portuguese decree called *Lei da Liberdade de Imprensa* [Law of Press Freedom] was issued, abolishing the censorship that had previously existed in Portugal. It included an article that recognized the rights of literary property. The provisions of the law were extended to Brazil, which was still a Portuguese colony. Three years after this decree and two years after Pedro I (1798–1834) had proclaimed the independence of Brazil from the old metropolis in 1822, the Constitution of the new nation adopted two positions of a liberal tendency:

(a) The abolition of the law of privilege, except where it served a public purpose, and the transfer of intellectual property rights to the inventors or creators of a literary work. It should be noted that in France the abolition of the law of privilege dates back to 1789, in the wake of the revolutionary events that led to the downfall of Louis XVI (1754–1793) and the court of Versailles, which marked the beginning of the modern democratization process in Europe. Although it may seem paradoxical, Pedro I, who had been trained to be an absolute monarch, endorsed, by means of the Constitution he approved, this liberalizing trend that was on the rise in parts of Europe, but had still not been tried out in Portuguese South America.

(b) The recognition that the inventors retain the intellectual property of their discoveries or inventions and are entitled to this right for some time. If this right was not respected or their works suffered from some form of vulgarisation, the law stated that the authors would be indemnified for their loss.

The privilege is thus transferred from the State to the author, assuring his or her ownership of the works produced. The Brazilian legislation did not adopt the progressive tone of the United States Federal Copyright Act (1790) but, to some extent, one can recognize in its formulation some of the points that emanated from it. Thus with regard to institutionalizing the author's rights, the Brazilian Constitution follows decisions to be found in the French and North American decrees.

Two key points can be highlighted with regard to the Constitution proclaimed by D. Pedro: the Brazilian State recognized — before Portugal — that the inventors and creators retain intellectual property rights concerning discoveries or works produced; the guarantee of intellectual property is not the object of any particular legislation but is included in articles from the Penal Code of 1830, which was also published during the reign of Pedro I. The Penal Code does not only refer to the violation of intellectual property rights. Inappropriate use of the press also includes the alleged 'abuse of the freedom to express one's thoughts', or when institutions such as the empire or the Constitution are attacked. These circumstances grant the State the right to exercise censorship. The Penal Code also mentions irregularities that may occur during the establishment of printing companies or their equivalent, which can be a punishable offence.

Article 261 refers explicitly to literary property, stating that it is considered a crime to seize possession of a written work or printed image from a Brazilian citizen during his or her lifetime or within ten years of their death. The penalty takes the form of the confiscation of volumes already published or the payment of a fine to the value of the pirated volumes. According to the legal expert J. M. Vaz Pinto Coelho (1836–1894), in an article published in *Revista Brasileira*, between 1880 and 1881, it was the Penal Code that expressed (albeit indirectly) the recognition of an author's rights to his intellectual property. He describes a case study from 1871, where the verdict, based on the clauses determined in Article 261, stipulated that the heirs of the author should be granted the rights to the work *Guia Médico-Cirúrgico*, by José Henriques de Proença, unlawfully published by another editor.[7]

Although in Portugal the article in the Constitution which grants inventors and authors 'the holding rights of their works and productions' was implemented later than similar measures in Brazil, the discussions regarding the regulation of the rights of authors preceded those that took place in the latter. The debates in Portugal started with the approval of the Constitution, and grew in intensity in the 1830s and 1840s, largely thanks to the energetic involvement of the then parliamentarian Almeida Garrett (1799–1854), and obtained final approval in 1851.

In Brazil, similar plans were consigned to oblivion, although at least three parliamentary initiatives were recorded. The first plan was formulated in 1856 by Aprígio Justiniano da Silva Guimarães (1832–1880), a congressman from Pernambuco; the second was presented a year later by another congressman, Bernardo Avelino Gavião Peixoto (1829–1912), with a similar view and, at first sight, identical content.[8] In 1859, Aprígio Guimarães published the booklet *Propriedade literária: histórico e sustentação de um projeto a respeito, apresentado à Câmara dos senhores deputados em 14 de agosto de 1856* [Literary property rights: the historical background of a plan supporting these rights presented to the honourable members of the Chamber of Deputies on 14 August 1856], but the booklet had a minimal effect and probably receiving nothing more than a reading by his parliamentary colleague Bernardo Peixoto.

The plan drawn up by the author José de Alencar (1829–1877) in 1875 and put forward to the Chamber of Deputies must have been equally unconvincing.[9] On this occasion, Alencar exercised his parliamentary mandate, but he was already a renowned national figure as a dramatist and above all as the acclaimed author of narratives about native Americans, historical novels and stories about urban life. Perhaps this dual capacity — political and literary — had paved his way to introduce legislation aimed at the protection of literary property rights.

In the first article of the project, Alencar defines what he understands by 'literary and artistic property', which enjoys the same materiality as 'property in general', meaning it should be given equal legislative guarantees so that it can be passed on to the heirs without 'time constraints' or 'distinction of nationality'. In the legal reasoning which accompanied the proposal, the congressman made clear what he understood by the materiality of the work as well as the inheritance transfer laws: 'Gold jewellery passed on in the family from generation to generation should not be regarded as more precious, nor as more their property than a poem by José Basílio da Gama, whose relatives are still alive.'

The second article is aimed at protecting the reproduction rights of works, which are to be held exclusively by the author and his successors, except when granted 'public contract'. The article also expresses the concept of work adopted by Alencar, reduced to their 'essence or substance', revealed by the 'title', when it is product of 'the invention of the author', by the 'form', understood as 'style', and by the 'plan', if it results from 'one's own creation'. Alencar shares a modern conception of literary works, characterized by originality which makes the work unique, insofar as it is produced by referred to a named author, his proprietor and /owner and his property of it.

The insistence of the two initial articles on the concepts of property and creativity are explained in Article 3, relating to the crime of counterfeiting, which was undermining the book industry in Brazil and was particularly harmful to authors who wanted to support themselves financially with the income generated by exercising their intellectual profession. Alencar had experienced this problem following the publication of *O guarani*, in 1857. The novel was a huge publishing success, but was the object of piracy in the same year that the book was launched in Rio de Janeiro.[10] However, it was not only this novelist who became victim of forgeries; they particularly affected Portuguese writers such as Almeida Garrett and Camilo Castelo Branco (1825–1890), whose books circulated in Brazil, usually as pirated works for which the authors received no remuneration. For this reason, pirated editions were often more profitable, though they led to a contraction of local production. However, the Brazilian State represented by Emperor Pedro II (1825–1891) did not react, because he adopted the position of Alexandre Herculano (1810–1877), who was opposed to the recognition of literary property and in favour of patronage.[11]

José de Alencar probably did not need to champion his own cause. One year before taking his proposal to parliament, he signed a contract with his publisher, Baptiste Louis Garnier (1823–1893) and was paid 'a sum of a hundred thousand *réis*' for the novels *Diva*, *Iracema* and *As minas de prata*, books which had previously been published in 1864, 1865 and 1866 respectively. However, José de Alencar was a political enemy of the emperor, who refused him a permanent senatorial position in 1870. Besides, he was probably concerned with providing for his family after his death, an anxiety that was justified in the light of testimonies about the wretched conditions that the widows of writers often had to face.[12]

Alencar did not limit himself to proposing Article 3, related to 'the crime of forgery', punishable with 'the penalties of theft', a matter which also troubled his precursors Aprígio Guimarães and Bernardo Peixoto. He also included the curious Article 11, which outlines who was able to judge those accused of the offence: a 'jury made up of three writers', a solution that suited the position of the proponent who, while being a congressman when the plan was drawn up, was an artist first and foremost. However, as was the case with the initiatives of Aprígio Guimarães and Bernardo Peixoto, José de Alencar's proposal was unsuccessful, remaining only in the memories of some intellectuals who, in 1877, upon the death of the novelist, drew up plans for the foundation of the Sociedade José de Alencar,[13] which aimed to defend the interests of writers; nevertheless, the project never materialized.

The legislation longed for during the reign of Pedro II was never put into effect and had to wait for the republican regime (1889) to be enacted. Even then it was only approved in 1898, following a series of petitions that lasted for more than five years. The first article in the Brazilian Law of 1898 did not show any significant differences in content from what had appeared in the Constitution of 1824. Despite this, it represented the first step towards recognition of the rights of the author and replaced the former concept of property, closing a debate that had taken place in Europe in the eighteenth century and lasted in Brazil throughout the nineteenth century, intensifying in the final decade. Thus, generally speaking, the chronological pattern of the disputes regarding the recognition of intellectual and literary property in Brazil lasted for approximately eighty years. After the abolition of the old privilege system, there had been strong endorsement for the view that the author was responsible for and possessor of his artistic or scientific creation, but it was only after 1898 that he could count on the legal protection that he had always lacked.

The granting of privileges is documented in works published in Brazil at the beginning of the nineteenth century when they were characterized as the legal way of sanctioning a type of economic bond between the author and the book containing his text. This is the particular case of *Corografia brasílica*, by Father Manuel Aires de Casal (1754–1821), who was granted the Royal Privilege to publish in 1817. In the text which declares that Aires de Casal was granted the licence to print and sell his *Corografia brasílica*, some passages stand out and exemplify the rights guaranteed by this concession. The document stipulates a time period during which it will remain in force — fourteen years — and the rights of succession: 'the same licence passes by the death of the petitioner to his heirs or whoever he leaves the work to, so long as this does not exceed the space of the stipulated fourteen years granted.'[14]

At the same time, and perhaps in an even more subtle way, it also suggests a time when the importing of books and their movement from one country to another was becoming standard practice, a situation possibly provoked by the long period when the existence of printing shops in Brazil had been banned. Since in 1817 both Brazil and Portugal formed part of the territory which the decree called 'my Kingdoms and Dominions', the need to explain this in the law could suggest that the legislators were aware of the clandestine traffic of books all over the world. In its turn, the granting of a privilege was fully justified because the work was 'the outcome of many years of work in which [the author] had invested a great deal'. But this was probably a very weak pretext because, as Lúcia Maria Bastos P. Neves makes clear, it was also used to grant the royal assent to Antônio José Osório de Pina Leitão (1762–18??), who wished to publish his epic poem, the *Alfonsíada*.[15]

In establishing the penalty for infractions, 'the culprit was deprived of all the copies that could be found, a half being given to the complainant and the other half to the captives'. This shows how in the nineteenth century legal measures survived that had originated in the Middle Ages: the 'half for the captives' mentioned in the privilege, originally represented a kind of tax that was exacted to ransom prisoners of war. That this sanction was a routine in this kind of document is suggested in the research study by Lúcia Maria Bastos P. Neves, when she writes about Monsenhor José de Souza Azevedo e Araújo Pizarro (1753–1830), author of

Memórias históricas do Rio de Janeiro, published in 1820. This book was protected by privilege which prevented its being sold, printed or obtained by another bookseller or typographer, under the penalty of the loss of copies that remained, 'half of them to the complainant and the other half to the captives.'[16] However, it can be assumed that the ostensible aim of a government directive is not always put into effect, and that the fraudulent use of a privilege might be in the interests of the State since it could benefit by imposing a heavy tax on it.

The reference in the old tax to the 'ransom of captives' is not the only archaic clause to be found in a nineteenth century document. The need for a publication to be regulated by privilege prolonged old practices that corresponded to a different era of books and printing. It should be stressed, however, that although the granting of privileges threatened the author with legal penalties, it also guaranteed that the end product — the book — would be given the protection of the State. The abolition of privileges and the end of state monopoly over the printing companies led to the introduction of a free enterprise system in the industrial field of the printing houses, which left the writers at the mercy of the market. In a country where illiteracy prevailed among the free population and the education of slaves of African origin was forbidden, securing the agreement of the typographers to publish a book was a thankless task for authors.

This is not to suggest that typography was not a good business. The typographers could print newspapers, notebooks, and even books which were mainly destined for the increasing school market, particularly in the Rio de Janeiro Court. For that reason printers born in Europe migrated to Brazil and set up flourishing businesses.[17] In the meantime, the authors, who had no doubts about what was their artistic property, had to resort to other measures to get their books published and later to seek readers (not necessarily real readers) to purchase their books. The two following cases illustrate the difficulty of their situation.

In 1829, Canon Januário da Cunha Barbosa (1780–1846) was not exactly unknown in the cultural and political milieu of Rio de Janeiro. He was a preacher in the Royal Chapel from 1808, the year when the Portuguese royal family arrived in Brazil, and professor of Moral and Rational Philosophy from 1814. He was a member of the Board of Directors of the *Impressão Régia* [Royal Press] and, before independence, had published, together with Gonçalves Ledo (1781–1847), the *Revérbero Constitucional Fluminense*, 'the most important political pamphlet of the time' according Carlos Rizzini.[18] He was awarded the Imperial Order of the Cross by Emperor Pedro I and in 1824 was appointed to the position of Canon of the Imperial Chapel as well as being elected deputy for Rio de Janeiro in 1826. Later, when he was not re-elected, he was appointed Director of the National Typography and of *Diario Fluminense*, the official newspaper that succeeded the *Gazeta do Rio de Janeiro*. However, all these credentials were not enough to spare him from having to resort to subscriptions as a way to publish his *Parnaso Brasileiro*, perhaps the first anthology of Brazilian poems published in the country.

The payment of subscriptions had been the alternative way of supporting periodicals since they first appeared in colonial Brazil and were dependent on the Portuguese crown. Diogo Soares da Silva de Bivar (1785–1865), the editor of *As*

Variedades, or Ensaios de Literatura, probably the first literary journal in the history of Brazil,[19] adopted this expedient when he launched the periodical in Bahia in 1811 through the typography of Manuel Antônio da Silva Serva. In announcing the first edition of *As Variedades*, he promised that 'the price of each booklet would be fixed at $480 *réis* [four hundred and eighty *réis*] for the subscribers, payable three months in advance, and $560 *réis* [five hundred and sixty *réis*] for non-subscribers.' As can be seen, customers were supposed to pay in advance for a service to be provided later.

In the opening pages of the first issue, Bivar attempted to justify the need for the reading public to accept the idea of paying in advance, pointing out at the same time a problem that would trouble Brazilian printers throughout the nineteenth century: printing costs were much higher in the colony than in Lisbon, which put the local industry in a weaker position when faced with foreign competition:

> If this publication is of some value both for its service and its novelty in this country, we hope that the public will rush out to sign up for the subscriptions that are being sold at the *Gazeta*'s shop, and that people will be convinced that without the assurance of regular sales it will be impossible for similar projects to be carried out, especially in a country where the printing costs greatly exceed those that are charged in Europe.[20]

Bivar was not successful in his undertaking: *As Variedades* did not go beyond the third issue (or the second double issue, according to Nelson Werneck Sodré).

Januário da Cunha Barbosa should not have had the same kind of problem because, at the time when his *Parnaso Brasileiro* was first launched, he was Director of the National Typography that succeeded the Royal Press founded by D. João. Nevertheless, the text on the back cover of the second volume (published in 1831) contradicts this hypothesis. In naming in the text the place where the subscriptions would take place, he suggested a partnership — profitable in the medium and long term — between authors and the establishments involved in printing and books: Veiga[21] and Plancher[22] were booksellers effectively established at the addresses mentioned, and the National Typography was the publishing house of *Parnaso*.

The advertisement even gives an approximate idea of the publication cost of a literary work in Brazil between the end of the 1830s and beginning of the 1840s. The subscription fee and the price of separate volumes of the *Parnaso* were higher than the corresponding price for *Variedades*. Diogo Bivar charged $480 *réis* [four hundred and eighty *réis*] per copy, paid in advance; after the printing, it would cost $560 *réis* [five hundred and sixty *réis*], an extra 16.7%. Januário requested $500 *réis* [five hundred *réis*] in advance for each volume (the subscription was budgeted at 2$000 *réis* [two thousand *réis*]), so long as 'they do not contain more than eight print sheets'; once it was published, the cost would rise to $600 *réis* [six hundred *réis*], which meant an extra 20%.

At that time, a junior Navy official earned monthly 12$000 *réis* [twelve thousand *réis*] as a government initiative to encourage men to pursue a career in the navy.[23] This salary was close to what, according to the federal decree issued on 14 June 1830, an elementary school teacher was paid annually, namely15$000 *réis* [fifteen thousand *réis*]. The director of the National Typography, the post filled by Januário da Cunha Barbosa at that time, earned 800$000 *réis* [eight hundred thousand *réis*] per year, plus a commission of 5% of the net company income.[24] It is clear, therefore, that the two thousand *réis* that Januário requested from the subscribers could have been a heavy burden for the household budget of a middle-class professional who depended on his annual salary.

The advertisement also refers to a typical practice in the book market of the period: it was up to the purchaser — in this case the subscriber — to keep himself informed of new publications by reading the newspapers. This practice is reported in many other advertisements that also tell us that books shared space with other merchandise in shops, and were probably not placed in the most prominent, visible position.

As the publication of the two volumes of *Parnaso brasileiro* extended over the period from 1829 to 1831, it can be supposed that the renowned canon did not find it easy to fulfil his aims. Even so, it can be presumed that he had more success than the poet Delfina Benigna da Cunha (1791–1853). Born in the town São José do Norte (Rio Grande do Sul), Delfina became blind when she was twenty months old. She must have received some education because in 1826 she dedicated a poem to Pedro I in which she appealed for his protection, stating that she had a double handicap, visual and financial:

Quem te fala, Senhor, quem te saúda
Não vê raiar de Febo a luz brilhante;
Dá-lhe pio agasalho um breve instante,
Seu fado imigo, em brando fado muda:
A sustentar o peso assaz lhe ajuda
De uma vida, que à morte é semelhante,
Não chegue a ser aflita mendigante
Quem um tal protetor roga lhe acuda.[25]

[The person who is speaking to you and greeting you, my Lord, is unable to see the shining light of the divine rays of Phoebus; give her your blessed protection for a brief moment, free her from her doom, and change it to a gentler fate. Help her support the burden of a life that is like death so she has never to endure the afflictions of a beggar, she who beseeches such a protector to help her.]

In another sonnet, the author gives thanks to D. Pedro I for his assistance, later maintained by Pedro II, as we learn from her fellow countryman Múcio Teixeira (1857–1926):[26]

Apenas o meu triste mal soubeste,
Egrégio Imperador d'alta memória,
Tornar-me venturosa, enfim, quiseste:[27]

[As soon as you knew of my sad affliction, your Exalted Highness of immortal memory, you did want to make me fortunate at last.]

However, the pension obtained was probably not enough for the young lady to overcome her dual condition of being a blind, poor poet. When her book was published, it was remarkable for its sincerity, since the author makes her dire financial situation and the need to sell copies to ensure her survival clear to her readers:

> It is not desire for fame that has led me to make this present publication: nor do I have any wish for praise; my work does not deserve it, I am well aware of that. What is it then that has spurred me on to have the audacity to offer my verses to the public? Readers — it is sheer necessity! — Necessity is my self-esteem; I cannot have any other. Daughter of Rio Grande, enduring the ravages of fate, I have suffered, I have suffered a great deal: I was forced to seek shelter again in Rio de Janeiro, but I have to live! I desperately need financial help and beg for this help by offering in exchange the only work that someone who has been blind from the cradle is able to offer! This is the only point that should be printed in the foreword of this work — as has been done.[28]

In his *História da literatura do Rio Grande do Sul*, Guilhermino Cesar (1908–1993) emphasizes the financial difficulties of Delfina Benigna da Cunha:

> The financial help of the Crown may not have been enough for the subsistence of the poet because on several occasions in Rio, there were shows for her benefit. In May 1840, in S. Januário, Delfina pleased the public when she said that she was there because she was afflicted with misfortune and in search of 'support, peace and life'.[29]

Guilhermino Cesar continues: 'in 1842 she suffers from new constraints and can be found in the same theatre imploring the Fluminense people to give her their charity'. The literary historian adds:

> It was then that she had to emigrate to the North. She spent some time in Rio; travelled to Bahia and to the Paraíba valley, which were places then dominated by 'the coffee aristocracy', where she could rest and enjoy the comforts of manor houses. In the towns of Parati, Lorena and Campos, she gathered more subscribers for the publication of her last book. In Parati alone she obtained about 130 subscribers while in her native province the total figure did not reach 200.[30]

The system of subscriptions lasted throughout the nineteenth century, as is illustrated by a project launched by the Livraria Americana of Porto Alegre in 1875. The firm was responsible on that occasion for the annual edition of Alfredo Ferreira Rodrigues's (1865–1942) *Almanaque Literário e Estatístico of Rio Grande do Sul*, an editorial practice in Europe since printing had been established and maintained on a regular basis in America in response to public interest. The proprietor of Livraria Americana also decided to invest in local authors by setting up a *Biblioteca Sul-riograndense*. To maintain this initiative depended, however, on adopting a subscription system which ensured further publications. This explains the measures described on the last page of the first book of the series, *Paisagens*, by Apolinário Porto Alegre (1844–1904), who wrote his books under the pseudonym 'Iriema':

> With this objective I undertook the task, for which I seek public protection.
>
> I will issue a monthly volume of 200 or more pages, with instructive and enjoyable reading.
>
> I begin my edition with PAISAGENS, a collection of stories from Iriema's learned, well-known and widely celebrated pen.
>
> [...]
>
> If, as well as the subscribers who spontaneously come to cheer me up, the

public responds to the appeal that I make to them — in brief I will carry out this useful publication.[31]

When the subscription system failed, a writer might be forced to peddle his books from door to door or publish them at his own cost either in newspaper's or government offices' printing presses, as is suggested in the case of Aquiles Porto Alegre (1848–1926), according to the memoirs of Augusto Meyer (1902–1970), his former student:

> I didn't know that old Aquiles was so understanding or so human. I've seen him at times in Praça da Matriz, dragging his feet along the pavement, carrying his suitcase full of books which he offered for sale from door to door: *Folhas caídas, Homens ilustres do Rio Grande do Sul, Flores entre ruínas, Através do passado, Paisagens mortas, Serões de inverno, Palavras ao vento, À sombra das árvores*. It was the first vivid image I had ever had with my own simple eyes of the destiny of a writer in our land — a melancholy image, but at the same time Homeric and picturesque, of the poor wandering poet, knocking on door after door and hearing vague mutterings that might be promises of promises:
> — Life is getting ever more expensive...[32]

These examples from the nineteenth century do not mean that writers in previous periods of history had not been remunerated for their literary works. But it was a question of sporadic payments independent of legislation. Alfredo Bosi, for example, records that in the second half of the seventeenth century Father Antônio Vieira (1608–1697) helped to give financial support to the Jesuit missionaries in Brazil with the income obtained from selling books of his sermons.[33]

In effect, the regular remuneration of writers was not standard practice before 1840. The receipt of fees is registered from 1841 onwards, when the Brazilian political regime became stable after the political separation from Portugal and the ascension of Pedro II to the Brazilian throne. In the same period, the country gradually pacified regional revolts that threatened the unity of the empire during the Regency government between 1831 and 1840. The Rio de Janeiro Court consolidated its position of national cultural supremacy, a position that was maintained until the end of the nineteenth century.

However, it was not until after 1860 that the system for remunerating writers in Brazil was consolidated. From observations of the period between 1858 and 1872, it is possible to confirm the hegemony of the bookseller Baptiste-Louis Garnier, who, from the mid 1840s onwards, managed the Brazilian subsidiary of his family business in Paris. In his catalogues, Garnier included authors of school books that were needed for secondary schools, which was an expanding market in the country, such as J. B. Calógeras (1810–1878), Justiniano José da Rocha (1812–1862) and the priest Joaquim Caetano Fernandes Pinheiro (1825–1876). Garnier also offered what seems to be a good contract to José de Alencar for the publication of his works, as the writer records in narrative memoir drafted around 1873: 'After working for 22 years in the field of printing, I finally found an editor — B. Garnier, who spontaneously offered me an advantageous contract in the mid 1870s.'[34]

Garnier did not restrict himself to well-known authors: in 1864 he invested in the young poet Machado de Assis (1839–1908), who had started his collaboration with the editor in the previous year through his involvement in the production of

Jornal das Famílias, a journal which appeared from 1863 to 1878. In 1864, Garnier and Machado de Assis signed a contract for the publication of *Crisálidas*, a book of poems, in which the author was offered $150 *réis* [one hundred and fifty *réis*] for each copy sold.[35] This sum was increased five years later when he launched *Falenas*, a second book of verses by Machado de Assis, who was paid $200 *réis* [two hundred *réis*] a copy, the same amount paid for *Contos fluminenses* published at the same time.

A prominent feature of the two contracts is that Garnier would acquire 'full and entire possession not only of the first but of all subsequent' editions, in such a way that the author gives up his writings. It should also be noted that in the case of *Crisálidas*, the editor began to make the payments only after the printing of the books and at the time when they were offered for sale. In the case of *Contos fluminenses* and *Falenas*, the situation changed: not only did Garnier increase the payment for each volume but he also paid for the first edition of 1,000 copies in advance; this meant that Machado de Assis was paid $200 *réis* [two hundred *réis*] for each of his books. These decisions might have meant that Garnier did not need to worry about marketing the first edition of the projected books, one of short stories and one of poems; but he reserved for himself the right to publish new editions, leaving the period of publication and the number of copies undefined. As these books were not republished before the beginning of the twentieth century, it can be presumed that Garnier knew the market reach of his publications and was not committed to their future in the medium term.

In the contracts signed between 1864 and 1869, Machado de Assis sold his literary property and renounced his rights to it. The practice is not unique to that writer and corresponds to the usual procedure for Brazilian intellectuals of the period. Calógeras is one of the few who escaped from this pattern because he was paid a fee for the first edition of his work, which shows that this was not expected to go beyond the printing of 2,000 copies. The historian is committed to not republishing the work so long as it remained in stock; for his part, Garnier paid him handsomely because he bought his product for '1 conto and 600$000 *réis* [one million six hundred thousand *réis*]'.

João Batista Calógeras, the author of *Compêndio da História da Idade Média* (a title abbreviated in the contract to *História Média*), was a European: he was born in Greece and educated in Paris, and settled in Brazil in 1841.[36] His provenance perhaps explains why the contract apparently gave fewer powers to the editor Garnier, who did not acquire the literary property of the author, and was limited to the first edition of 2,000 copies. On the other hand, Calógeras was to some extent a hostage to the entrepreneur because the precious '1 conto and 600$000 réis [one million and six hundred thousand *réis*]' would be used to pay off a debt to the publisher: 'the sum [...] that is retained as payment of the standing amount that is owed to Garnier.'[37]

Anyhow, the unequal treatment employed to make a contract with João Batista Calógeras on the one hand, and Machado de Assis on the other, suggests a distinction in the conception of the relationship between the author and his artistic or intellectual creation. Calógeras did not lose his rights because the next editions would be negotiated with Garnier or any other publisher; Machado de Assis, like most of his contemporaries, sold his property by renouncing the possession of the texts.

In Brazil in the nineteenth century, as occurred in Europe at the end of the eighteenth century and beginning of the nineteenth, two concepts were in force which were not synonymous — the concept of *literary property* and that of *authorial rights*. The former predominated in the period, at least in Brazil, because the latter had still not been consolidated. This only took place when Law 496, which defined and guaranteed authorial rights, was enacted on 1 August 1898.

In an essay about the history of authors' rights, Anne Latournerie noted that the expression 'authors' rights' appeared very late. It was in 1838 that, according to the researcher, the first book that used the expression 'authors' rights' in the title was published: it is the *Traité des droits d'auteurs, dans la littérature, les sciences et les beaux-arts*,[38] by A.-C. Renouard (1794–1878):

> The use of this word, invented by the doctrine, would thus be generalized and adapted throughout the second half of the nineteenth century, even though this did not prevent the simultaneous use of the notion of literary and artistic 'property'. The nuances of the expression also conceal the debate the lies behind the philosophy and real nature of the rights at stake.[39]

Calógeras seems to have had a card up his sleeve in his editorial dealings: his work had been approved by the Board of Public Education, as the contract shows, a circumstance which perhaps explains why the price of a book destined for school was so much higher than a book of poems. Both being commodities, they were aimed at distinct types of consumers. The work with teaching material depended on a captive public and could be produced in greater quantities. That is why the historian J. B. Calógeras could be paid 1,600,000 *réis* for his compendium which had 2,000 copies, an impressive figure when we think that works like *Meandro poético*, by Fernandes Pinheiro, a collection of Brazilian verses that already formed a part of the literary canon and was designed for college students, did not exceed a thousand copies when it was first published.

After being printed, Calógeras's book proved to be profitable because its two bound tomes were offered for sale, in 1865, for 6$500 *réis* [six thousand five hundred *réis*] which meant selling 25% of the copies was enough to recoup the sum paid to the author.[40] It should be remembered that it was not cheap to produce books in Brazil in the nineteenth century, and that since 1862 Garnier had printed his publications in Paris, a decision that infuriated typographers,[41] but was praised by Machado de Assis:

> Another volume has just been published in the important House of Garnier: *Meandro poético*, a collection of poems from the first Brazilian poets for the use of college students. It is compiled by Sr. Dr. Fernandes Pinheiro. This work is embellished with biographical sketches and a large number of historical, mythological and geographical notes.
>
> [...]
>
> The printing, which was carried out in Paris, is similar to the last impressions of the House of Garnier: excellent.
>
> In a country where there are no publishers, there is a need to encourage those that are committed, like Garnier, to facilitate the publishing of books.[42]

It can be estimated that the profits of the editor corresponded to roughly 50% of the market price, which was enough to make him rich. Two factors can be added to this: first, his gains were not restricted to Calógeras's book: a similar calculation can be made for works like those of Justiniano José da Rocha and Fernandes Pinheiro; furthermore, the editor remunerated his authors unevenly, even when they were aimed at the same market niche, as in the case of the school books. Thus, Justiniano José da Rocha was paid less than Calógeras, and Fernandes Pinheiro earned more money when he devoted his works to religious subjects than when he wrote about Brazilian literature: the *Catecismo de doutrina cristã* yielded him 1,800,000 *réis*, in contrast with *Meandro poético*, for which Garnier paid him 300,000.

Equally significant is the nature of the contracts signed with Brazilian writers, especially those who lived in the second half of the nineteenth century and the publishers based in Rio de Janeiro, where the main national companies linked to the book industry were found.

It is worth pointing out an interesting example of a contract drawn up in 1872 between Bernardo Joaquim da Silva Guimarães (1825–1884) and Garnier.[43] The publisher already had a novel in his catalogue, *O garimpeiro*, by Bernardo Guimarães. The documents refer to 'author' and 'editor' to specify the contracting parties, terms not used in previous contracts. It can also be observed that, in the first lines, the two documents provide a kind of map of the Brazilian book world of the time: an author who resides in Ouro Preto, a town in of the Province of Minas Gerais, resorts to an editor in Rio de Janeiro, where the national government was based, for the publication of his works.

The contract of 1872 puts the expressions 'property' and 'authors' rights' side by side and adds the possessive pronoun 'their' to the noun 'works'. This wording suggests that the two concepts — 'property' and 'authors' rights' — overlapped and, as has been previously observed, they governed the debates about what kind of prerogative writers have concerning their literary works. The contract signed by Bernardo Guimarães shows how the 'works' are conceived: while 'the property' of the author, by virtue of being his possession, it can be sold by him. At the same time, to the extent that the sale outlined by the contract includes the 'author's rights', it constitutes a recognition of the existence of these rights, as a kind of legislation that regulates rights and responsibilities regarding the possession of a work.

The amount stipulated for the acquisition of two works — 600$000 *réis* [six hundred thousand *réis*] — is equal to what Machado de Assis was paid in 1876, for the sale of his novel *Helena*, and more than Bernardo Guimarães earned from the first edition of *O garimpeiro*, sold to Garnier for 500$000 *réis* [five hundred thousand *réis*]. The payment conditions, 'at the first request of the author', seem to detach the remuneration of the writer from the effective launching of the work, a situation, however, that Machado de Assis had managed to overcome. Yet the contract of 1872 does not mention the later works of Bernardo Guimarães, while in the contracts signed in 1869 by Machado de Assis, there is a clause that refers to new editions, which is also envisaged in the document relating to the other Bernardo de Guimarães novel, *O garimpeiro*. Perhaps Garnier had ceased to believe that Brazilian books could ever warrant new editions; or else he was beginning to adopt the practice that the novelist Coelho Neto (1864–1934) accused him of, via one of the characters in his novel *A conquista*, in 1898: indefinitely reprinting the works of his publications without giving any explanation.[44] Anyway, by 1872, the Brazilian publishing world seemed to be far beyond the times of 'privileges'. Despite this, the practice of establishing a fixed period during which the contract that regulates rights and responsibilities of authors and publishers to their heirs and successors remained in force, even at the beginning of the twentieth-first century.

On 18 July 1874, a receipt signed by Bernardo Guimarães records the sum paid for another of his books, *A captiva Isaura*: 600$000 *réis* [six hundred thousand *réis*], which suggests that in the 1870s there was a degree of stability in the price of books contracted by Garnier. In 1878, another agreement signed between Bernardo Guimarães and Garnier included, among the books mentioned in the document, *O pão de ouro*, the book which is referred to in the 1872 contract. In the 1878 document, the opening clause gives a discharge value that is adjusted to the value of two works: 600$000 *réis* [six hundred thousand *réis*], which is specified in what follows as 'already paid', an expression that contradicts the 1872 clause that records that 600,000 *réis* 'will be paid on the first request of the author'.

The reason for this might have been that the author and editor lived very far from each other in geographical terms. This is suggested by a letter from Bernardo Guimarães to Garnier, written in Ouro Preto and dated 25 February 1870, in which he declares that he accepts the conditions proposed for the publication of *O garimpeiro*.[45] According to the document, the letter was sent together with a copy of the contract he signed. He also authorizes the delivery of 'the sum of 500$000 *réis* [five hundred thousand *réis*]' to João Antônio de Mattos e Cia., 'by the care of Sr. Moritz Mayer Sohn', who is entrusted with this business. Apparently, Bernardo Guimarães was paid twice for *O pão de ouro*, since this book of short stories was published only in 1879. However, *A captiva Isaura*, launched in 1875, with the title *A escrava Isaura*, was at that time — and still is — a huge editorial success, which probably put the author in a strong bargaining position with the publisher.

Even though the documents regarding the relationship of Bernardo Guimarães with Garnier represent a considerable advance regarding the conditions that prevailed at the time of Aires Casal (1817), Januário da Cunha Barbosa (1829–31) and Delfina Benigna da Cunha (1834), they do not go into great detail about the rights and responsibilities of editors and authors.

Prices and contracts stabilized in the 1870s, and around 600$000 *réis* [six hundred thousand *réis*] were paid by Garnier for one or more works. In the following decade, the most highly regarded Brazilian editor apparently reduced the rate of his advances and made further demands. A receipt signed by Machado de Assis suggests that the editor was only responsible for the purchase of the first edition and entailed a clear commitment on the part of the author not to republish the work before the stock of books for sale had run out.

Machado de Assis was paid 300$000 *réis* [three hundred thousand *réis*] for his *Histórias sem data*, an amount lower than he had been offered for *Helena* in 1876 (600,000). There are several hypotheses with regard to this: at that time, Garnier practically had the monopoly of the Brazilian book industry because his competitors were largely devoted to the school book market or were mere typographers who only printed the books at the authors' own expense, which made it difficult for them to bargain with the publishers. Machado de Assis himself was not published by Garnier after 1876, the year when *Helena* had been first published. His following books — *Iaiá Garcia*, in 1878, *Memórias póstumas de Brás Cubas*, in 1881, and *Papéis avulsos*, in 1882 — were printed, respectively, by *O Cruzeiro*, the typography responsible for the newspaper when the *feuilleton* first appeared,[46] the National Typography, a State company since the time of Januário da Cunha Barbosa, and Lombaerts, the firm of the Belgian Jean-Baptiste Lombaerts (1821–1875) and his son Henri Gustave Lombaerts (1845–1897), to whom homage was paid by the novelist in a moving obituary.[47] Since 1878, Machado had ceased to participate in the *Jornal das Famílias*, which was no longer in circulation from that year on, and became more involved as a short-story writer, particularly with *A Estação*. This was a magazine that had superior typographic quality, produced by Lombaerts, and was on a par with European standards; it published texts destined for the female readers in the Court élite.[48]

In 1884, perhaps the writer wished to reattach his ties with his first editor, and accepted a lower sum for his book of short stories, most of which had been published earlier in the *Gazeta de Notícias* and *A Estação*. However, it is possible that the decision to bring out an anthology of short stories at a time when the short story was not a prestigious literary genre may have been the reason for the lower assessed value of the work, compared to the novels *O seminarista*, *A captiva Isaura* and *Helena*.

The hypothesis that there are distinct prices for different literary genres and writers that are distinctly placed in the hierarchy of the literary system is supported by an older document: the receipt which shows how, in 1860, Francisco Leite Bittencourt Sampaio (1834–1895) offered a book of poems for sale for 200$000 *réis* [two hundred thousand *réis*]. Although the genre of the work and the historical time of the contract can explain the amount offered to the author, it is worth mentioning that Bittencourt Sampaio was someone of political and intellectual prestige. Born in Sergipe and a follower of Spiritism, he was governor of the Province of Espírito Santo, lyricist for the music of Carlos Gomes (1836–1896) and director of the National Library; however, it should also be noted that the book was published in 1860, when Sampaio was only twenty-six years old. Perhaps the comparative youth of the author accounts for the fact that for his book of poems he was only paid a third of the amount that his novelist colleagues received; but the genre chosen may not have warranted him a higher payment.

With regard to poetry, there are some documents in the mid-nineteenth century that provide a more detailed view of the opportunities that the world of books opened up for enabling intellectuals to pursue professional careers. There are two receipts that no longer show the name of the author of the book, but that of the organizer or compiler (a practice that still occurs today).

One of these receipts, dated 1880, introduces to the scene Alfredo do Vale Cabral (1851–1894), who appears here not as the Head of the Manuscripts Section in the National Library, the position that the traditional history of reading in Brazil reserves for him, but as a compiler of the poems of Laurindo Rabelo (1826–1864). The background of the document suggests an interesting plot: Garnier had published a book by Laurindo Rabelo, who had died and left some works which the editor was interested in publishing. The amount mentioned in the receipt, higher than what Bittencourt Sampaio received twenty years earlier, paid for the research and compilation of the unpublished works of Rabelo, whose ballads Vale Cabral had already made known in *Revista Brasileira*, in 1880.[49]

A similar task, but apparently more complex than that which was commissioned to Vale Cabral, is that regarding the work of the romantic poet Fagundes Varela (1841–1875), for which Visconti Coaracy (1837–1892) four years later was paid 150$000 *réis* [one hundred and fifty thousand *réis*], an lower amount than that offered to Cabral: Cabral had to select texts that 'were not included in the publishing house of Sr. Garnier',[50] while Coaracy should assemble all poems of Varela as a single book which came out in two volumes in 1892.

The issue becomes more interesting when the document of 1884 is compared with another from 1880 signed by the widow of Fagundes Varela, who was paid 726$000 *réis* [seven hundred and twenty six thousand *réis*] for 605 copies of her husband's work: *O evangelho*, probably *Anchieta ou o Evangelho nas selvas*, a posthumous publication (1875) produced by the Livraria Imperial and printed by Typ. de Brown & Evaristo with an introduction by the editor. The most likely explanation is that Garnier, having bought the stock of books from Livraria Imperial in an auction, had purchased the rights to the titles from the widow. Garnier's edition of the complete works of Fagundes Varela (1892), mentioned earlier, states that it is a question of an 'organized and revised edition, preceded by a biographical note by Visconti Coaracy and a critical study by Dr Franklin Távora'.[51] This makes clear the meaning of the expression 'compilation of the works of Fagundes Varela' inserted in the receipt signed by Coaracy. At the same time, it points that the transaction between the poet's widow and Garnier came into effect because, from now on, the rights of an author should be passed on to the heirs.

There were alterations to the pattern of contracts and payment to writers that occurred in the last decade of the nineteenth century. Despite the changes, again Machado de Assis does not seem to have been fairly remunerated. In the case of *Quincas Borba*, the novelist reverted to the level of 600,000, which he had reached fifteen years earlier; for the new edition of 1896, he was paid the sum of 250$000 *réis* [two hundred and fifty thousand *réis*]. In the case of *Memórias póstumas de Brás Cubas*, the first edition having been sponsored by the National Typography, as mentioned earlier, the figure was the same — two hundred and fifty thousand as well as the novel *Iaiá Garcia*, republished in 1897. However, the Garnier who signed contracts at the end of the century is someone else: Baptiste-Louis died in 1893, and was also paid a tribute in his obituary by the most famous writer he published — Machado de Assis[52] — but this was not enough for Hippolyte (1816–1911), the brother and heir of the deceased, to offer him more beneficial contracts.

It was to Hippolyte Garnier that, in January 1899 (shortly after legislation had been approved with regard to authors' rights), Machado de Assis sold 'the entire and intact property' of his works which up to that year comprised: *A mão e a luva*,

Americanas, *Brás Cubas*, *Contos fluminenses*, *Crisálidas*, *Dom Casmurro*, *Falenas*, *Helena*, *História da meia-noite*, *História sem data*, *Iaiá Garcia*, *Páginas recolhidas*, *Papéis avulsos*, *Quincas Borba* and *Ressurreição*, as shown in the contract where they are identified and put in alphabetical order. The writer was paid eight *contos* [8 million *réis*] for this set of works, which may seem a large amount but represents less than 600$000 *réis* [six hundred thousand *réis*] per title, less than he had been paid in previous contracts. Besides, two years before, the novelist Aluísio Azevedo (1857–1913) was paid ten *contos* (also by Hippolyte Garnier), in return for granting the 'entire and perpetual property' of *Filomena Borges*, *Memórias de um condenado*, *O cortiço*, *O Coruja*, *O mulato*, *Pegadas* and *Uma lágrima de mulher*. Thus, Aluísio gave up seven titles at more than one *conto* of *réis* [one million *réis*] for each one, and still did not sell his whole portfolio, as novels as renowned as *Casa de pensão* were not included in this list.

After that, Machado de Assis produced new works, which required supplementary contracts. The contract of 1900 refers to the edition of *Poesias completas*, which included *Crisálidas*, *Falenas* and *Americanas*, which under the terms of the agreement already belonged 'to Mr. H. Garnier', and the then new *Ocidentais*. As a result of this new negotiation, the author was paid 800$000 *réis* [eight hundred thousand *réis*], which suggests a small degree of progress in the financial dealings of the editor, but to reach this point, the author had to accept one restriction: to renounce 'the rights and benefits granted to the authors by the new law that allowed the property of works to be recovered provided that the publisher was reimbursed with an amount that correspond to their value'. The law had not been yet implemented, as its regulation had to wait until the following decades, that is, well into the twentieth century. Nonetheless, the businessmen, even when operating from a distance like Hippolyte Garnier, who resided in Paris, were on their guard and imposed draconian rules on the writers in their catalogues.

However, Machado de Assis seemed to adapt easily to these norms as, in 1902, he attempted to sell Hippolyte the volume of *Várias histórias*, published in 1894 by Laemmert, which he sold, probably at a good profit, for 3$000 *réis* [three thousand *réis*], in 1896, according to information supplied by Olavo Bilac (1865–1918). In a letter dated 1902, Machado de Assis offered him the work for one million two hundred thousand *réis*, but settled for one million. This is not to say that the storyteller was not worried about his book. In a letter of 10 July 1903, Machado de Assis sent the editor a carefully revised version of *Várias histórias*. This attention can be explained by the fact that, in the words of the author, the collection was to be adapted for use in schools, and the number of typographical errors in the original edition could affect this.

Alterations in the Brazilian editorial board at the end of the nineteenth century led to the introduction of a new editor devoted to fiction: Domingos de Magalhães, the proprietor of Livraria Moderna, in Rio de Janeiro, who gave prominence to the emerging generation of fiction writers affiliated with the Naturalism movement. In 1893, Adolfo Caminha (1867–1897) had his novel *A normalista* published by that editor, who in 1894 also launched *No país dos ianques*, by the same author who was paid 400$000 *réis* [four hundred thousand *réis*]. The writer from Ceará was paid 2 million for 5,000 copies of *O bom crioulo*, and both his readership and number of copies printed were higher than those his contemporaries were accustomed to achieving. Domingos de Magalhães still included Coelho Neto in his catalogue, and offered him a salary for five years of 400$000 *réis* [four hundred thousand *réis*] per month.

It is not known if the contract provided the author with exclusive rights. This does not seem to be the case, since a letter by Coelho Neto sent to another important bookseller and publisher of the period, Francisco Alves (1848–1917), suggests sharing plans for book publication. In this letter, the novelist invited the editor to have lunch with him together with the co-author of the book, José Veríssimo (1857–1916). Was this a kind of *preview* of a book, promised in the meeting of Coelho Neto, José Verissimo and Francisco Alves, that was going to be launched? Or was it a crude exposure of the author's lack of modesty, shown by the high value that Coelho Neto attached to his own work, which he regarded as 'the most original that has been carried out among us?' Or was it a celebration of a final editorial order?

Two years later, another letter, also written by Coelho Neto to Alves, suggests that relations may have become a little strained between the author and editor:

> Rio, 29–08–98
>
> My dear Alves:
>
> I'm going back to my point. It is not just a question of insistence and importunity; it is a real emergency and cannot be put off — the guarantee of my strength. It is not fair that I should have to forfeit what I have begun to accumulate at such a heavy cost. My insurance policy matures on the 31st and I see myself having difficulties in paying off the policy because this month, with the birth of my son, there are constant expenses and they are taking up everything I earn. I beg you, if you are unable to accept my suggestion, that you pledge this same work or another of your choice as security, that you lend me the sum of 1,000,000 until October 6th when it will be repaid without fail. In this way, I will be able to save my capital, which is at risk if Alberto Torres fails to fulfil the promise that he has made for September 15th, and make the payment for *Terra Fluminense*.
>
> You know that I am a man of my word, especially when it comes to sensitive matters like money.
>
> Yours as ever,
>
> Friend

Here in August 1898, the asymmetry and inequality of the relationship between the two is made apparent. Right at the beginning of the letter the writer implies that he is responding to a previous request made by the author in negative terms ('I'm returning to my point'); in what follows, the seriousness of the situation is outlined in what the writer tells the editor. Throughout the letter, the figure of Francisco Alves acquires the image of a capitalist or banker, while also having an intimidating effect on the professional image of the writer who suggests mortgaging one of his works ('that you pledge this same work or another of your choice as security, the sum of ...') as a way of helping him out of this urgent situation.

Francisco Alves is the last major editor of nineteenth century Brazil. Like his predecessors Garnier, Laemmert (financed by the brothers Eduardo (1806–1880) and Henrique (1812–1884), of German origin) and Lombaerts, Alves was not born in Brazil, but emigrated there in 1863. He went back to Portugal, but returned in 1876 at the invitation of his uncle, Nicolau Antônio Alves (1827–1902), the owner of Livraria Clássica, founded in 1854. He became the director of the shop around 1882, and, from 1890 onwards, devoted himself to the industrial branch and concentrated on the school sector that was expanding in this period.

In these circumstances, the Francisco Alves publishing house took on responsibility for producing teaching material prepared by the generation of Coelho Neto, including names which constituted the fin-de-siècle canon in Brazil such as Alberto de Oliveira (1857–1937), José Veríssimo, Júlia Lopes de Almeida (1862–1934) and Olavo Bilac. Since the investment in school books ensured a significant financial return for the authors and publishers, writers were happy to take part in the enterprise that gave them long-running best-sellers like *Poesias infantis*, by Olavo Bilac, *Contos pátrios*, by Olavo Bilac and Coelho Neto, and *Através do Brasil*, by Olavo Bilac and Manuel Bonfim (1868–1932). Alves had the most prestigious writers that were producing books at that time at his service including, among others, Abílio César Borges (1824–1891), the famous Barão de Macaúbas, João Kopke (1852–1926) and Felisberto de Carvalho (1850–1898).

At the same time, the situation increasingly made the writers beholden to the editors, as is reflected in the exchange of correspondence between Coelho Neto and Alves. In their dispute, there are clear signs of the fragility of the economic system on which intellectual production was based, as is evident from the mention of the irregularity of the payments promised by Alberto Torres (1865–1917), an intellectual who at that time was President of the Province of Rio de Janeiro, a position to which he had been elected. The work mentioned in the correspondence is *Terra fluminense*, by Coelho Neto and Olavo Bilac, aimed, as the sub-title ('for Civic Education') shows, at schools and only published in 1898 by the National Press, the successor to the National Typography, which had operated as the Royal Press in the times of D. João.

Therefore, when Brazil inaugurated a republican system of government towards the end of the century (in 1889), the initial problems remained, which explains a series of demands and complaints that come under the heading of the following topics:

(a) The reduced number of readers and particularly consumers of printed material, as was pointed out by Machado de Assis in a chronicle in 1866, which endangered the future of the book-publishing industry;

(b) The difficulties experienced by writers who wished to make a living from intellectual work, as revealed by José de Alencar;

(c) The inequitable competition with imported books, due to the fact that the price of printed paper was lower than 'smooth paper simply used for writing', as F. Conceição makes clear in an essay published in *Revista Brasileira*;[53]

(d) The lack of regulation of authorial rights which affected both Brazilian and Portuguese writers who were read in the country, according to a criticism made by the Portuguese dramatist, Manuel Pinheiro Chagas (1842–1895), in a letter addressed to Pedro II.[54]

The Brazilian writers' claims began to be formulated at the end of the Monarchy and gathered intensity in the first ten years of the new republican regime. The regime had come to power in the name of modernization, and the intellectuals who had struggled for its establishment were the same ones who had proclaimed the need for recognition of the value of the kind of work that they were capable of producing. The socialist Pardal Mallet (1864–1894) was one of the first to declare his position on behalf of a recognition of 'authors' rights', a concept he favoured over the standard, commonly used expression 'literary property', which, in his view, reflected the outlook of a capitalist world. The young champion of the writers' cause formulated the question in terms of the relationship between the owner of the means of production and the workers subjected to the exploitation of the capitalists.[55]

Although not all intellectuals adopted the clearly stated political attitude of Pardal Mallet, they were unanimous on one point which is made clear by Adolfo Caminha[56] and Olavo Bilac: the editors used foreign labour and this gave their companies a great commercial advantage. Nothing makes it clearer than a text of Bilac's of 24 August 1900. In the opening paragraph, the mention of Artur de Azevedo (1855–1908) states the current concern with the subject in the title of his article: 'Authorial rights'.[57] In the development of his argument, Bilac provides a historical sketch of the situation experienced by writers in Brazil and, with great irony, conveys the ideological and metaphorical senses of the expression 'bread of the spirit' through which the economic claims of intellectuals and writers are usually undermined.

The figure of the editor does not escape unscathed by the irreverent pen of the poet: the noun which is employed to characterize his activities ('piracy') and his agent ('a pirate') testifies to the precarious situation of the writers. He settles the question by revisiting the 'bread of the spirit' metaphor in an amusing comparison with commercial production, with 'bakers and suppliers' representing writers, editors and compilers.

Finally, towards the end of this chronicle, the question is put in an international context. Lying within the text ('the misprint of our poems come together with the low payment for our prose') is the question of the complex literary field and the materiality of literature. These factors become extremely contemporary and are relevant to the twentieth-first century when certain aspects of literary studies are being viewed afresh, and attention is being paid to the links between literature and society.

Translated by Frank Hanson

Notes to Chapter 10

1. Nelson Werneck Sodré, *História da imprensa no Brasil* (São Paulo: Intercom; Porto Alegre: Edipucrs, 2011), p. 28.
2. Max Fleuiss, 'Subsídios para a história da imprensa no Brasil', in *Páginas de história*, 2nd edn (Rio de Janeiro: Imprensa Nacional, 1930), p. 597.
3. The only exception was the typography of Manuel Antonio da Silva Serva (?–1819), whose establishment in Bahia was officially sanctioned by D. João in 1811. See Renato Berbert de Castro, *A Tipografia Imperial e Nacional, da Bahia* (São Paulo: Ática, 1984).

4. José Martínez de Sousa, *Pequeña historia del libro*, 3rd edn (Gijón: Trea, 1999), p. 152.
5. Artur Anselmo, 'Da edição à transgressão', in *Estudos de história do livro* (Lisbon: Guimarães, 1997), p. 14.
6. See Martha Woodmansee, *The Author, Art, and the Market: Rereading the History of Aesthetics* (New York: Columbia University Press, 1994); and Lucy Newlyn, *Reading, Writing, and Romanticism: The Anxiety of Reception* (Oxford: Oxford University Press, 2003).
7. See J. M. Vaz Pinto Coelho, 'Da propriedade literária no Brasil (Memória)', *Revista Brasileira*, Rio de Janeiro, 2nd series, vol. 6, October 1880, and vol. 8, April 1881. See also Laurence Hallewell, *O livro no Brasil: sua história*, trans. by Maria da Penha Villalobos, Lólio Lourenço de Oliveira and Geraldo Gerson de Souza, 2nd edn (São Paulo: Editora da Universidade de São Paulo, 2005), p. 244.
8. See Lúcia Maria Bastos P. Neves, 'Do privilégio à propriedade literária: a questão da autoria no Brasil imperial (1808–1861), <http://www.livroehistoriaeditorial.pro.br/pdf/luciabastosneves.pdf> [accessed 15 December 2011]; Cilza Carla Bignotto, *Novas perspectivas sobre as práticas editoriais de Monteiro Lobato (1918–1925)* (Campinas: Universidade Estadual de Campinas, 2007).
9. We would like to express our gratitude to Valéria Augusti, who supplied us with the data related to the José de Alencar project.
10. See Antonio Hohlfeldt, *Deus escreve direito por linhas tortas: o romance-folhetim dos jornais de Porto Alegre entre 1850 e 1900* (Porto Alegre: EdiPUCRS, 2003), p. 299.
11. See Alexandre Herculano, 'Da propriedade literária e da recente convenção com a França', in *Garrett, Herculano e a propriedade literária*, ed. by Luiz Francisco Rebello (Lisbon: Publicações Dom Quixote; Sociedade Portuguesa de Autores, 1999).
12. See Marisa Lajolo and Regina Zilberman, *O preço da leitura* (São Paulo: Ática, 2001), p. 79.
13. See Raimundo Magalhães Júnior, *Arthur Azevedo e sua época*, 3rd edn (Rio de Janeiro: Civilização Brasileira, 1966), p. 72.
14. Manuel Aires de Casal, *Corografia brasília ou Relação histórico-geográfica do reino do Brasil* (Rio de Janeiro: Impressão Régia, 1817).
15. See Lúcia Maria Bastos P. Neves, 'Do privilégio à propriedade literária', p. 4.
16. Ibid.
17. See Marisa Lajolo and Regina Zilberman, 'A leitura no Brasil: um grande negócio', in *A leitura rarefeita* (São Paulo: Ática, 2002).
18. Carlos Rizzini, *Hipólito da Costa e o Correio Brasiliense* (São Paulo: Nacional, 1957), p. 166.
19. See Nelson Werneck Sodré, *História da imprensa no Brasil.*
20. *As Variedades, ou Ensaios de Literatura*, facsimile reprint (Salvador: Arquivo do Estado, 1992).
21. The brothers João Pedro and Evaristo da Veiga (1799–1837) purchased the Silva Porto bookstore, located in Rua da Quitanda. Later on, the brothers separated, each of them setting up his own bookshop.
22. From 1824, Pierre Plancher, a French emigrant, kept a graphics and book shop on the Rua do Ouvidor.
23. See *Autobiographia de C. C. Ottoni*, in <http://doc.brazilia.jor.br/HistDocs/Ottoni/Ottoni Autobiographia04.htm> [accessed 16 December 2011].
24. See Marisa Lajolo and Regina Zilberman, *A formação da leitura no Brasil* (São Paulo: Ática, 1996), p. 313.
25. Delfina Benigna da Cunha, Soneto, 'À S. M. I. o Senhor D. Pedro I', *Poesias: oferecidas às senhoras rio-grandenses*, 3rd edn (Porto Alegre: Instituto Estadual do Livro, 2001), p. 42.
26. Múcio Teixeira wrote: 'On the death of the father of our poetess, D. Pedro I provided her with an allowance that granted her to live in a modest way; this pension was generously maintained by D. Pedro II, who Delfina honoured in more than one of her inspired poems.' In Múcio Teixeira, *Os gaúchos* (Rio de Janeiro: Leite Ribeiro & Maurillo, 1921), II, 87.
27. Delfina Benigna da Cunha, op. cit., p. 43.
28. Id., p. 27.
29. Guilhermino Cesar, *História da literatura do Rio Grande do Sul* (Porto Alegre: Globo, 1956), p. 98.
30. Id. p. 99.
31. J. J. da Silva, 'Duas palavras', in 'Iriema' (Apolinário Porto Alegre), *Paisagens* (Porto Alegre: Imprensa Literária, 1875), pp. 262–63.

32. Augusto Meyer, *No tempo da flor* (Rio de Janeiro: O Cruzeiro, 1966), p. 64.
33. See Alfredo Bosi, 'Introdução. Antônio Vieira: vida e obra. Um esboço', in Antônio Vieira, *Essencial Padre Vieira* (São Paulo: Penguin Classics, Companhia das Letras, 2011), p. 104.
34. José Alencar, *Como e porque sou romancista* (Campinas: Pontes, 1990), p. 70.
35. For the contracts of Machado de Assis, see Ministério da Educação e Saúde, *Exposição Machado de Assis: centenário do nascimento, 1839–1939* (Rio de Janeiro: Ministério de Educação e Saúde, 1939).
36. See Patronos, 'Cadeira 12', Instituto Histórico e Geográfico de Santos, <http://www.ihgs.com.br/cadeiras/patronos/joaopandia.html> [accessed 17 December 2011].
37. Marisa Lajolo and Regina Zilberman, *O preço da leitura* (São Paulo: Ática, 2001), p. 97.
38. Cf. Augustin-Charles Renouard, *Traité des droits d'auteurs dans la littérature, les sciences et les beaux-arts* (Paris: Jules Renouard & Cia., 1838), 2^{v}.
39. Anne Latournerie, 'Petite histoire des batailles du droit d'auteur', *Multitudes. Revue politique artistique philosophique*, <http://multitudes.samizdat.net/article.php3?id_article=168> [accessed on 25 November 2011].
40. See 'Livros à venda na mesma livraria', a separate appendix to the fifth volume of the *História da fundação do império brasileiro*, by J. M. Pereira da Silva (1817–1898), published by Garnier, in 1865. The comparable titles, *Compêndio de história antiga* and *Compêndio de história da Idade Média*, by Justiniano José da Rocha, were also contracted by Garnier, and sold in bound editions, the price of each copy being 2$400 *réis* [two thousand four hundred *réis*].
41. See Laurence Hallewell, *O livro no Brasil*, pp. 201–03.
42. Machado de Assis, *Crônicas*, vol. II (São Paulo: Mérito, 1959), pp. 245–46. First published in *Diario do Rio de Janeiro*, 22 November 1864.
43. The contracts mentioned can be found at <http://www.bn.br/bndigital/manuscritos_G.htm>.
44. See Coelho Neto, *A conquista* (Rio de Janeiro: Civilização Brasileira, 1985).
45. Cf. <http://bndigital.bn.br/scripts/odwp032k.dll?t=nav&pr=fbn_dig_pr&db=fbn_dig&use=cs0&rn=13&disp=card&sort=off&ss=22351800&arg=contrato> [accessed 26 December 2011].
46. See Daniele Maria Megid, 'A literatura na imprensa: uma análise de *Iaiá Garcia* no jornal *O Cruzeiro*', <http://www.anpuhsp.org.br/downloads/CD%20XIX/PDF/Paineis/Daniele%20Maria%20Megid.pdf>.
47. See Henrique Lombaerts, in Machado de Assis, *Obra completa*, vol. III (Rio de Janeiro: Aguilar, 1958), p. 1019.
48. With regard to *A Estação* and the involvement of Machado de Assis in this publishing venture, see Ivan Teixeira, *O altar & o trono: a dinâmica do poder em 'O alienista'* (São Paulo: Ateliê, 2010).
49. See *Revista Brasileira*, Tomo VI, ano II, p. 262; p.492.
50. This concerns *Obras poéticas*, by Laurindo Rabelo, arranged by Joaquim Norberto de Sousa Silva (1820–1891) and published by Garnier in 1876.
51. See *Obras completas de L. N. Fagundes Varela* (Rio de Janeiro: Garnier, 1892).
52. See Machado de Assis, *A Semana*, vol. I (São Paulo: Mérito, 1959), p. 395.
53. See F. Conceição, 'Os livros e as tarifas alfandegárias', *Revista Brasileira*. Ano I, Tomo 1, 1879. pp. 607–11.
54. See Manuel Pinheiro Chagas, *A propriedade literária: Carta a Sua Majestade o Imperador do Brasil* (Porto and Braga: Ernesto Chardron, 1879).
55. See Pardal Mallet, 'Direito autoral, Carta aberta a Benjamin Constant', *Gazeta de Notícias*, Rio de Janeiro, 26 April 1890 — 9 May 1890.
56. See Adolfo Caminha, *Cartas literárias* (Rio de Janeiro: n.pub., 1895).
57. Olavo Bilac, 'Direitos autorais', in *Registro: crônicas da Belle Époque carioca*, ed. by Alvaro Santos Simões Jr. (Campinas: Ed. da Unicamp, 2011), pp. 50–51.

CHAPTER 11

Print Technologies, World News and Narrative Form in Machado de Assis[1]

Jussara Menezes Quadros

As a writer who published in newspapers and literary magazines throughout the second half of the nineteenth century, Machado de Assis (1839–1908) was a close witness of the emergence of new media technologies. The innovations of Machado's youth were the steam-powered printing press, the expansion of lithographic reproduction, and the advent of photography. In a letter written in November 1866 to his friend Quintino Bocaiúva (1836–1912), a Brazilian journalist then in New York City, the writer shows curiosity and enthusiasm for a metropolis that he imagined from a distance, as though it were a place pertaining to another dimension of time, a 'time of telegraph wires':

> I am anxious to see letters from you and to know what your impressions were upon entering that great world: what it all seems like to you, what it is like in reality. Should you have the leisure to recount all this to me, know that you will give me infinite pleasure in doing so. At the least, I will find enjoyment through your letters, which will give me satisfaction here in the midst of the profound boredom in which I live. Oh, time of telegraph wires, of meetings,[2] time of finance,[3] in short, your time! I am in the hands of Lord Spleen. Adieu, write to me, do not forget me.[4]

This letter addressed to the friend in a distant country puts two temporalities into contrast: the subjective time of 'spleen', the romantic malaise that Machado de Assis identifies as his mood, and the expectation of time's acceleration and the shortening of distances as promised by the recent expansion of telegraph technology. The intimate codes of the personal letter and the delivery times of the postal system are conjoined with a longing for broader public connections, such as those being unveiled at the time by the new technologies of communication. And although the writer says he is 'in the hands of Lord Spleen', thereby foregrounding a literary positionality, his letter also emphasizes the links between technological advances and the democratization of public space. In his letter of 1866, subjective experience, material modernization, and progressive political ideas are combined in an ambivalent, yet non-conflicting, way.

Nonetheless, some years later, in a *crônica* published in 1876,[5] he stated: 'what I draw from all that reaches us via submarine cable and transatlantic steamships is that the Orient has come to an end and poetry with it'.[6] Machado is referring to news of the Ottoman Empire's apparent adoption of a parliamentary system. His comment is ironic, signalling the moment of the Orient's incorporation into the space-time of modernity, while at the same time announcing the decline of an oriental imaginary that Romanticism had transformed into myth. Machado the chronicler often played with orientalist stereotypes — harems, concubines, and eunuchs — with satirical intent, mocking not Islamic traditions themselves, but the Westernization that threatened them.

In another of his *crônicas* from the 'Quinze Dias' series published in the magazine *Illustração Brasileira*, the writer draws from articles in the daily papers to comment on a report of a *coup d'état* in Turkey and the sudden reversal in the expectations of constitutional reforms:

> Turkey is aping Bolivia in a most scandalous way: it changes sultans like Bolivia changes presidents and a reader changes shirts. A Turkish sultan is equivalent to a paper collar, lasting for only a single outing. Yet the collar lasts longer than the constitutional project, of which nothing is any longer being said, fortunately for the Koran.[7]

Machado showed a genuine interest in world politics, but the oblique writing of his *crônicas* used intentional irony and humour to provoke unexpected inversions of perspective and points of view. His concern with the eastern upheavals assumes a farcical tone when he compares the events in Turkey to a mistranslation of a Wagnerian opera. The disparate intermingling of world events and cultural references in the *crônica* comically exaggerates the realities of the overcoming of boundaries, the cross-national dimension, and the effect of simultaneity in the transmission of news by cable telegraphy.

World news, submarine cables and the end of poetry are juxtaposed and confronted in Machado's *crônicas*, as aspects of an emerging modernity to which the writer seems to react with an ironic distancing. The sense of the end of poetry referred, above all, to the demise of romantic poetry, a romanticism which had nurtured his own generation, but it also reflected the writer's awareness of broader technological shifts that would transform social and cultural perceptions, as well as literary techniques.

The perception that change was occurring more rapidly, threatening to destabilize cultural and political models or traditional literary genres such as poetry, was accentuated in the 1870s, when peripheral regions such as the Orient and peripheral nations such as Brazil were integrated into a global system of communications that resulted from the industrialization and economic expansion of the European powers.

The Emergence of Global Telegraph Networks

With the inauguration of the transatlantic cable between Brazil and Europe in 1874, the British Empire, financiers, and cartels of international companies were finally close to achieving their goal of wiring the world. Following many unsuccessful attempts, the transformation of national telegraph systems into a global network became possible when an Anglo-American submarine cable between the United States and Europe was finally laid in 1866, the year Machado de Assis wrote to his friend Quintino Bocaiúva in New York and hailed the new 'time of telegraph wires'. By 1865, two submarine telegraph cables had already connected Europe and India: a main line crossing the Ottoman Empire and Persia, and a second line extending further to the north, through Russia. In 1870, a new company directed by the German Charles Siemens (1823–1883) and Julius Reuter (1821–1889) laid a cable system that extended from London via Berlin to Warsaw and Odessa, passed under the Black Sea, and then connected to the telegraph cables of the Persian Gulf through Tehran. Another important telegraph network, constructed and administered by the Greater Northern Company, shortened communications between Europe and the Orient in a vast extension of telegraph networks that crossed Russia to reach Japan, China, and Hong Kong.[8]

Brazil's incorporation into this global communication system came relatively late. In 1871, Brazilian industrialist and financier Irineu Evangelista de Sousa, the Baron of Mauá (1813–89), lamented that Brazil remained 'segregated from the civilized world and excluded from the enjoyment of the most sublime invention of the nineteenth century'.[9] The wealthiest man in the Brazilian Empire and a rare paragon of the new capitalist drive in a slave-owning society, the Baron of Mauá played a key role in the negotiations that led to the expansion of telegraphy in Brazil. In his association with the two largest British telegraph companies — the British Telegraph Construction and Maintenance Company and the British Indian Rubber, Gutta Percha, and Telegraph Company — he was instrumental in obtaining government concessions and subsidies for his foreign partners in Brazil and Uruguay. Already by 1865, this alliance of capitalists had created the River Plate Telegraph Company of London, which would be responsible for the construction and maintenance of a telegraph cable in Montevideo that linked up to Brazil. The Baron's prestige and influence would subsequently guarantee that the British companies would be granted the concession for constructing the submarine telegraph cable between Brazil and Europe, thanks to monopoly rights given for the operation of an extensive coastal telegraph network linking Rio de Janeiro with the main provinces of the north and south of the nation.[10]

Emperor D. Pedro II would announce the construction of the new cable lines in his Throne Speech of 1872:

> I rejoice in announcing that, with the agreement of the Portuguese government, the installation of an electric cable between Europe and Brazil has been contracted. In the course of 1874 we will now be able to make use of this most marvellous instrument of our century in our relations with that continent. At the same time, we will also work with the greatest efforts to link an exclusively Brazilian landline to the transatlantic cable.[11]

Although plans had been set since 1852 to roll out a national system of telegraph wires, the few lines constructed by the 1860s were restricted to Rio de Janeiro and used almost exclusively for transmitting official messages between the imperial court and the interior provinces. However, the outbreak of war with Paraguay hastened the construction of a network of inter-regional telegraph lines for military-strategic use, linking Rio de Janeiro with the southern battlefields. It was not until the 1870s that the telegraph became a regular service accessible to the public; by the end of 1879, telegraph landlines linked thirteen of the Empire's twenty provinces with Rio de Janeiro. Meanwhile, the emperor's 1872 promise of an 'exclusively Brazilian' telegraph system would fail to be realized, despite the efforts of engineer Guilherme S. de Capanema (1824–1908), director of the empire's Bureau of Telegraphic Services, who continued to advocate a national, state-monopoly system up to the end of the nineteenth century. Despite his efforts, the strategic and more lucrative flow of communications between Brazil and Europe, as well as among the major Brazilian coastal cities, remained under the control of British companies. In 1873, the twenty-year concession that had been granted to the Baron of Mauá for the construction of the submarine cable between Brazil and Portugal was transferred to the Brazilian Submarine Telegraph Company, a subsidiary of the Eastern Telegraph Company. At the same time, the sixty-year monopoly given to the Telegraph Construction and Maintenance Company (Telcon) for the installation and maintenance of the coastal submarine line was also transferred to another British subsidiary, the Western & Brazilian Telegraph Company.[12]

In June of 1875, less than a year after the transatlantic line went into operation, the international news agencies Reuters and Havas opened joint bureaux in Recife, Salvador, Rio de Janeiro, Montevideo and Buenos Aires.[13] Prior to the era of the submarine cable, foreign news, financial information, government communications and private correspondence had been dependent on the slow rhythm of transatlantic ships, whose journeys took a month or more. Suddenly, with the advent of telegraphs and cable dispatches, messages could now be transmitted and received in a matter of a few hours. World news began to circulate more rapidly, and the integration of the news with the global circuits of capitalist exchange, via the mediation of international news agencies, was now redefining the very notion of 'news'.[14]

International News Agencies: The Chronicler's Suspicions

Machado de Assis satirized the global expansion of news agencies using the image of a mythical ocean relegated to the function of a mere reporter of the Havas agency:

> Father Ocean is losing all the prestige that poetry and superstition had bestowed on him; today he is barely a reporter, sometimes bold, but extremely faithful — thus says the Havas agency.[15]

In the ocean's metamorphosis into a reporter, new achievements of technology, such as the submarine cable, triumphed over a disenchanted nature. Thanks to technological progress, the ocean lost its prestige and mystery, surrendering its ancient powers to the new forces of production. And once again, Machado de Assis opposes poetry to the new phenomena of modernization, evoking it by antithesis to the values of utilitarianism. In his allusion to the Havas agency's pretentions to universality, he foresaw what Mallarmé would later criticize as the effect of the intensified instrumentalization of language in the nineteenth century; the unrestrained expansion of a 'reportage universel'.[16] Machado's proximity to the French symbolist poet in this sense is not fortuitous; both writers maintained a contentious stance toward the apologetic modernizing discourses of the second half of the nineteenth century, responding to them with a marked critical distancing.

In his caricature of the Ocean-as-reporter, Machado emblematizes the decline of classical myths, and of literature, in the face of the rising prestige of the new regime of information represented by the Havas agency. In the same way, his use of 'fidelíssimo' [extremely faithful] in the text serves to sharpen the reader's mistrust by implying the possibility of a non-fidelity or non-reliability on the part of the Havas agency's telegraph dispatches.

In the same *crônica*, parodying a so-called 'cable style', he once again counters the belief in the accuracy of telegraphic information:

> vague, yet dubious hypotheses about events which are unlikely to occur or perhaps never will, insofar as earlier facts induce one to have slight suspicions, without, however, prejudging occurrences that are presumable and not improbable, although thus far uncontainable.[17] Apologies to the cable if I copy its style.[18]

The frequent interruptions in transatlantic cable transmissions were also susceptible to comic and dismissive remarks on the inefficiency of the new medium:

> Poor cable! Born to inform one side of the Atlantic or the other of the price of coffee or the exchange rate, and little, very little, extremely little, about Gladstone's theological sneezes and other events of a similar sort, it has spent its days saying nothing at all. Every month, there is an interruption.[19]

The comic scale of the diminutives — the 'pouco, muito pouco, pouquíssimo' [little, very little, extremely little] of information that the cable provides, the demoralizing image of Gladstone's ideas turned into less than words, into 'sneezes'[20] — and the cable's failure to say anything at all allude to the brevity of telegraphic information, a brevity conditioned by the economic laws of the technical medium, by the constraints of its standardized word fees. But the target of the chronicler's ironic commentaries was also the unrivalled British monopoly on transatlantic submarine cable operations, and the fact that the supply of foreign news by European news agencies to South America would inevitably pass through Britain. In another *crônica* from August 1877, Machado de Assis once again assails the telegraph, denouncing the influence of British interests on the tenor of the news transmitted by the Havas agency in Brazil:

> The telegraph's vocation is a fraud. Often it is correct or approximates the truth, yet fraud is its vocation. This fortnight the fraudulence concerned the four thousand pounds of the English parliament. When the Havas agency gravely told us that the English government had proposed 4,000 pounds for [the Brazilian province of] Ceará, there was astonishment and gratitude on every face. The gesture was unprecedented; but the disasters of Ceará are hardly trivial. Everyone trusted the agency's word, whose gravity, veracity, and universality are well-known. But wouldn't you know, it was then discovered that there had been no behest made to the English, no English pounds requested from the English parliament. It was the opposite of our adage. The telegram was only for Brazilians to see.[21] Certainly, the Havas agency has not yet provided an explanation in this regard; but we must recognize that if we were astonished by the declaration, the agency must have been astonished by the correction, and the effect on it must be greater.[22]

The accusation was a serious one, since it related to the devastating drought of 1877 in Ceará; shocking images of starving women and children had circulated via lithographs throughout world newspapers that year.[23] The tragedy's universalization as a sensational news story rendered plausible the hypothesis of financial aid from the British Empire. Denouncing the hoax, Machado's irony also insinuates that the European news agency's universality gave an even more negative scope to the telegraph 'vocation of fraud' and vice versa.

Machado de Assis was by no means the first to launch invectives against the Havas agency. That role perhaps corresponded to Balzac, who in 1840 warned against the monopolistic nature of Charles Havas's journalistic enterprises: 'The public perhaps believes that there are many (French) newspapers, but in reality there is only one: The Havas agency.'[24]

In 1835, Charles Havas (1783–1858) opened an office dedicated to the translation of foreign news, focusing initially on trade news, but his business later grew to include news services and, with telegraphy's expansion, news agencies with correspondents and translators located throughout Europe. The global expansion of his enterprise accompanied the extension of the new networks of transcontinental submarine cables, and in 1870 the three largest European news agencies — the French Havas Agency, Julius Reuter's agency headquartered in London, and the agency led by Bernhard Wolff in Germany — formed a cartel, entering into an agreement to divide the world into zones, each agency being granted exclusive operating rights within its corresponding territories. The Reuters Telegraph Company claimed the entire British Empire, Turkey, India, and the Far East, and maintained joint bureaus with the Havas agency in South America. The Havas agency held monopoly rights over the distribution of international news in France, Sweden, Italy, the Iberian Peninsula, and Central America, as well as joint rights with Reuter in South America and Egypt. For Wolff's Continental Telegraphen Compagnie were reserved exploration rights for a network of agencies and correspondents encompassing Germany, Austria, Scandinavia, Russia, the Balkans, and the Nordic countries.[25]

Concerns were raised over this concentration into so few agencies of so much power and control over the flows of global information. As a Vanity Fair journalist warned in 1872, 'As foreign news is now managed, it is not too much to say that he who has control of telegrams has control of public opinion in foreign affairs'.[26] The linkages between the news agencies, global telegraph networks, and the political-economic strategies of the European powers did not go unnoticed. The news agencies revolutionized print technologies, but their practices and effects did not cease to generate controversy. Thanks to them, the production of news assumed an industrial rhythm mediated by the speed of telegraphic transmission itself. It was a massive, rapid, and daily production with unprecedented global reach, yet standardized due to the brevity of the telegraph and its high costs.

The imposition of telegraphic language on the journalistic news account was frequently criticized by Machado de Assis. Against the news agency telegrams, he defended the 'prose of events', world news that arrived with foreign newspapers via steamship and was not subjected to the limits of telegraphic messages:

> This substitute for the mail is destined to frequently perturb human brains. Its merit is speed; its defect is concision and confusion. It is obliged to say things by half words, at times by shadows of words; and the result is often that of saying something else.
>
> Be that as it may, I am now sceptical of the telegraph news from Europe. Telegraph news from the north of the [Brazilian] Empire is always accurate, because it is free of charge. A free telegraph cannot err, because it does not suppress half of the message; it says everything that is necessary. But a charged telegraph is a different story, and as we know, transatlantic telegraphs are paid.[27] [...] For this reason, I no longer trust telegrams. I want to see news in good, scattered prose, as in the time when steamers brought us the news, brand new, in the papers.[28] The agency can tell me what it thinks. I want to give credence to the victories of the Turks, but how can I, after the English pounds? It is better to appeal from the telegraph to the steamship;[29] in this way I do not offend progress: both are its children.[30]

The chronicler directs his arguments of resistance against the new regime of information founded on the speed of telegraphic communication. It is true that an information-based journalism, properly speaking, would only become predominant in the Brazilian press after the turn of the century. Nevertheless, already by 1870, as demonstrated by Machado de Assis's *crônicas* from this period, the first stages of its establishment were already becoming evident, although not without generating tensions and oppositions. The primacy of factuality encountered a tenacious adversary in Machado, who for decades insisted on questioning the legitimacy and authenticity of telegraph news. For Machado, the technologically conditioned precision of telegraphy did not guarantee objectivity. To the semantic impoverishment of language were added risks of distortion, confusion, error, or even a propensity toward equivocation and fraud. In his view, telegraphy represented the antonym of the ideal of perfectibility so avidly pursued by nineteenth-century technology.

Nonetheless, in his *crônica* of August 1877, Machado makes a distinction between the telegraph news from Europe, transmitted by the Havas agency via transatlantic cable, and news from the north of the Brazilian Empire, transmitted at no charge by state landlines connecting Rio de Janeiro to the northern provinces. Without appealing to a nationalist rhetoric, Machado de Assis nonetheless takes sides in favour of the national telegraph system, whose networks had no telegraph connection with Europe, although in the north, in Pará, those networks were in communication with steamships on the route to Lisbon and Liverpool. Machado was aware that the national network was unable to compete with the British telegraph companies that administered the coastal telegraph line and the transatlantic cable. Nonetheless, his *crônica* stresses the economic aspects of telegraph communication in order to caution readers that European telegraph news had a price but not necessarily value:

> Even before the cable's inauguration, I harboured serious doubts about Rio de Janeiro newspaper subscribers. I would not say that these subscribers were indifferent to the price of potatoes or rice; that is not what I am saying. But in my opinion, they desired no more than this. The *Jornal do Commercio*, which I assume is the only subscriber to the Havas-Reuters agency, still gives us little more than the dregs of London exchange rates or the price of coffee in

> Antwerp. We do not demand more. [...] There are simpletons who ever since the inauguration of the cable are fully convinced of the uselessness of packet boats with regard to news. [...] Never were packet boats more necessary than they are today. Less cable was not to belittle the cable:[31] it was at most a pun.[32]

Machado is being didactic here: for the 'simpleton' reader, his *crônica* not only reveals that news reports are a merchandise, but it also demonstrates that newspaper subscribers are implicated in the relations between the local press market ('potatoes or rice') and the global news market represented by Havas-Reuters ('London exchange rates or the price of coffee in Antwerp'). The chronicler's artful reasoning is a play on suspicions that targets the reader's credulousness. While seeking to discredit the Havas agency it also sows doubts regarding the reader's capacity to judge the meaning and value of the news, or furthermore, to comprehend the new realities of competition alluded to in the *crônica*. The services of the Havas agency were costly and commercially disadvantageous for Brazilian newspapers at the time, with the exception of the most influential newspaper in the country, the *Jornal do Commercio*, which by this time was already employing a large number of foreign correspondents.[33]

The regular steamship lines supplied the local press with foreign newspapers, the main source of 'the prose of events' defended by Machado de Assis in his opposition to the commercialized brevity of telegraph dispatches. A conflict of interests had arisen between the press and the modernization of the communication system. For the local press, subscribing to foreign newspapers meant having access to many different news sources from which stories could be drawn and rewritten. Furthermore, in contrast with the telegraphic news, selectively mediated by the Havas agency, newspaper reports still maintained traces of their origin in a public sphere. News agencies like Havas, due to their transnational character and the high degree of technical specialization of their practices, were turning the news into remarkably decontextualized information depleted of prose, a product more of telegraphy itself and of the emergent information market it was helping to expand, than of the social demands and mediations of a public sphere.

In emphasizing the importance of prose, of a full-length written account or the narrativization of events, Machado's *crônica* betrays a certain anxiety. The change in the status of news that was taking shape would eventually destabilize the strong link between literature and journalism. But another notable aspect of this writer's diatribe against the Havas agency and telegraphy was his concern that the compressed form of messages and the commodification of telegraph news could also threaten the substantial value of opinion. The chronicler not only sought to provoke and persuade the reader to change his naive opinion; it also suggested that an enlightened opinion depended on the reading of the 'good and scattered prose', or 'abundant prose' ('boa e esparramada prosa') of newspapers and on a sceptical reception of telegraph news.[34]

In these *crônicas* of 1877, one already notes a pronounced ironic tendency toward suspicion, together with a tactic of provocative interpellation of the reader. This combination would become a structural device in the so-called 'second-phase' novels of Machado de Assis's literary work, starting with *The Posthumous Memoirs of Brás Cubas* (1880). In the wake of John Gledson's groundbreaking work, recent critical studies have shown that Machado's *crônicas* and short stories from the 1870s served as an experimental field for the formal innovations of his 1880 novel, although acknowledging this line of continuity should not cause us to forget the surprising rupture that *The Posthumous Memoirs of Brás Cubas* represented.

Numerous points of dialogue and formal procedures link Machado's novels to his *crônicas*. Nonetheless, the level of complexity of his writings in both genres frustrates attempts toward their reciprocal elucidation while at the same time making it more productive to problematize their differences. The most important commonality between Machado's *crônicas* and the sequence of novels inaugurated by *The Posthumous Memoirs of Brás Cubas* would be the ironic enunciation. In the case of the texts we are examining here, it is clear that irony made the communicative pact of the *crônicas* ambiguous, and that suspicion in these texts serves as a rhetorical weapon in the service of a critique of modernizing processes. As already shown, this critique was aimed at specific transformations that telegraphy and its new system of communication was effecting on the press, on journalistic discourses, on prose, and on language — in addition to the important fact that, over the long term, telegraphy would also transform readers themselves. And here Machado's irony would hold the irresolution of its paradox in suspense: that irony viewed Rio de Janeiro subscribers — readers of newspapers — with suspicion, due to their naivety and their unreflective fascination for new technologies; but at the same time, it also sought to enlist those readers in the critical exercise of suspicion itself.

Machado the chronicler demonstrates an almost aggressive mistrust of readers' competence at the same time that he seeks to soften that mistrust in order to position (or reposition) readers within the new realities of competition that had arisen between the telegraph and the newspaper. And his interpellations of readers not only confront them but seek to insert them in a public discussion of the effects of telegraphy, a discussion constructed on the binaries of oppositions (true vs. false foreign news; journalistic news vs. telegraph messages; steamship vs. submarine cable) and which incite readers to reflect and deliberate, should they wish to refute their characterization as simpletons by which Machado baits them. Thus, the interpellations of the readers of the *crônica* take on a diverse function that would later be carried out more overtly in his novel of the 1880s, in which, as Roberto Schwarz has observed, 'the games with the reader do not aim to create but to destroy the idea of an enlightened understanding with the reading public'.[35]

Treating the innumerable differences between Machado's *crônicas* and his novels is not the concern here, but rather pointing out the striking difference between the autobiographical enunciation — the individual and private voice of the character-narrator Brás Cubas, with his hierarchical class codes — and the performance of the narrative voice(s) in Machado's *crônicas*, a performance which is inseparable from the collective enunciation of the newspaper and the social-symbolic exchanges of the public sphere as mediated by print discourses. Of course, social and public voices are also at work in *The Posthumous Memoirs* of *Brás Cubas*, and one of this novel's innovations, among others, was its destabilization of the authorial voice through the strategic device of a posthumous narrator-author's double. But even though irony lends the voice(s) in Machado's *crônicas* certain superiority, it never elevates that voice from the ground of a public and contingent everydayness; and likewise, the chronicler's frequently conversational, familiar, and intimate tone is articulated in the double horizon of the newspaper and the city, and deeply rooted in them. Due to their closer links with public space, Machado's *crônicas* thus preserve a communicative pact — although submitting it to the ambivalences of irony — that would be undermined by derision in *The Posthumous Memoirs*.

In the protocols of reading, the implicit readers of the *crônicas* and those of the novel would not be the same, but both genres internalized a critique of the reader, a critique that was conceived and transformed by Machado de Assis into a stylistic device. This occurred first in his *crônicas*, during the 1870s, at a time when telegraphy threatened to drastically change the modes of reception of the news as well as reader expectations. In the new regime of telegraphic information, what was new was not merely the temporal primacy accorded to the present, but the fact that the present was now measured in hours, creating an expectation not only for the current but for the latest news, which could arrive at any moment of the day.

Machado de Assis would mock this new temporal imperative in a *crônica* of days lived entirely in the expectation of news of a revolution in the Brazilian south. With minute-by-minute precision, the chronicler registers, not the arrival of the news, but the time of the irruption of rumour and gossip, unleashed by the ambivalence of an initial, misinterpreted, telegram:

> Day 10 brought a news item in its pocket: nothing less than the departure of the president of Rio Grande. Why had he departed? This question was repeated, heard, commented, throughout the twenty-four hours of the aforementioned day 10, and not a charitable soul was able to give it a worthy response. [...] The telegrams came in pairs, pairs went after the telegrams (if I can be granted licence for the antithesis), and nothing was known.[36] [...] At ten thirty on day 11 [...] it was learned that a revolution had broken out in Rio Grande, that General Osório was in the office of the presidency of the republic; that a general, leading the lawful forces, was battling the forces of the revolution [...].[37]

This mock news bulletin satirizes the public expectation of a revolution; out of the uncertainty of the first telegram, circuits of rumours proceed to activate circuits of opinion which feed off of one another in judging the revolution to be imminent, and in imagining, from a distance, its unfolding:

> At midday, the imperial president was now completely vanquished, with the installation of the republic [...]. At 1:12 news began to spread that an assembly had been elected [...]. Just as this news had begun to run through the space between the Garnier house and the bonnets store (all along Rua do Ouvidor) came a new bombshell: — the bombshell of the alliance; the young republic was signing treaties with all the sister countries of the River Plate region and the Pacific. It was now five in the afternoon.[38]

In this telegraphic comedy of errors, news rumours run faster and seem to have better timing than telegrams, rumours construct and reconstruct events in the intervals between news reports, or make and unmake revolutions that emerge from the ambiguities of telegraphic codified brevity. The *crônica* portrays with subtle humour the transfigurations that news undergoes in its reverberations through the social space of the city, and its textual rhythm reproduces the anxieties of a collective expectation that then becomes temporarily oriented by up-to-the-minute news. In the end, however, the chronicler reverses these expectations, demonstrating that the revolution had been no more than an illusion generated by the unreliability of telegraph technology. And when the daily newspaper is delivered to subscribers' doorsteps, it undoes the misreadings of the telegraph, completely debunking the rumours of a revolution:

> At five forty-five, the assembly ceased to exist, dissolved by the president; at six twenty the president fell in a vote of the new assembly. The latter succumbed after a quarter hour of work, leaving a president who likewise succumbed after five minutes of idleness [...]. Early in the morning on day 12, [...] the newspaper delivery personnel left the paper under the doors. The most curious got up, read, and were left knowing that there had been no revolution or anything of the sort.[39]

Machado's text mocks the telegraph's pretentions to objectivity by associating it with rumour and street gossip, but it also suggests the risks of telegraphy's political instrumentalization. Concerns over the potential for dissemination of telegraph messages, given the wide reach of their rapid transmission over regional and international networks, would be a constant throughout the century. Writing in 1893, Joaquim Nabuco (1849–1910) would describe the telegraph as 'the most important of the political machines', imagining the hypothesis of a situation quite similar to the fictional one described by Machado: 'an operator, lord of the wires in this city, who wished to have some fun, could overthrow in the morning and by nightfall re-establish the governments of all the states of the Union'.[40]

In Machado's *crônica*, and in Joaquim Nabuco's observation, the same anxiety arises regarding the possibility that the telegraph could break the central order of political power. Both writers conceive telegraph technology as an external agent as well as a factor exogenous to political representation and its mediations, wholly opposing the economy of the telegraphic abbreviated language to the discursive protocols of political eloquence and journalistic discourse.

These writers' objections to the telegraph extend even to the uncertain authenticity of the telegraph message, as if the medium in itself were more susceptible than other technologies of communication to the propagation of unreliable messages; as though behind the codified information of telegrams and cable dispatches the sender could more easily conceal his deceptive intentions. The risk, which Machado de Assis's *crônicas* warned against, was that telegraph messages and news might be accorded an automatic truth value, when they constituted nothing more than impoverished forms of writing and language, a 'stuttering'. This is suggested in Machado's *crônica* of 25 June 1889, in which, starting with a mistranslation, and through a dialogue between the chronicler and an official of the British telegraph company, a local branch of the international news market is portrayed in a debased manner as a mere telegraph desk. The chronicler follows the opposite itinerary to that of a reporter, not heading out in search of news, but going to the telegraphic counter to investigate its meaning:

> In Venezuela (according to a telegram from New York received on the 25th, published on the 26th) the party of General Guzmán Blanco was dissolved. I reacted as you could not imagine, such that I did not have time to congratulate you, dear reader, as I desired. I ran to the telegraph company office to see if there had been an error in the telegram's translation. Perhaps 'party' was 'patrol', or 'dance party', or 'battalion'. We did dissolve battalions. 'Party' is what I found...
>
> — Here is telegram, sirr, the Englishman informed me, looking down at me with an air of excess; sirr can eksamine it and see Company have no interest in invent telegrams.
>
> — You must forgive me, but the Prince of Bismarck is of the contrary opinion.
>
> — Contrary to Company?
>
> — No, to telegrams. He once commented to an orator of the Chamber, in an aside: 'Oh Mr. Deputy, you lie like a telegram'. But I do not go so far; telegrams don't lie, but they can stutter.
>
> — Sirr is speaking Latin; I am leaving, sirr...
>
> And the Englishman withdrew; I descended the stairs and went out onto the street, disoriented and ever more curious to find an explanation for the news, which seemed ludicrous to me. It was difficult to understand how a party could be dissolved in such a way, on a given day, like a decree being issued. I understand that a family reunion can dissolve at a certain hour; [...] But a party, a political vegetation? That was difficult for me to absorb.[41]

Machado de Assis's intention to disqualify the 'Company' — the never-mentioned Western and Brazilian Telegraph Company — is clear. However, more significant is the fact that he carries this out entirely through metalinguistic wordplays yet within a specific framing context. The parody of the Portuguese spoken by the British company official serves to emphasize the analogy between the man's short phrases, replete with errors, and the language of telegrams. Machado's criticism partly denounces and partly uses as a comic device the disproportion between the brevity of the telegraphic enunciation and the possible effects that simple verbal substitutions or semantic slippages can provoke in reality. Telegrams in themselves did not dissolve parties, but mistranslation could acquire ambiguous political connotations in the context of the Brazilian parliamentary crisis of 1889, which was the underlying target, the political subtext of the chronicler's malice. The analogy is pertinent, since it focuses on the crisis of another liberal party, in Venezuela. Nonetheless, the explicit criticism of the 'Company' was perhaps also aimed at the Western and Brazilian Telegraph Company's monopoly on telegraph communications in South America, which gave it considerable control over the continental flow of information.

The fact that Machado de Assis was, in addition to a writer, a high official in the Ministry of Agriculture, Commerce and Public Works may have contributed to his criticism of the telegraph companies. Although he worked in the Office of Agriculture, it was quite unlikely he would have been unaware of matters handled by other branches of the ministry, which during the second half of the century were responsible for decisions regarding modernizing projects for the nation's infrastructure, including railways, ports, the postal system and telegraphy, urban transport and illumination, most of which, even when administered by the state, relied on the expertise of British companies.[42] Machado de Assis's privileged position as a state official made his resistance as a writer to processes of modernization even more significant. The disqualification of progress through irony, mistrust, and even silence, is one of the paradoxically modern traits of the work of Machado de Assis. As a writer who distanced himself of Brazilian literature's extolling of Brazilian nature and exoticism, Machado did not express enthusiasm in the face of the technological advances of his time either. He treated them instead with reticence, and strove to discredit them. If he once let slip a sign of admiration for a monumental project like the Suez Canal, that admiration was qualified by ambivalence due to its articulation in the context of the corruption scandal involving Lesseps and the construction of the Panama Canal.[43]

And if out of all the new technologies of the century the writer reserved his most explicit critiques for the telegraph, it was because he felt that this new medium imposed extreme constraints on language and threatened to change the discursive practices of journalism, on which literature was dependent. In Machado's *crônicas*, narrative strategies and the ironic perspective confronted the unchartered referential authority that technology granted to telegraphic news. The anti-informative gesture of Machado's *crônicas*, his rewriting and fictionalization of the news, worked to safeguard the indeterminacy of the event and its meaning, against the economic abbreviation — temporal as well as semantic — of the emergent regime of information.

In contrast to the imperative of the current and standardized time of telegraphic news, for Machado de Assis the time of the event can never coincide with the technological materiality of the news register or be assimilated to it. Machado did not think the event in accordance with the new factual models of the present; in his *crônicas* and novels no events are mentioned which are not in some way touched and mediated by memory (and its loss): social and collective memory, private memory. As was said in the nineteenth century, reporters have legs, chroniclers have reminiscences.

Notes to Chapter 11

1. This essay was translated by Carl Good.
2. Machado de Assis uses the Anglicism 'meeting' in his text. The term was incorporated into Portuguese in the nineteenth century and used mainly to refer to public meetings, public assemblies and rallies. It is possible, that when writing his letter, Machado de Assis still had in mind the abolitionist meetings that preceded the end of slavery in the United States in 1865.
3. Machado de Assis uses the word *praça* in the sense, still current in the nineteenth century but now in disuse, of a district in a metropolitan urban centre where commerce, banking and the stock exchange were concentrated. The word also referred to the totality of a city's commerce and banking (for example, 'a praça do Rio de Janeiro'). The term remained in use in popular expressions such as 'ter bom nome na praça', which means 'to have good credit, without financial debts'. We have translated *tempo da praça* as 'time of finance' here, but the expression could also be rendered as 'time of the market' or 'time of the stock and exchange'.
4. Letter from Machado de Assis to Quintino Bocaiúva, November 1866, in Machado de Assis, *Correspondência (1860–1869)*, ed. by Sergio Paulo Rouanet, notes by Irene Moutinho and Silvia Eleutério (Academia Brasileira de Letras: Rio de Janeiro, 2008), pp. 19–20. Quintino Bocaiúva

(1836–1912), was a journalist and republican publicist, one of the founders of the Republican Party in 1870, editor of several Rio de Janeiro newspapers, and at the end of the century, under the republican regime, a senator and Minister of Foreign Affairs (1890–91). In 1860, when Bocaiúva was editor of the *Diario do Rio de Janeiro*, he invited Machado de Assis to become a regular contributor to the daily. From 1866 to 1867, Bocaiúva was posted to New York as a government representative for immigration affairs of the Brazilian Empire. All citations from Machado have been translated for this essay, unless otherwise indicated.

5. Machado de Assis wrote weekly and biweekly *crônicas* for several newspapers, from the 1860s to the turn of the century. He became a master of this minor genre by taking advantage of its hybridity and flexibility, and was able to turn it into a medium for narrativizing the news while experimenting with formal literary devices. For a generic definition of the *crônica* see Chapter 9, by Lúcia Granja, and John Gledson's introductions to Machado de Assis, *Bons Dias!, crônicas (1888–1889)*, ed. and notes by John Gledson (Editora Hucitec/Editora da Unicamp: São Paulo, 1990), pp. 11–27, and Machado de Assis, *A Semana, crônicas (1892–1893)*, introduction and notes by John Gledson (Editora Hucitec: São Paulo, 1996), pp. 11–34. On the relevance of the *crônica* for Brazilian nineteenth-century social history see *História em cousas miúdas: capítulos de história social da crônica no Brasil*, ed. by Sidney Chalhoub, Margarida de Sousa Neves and Leonardo Affonso de Miranda Pereira (Editora da Unicamp: Campinas, 2005).
6. 'História de Quinze Dias', *Illustração Brasileira*, 15 August 1876, in Machado de Assis, *História de quinze dias*, ed. by Leonardo Affonso de Miranda Pereira (Editora da Unicamp: Campinas, 2009), p. 61.
7. 'História de Quinze Dias', *Illustração Brasileira*, 1 September 1876, in Machado de Assis, *História de quinze dias*, pp. 89–95. Machado de Assis's *crônica* probably refers to the two *coups d'état* of 30 May 1876 and of August 1876 which dethroned first the sultan Abdülaziz and then his successor, his nephew Murad V. The depositions were supported by the elites, by the Young Ottomans who called for reforms and the establishment of a constitutional monarchy to rule the Ottoman Empire. The new sultan Abdülhamid II did approve the introduction of a parliament and a new constitution, the latter being promulgated on 23 December 1876 but repealed only a few months later, on Russia's entry into the war in the Balkans in 1877. The parliament was later dissolved, in 1878. See James J. Reid, *Crisis of the Ottoman Empire: Prelude to Collapse, 1839–1878* (Steiner: Stuttgart, 2000), pp. 317–18, and Charles and Barbara Jelavich, *The Establishment of the Balkan National States, 1804–1920* (Seattle: University of Washington Press, 1977), pp. 110–13.
8. Cf. Dwayne R. Winseck and Robert M. Pike, *Communication and Empire: Media, Markets, and Globalization, 1860–1930* (Durham, NC: Duke University Press, 2007), pp. 29–38.
9. Cf. Irineu Evangelista de Sousa, Visconde de Mauá, *Autobiografia* (Rio de Janeiro: Zélio Valverde Ed., 1942), p. 207.
10. The coastal telegraph lines linked Rio de Janeiro, the capital of the empire, to Bahia, Recife (Pernambuco), Ceará, Maranhão and Pará to the north, and to Santos, São Paulo, Santa Catarina and Rio Grande do Sul to the south. See Victor M. Berthold, *History of the Telephone and Telegraph in Brazil, 1851–1921* (New York: American Telephone and Telegraph Company, 1922), pp. 7–13, and Winseck and Pike, *Communication and Empire*, pp. 65–69.
11. Cf. *Falas do trono: desde o ano de 1823 até o ano de 1889, acompanhados dos respectivos votos de graça* (Brasília: Instituto Nacional do Livro, 1977), pp. 409–10.
12. Cf. Berthold, *History of the Telephone and Telegraph in Brazil*, pp.12–13 and pp. 34–36.
13. Cf. Winseck and Pike, *Communication and Empire*, pp. 68–69. See also Donald Read, *The Power of News: The History of Reuters, 1849–1989* (Oxford: Oxford University Press, 2000).
14. For a discussion of the global hegemony of the Victorian telegraph system, see Armand Mattelart, *Networking the World, 1794–2000* (Minneapolis: University of Minnesota Press, 2000), pp. 8–11.
15. 'Notas Semanais', *O Cruzeiro*, 23 June 1878, in Machado de Assis, *Notas Semanais*, ed. by John Gledson and Lúcia Granja (Campinas: Editora da Unicamp, 2008), p. 124.
16. In his 'Crise de vers' (1886, 1892, 1896), Mallarmé (1842–1898) criticized the universalization of a language instrumentalized for the reporting of facts ('l'universel reportage'), also relating this universalization to monetary circulation and exchange: 'One of the undeniable ideals of our time is to divide words into two different categories: the first is for narrative, instruction

or description (even though an adequate exchange of human thoughts might well be achieved through the silent exchange of money). The elementary use of language involves that universal journalistic style (*l'universel reportage*), which characterizes all kinds of contemporary writing, with the exception of literature'. See 'Crisis in Poetry', in Mallarmé, *Selected Prose Poems, Essays and Letters*, trans., with introduction, by Bradford Cook (Baltimore, MD: Johns Hopkins University Press, 1956), pp. 42–43. For an excellent interpretation of the implications of 'journalism' in Mallarmé's prose, see Barbara Johnson, 'Erasing Panama: Mallarmé and the Text of History', in Barbara Johnson, *A World of Difference* (Baltimore, MD: Johns Hopkins University Press, 1987), pp. 58–67.

17. The writer is playing with a meaning of the word *incoercível* (translated as 'uncontainable') which has now fallen into disuse: 'that which is uncompressed' or 'that which cannot be compressed'. In this context, it alludes to events or news that could not be 'compressed' to fit into the predetermined ciphers or abbreviated forms of telegraphy. Because *incoercível* also signifies 'irrepressible' or 'uncontainable' the word is being translated here in its more contemporary sense for the sake of legibility, but one should keep in mind that in the nineteenth century Machado's readers would have been well aware of the word's double meaning.
18. 'Notas Semanais', *O Cruzeiro*, 23 June 1878, in Machado de Assis, *Notas Semanais*, ed. by Gledson and Granja, p. 124.
19. 'História de Quinze Dias', *Illustração Brasileira*, 1 February 1877, in Machado de Assis, *História de quinze dias*, ed. by Leonardo Affonso de Miranda Pereira (Campinas: Editora da Unicamp, 2009), pp. 161–63.
20. When Machado's column was published (1877), William Ewart Gladstone (1809–98) had already completed his first term as British prime minister (1868–74) and stepped down as leader of the Liberal Party. The 'theological sneezes' referred to by Machado probably allude to Gladstone's pamphlets against the doctrine of papal infallibility — 'The Vatican Decrees in their Bearing on Civil Allegiance' (1874) and 'Vaticanism: An Answer to Reproofs and Replies' (1875) — and the controversies they provoked.
21. Machado de Assis is inverting the popular saying, 'só para inglês ver' ('only for the English to see'), an expression coined in reference to the Law of 7 September 1831 that abolished the trafficking of slaves in Brazil but which remained unenforced until the 1850s, being popularly considered a deceitful 'façade law' to be maintained only 'for the English to see', i.e. merely to satisfy the British pressures for the cessation of the slave trade. Almost twenty years later, in 1849 and 1850, the British government ordered slave ships to be attacked even within Brazilian territorial waters. Under the threat of a naval blockade of Brazilian harbours, the Brazilian government acceded to an effective suppression of the slave traffic, but between 1831 and the passage of the Eusébio de Queirós Law of 4 September 1850, half a million slaves had been illegally imported to Brazil.
22. 'História de Quinze Dias', *Illustração Brasileira*, 15 August 1877, in Machado de Assis, *História de quinze dias*, p. 229.
23. For an account of the Ceará drought in the context of the great global famines of 1876–78, see Mike Davis, *Late Victorian Holocausts: El Niño Famines and the Making of the Third World* (London and New York: Verso, 2001), pp. 79–90.
24. Honoré de Balzac, *Revue Parisienne*, no. 2, 25 August 1840, in *Œuvres*, 24 vols (Paris: Michel Lévy Frères, 1868), XXIII, 672.
25. See Alex Nelbach, '"The Software of Empire": Telegraphic News Agencies and Imperial Publicity, 1865–1914', in *Imperial Co-Histories: National Identities and the British and Colonial Press*, ed. by Julie F. Codel (Cranbury, NJ: Associated University Presses, 2003), pp. 68–94. See also John Hohenberg, *Foreign Correspondence: The Great Reporters and their Times* (New York: Columbia University Press, 1965), pp. 7–10. For a general history of news agencies, see Antoine Lefébure, *Havas. Les Arcanes du pouvoir* (Paris: B. Grasset, 1992), and Donald Read, *The Power of News*.
26. Quoted in Alex Nelbach, '"The Software of Empire"', p. 77.
27. The word *retribuição* in Portuguese, like the French *rétribution*, means 'remuneration' or 'pay'.
28. Machado is playing with the homophony between the expression 'novos em folha' (brand new) and 'nas folhas' (in the papers, in the newspapers).

29. In this last sentence there is also a tricky twist of meaning in the use of the term 'apelar' (appeal). The chronicler's intention is to reinstate the value of sea transport and its links to the postal system, a cheaper and more reliable channel of transatlantic communications, against the appeal of the faster but more costly transmission of information by submarine cable telegraphy.
30. 'História de Quinze Dias', *Illustração Brasileira*, 15 August 1877, in Machado de Assis, *História de quinze dias*, p. 230.
31. Machado de Assis is playing with the splitting of the word 'menoscabo' (contempt), translated here as 'belittle the cable' and its homophony with 'menos cabo' (less cable).
32. 'História de Quinze Dias,' *Illustração Brasileira*, 1 July 1877, in Machado de Assis, *História de quinze dias*, pp. 217–18.
33. An account of the 1873 World Exposition in Vienna provides important additional information about the *Jornal do Commercio*: at that time, the paper had a daily press run of 15,000 copies and employed eight editors, both domestic and foreign, as well as eighty correspondents working in Europe, the United States and the Brazilian Empire. Cf. *O Império do Brazil na Exposição Universal de 1873, em Vienna d'Austria* (Rio de Janeiro: Tipographia Nacional, 1873), p. 324. For more on the history of the *Jornal do Commercio*, from its founding by French publisher Pierre François Plancher, who arrived in Brazil in 1823, to its administration by the journalist José Carlos Rodrigues at the end of the nineteenth century, see Laurence Hallewell, *O Livro no Brasil (sua história)* (São Paulo: EdUSP, 2005), pp. 137–50.
34. 'Abundant prose' would be a little closer to the intended meaning of Machado de Assis's expression. He was praising the length and style of the periodical article and its identification with literary prose, in contrast with the brevity and dry language of the cable dispatches.
35. Roberto Schwarz, *A Master on the Periphery of Capitalism: Machado de Assis*, trans., with introduction, by John Gledson (Durham, NC: Duke University Press, 2001), p. 122. Originally published as *Um mestre na periferia do capitalismo: Machado de Assis* (São Paulo: Duas Cidades, 1990), p. 172.
36. The sentence is puzzling, but it could refer to the simultaneous arrival and sending, the crisscrossing of telegrams between the south and the capital, as well to the 'pairs/peers' of senders and receivers located in both places. Technically, a telegram will always engender a copy, a doubling, a duplicity, and delusion that Machado's *crônica* comically explores.
37. 'História de Quinze Dias', *Illustração Brasileira*, 15 October 1876, in Machado de Assis, *História de quinze dias*, pp. 115–16.
38. Ibid., pp. 116–17.
39. Ibid., pp. 116–17.
40. Joaquim Nabuco, *A revolução estrangeira durante a Revolta de 1893* (Brasília: Edições do Senado Federal, 2003), p. 43.
41. 'Bons Dias!', *Gazeta de Notícias*, 29 June 1889, in Machado de Assis, *Bons Dias!*, ed. by John Gledson, pp. 197–98.
42. On Machado's career as a public official in the Ministry of Agriculture, Commerce and Public Works, see Sidney Chalhoub, *Machado de Assis historiador* (São Paulo: Companhia das Letras, 2003), pp. 203–65, and R. Magalhães Júnior, *Machado de Assis, vida e obra*, 4 vols (Rio de Janeiro/São Paulo: Editora Record, 2008), II, 273–83. The fundamental study of the British influence on Brazilian modernization during the nineteenth century is Richard Graham's *Britain & the Onset of Modernization in Brazil, 1850–1914* (Cambridge: Cambridge University Press, 1972).
43. 'A Semana', *Gazeta de Notícias*, 11 December 1892, in Machado de Assis, *A Semana*, ed. by Gledson, pp. 165–66.

CHAPTER 12

The Brazilian Book Market in Portugal in the Second Half of the Nineteenth Century and the Paradigm Change in Luso-Brazilian Cultural Relations

Patrícia de Jesus Palma[1]

> [...] the face of the world had begun to change: the old barriers which politics and preconceptions had erected between peoples had almost disappeared; mutual needs and even luxury brought about almost indispensable changes in the business world; and through business nations became like brothers.
>
> People began to learn each other's languages and language study became widespread: the work of wise men then began to circulate in every country: good books now became the province of all languages; and within every country a new state developed (without the disadvantages of having a *state within a state* as with the Catholic Church) — a state which, with justice and rigour obtained the richly deserved name of the '*Republic of Letters*' which is one and universal, without danger of schism.[2]

Brazilian Books in Portugal: from Silence to Commercialization

'Lack of understanding', 'contempt', 'indifference' and 'silence' are some of the words frequently used by nineteenth-century writers to describe the attitude of the Portuguese towards intellectual works from Brazil. Moreover, this was frequently seen in the laments of both Brazilian and Portuguese intellectuals who were interested in the culture of letters and sciences stemming from overseas. Among the Portuguese were Almeida Garrett, Alexandre Herculano, Camilo Castelo Branco, Manuel Pinheiro Chagas, Rodrigo Veloso, Guimarães Fonseca, Gervásio Lobato, Luciano Cordeiro, José Silvestre Ribeiro and Inocêncio Francisco da Silva, to name but a few.[3] Some welcomed the discovery of new talent, predicting a happy future — e.g. Alexandre Herculano, Rodrigo Veloso, Guimarães Fonseca, Camilo Castelo Branco and Gervásio Lobato — while others took pleasure in circulating detailed bibliographic studies on contemporary Brazilian writers — e.g. Inocêncio da Silva and Pinheiro Chagas.

With regard to this plethora of writers, it can be said that Brazil was indeed of interest to some of the most distinguished Portuguese intellectuals, whether in the name of the 'Republic of Letters' or for rather more obvious interests in the Brazilian market. However, according to Cordeiro, they all supported the idea of the existence of 'a wall of contemptuous and unjust silence'.[4]

Recent studies on Portuguese–Brazilian relations have confirmed this, highlighting the fact that this dissemination, according to Valéria Augusti, tried to 'strengthen ties between Brazilian authors and the old metropolis, emphasizing the role of the latter in its development', in an effort also to maintain spiritual leadership over Brazil, which often justified Portuguese censorship of linguistic innovations by Brazilian writers.[5] This was the case with the development of home-grown literature, the focus of heated discussion among Brazilian writers, and between Portuguese and Brazilian writers.[6]

One of the emblematic examples of this cultural relationship and which introduces the topic that is being developed here — the Brazilian book market in Portugal — is the *Diccionario Bibliographico Portuguez*, the product of continual work by Inocêncio Francisco da Silva. In spite of his efforts, his results were not spared the criticism of the German scholar Ferdinand Wolf who, in 1863, lamented the paucity of information on Brazilian authors in his *Brésil littéraire*. Inocêncio responded by referring to the first few pages of Volume I, in which he had apologized for any lack of information, and then went on to explain the reason for such a gap:

> As I said, the decision to go to press had already been taken, and printing was about to get underway, when I decided to broaden the scope of the work, by combining Portuguese writers with Brazilian writers born after the period of separation and independence from the empire. *However, grants for this work had been small and scarce*, only flowing in greater abundance after the publication of Volume II, and increasing successively and significantly, thanks to the passionate and equally obliging and disinterested cooperation of two of our noble residents in Rio de Janeiro [...].[7]

Even so, Inocêncio was to commit himself to paying back the public, and in the *Revista Contemporânea de Portugal e Brazil* and in the *Archivo Pittoresco* he published bibliographical sketches of Brazilian authors. In the *Revista Contemporânea de Portugal e Brazil*, in which he succeeded the Brazilian writer João Francisco Lisboa, Inocêncio dedicated a study to Gonçalves de Magalhães, condemning what was, at the time, the greatest obstacle to be overcome, namely access to Brazilian books.[8]

On page 292, the learned bibliographer tells us that:

> [...] the first signs of his poetic vocation appeared, which were published in a book that was printed in Rio in 1832, and which, in the form of essays and youthful experiments, under the title *Poesias* [Poems], was a collection of early inspirations from the muse which had nurtured it.
>
> *We have tried in vain to find this volume, which today appears to be extremely rare, even in Brazil* [...].[9]

Later, he refers to the *Confederação dos Tamoyos* [The Tamoio Confederation], stating that:

> It is felt, indeed, that the scope and extent of this essay leaves us room to dedicate more time to this poem, *which few Portuguese readers will have read, since perhaps only ten or twelve copies have ever reached Portugal!*'[10]

In the supplementary information on Domingos J. Gonçalves de Magalhães, published in Volume IX of the *Diccionario*, Inocêncio gives us much more important news: as a result of its 'extreme scarcity in the market' and in light of the 'work's merit', the editor of the newspaper *Aurora do Cávado*, Rodrigo Veloso, had released a second limited edition of the aforementioned poem, which was published in 1864 in the *Imprensa Literária de Coimbra*.[11] At the same time, the poet made corrections and additions to what would become the actual second edition, printed in Vienna, Austria.[12] This was, however, completely unknown to Rodrigo Veloso, who, under the title of 'News from the Editor', justified this initiative by providing a framework for it within a more ambitious project to publish Brazilian literature in Portugal, in order to address the issue of its scarcity and the prohibitive prices charged. The Barcelos editor stated:

> The first and only edition to date of *Confederação dos Tamoyos* was published in Rio de Janeiro in 1857, at the expense of the Emperor Pedro II, and supply has long since been exhausted, as very few were brought to Portugal.
>
> Gain was not the motive that has led us to reprint such a magnificent poem, since only a limited number of copies were made, but rather the sole desire to pay tribute to the lovers of Brazilian Letters, among which the *Confederação dos Tamoyos* clearly stands out due to its highly American character and features, and its countless beauties. If the public response to this first attempt is favourable, then it will not be only one. More masterpieces of Brazilian Literature will then be published, which are so little known, or perhaps even disdained by us, and yet with so much to discover and admire. The truth is that we can perhaps be forgiven for not knowing about overseas literature, given the excessive, exorbitant prices of Brazilian editions and their rarity.
>
> It may be, perhaps, that we shall seek a remedy for these two difficulties in the future.[13]

This was published in 1864, and Rodrigo Veloso was no longer able to continue with the business to which he had aspired. Nevertheless, already in the texts of the 1860s, Inocêncio had highlighted the invaluable services of Baptiste-Louis Garnier to Brazilian culture, by publishing old and contemporary books, and promoting 'a liking for books and the business of selling them', which would make him a solid commercial player.[14]

With a national literature developing and the editorial market expanding, Brazil became above all a privileged place for the creation of Portuguese works. It is worth pointing out that in the case of publications, with very few exceptions, the subheading 'Portugal and Brazil' was added to the title to show the book was being distributed in these two countries, and did not signify mutual collaboration between writers from both sides of the Atlantic or even news from Brazil. But this situation was not to continue *ad infinitum*, as Alexandre Herculano had predicted in 1847, in his famous article 'Futuro litterario de Portugal e do Brazil', dedicated to Antonio Gonçalves Dias.[15]

From Advertising to Marketing

Who initiated the paradigm shift in the cultural exchanges between Portugal and Brazil, and how and when was it initiated, to thus become reciprocal? And what was the reading public which supported them?

With regard to the '*how*', here are some points to consider: from time to time, there was a complaint that this was a literature which was condemned to 'unjust silence' from the Portuguese, and the space set aside for this or that more worthy Brazilian author gradually increased in the press.

The year 1874 saw what I would describe as a pioneering action within the context set out here. In January of that year, the director of the *Revista de Portugal e Brazil*, Luciano Cordeiro, Professor of Philosophy and Literature, complained about what he called the 'conspiracy of silence' and made an impassioned appeal for a change in attitude in the relations between the two countries:

> Brazil, which ceased to be our colony at a political level so many years ago, is seen by many still to be so at a literary level. In our own literature there has been a wall of contemptuous and unjust silence.
>
> Let us consider: who knows or who has spoken about Alencar, Varela, Macedo, Bernardo Guimarães, Teixeira de Sousa, Joaquim Celso, Rosendo Moniz or of Guimarães Júnior?
>
> Who here noticed Gonçalves Dias, Guilherme d'Azevedo, Junqueira Freire or Casimiro d'Abreu before fame brought them to our attention, and forced us to face up to the bare truth, without seeking to justify it to ourselves through the serene legitimacy of critical analysis? [...]
>
> It is natural for some to bear good and others ill-will in our arguing in front of that very vigorous child called — Brazil — to whom we mete out a stepfather's rough justice instead of a loving father's affections, and whom we believed was destined for the sole purpose of providing manpower and raw materials to the benefit of our rich and greedy nobility.
>
> [...].
>
> Let us then look forthrightly and happily at their progress and courage — let us continue to be grateful for their good intentions and let us receive with the impartiality of honest criticism, the products of those talents, the works of those workers, which are also Portuguese works.
>
> And some of which are remarkable works.
>
> Let us break with and end this unjust, hateful and petulant action by literary circles, as it has been broken and attacked by others; an action whose most genuine contribution has been the *conspiracy of silence*, this ridiculous thing which, as Hoppe said recently at one of the early science conferences in Europe, 'is the extreme resort of dogmas and schools of thought that are condemned and no longer valid.'[16]

This quotation is as long as it is instructive. In fact, his appeal was to be effective. Three months later, in April 1874, Camilo Castelo Branco included a chapter entitled 'Brazilian Literature' in issue no. 4 (of twelve) of his monthly publication, *Noites de insomnia offerecidas a quem não póde dormir*, which started in the following way:

> For a long time, scholars have complained about the neglect of Portuguese booksellers concerning the supply of Brazilian books. Writers from outside the

> empire would be referred to by hearsay, and their work would be seen on few bookshelves. In public libraries, it was pointless looking for them. Conversely, there were many rare editions of secular works which no one looked at.

With his diagnosis having been completed, Camilo Castelo Branco announced that:

> The Brazilian book market in Portugal opened a few months ago. We owe it to the intelligent endeavour of Mr Ernesto Chardron. It was he who first published a catalogue of varied literature in which the names of the most popular writers in that flourishing country have been highlighted. [...]
>
> The catalogue of the Chardron Bookshop was replete with details on various sciences, elementary books, lexicology and even religious motifs.[17]

Camilo continued to make recommendations and to leave critical notes on the work of some of the authors included, without forgetting Garnier's decisive role:

> Let us not forget, however, that the driving force of this brilliant literary movement in Rio de Janeiro, and consequently throughout the empire, is the book publisher Garnier, this entrepreneurial spirit who makes the talented writers he publishes shine, benefiting in turn from the honour of making them known and lauded.

Given that, at the time, Camilo Castelo Branco was published by the International Bookshop of Ernesto Chardron, located at Nos. 96 and 98 in the Largo do Clérigos, in Porto, can we consider the assertion made about the French bookseller and publisher Ernesto Chardron being the top importer and seller of Brazilian Literature to be objective? Or is this the impressionism of the language of advertising?[18]

The answer to these questions requires a chronological analysis of the catalogues of the various contemporary booksellers. Using available resources, I compiled a *corpus* of catalogues, encompassing the period between 1852 and 1895, in total twenty-five catalogues from sixteen booksellers located in Lisbon, Coimbra and Porto, as set out in Table 12.1.

Let us begin with Ernesto Chardron's catalogue, which earned applause from Camilo (see Table 12.1, 7, 1874). It was the third from the 'Livraria Internacional'[19] and was edited, not as a supplement or an extract, but as an independent piece, dedicated solely to Brazilian publishing, entitled *Catalogo das publicações brazileiras recebidas pela Livraria Internacional de E. Chardron. Porto e Braga* — to which he added: 'Every month Ernesto Chardron's International Bookshop receives material which has been published in the Empire of Brazil and dispatches any order made with it in the certainty that our prices are the lowest possible'.[20]

For the most part, it included contemporary authors, translations (by Brazilian writers), newly released editions, and also Portuguese authors published there, such as António Feliciano de Castilho and José Feliciano de Castilho.

It was well laid out, with a variety of print types, pages of this or that publication highlighted, and was impeccably organized and divided into the following sections: uncategorized (pp. 1–3), 'Classic Bookshop: excerpts from the leading well-regarded authors' (pp. 4–6); 'Pocket Library' (p. 7); 'Literature, Novels, Poetry, Etc.' (pp. 9–14); 'Religious Books' (pp. 14–16); 'Jurisprudence, Trade, Medicine, etc.' (pp. 16–19); 'Elementary books, instruction, etc.' (pp. 19–20); 'Board Games' (back cover).

Corpus of Catalogues: 1852–1895[21]			
No	Booksellers	Date	Location
1	Livraria Viúva Bertrand e Filhos	1852, 1859, 1876, no date [>1875, <1878] 1881	Lisbon
2	A. J. F. Lopes, Livreiro	1856	unknown
3	Empresa Editora Gonçalves Lopes	1865	Lisbon
4	Livraria de J. L. Bordalo	1866	Lisbon
5	*Commercio do Porto*	1867	Porto and Lisbon
6	Campos Junior	1868	Lisbon
7	Livraria Internacional de Ernesto Chardron	1873, 1874, 1879–83, 1888	Porto and Braga
8	Matos Moreira & C.ª	1877	Lisbon
9	Francisco Artur da Silva	1877, 1880	Lisbon
10	Nova Livraria Internacional	1877, 1881	Lisbon
11	Livraria Magalhães & Moniz Editores	1881	Porto
12	Casa Editora David Corazzi	1884	Lisbon
13	*Diario Ilustrado*	1895	Lisbon
14	Livraria Luso-brasileira Editora	1895	Porto
15	Biblioteca Moré	No date	Porto and Coimbra
16	Biblioteca dos Dous Mundos	No date	Lisbon

Table 12.1. *Corpus* of Catalogues (1852–1895)

Entries were personalized with the name of the author which was highlighted in the centre in boldface. The titles were accompanied, when applicable, by the names of annotators, commentators or biographers. The information given included: number of volumes, size, and at times, the edition number, and the respective prices, which were similar to the prices of Portuguese publications.

Here, the Portuguese public could establish contact in their own individual and independent way with Brazilian publications and their authors, whose names were highlighted regardless of their popularity: Gonçalves de Magalhães, A. A. de Sousa Carvalho, Cónego Fernandes Pinheiro, A. J. de Mello Moraes, Manuel António Álvares de Azevedo, Augusto de Castro, António Gonçalves Dias, Augusto Emílio Zaluar, Casimiro d'Abreu, B. J. Silva Guimarães, Junqueira Freire, Bruno Seabra, Manuel Inácio da Silva Alvarenga, Ignacio Francisco Silveira Motta, Alvarenga Peixoto, Rosendo Moniz, Manuel Araújo Porto-Alegre, Sílvio Dinarte, José de Alencar, Machado de Assis and many, many others, amounting to a provisional total of 132 authors. Similarly, there were Brazilian translations of French authors, such the Younger Dumas, Octave Feuillet, Paul Féval and Jules Verne; in the case of the latter author, these were the first of his titles to be translated into the Portuguese language in circulation in Portugal.[22]

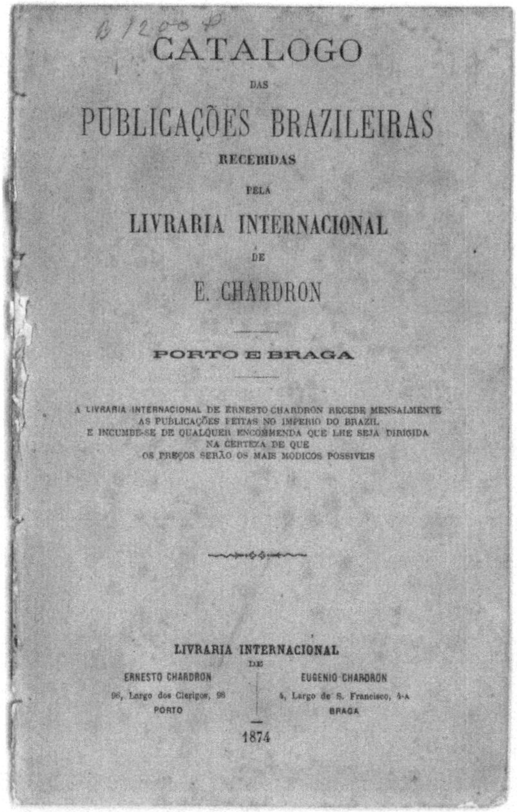

CATALOGO

DAS

PUBLICAÇÕES BRAZILEIRAS

RECEBIDAS

PELA

LIVRARIA INTERNACIONAL

DE

E. CHARDRON

PORTO E BRAGA

A LIVRARIA INTERNACIONAL DE ERNESTO CHARDRON RECEBE MENSALMENTE
AS PUBLICAÇÕES FEITAS NO IMPERIO DO BRAZIL
E INCUMBE-SE DE QUALQUER ENCOMMENDA QUE LHE SEJA DIRIGIDA
NA CERTEZA DE QUE
OS PREÇOS SERÃO OS MAIS MODICOS POSSIVEIS

LIVRARIA INTERNACIONAL

DE

ERNESTO CHARDRON
96, Largo dos Clerigos, 98
PORTO

EUGENIO CHARDRON
4, Largo de S. Francisco, 4-A
BRAGA

1874

Figure 12.1 Reproduction of the cover of the *Catalogo das Publicações Brazileiras* [Catalogue of Brazilian Publications]. © National Library of Portugal LP 195.

Following the editor Ernesto Chardron, there is the *Bibliographia portugueza e estrangeira* (see Table 12.1, 7, 1879–83). This was a bibliographic publication published monthly between 1879 and 1883 (with a break in 1882), which was coordinated by Camilo Castelo Branco. Here too, we can see the same respect for Brazilian cultural independence, with the news regarding its publications duly identified alongside Portuguese, French and Spanish publications.

However, this data do not confirm that Ernesto Chardron was the top importer of Brazilian books. Were overseas publications in circulation in Portugal before then?

After comparing catalogues, we can conclude that Brazilian publications did not arrive to the Portuguese market before the 1870s, with only a very tiny amount available in Portuguese inventories. In the decade prior to 1874, only the 1859 catalogue from the Bookseller *Viúva Bertrand & Filhos*, Lisbon, carried reports regarding Brazil. Of the twenty-four pages of titles offered to readers, only eight items related to Brazil, three of which made no mention of the publisher's location, four being printed in Paris and only one being published in Brazil, and, more specifically, printed in Pernambuco. The 1876 *Catalogo (extracto) de Livros portuguezes antigos e modernos á venda nesta livraria* (*Viúva Bertrand & Filhos* Bookseller), consisting of 86 pages, certainly presents a very different picture (See Table 12.1, 1, 1876). Organized alphabetically and by titles, it was divided into four sections ('Miscellaneous', pp. 3–53; 'Religious', pp. 53–66; 'Romance' pp. 66–79; and

'Theatre', pp. 80–86), with a total of 257 entries for Brazilian publication titles to be found in all the categories.[23] With regard to the Brazilian and French modern publications on sale at the Bertrand bookshop, one page had a list of titles on sales, organized according to author (see Table 12.1, 1). This page is undated, but it was certainly published between 1875 and 1878, given that it included Machado de Assis's *Americanas* (first edition, 1875) and an advertisement for the periodical *Jornal das famílias*, which was published between 1863 and 1878.

Brazilian publications total 332 titles. A section on 'Religious and Ecclesiastic Works' is included. Interestingly, in a later catalogue, *Edições e diversas obras*, printed in 1881 and on sale at the same bookshop, there was no mention to Brazilian publications. This does not mean, however, that the bookshop stopped selling them or that they were not included in other more comprehensive catalogues.

After 1874, there was no mention to Brazilian publications in the remaining eleven catalogues studied, except for the 1881 *Nova Livraria Internacional*, Lisbon, which included *A litteratura brazileira e a critica moderna* by Sylvio Romero, published the previous year in Rio de Janeiro.[24] In contrast, all the catalogues in Portuguese bookshops gave good coverage of French authors, in both luxury and economical editions.

Ernesto Chardron and Cultural Reciprocity between Brazil and Portugal

Ernesto Chardron may not have been the first bookseller to market Brazilian books, but he was certainly the first to recognize the independence of Brazilian literature and literary works, and make a significant contribution in this regard by publishing a catalogue exclusively devoted to Brazilian publications. It should be remembered that when the other catalogues marketed Brazilian books, they did so by including them in the group of 'Portuguese books', without any further reference. Chardron was a business pioneer in this new way of thinking, which was marked by the respect and appreciation shown for overseas intellectual works. In Portugal, his attitude could be interpreted as the beginning of a change in mentality towards the intellectual and creative work to emerge from a former colony and, in Brazil, it could be seen as a symbol of the stabilization and recognition of the independence of its literary, editorial and commercial system.[25]

Who was Ernesto Chardron? Which conditions shaped the profile of this bookseller and publisher, who opened the doors to the Brazilian book market in Portugal? According to Fernando Guedes, in his study 'Três livreiros centenários de origem francófona', 'Ernesto Chardron was certainly the last of the French booksellers, in the middle of the nineteenth century, to demand that Portugal commit itself to the book business and industry'.[26] Chardron was born in the Ardennes in France on 9 August 1840 and died in Porto in 1885. He attended a business school for twelve years, and then worked in agriculture. His dream was to be a great industrialist. Through the intervention of an uncle who had contacted Nicolau Moré, a bookseller based in Porto, the would-be 'industrialist' arrived in that city in 1858 to work as a bookkeeper in the bookshop. There he spent eleven years not only learning the language, but also the book industry; he established

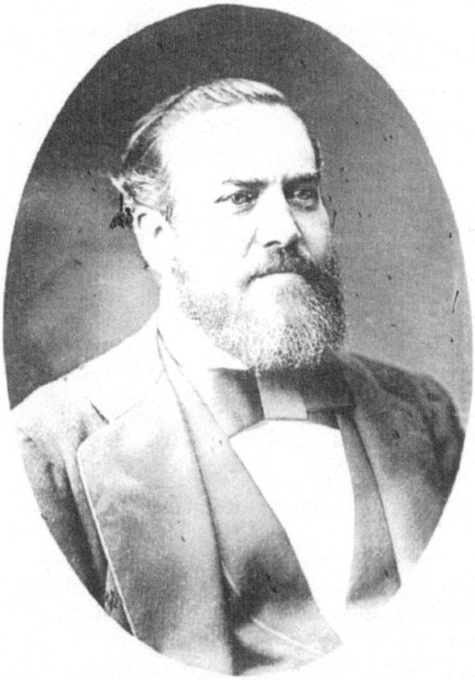

FIG. 12.2. Photograph of the bookseller and publisher Ernesto Chardron (Ardennes, 1840–Porto, 1885). *Commercio e Industria. Sciencias, Artes e Lettras. Galeria Biographico-Contemporanea*. Lisbon, n. 8, 1881. © National Library of Portugal, J. 2346 M.

relations with other booksellers, with printers, customers, and finally made a robust entry into the publishing world.[27]

In 1869, with two titles by Camilo already published at his own expense,[28] Ernesto Chardron took a big step and set up his own bookshop on Largo dos Clérigos, nos. 96 and 98, in Porto; and in 1871, his brother, Eugénio Chardron, opened another branch of the 'Livraria Internacional' on Largo de S. Francisco, n. 4 and 4A, in Braga, which he presumably managed until his death in 1881. The enduring image of this bookseller-publisher to emerge from the press of the period and the memory of those who lived with him is that of a tireless worker with exceptional vigour, audacity and, above all, a love for gastronomy. Beldemónio (the pseudonym of Eduardo Barros Lobo), the editor of *O Arauto*, portrayed him thus:

> He was a *rude gaillard* (strapping lad) with a big Flemish appetite and Gallic joy, loving life above all else and in all its manifestations, with an exuberance of energy which gave him his sanguine temperament. Tall, stout, with reddy-blonde hair, very blue eyes — a Delft blue — , deep chested, and neck placed solidly on his shoulders, Ernesto Chardron was the kind of hardy adventurer of the North who went out every day to conquer life wherever there was a fortune to be made or glory to be won. Intelligent, hard-working, with a small dose of ruthlessness, which is necessary to every upright man in the fight for existence, bold in speculation, and full of confidence in his destiny, *he became a publisher, at a time when all the other publishers were going out of business; and triumphed through a stroke of audacity which, in this vicious environment, can be summed up as providing books for a country which did not know how to read, teaching them to read and enabling them to buy books.*[29]

His dynamism was forged in the publications he released: first of all, Portuguese writers, renowned writers, then translations, religious books, education, and 'finally, works of all genres, and in all and varied branches of human knowledge', according to Magalhães Lima,[30] expanding the market to Brazil, the Islands and Africa, and 'to any corner of the world where a person can spell a Portuguese word'.[31] The extent of his activity can be assessed through the large amount of material sent to the various print shops. As Magalhães Lima said:

> In Porto, he was known to have provided enough work to keep six print shops busy, among them that of António José da Silva Teixeira, who spent nine years busily working exclusively for that establishment, supported regularly by 25–30 workers a day.[32]

Alberto Pimentel also speaks of the time when he established a working relationship with Chardron, remembering: 'He told me about the works he was printing; there was certainly more than twenty. His shop looked small just for the amount of volumes it was publishing, never mind the others!'[33]

Ramalho Ortigão thought that Chardron had a nose for business, but not its ideology:

> Where making a decision on a specific set of ideas as far advertising was concerned; or in the chaotic day-to-day fray, and distinguishing and bringing those around him who were going to be the winners and leaders of the new movement, Chardron did not have a clue.[34]

Alberto Pimentel paints a similar picture:

> Ernesto Chardron did a perfect job on the publication of one of those books, *O guia do viajante* which was bound in Paris. And for an interesting reason. He heard it being read; the only thing that he knew about the whole book, a little story which I included in the *Guia* as a narcotic for some insomniac tourist: *Verídicas aventuras de um viajante alegre*. This traveller is a Frenchman, called Jules Bréton, whom Chardron liked. This was the reason for his choice.[35]

In letters to António Feliciano de Castilho, Camilo Castelo Branco also refers to the industrial acumen of Ernesto Chardron, whose work he considered to be less tidy and more businesslike than those of Moré's publishing company[36]: 'this publisher is blissful in his ignorance. He sells everything, and prospers with works which would ruin another publisher'.[37]

As a businessman, a would-be industrialist, a contemporary man, a 'publisher of the future', as José Gomes Monteiro, manager of the Moré Bookshop, once predicted, I am certain that his development owed much to the professional training he received from that publishing house, and to his assiduous personal contact with writers and, in particular, the protective figure of Camilo to whom the founding of Chardron's publishing house was inextricably linked.

His *curriculum* of catalogues shows the attention given to new Portuguese and foreign listings, with statements like 'new Portuguese and foreign publications' and 'this year's' works, even though it may be true to say that the bookshop was more conservative, as separate catalogues on religious literature indicate. The innovative attitude that characterizes Ernesto Chardron's business and publishing activity should be understood in the light of his period at the Viúva Moré publishing house, as I mentioned above. Fernando Guedes, who analysed the catalogues of Moré's publishing house, concluded

> they display a focus on modernization; furthermore, the very entries made in both catalogues announce this intention: a mixture of type fonts and the layout of the text in the space reveal modern characteristics, linked to Romanticism, now very widespread among us.
>
> In the French catalogue, which is completely personalized with the names of the authors of the works, there is no shortage of names of great writers of modern French literature from the first half of the nineteenth century [...].[38]

On the catalogue of books in Portuguese, he concluded

> the novella and the novel clearly predominate, mainly of a literary level that is more popular than that of the French catalogue [...].
>
> Finally, the publications featured were generally new, the vast majority having been printed after 1834.[39]

In truth, even in the titles of the catalogues, Viúva Moré's publishing house was a pioneer in establishing a new way of communicating with its customers. In addition to the standard formulae ('books on sale in' and 'books printed at the expense of') it added the central theme of the books (1863 catalogue) and, thereafter, specified the language variety (1865 catalogue).[40] In the 1870s, this formula became more widespread and, by the end of the century, the use of synopses again became more predominant. Hence, Ernesto Chardron's spirit was honed within a context of innovation, through constant contact with modern French and Portuguese literature and, in general terms, with the publication of Romantic works; independent, if not yet commercially, at least ideologically, of the conservative bonds of religious literature.

Then, there is the figure of Camilo Castelo Branco, whose influence cannot be overlooked in this respect. Camilo worked hand in hand with the publisher between 1868 and 1883. The interests of the one were, in part, the interests of the other. A professional man of letters, popular among Brazilian readers, Camilo had clear interests in the market where some of his works were published for the first time,[41] and where counterfeits of others were being made.[42] Ernesto Chardron, who above all else wanted to expand his field of action, actually felt hampered by the issue of counterfeiting in Brazil and published texts on the matter, of which the one by Manuel Pinheiro Chagas is the most well-known.[43] Magalhães Lima highlighted the effects of this:

> The lack of a literary agreement with Brazil has been extremely detrimental to all the publishers in the country. Ernesto Chardron is even now among the most affected, as everyone knows. For this reason, he has committed all his good will, so that the interests of Portuguese authors may flourish above all else, and that a principle so urgently demanded by the very special circumstances in our literature and by our men of letters, will always be safeguarded.[44]

This very practical reason may also have been a significant factor in the importation of Brazilian literature. By establishing a commercial agreement with the main Brazilian publisher of the period, thereby marketing and promoting Brazilian literature there in Portugal, Chardron might have been expecting the same treatment on the other side of the Atlantic, thus helping to reduce the harm caused by the counterfeiting market.

Finally, the last question: with Brazilian literature neglected in Portugal, as highlighted by the literary elite, which public did Chardron expect to address? The 'International Bookshop' was first established in Porto and then in Braga, and therefore was located in the North-West of Portugal. This was an area which had seen considerable emigration to Brazil and, in the 1870s, some returns, with some leaving behind businesses and interests in Brazil which they continued to run from Portugal. The 'Returning Brazilian' became a notable feature in the landscape of the region, as is well demonstrated in the work coordinated by Joaquim Romero Magalhães.[45] This was, in reality, a region with a different sort of relationship with Brazil, as noted in 1862 by João Francisco Lisboa, a Brazilian residing in Portugal, when he compared interest in the press in Lisbon with that in Porto:

> The truth is that there is another noticeable aspect in the journalism in Porto, which in this regard, as in others, has a well-known advantage over Lisbon; however, Porto does not set the tone for the entire kingdom; and *this fact is further explained by the circumstance in which this 'Capital of the North', in a case of role reversal, is today a kind of Brazilian colony*, which only provides manpower that is surplus to requirements and which its poor soil can barely sustain, in exchange for the large amounts of capital which it receives from there, and which nourish, enrich and beautify it with an expansion that is as rapid as it is wonderful.[46]

There was consequently a very considerable number of readers interested in Brazilian affairs; this was not confined to the North West alone. It expanded, for example, to the southernmost province, the 'Kingdom of the Algarve', where, immediately after the *Catalogo das publicações brazileiras* had been published, the editor of the *Gazeta do Algarve* added his voice to Camilo's applause regarding the efforts of Ernesto Chardron, declaring it 'to be a true confession as to how greatly we, and our brothers in Brazil, are indebted to Mr Chardron in respect of the literature of that empire'.[47] This recognition is an indication that Brazil was, in fact, a topic of interest that was even more important and more valued in Portuguese society than elitist paternalistic discourse would lead us to believe.

Consequently, Ernesto Chardron played a decisive part in the field of Portuguese and Brazilian literary communication systems, as his catalogues and other bibliographic publications represent not only refined instruments of advertising and socio-professional self-promotion, but also a precious contribution in changing the paradigm in Luso-Brazilian cultural relations, which was hitherto one-way. However, this leading role was shared with the bookseller and publisher Baptiste-Louis Garnier, who made a decisive contribution to the professionalization, promotion and publication of Brazilian writers both in Portugal and internationally, thus initiating the export of Brazilian publications and literature, and thereby affirming the independence of Brazilian intellectual production.

Garnier and Chardron are therefore the perfect example of the epigraph chosen to conclude these remarks: 'and through business nations became like brothers'.

Notes to Chapter 12

1. This chapter benefited from various types of support. I am grateful to Prof Dr Artur Anselmo for having provided me with his documentation on Portuguese publishers of the nineteenth century and Dr Luís Farinha Franco for bibliographical suggestions in this regard. Translation and review of the text received financial support from the Cultural History Centre (School of Humanities and Social Sciences, New University of Lisbon), and I would like to thank the Centre and its director, Prof Dr João Luís Lisboa, for this. The translation of this text was performed by Inpokulis Translations and the proofreading by David Hardisty.
2. Almeida Garrett, 'Bosquejo da história da poesia e lingua portugueza', in *Parnaso Lusitano ou poesias selectas dos autores portuguezes antigos e modernos, ilustradas com notas* (Paris: J. P. Aillaud, 1826), pp. xxxvii–xxxviii.
3. Almeida Garrett, 'Bosquejo da história da poesia e lingua portugueza', pp. vii–lxvii; Alexandre Herculano, 'Futuro literário de Portugal e do Brazil: por occasião da leitura dos *Primeiros Cantos: Poezias* do Sr. A. Gonçalves Dias', in A. Gonçalves Dias, *Cantos: Collecção de Poezias*, 2nd Edition (Leipzig: F. A. Brockhaus, 1857 [1847/48]), pp. viii–xviii. Article initially published in the *Revista Universal Lisbonense*, Volume 7, page 5; Camilo Castelo Branco, *Noites de insomnia offerecidas a quem não póde dormir* (Porto and Braga: Livraria Internacional de Ernesto Chardron e Eugênio Chardron, 1874), n. 4 and 6; M. Pinheiro Chagas, 'A. Gonçalves Dias', in *Ensaios críticos* (Porto: Viúva Moré — Editor, 1866 [1865]), pp. 161–80. First published in the *Revista Contemporânea de Portugal e Brazil*, 5th Year, Lisbon; Rodrigo Veloso (ed.), 'Aviso do editor', in Domingos José Gonçalves Magalhães, *Confederação dos Tamoyos: poema por Domingos José Gonçalves de Magalhães* (Coimbra: Imp. Litteraria, 1864), p. [3]; Guimarães Fonseca, 'Luiz Guimarães', *Diario Illustrado* (Porto, 1874) n. 761, 10 Nov; Gervásio Lobato, 'Lyrica: Sonetos e Rimas de Luiz Guimarães Júnior', *Bibliographia de Portugal e Brazil* (1st year, n. 5, 29 Oct, 1881), pp. 39–41; Luciano Cordeiro, 'Factos Artisticos do Brazil', *Revista de Portugal e Brazil* (Lisbon: Empresa *Revista de Portugal e Brazil*, 1874), n. 7, Jan, pp. 125–26; José Silvestre Ribeiro, 'O *Resumo de Historia Litteraria* do Conego Doutor Joaquim Caetano Fernandes Pinheiro', *Revista de Portugal e Brazil* (Lisbon: Empresa *Revista de Portugal e Brazil*, 1874), pp. 206–08; Inocêncio Francisco da Silva, 'Domingos José Gonçalves de Magalhães', *Revista Contemporanea de Portugal e Brazil*, 5th Year (Lisbon: Typ. Franco-Portugueza, 1865), pp. 285–301.
4. Luciano Cordeiro, 'Factos Artisticos do Brazil', *Revista de Portugal e Brazil*, p. 125.
5. Valéria Augusti, 'Biografias de escritores brasileiros em publicações portuguesas (1860–1890)', *Boitatá. Revista do GT de Literatura Oral e Popular da ANPOLL* (n. 7, Jan–Jun, 2009), p. 78, <http://www.uel.br.> [accessed 26 September 2011].
6. Cf. Marcelo Peloggio, 'Santiago Nunes Ribeiro e José de Alencar: filhos presentes da literatura brasileira', *Revista dos Encontros Literários Moreira Campos* (Universidade Federal do Ceará: Departamento de Literatura), 1 (Apr–Jul 2008), pp, 1–5 <http://encontrosliterarios.ufc.br.> [accessed 26 September 2011].
7. The two 'noble residents in Rio de Janeiro' are Joaquim and Manuel da Silva Mello Guimarães. Inocêncio Francisco da Silva, 'Apontamentos para a vida e trágica morte do insigne poeta brasileiro António Gonçalves Dias', *Archivo Pittoresco* (Semanário Illustrado), vol. X (Lisbon: Castro Irmão & C.ª, Editores Proprietários, 1867), p. 207 (my emphasis).
8. João Francisco Lisboa was born in Maranhão in 1812, and died in Lisbon on 26 April 1863. He was a Commander of the Imperial Order of the Rose. In his only article, published in the *Revista*'s 4th year of publication (1862, pp. 329–53), dedicated to Manuel Odorico Mendes (1799–1864), João Francisco Lisboa wrote an interesting review of the state of Brazilian Literature in Portugal, clearly expressing Brazilian dissatisfaction with the state of things. In fact, with the *Revista* having made room for Brazilian affairs in its third year of existence, specifically the section 'Correspondência do Brasil', by F. X. de Novaes, it was only in its fifth and final year of publication that greater balance could be seen in its contents, with the articles of Inocêncio F. da Silva, dedicated to Domingos José Gonçalves Magalhães and the Viscount of Uruguay, Paulino José Soares de Sousa; with M. Pinheiro Chagas's article on Antonio Gonçalves Dias, and publications by Brazilian writers: *Versos a Corina* by Machado de Assis, and *A noiva de Messina* by A. Gonçalves Dias.

9. Inocêncio Francisco da Silva, 'Domingos José Gonçalves de Magalhães', *Revista Contemporanea de Portugal e Brazil* (5th year, Lisbon: Typ. Franco-Portugueza, 1865), p. 298 (my emphasis).
10. Inocêncio Francisco da Silva, 'Domingos José Gonçalves de Magalhães', p. 298 (my emphasis).
11. Cf. Inocêncio Francisco da Silva, *Diccionario Bibliographico Portuguez*, Volume IX (second Supplement) (Lisbon: Imprensa Nacional, 1870), pp. 142–44.
12. Domingos José Gonçalves de Magalhães, *Obras de D. J. G. de Magalhães, Tomo V, A Confederação dos Tamoyos: segunda edição revista, correcta e acrescentada pelo auctor* (Rio de Janeiro: Livraria de B. L. Garnier, 1864) (Vienna, Austria: Imperial e Real Typographia), 354 pp.
13. Rodrigo Veloso, 'Aviso do editor', in Domingos José Gonçalves Magalhães, *Confederação dos Tamoyos: poema por Domingos José Gonçalves de Magalhães* (Coimbra: Imp. Litteraria, 1864), p. 3.
14. Inocêncio Francisco da Silva, 'Domingos José Gonçalves de Magalhães', p. 299.
15. Alexandre Herculano, in his famous article *'Futuro litterario de Portugal e do Brazil'*, originally published in the *Revista Universal Lisbonense*, Volume 7, Year 1847–48, acknowledged Brazilian development efforts, reporting that it surpassed that of the former metropolis: 'The press in old Portuguese America, which was limping along only two days ago, is now overtaking that of the former metropolitan nation. Periodical publications, the first expression of a developing intellectual culture, became associated with more encouraging compositions — books. In addition, Brazil is the major market for what little is printed here, and it is easy to predict that in the area of letters, as in its importance and prosperity, our emancipated colonies will quickly get the better of us.' (1857 [1847/8: XV]).
16. Luciano Cordeiro, 'Factos Artisticos do Brazil', pp. 125–26.
17. Camilo Castelo Branco, *Noites de insomnia offerecidas a quem não póde dormir*, no. 4 (Porto and Braga: Livraria Internacional de Ernesto Chardron e Eugénio Chardron), p. 3.
18. The International Bookshop of Ernesto Chardron was founded in 1869 and it was managed by him until his death in 1885.
19. The above-mentioned two catalogues date back to 1873. *Bibliographia geral (n. 1) da livraria internacional de Ernesto Chardron, 96, Largo dos Clérigos, 98, Porto; e Eugénio Chardron, 4, Largo de S. Francisco, 4-A, Braga. Esta publicação sahirá mensalmente, dando os títulos e os preços das novas publicações portuguezas e estrangeiras, que se encontram á venda nas livrarias acima. Todas as obras annunciadas n'este numero são publicações d'este anno* (Porto: Typ. de António José da Silva Teixeira) 16 pp. (copy not found); 'Publicações feitas pela Livraria Internacional de Ernesto Chardron desde o principio do seu estabelecimento até hoje, 1870–1873', in *Almanach da Livraria Internacional para 1874, Primeiro anno da sua publicação, coordenado por Alberto Pimentel* (Porto / Braga: Livraria Internacional de Ernesto Chardron e Eugénio Chardron, 16 pp).
20. Porto and Braga, Livraria Internacional de Ernesto Chardron e Eugénio Chardron, 1874, 20 pp. A six-page extract was taken from it.
21. This is a sample; the results presented here may be corrected in the future after following the enlargement of the analysed *corpus*. This does not however constitute a reason for not presenting the conclusions which have been obtained thus far, through the analysis and rigorous study of the book lists.
22. David Corazzi's Company *Horas Românticas* also started a translation of Jules Verne's works in 1874, through the weekly publication of a 32-page issue. The first title to be printed was *Da Terra à Lua* [*From the Earth to the Moon*], cf. A. J. Ferreira, 'Como Jules Vernes conquistou Portugal', *Jornal Infantil Português Ilustrado* (Jul–Nov 1994) <http://jvernept.blogspot.com>, [accessed 30 September 2011]; meanwhile, Ernesto Chardron was already marketing *A volta ao mundo em 80 dias* [*Around the World in 80 Days*], *Viagem ao centro da terra* [*Journey to the Centre of the Earth*] and *Os Filhos do Capitão Grant* (América do Sul, 'Austrália' e 'Oceano Pacífico') [*The Children of Captain Grant*, chapters 'South America', 'Australia', and 'New Zealand').
23. This number may actually be higher, since works are identified by their place of publication, when stated, or by authorship and date of publication.
24. See Table 12.1. 1: 1876, 1881; 8: 1877; 9: 1877, 1880; 10: 1877, 1881; 11: 1881; 12: 1884; 13: 1895; 14: 1895.
25. I have not ruled out the possibility that this repertoire was a contractual condition established by Baptiste-Louis Garnier, which merely emphasizes his own commercial ability as a publisher and the maturity of the Brazilian book market. This and other questions can only be properly clarified either by locating the publisher's collection which, for now, remains untraceable, or by

perusing B. L. Garnier's collection, which has not yet been carried out. I wish to express my thanks to Dr. Paulo Samuel for information on Ernesto Chardron's collection.

26. Fernando Guedes, 'Três livreiros centenários de origem francófona', in *O livro e a leitura em Portugal: subsídios para a sua história, séculos XVIII e XIX* (Lisbon and São Paulo: Editorial Verbo, 1987), p. 61.
27. Cf. Beldemónio, 'Os Grandes Editores: Ernesto Chardron', *O Arauto* («Semanal») (Lisbon, 1886) n. 3, 21 Jan.
28. Fernão Rodrigues Lobo Soropita, *Poesias e Prosas Inéditas*, Preface by Camilo Castelo Branco (Porto: Typographia Lusitânia, 1868) and João de São José Queirós, *Memórias de Fr. João de S. Joseph Queiroz Bispo do Grão Pará*, introduction and notes by Camilo Castelo-Branco (Porto: Typographia da Livraria Nacional, 1868). The publication of these volumes was initially attributed to João de Mendonça until Henrique Marques revealed, in great detail, the agreement between Camilo and Ernesto Chardron to publish the two volumes. On this subject, see Henrique Marques, *Os editores de Camilo: alguns subsídios para a história da livraria em Portugal com retratos de Camilo e de 22 dos seus editores* (Lisbon: Empresa da História de Portugal, 1925), pp. 82–95.
29. Beldemónio, 'Os Grandes Editores: Ernesto Chardron', n. 3 (my emphasis).
30. Magalhães Lima, *Commercio e industria, sciencias, artes e lettras, galeria biographico-contemporanea* (Lisbon, 1881) n. 8, 4 pp.
31. Beldemónio, 'Os Grandes Editores: Ernesto Chardron', n. 3.
32. Magalhães Lima, *Commercio e industria, sciencias, artes e lettras, galeria biographico-contemporanea*, n. 8.
33. Alberto de Pimentel, 'O editor Chardron', in *Atravez do Passado* (Paris and Lisbon: Guillard Aillaud & C.ª, [1888]) p. 36.
34. Ramalho Ortigão, 'Ernesto Chardron', in *As Farpas: o país e a sociedade portuguesa*, tomo III (Lisbon: Livraria Clássica Editora, 1943), p. 143.
35. Alberto de Pimentel, 'O editor Chardron', p. 37.
36. Alexandre Cabral, *Obras de Alexandre Cabral: correspondência de Camilo Castelo Branco com António Feliciano de Castilho — II, Eugénio de Castilho, Júlio de Castilho*, vol. IV (n.p.: Livros Horizonte, 1985), p. 137.
37. Alexandre Cabral, *Obras de Alexandre Cabral*, p. 100.
38. Fernando Guedes, *O livro e a leitura em Portugal*, pp. 140–41.
39. Fernando Guedes, *O livro e a leitura em Portugal*, pp. 141–42.
40. Cf. inventory carried out by Martinho Fonseca, 'Catalogos de livreiros', *Boletim da Sociedade de Bibliophilos Barbosa Machado*, vol. II (Lisbon, 1913), pp. 134–66.
41. *Agulha em Palheiro*, 1st edition (Rio de Janeiro: Typ. do Correio Mercantil, 1863).
42. An example being *Doze Casamentos Felizes* (Rio Grande, Typ. do «Artista», 1866).
43. Manuel Pinheiro Chagas, *A propriedade litteraria: carta a sua magestade o imperador do Brazil* (Porto: Livraria Internacional de Ernesto Chardron, 1879).
44. Magalhães Lima, *Commercio e industria, sciencias, artes e lettras, galeria biographico-Contemporanea*, n. 8.
45. Cf. Joaquim Romero Magalhães, *Os brasileiros de torna-viagem no noroeste de Portugal* (Lisbon: Comissão Nacional para as Comemorações dos Descobrimentos Portugueses, 2000).
46. João Francisco Lisboa, 'Manuel Odorico Mendes', *Revista Contemporanea de Portugal e Brazil*, 4th Year (Lisbon: Typ. Franco-Portugueza, 1862), p. 330 (my emphasis).
47. Augusto Feio Soares de Azevedo, *Gazeta do Algarve*, n. 69 (Lagos: Typographia da *Gazeta do Algarve*, 1874) 22 Apr, p. 1.

CHAPTER 13

Popular Editions and Best-sellers at the End of the Nineteenth Century in Brazil

Alessandra El Far

Books for the General Public

There was a good deal of discussion among intellectuals at the end of the nineteenth century and beginning of the twentieth century about whether or not there was a significant reading public in Brazil. Some writers pointed to the data from census surveys as a reminder of the fact that vast numbers of men and women throughout the country were illiterate, whereas others stressed that it was becoming increasingly evident that there was a large supply of cheap books which could be found in the shop-windows of book stores and among the wares of itinerant traders.[1]

From the 1870s on, long lists of books at tempting prices could readily be found in advertising columns of Rio de Janeiro's newspapers, at that time the capital of the Empire of Brazil. In spreading the word about their collections, the booksellers themselves told their readers that there was no point any longer in 'falling back on the excuse that they can't read because books are too expensive'.[2] Owing to new printing technologies and the business acumen of editors, who did everything to make the printed volume a commodity that was more accessible to the general public, people from working-class and other low-income groups could be seen (at least in Rio de Janeiro) with a book between their hands.

In commenting on the last gasp of the nineteenth century, A. Aguiar, a newspaper columnist for the *Jornal do Brasil*, gave an appraisal of the extraordinary changes that the world had undergone with the arrival of the telegraph, trains, electricity and books designed for the working-classes. 'Instruction', he wrote, 'has been disseminated to the most distant corners of the nation. Books have become widespread; they have ceased to be rare, expensive objects and have even reached the poor'.[3]

With regard to Brazil as a whole, which had only a 20% rate of literacy, this situation was clearly a long way from becoming a reality. However, in the case of Rio de Janeiro, where 50% of the people were considered to be potential readers, it can be said that, although education was very far from reaching the 'obscure social classes',[4] as the reporter underlined, books had ceased to be the exclusive preserve of a privileged and wealthy public, but now catered to a significant number of mass consumers who were becoming increasingly literate and more noticeable in the everyday life of the city.[5]

In search of items for his newspaper column, João do Rio, the pseudonym used by Paulo Barreto (1881–1921), became acquainted with Arcanjo, an illiterate Italian newsvendor and bookseller. João do Rio used to relate that there were many other people like Arcanjo, 'of all colours, shapes and sizes, from old weirdoes to idle youths and faith disseminators'.[6] These 'booksellers', he used to say, 'are a swarming rabble that are scattered round the city. Every morning, they go into the warehouses, climb up the hills, wander through the suburbs and then take up a stand at any place where there are people moving about'.[7] João do Rio stated that since such vending provided a reasonable profit, the profession was thriving and attracting new followers every day. As well as 'forged' editions of the classical authors of Brazilian literature, these traders sold volumes that were 'soaked in crime and lunacy' which were read 'voraciously' in prisons, humble shacks and centres for vagrants by 'primitive men'.[8]

Despite all his criticism of the kind of literature consumed by the most impoverished classes in the city of Rio de Janeiro, João do Rio clearly shows us that for a long time books had ceased to be an expensive item or confined to the erudite knowledge of a small intellectual elite. By being made popular, the printed volume with its paperback cover and cheap binding became accessible to a huge and heterogeneous social class, which was particularly located in the main urban centres of the country.

The 'carioca' editors lost no time in catering to the needs of this new public readership. They were constantly launching new titles, so-called 'books for the people', with great ostentation. A wide assortment of titles could be found in the catalogues of bookstores, the advertisements in magazines and even among the wares of street traders. These included: *Orador do povo*, *Médico do povo*, *Trovador do povo*, *Lira popular*, *História Natural Popular*, *Mistérios do povo*, *Cozinheiro popular* and *Livro do povo ou o silabário brasileiro* — this final item being a compendium of teaching material designed 'to reach those whom fortune had disinherited'.[9]

The editors, who up to that time had prepared books in expensive well-bound editions, began to offer their collections at affordable prices. Baptiste Louis Garnier, the brother of the famous Parisian bookseller, who became renowned in the Rio de Janeiro book market for publishing well-printed volumes by authors that had been praised by Brazilian literary critics, never gave up selling luxury editions. However, in 1873, he announced the launch of twenty volumes of his 'Biblioteca da Algibeira' ('Pocket Library'). As a journalist of the time pointed out in the small newspaper *O Mosquito*, these works, which were in 'a format that could fit into any pocket other than the waistcoat', placed the literature of José de Alencar (1829–1877) and Bernardo Guimarães (1825–1884) alongside the recognized names of contemporary French literature such as Octave Feuillet (1821–1890), Jules Sandeau (1811–1883) and Edmond About (1828–1885). In his view, even this famous library had 'to cater to the taste of the reader and ensure that good books were placed within everyone's reach'.[10]

In this context, similar undertakings to those of Baptiste Louis Garnier began to be increasingly common. In the *Almanak Laemmert* of 1875, the editors Felix Ferreira & Co. gave the following information: 'A library for everyone: publications of novels, short stories, poetry, history and popular science in volumes of 250 and 300 pages'. The editors even stated that the orders could be sent 'to any part of the Empire'.[11] In 1878, the newspaper *O Besouro* also attempted to spread its 'Biblioteca econômica' [Economical Library], which comprised translations of weighty novelists like Victor Hugo (1802–1885). According to the editor of the periodical, by buying these works people would definitely be able to economize since after all this was their main aim.[12]

After a period of time, the editors began to improve their advertising strategies. On several occasions, Pedro da Silva Quaresma, who opened the Livraria do Povo [Bookstore of the People] in Rua São José in the centre of Rio de Janeiro, published lists of works in the *Gazeta de Notícias* with the purpose of showing the huge range of his stock. Under the banner 'the cheapest books' written in bold letters, the bookseller used to say 'everything is good and cheap'. 'Even the corpses will rise up', said Quaresma with a certain exaggeration, 'to take advantage of the bargains for sale in the Livraria do Povo'.[13]

In 1899, Pedro da Silva Quaresma, who was seeking a wider readership and also edited books, recommended that the latest edition of *Mãe e mártir* should be for 'the whole of the public in general', for 'everybody', for the 'minds who are well prepared for them, pure and noble hearts, romantic girls, fiancés and simple people'. In other words, they should be 'for every social class, from the highest to the lowest, who likes to read and can appreciate a good story'.[14] Quaresma, like other editors of this period, sought to surmount any social or economic barriers and pursue his aim of obtaining the maximum number of readers by stressing that he did not wish just to please a particular type of reader. His books were above all for 'the people without any distinctions being made'.[15]

But were these books for the general public really cheap? Throughout the 1880s, the price of a popular work varied from $100 [a hundred *réis*] to 2$000 [two thousand *réis*], depending on the number of pages, the final shape of the book and the genre in question, whereas a novel printed with paper of good quality and sold by the prestigious Garnier bookstore could sell for 3$000 [three thousand *réis*] or 4$000 [four thousand *réis*]. This means that at the end of the nineteenth century, a normal worker, such as a blacksmith, for example, who earned an average of 3$000 [three thousand *réis*][16] per day, could spend less than half of what he earned in a day's work to buy a best-selling popular novel. And to obtain a story that was relatively unknown he might lay out just a few coins of $100 [a hundred *réis*] or $200 [two hundred *réis*]. The civil servants working for the city council, such as office employees and clerks, who earned between 60$000 [sixty thousand *réis*] and 100$000 [one hundred thousand *réis*] per month, had a much wider margin for additional expenditure, and could thus purchase more than one book.[17] This is to say that, to a certain extent, the publications that were printed at low cost were already proving to be accessible to a wide range of social classes.

In addition, editors saw with their own eyes the growth that was taking place on a day-to-day basis in the streets of the cities, among a public that was becoming literate and a potential consumer market, owing to the abolition of slavery, the arrival in the country of immigrant manpower, and the development of a home market in Brazil. In view of this, they shrewdly took every step to cater to the taste of the public. This involved highlighting everything possible to attract the attention of the potential reader: information, entertainment, fun, highly sensational storylines, and inevitably, daring and spicy stories, more commonly known in the period as 'men's only novels'.

Sensation Novels

In 1895, Adolfo Caminha (1867–1897), the author of *A Normalista* (1893) and *O Bom-Crioulo* (1895), wrote a scathing article in *Cartas Literárias* in which he warned the readers of the difficult situation of 'writers of talent', who in his view were often driven to obscurity due to the ambitions of their editors. As a way of illustrating this situation, Caminha wrote a fictitious dialogue between an editor who was blinded by his thirst for profit and a serious man of letters who was searching, without much success, for a way to publish his manuscripts. Caminha wrote:

> The discourse is the same as ever: there are no readers and, additionally, the novel is not of a kind that 'our people' like and such stuff....
>
> But look at this, it's a good book Sr. F., it has style, it's worth reading.
>
> 'My friend, you're fooling yourself', said the other, 'we — editors — prefer a bloodcurdling story full of mystery and overwhelming emotions to style or the artistry of a good plot! It's this that the public likes and we, with regard to literary taste, we only know the public'.[18]

Nonetheless, there were many writers who were willing to cater to this popular literary demand and managed to publish their stories that in general were easy to read and full of dramatic and intriguing adventures. Luiz Edmundo, a famous chronicler of that period, wrote that these plots recounted 'formidable' stories, 'as if they were written with the point of a knife or dagger', and were designed to lacerate the human heart.[19]

As a result of their capacity to stir up strong feelings in their readers, these narratives, also called 'sensation novels', rapidly captured the attention of the public at large. Very quickly in the first pages, the characters, who were victims of some misfortune, found they were forced to abandon the safety and tranquillity of a peaceful life to be submerged in a succession of dramatic incidents that were astonishing, full of injustices, and bloodthirsty. At the end of the nineteenth century, any literate person who saw the word 'sensation' written under the title of a book immediately recognized the nature of the plot that he would encounter.

It was not by chance that Machado de Assis (1839–1908), in *Dom Casmurro* (1899), gave the name 'Sensações alheias' ['Other people's sensations'] to the chapter in which Bentinho speaks about Capitu to an older cousin who, cunningly, encourages him to continue the narrative. While the young lover expresses his feelings, his cousin is submerged in a world that does not belong to her, but in some way is painted in more vivid colours. 'Only then did I feel', says Bentinho, 'that, as I was speaking, cousin Justina's eyes seemed to touch me, hear me, smell me, taste me: they seemed to stand in for all the other senses'. 'I think', he continues, 'cousin Justina found a vague reawakening of her own sensations from watching those of others. Lips can give pleasure merely by narrating'.[20]

When faced with the opportunity to entertain the public with pleasurable experiences and strong emotions as a result of the power inherent in literary narrative, the editors were attracted to the plots of sensation novels published at the end of the nineteenth century. These generally tended to be stories of girls who had lost their virginity before marriage, youngsters kidnapped by cruel men, children abandoned by their parents, unexpected voyages to distant continents, unusual reunions and even apparitions of ghosts who returned to demand the fulfilment of promises that had been broken or forgotten. By employing a direct style of writing, it was expected that readers would be fascinated by these twists and turns of the stories, and in this way, become a captive audience for this type of narrative.

For example, in announcing the spectacular nature of the plot of *O monge de Olinda ou o frade perseguido pela polícia*, which told the story of a monk hunted by the police, the editor Pedro da Silva Quaresma said that it was a typical 'sensation novel'.[21] The same thing occurred with *O Primo Basílio* (1878) by Eça de Queiroz (1854–1900), which was called 'a modern novel of sensations';[22] and *O fruto de um crime*, 'a novel of sombre feelings;[23] while *A madrasta* was a 'realistic novel' about a stepmother full of 'new sensations', which on some occasions was accompanied by the following brief summary: 'a sublime novel about a woman who loved her stepdaughters and was bigamous'.[24]

At times it was the author himself who emphasized the sensational character of his narrative. In the view of its author, Abílio Soares Pinheiro, *Os estranguladores do Rio ou o crime da rua Carioca*, a book about a famous crime that was committed in the city, which had the subtitle 'Sensational novel about the hidden Rio', contains all the features of a book of its kind. It was dedicated to the lovers of 'strong sensations', promised to keep a distance from the 'cold stiffness of the legal reports' and strive to represent a faithful study of Rio de Janeiro society, where crime is 'so near to us', has struck 'its intended blows' and 'is sowing the seeds of dread and death.'[25]

As is well known, narratives of sensation were not a Brazilian literary invention. Both the stories published in newspapers and the many French and English novels sold in the form of cheap books — with their masterly plots and dramatic scenes — were widely read by the Brazilian public throughout the nineteenth century.[26] Aware of this taste, the Rio de Janeiro editors attempted to offer their readers narratives with the same themes, but based in settings that were more suited to local wishes and expectations. It was not by chance that the advertisements published in daily newspapers underlined: here a 'Brazilian novel' or there a 'novel set in the Botafogo district'. By these means it was expected that the Brazilian public would be able to identify with the settings of the incidents and origins of the characters, and thus be able to follow more closely the vagaries of fortune embedded in the plot.

Many of the 'sensation novels' written by Brazilian authors at the end of the nineteenth century achieved sales of thousands of copies and thus ran into several editions. Titles like *Elzira, a morta virgem*; *Fruto de um crime*; *Mãe e mártir*; *Maria, a desgraçada*; and *Casamento e mortalha*, among others, that sound strange to the ears of a contemporary reader, were read, re-read and enjoyed by countless readers, and remained on the shelves of bookshops for many decades.

The novel *Elzira, a morta virgem*, which has since been forgotten by the anthologies of the history of Brazilian literature, stirred the emotions of readers throughout the entire country for several decades and was even adapted by writers of *cordel* (chapbook) literature. Written by Pedro Ribeiro Vianna, this novel was first published in 1883 in a volume of 100 pages by the Serafim José Alves bookstore in Rio de Janeiro. By the beginning of the 1890s, this small novel was being printed by Pedro Quaresma's Livraria do Povo, and by 1913 it had already undergone several editions. In 1916, it was once again kept afloat by obtaining the editorial seal of A. de Azevedo & Costa, and in 1924 it was picked up by Livraria Editora Pauliceia in São Paulo.

But why did these novels achieve such success? This is a difficult question to answer with any precision. Nonetheless, it can be said that in some way these novels made sense to readers at the end of the nineteenth century and beginning of the twentieth century and spoke directly to their expectations, fears and dreams. It is thus no coincidence that these plots deal with some important subjects of the time, such as marriage and the purity of young maidens. However, as a means of ensuring that the narratives contained a significant amount of melodrama, these young people inevitably undergo distressing and painful experiences, unexpected separations, misunderstandings and quite often a premature death.

The novel *Elzira, a morta virgem*, which would probably go unnoticed today, stirred the imagination and feelings of countless readers of the period. In Pedro Vianna's book, Elzira becomes acquainted with Amâncio on the festival of São João, in 1874. They immediately fall in love with each other and declare their ties indissoluble. In the first stages of their passion, they exchange glances, letters, visits and promises. However, the proposal of marriage made by Amâncio triggers an endless series of fights and conflicts in Elzira's home, since her mother, D. Cândida, wants her daughter to marry a man from a wealthy family. Subjected to endless suffering, it is not long before Elzira falls ill. The young girl, who had every prospect of enjoying a long-lasting and true loving relationship, keeps saying to her mother: 'I would rather die than not be allowed to choose the person I love and who loves me'.[27] The young girl loses her appetite, sleeps very little and fades away before the very eyes of her family. When her parents finally decide to comply with Elzira's wishes, it is already too late. Deeply in love and still a virgin, the girl dies in Amâncio's arms.

The success of the story of Elzira was probably due to the sensations aroused in readers, who followed the deprivations of a character with everything to look forward to. Contrary to expectations, though, the beautiful and much sought after Elzira suffers the wretchedness and bitterness of a sad existence. Her family, the very image of a well-to-do bourgeois home, had to face up to Elzira's suffering. This conflict must have seemed quite interesting in the eyes of readers, who were used to being given the example of a strict code of behaviour and a kind of obedience that was unacceptable to the heroine. The breakdown of the predictable, the image of a father without an authoritative voice and a mother criticized for her mercenary actions, combined with a glimpse of new perspectives, captivated the feelings of a significant number of readers, who, to a certain degree, had recognized from a young age the remote chance of fulfilling their own desires and wishes.

Unlike many young girls of her time, Elzira had enough courage to oppose the wishes of her parents. Although this small drama reasserted the values of marriage, virginity and the family, its climax occurred at the exact time when all these conventions were losing their stable and secure foundations. This is to say it was precisely when the social order was revealing its fractures and weaknesses that we see the plot become sensational, and the book exploit to the maximum the acute distress and courage displayed by the characters.

Another novel that had great success in the period was Alfredo Elisiário da Silva's *Maria, a desgraçada*, which reached its eighth edition in 1898 and remained in the catalogue of the Livraria do Povo until at least 1923. This paperback of about 130 pages had short chapters with explanatory titles, and was easy to read. It had a narrative that was full of torments and suffering, and showed the public the thin line that divides a virtuous life guided by good customs from the ever-present possibility of a complete reversal of fortunes. In the catalogue of the Livraria do Povo, Pedro Quaresma explains the substance of the plot in succinct terms:

> [...] a sentimental novel about a young girl who is kidnapped on the eve of the day when she is going to marry a young man she is devoted to: throughout the slow martyrdom of this unfortunate girl kept in forced confinement by her executioner; her anguish, her despair, the agony and despair of her fiancé, — this comprises the novel *Maria, a desgraçada.*[28]

The novel, set in Portugal, tells the story of the beautiful and chaste Maria with an angel face, who lives in a simple way with her mother and sister in the country. One morning, Maria is saved from a sudden fall from the top of a tree by a young man named Alberto, a twenty-year-old orphan from the capitalist class and heir to a large fortune, who at once falls in love with her. Feeling immensely happy, Alberto seeks the hand of Maria from her mother D. Elisia. However, on the eve of the expected wedding day, Alberto pays a surprise visit to Maria's house with the purpose of delivering her wedding dress. Dazzled by the splendour of the garment, the young girl decides to try it on; likewise Alberto, in the adjoining bedroom, puts on his expensive wedding suit.

When they see each other so elegantly dressed, the fiancés stop thinking clearly. As if in a hallucination, they give themselves to each other. Alberto 'ran to her mad and reckless with eyes aflame and took her in his arms!'[29] Then with an altered voice, he cries out: 'Maria! earthbound angel!... let's anticipate our happiness by one day.... only one! Do you see that I'm dying... if I don't satisfy the desire that is gnawing my soul...'[30] At first, Maria tries to run away, but after some time is unable to resist: 'she lost her head and threw herself into her lover's arms'.[31] In a few words, the author says:

> Then he seized her by force and took her to her virginal bed.
> . . . .
> . . . .[32]

In the literature of the nineteenth century, the dotted lines stood for scenes or comments that were regarded as inappropriate by the moral standards of the time, allowing readers to imagine for themselves the part left out by the narrator.[33] What could not be expressed in verbal terms came in the form of omission points. Faced with this, the reader could be sure that the characters had put aside their modesty so that they could be submerged in a world of pleasure and intense sexuality.

Tormented by his powerful emotions after completing the sexual act, Alberto abandons Maria, who has been seduced in her bridal bed. Maria, who until then had been a pure and virtuous girl, becomes a disgraced victim after losing her virginity before the marriage. However, her misfortunes do not end there. After having been left by Alberto, Maria is kidnapped by a cruel neighbour, who keeps her locked up for years in a dingy and frightening dungeon. Maria only manages to secure her freedom after killing her enemy, but then, torn apart by so much suffering, the young girl soon dies. Or in other words, injury and horror prevailed where once harmony and proper moral standards had reigned.

The readers at the end of the nineteenth century, who followed the adventures of the unfortunate Maria, had a genuine sensation novel on their hands. It was a book based on exacerbated sentimentalism carried to excess in a constant conflict between good and evil, which highlighted the bitter experiences endured by its characters. Like so many other narratives of this period, these adventures had the same objective in common: to excite powerful feelings in their readers.

Novels for Men

In addition to 'sensation novels', the so-called 'novels for men' achieved an extraordinary popularity in the world of popular literature in the second half of the nineteenth century in Brazil. Throughout their pages, these publications contained pornographic stories in the midst of an endless series of pleasure.

The expression 'novels for men' openly sought to steer the reader toward the exclusive preserve of the male public, owing to the possible harmful effects on the character of women, who in that epoch were viewed as weak and thus susceptible to the temptations of narratives.[34] This prohibition, which was not based on legal codes but rather on the moral assumptions in vogue, did not always prove to be effective. This was owing to the determined capitalistic spirit of the bookstore and the curiosity of women, who could get hold of these books in any bookstore in the city after dodging the vigilant glances of their parents or husbands.

Under the influence of these stories, women ran the risk of setting social conventions aside and going out in search of emotions and feelings that were far removed from the reality of their world. Alternatively, since it was believed that men were able to distinguish between the world of fiction and everyday conventions and customs, they could, in the opinion of the doctors and legal experts of that time, have unrestricted access to these books.

There were a considerable number of men from the world of science who warned parents and husbands of the dangers of pornographic literature on the female imagination. What might women get up to 'with their feeble minds, if they surrendered themselves with abandon to reading novels full of the perfume and treachery of eroticism?', asked Gilberto Sabóia, an eminent lawyer of that epoch.[35] Viveiros de Castro, a well-known Professor of Criminal Law, offered a similar argument in his book *Atentados ao pudor*. From his perspective, these works aroused

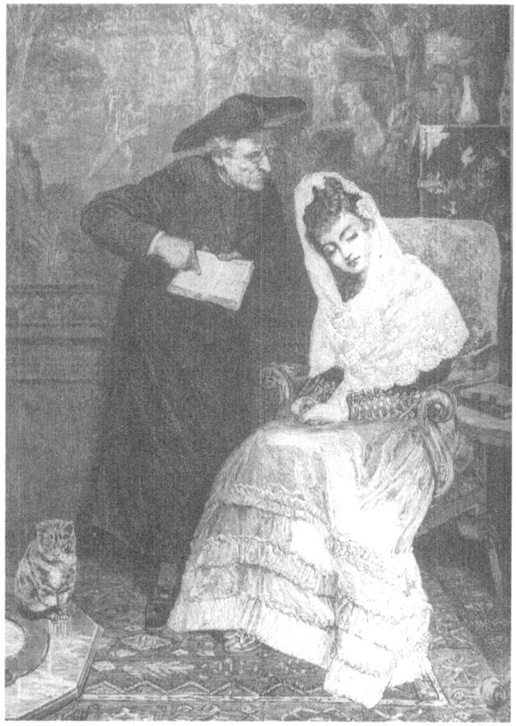

Figure 13.1. 'The forbidden book', *Ilustração Brasileira*, 1 September, 1877 © National Library of Rio de Janeiro

'a terrible state of curiosity' in women. 'Two friends', he said, 'meet and talk about the novel they have both read; they then experiment in their own lives with the new sensations the writer has so passionately written about and find they like the experience and then pass on their new discoveries to others'.[36]

While men were free to enjoy their literary musings, women not only had to bear the constant prying of their families, but also had to face the warnings of medical treatises. Indeed, the specialists were concerned both with the fact that these works encouraged sex outside marriage and that women might be tempted to seek pleasure on their own — a practice at that time referred to as 'clitorism'. Pires de Almeida, a famous clinician in Rio de Janeiro, listed the terrible consequences endured by women who indulged in this practice: flaccid breasts, bad breath, discoloured gums and lips, loss of moisture in the eyes, freckles, spots, blotches on the face and a loss of muscular strength. Over a period of time, the doctor said, it would inevitably lead to a loss of memory and of sanity, and finally result in a lingering, painful death.[37]

In this context, the bookstores could not — at least in theory — count on a female readership. However, this did not seem to matter much since at the end of the nineteenth century there were many single men confident that they could find a way to satisfy their fantasies in brothels or in the purchase of 'novels for men'. The census of Rio for 1890 shows a distinct numerical imbalance between the sexes. Whereas the male population consisted of 293,657 people, women only made up 228,994, giving a surplus of nearly 65,000 males. By 1906, the survey showed that there were 463,453 males and 347,990 females, a surplus of over 115,000 males, a good number of whom would have been adult men without a female partner.[38]

This disproportion between men and women was caused by the arrival of foreign immigrants, mainly Portuguese, in search of work. In general, they were young and single, between fifteen and thirty years of age. Together with the veterans, who were acclimatized to the tropical land, they sought to take part in the amorous intrigues, games of seduction and sexual conquests that are always present in the urban setting of a metropolis. In addition, apart from having to face clear inequality in numerical terms when seeking to satisfy their sexual desires, the males of Rio also had to cope with the problem that a significant number of girls were virgins and chaste, religious women fearful of the chastisement of the church, and faithful wives. Unlike illiterate people, those who knew how to read could at least count on pornographic paperbacks at low prices.

The plots of the 'novels for men' explored different themes and tastes. In political areas, there were a considerable number of governors, aristocrats and representatives of public life who forgot their social responsibilities and were happy to seize the chance to have an uninterrupted series of secret meetings and ardent delights. At least this is what the authors sought to convey to their readers in works such as *Cartas pornográficas de D. Pedro I*; *Carta de Napoleão à sua querida* and *Os amores secretos de Pio IX ou os escândalos praticados atrás dos reposteiros do Vaticano*.[39]

Priests and friars appeared in these pornographic plots in the figure of eminent seducers and lords of an insatiable sexuality. This obliterated any idea of serenity, meditation and faith that might exist within the walls of convents and monasteries. Amidst hostile criticism, these books testify to the hypocrisy of the religious environment and describe an everyday life charged with eroticism, as can be read in the following titles of the period: *Suspiros de um padre ou a crioula de baixo da cama*; *A mulher e o padre, grande exercício em um convento, afrodisíaco indispensável*; *Serões do convento*; *João e Francisco: os frades e as freiras num convento*; *Frei João da Boa Hora*; *Padre Soriano* and *O padre Antonio*.[40]

In the varied lists of 'novels for men', some editions attempted to explain the spicy contents through provocative titles, which dispensed with the need for any further explanations. Among these were *Volúpias*; *Luxuriosas*; *Sensuais*; *Afrodisíacas*; *Gotas de amor*; *Lúbricas*; *Remédio para impotentes*; *Remédio para matar paixões*; *Ele e ela escondidos no quintal*; *Os prazeres do vício*; *Rédea solta*; *Sensualidade e amor*; *Contos nervosos que produzem calafrios na espinha dorsal*; *Gritos da carne* and *Sensações fortes*.[41]

And finally, there were matters related to women — whether they be adultery, virginity, inquisitiveness or the question of belonging to the sophisticated milieu of prostitution. In general, these were narratives in the first person, which described in great detail a wide range of amorous adventures of female characters. Examples of these are *Clarita*; *Beatriz*; *Alva*; *Branca*; *Clara*; *Miss Mary*; *Eva*; *Carmem*; *Judith*; *Isaura*; *Suzana*; *Gabriela ou uma cortesã dos tempos coloniais*; *Celestina ou a adúltera na noite do casamento* and *Júlia de Milo, perfil de uma mulher desonesta*.[42]

Clearly these novels have a wide range of narrative styles. Whereas some make excessive use of explicit descriptions of sexual activities, others only offer the reader discreet kisses and innuendos of love. Even so, both were listed in the newspaper advertisements as 'novels for men' because they breached the prevailing standards of modesty and good conduct.

The Local Colour of Pornographic Plots

At the beginning of the second half of the nineteenth century, there was a large number of 'novels for men' sold in Rio de Janeiro that used translations of well-known titles from the European Enlightenment, such as *Thérèse Philosophe* (1788), *Historie de Dom B.* (1740) and *Fanny Hill* (1748) which was known by the cariocas of the time as *Vôo da inocência ao auge da prostituição ou memórias de Miss Fanny.*[43] From the 1870s onwards, with the dynamic growth of publishing houses and readers and purchasers of books in the country, there were a much larger number of plots created by Portuguese and Brazilian writers. This was the case with *Os serões do convento*, signed with the initials M.L., a compilation of pornographic stories told by a group of lesbian nuns at the end of the afternoon. This book remained on the shelves of bookstores and among the wares of wandering book traders for more than four decades. The three small volumes, in the format of a pocket book, that comprised *Os serões do convento* were mainly sold in the city of Rio de Janeiro, although they were also printed in Lisbon.[44]

The first two volumes brought together a range of episodes: lay officials who lived lecherous lives with nuns inside convents, friars who seduced women in the confessionals of churches, cuckolded husbands, hermits who broke their vows of chastity to deflower young maidens, paradisiacal harems and carnival balls where the main fantasy consisted of love potions that light up the genital organs. At the end of each evening, the nuns, excited by their series of successful couplings, exchange kisses, hugs and sighs, and then wander off to their cells in pairs or groups of three with the purpose, according to the author, of practising what they have learnt from these episodes.

The third tome, in its turn, includes a long story of 'Roberto do Diabo', a youth used to playing small and amusing tricks on people with the aim of putting his demonic sexual forays into practice. Roberto is the son of an abbot and a lace-maker, who early in life began an interminable series of successful sexual encounters. In the house of his teacher, Domingos Engrácio, Roberto managed without much effort to seduce the housewife and her maid, and with these two, he devises sexual stratagems that can satisfy everybody. 'As you see,' said Roberto, 'I only have one instrument — however, I have two hands which can also serve. Come here and do what I tell you!'[45]

After some time, Roberto decides to spend his final years of life in a convent, disguised as Sister Angela. According to the narrator, Angela's behaviour in the cloisters was so exemplary that after a short time they made her 'Directress of the Novitiate'. In his words, all the novitiates were mad about her and she about them, each one in turn.[46] On reaching the age of fifty, she died, which caused great consternation in the convent. According to the narrator, her companions acted as if they had become widows and for many years they remembered her as a saint and a real angel.

From the 1880s onwards, despite the reluctance of the authors to accept it, a lot of work inspired by the literary school of naturalism, in particular the novels of Emile Zola, were relegated to the category of 'novels for men' in Brazil. This was because those works gave a significant amount of space to detailed descriptions of the female body and sexual encounters. *A carne*, by the eminent philologist Julio Ribeiro (1845–1890), appeared in the wake of books that were often advertised in the newspapers of the period as 'hot', 'scorching' books or even novels of 'fire'. From the time when it was first published, *A carne* aroused strong reactions in the press. Several critics, whether under the protection of pseudonyms or not, said that the novel 'was a real enemy of the soul',[47] 'written with a pornographic aim',[48] and often pleaded with the author to return his attention solely to the Portuguese language.

A carne tells the story of Lenita, a girl aged twenty-two, who has lost her father. She leaves her home in the city to live on a farm that belongs to an old friend of the family. Once close to nature, the character feels like someone else and discovers her 'femininity' by being attracted to a more rugged, 'macho' model of masculinity. The sensations of Lenita increase in intensity with the arrival at the farm of the young Barbosa. Both characters are readers of Charles Darwin and Herbert Spencer and admirers of progress in science. Gradually the ties of friendship draw them closer together. This continues until one night Lenita is overwhelmed with a feeling of desire and the promptings of the flesh. She runs to Barbosa's bedroom and throws herself into his arms:

> Barbosa's robust arms restrained her. His kisses multiplied on her face, her eyes, her neck: and these ardent, hungry kisses burned her skin, turned her blood to glowing lava, whipping her nerves, torturing her flesh.
>
> Growing bolder, more uncontrolled by the minute, he moved down her throat, reached her firm, swollen, panting breasts. He mouthed and kissed them, at first respectfully, fearfully, like one committing an act of sacrilege; then insolently, lasciviously, bestially, like a satyr. In growing exaltation he sucked and bit the erect nipples.[49]

A few years after the publication of *A carne*, the Livraria do Povo took advantage of the public interest in the literary genre and announced the launching of *O aborto* by Figueiredo Pimentel, a story written 'in plain language' in the manner of Zola. In the short period of fifteen days, *O aborto* had sold 5,000 copies; 'it's never happened before', exclaimed the editor Pedro Quaresma, the owner of Livraria do Povo. In the following weeks, the sales of the book continued to rise. In the further words of Quaresma, *O aborto* was 'a huge success — the greatest success in Brazilian Literature! Almost 7,000 copies were sold in 3 months! It is thought a 2nd edition is going to be published!'[50]

When faced with the repercussions of this publication, several journalists attempted to understand the reasons for its success and stated that to this end they needed to stray from 'the terrain of what is strictly speaking that of letters, to fall into the domain of pseudo-literature, which is industrial and pornographic!'[51] They felt they had to digest 'the disgusting and poisoned fare' of these books so that they could ascertain the reason why the public, 'at such a serious and defining moment of our history', was so avid to purchase 'edition after edition' of *O aborto*.[52] The journalist Magalhães de Azevedo (1872–1963), who wrote two reviews of Pimentel's book, made clear to readers the reasons for his choice when he said: 'some days ago, all of a sudden, a copy of *O aborto* arrived with the ink still wet on the printing-press — the six thousandth copy! I decided to buy it and take it home with the sole aim of discovering the qualities that could explain the amazing success of a book that was amazingly awful!'[53]

Since abortion was a practice that was condemned in the nineteenth century, Pimentel, who was probably in search of a controversial subject that could allow him to make his mark in the world of letters, decided to write about this issue. The book tells the tragic fate of Maricota, 'a genuine type of Brazilian woman', with brunette, dark hair, and 'perhaps with a sixth part of African blood'.[54] She seduces her cousin Mario, becomes pregnant, and then dies while undergoing an abortion that he has arranged. Mariota, as an avid reader of *Serões do convento*, admires women who live in a world of luxury and pleasure. In the words of the teenager, she was eager to have a life of fleeting pleasures and dreamt about being the public woman who was most sought after in her time. Mariota said 'when I can pass through the streets in an open carriage, dressed in silk and covered with jewellery, they will call me a fallen woman but they will still envy me'.[55]

In an attempt to achieve the same success as *O aborto*, many 'novels for men' appeared at the end of the nineteenth century and remained on the shelves of bookshops until at least the first decade of the twentieth century. Even though these books had been censured by journalists and men of letters, and were regarded as part of a minor genre literary, they existed alongside many other novels of a popular kind during that period, greatly assisting the growth of the Brazilian publishing industry and also forming a part of the variegated literary scene in Brazil. This is to say that, in addition to writers of critical acclaim, there were others who took part in the Brazilian literary world and managed to disseminate their texts and narrative tendencies with a significant degree of success.

Furthermore, I would like to underline that the experience of reading in that period was not confined to writers in the literary canon that can currently be found in the anthologies of Brazilian literature. In those years, people did read Machado de Assis, Aluísio de Azevedo (1857–1913) and Raul Pompéia (1863–1895), but they also read a wide range of other writers, especially those who published stories full of adventure, mystery and endless pleasures.

In the hope of bringing these books to light again, I have given in this chapter a brief account of some of these titles. Without doubt, they represent a small sample of the different narrative genres that formed the world of popular literature that emerged from the publishing houses of Rio de Janeiro and were sold in other states in Brazil. Amid so many books, it can be said that in that period they reflected a common concern among booksellers and editors, namely to publish works for a broad public that could please *all* those that were free from the handicap of not knowing how to read.

Notes to Chapter 13

1. For a fuller discussion of the popular books, printing and low-cost publishing at the end of the nineteenth century, see Alessandra El Far, *Páginas de sensação: literatura popular e pornográfica no Rio de Janeiro (1870–1924)* (São Paulo: Companhia das Letras, 2004).
2. *Gazeta da Tarde*, 22 June 1896.
3. 'O século que finda', *Jornal do Brasil*, 31 December 1900.
4. 'O século que finda', *Jornal do Brasil*, 31 December 1900.
5. The percentage rate of literacy in the federal capital rose from 35.2% in 1872 to 50.8% in 1890 and 61.1% in 1920. For further information about the indices, see Sylvia Damazio, *Retrato social do Rio de Janeiro na virada do século* (Rio de Janeiro: Ed.UERJ, 1996), pp. 121–23.
6. João do Rio, 'Os mercadores de livros e a leitura das ruas', in *A alma encantadora das ruas* [1st edn 1908] (Rio de Janeiro: Secretaria de Cultura do Rio de Janeiro, 1991), p. 47.
7. João do Rio, 'Os mercadores de livros e a leitura das ruas', p. 47.
8. João do Rio, 'Os mercadores de livros e a leitura das ruas', pp. 48–49.
9. *Gazeta da Tarde*, 4 November 1895.
10. 'A biblioteca da Algibeira', *O Mosquito*, 12 July 1873.
11. *Almanak Administrativo, mercantil e industrial da corte e província do Rio de Janeiro para o ano de 1875* (Rio de Janeiro: E. & H. Laemmert), p. 1023.
12. *O Besouro*, 27 June 1878.
13. *Gazeta de Notícias*, 4 September 1882.
14. *O País*, 15 March 1899.
15. Elysario Silva, 'Ao leitor', *Maria, a desgraçada* (Rio de Janeiro: Quaresma & Cia, 1898).
16. Sylvia Damazio, *Retrato social do Rio de Janeiro na virada do século*, pp. 48–50.
17. Ibid.
18. Adolfo Caminha, *Cartas literárias* (Rio de Janeiro: n.pub., 1895), p. 150.
19. Luiz Edmundo, *O Rio de Janeiro do meu tempo*, 3 vols (Rio de Janeiro: Imprensa Nacional, 1938), II, 739.
20. Machado de Assis, *Dom Casmurro*, trans. by John Gledson (Oxford: Oxford University Press, 1997), p. 45.
21. 'Livros baratíssimos', *Gazeta de Notícias*, 10 March 1884. Most of the titles cited were advertised in the newspapers of the period without any more specific bibliographical references.
22. 'Livros baratíssimos', *Gazeta de Notícias*, 6 March 1885.
23. 'Livros baratíssimos', *Gazeta de Notícias*, 12 May 1884.
24. 'Livros baratíssimos', *Gazeta de Notícias*, 12 May 1884.
25. Abílio Soares Pinheiro, *Os estranguladores do Rio ou o crime da rua Carioca: romance sensacional do Rio oculto* (Rio de Janeiro: Typ. Luiz Miotto, 1906), p. 6.
26. I cite here the precursor study of Marlyse Meyer, *Folhetim: uma história* (São Paulo: Companhia das Letras, 1996); also Sandra Guardini T. Vasconcelos, 'Caminhos do romance inglês no Brasil do século XIX', in *Cultura letrada no Brasil: objetos e práticas*, ed. by Márcia Abreu and Nelson Schapochnik (Campinas: Mercado de Letras, 2005).
27. Pedro Ribeiro Vianna, *Elzira, a morta virgem* (Rio de Janeiro: Quaresma & Editores, 1913), p. 63.
28. 'Catálogo da Livraria Quaresma', *Trovador de esquina ou repertório do capadócio* (Rio de Janeiro: Quaresma & C., 1901), p. 16.
29. Elysiario da Silva, *Maria, a desgraçada* (Rio de Janeiro: Quaresma & C., 1898), p. 74.
30. Silva, p. 74.
31. Silva, p. 75.
32. Silva, pp. 74–75.
33. In *Epitaph of a Small Winner* (1881), the famous writer Machado de Assis, with considerable irony, had recourse to omission points, with the addition of interrogation and exclamation marks. This device was employed to inform the reader, throughout the chapter that has the title 'The venerable dialogue of Adam and Eve', of the nature of the thoughts exchanged between the lovers Brás Cubas and Virgilia. Joaquim Maria Machado de Assis, *Epitaph of a Small Winner*, trans. by William L. Grossman (New York: Farrar, Straus and Giroux, 2009).

34. Ever since their appearance in Europe in the eighteenth century, novels had been regarded as dangerous reading for the female sex. Society feared that if women became intoxicated with impossible amorous adventures they might abandon the good moral standards. In the case of the 'novels for men' the risk to women was greater still, since the main narrative appeal of these books was in their explicit descriptions of sex scenes.
35. Gilberto Ribeiro de Sabóia, *O lenocínio* (Rio de Janeiro: Typ. de Carlos Schmidt, 1896), p. 20.
36. Francisco Viveiros de Castro, *Atentados ao pudor: estudos sobre as aberrações do instinto sexual* (Rio de Janeiro: Livraria Moderna, 1895), p. 238.
37. José Ricardo Pires de Almeida, *Higiene moral — homossexualismo — a libertinagem no Rio de Janeiro* (Rio de Janeiro: Laemmert, 1906), p. 198.
38. Sidney Chalhoub, *Trabalho, lar e botequim* (São Paulo: Brasiliense, 1986), p. 26.
39. The titles cited below were advertised in the newspapers of the period without any more specific bibliographical references. They were published in Portuguese but the titles can be translated as follows: *The pornographic letters of D .Pedro I, The letters of Napoleon to his lover, The secret love of Pope Pius IX or the scandals practised behind the curtains of the Vatican.*
40. These books were also published in Portuguese and their titles can be translated as follows: *Sighs of a priest or creole under the bed, The woman and the priest, Much exercise in a convent: An indispensable aphrodisiac, Evenings in a convent, João and Francisco: The friars and nuns in a convent, Good time Friar João, Friar Soriano*, and *The priest Antonio.*
41. The titles in English are as follows: *Lustful pleasures, Lusts, Sensual people, Aphrodisiacs, Drops of love, Lascivious women, Remedies for impotence, Remedies for sudden passions, He and she hidden in the yard, The pleasures of addiction, Free rein, Sexuality and love, Thrilling stories that cause a shiver down the spine, Cries of flesh and overwhelming sensations.*
42. The translation of these titles is: *Gabriela or a courtesan in colonial times, Celestina or adultery on the wedding night, Julia de Milo — picture of a dishonest woman.*
43. Many of the erotic novels of the French Enlightenment were published anonymously or by means of pseudonyms. For a fuller discussion of these titles, consult the books of Robert Darnton, in particular *The Forbidden Best-Sellers of Pre-Revolutionary France* (New York: W. W. Norton & Company, 1995), and Jean-Marie Goulemot, *Ces livres qu'on ne lit que d'une main* (Paris: Minerve, 1994).
44. According to the advertisements of the epoch, some editions of *Serões do convento* are still made up of four or more volumes.
45. M.L., *Os serões do convento*, 3 vols (Lisbon: Typographia do Bairro Alto, s.d.), III, 71.
46. Idem, p. 220.
47. *Revista Ilustrada*, 29 November 1888.
48. *Diario Mercantil*, 12 August 1888.
49. Júlio Ribeiro, *Flesh* [1888], trans. by William Barne, MHRA New Translations, 2 (London: Modern Humanities Research Association, 2011), pp. 113–14.
50. *O País*, 27 June 1893.
51. *Gazeta de Notícias*, 19 June 1893; *Gazeta de Notícias*, 3 July 1893.
52. *Gazeta de Notícias*, 19 June 1893.
53. *Gazeta de Notícias*, 19 June 1893.
54. Figueiredo Pimentel, *O aborto* (Rio de Janeiro: Quaresma & Comp., 1893), p. 21.
55. Pimentel, p. 123.

CHAPTER 14

❖

The Brazilian Publishing Industry at the Beginning of the Twentieth Century: The Path of Monteiro Lobato

Cilza Bignotto and Milena Ribeiro Martins

José Bento Monteiro Lobato (1882–1948) holds a prominent position in both the history of the book and that of reading in Brazil. His activities as a publisher between 1918 and 1925 revolutionized the country's then stagnant publishing industry and created the opportunity to modernize the sector in the following decades.[1] A great part of his success in the field of publishing was linked to the success he achieved as a writer with *Urupês*,[2] a book of short stories that practically launched his publishing business, becoming a success among critics and readers soon after it was published.[3]

The point of departure for his publishing activities was the journal *Revista do Brasil*, which, as will be shown below, already enjoyed considerable prestige among Brazilian intellectuals when it was acquired by Lobato. The nationalist ideology of the journal was consistent with the literary project supported by the writer, for which the main guidelines were the recognition of the importance of both national themes and popular culture and a desire to combat what he viewed as an imitation of European cultural tendencies.[4]

These were the lines that directed both Monteiro Lobato's work as a writer and the editorial policies of his company. Brazil — and especially its social, political, economic and artistic obstacles — was the main theme of the books he published in those years, all of which were bestsellers at the time. However, before coming to a better understanding of his project, the nature of the influence of European literature (especially French and English literature) on the development of the intellectual Monteiro Lobato must be determined.

His *Complete Works* and the hundreds of letters sent throughout his life to many different addressees contain numerous references to English and French works.[5] This chapter will examine some of the influences of these works on the Brazilian cultural field and on the intellectual formation of Monteiro Lobato, in particular, those more closely linked to the literary project that guided his activities as an author and a publisher. In view of this, it is necessary to trace his path through the Brazilian literary field to the newsroom of *Revista do Brasil*.

The Editorial Scene

In the first years of the twentieth century, the prospects for a young Brazilian writer wishing to publish books were 'not very auspicious', according to Laurence Hallewell.[6] The most important company in the publishing industry was Garnier, which was based in Rio de Janeiro. This publishing house was founded in 1844 and it can be seen as the main player at the beginning of the development of Brazilian publishing. Its proprietor, Baptiste Louis Garnier, belonged to a family of booksellers established in Paris. The family owned a bookstore and publishing house named Garnier Frères, founded in 1833 by Baptiste Louis's older brothers, Auguste and Hyppolite. After the death of Baptiste Louis in 1893, control of the company passed to Hippolyte, who avoided publishing new authors.

Garnier's main competitors in Brazil were Laemmert, who published just a few literary titles, and Francisco Alves, a specialist in educational books. The doors of both publishing houses were not easily opened for novice writers. Faced with this discouraging scene, men of letters turned to the Portuguese publishers. According to Hallewell, a significant number of Brazilian books were published in Portugal by the beginning of the Republic (1890–1910).[7] However, before seeking these publishers, whether home-based or foreign, both novice and established writers sought first to publish their works in the pages of the Brazilian newspapers and magazines.

As Nelson Werneck Sodré states, the turn of the century was marked by 'the transition from the small to the large press'.[8] The rise of the press companies, which replaced the few small newspapers, was linked, among other factors, to the rise of the bourgeoisie and to the progressive establishment of capitalist relationships in the country. The transformation of newspapers into business conglomerates was characterized by changes that involved importing more modern and suitable graphic printing equipment, and also paying salaries to writers who worked as regular columnists.

Sodré sums up the importance of the newspapers for the literary field in this period:

> The men of letters sought to find in newspapers what they could not find in books: fame in the first place; and a little money, if possible. The newspaper *Jornal do Commercio* paid its contributors between thirty and sixty thousand *réis*; *Correio da Manhã*, fifty. In 1907, Bilac and Medeiros e Albuquerque were paid a monthly wage for the newspaper columns that they wrote for *Gazeta de Notícias* and *O País*, respectively; in 1906, Adolfo Araújo offered to pay 400 thousand *réis* per month for Alphonsus de Guimaraens to write for *A Gazeta*, in São Paulo. In an inquiry conducted by Paulo Barreto, the results of which were later collated in the volume *O momento literário*, one of the questions was: 'Is journalism, particularly in Brazil, a good or a bad factor for the literary art?' Of course, most of them replied that it was a good one.[9]

The newspapers that Sodré refers to were based in Rio de Janeiro, the capital of Brazil at the time, and home to the country's most renowned writers, such as Olavo Bilac, Medeiros e Albuquerque (both poets who also wrote prose, mainly for the periodicals), and Paulo Barreto, a journalist, columnist and novelist, better known by the pseudonym João do Rio. The newspaper column and literary inquiry, as well as reports and interviews, were genres that had been introduced into the country by the European press, particularly by the French, and which the national writers attempted to follow.[10]

In that period, Monteiro Lobato was a public prosecutor and, in his spare time, a novice writer; like so many others, he began his literary career by writing for minor newspapers and magazines. His first works were published when he was a law student, a conventional career of the Brazilian elite — even for the decadent elite, of which his own family was a part.[11] Among his early writings are two short stories with French titles: 'D'Après Nature' [Painted from life], published in 1903 in *Educação* [Education], a periodical from São Paulo, and 'Gens ennuyeux' [Boring people], the winner of a competition held by the Student Union of the Law School and published in the institution's magazine *Onze de Agosto* [August Eleventh].[12] This short story was subsequently included in the book *Cidades Mortas* [Dead Cities] (1919).[13]

The French titles can be understood as an example of what Sérgio Miceli called the 'francomania' experienced by writers and readers in that period.[14] Monteiro Lobato shared the general passionate feelings of Brazilian intellectuals for France and French products, which included literature itself. In a letter dated 30 September 1915, he admitted to Godofredo Rangel the breadth of his reading in French:

> When I reached puberty, aesthetically speaking, and my mental curiosity was awakened, I began to apply myself to reading — but only in French, until I was twenty-five years old. Up to this time, I could count on my fingers how many books I had read in our own language: some Eça [de Queirós], five volumes by Camilo [Castelo Branco], half of Machado de Assis's works. And Euclides [da Cunha] and some newspapers. As you can see, I was fatally infected with the French scabies. The reaction came with the period of the *Velha Praga*.[15] I'm still the old version of myself there. The ricocheting flashes of Camilo [Castelo Branco] appear in *Urupês*; the great Camilo who *revealed* to me the Portuguese language and allowed me to see the limits between it and the trashy language of the newspapers and deputies — the kaffir language for kaffir stuff, said Camilo.[16] Since *Urupês* I have been groping, attempting to jump to the other side in the struggle of transitions. This step is not anything like a gymnastic leap; it is a metaphorical step, the imperceptible leap of the hand of a watch. I am with one foot in the land of the kaffirs and the other in the air, coming down slowly and afraid of the real Lusitanian language. I hope to succeed in my jump. I will jump.[17]

When referring to the great impact that French literature had on his education, Lobato uses the metaphor of a disease — scabies, an infection caused by a parasitic mite that burrows under the skin of the host. One of the symptoms of contact with the French language would be the constant grammatical mistakes made when writing in Portuguese, as he states in the same letter. Ironically, the Portuguese language in its turn seems to have interfered in his attempts to write in French. The original title of the story '*Gens ennuyeux*' was '*Gens ennuyeuses*', a mistake of agreement soon pointed out by one of the judges of the competition in which it was awarded first prize in 1904.[18] In French, *gens* is masculine, while in Portuguese *gente* is feminine — which is presumably what caused the mistake.

Another metaphor worth noting is that used in the expression 'Kaffir language for kaffir stuff', by the Portuguese writer Camilo Castelo Branco. The expression was probably read by Lobato in the preface to the second edition of the romantic story *O bem e o mal* [Good and evil], published in 1868, where the Portuguese writer seeks to explain the disappointing sales of the book:

> The story did not lose anything by being badly written but by being badly thought out. As far as the language is concerned, I constructed that with the same craftsmanship that I used when I created its two sisters. Errors are inevitably made when you have to write a great deal in a hurry and only then take your time to finish your work. In Portugal one has to do this.[19]
> The flaw in this book is the plethora of virtues that bore readers who exercise the same or greater virtues every day. Thank goodness! The individual who wants fame and glory must paint and spatter his panels with blood and mud. Gaining the close attention of readers is only allowed to those who furnish them with news about things that are unknown or have never been tried out. Virtue is the rancidity of those bloated souls of our country. The crimes of kaffirs must be reported in a kaffir-like language.[20]

The complaints of Camilo Castelo Branco about work written in haste for newspapers and the supposed lack of virtues in the readers are common among nineteenth-century writers; they resemble those uttered by Monteiro Lobato several decades later.[21] In letters dating from the 1910s, Lobato records his repudiation of the periodicals — mainly owing to the language in which they were written — and his desire to cease collaborating with them. Lobato's pathway to becoming a professional writer was similar to the steps taken by Camilo Castelo Branco, on the other side of the Atlantic, as he noted in a letter of 7 February 1916:

> I have come to understand our public. If you want to interest them, you must come with bombs in your hands and let them off in someone's nostrils or make them laugh, poking fun at any important political figure [...] — or then talk about the *caboclo*. If you have a *caboclo* on the scene the public will lap up all of it.[22]

It should be noted that the model of the polemicist, as Lobato states in another passage from the letter, was Camilo Castelo Branco.[23] The Portuguese writer often used the term 'cafra' [kaffir] to talk about Brazilian intellectuals in a pejorative way, those who were accustomed to being called half-castes, Botocudo Indians, and monkeys — which is what makes so ambiguous the appropriation of the expression 'Língua de Cafra' [Kaffir language] by Lobato. His move seems to have led him, mainly in the works he published after 1914, to plant both feet in 'Cafra' [the kaffir language] — or at least to draw away from 'the pure Lusitanian language of Portugal' and to adopt features of Brazilian orality.

However, 'francomania' infected the intellectuals of the 1910s, just as 'anglomania' had infected the men of letters in the preceding generations. In the opinion of Sérgio Miceli, who has analysed the formation, development and rules of the Brazilian literary scene, the men of letters of the generation of the 1870s (the main exponent of which was Machado de Assis) had tried out the attractions of English literature and the British political model:

> This 'anglomania', as a peculiar form of dependence, can be explained by the greater degree of autonomy held by writers of that generation in the field of power, where they were both intellectuals and public figures at the same time. In the case of the 'Anatolians', the imprint of French literature, particularly of its more mundane exponents, as well as the importing of new Frenchified genres and the fascination for Paris, all this was the symbolic reversal of their objective position; the employees of the mainstream press were no longer in a suitable position to plan a 'personal' work as a unique 'creation' by an individual artist; on the other hand, the arena they worked in did not release them from their involvement in the most palpable and brutal world of political ambitions.[24]

Miceli used the term 'Anatolians' to refer to the men of letters who adopted Anatole France as the main cultural model in their biographies and memoirs. Monteiro Lobato was not only a member of this group, but would have liked to have been the 'Anatolian' with 'greatest commercial and intellectual success in the 1920s in São Paulo'.[25] Like a few other contemporary writers, he adopted a half-way position between the models offered by the generation of Machado de Assis, to which he was already having difficulties adjusting, and the models offered by the literary vanguard of the period.

In the opinion of Miceli, intellectuals like Lobato lacked the cultural capital necessary to import an aesthetic, ethical and political program from the European vanguards and ended up by renouncing it. There was a high price in making this renunciation: the artistic 'choices' of Lobato, like those of other 'Anatolians', were later regarded as 'reactionary' by a significant part of the Brazilian critical establishment, when compared with the choices made by the 'modernists'.[26]

In fact, the cultural models most often mentioned by Monteiro Lobato in his autobiographical documents, like the letters to Rangel, are the authors of the nineteenth century or previous periods. In a letter dated 23 October 1914, he imagines what his first book would be like: 'Perhaps a mixture of [Laurence] Sterne, Machado [de Assis], Camilo [Castelo Branco] etc.'[27] From what can be read in other letters, the 'etc.' covered the French writers Alphonse Daudet and Émile Zola, the Portuguese Fialho de Almeida and Eça de Queirós, and the English Shakespeare and Charles Dickens. The most widely praised writers of his time seem to have been Anatole France and Rudyard Kipling.

The importance of English literature in the education of Lobato can be measured by the contrast he makes with French literature, in a letter dated 5 June 1917:

> I think reading English writers is of immense value: it frees us from having to absorb the syphilitic infection of the French: the mental pox which is draining away our letters and turning us into just a French moonshine. And apart from the English, I read Camilo; I don't spend a day without looking at some of his pages.[28]

Again, the influence of French literature on the Brazilian literary scene is regarded as a disease which is not combated by reading national authors, but only by reading English and Portuguese writers instead. At the same time, *O Saci-Pererê: resultado de um inquérito* [Saci-Pererê: aftermath of an inquiry] was the first book edited by Lobato and also the first printed in the workshop of the newspaper *O Estado de S. Paulo*. Only then did he prepare the stories that went into *Urupês*, some of them already published by *Revista do Brasil*, which came to be his first publishing house. These works offered a new formula for caring for the health of the national literature.

The Stage and the Door

Before becoming the proprietor of *Revista do Brasil*, Monteiro Lobato had been closely involved with it from the point of its founding, in 1916, and had published his writings in it from its third number onwards. The importance of the journal in the cultural setting of Brazil of the time derives, among other factors, from the group that brought about its existence: some shareholders of *O Estado de S. Paulo*, with which Lobato maintained a close relationship.

O Estado de S. Paulo was then regarded as one of the most important newspapers in the country. By 1915 it had a circulation of forty thousand copies and the number of its readers was estimated to be one hundred thousand.[29] Its director, Júlio de Mesquita (1862–1927), was 'held by his contemporaries to be dynamic, lively and capable of innovating, [...] while always being aware of the latest technology'.[30] In that decade, the paper significantly increased its technical equipment by purchasing real estate and machinery that could serve the requirements of the 'books section'. The new administrative headquarters also included a theatre-house. *O Estado de S. Paulo* was, then, much more than just a newspaper: it became a capitalist enterprise, with all the many ramifications that entailed.[31]

In the midst of these innovations, the *Revista do Brasil* took shape and was launched on 25 January 1916, symbolically the same day as the anniversary of the city of São Paulo, which then had about half a million inhabitants. In the view of Ana Luiza Martins, this launching 'ushered in a new trend for periodicals in Brazil':

> In opposition to the amateurish approach that prevailed in previous enterprises born out of the enthusiasm and idealism of the bohemian people in pastry shops at the time of the initial Republic of Letters, the launching of *Revista do Brasil* was carefully planned and had an editorial policy and guidelines that were well thought out. Finally, the enterprise envisaged carrying out *a diagnosis for the nation*.[32]

In its first number, the journal published a list of its sixty-six shareholders, who were representatives of the São Paulo elite. Some of the shareholders — like Veiga Miranda, Ricardo Gonçalves and Valdomiro Silveira — were men of letters who later had their works published by Monteiro Lobato.

Although Lobato collaborated with the newspaper, he did not take part in the enterprise, apparently because he did not have the liquid assets available to afford the 300$000 [300,000 *réis*] necessary. In spite of this, the writer believed so much in the enterprise that he insisted that Godofredo Rangel be involved in the group.[33]

In January 1915, Lobato remarked in a letter that his personal relations with *Estado* were very good indeed: he continued publishing in the paper and was invited by the Director-General Pinheiro Júnior to take part in a series of conferences of the Society of Artistic Culture. He wrote to Rangel: 'São Paulo is already something and it's worth entering the stage through this door. And we will go together.'[34] There are two important metaphors in this sentence — the stage and the door — which are employed by Lobato to refer to his desire to enter the world of letters with the help of the newspaper *O Estado de S. Paulo*. He was already part of its world, and he was publishing in other periodicals as well, but he had not yet had the visibility that he planned to get when publishing in *O Estado de S. Paulo*. The periodicals published by the *Estado* group were the ideal stage for Lobato to display his literary works due to the number of their readers and their prestige in the literary field.

The interest was reciprocated. *O Estado de S. Paulo* also wanted Lobato; he had been collaborating with that newspaper for a long time and his name was in the ascendant in the literary scene. As far as can be ascertained, his first works for newspapers were contracted translations of articles from *The Weekly Times*, published in London, back in 1908.[35] From 1913, he began to write articles for *O Estado de S. Paulo*.[36] The article 'Velha Praga', which some critics tend to link to the beginning of his career as a known writer, was published by the newspaper in November 1914.

The characters Jeca Tatu, Chico Marimbondo, and Manuel Peroba appeared for the first time in 'Velha Praga'. Those were names invented by Lobato to describe the 'caboclos' [countryside men], who would be responsible for starting fires as dangerous as the ones in Europe in World War I, according to the writer. 'Urupês', an article in which the character Jeca Tatu and the social group that he represents are scrutinized, came out in December of the same year. The articles resonated widely.[37] In the following months, Lobato's collaborations with *O Estado de S. Paulo* increased, and his bonds with Pinheiro Júnior and other journalists were strengthened.

A National Literary Project in *Saci-Pererê*

O Saci-Pererê is emblematic of the changes Monteiro Lobato had in mind for the Brazilian publishing industry. In this book, the editor recognizes the value of popular culture, especially of those elements of Indigenous or African origin.

The *Revista do Brasil* of December 1917 included in its 'New Books' section a short note with the title 'A aparecer' [Coming soon], which advertised two forthcoming books: *O Saci-Pererê*, by 'an amateur Demonologist', and *Dez mortes trágicas* [Ten tragic deaths], 'short stories by Monteiro Lobato, an edition by "Revista do Brasil"'.[38] In that month, Lobato was already living in São Paulo with his family. He had sold the farm he had inherited from his grandfather, a property which he had looked after since 1911. He was also thinking about how he was going to spend the money he had acquired, and amongst other things planned to go to Portugal — a wish that was prevented by the war.

In February 1918, the *Revista do Brasil* recorded the appearance of *O Saci-Pererê* and commented that Monteiro Lobato put together in a single volume the testimonies regarding the Brazilian goblin, the legendary one-legged black boy called 'Saci',

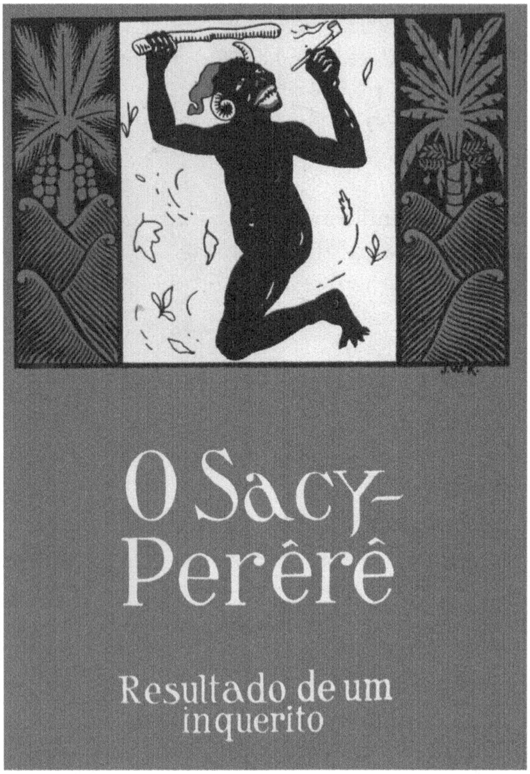

Figure 14.1. Book cover of Monteiro Lobato's *O Sacy-Pererê:* resultado de um inquérito (São Paulo: Seção de Obras d'O Estado de S. Paulo, 1917). © Monteiro Lobato's Family Archive.

which had been the subject of a survey organized by *Estadinho*, the evening edition of the newspaper *O Estado de S. Paulo*.

The testimonies of Lobato's survey on the Brazilian goblin were brought together in a book that was financed by himself and by companies that advertised on the pages of the Books Section of *O Estado de S. Paulo*. It was common for books to be published in the workshops of the newspapers, because Brazil did not have suitable printing houses to meet the demands made on the publishing industry.[39] Monteiro Lobato was the 'amateur demonologist' who signed the book:

> [...] My Saci is ready, that is, it has been constructed; it only needs to be printed. I flip through the book and then buck like a spirited donkey at the preface, the prologue, the introductory preamble, the dedication, the notes, and the epilogue; all with a good deal of rudeness and impudence. Yesterday, I wrote the epilogue and it was the most mine of all the things I've already written — and today I end it with the apology of Jeca. I'm becoming a turncoat. I'm convinced that Jeca Tatu is the only worthy thing in this country. [40]

O Saci is emblematic of the changes Monteiro Lobato had in mind for the Brazilian publishing industry. The book was the outcome of an inquiry that was published in the newspaper and which gathered immense support among the readers. In material terms, it highlights once more that the illustrated periodicals were very successful with the public because they had beautifully coloured covers, reproductions of works of art, and innovative advertisements.[41] Even more innovative was the national art project displayed by Lobato in the epilogue of the book, of which the following extract is one of its highlights:

> This book means a little more than what appears at first sight. It reveals 'where' and 'how' we should seek the means of studying and understanding ourselves. Even today we still follow the opposite path. If we want to do something new, we take steps as an inhabitant of the moon. We never look at ourselves, and all our faults are centred on this mistake. The country is split into two social sectors: a plagiaristic one and the other.
>
> The plagiaristic zone shows itself off as the civilized one because it has mounted by the seashore a mix of pillaged civilizations, and it constantly *épate* itself [...] and continues to *épater* itself by the use and abuse of ideas, alcohol, feelings, and other mixtures foisted on it by Europe in exchange for coffee, rubber, and cocoa, which the *other zone* produces. The plagiaristic zone can afford European luxuries, including the lost art of morphine addiction, pretending to be *boulevardière*. This small civilization sees itself as an exquisite whisky of refined taste; however, according to those of refined palates, it is nothing more than an insipid syrupy drink. Syrup with starch, at most. Sticky syrup ah! ah! ah![42]

This epilogue is extremely important in showing the direction of the literary and publishing career of Monteiro Lobato. He uses it to bring together and improve his ideas regarding the national culture, especially in the field of the arts; ideas which have been sketched out since the publication of his articles 'Velha Praga' and 'Urupês'.[43] According to Tadeu Chiarelli, although this text cannot be seen as a 'manifesto' in the manner that such a thing is carried out by the European vanguard, Lobato, like some European artists, 'nursed a project involving a radical aesthetical change of the Brazilian reality'.[44]

The analysis of the literary background is conducted in an inventive, good-tempered, and colloquial style that seems to foreshadow the language and style of the future modernist manifestos:

> Byron emerged in England as an Apollonian Saci. We have become Byronized on a large scale, transforming the River Tamanduateí into the Hellespont and Creole women into Lady Hamiltons and Countess Guiccíollis. Heredia came along, then came Lecomte. We acted like Heredia licentiously and we made everything like Lecomte with the same seriousness... [...] All the countries dress up as they wish — except us. We don't have enough courage to cover our heads with an embellished gourd and go to a diplomatic reception with our heads up.[45]

In his attempt to combat European trends, Lobato sought to recognize the value of popular culture, especially of those elements of Indigenous or African origin — in this way, he completed the jump announced in 1915, when he stated that he was planting both feet in the Kaffir land. He went back to writing about Jeca Tatu, a character already well-known as a result of his article 'Urupês', and turned him into a national symbol:[46]

> The truth is this: Jeca is our only statement of an individuality that is not besmirched by any kind of mockery. [...] This raises a dilemma: either to be Jeca, or sticky syrup with shots of *whisky*. Being Jeca is to take the adaptation of the individual to their environment to its final conclusion; the other option

> is to be a *cocktail*, *puzzle*, *side dish*, a sort of nationality that wears a used dress with a greasy collar.[47]

The article ends with the conclusion that being able to solve the dilemma raised here has only discouraging prospects. Throughout, the voice of Capilé — the syrup — joins the discussion and argues against the ideas defended by the author. In the end, this voice prevails for one last time:

> But Saci... he is a revealing sample, we can say, a sign that this earth has a soul. Was it worth calling him to the city? Does the city understand what this means?

She doesn't understand anything... Her eyes are bemused by all the astonishing costumes around:

> — How lovely! The collar is worn like this, just like this. Poetry, can you see? It's worn in a symbolist way. The upper part of the boots must be made of grey wool. How wonderful to have all of this psychology in the novel! Oh! *Gourmont, Gourmont*! How clearly you foresaw our modern mental attitude!
> — But, Saci...
> — Pff! Regionalism![48]

Lobato might have imagined that the readers of the book would be like Capilé in their resistance to the suggestions in the epilogue. By incorporating, in the text, the voice that he imagines for his readers, he establishes one of the guidelines of his literary project — a dialogue with the reading public. As a writer and a publisher, Lobato was always paying attention to the reception of his books by the readers, whether real or imagined. One hypothesis is that his aesthetic choices were not made as a result of a lack of cultural capital, as Sérgio Miceli argues, but by an excessive concern with entering into a dialogue with potential (or imagined) readers. This is what is indicated, for example, in a letter he sent to the Portuguese writer Ana de Castro Osório, on 14 May 1925, two months before he filed for bankruptcy on his publishing house:

> Our publishing company is at this time out of the market and only concerned with printing works that are already in the public domain, the melodramas and 'blood and thunder' plays of Escrich, Ponson, Dumas, etc., which are the only things that are read in Brazil.[49]

That figure of the reader foreshadowed in the epilogue of *O Saci*, dazzled by European literature and especially that of the nineteenth century, begins to crop up again in the comments of Monteiro Lobato, this time as a publisher on the brink of bankruptcy.[50] However, before going bankrupt, Lobato invested heavily in establishing other cultural ties, in addition to those with Europe, that were aimed at enabling Brazilians to achieve the desired understanding of themselves. These investments were carried out through *Revista do Brasil* and Monteiro Lobato & Company publishing house, as will be demonstrated below.

The World of Books According to *Revista do Brasil*

From the time when it was acquired by Lobato in 1918, the *Revista do Brasil* began to play a new role in addition to the one it already had. It advertised books from publishers throughout the country, as well as some published in other countries.[51] At the same time, it worked as a platform for discussion about the path of the Brazilian publishing industry; it opened up an important space for debating ideas related to the world of books, that is, to different aspects involved in the production and reception of books, which included the following: the conditions for writing a book — its material production, its distribution and sales; the conditions for reading books — in libraries or through private purchase; the financial situation and the degree of literacy among the reading public; cooperation or competition with other means of communication; and the reasons for consecrating literature.[52]

Very often, the purpose of the articles or critical texts that dealt, for example, with Brazilian books published overseas was to discuss the destination of the national publishing industry and to draw attention to problems faced by Brazilian publishers. An example of this was the knowledge that *O Guarani*, by José de Alencar, had been published in Portuguese in Milan in a sub-standard edition, full of errors and omissions. The writer attributed the problem to the price of national books:

> They complain that we do not have any literature. They complain that the little that we have is not known or praised as it should be. And the reasons are obvious. We do not have publishers that can place books within reach of the public, in cheap editions — that is, at a reasonable and fair price.
>
> But while the makers of books in Brazil are always falling behind, the foreign publishers advance with resolute determination in our market, selling our own books. And in what a way![53]

This piece of information provides ammunition for the campaign in favour of bringing down the price of national books, particularly by lowering taxes on imported paper. It also draws attention to the existence of a consumer market for national classics in view of the fact that the Italian edition, although full of cuts and errors, had a significant number of readers in Brazil.

This market niche would soon be exploited by Lobato, who, even in the 1920s, invested in national and foreign classics, and assumed the right to alter the original texts, by changing the vocabulary or making stylistic amendments. After this, especially during the 1930s, Lobato invested as never before in translating and adapting foreign works, many of which were in English. The lack of good foreign works translated for the Brazilian public, especially for children, was also noted by Gilberto Amado, who, in an article reproduced in *Revista do Brasil* in December 1923, outlined plans for improving the standard of Brazilian school textbooks and basically suggested that a series of titles from foreign literature and history should be translated into Portuguese, including some works by Shakespeare, Dickens, Andersen, Defoe and others.[54] Lobato noted this gap too and devoted himself to translating and adapting several British and American titles, among which were many of the works mentioned by Amado.[55]

Thus the Brazilian relationship with the European literature continued to be in

Lobato's sights as a writer and a publisher. Yet what is of great importance is the clearly expressed desire (of the publisher and of many intellectuals in his circle) for building a national publishing industry and cutting the ties of dependence, particularly on the Portuguese and French markets, which were regarded as harmful to the autonomy of Brazilian literature and its book industry.

Contemporary comments regarding the difficulties that Brazilian writers faced in getting published in Portugal are symptomatic of this. After noting the disdain from the old country for the writers of the former colony, one writer asks for the books by Brazilian authors to be sold in the Brazilian market, even when published in Portugal:

> Our Portuguese friends are intelligent enough to understand that we are not a simple colony and that we should treat each other as equals. They should cease attempting to foist those insipid novels on us, of which the writers on the other side of the Atlantic have become such masters in the *post* Eça [de Queirós] and Fialho [de Almeida] period.[56]

In a similar tone, the same 'Bibliography' section shrugs off a good part of the culture of Portugal from the beginning of the twentieth century by disparaging the dramatic poem *Jesus*, written by D. João de Castro. On this, Lobato wrote:

> He is a good Portuguese poet, but how can one put up with the poem *Jesus*? In fact, we should distance ourselves from the original pattern of the old country. None of the mystical feeling of these verses vibrates in any fibre of our being [...]. To conclude, while our soul has broken away from the soul of Portugal, our culture has followed a host of different paths, which means that this kind of art is no longer congenial to us. [57]

This contempt for Portuguese work is also reflected in the increasingly lower number of Portuguese works (and French ones) in the pages of *Revista do Brasil*. They can be found in a significant number during the first years of the journal, but they later give way to publications from other countries, particularly from Hispanic-American countries: during the year 1922, *Revista do Brasil* promoted fifteen Argentinian books and only one Portuguese.[58] This drawing together of the Brazilian and Argentinian publishing industries was encouraged by Lobato: the advertisements for Argentinian books were followed by the information that requests should be made to *Revista do Brasil* or to Monteiro Lobato & Company, which suggests that the journal and the publisher also operated as a point of sale for books published by third parties.

It is worth remembering that the representative of *Revista do Brasil* in Buenos Aires was Braulio Sánchez-Sáez, one of the most important translators of Brazilian writers, among whom Lobato himself figured. In 1922, *Revista do Brasil* published the results of an inquiry carried out by Sánchez-Sáez amongst South American writers, concerning the relationship between the Brazilian and the Hispanic-American publishing industries. The objective of the survey was 'to lay the groundwork for a larger literary exchange than that which already exists'.[59] The interviewer encouraged the drawing together of Brazilian and other South-American literatures, and, for this 'cultural crusade', he sought the involvement of South-American intellectuals. The inquiry seems to have operated as a kind of market research and showed a serious gap in the Hispanic-American publishing industry, since all the interviewees welcomed the suggested exchange. Running in parallel with the investigation, and probably resulting from it, too, was the establishment of some real kinds of exchange through the translation and publishing of South-American works. In Brazil, this initiative was taken by the publishing house Monteiro Lobato & Company, whose first volume — *Facundo* by Domingo Sarmiento — ushered in a collection called 'American Library', which would gather together other translations published by Lobato in the following years.[60]

When announcing this new venture, *Revista do Brasil* praised the role played by the translators and the publishers:

> We hope that the American Library will keep going on and will not depart from the criterion that presided over the choice of the first volume. All high-minded men are in agreement that the resentments and petty rivalries between South-American peoples result from a lack of mutual knowledge. This knowledge can only be possible and effective through the vulgarization of works of art that have a representative status — in a way, that will be the task of translators and publishers to bring about the peace and reconciliation of America. [61]

So the editorial initiative was now seen as pertaining to cultural politics. In this pacifist and diplomatic venture, the nationalism of *Revista do Brasil* and its editor developed into an Americanized discourse. In the same edition of the journal, the editorial staff also commented on the Argentinian edition of Horácio Quiroga's *Historia de un amor turbio* (1923), and complained about the fact that Quiroga was unknown in Brazil:

> What a pity for Brazil that the world is France and only France! [...] There is just a single reason that we do not know Quiroga in Brazil: he does not come from Paris, he is not called Horace Quirot....[62]

As it can be seen, the proximity to South-American literature and its publishing industry was seen not only as a marketing action, but as a movement towards Brazilian and South-American cultural independence.[63] It is known that Lobato's literary and publishing activities had consequences in Argentina, where he not only had books published and adopted by the government, but also founded the Acteon publishing house. These activities in Brazil's neighbouring country can be regarded as a development of what he had witnessed and been actively involved in when he managed *Revista do Brasil.* This investment in the South-American market is a further factor suggesting that the relationships forged by Lobato allowed him to act as an intermediary in *Revista do Brasil* and that its publishing activities were of great importance in consolidating the Brazilian (and South-American) literary scene in the 1920s. This was not only because of the success of its books, the sales of its editions, the revolutionary forms of distribution, and the contracts signed with writers. It was also due to the complexity and the extent of the networks of relationships he developed, which greatly contributed to the literary scene.

Notes to Chapter 14

1. Laurence Hallewell, *O livro no Brasil: sua história* (São Paulo: EdUSP, 2005), p. 326.
2. Monteiro Lobato, *Urupês* (São Paulo: Edição da Revista do Brasil, 1918).
3. Milena Ribeiro Martins, 'Lobato edita Lobato: história das edições dos contos lobatianos' (unpublished doctoral thesis, Campinas State University, 2003).
4. Ènio Passiani, *Na trilha do Jeca: Monteiro Lobato e a formação do campo literário no Brasil* (Bauru, SP: EdUSC, 2003), p. 61.
5. Most of these references have not yet been investigated in detail. There is already a survey of the French influence in the letters exchanged between Monteiro Lobato and his friend Godofredo Rangel over a period of forty years. See Ana Luiza Reis Bedê, *Monteiro Lobato e a presença francesa em 'A barca de Gleyre'* (São Paulo: Fapesp, Annablume, 2007).
6. Hallewell, *O livro no Brasil*, p. 263.
7. Ibid. For more information about the Brazilian book market in Portugal at the end of the nineteenth century, see Patrícia Palma's discussion in this book (Chapter 12).
8. Nelson Werneck Sodré, *História da imprensa no Brasil*, 4th edn (Rio de Janeiro: Mauad, 1999), p. 275.
9. Sodré, *História da imprensa no Brasil*, p. 292.
10. Sérgio Miceli, 'Poder, sexo e letras na República Velha (estudo clínico dos anatolianos)', in *Intelectuais à brasileira* (São Paulo: Companhia das Letras, 2001), p. 17.
11. Lobato began studying law in 1900. See *Monteiro Lobato: furacão na Botocúndia*, ed. by Carmen Lucia de Azevedo, Marcia Camargos and Vladimir Sacchetta (São Paulo: Editora Senac, 1998), p. 31.
12. The story '*D'Après Nature*' was not included by Lobato in his *Complete Works* and remained forgotten for almost a century until it was rediscovered in 1999. See Cilza Carla Bignotto, 'Personagens infantis da obra para adultos e da obra para crianças de Monteiro Lobato: convergências e divergências' (unpublished master's thesis, Universidade de Campinas, 1999), p. 79.
13. Monteiro Lobato, '*Gens ennuyeux*', in *Cidades Mortas* (São Paulo: Globo, 2007), pp. 98–105.
14. Miceli, 'Poder, sexo e letras na República Velha', pp. 58–63.
15. 'Velha Praga' [Old Plague] was a famous article published in *O Estado de S. Paulo* in 1914, and later included in *Urupês* (1918).
16. The word 'kaffir' was originally used by the Portuguese author to refer to people from the poor non-Muslim world of South-East Africa; by extension, it came to mean anybody who was black. On the pejorative way that Camilo Castelo Branco applied it to Brazilian writers, see Camilo Castelo Branco, *Polêmicas em Portugal e no Brasil*, ed. by Costa Rego (Rio de Janeiro: Dois mundos, n.d.), pp. 97–139.
17. Monteiro Lobato, *A barca de Gleyre: quarenta anos de correspondência literária entre Monteiro Lobato e Godofredo Rangel*, 2 vols (São Paulo: Brasiliense, 1948), II, 50.
18. Lobato records the incident concerning the mistake in a letter to Rangel on 3 November 1904. See *A barca de Gleyre*, I, 75.
19. In Portugal, the writer of the *feuilleton* had to produce as many chapters as he could at the start, so he could get the money for his work right away. As a result of this haste, many stories had structural problems.
20. Camilo Castelo Branco, *O bem e o mal*, 19th edn (Lisbon: Parceria A. M. Pereira, 1971), p. 3.
21. On the way Portuguese and Brazilian writers became professionals in the nineteenth century, and their relationship with newspapers and readers, see Marisa Lajolo and Regina Zilberman, *O preço da leitura* (São Paulo: Ática, 2001), pp. 122–53, and also their discussion in this book (Chapter 10).
22. *A barca de Gleyre*, II, 68. *Caboclos* are people of mixed American Indian and European ancestry. This term has many meanings in the Brazilian culture; here it also means the men of the countryside.
23. *A barca de Gleyre*, II, 68.
24. Miceli, 'Poder, sexo e letras na República Velha', p. 60.
25. Miceli, 'Poder, sexo e letras na República Velha', p. 98.

26. Miceli, 'Poder, sexo e letras na República Velha', p. 60.
27. *A barca de Gleyre*, II, 56.
28. *A barca de Gleyre*, II, 139.
29. Ana Luiza Martins, *Revistas em revista: imprensa e práticas culturais em tempos de República* (São Paulo: EdUSP; Fapesp; Imprensa Oficial do Estado, 2001), p. 67.
30. Tânia Regina de Luca, *A Revista do Brasil: um diagnóstico para a (N)ação* (São Paulo: Fundação Editora da Unesp, 1999), p. 37.
31. Tânia Regina de Luca, *A Revista do Brasil*, p. 38.
32. Ana Luiza Martins, *Revistas em revista*, p. 67.
33. *A barca de Gleyre*, II, 49.
34. *A barca de Gleyre*, II, 11.
35. Azevedo, Camargos, and Sacchetta, *Monteiro Lobato*, p. 91.
36. Azevedo, Camargos, and Sacchetta, *Monteiro Lobato*, p. 102.
37. This resonance increased with the launching of his book *Urupês*. See Marisa Lajolo, *Monteiro Lobato: um brasileiro sob medida* (São Paulo: Moderna, 2000), pp. 53–57.
38. Anon. *Revista do Brasil*, no. 24, vol. 6. São Paulo, 1917, p. 573.
39. Mário de Camargo, *Gráfica: arte e indústria no Brasil: 180 anos de história*, 2nd edn (São Paulo: EdUSC: Bandeirantes Gráfica, 2003), pp. 49–50.
40. *A barca de Gleyre*, II, 160–61.
41. On *O Saci-Pererê*, see Marisa Lajolo, 'Os anõezinhos fora de lugar', in *Projeto Monteiro Lobato (1882–1948) e outros modernismos brasileiros*, <http://www.unicamp.br/iel/monteirolobato/outros/lobatoanoezinhos.pdf> [accessed 4 February 2012].
42. In the original excerpt, Lobato created a new word from the French verb *épater* (to shock), which stressed the idea that the Brazilian bourgeoisie used to copy French habits. Monteiro Lobato, *O Saci-Pererê: resultado de um inquérito* (São Paulo: Seção de Obras d'*O Estado de S. Paulo*, 1917), pp. 282–83.
43. Monteiro Lobato had already published articles in which he defended a Brazilian art that was opposed to the imported 'isms'. One of these articles, 'Regarding Malfatti's exhibition', published in *Estadinho* on 20 December 1917, ignited the controversy with the nascent group of modernists. On the implications of this article, one of the most studied in Brazilian literature, see Passiani, *Na trilha do Jeca*, 2003.
44. Tadeu Chiarelli, *Um jeca nos vernissages* (São Paulo: EdUSP, 1995), pp. 188–89.
45. Monteiro Lobato, *O Saci-Pererê*, p. 286.
46. Lobato also wrote about Jeca in a series of articles published in *O Estado* at the beginning of 1918, which were later brought together in the book *O problema vital* (1918). The book has this epigraph: 'Jeca is not *always* like this: he is like this *now*'. The articles seek to show that the misfortunes of Jeca were the result of poverty and a lack of sanitation, among other problems.
47. Monteiro Lobato, *O Saci-Pererê*, p. 290.
48. Monteiro Lobato, *O Saci-Pererê*, p. 291.
49. The letter is reproduced in Marisa Lajolo, 'Correspondência entre Anna de Castro Osório e Monteiro Lobato', in *Projeto Monteiro Lobato (1882–1948) e outros modernismos brasileiros*, <www.unicamp.br/iel/monteirolobato/outros/AnnaOsoriodeCastro.pdf> [accessed 5 February 2012].
50. On the relationship between the editor Monteiro Lobato and the reading public, see Cilza Carla Bignotto, 'Novas perspectivas sobre as práticas editoriais de Monteiro Lobato (1918–1925)', (unpublished doctoral thesis, Campinas State University, 2007).
51. The magazine advertised and critiqued books published by Renascença Portuguesa (Porto), Aillaud & Bertrand (Lisbon), Gauthier-Villars & Cie. (Paris), Garnier (Paris and Rio de Janeiro), Editorial Cervantes (Barcelona), Editora Renacimiento (Madrid), and Cia. Editorial Limitada (Buenos Aires), among others.
52. Martins, 'Lobato edita Lobato', pp. 29–95.
53. [Monteiro Lobato] 'Um Guarany em geringonça', in *Revista do Brasil*, no. 49. São Paulo, January 1920, p. 81. The article is unsigned but was subsequently published in Monteiro Lobato, *Críticas e outras notas* (São Paulo: Brasiliense, 1965), pp. 44–46.
54. Gilberto Amado, 'Livros para crianças', in *Revista do Brasil*, no. 96. São Paulo, December 1923, pp. 366–68.

55. Cf. John Milton, 'Monteiro Lobato and translation: 'Um país se faz com homens e livros', DELTA [online] special issue 19 (2003), pp. 117–32, <http://www.scielo.br/pdf/delta/v19nspe/08.pdf > [accessed 10 January 2012].
56. Anon., 'Bibliografia', in *Revista do Brasil*, no.105. São Paulo, September 1924, pp. 55–60. (On the edition of *O vigia da casa grande*, by Mário Sette and printed at Lello & Brothers in Porto in 1924.)
57. 'Bibliografia', in *Revista do Brasil*, no. 56. São Paulo, August 1920, pp. 326–30.
58. Among the books published in Argentina, the following should be highlighted: *Anaconda* (1921) by Horacio Quiroga; *Tierra Adentro* (1922) by Victoria Gucovsky; *La tragedia de un hombre fuerte* (1922) by Manuel Galvez. The book published in Portugal is *Perpétua Metrópole* (1922) by the Brazilian Almachio Diniz (Porto: Ed. Portugal-Brasil Ltda).
59. 'Inquérito literário sul-americano', in *Revista do Brasil*, no. 91. São Paulo, July 1923, pp. 193–205.
60. Domingo Sarmiento, *Facundo*, trans. by Carlos Maul (São Paulo: Monteiro Lobato & Cia., 1923).
61. Anon., 'Bibliografia', in *Revista do Brasil*, no. 97. São Paulo, January 1924, pp. 57–69.
62. Idem.
63. For other data regarding the bilateral relationship between Brazil and Argentina, see Martins, 'Lobato edita Lobato', esp. Chapters 1 and 4, and Thaís de Mattos Albieri, 'São Paulo-Buenos Aires: a trajetória de Monteiro Lobato na Argentina' (unpublished doctoral thesis, Campinas State University, 2009).

BIBLIOGRAPHY

Abreu, Márcia, 'Os lugares dos livros: o comércio livreiro no Rio de Janeiro Joanino', in *História do livro e da leitura*, special issue of *Floema*, 5A (October 2009), 7–30

—— *Os caminhos dos livros*, Campinas: ALB/Mercado de Letras; São Paulo: FAPESP, 2003

Abreu, Martha, 'Tipografias', in *Dicionário do Brasil imperial*, ed. by Ronaldo Vainfas, Rio de Janeiro: Objetiva, 2002, pp. 697–98

Agulhon, Maurice, *La Cercle dans la France bourgeoise 1810–1848. Étude d'une mutation de sociabilité*, Paris: Armand Colin, 1977

Albieri, Thaís de Mattos, 'São Paulo-Buenos Aires: a trajetória de Monteiro Lobato na Argentina' (unpublished doctoral thesis, Campinas State University, 2009), in *Biblioteca Digital da Unicamp* <http://cutter.unicamp.br/document/?code=000772097> [accessed 25 February 2011]

Alencar, José de, *Como e porque sou romancista*, adaptação ortográfica de Carlos de Aquino Pereira, Campinas: Pontes, 1990

Algranti, Leila Mezan Algranti, 'Censura e comércio de livros no período de permanência da corte portuguesa no Rio de Janeiro (1808–1821)', *Revista Portuguesa de História*, 23.1 (1999), 631–63

—— 'Política, religião e moralidade: a censura de livros no Brasil de D. João VI (1808–1821)', in *Minorias silenciadas: história da censura no Brasil*, ed. by Maria Luiza Tucci Carneiro, São Paulo, EdUSP/Imprensa Oficial do Estado/FAPESP, 2002

Almeida, Manuel Antonio de, *Memoirs of a Militia Sergeant*, trans. by Ronald W. Sousa, New York: Oxford University Press, 2000

Amaral, Azevedo, 'Álvares de Azevedo, o único poeta romântico', *Revista Nova*, 1 (1922), 2–28

Anselmo, Artur, 'Da edição à transgressão', in *Estudos de história do livro*, Lisbon: Guimarães, 1997

Armitage, John, *History of Brazil from the Arrival of the Braganza Family in 1808, to the Abdication of Don Pedro the First in 1831*, 2 vols, London: Smith, Elder and Co., 1836

Augusti, Valéria, 'Biografias de escritores brasileiros em publicações portuguesas (1860–1890)', *Boitatá. Revista do GT de Literatura Oral e Popular da ANPOLL*, n. 7, Jan–Jun, 2009, pp. 69–80 <http://www.uel.br.> [accessed 26 September 2011)]

Azevedo, Álvares de, *Cartas de Álvares de Azevedo*, São Paulo: Academia Paulista de Letras, 1976

Azevedo, Carmen Lúcia de, Márcia Camargos and Wladimir Sacchetta, *Monteiro Lobato: furacão na Botocúndia*, São Paulo: Ed. SENAC, 1997

Azevedo, Vicente de, *A vida de Álvares de Azevedo*, São Paulo: Revista dos Tribunais, 1931

Badaró, Libero, 'Liberdade de Imprensa', *Revista do Instituto Histórico e Geográfico de São Paulo*, 28 (1930), 24–82

Balzac, Honoré de, *Œuvres*, 24 vols, Paris: Michel Lévy Frères, 1868

Baratin, Marc, and Christian Jacob (eds), *Le Pouvoir des bibliothèques. La Mémoire des livres en Occident*, Paris: Albin Michel, 1996 [Portuguese edn, *O poder das bibliotecas: a memória dos livros no Ocidente*, Rio de Janeiro: EdUFRJ, 2000]

BARBIER, FRÉDÉRIC BARBIER, 'Le Commerce international de la librairie française au XIXe siècle (1815–1913)', *Revue d'Histoire Moderne et Contemporaine*, 28 (January–March 1981), pp. 94–117

BARTHES, ROLAND, *The Fashion System*, New York: Hill and Wang, 1983

BAY, ANDRÉ, 'La Littérature enfantine', in *Histoire des littératures*, Encyclopédie de la Pléiade, Paris: Gallimard, 1967, tome III, p. 1608

BEDÊ, ANA LUIZA REIS, *Monteiro Lobato e a presença francesa em 'A barca de Gleyre'*, São Paulo: Fapesp, Annablume, 2007

BEETHAM, MARGARET, *A Magazine of Her Own?: Domesticity and Desire in the Woman's Magazine, 1800–1914*, New York: Routledge, 1996

BELDEMÓNIO, 'Os Grandes Editores: Ernesto Chardron', *O Arauto* («Semanal»), Lisbon, n.º 3, 21/Jan, 1886

BERTHIER, PATRICK, *La Presse littéraire et dramatique au début de la Monarchie de Juillet (1830–1836)*, Villeneuve-d'Ascq: Presses Universitaires du Septentrion, 2001

BERTHOLD, VICTOR M., *History of the Telephone and Telegraph in Brazil, 1851–1921*, New York: American Telephone and Telegraph Company, 1922

BESSONE, TANIA MARIA, *Palácios de destinos cruzados: bibliotecas, homens e livros no Rio de Janeiro, 1870–1920*, Rio de Janeiro: Arquivo Nacional, 1999

BIGNOTTO, CILZA CARLA, 'Personagens infantis da obra para adultos e da obra para crianças de Monteiro Lobato: convergências e divergências' (unpublished masters's thesis, Universidade de Campinas, 1999), in *Biblioteca Digital da Unicamp* <http://www.bibliotecadigital.unicamp.br/document/?code=vtls000224320> [accessed 25 February 2011]

——'Novas perspectivas sobre as práticas editoriais de Monteiro Lobato (1918–1925)' (unpublished doctoral thesis, Campinas State University, 2007), in *Biblioteca Digital da Unicamp* <http://cutter.unicamp.br/document/?code=vtls000410260> [accessed 25 February 2011]

BILAC, OLAVO, *Registro: crônicas da Belle Époque carioca*, ed. by Alvaro Santos Simões Jr, Campinas: Ed. da Unicamp, 2011

BLAKE, AUGUSTO VICTORINO ALVES SACRAMENTO, *Diccionario bibliographico brazileiro*, 7 vols, Rio de Janeiro: Typographia Nacional; Conselho Nacional de Cultura, 1970 (1st edn 1883–1902)

BOSI, ALFREDO, 'Introdução. Antônio Vieira: vida e obra. Um esboço', in Antônio Vieira, *Essencial Padre Vieira*, São Paulo: Penguin Classics, Companhia das Letras, 2011

BOYVEAU-LAFFECTEUR, *Observations sur l'histoire et les effets du rob anti-syphilitique*, Paris: Chez l'Auteur, 1810

BRAGANÇA, ANÍBAL, 'Uma introdução à História editorial brasileira', *Centro de História da Cultura*, Lisbon: Universidade Nova de Lisboa, 14 (2002), 57–83

BRANCO, CAMILO CASTELO, *Noites de insomnia offerecidas a quem não póde dormir*, Porto and Braga: Livraria Internacional de Ernesto Chardron e Eugénio Chardron, 1874, nos. 4 and 6

——*Polêmicas em Portugal e no Brasil*, ed. by Costa Rego, Rio de Janeiro: Dois mundos, n.d.

——*O bem e o mal*, 19th edn, Lisbon: Parceria A. M. Pereira, 2007

BRANTLINGER, PATRICK, *The Reading Lesson: The Threat of Mass Literacy in Nineteenth-century British Fiction*, Bloomington: Indiana University Press, 1998

BROCA, BRITO, 'O que liam os românticos', *Revista do livro*, 4 (1959), 163–72

BRUNO, SAMPAIO, *A geração nova*, Porto: Lello & Irmão, 1984

BUITONI, DULCÍLIA SCHROEDER, *Mulher de papel*, São Paulo: Edições Loyola, 1981

——*Imprensa feminina*, São Paulo: Editora Ática, 1986

BURKE, ULICK RALPH, and ROBERT STAPLES JR, *Business and Pleasure in Brazil*, London: Field and Tuer, n.d.

CABRAL, ALEXANDRE, *Obras de Alexandre Cabral: correspondência de Camilo Castelo Branco com António Feliciano de Castilho — II, Eugénio de Castilho, Júlio de Castilho*, vol. IV: Livros Horizonte, 1985

CAEIRO, F. DA GAMA, 'Livros e livreiros franceses em Lisboa, nos fins de setecentos e no primeiro quartel do século XIX', *Dispersos*, 2 vols, Lisbon: Imprensa Nacional — Casa da Moeda, 2000, pp. 133–56

CAMARGO, MÁRIO DE, *Gráfica: arte e indústria no Brasil: 180 anos de história*, 2nd edn, São Paulo: EdUSC, Bandeirantes Gráfica, 2003

CAMARGOS, MÁRCIA, *Villa Kyrial: crônica da belle époque paulistana*, São Paulo: Senac, 2001

CAMINHA, ADOLFO, *Cartas literárias*, Rio de Janeiro: n.pub., 1895

CANDEIAS, ANTÓNIO, and EDUARDO SIMÕES, 'Alfabetização e escolar em Portugal no século XX: Censos Nacionais e estudos de caso', *Análise Psicológica*, 1 (1999), 163–94

CANDIDO, ANTONIO, *Formação da literatura brasileira (momentos decisivos)*, 4th edn, 2 vols, São Paulo: Livraria Martins Editora, 1971

——*Educação pela noite e outros ensaios*, São Paulo: Ed. Ática, 1987

——*Formação da literatura brasileira: momentos decisivos*, 7th edn, 2 vols, Belo Horizonte: Itatiaia, 1993

——*Recortes*, São Paulo: Companhia das Letras, 1993

—— 'Dialectic of Malandroism', in *On Literature and Society*, trans., ed. and intro. by Howard S. Becker, Princeton, NJ: Princeton University Press, 1995

——*On Literature and Society*, trans., ed., and intro. by Howard Becker, Princeton, NJ: Princeton University Press, 1995

CASAL, MANUEL AIRES DE, *Corografia brasília ou Relação histórico-geográfica do reino do Brasil*, Rio de Janeiro: Impressão Régia, 1817

CASTRO, RENATO BERBERT DE, *A Tipografia Imperial e Nacional, da Bahia*, São Paulo: Ática, 1984

CESAR, GUILHERMINO, *História da literatura do Rio Grande do Sul*, Porto Alegre: Globo, 1956

CHAGAS, M. PINHEIRO, 'A. Gonçalves Dias', in *Ensaios críticos*, Porto: Viúva Moré — Editora, 1866 [1865], pp. 161–80. First published in the *Revista Contemporânea de Portugal e Brazil*, 5th Year Lisbon

——*A propriedade litteraria: carta a sua magestade o imperador do Brazil* Porto: Livraria Internacional de Ernesto Chardron, 1879

CHALHOUB, SIDNEY, *Trabalho, lar e botequim*, São Paulo: Brasiliense, 1986

——*Machado de Assis Historiador*, São Paulo: Companhia das Letras, 2003

——, MARGARIDA DE SOUSA NEVES and LEONARDO AFFONSO DE MIRANDA PEREIRA (eds), *História em cousas miúdas: capítulos de história social da crônica no Brasil*, Editora da Unicamp: Campinas, 2005

CHAPPLE, J. A. V., *Science and Literature in the Nineteenth Century*, London: Macmillan, 1986

CHARTIER, ROGER, *Le Livre en révolutions*. Entretiens avec Jean Lebrun, Paris: Éditions Textuel, 1970 [Portuguese edn, *A aventura do livro*, São Paulo: Ed. Unesp, 1998]

CHAVES, CLÁUDIA MARIA DAS GRAÇAS, 'O outro lado do Império: as disputas mercantis e os conflitos de jurisdição no Império Luso-Brasileiro', *TOPOI*, 7.12 (Jan–Jun 2006), 147–77

CHIARELLI, TADEU, *Um jeca nos vernissages*, São Paulo: EdUSP, 1995

CITRON, PIERRE, introduction to Honoré de Balzac, *La Comédie humaine*, 12 vols, Paris: Gallimard, 1979, v, 54–58

COELHO NETO, HENRIQUE MAXIMIANO, *A conquista*, Rio de Janeiro: Civilização Brasileira, 1985

CONCEIÇÃO, F., 'Os livros e as tarifas alfandegárias', *Revista Brasileira*. Ano I, Tomo 1, 1879, pp. 607–11

Cordeiro, Luciano, 'Factos Artisticos do Brazil', *Revista de Portugal e Brazil*, Lisbon: Empresa *Revista de Portugal e Brazil*, 7 (1874), pp. 125–26

Cristóvão, Fernando Alves, 'Presença de Fénelon no espaço literário luso-brasileiro: subsídios para um estudo', Paris: Fondation Calouste Gulbenkian, Centre Culturel Portugais, 1983, pp. 135–50

Curto, Diogo Ramada, Manuela Domingos, et al., *As gentes do livro: Lisboa século XVIII*, Lisbon: Biblioteca Nacional, 2007

d'Alcochete, Nuno Daupiás, 'Les Pamphlets portugais anti-napoléoniens', *Arquivos do Centro Cultural Português*, 11 (1977), 7–16

Damazio, Sylvia, *Retrato social do Rio de Janeiro na virada do século*, Rio de Janeiro: EdUERJ, 1996

Darnton, Robert, *The Forbidden Best-Sellers of Pre-Revolutionary France*, New York: W. W. Norton & Company, 1995

Davidson, Cathy N., 'The Life and Times of *Charlotte Temple*: The Biography of a Book', in *Reading in America*, ed. by Cathy N. Davidson, London and Baltimore, MD: Johns Hopkins University Press, 1989, pp. 157–79

Davis, Mike, *Late Victorian Holocausts: El Niño Famines and the Making of the Third World*, London and New York: Verso, 2001

Deaecto, Marisa Midori, 'Anatole Louis Garraux e o comércio de livros franceses em São Paulo (1860–1890)', *Revista Brasileira de História*, 55 (2008), <http://www.scielo.br/scielo.php?script=sci_arttext&pid=S0102–01882008000100005&lng=en&nrm=iso> [accessed 7 February 2012]

—— 'Os primórdios da imprensa paulista: Costa Carvalho e o *Farol Paulistano* (1827–1831)', *Revista de História Regional*, 12 (2008), pp. 29–50

—— *O império dos livros: instituições e práticas de leituras na São Paulo oitocentista*, São Paulo: EdUSP; Fapesp, 2011

—— and Lincoln Secco, 'A São Paulo de Libero Badaró', *Notícia Bibliográfica e Histórica* (PUCCAMP), 189 (2003), 151–78

Donegá, Ana Laura, 'Publicar ficção em meados do século XIX: um estudo das revistas femininas editadas pelos irmãos Laemmert' (unpublished MPhil dissertation, Campinas: UNICAMP, 2013)

Drabble, Margaret, *The Oxford Companion to English Literature*, 2nd edn, Oxford: Oxford University Press, 1996

Dumasy, Lise (ed.), *La Querelle du roman-feuilleton. Littérature, presse et politique, un débat précurseur (1836–1848)*, Grenoble : ELLUG, 1999

Eagleton, Terry, *Literary Theory*, Oxford: Basil Backwell Publisher, 1983

Ebel, Ernest, *Rio de Janeiro und seine Umgebungen im Jahre 1824 in Briesen eines Rigaer's*, St. Petersburg: Gedruckt bey der Kayserlichen Akademie der Wissenschaften, 1828 [Portuguese edn, *O Rio de Janeiro e seus arredores em 1824*, São Paulo: Nacional, 1972]

Edmundo, Luiz, *O Rio de Janeiro do meu tempo*, 3 vols, Rio de Janeiro: Imprensa Nacional, 1938

El Far, Alessandra, *Páginas de sensação: literatura popular e pornográfica no Rio de Janeiro (1870–1924)*, São Paulo: Companhia das Letras, 2004

Elwes, Robert, *A Sketcher's Tour Round the World*, London: Hurst and Blackett, 1854

Espagne, Michel, 'Transferts culturels et histoire du livre', in *Histoire et civilisations du livre. Revue internationale*, 5 (2009), 202–18

Falas do trono: desde o ano de 1823 até o ano de 1889, acompanhados dos respectivos votos de graça, Brasília: Instituto Nacional do Livro, 1977

Faoro, Raymundo, *O debate político no processo da independência*, Rio de Janeiro: Federal Council of Culture, 1973

Feijó, Elias J. Torres, 'Camilo Castelo Btranco', in M., *Dictionary of Literary Biography: Portuguese Writers*, ed. by Rector, Monica and Clark, Fred, Detroit, MI: Bruccoli Clark Layman, 2003, pp.58-74

Ferraro, Alceu Ravanello, 'Analfabetismo e níveis de letramento no Brasil: o que dizem os censos?', *Educ. Soc.* [online], 23.81 (2002), 21–47 <http://www.scielo.br/pdf/es/v23n81/13930.pdf> [accessed 10 July 2012]

Ferreira, A. J., 'Como Jules Vernes conquistou Portugal', *Jornal Infantil Português Ilustrado*, Jul–Nov 1994 <http://jvernept.blogspot.com> [accessed 30 September 2011]

Ferreira, Orlando da Costa, *Imagem e letra*, São Paulo: EdUSP, 1994

Ferreira, Tânia Bessone da C. Ferreira and Lúcia Maria Bastos P. das Neves, 'Livreiros franceses no Rio de Janeiro, 1808–1823', *História hoje: balanço e perspectivas*, IV Encontro Regional da ANPUH-RJ, Rio de Janeiro: Associação Nacional dos Professores Universitários de História, 1990, pp. 190–202

Fleuiss, Max, 'Subsídios para a história da imprensa no Brasil', in *Páginas de história*, 2nd edn, Rio de Janeiro: Imprensa Nacional, 1930

Flint, Kate, *The Woman Reader, 1837–1914*, Oxford: Clarendon Press, 1995

Fonseca, Guimarães, 'Luiz Guimarães', *Diario Illustrado*, Porto, 1874, n. 761, 10 Nov

Fonseca, Martinho, 'Catalogos de livreiros', *Boletim da Sociedade de Bibliophilos Barbosa Machado*, vol. II, Lisbon, 1913, pp. 89–184

Freyre, Gilberto, *Um engenheiro francês no Brasil*, 2nd edn, 2 vols, Rio de Janeiro: José Olympio, 1960 [1st edn, 1940]

—— *Ingleses no Brasil: aspectos da influência britânica sobre a vida, a paisagem e a cultura do Brasil*, 3rd edn, Rio de Janeiro: Topbooks, 2000

Gallo, Ivone, 'O Brasil e o socialismo do século XIX: fourieristas no Saí', in *Franceses no Brasil (séculos XIX–XX)*, ed. by Tania Regina de Luca and Laurent Vidal Vidal, São Paulo: Fundação Editora Unesp, 2009, pp. 147–60

Garrett, Almeida, 'Bosquejo da história da poesia e lingua portugueza', in *ParnasoLusitano ou poesias selectas dos autores portuguezes antigos e modernos, ilustradas com notas*, Paris: J. P. Aillaud, 1826, pp. VII–LXVII <http://purl.pt/25> [accessed 30 July 2014]

Gay, Peter, *The Cultivation of Hatred*, New York: W. W. Norton, 1993 [Portuguese edn, *A cultura do ódio*, São Paulo: Companhia das Letras, 1995]

—— *The Naked Heart*, New York: W. W. Norton, 1995 [Portuguese edn, *O coração desvelado*, São Paulo: Companhia das Letras, 1999]

Gledson, John (ed.), *Conversa de burros, banhos de mar e outras crônicas exemplares*, Curso Breve de Literatura Brasileira, 14, Lisbon: Editora Cotovia, 2006

Gonçalves, Adelaide, 'Comunidades utópicas e os primeiros sinais de socialismo no Brasil', *E-topia: Revista Eletrônica de Estudos sobre a Utopia*, 2 (2004) <http://ler.letras.up.pt/uploads/ficheiros/artigo10561.pdf> [accessed 30 July 2014]

Goulemot, Jean-Marie, *Pratiques de la lecture*, ed. by Roger Chartier, Paris: Payot & Rivages 1993 [Portuguese edn, *Práticas da leitura*, São Paulo: Estação Liberdade, 1996]

—— *Ces livres qu'on ne lit que d'une main*, Paris: Minerve, 1994.

Graham, Richard, *Britain & the Onset of Modernization in Brazil, 1850–1914*, Cambridge: Cambridge University Press, 1972

——'Clientelismo na cultura política brasileira: toma lá dá cá', Braudel Center Papers, 15 (1997) <http://pt.braudel.org.br/publicacoes/braudel-papers/downloads/portugues/bp15_pt.pdf> [accessed 28 March 2014]

Granja, Lucia, 'Antes do livro, o jornal: *Conto Alexandrino*', *Luso-Brazilian Review*, 46 (2009), 106–14

Guedes, Fernando, *O livro e a leitura em Portugal: subsídios para a sua história, séculos XVIII e XIX*, Lisbon and São Paulo: Editorial Verbo, 1987

—— *Os livreiros franceses em Portugal no século XVIII: tentativa de compreensão de um fenómeno migratório e mais alguma história*, Lisbon: Academia Portuguesa da História, 1998

Guerra, F.-X., Annick Lempérière et al., *Los espacios públicos en Iberoamérica: ambigüedades y problemas. Siglo XVIII–XIX*, Mexico: Fondo de Cultura Económico, 1998

Guizot, F., *A democracia na França*, trans. by ***, Paris: Typ. de E. Thurnot et Cie., 1849

Habermas, Jürgen *The Structural Transformation of the Public Sphere: An Inquiry into a Category of Bourgeois Society*, Cambridge, MA: MIT Press, 1989

——*L'Espace public. Archéologie de la publicité comme dimension constitutive de la société bourgeoise*, trans. by Marc B. de Launay, Paris: Payot, 2008

Hall, David D., *Cultures of Print*, Amherst: University of Massachusetts Press, 1996

Hallewell, Laurence, *Books in Brazil*, London and Metuchen, NJ: The Scarecrow Press, 1982 [Portuguese editions: *O livro no Brasil: sua história*, São Paulo: T. A. Queiroz/ EdUSP, 1985, and *O livro no Brasil: sua história*, trad. by Maria da Penha Villalobos, Lólio Lourenço de Oliveira and Geraldo Gerson de Souza, 2nd edn, São Paulo: Editora da Universidade de São Paulo, 2005]

Heaton, Herbert, 'A Merchant Adventurer in Brazil 1808–1818', *The Journal of Economic History*, 6.1 (May 1946), pp. 1–23

Herculano, Alexandre, 'Da propriedade literária e da recente convenção com a França', in *Garrett, Herculano e a propriedade literária*, ed. by Luiz Francisco Rebello, Lisbon: Publicações Dom Quixote; Sociedade Portuguesa de Autores, 1999

——'Futuro literário de Portugal e do Brazil: por occasião da leitura dos *Primeiros Cantos: Poezias* do Sr A. Gonçalves Dias', in *Cantos: Collecção de Poezias*, ed. by A. Gonçalves Dias, 2nd edn, Leipzig: F. A. Brockhaus, 1857 [1847/48], pp. VIII–XVIII. Article first published in the *Revista Universal Lisbonense* Volume 7, page 5

Hill, Christopher, *The World Turned Upside Down*, London: Penguin, 1991

Historia Completa da Revolução Franceza desde 1789 a 1815 e precedido por um resumo da Historia da França por um brazileiro, Rio de Janeiro: Laemmert, 1877

Hohenberg, John, *Foreign Correspondence: The Great Reporters and their Times*, New York: Columbia University Press, 1965

Hohlfeldt, Antonio, *Deus escreve direito por linhas tortas: o romance-folhetim dos jornais de Porto Alegre entre 1850 e 1900*, Porto Alegre: EdiPUCRS, 2003

Ipanema, Marcello, and Cybelle de Ipanema, *Silva Porto: livreiro na Corte de D. João — Editor da Independência*, Rio de Janeiro: Capivara, 2007

——'Imprensa na Regência: observações estatísticas e de opinião pública', *Revista do Instituto Histórico e Geográfico Brasileiro*, 307 (April–June 1975), 91–95

——'Subsídios para a história das livrarias', *Revista do Livro*, 11[32] (1968), 23–31

Irineu Evangelista de Sousa, Visconde de Mauá, *Autobiografia*, Rio de Janeiro: Zélio Valverde Ed., 1942

Jacob, Christian , 'Préface', Marc Baratin & Christian Jacob, *Le pouvoir des bibliothèques. La mémoire des livres en Occident*, Paris: Albin Michel, 1996

Jelavich, Charles, and Barbara Jelavich, *The Establishment of the Balkan National States, 1804–1920*, Seattle: University of Washington Press, 1977

Johnson, Barbara, *A World of Difference*, Baltimore, NJ: Johns Hopkins University Press, 1987

Jones, Kathleen, *La Revue Britannique, son histoire et son action littéraire (1825–1840)*, Paris: Librairie E. Droz, 1939

Kawamura, Yuniya, *Fashion-ology*, Oxford: Berg Publishers, 2004,

——*The Japanese Revolution in Paris Fashion*, Oxford: Berg Publishers, 2006

Kidder, Daniel Parish, and James C. Fletcher, *Brazil and the Brazilians Portrayed in Historical and Descriptive Sketches*, Philadelphia, Childs & Peterson; New York, Sheldon, Blakeman & Co., 1857 [Portuguese edn, *O Brasil e os brasileiros*, São Paulo: Nacional, 1941]

Klancher, Jon P., *The Making of English Reading Audiences, 1790–1832*, Madison: Wisconsin University Press, 1985

Koselleck, R., *Futures Past: On the Semantics of Historical Time*, Cambridge, MA: MIT Press, 1985

Kury, Lorelai (ed.), *Iluminismo e Império no Brasil: O Patriota (1813–1814)*, Rio de Janeiro: Fiocruz, 2007

LaCapra, Dominick, 'History and Novel', *History and Criticism*, Ithaca, NY: Cornell University Press, 1985

Laffont-Bompiani, *Dictionnaire des Œuvres de tous les temps et tous les pays*, 4th edn, Paris: Société d'Édition de Dictionnaires et Encyclopédies, 1962

Lajolo, Marisa, *Monteiro Lobato: um brasileiro sob medida*, São Paulo: Moderna, 2000

——'Correspondência entre Anna de Castro Osório e Monteiro Lobato', in *Projeto Monteiro Lobato (1882–1948) e outros modernismos brasileiros*, 2003, <www.unicamp.br/iel/monteirolobato/outros/AnnaOsoriodeCastro.pdf> [accessed 5 February 2012]

——'Os anõezinhos fora de lugar', in *Projeto Monteiro Lobato (1882–1948) e outros modernismos brasileiros*, 2003, in <http://www.unicamp.br/iel/monteirolobato/outros/lobatoanoezinhos.pdf> [accessed 4 February 2012]

——'Projeto temático: Monteiro Lobato (1882–1948) e outros modernismos brasileiros', 2003, in <http://www.unicamp.br/iel/monteirolobato/home.htm> [accessed 16 March 2011]

——and Regina Zilberman, *A formação da leitura no Brasil*, São Paulo: Ática, 1996

——and Regina Zilberman, *A leitura rarefeita*, São Paulo: Ática, 2002

——and Regina Zilberman, *Literatura infantil brasileira: história & histórias*, São Paulo: Ática, 1985

——and Regina Zilberman, *O preço da leitura: leis e números por detrás das letras*, São Paulo: Ática, 2001

——and Regina Zilberman, *Um Brasil para crianças: para conhecer a literatura infantil brasileira: histórias autores e textos*, São Paulo: Global Editora, 1986

Larousse, Pierre, *Grand Dictionnaire Universel du XIXè Siècle. Français, Historique, Géographique, Mythologique, Bibliographique, Littéraire, Artistique, Scientifique etc.*, Geneva and Paris: Slatkine, 1982 (reprint of Paris edn of 1866–1879)

Latournerie, Anne, 'Petite histoire des batailles du droit d'auteur', *Multitudes. Revue politique artistique philosophique*, <http://multitudes.samizdat.net/article.php3?id_article=168> [accessed 25 November 2011]

Leef, Nathaniel H., *Subdesenvolvimento e desenvolvimento no Brasil: estrutura e mudança econômica, 1822–1947*, Rio de Janeiro: Expressão e Cultura, 1991

Lefébure, Antoine, *Havas. Les Arcanes du pouvoir*, Paris: B. Grasset, 1992

Leithold, Theodor von, and Ludwig von Rango, *O Rio de Janeiro visto por dois prussianos em 1819*, ed. and trans. by Joaquim de Sousa Leão Filho, São Paulo: Companhia Editora Nacional, 1966

Leonard, Irving A., *Books of the Brave: Being an Account of Books and of Men in the Spanish Conquest and Settlement of the Sixteenth-Century New World*, Berkeley, Los Angeles, Oxford: University of California Press, 1992

Lima, José Ignacio de Abreu, *Socialismo*, Recife: Typographia Universal, 1855

Lima, Magalhães, *Commercio e industria, sciencias, artes e lettras, galeria biographico-Contemporanea*, Lisbon, 1881, n. 8, 4 pp

Lisboa, Eugénio, *Dicionário cronológico de autores portugueses*, Mem Martins: Europa-América, 1990

Lisboa, João Francisco, 'Manuel Odorico Mendes', *Revista Contemporanea de Portugal e Brazil*, 4th year, Lisbon: Typ. Franco-Portugueza, 1862, pp. 329–53

Lobato, Gervásio, 'Lyrica: Sonetos e Rimas de Luiz Guimarães Júnior', *Bibliographia de Portugal e Brazil*, 5 (29 Oct 1881), pp. 39–41

Lobato, Monteiro, *O saci-pererê: resultado de um inquérito*, São Paulo: Seção de Obras d'O *Estado de S. Paulo*, 1917

——*O problema vital*, São Paulo: Edição da *Revista do Brasil*, 1918

——*Urupês*, São Paulo: Edição da *Revista do Brasil*, 1918
——*A barca de Gleyre: quarenta anos de correspondência literária entre Monteiro Lobato e Godofredo Rangel*, 2 vols, São Paulo: Brasiliense, 1948
——*Críticas e outras notas*, São Paulo: Brasiliense, 1965
——*Cidades Mortas*, São Paulo: Globo, 2007
LOPES, HÉLIO, *A divisão das águas: contribuição ao estudo das revistas românticas 'Minerva Brasiliense' (1843–1845) e 'Guanabara' (1849–1856)*, São Paulo: Conselho Estadual de Artes e Ciências Humanas, 1978
LUCA, TÂNIA REGINA DE, *A Revista do Brasil: um diagnóstico para a (N)ação*, São Paulo: Fundação Editora da Unesp, 1999
LYONS, MARTYN, *Histoire de la lecture dans le monde occidental*, ed. by Guglielmo Cavallo and Roger Chartier, Paris: Éditions du Seuil, 1997 [Portuguese edn, *História da leitura no mundo ocidental*, 2 vols, São Paulo: Ática, 1999]
MACEDO, JOAQUIM MANUEL DE, *Memórias da Rua do Ouvidor: publicações em folhetins do 'Jornal do Commercio'*, Rio de Janeiro: Tipografia Perseverança, 1878
MACHADO DE ASSIS, *Chronicas*, Rio de Janeiro: W. C. Jackson, 1958
——*Obra completa*, Rio de Janeiro: Aguilar, 1958
——*Crônicas*, São Paulo: Mérito, 1959
——*A Semana*, São Paulo: Mérito, 1959
——*Obra completa*, 4 vols, Rio de Janeiro: Nova Aguilar, 1986
——*Bons Dias!: crônicas (1888–1889)*, intro. and notes by John Gledson, São Paulo: Editora Hucitec/Editora Unicamp, 1990
——*A Semana*, intro. and notes by John Gledson, São Paulo: Editora Hucitec, 1996
——*Dom Casmurro*, trans. by John Gledson, Oxford: Oxford University Press, 1997
——*Correspondência (1860–1869)*, ed. by Sergio Paulo Rouanet, notes by Irene Moutinho and Silvia Eleutério, Academia Brasileira de Letras: Rio de Janeiro, 2008
——*Notas Semanais*, ed. by John Gledson and Lúcia Granja, Campinas: Editora da Unicamp, 2008
——*Epitaph of a Small Winner*, trans. by William L. Grossman, New York: Farrar, Straus and Giroux, 2009
——*História de quinze dias*, ed. by Leonardo Affonso de Miranda Pereira, Campinas: Editora da Unicamp, 2009
MAGALHÃES JÚNIOR, RAIMUNDO, *O império em chinelos*, Rio de Janeiro: Civilização Brasileira, 1957
——*Arthur Azevedo e sua época*, 3rd edn, Rio de Janeiro: Civilização Brasileira, 1966
——*Machado de Assis: vida e obra*, 4 vols, Rio de Janeiro: Editora Record, 2008
MAGALHÃES, JOAQUIM ROMERO, *Os brasileiros de torna-viagem no noroeste de Portugal*, Lisbon: Comissão Nacional para as Comemorações dos Descobrimentos Portugueses, 2000
MALERBA, JURANDIR, *A corte no exílio: civilização e poder no Brasil às vésperas da Independência (1808 a 1821)*, São Paulo: Companhia das Letras, 2000
MALLARMÉ, *Selected Prose Poems, Essays and Letters*, trans., with intro. by Bradford Cook, Baltimore, MD: Johns Hopkins University Press, 1956
MARROCOS, LUÍS JOAQUIM DOS SANTOS, *Cartas do Rio de Janeiro, 1811–1821*, Lisbon: Biblioteca Nacional de Portugal, 2008
MARTINS, ANA LUIZA, 'As Leituras às Vésperas da República', in Suplemento de Cultura, *O Estado de São Paulo* 7 (no. 486), 18 November 1989, pp. 4–6
——*Gabinetes de leitura da província de São Paulo: a pluralidade de um espaço esquecido (1847–1890)*, São Paulo: FFLCH/USP, 1990
——*Revistas em revista: imprensa e práticas culturais em tempos de República*, São Paulo: EdUSP; Fapesp; Imprensa Oficial do Estado, 2001
MARTINS, MILENA RIBEIRO, 'Lobato edita Lobato: história das edições dos contos lobatianos' (unpublished doctoral thesis, Campinas State University, 2003), in *Biblioteca*

Digital da Unicamp <http://cutter.unicamp.br/document/?code=vtls000301166> [accessed 25 January 2012]

MARTINS, OLIVEIRA, *Portugal contemporâneo*, Lisbon: Guimarães Editores, 1952

MARTINS, WILSON, *A idéia modernista*, Rio de Janeiro: Academia Brasileira de Letras; Topbooks, 2002

MASSEAU, DIDIER, *L'Invention de l'intellectuel dans l'Europe du XVIII siècle*, Paris: PUF, 1994

MATHIEZ, *História da Revolução Francesa*, São Paulo: Atena, n.d.

MATTELART, ARMAND, *Networking the World, 1794–2000*, Minneapolis: University of Minnesota Press, 2000

MATTOS, ILMAR ROHLOFF DE, *O tempo saquarema: a formação do estado imperial*, 5th edn, São Paulo: Hucitec, 2004

MAY, GEORGES, *Le Dilemme du roman du XVIIIe. siècle. Étude sur les rapports du roman et de la critique (1715–1767)*, Paris: PUF, 1963

MAYO, ROBERT D., *The English Novel in the Magazines, 1740–1815. With a Catalogue of 1375 Magazine Novels and Novelettes*, London: Oxford University Press; Evanston, IL: Northwestern University Press, 1962

MCKITTERICK, DAVID, 'La Bibliothèque comme interaction. La Lecture et le langage de la bibliographie', in *Le Pouvoir des bibliothèques. La Mémoire des livres en Occident*, sous la dir. de Marc Baratin et Christian Jacob, Paris: Albin Michel, 1996 [Portuguese edn, 'A biblioteca como interação: a leitura e a linguagem da bibliografia', in *O poder das bibliotecas: a memória dos livros no Ocidente*, ed. by Marc Baratin and Christian Jacob, Rio de Janeiro: EdUFRJ, 2000]

MEGID, DANIELE MARIA, 'A literatura na imprensa: uma análise de *Iaiá Garcia* no jornal *O Cruzeiro*', <http://www.anpuhsp.org.br/downloads/CD%20XIX/PDF/Paineis/Daniele%20Maria%20Megid.pdf> [accessed 30 July 2014]

MENEZES, D., *O Brasil no pensamento moderno*, Rio de Janeiro: INEP, 1957

MENEZES, LENÁ MEDEIROS DE, 'Francesas no Rio de Janeiro: trabalho, sonhos e ousadia (1816–1822), *Caderno Espaço Feminino*, 12.15 (Aug–Dec 2004), pp. 61–82

MEYER, AUGUSTO, *No tempo da flor*, Rio de Janeiro: O Cruzeiro, 1966

MEYER, MARLYSE, 'O que é, ou quem foi *Sinclair das Ilhas?*', *Revista do Instituto de Estudos Brasileiros*, 14 (1973), 37–63

—— *Caminhos do imaginário no Brasil*, São Paulo: EdUSP, 1993

—— *Folhetim: uma história*, São Paulo: Companhia das Letras, 1996

MICELI, SÉRGIO, 'Poder, sexo e letras na República Velha (estudo clínico dos anatolianos)', in *Intelectuais à brasileira*, São Paulo: Companhia das Letras, 2001

MILLER, RORY, *Britain and Latin America in the Nineteenth and Twentieth Centuries*, London: Longman, 1993

MILTON, JOHN, 'Monteiro Lobato and translation: "Um país se faz com homens e livros" ', *DELTA* [online], special issue 19 (2003), 117–32 , <http://www.scielo.br/pdf/delta/v19nspe/08.pdf> [accessed 10 January 2012]

MINISTÉRIO DA EDUCAÇÃO E SAÚDE, *Exposição Machado de Assis: centenário do nascimento. 1839–1939*, Rio de Janeiro: Ministério de Educação e Saúde, 1939

MOLLIER, JEAN-YVES, *L'Argent et les Lettres. Histoire du capitalisme d'édition (1880–1920)*, Paris: Fayard, 1988

——, MARTINE REID and JEAN CLAUDE YON (eds), *Repenser la Restauration*, Paris: Nouveau Monde Éditions, 2005

MONTEVERDE, JOSÉ MARTÍ, *La poética del café*, Barcelona: Anagrama, 2007

MORAES, RUBENS BORBA DE, *Livros e bibliotecas no Brasil colonial*, Rio de Janeiro: LTC, 1979

—— *O bibliófilo aprendiz*, 3rd edn, Brasília: Briquet de Lemos; Rio de Janeiro: Casa da Palavra, 1998

MOREL, MARCO, *As transformações dos Espaços Públicos. Imprensa, atores políticos e sociabilidades na cidade Imperial (1820–1840)*, São Paulo: Hucitec, 2005

MORETTI, FRANCO, *Atlas of the European Novel, 1800–1900*, London: Verso, 1998
——'Conjectures on World Literature' *New Left Review*, 1 (Jan–Feb 2000), 54–68
——'More Conjectures', *New Left Review*, 20 (Mar–April 2003), 73–81
MORRIS, R. J., 'Voluntary Societies and British Urban Elites, 1780–1850: An Analysis', *The Historical Journal* 26 (1983), 95–118
MORSE, RICHARD, *Formação histórica de São Paulo*, São Paulo: Difel, 2001
NABUCO, JOAQUIM, *Minha formação*, São Paulo: Instituto Progresso Editorial, 1947
——*A revolução estrangeira durante a Revolta de 1893*, Brasília: Edições do Senado Federal, 2003
NELBACH, ALEX, '"The Software of Empire": Telegraphic News Agencies and Imperial Publicity, 1865–1914', in *Imperial Co-Histories: National Identities and the British and Colonial Press*, ed. by Julie F. Codel, Cranbury, NJ: Associated University Presses, 2003
NERVAL, GÉRARD DE, *Voyage en Orient*, Paris: Club des libraires de France, 1955
NEVES, LÚCIA MARIA BASTOS PEREIRA DAS, 'Comércio de livros e censura de idéias: a actividade dos livreiros franceses no Brasil e a vigilância da Mesa do Desembargo do Paço (1795–1822)', *Ler História*, 23 (1992), 61–78
——'Tipografias', in *Dicionário da história da colonização portuguesa no Brasil*, ed. by M. Beatriz Nizza da Silva, Lisbon: Verbo, 1994, pp. 788–91
——*Acervo*, 8.1–2 (1995), 123–38
——'Corcundas e constitucionais: a cultura política da independência, 1820–1822', Rio de Janeiro: FAPERJ/Revan, 2003
——'Do privilégio à propriedade literária: a questão da autoria no Brasil imperial (1808–1861)', I Seminário Brasileiro sobre Livro e História Editorial, 8 a 11 de novembro de 2004, Casa de Rui Barbosa, Rio de Janeiro <http://www.livroehistoriaeditorial.pro.br/pdf/luciabastosneves.pdf> [accessed 15 December 2011]
——*Napoleão Bonaparte: imaginário e política em Portugal* (São Paulo: Alameda, 2008)
——'A missão artística francesa', <http://redememoria.bn.br/2012/01/a-missao-artistica-francesa/> [accessed 23 June 2014]
NEWLYN, LUCY, *Reading, Writing, and Romanticism: The Anxiety of Reception*, Oxford: Oxford University Press, 2003
NOVAES, F. X. DE, 'Correspondência do Brazil', *Revista Contemporanea de Portugal e Brazil*, 3rd year, Lisbon: Typ. Franco-Portugueza, 1861, pp. 320–23 and 426–29
O Império do Brazil na Exposição Universal de 1873, em Vienna d'Austria, Rio de Janeiro: Tipographia Nacional, 1873
OLIVEIRA, CARLOS EDUARDO FRANÇA DE, 'Tipógrafos, redatores e leitores: aspectos da imprensa periódica no Primeiro Reinado', *Revista Brasileira de História & Ciências Sociais*, 2.3 (July 2010) <www.rbhcs.com> [accessed 10 March 2013]
OLIVEIRA, PAULO MOTTA, 'Dumas, Hogan, Camilo: um romance mediterrânico e seus desdobramentos', in *Portogallo e Mediterraneo. Atti del Congresso Internazionale*, Naples: Il Torcoliere, 2009, pp. 193–206
——'Um sucesso quase mundial: *A mão do finado* ou as metamorfoses de um conde', in *Veredas*, 13 (2010), 7–24
——'Alexandre Herculano', in M., *Dictionary of Literary Biography: Portuguese Writers*, ed. by Rector, Monica and Clark, Fred, Detroit, MI: Bruccoli Clark Layman, 2003, pp.133–42
ORTIGÃO, RAMALHO, 'Ernesto Chardron', in *As Farpas: o país e a sociedade portuguesa*, Volume III, Lisbon: Livraria Clássica Editora, 1943, pp. 139–43
PARENT-LARDEUR, FRANÇOISE, *Lire à Paris au temps de Balzac. Les Cabinets de lecture à Paris, 1815–1830*, 2nd edn, Paris: Éditions de l'École des Hautes Études en Sciences Sociales, 1999
PASSIANI, ÊNIO, *Na trilha do Jeca: Monteiro Lobato e a formação do campo literário no Brasil*, Bauru, SP: EdUSC, 2003
PELOGGIO, MARCELO, 'Santiago Nunes Ribeiro e José de Alencar: filhos presentes da literatura brasileira', *Revista dos Encontros Literários Moreira Campos*, 1 (Apr–Jul, 2008), pp. 1–10 <http://encontrosliterarios.ufc.br.> [accessed 26 September 2011]

PERROT, VÉRONIQUE, 'Le Cercle de la *Revue Britannique* (1825–1901). Histoire d'une revue', 2 vols (unpublished doctoral thesis, Université de Picardie Jules Verne, Faculté des Lettres, 2002)

PIMENTEL, ALBERTO DE, 'O editor Chardron', in *Atravez do Passado*, Paris and Lisbon: Guillard Aillaud & C., [1888], pp. 32–40

PINASSI, MARIA ORLANDA, *Três devotos, uma fé, nenhum milagre: Nitheroy, revista brasiliense de ciências e artes*, São Paulo: Fundação Editora da UNESP, 1998

PINSON, GUILLAUME, *Fiction du monde. De la presse mondaine à Marcel Proust*, Montreal; Presses Universitaires de Montréal, 2009

PIRES DE ALMEIDA, JOSÉ RICARDO, *Higiene moral — homossexualismo — a libertinagem no Rio de Janeiro*, Rio de Janeiro: Laemmert, 1906

POCOCK, J. G. A., *Virtue, Commerce, and History*, Cambridge: Cambridge University Press, 1988

PRADO JR., CAIO, *Evolução política do Brasil e outros estudos*, 3rd edn, São Paulo: Brasiliense, 1961

PRADO, DÉCIO DE ALMEIDA, *História concisa do teatro brasileiro*, São Paulo: EdUSP, 2003

QUADROS, JUSSARA MENDES, 'Estereotipias: literatura e edição no Brasil da primeira metade do século XIX, 1837–1864', unpublished doctoral thesis, Campinas, Unicamp, 1993

RABELO, LAURINDO, *Obras poéticas*, Rio de Janeiro: Garnier, 1876

RAINHO, MARIA DO CARMO TEIXEIRA, *A cidade e a moda: novas pretensoẽs, novas distinções: Rio de Janeiro, século XIX*, Brasília: Editora UNB, 2002

RAMA, ANGEL, *The Lettered City*, trans. by John Charles Chasteen, Durham, NC: Duke University Press, 2006

RAMICELLI, MARIA EULÁLIA, *Narrativas itinerantes: aspectos franco-britânicos da ficção brasileira, em periódicos da primeira metade do século XIX*, Santa Maria: EdUFSM, 2009

RAMOS, JULIO, *Divergent Modernities: Culture and Politics in Nineteenth-Century Latin America*, trans. by John D. Blanco, Durham, NC: Duke University Press Books, 2001

REBELLO, LUIZ FRANCISCO, 'Alfredo Hogan', in Dicionário do Romantismo literário português, ed. by Buescu, Helena Carvalhão, Lisbon: Carninho, 1997, p. 233

READ, DONALD, *The Power of News: The History of Reuters, 1849–1989*, Oxford: Oxford University Press, 2000

REID, JAMES J., *Crisis of the Ottoman Empire: Prelude to Collapse, 1839–1878*, Steiner: Stuttgart, 2000

REISEWITZ, MARIANNE, 'Dom Fernando José de Portugal e Castro: prática ilustrada metropolitana na colônia (1788–1801)', unpublished Master's dissertation, FFLCH, USP, 2001

RENOUARD, AUGUSTIN-CHARLES, *Traité des droits d'auteurs dans la littérature, les sciences et les beaux-arts*, Paris: Jules Renouard & Cia., 1838

RIBEIRO, JOSÉ SILVESTRE, 'O *Resumo de Historia Litteraria* do Conego Doutor Joaquim Caetano Fernandes Pinheiro', *Revista de Portugal e Brazil*, Lisbon: Empresa *Revista de Portugal e Brazil*, 1874, pp. 206–08

RIBEIRO, JÚLIO, *Flesh*, trans. by William Barne, MHRA New Translations, 2, London: Modern Humanities Research Association, 2011

RIBEIRO, MARIA APARECIDA, *Literatura Brasileira*, Lisbon: Universidade Aberta, 1994

RIO, JOÃO DO, *A alma encantadora das ruas*, Rio de Janeiro: Secretaria de Cultura do Rio de Janeiro, 1991 [1st edn 1908]

RIOS FILHO, ADOLFO MORALES DE LOS, *O Rio de Janeiro Imperial*, 2nd edn, Rio de Janeiro: Topbooks and UniverCidade Editora, 2000

RIZZINI, CARLOS, *Hipólito da Costa e o Correio Brasiliense*, São Paulo: Nacional, 1957

RODARTE, MARIO MARCOS SAMPAIO, and JOSÉ MARIA DOS SANTOS JÚNIOR, 'A estrutura ocupacional revisitada: uma proposta de correção dos dados do Recenseamento Geral do Império de 1872', XVI Encontro Nacional de Estudos Populacionais, Caxambu, MG, Brazil, 29 September–3 October 2008 <http://www.abep.nepo.unicamp.br/encontro2008/docsPDF/ABEP2008_1854.pdf> [accessed 10 July 2012]

RODRIGUES, A. GONÇALVES, *A novelística estrangeira em versão portuguesa no período pré-romântico*, Coimbra: n.pub., 1951
——*A tradução em Portugal*, Lisbon: Imprensa Nacional–Casa da Moeda, 1992, vol. 1: *1495–1834*
——*A tradução em Portugal*, Lisbon: ISLA, 2003
ROSSINI, GABRIEL ALMEIDA ANTUNES, 'As pragmáticas portuguesas de fins do século XVII: política fabril e manufatureira reativa', *Saeculum. Revista de História* 22 (Jan– Jun 2010), 117–35
SAINTE-BEUVE, CHARLES-AUGUSTIN, 'Des jugements sur notre littérature contemporaine à l'étranger', *Revue des Deux Mondes*, 15 June 1836, pp. 749–56
SAINT-HILAIRE, AUGUSTE DE, *Viagem à província de São Paulo e resumo das viagens ao Brasil, província Cisplatina e missões do Paraguai*, trans. by Rubens Borba de Moraes, 2nd edn, São Paulo: Martins, 1945
SALLES, DAVID (ed.), *Primeiras manifestações da ficção na Bahia*, ed. by David Salles, São Paulo: Cultrix-INL-MEC, 1979
SARAIVA, ANTÓNIO JOSÉ, and ÓSCAR LOPES (eds), *História da Literatura Portuguesa*, Porto: Porto Editora, 1982
SARAIVA, ARNALDO, 'A causa da literatura brasileira em Portugal', *Revista do Centro de Estudos Brasileiros*, Porto: Universidade do Porto — Faculdade de Letras/Centro de Estudos Brasileiros, 2002, pp. 7–14 <http://ler.letras.up.pt> [accessed 1 December 2010]
SCHAPOCHNIK, NELSON, 'Contextos de leitura no Rio de Janeiro do século XIX: salões, gabinetes literários e bibliotecas', in *Imagens da cidade, séculos XIX e XX*, ed. by Stella Bresciani, São Paulo: ANPUH-SP/Marco Zero/FAPESP, 1994, pp. 147–62
——'Os jardins das delícias: gabinetes literários, bibliotecas e figurações da leitura na corte imperial', unpublished doctoral thesis, Universidade de São Paulo, 1999
SCHWARZ, ROBERTO, *Misplaced Ideas: Essays on Brazilian Culture*, trans. by John Gledson, London, Verso, 1992
——*A Master on the Periphery of Capitalism: Machado de Assis*, trans., with intro., by John Gledson, Durham, NC: Duke University Press, 2001
SERRÃO, JOEL, *Liberalismo, socialismo, republicanismo*, 2nd edn, Lisbon: Livros Horizonte, 1979
SEVCENKO, NICOLAU, *A corrida para o século XXI: no loop da montanha-russa*, São Paulo: Companhia das Letras, 2001
SILVA, ANA CLÁUDIA SURIANI DA, *Machado de Assis's 'Philosopher or Dog'? From Serial to Book Form*, Oxford: Legenda, 2010
SILVA, ANTONIO DE MORAES, *Diccionario da lingua portuguesa*, 2nd edn, Lisbon: Tip. de M. P. de Lacerdina, 1813 (facsimile: Rio de Janeiro, 1922)
SILVA, CAMILA BORGES DA, *O símbolo indumentário: distinção e prestígio no Rio de Janeiro (1808–1821)*, Rio de Janeiro: Arquivo Geral da Cidade do Rio de Janeiro, 2010
SILVA, INNOCENCIO FRANCISCO DA, *Diccionario Bibliographico Portuguez*, Lisbon: Imprensa Nacional, 1858, 1861, 1867, 1870, 1923
——'Domingos José Gonçalves de Magalhães', *Revista Contemporanea de Portugal e Brazil*, 5 (1865), pp. 285–301
——'Apontamentos para a vida e trágica morte do insigne poeta brasileiro António Gonçalves Dias', *Archivo Pittoresco* («Semanário Illustrado»), vol. x, Lisbon: Castro Irmão & C.ª, Editores Proprietários, 1867, pp. 206–08, 230–31, 243–44, 377–79, 293–94
SILVA, J. M. PEREIRA DA, *História da fundação do império brasileiro*, Paris: Garnier, 1865
SILVA, MARIA BEATRIZ NIZZA DA, 'Livro e sociedade no Rio de Janeiro (1808–1821)', *Revista de História*, 46.94 (April–June, 1973), 441–57
——*Cultura no Brasil colônia*, Petrópolis: Vozes, 1981
——*Movimento constitucional e separatismo no Brasil, 1821–1823*, Lisbon: Livros Horizonte, 1988

——*A Gazeta do Rio de Janeiro (1808–1822): cultura e sociedade*, Rio de Janeiro: EdUERJ, 2007
Silva, Nicoláo Duarte e, *Libero Badaró (1830–1930)*, São Paulo: Edição do Autor, 1931
Sobreira, Luís, 'Uma imagem do campo literário português no período Romântico: contributo para a história da literatura produzida em Portugal entre 1840 e 1860', unpublished master's thesis, Faculty of Arts, University of Lisbon, 1998
Sobrinho, Barbosa Lima (ed.), *Os precursores do conto no Brasil*, Rio de Janeiro: Editora Civilização Brasileira, 1960
Sodré, Nelson Werneck, *História da imprensa no Brasil*, Rio de Janeiro: Civilização Brasileira, 1966
Sousa, José Martínez de, *Pequeña historia del libro*, 3rd edn, Gijón: Trea, 1999
Sousa, Octávio Tarquínio de, *Evaristo da Veiga*, Belo Horizonte: Itatiaia; São Paulo: Editora da Universidade de São Paulo, 1988
——*Fatos e personagens em torno de um regime*, Belo Horizonte: Itatiaia; São Paulo: EDUSP, 1988
Souza, Gilda de Mello e, *O espírito das roupas: a moda no século XIX*, São Paulo: Companhia das Letras, 1987
Spix, Johann Baptiste von, and, Karl Friedrich Philipp von Martius, *Viagem pelo Brasil (1817–1820)*, pref. Mário Guimarães Ferri, trans. by Lúcia Furquim Lahmeyer, notes by Basílio de Magalhães, 3 vols, São Paulo: EdUSP, 1981
Stendhal, *Le Rouge et le Noir*, ed. by Henri Martineau, Paris: Garnier, 1950
Steward, C. S., *A Visit to the South Seas, including Notices of Brazil, Peru, Manilla, the Cape of Good Hope and St. Helena*, New York: John P. Haven, 1833
Streeter, Harold, *The Eighteenth-century English Novel in French Translation: A Bibliographical Study*, New York: Institute of French Studies, 1963
Subercaseux, Bernardo, *Historia del libro en Chile (Alma y Cuerpo)*, Santiago: Editorial LOM, 2000
Tavares, J. N., *Marx, o socialismo e o Brasil*, Rio de Janeiro: Civilização Brasileira, 1983
Teixeira, Ivan, *Mecenato pombalino*, São Paulo: FAPESP/EdUSP, 1999
——*O altar & o trono: a dinâmica do poder em 'O alienista'*, São Paulo: Ateliê, 2010
Teixeira, Múcio, *Os gaúchos*, 2nd edn, 2 vols, Rio de Janeiro: Leite Ribeiro & Maurillo, 1921
Thérenty, Marie-Eve, *La Littérature au quotidien. Poétiques journalistiques au XIXe siècle*, Paris: Seuil, 2007
——and Alain Vaillant (eds), *1836, l'an I de l'ère médiatique. Analyse littéraire et historique de 'La Presse' d'Émile de Girardin*, Paris: Nouveau Monde, 2001
Tocqueville, Alexis de, *L'Ancien Régime et la Révolution*, Paris: Calmann-Lévy, 1856
——*Souvenirs*, Paris: Gallimard, 2004
Todd, Janet (ed.), *Dictionary of British Women Writers*, London: Routledge, 1991
Trilling, Lionel, *The Liberal Imagination*, New York: New York Review Books, 2008 [Portuguese edn, *Literatura e sociedade*, Rio de Janeiro: Lidador, 1965]
Varela, L. N. Fagundes, *Obras completas*, Rio de Janeiro: Garnier, 1892
Vasconcelos, Sandra Guardini T., 'Caminhos do romance inglês no Brasil do século XIX', in, and *Cultura letrada no Brasil: objetos e práticas*, ed. by Márcia Abreu and Nelson Schapochnik, Campinas: Mercado de Letras, 2005
Veloso, Rodrigo (ed.), 'Aviso do editor', in Domingos José Gonçalves Magalhães, *Confederação dos Tamoyos: poema por Domingos José Gonçalves de Magalhães*, Coimbra: Imp. Litteraria, 1864
Venturi, Franco, *Utopia e reforma no Iluminismo*, trans. by Modesto Florenzano, São Paulo: EdUSC, 2003 (English edition: Franco Venturi, *Utopia and Reform in the Enlightenment*, Cambridge: Cambridge University Press, 1971)
Vianna, Pedro Ribeiro, *Elzira, a morta virgem*, Rio de Janeiro: Quaresma & Editores, 1913
Villalta, Luiz Carlos, 'O que se fala e o que se lê: língua, instrução e leitura', in *História*

da vida privada no Brasil, ed. by Laura de Mello e Souza, 3 vols, São Paulo: Companhia das Letras, 1997, I, 331–85

——'Bibliothèques privées et pratiques de lecture au Brésil colonial', in *Naissance du Brésil moderne (1500–1808)*, ed. by K. M. de Queirós Mattoso et al., Paris: Presses de l'Université de Paris-Sorbonne, 1998, pp. 319–36

VIVEIROS DE CASTRO, FRANCISCO, *Atentados ao pudor: estudos sobre as aberrações do instinto sexual*, Rio de Janeiro: Livraria Moderna, 1895

WALSH, ROBERT, *Notices of Brazil in 1828 and 1829*, London: Westley, 1830 [Portuguese edn, *Notícias do Brasil, 1828–1829*, São Paulo: EdUSP; Belo Horizonte: Itatiaia, 1985]

WATT, IAN, *The Rise of the Novel*, London: Chatto and Windus, 1957

—— *The Rise of the Novel*, 2nd US edn, Berkeley and Los Angeles, University of California Press, 2001

WELLS, JAMES W., *Exploring and travelling three thousand miles through Brazil from Rio de Janeiro to Maranhão*, London: Sampson Low, Marston, Searle & Rivington, 1887 [Portuguese edn, *Explorando e viajando três mil milhas através do Brasil. Do Rio de Janeiro ao Maranhão*, Belo Horizonte: Fundação João Pinheiro, Centro de Estudos Históricos e Culturais, 1995]

WINSECK, DWAYNE R., and ROBERT M. PIKE, *Communication and Empire, Media, Markets, and Globalization, 1860–1930*, Durham, NC: Duke University Press, 2007

WOLBERS, MARIAN FRANCES, *Uncovering Fashion: Fashion Communications across the Media*, New York: Fairchild, 2009

WOODMANSEE, MARTHA, *The Author, Art, and the Market: Rereading the History of Aesthetics*, New York: Columbia University Press, 1994

INDEX

❖

About, Edmond 231
Abreu e Lima, General 60
Abreu, Casimiro de 218, 220
Academy of Law 54, 55, 64, 65 n. 15
Academy of Sciences [in Lisbon] 45
Adet, Emílio 82
ad usum 15, 20, 21, 29 n. 10
  ad usum delphini 15, 20, 26
  ad usum scholarum 15
  ad christianae juventutis usum 15
  Horace, *ad usum* 15, 18, 23
  Ovid, *ad usum* 15
  Virgil, *ad usum* 15
Aesop, *Fables* 14, 23
Aguiar, A. 230
Ainsworth, William Harrison 76, 105
Alencar, José Martiniano de 75, 79, 82, 83, 85 n. 32, 168–69, 170, 173, 174, 179, 180, 186, 195, 216 n. 6, 218, 220, 231, 255
  Asas de um anjo 83
  Cinco Minutos [*Five Minutes*] 168
  Como e porque sou romancista [*How and why I'm a writer*] 82, 164
  Diva 180
  O Guarani 82, 168, 180, 255
  Iracema 82, 180
  Lucíola 79
  As minas de prata 180
  Senhora [*Senhora: Profile of a Woman*] 79
  A viuvinha [*The Little Widow*] 168
Algranti, Leila 4
Almanach Litterario de São Paulo 53
Almanak Laemmert 7, 92, 93, 95, 231
Almanaque Plancher 43, 45
Almanaque do Rio de Janeiro 36, 43
Almeida, Father Theodoro de, *O Feliz independente do mundo e da fortuna* 14, 17, 18, 23
Almeida, Fialho de 249, 256
Almeida, Júlia Lopes de 76, 195
Almeida, Manuel Antonio de 79, 81, 86 n. 49
  Memórias de um Sargento de Milícias [*Memoirs of a Militia Sergeant*] 3, 82
Almeida, Pires de 238
Alvarenga, Manuel Inácio da Silva 72, 220
Alves, Francisco 194–95, 246
Alves, Serafim José 58, 235
Amado, Gilberto 255
L'ami des enfants 25
Anais Fluminenses 38
Andersen, Hans Christian 104, 255
The Anglo-Brazilian Times 94, 109, 111, 117 n. 47
Anglomania 13, 248–49
Antonio Candido 3, 68, 78, 79, 81, 82, 123, 135, 164, 174
Araújo, Adolfo 246
Arcanjo 231
Archivo das Famílias 156
Armitage, John 55
Armstrong, John 43
Arrabida, Francisco de Paula da 21
Arthur, Joseph 52
Athanassoglou-Kallmyer, Nina 137
Aulard, François Victor Alphonse 63
Azevedo, Aluísio de 242
Azevedo, [Manuel Antonio] Álvares de 52, 56–61, 66 n. 31, 67 n. 33, 220
Azevedo, Guilherme d' 218
Azevedo, Magalhães de 242
Azevedo & Costa, A. de 235

Badaró, Libero 54–56, 64
Balzac, Honoré de 68, 82, 84 n. 19, 204
Barros, João de, *Crônica do Imperador Clarimundo* 18
Barthélemy, Jean-Jacques, *Voyage du Jeune Anacharsis en Grèce* 21, 22
bas de page 163, 170, 171, 172, 173, 174
Bastos, José Rodrigues, *A Virgem da Polônia* 118, 119
Beaumont, Mme Leprince de:
  Instructions pour les jeunes dames 24
  Magazin des adolescentes, 24, 25
  Magasin des enfants 18, 23, 24, 25
  Thesouros de meninas 23
The Beauty and the Beast 24
Beckford, William, *Vathek* 76
Beldemónio *see* Lobo, Eduardo Barros
Bellegarde, Pedro de Alcântara de Niemeyer 133, 135, 137, 140
Bello, Pedro Antonio de Campos 43
Berthier, Patrick 139, 147 n. 22
Berton, Jean-Michel 147 n. 16
Bertrand (editors) 17
Bertrand *see* Viúva Bertrand e Filhos
O Besouro 232
Biblioteca da Algibeira 231
Biblioteca dos Dous Mundos 220
Biblioteca Econômica 232

Bilac, Olavo 246
Biographie de jeunes gens 25
Blackwood's Magazine 101,141
Blake, Sacramento 63
Blanchard, Pierre *Le Buffon de la jeunesse* 18, 23
see also Costa, Matheus José da, *Thesouro de meninos*
Bloomfield, Robert 43
A boa mãi 263
Bocage, Manuel Maria l'Hedoux Barbosa du 17, 45
Obras 18, 23
Rimas 14
Bocaiúva, Quintino 199, 201, 211–12 n. 4
Bodin, Felix 63
Boileau, *Oeuvres* 21–23
Bompard, Jean Baptiste 39, 41, 43, 47
Bonaparte, Napoleon 2, 41, 44, 122, 137, 149, 150, 177
book trade:
in Brazil 4, 35–43, 46–47, 70, 72, 230–31
in Portugal 219
Bordalo, J. L. 220
Borel, Diogo 52
Bourbon dynasty 54
Bourgeois, João Roberto 38, 40, 42, 44, 45, 49 n. 28
Branco, Camilo Castelo 119, 130 n. 2, 180, 215, 218, 219, 221, 224, 225, 247–49, 258 n. 16
Amor de perdição 118
Maria não me mates, que sou tua mãe 119
O Brasil Elegante 156
Brazilian Empire 44, 46, 47, 52, 150, 164, 171, 174, 186, 202, 205, 219, 230
British Amateur Athletic Association 94
British Benevolent Fund 89, 91, 97
British Burial Ground Fund 89, 91, 94
British Church Fund 91
British Episcopal Church 89, 91, 92
British Empire 101, 109, 137, 200, 204
British Subscription Library, Rio de Janeiro, *see also* Circulating Libraries 2, 5, 74
addresses 94–95
annual fee and subscriptions 89
1842 Catalogue 98–101
1882 Catalogue 102–08
directorship 93
donations 94, 98
features and hierarchy 91–93
members 88, 89, 91, 92, 93, 94, 95, 97, 98, 103, 104, 108, 109, 112, 113
mistaken classification 110
novelists in 1882 Catalogue 104–06
opening hours 95
poetry and drama in 1882 Catalogue 106–07
sociability 87, 88–89, 96, 114
social status 91, 96
statutes 92, 102, 113
Brito, Paula, *O Enjeitado* 80–81
Broca, Brito 59
Brockhaus 53
Brotero, Felix de Avellar 24
Bruno, Sampaio 120
Buget, Nicolas 17
see also Fénelon, François de Salignac de la Mothe
Bulwer-Lytton, Edward 76, 105
Burdett, Charles 17
see also Fénelon, François de Salignac de la Mothe
Burney, Fanny 75, 76
Byron, Lord 52, 253

Le Cabinet des enfants 25
Cabral, Alfredo do Vale 191–92
Cabral, J. E. S. 134
Caieiro, Gama 36
Calógeras, João Batista 186, 187–88, 189
Camacho, M.A. 128, 129
Caminha, Adolfo 196
O Bom-Crioulo 193, 233
Cartas Literárias 233
A Normalista 193, 233
Camões, Luís de 17, 19, 23
Os Lusíadas 17, 19
Obras 14, 18
Rimas 17
Campos Junior 220
Campos, Luís Caetano de, *Viagens de Altina* 14, 17, 23
Le capitaine Paul (Captain Paul) 164
Cardoso, Vicente Licínio, 64
Carneiro, Gertrum 127, 128, 129
Cartas de Ovídio [Ovid's Letters] 15
Carvalho, A. A. de Sousa 220
Carvalho, José da Costa 65
Carvalho, Nunes 127
Castilho, António Feliciano de 219, 224
Castilho, José Feliciano de 219
Castro, Augusto de 220
Castro, D. João de 256
Castro, Francisco Viveiros de, *Atentados ao pudor* 237
Celso, Joaquim 218
censorship 2, 3, 4, 13, 16, 19, 21, 22, 24–26
Cervantes, Miguel de, *Don Quixote de la Mancha* 14, 16, 21, 23, 25, 100
Chagas, Manuel Pinheiro 195, 215, 225
Chardron, Ernesto 219, 220, 221, 222–26
Chardron, Eugénio 223
Charles X 55
Chasles, Philarète 141–42
Chateaubriand, François-René de 68
Atala, ou Amores de Dois Selvagens 73
Chiarelli, Tadeu 253
children's books 23, 24, 27, 255
Children's books A B C 25
Chompré, Pierre, *Selecta Latini* 14, 15, 18, 20
chronique 166, 167, 169, 170
Cicero:
Ciceronis Opera omnia cum delectu commentariorum 21
Ciceronis Opera, quae supersunt omnia 21

Epístolas [*Epistles*] 15
Obrigações [*On Obligations*] 15
Orações [*Orations*] 15
Circulating Libraries 70, 71, 72, 74, 76
Biblioteca Fluminense 5, 74
see British Subscription Library, Rio de Janeiro
Gesellschaft Germania 2, 5, 88
Real Gabinete Português de Leitura 2–3, 5, 74
clientelism 3, 11 n. 11
Cochin, Augustin 63
Coelho Neto, Henrique Maximiniano 190, 194, 195
Coleção de Leis e Decretos do Império do Brasil 46
Coleção dos Retratos e Elogios dos Varões e Damas Portugueses com memórias históricas de suas Vidas 37
Collection Complete des Ouvrages publiés sur le gouvernement représentatif de la Constitution de la France 46
Colonial Pact 52
Commercio do Porto 220
Commune of Paris 62
Comte, Auguste 59
Constant, Benjamin 45, 46
1824 Constitution 3, 39, 178, 179, 181
Le Constitutionnel 66 n. 18
Contes a mes jeunes amis 25
Les contes de fées 25
contracts between publishers and writers 189–90, 194–96
Corazzi, David 220, 228 n. 22
Cordeiro, Luciano 215, 218
Cordes, Nelly 129
Corneille, *Oeuvres* 21, 22, 23
Cornelius Nepos 15
Correia, José Lucio 58
Correio das Modas 149, 151, 154, 155, 157–60
Costa, Matheus José da, *Thesouro de meninos* 18, 24
see also Blanchard, Pierre, *Le Buffon de la jeunesse*
Count of Gobineau 52
Cours de Politique Constitutionnelle 46
Cousin, Victor 59
crônica 164, 165, 166, 167–75
O Cronista 133
Cruz e Silva, António Diniz da, *Odes pindáricas* 18
Cunha, Euclides da 247

Dalbin, Pierre Constant 37
Dâmaso, Joaquim 37
Darwin, Charles 108, 241
Daudet, Alphonse 249
Defoe, Daniel 73, 74, 75, 104, 109, 255
The Life and Strange Surprizing [sic] *Adventures of Robinson Crusoe* 20, 21, 25, 75
Vida e aventuras admiráveis de Robinson Crusoé 20, 73
Diario do Rio de Janeiro 2, 35, 38, 41, 44
Diario Ilustrado 220
Dias, [Antonio] Gonçalves 134, 217, 218, 220
Dickens, Charles 76, 104, 105, 110, 113, 249, 255
Diderot, Denis, *Jacques le fataliste* 72
Dinarte, Sílvio 220
Direito das Gentes [The Rights of Man] 58
Dom João [Prince Regent, afterwards Dom João VI] 39, 44,52, 77, 154, 177, 183, 195
Dom Pedro I 39, 42, 44, 45, 54–56, 143, 178, 182, 184
Dom Pedro II 39, 143, 180, 181, 186, 195, 201, 217
Dom Pedro IV 56
Dondey-Dupré, Prosper 147 n. 16
Dondey-Duprés firm 138, 147 n. 19
As duas desafortunadas 26
Dumas, Alexandre 68, 104, 118, 129, 163, 164, 170
The Count of Monte Cristo 119–29
Dieu dispose (*God disposes*) 170, 172
Obras de Alexandre Dumas 122
Durand, Carlos 22
Durão, Santa Rita, *Caramuru* 18
Dutra e Mello 77, 83

Ebel, Ernest 88
Edgeworth, Maria, *Tales of Fashionable Life* 21, 22, 104
Edinburgh Review 90, 101, 136, 142
Elwes, Robert 96
Enciclopedia da Infancia 25
Les enfans (contes) 25
Les enfants célèbres 25
Engels, Friedrich 60
Ensaio Filosófico 58
Ensayo de Meninos 25
Les escoliers en Vacance 25
O Espelho 155, 166
O Espelho Diamantino 151, 154, 155, 157, 159
Espelho Fluminense 155
O Estado de S. Paulo 250–52
A Estação 156, 191
Estudes [sic] *de demoiselles* 25
Etrennes a mon fille 25
Empresa Editora Gonçalves Lopes 220

Faculty of Law of São Paulo 52
O Farol Paulistano 65 n. 15
fashion:
fashion system 148, 149, 151–54, 158
fashion professionals based in Rio 150, 151
Favre, Jules 62
fees paid to writers 189–93
Felix Ferreira & Co 231
Fénelon, François de Salignac de la Mothe:
Aventuras de Telémaco em verso portugues, by Joaquim José Caetano Pereira e Sousa 17
Les Aventures de Télémaque 14, 16, 18, 19, 20, 21, 25, 26
Aventuras finaes de Telemaco 17
Il Telemaco in ottava rima, by Flamino Scarselli 17
Telemachus versified, by Charles Burdett 17
Le Télémaque mis en vers, by Nicolas Buget 17
Fernandes, Antônio Luís 36

Ferreira, Simão Tadeu 40
Feuillet, Octave 220, 231
feuilleton 68, 76, 78, 191, 258 n. 19
feuilleton-varietés 164
Féval, Paul 68, 220
Fielding, Henry 75, 81, 82
Tom Jones 73
Figueiredo, Antonio Pedro de 60
First Reign [*also* Empire] [1822–1831] 39, 44, 55, 56, 77
folhetim-variedades 164, 165, 167–74
Folhinhas de Algibeira e de Porta 45
Fonseca, Guimarães 215
Fourier 60
France, Anatole 249
Franco-Prussian War 61
Freire, Junqueira 218, 220
French Constitution 52
French Revolution 52, 56, 59, 60, 63, 64
French Third Republic 63
Freyre, Gilberto 60, 74
Frias, Joaquim Ignácio de 23

O Gabinete de Leitura 80
Galerie des enfans [sic] 25
Galland, Antoine, *Les Mille et Une Nuits* 18, 19
Gama, José Basílio da Gama, *O Uraguay* 14, 31 n. 34
Garcez, Antônio Joaquim da Silva 38, 39
Le garçon sans souci 25
Garnier, Baptiste-Louis 4, 156, 180, 186, 187, 188–93, 208, 217, 219, 226, 231, 232, 246
Garnier, Hyppolite 246
Garraux, Anatole Louis 61
Garrett, Almeida 179, 180, 215
Gautier, Théophile 173
Gazeta de Notícias 191, 232, 246
Gazeta do Rio de Janeiro 35–38, 41, 42, 44, 72–73, 150, 151
General Census of the Empire 1, 2
Girardin, Émile de 163
Gladstone, William Ewart 203, 213 n. 20
Gledson, John 164, 207
O Globo 60
Godwin, William 75
Goethe, Johann Wolfgang von 52, 68, 52, 107
Faust 101
Werther [*The Sorrows of Werther*] 45, 100
Wilhelm Meister 100
Gomes, Agostinho 52
Gomide, Councillor 55, 66 n. 24
Gonçalves, Adelaide 60
Gonçalves, Ricardo 250
Gonzaga, Thomas Antonio, *Marilia de Dirceu* 18, 19, 23
O Gosto 155
Gresset, *Oeuvres* 21, 22
Guanabara 134–35
Guedes, Fernando 222, 225
Guerreiro, Miguel do Couto *see* Ovid's letters
Guimarães, Aprígio Justiniano da Silva 179, 180
Guimarães Junior, Luiz 218
Guimarães, Bernardo [Joaquim da Silva] 189, 190, 218, 220, 231
A escrava Isaura 190, 191
O garimpeiro 189
Guimarães, Jerônimo G. [J. G.] 36, 38
Guizot 57–59, 63, 65 n. 12
Gutiérrez, Ricardo Padilla 122

Hallewell, Laurence 5, 19, 39, 41, 72, 246
Havas agency 202–06
Havas, Charles 204
Helme, Elizabeth:
Alberto, ou o Deserto de Strathnavern 72
Luiza, ou o Cazal [sic] *no Bosque* 73
Sinclair das Ilhas [*St Clair of the Isles, or the Outlaws of Barra*] 76, 85 n. 32, 164
Herculano, Alexandre 119, 130 n. 5, 180, 215, 217, 228 n. 15
Hervey, James, *Meditations and Contemplations* 14, 20
Histoire des Cent jours en forme de lettres 46
Historia da Donzella Theodora 26
História do Imperador Carlos Magno e dos doze pares de França 14, 18, 23
História verdadeira da princeza Magalona 26
Hogan, Alfredo:
A Mão do finado 119–30
Os Mistérios de Lisboa 125
Horace 15, 20, 77
ad usum 15, 18, 23
Odes 15
Horta, Theresa Margarida da Silva, *Aventuras de Diófanes* 18
Hugo, Victor 104, 118, 232

Illustração da Moda 156
Ilustração Brasileira 238
Inchbald, Elizabeth 76
Inconfidência Mineira [the Minas Conspiracy] 31 n. 32

Jacob, Cap. André 38
Japyassu, Candido 54, 55
Jaurès, Jean 63
João do Rio [Paulo Barreto] 231, 247
Johnson, Samuel, 104
Rasselas 76
Jornal das Famílias 156, 191
O Jornal das Senhoras 155
Jornal do Brasil 230
Jornal do Commercio 2, 35, 38, 74, 80, 92, 101, 121, 148, 164, 165, 170–73, 205, 206, 214 n. 33, 246
Journal des Débats 136, 165
Junqueira, João José de Oliveira 62
Juvenile Games 25

Kidder and Fletcher 101, 108
Kipling, Rudyard 249

La Fontaine, Jean de, *Fables de La Fontaine* 21
La Presse 163, 166, 168, 170
Laemmert [publishing house] 149, 155, 158, 193, 194, 246
Lafayette 65 n. 12
Lailhacar, De 61
Lamartine, Alphonse de 66 n. 33, 104
  L' Histoire des girondins 57
  Raphael 57
Laporte, Joseph de, *Le Voyageur François* 14, 23
Larousse, Pierre, *Grand Dictionnaire Universel du XIXe Siècle* 137
Le-Cor, Luis Pedro, *Livro de educação de meninos* 24
Lee, Sophia 76
Leithold, Theodor von 35
Lembranças de 1848 59
Lennox, William 37, 48 n. 13
Lermina, Jules, *The Son of the Count of Monte Cristo* 122
Lesage, Alain René 23
  Histoire de Gil Blas de Santillane 14, 18, 21, 72, 100
  O Diabo Coxo 26, 41, 73
  Oeuvres 22
Liberal Revolution in Portugal (1820) 39, 56
Lima, Magalhães 224, 225
Lisboa, João Francisco 216, 226, 227 n. 8
Livraria do Povo 232, 235, 236, 241
Livraria Editora Pauliceia 235
Livraria Internacional 219, 220, 223
Le livre des Enfans Laborieux 25
Lobato, José Bento Monteiro:
  as translator 255
  Jeca Tatu 251–53
  Saci 251, 253–54
  O Saci-Pererê: resultado de um inquérito 249, 251, 252, 254
  short stories 245, 247, 251
  'Urupês' (article) 251, 253
  Urupês 245, 247, 250
  'Velha Praga' 247, 251, 253, 258 n.15
  see also Monteiro Lobato & Company
Lobato, Gervásio 215
Lobo, Eduardo Barros 223
Le loisir de l'enfant 25
Lopes, A. J. F., Livreiro, 220
Lopes, Hélio 133–34
Louis XVI 64, 152
Luiz, Edmundo 233
Luso-brasileira Editora 220

M. L., *Os serões do convento* 239, 240, 242
Macedo, Joaquim Manuel de 74, 77, 79, 85 n. 28, 134, 148, 149, 150, 152, 218
  Os Dois Amores 79
  Memórias da Rua do Ouvidor 148
  A Moreninha 74, 77, 82, 83, 130 n. 6
  Vicentina 77
Machado de Assis, Joaquim Maria 1, 2, 81, 82, 87, 165, 166, 167, 168, 169, 170, 173, 174, 186, 187, 188, 189, 190, 191, 192, 193, 195, 220, 222, 233, 242, 247, 248, 249
  foreign news 200, 202–06
  cable telegraphy 200–03, 205, 209
  crônicas 1, 5, 165, 166, 168, 169, 171, 173, 199–200, 205–09, 211, 212 n. 5
  Dom Casmurro 193, 233
  Havas news agency 202–06
  Helena 189, 190, 191, 193
  Iaiá Garcia 192
  irony 87, 167, 172, 200, 204, 207–08, 211, 243 n. 33
  A Mão e a Luva [*The Hand and Glove*] 1, 192
  Memórias Póstumas de Brás Cubas [*Posthumous Memoirs of Bras Cubas* or *Epitaph of a Small Winner*] 1, 206–07, 208, 243 n. 33
  Poesias Completas 193
  Quincas Borba 192, 193
  Resurrection [*Ressurreição*] 1, 193
  telegraphic brevity 203, 205, 204, 206, 208–10, 213 n. 17, 214 n. 34
  unreliability of telegraph technology 203, 205–06, 208–10
  wordplay 210, 211, n. 2, n. 3, 213, n. 17, n. 21, n. 28, 214 n. 29, n. 34, n. 36
Magalhães & Moniz Editores 220
Magalhães Junior, Raimundo 121, 127, 128
Magalhães, Domingos José Gonçalves de 216, 217, 220
Mallarmé, Stéphane
  'universel reportage' 202, 212 n.16
  'crise de vers' 212–13 n. 16
Mandillo, Francisco Nicolau 38
Mandillo, Manuel [*also* Manoel] 37, 38, 42
Marcet, Jane 141
Marmontel, Jean-François:
  Belizario 73
  Memoires d'un Père a ses enfants 25
Marquis of Pombal 14
Marrocos, Luís Joaquim dos Santos 35, 37, 40
Martin, Paulo *also* Paulo Agostinho, Paulo Augusto, Paulo Martin Filho 38–42, 44, 45, 47, 49 n. 39
O Martinho 155
Martins Pena, Luís Carlos 165
Martins, Ana Luiza 76, 250
Martins, Oliveira 54
Mascarenhas, Henrique Leitão de Sousa 20
Mathiez, Albert 63
Matos Moreira & C.ª 220
Mattos, Ilmar Rohloff de 143, 146
Mattos, João Xavier de, *Rimas* 14, 17, 23
Medeiros e Albuquerque 246
Meireles, Zeferino Vito 2
Melo, José Alexandre Teixeira de 134, 146 n. 8

Mendes, Manuel Odorico 133, 227 n. 8
Le menthor des enfants 25
Mercúrio Histórico 36
Mesa do Desembargo do Paço [The Appelate Court] 21, 22, 24, 26, 35, 38, 41, 43, 45
Mesquita, Júlio de 250
Meus meninos 25
Meyer, Marlyse 72, 76, 78, 85 n. 3, 164
Miceli, Sérgio 247, 248–49, 254
Mignet, François Auguste Marie 64
Miller, Henry 43, 92, 93, 94
Milton, John 14, 15, 43
  Paradise Lost 15–16, 20, 23
Minerva Brasiliense 77, 83, 134
Miranda, Sá de, *Obras* 18
Miranda, Veiga 250
mistranslation 200, 209, 210
Modellos das meninas 25
Molière, *Oeuvres* 21, 22, 23
Moniz, Rosendo 218, 220
Monroy y Ros, D Felix Moreno de, *Lances da Ventura, acasos da desgraça e heroísmos da virtude* 14, 17, 18, 23
Monteiro Lobato & Company 254, 256, 257
Monteiro, José Gomes 224
Montolieu, Baroness Isabelle de [Elisabeth Jeanne Pauline Polier de Bottens], *Caroline de Lichtfield* 14, 23
Moraes, A. J. de Mello 220
Moraes, Rubens Borba de 11 n. 7, 41
Morale en action 25
Moré, Nicolau 222, 224, 225
  Biblioteca Moré 220
Moreira & Garcez Typography 39
Morris, R J 89
Moreira, José de Cristo 39
Moretti, Franco 70
O Mosquito 231
Mota, José Inácio Silveira da 62
Motta, Ignacio Francisco Silveira 220
A Mulher do Simplício ou A Fluminense Exaltada 154, 155, 157, 158
Municipal Chamber 55
Mureau, L A Milet, *Voyage de La Pérouse au tour du Monde* 21, 22
Musée de la Jeunesse 25
Les mystères de Paris 165
Mytologie de la jeunesse 25
Mauá, Baron of *see* Sousa, Irineu Evangelista de

Nabuco, Joaquim 61, 62, 209
Nagis, Imbert de 37
Napoleon III 62
national consciousness 78, 82
Naval College 46
Nerval, Gérard de 53
newspaper column(s) 148, 165, 167, 168, 169, 170, 231, 246, 247
Niterói 134, 135, 144
Noé, Pierre René François de la 41
Nova Livraria Internacional 220, 222
A Nova Minerva 134
novel(s) 26, 27, 33, n. 57, n. 58, 69–72, 130 n. 6
  characteristics of 75
  dangers of 76–77
  founders of 75
  for men 237–40
  gothic 75, 80, 86 n. 50, 105
  justification of 77–78
  sensation novels 233–37
  serialized novels 163, 164, 165, 168, 170, 171, 172, 173 , 174
  sub-genres 73, 75–76, 105
  techniques 79
  verisimilitude 79–80
Novo Correio de Modas 155
Les nuits enfantines 25

O Observador Constitucional 54, 55
Olaya e Júlio, ou A Periquita 79
Oliveira, João Gomes de 19
Oliveira, Joaquim Antonio de 38
Ortigão, Ramalho 224
Osório, Ana de Castro 254
Otaviano, Francisco 165
Otoni, José Elói 133

Palacios, José Manuel Valdez 134
O Pantheon 156
Passatempo da Mocidade 25
patrimonialism 3, 11 n. 11
O Patriota 38
Peixoto, Alvarenga 220
Pereira, José Manoel Ribeiro 17
Pereira, José Saturnino da Costa, *Leitura para os meninos* 25
A Perjura 80
Phaedrus, *Fables* 15
Pigoreau, A. N. 71, 72, 84 n. 19
Pimentel, Alberto 224
Pimentel, Figueiredo, *O aborto* 241, 242
Pinassi, Maria Orlanda 143, 144
Pinheiro, Abílio Soares, *Os estranguladores do Rio* 234
Pinheiro, Joaquim Caetano Fernandes 77, 186, 188, 189, 220
Pinheiro Júnior 250, 251
Pinho, José Borges de 42
Plancher, Pierre 2, 38, 39, 41, 45, 46, 49, 74, 154, 164, 197 n. 22
Plancher Imperial Typography 39
Pompéia, Raul 242
Porto-Alegre, Manuel de Araújo 134, 220
Porto, Manoel de Joaquim da Silva 37, 38, 39, 42–43, 44, 45
pragmatic sanctions 149

Prevost, *Oeuvres* 21, 22
A Primavera 156
printing privileges 177
O Progresso 60
property rights, legislation 178–79, 188, 189, 190, 192, 193, 194, 195, 196
Proudhon, 60

Queirós, Eça de 247, 249, 256
Quiroga, Horácio 257
Quita, Domingos dos Reis, *Obras poéticas* 18

Racine 23
Athalie 22
Oeuvres 21, 22
Phèdre 22
La Religion (*Le poeme sur la religion*) 21, 22
Théâtre 22
Radcliffe, Ann 74, 75, 85 n. 29
L'Italien, ou le confessional des pénitents noirs 72
Rangel, Godofredo 247, 249, 250–51, 258 n. 5
Real Junta do Comércio, Agricultura, Fábricas e Navegação 42
Real Mesa Censória [Royal Censorship Board] 14, 18, 28 n. 2
Recreio do Bello Sexo 155
Reeve, Clara 75
Rego, M. G. de S. 60
'A Ressurreição do Amor' 80
Restoration 4, 41, 56, 59, 61, 63, 65 n. 12, 66 n. 18, 137, 150
Reuter, Julius 201
Reuters 202, 204, 206
Revista Popular 156
Revista da Sociedade Filomática 133, 134
Revista do Brasil [periodical] 245, 250, 251, 254–57, 259 n. 51
Revista do Brasil [publishing house] 251
Revista Nacional e Estrangeira 133–37, 139–46
Revista do Instituto Histórico e Geográfico Brasileiro 134
Revue Britannique 70, 135, 136–46, 147 n. 16, n. 23, n. 28
Revue des Deux Mondes 169
Revue Germanique 138, 147 n. 19
Reycend, João Baptista [*also* Jean] 17, 36
Ribeiro, Bernardim, *Menina e Moça* 18
Ribeiro, Francisco Bernardino 133
Ribeiro, José Silvestre 215
Ribeiro, Julio, *A carne* 241
Richardson, Samuel 75, 79, 81, 82, 84 n. 14
Clarissa Harlowe 73, 82
Pamela, or virtue rewarded 71, 79, 82
Rio British Cricket Club 97
The Rio News 94, 95,109, 112–14
Rios Filho, Adolfo Morales de los 133
Rocha, Justiniano José da 165, 186, 189, 198 n. 40
Roche, Regina Maria, *Amanda e Oscar* [*The Children of the Abbey*] 76, 164
Rodrigues, A. A. Gonçalves 118
Rodrigues, Antonio Coelho 62
Rolland, Francisco 16, 17, 19, 36, 40
Romero, Sylvio 222
Rosa, José Vicente da 37
Rousseau, Jean-Jacques, *La Nouvelle Héloïse* 14
Royal Library 37
Royal MilitaryAcademy 46
Royal Press [Impressão Régia]:
Lisbon 20, 21, 24
Rio de Janeiro 2, 13, 19, 25, 26, 35, 39, 41, 48 n. 20, 154, 177, 182, 183, 195
Rub Antisyphilitique 37, 48 n. 12

Sabinus 15
Sabóia, Gilberto 237
Sainte-Beuve, Charles-Augustin 138, 169
Saint-Hilaire, Auguste de 53
Saint-Pierre, Jacques-Henri Bernardin de :
A Choupana Índia 73
Paul et Virginie 16, 21
Paul and Virginia 16
Paulo e Virgínia 26, 45, 73
Saint Simon [Count of] 59
Sánchez-Sáez, Braulio 256
Sandeau, Jules 231
Santos, Quirino dos, *Gazeta de Campinas* 75
Sarmiento, Domingo, *Facundo* 257
Saulnier, Louis-Sébastien 137–38, 147 n. 16
Schmidt, Afonso 129
School of Surgeons 46
Schwarz, Roberto 68, 69, 70, 118, 207
Scott, Sir Walter 69, 73, 74, 75,76, 81, 104, 105, 106, 108, 113
Seabra, Bruno 220
Second Reign [*also* Empire] [1840–1889] 55, 60, 143
Semana Familiar 156
Semiond, Estevão 16
serials 98, 105, 126, 159, 160, 163, 164, 166, 168, 169, 170–74
Serva, Manuel Antônio da Silva 39, 42, 183
Shakespeare, William 82, 107, 249, 255
Sidronius 15
Le Siècle 165, 174 n. 2
Silva, Alfredo Elisário da, 234
Maria, a desgraçada 236, 237
Silva, António Manuel Policarpo da, *O Piolho Viajante* 18, 19, 23
Silva, Father José Amaro da 16
Silva, Firmino Rodrigues da 133
Silva, Francisco Artur da 220
Silva, Inocêncio Francisco da 63, 215, 216
Silva, João Manuel Pereira da 133–34, 135, 137, 140–41, 146 n. 5, 147 n. 32
Silva, José Antonio da 38
Silva, Josino do Nascimento 133, 135, 137, 146 n. 5
Silva, Machado Freire Pereira da, 62

Silva, Manuel Jorge da 38
Silva, Maria Beatriz Nizza da 37
Silveira, Valdomiro 250
Slavery 3, 144, 145, 201, 213 n. 21, 232
  slave owners 64
  slaves 2, 3, 11 n. 9, 27, 38, 44, 62, 76, 81, 144, 147 n. 31, 153, 183
  slave trade [*also* traffic] 72, 144, 145
Smith & Elder 97, 98, 110, 115 n. 26
Sobreira, Luís 119
O Socialista da Província do Rio de Janeiro 60
Society of Artistic Culture, 251
Sodré, Nelson Werneck 78, 183, 246
Soulié, Frédéric 68, 169–70
Sousa, Antonio Gonçalves Teixeira e 77, 86 n. 42, 130 n. 6, 218
Sousa, Irineu Evangelista de [Baron of Mauá] 201–02
Sousa, Joaquim José Caetano Pereira e 17
  see also Fénelon, François de Salignac de la Mothe
Sousa, Manuel de 17
  see also Fénelon, François de Salignac de la Mothe
Souvestre, Emile 68, 104, 118
Souza, Manoel Dias de, *Livro para meninos* 24
Spencer, Herbert 241
Staël, Mme de 64
Stendhal, 66 n. 18
Sterne, Laurence 75, 87, 104, 108, 249
  Sentimental Journey 11 n. 7
Stewart, Reverend C. S. 90
Streeter, Harold 72
subscription system 182–86
Sue, Eugène 68, 118, 163, 165
  Os Mistérios de Paris [*The Mysteries of Paris*] 126
sumptuary laws 149, 152
Swift, Jonathan 108
  Gulliver's Travels 11 n. 7
  Viagens de Gulliver 73

Taine, Hippolyte 63
Tasso, Torquato, 107
  Jerusalem délivrée 23
  Jerusalem [*delivered*] 101
  Jerusalem liberata 21
Teixeira, António José da Silva 224
telegraphy:
  and news agencies 202, 203, 204–06
  British telegraph companies 201–02, 209
  cable telegraphy (*see* Machado de Assis)
  in Brazil 201–03, 205, 210
  global networks 200–02, 204
  submarine cable 199, 200, 201, 202, 203, 204, 207
  transatlantic cable 200, 201, 203, 205
Thiers, Louis Adolphe 62, 63
Tocqueville, Alexis de, *Lembranças de 1848* 59
translation(s) 15, 16–17, 19, 23, 28 n. 5, 58, 68, 69, 71, 74, 76, 99, 118, 128, 129, 137, 139, 142, 145, 147 n. 32, 154, 170, 204, 210, 219, 220, 224, 232, 240, 252, 257
translator(s) 15, 16, 17, 20, 23, 24, 63–64, 69, 72, 99, 128, 139, 144–45, 147, n. 23, n. 32
Le trou de l'enfer 172

utile dulci 77, 78, 141

Valles, Esteban 39
Varela, Luís Nicolau Fagundes 192, 218
Varnhagen, Francisco Adolfo de [Visconde do Porto Seguro] 63
Vauthier [Louis Léger] 60
Veiga, Evaristo da 39, 41, 197 n. 21
Veiga, Francisco Luiz Saturnino da 36, 37, 42, 47
Veiga, João Pedro da 43, 47, 50 n. 48, 197 n. 21
Veloso, Rodrigo 215, 217
Venturi, Franco 53
Verne, Jules 104, 220, 228 n. 22
Vianna, Pedro Ribeiro:
  Elzira, a morta virgem 234, 235–36
Vicente, Gil 18
Villalobos, João Rosado de, *Livro dos meninos* 24
Virgil 23
  ad usum 15
  Opera 21
Viúva Bertrand e Filhos 220, 221–22
Voltaire 23
  La Henriade 21, 22

Walpole, Horace 75, 79
War of the Triple Alliance, 62
Warren, Samuel, *Passages from the Diary of a Late Physician* 141
Washington, George 54
The Weekly Times 251
Wolcott, John 43
Wolf, Ferdinand 216
Wolff, Bernhard 204
Wollstonecraft, Mary 73, 74
women novelists 76
women readers 76, 77, 106
writers' remuneration 177, 178, 180, 186–89

Young, Edward 23,107
  Night Thoughts on Life Death and Immortality 14, 23

Zaluar, Augusto Emílio 220
Zola, Émile 241, 249

For Product Safety Concerns and Information please contact our EU representative GPSR@taylorandfrancis.com Taylor & Francis Verlag GmbH, Kaufingerstraße 24, 80331 München, Germany

Printed and bound by CPI Group (UK) Ltd, Croydon, CR0 4YY
16/10/2025
01977775-0019